HEARINGS

BEFORE

ADMINISTRATIVE TRIBUNALS

by
ROBERT W. MACAULAY, Q.C.
and
JAMES L.H. SPRAGUE, B.A., LL.B.

CARSWELL
Thomson Professional Publishing

Canadian Cataloguing in Publication Data
Macaulay, Robert W. (Robert William), 1921-
    Hearings before administrative tribunals

Originally issued as chapts. 12, 17 and 22 of: Practice and procedure before administrative tribunals.

Includes index.
ISBN 0-459-56057-3

1.   Administrative courts – Canada.
2.   Administrative procedure – Canada.   I. Sprague, James L.H.   II. Title.

KE5029.M23 1996   342.71'0664   C96-930071-9
KF5417.M23 1996

CARSWELL
Thomson Professional Publishing

One Corporate Plaza, 2075 Kennedy Road, Scarborough, Ontario M1T 3V4
Customer Service:
Toronto 1-416-609-3800
Elsewhere in Canada/U.S. 1-800-387-5164
Fax 1-416-298-5094

FOREWORD

This practical book should prove very useful to tribunal members and administrative law practitioners. The material, originally found in the three-volume *Practice and Procedure before Administrative Tribunals* by Macaulay and Sprague, has been rewritten and expanded but it maintains the practical approach and robust style of the original. This is the only place where one can find an exhaustive treatment of administrative law principles together with practical information on subjects such as the issuance of subpoenas, the physical set-up of a hearing room, electronic systems and record keeping, the pre-hearing conference, the use of written evidence, the rights of witnesses, the power to cite for contempt and, not least, when to give reasons and how to write them. It is a treasure trove of practical information and guidance. The distinguished authors have produced a handy bench book which will be useful for lawyers and tribunal members and staff.

Brian A. Crane, Q.C.
Ottawa, January 1996

FOREWORD

As a legal academic, I have witnessed over the last thirty years a growing level of sophistication in Canadian administrative law. For example, restrictive rules governing natural justice have been replaced by flexible principles of fairness; institutional decision-making and administrative fact finding processes have been more clearly identified; the comparative qualifications and roles of agencies and courts have been explored in the context of statutory interpretation and jurisdictional review and access to the courts has been made much easier as a result of wide-ranging remedial reforms.

Overall, this has been a very desirable development as the law must always seek to keep up with the pervasive high ambition of modern government. But there has been a price for this greater legal sophistication in that a growing gap has been created between the administrative law of legal experts and the administrative practice of most of those who actually run administrative agencies. This book seeks to close this gap.

Fortunately, there has also been a steady upgrading in the level of professionalism in the agencies themselves. As one who studied Ontario agencies in the late 1960's and early 1970's, and who worked for the Law Reform Commission of Canada's Administrative Law Project in the mid-1970's, and has remained very much involved in administrative law ever since on an academic level and occasionally on a more immediately practical basis, I have seen encouraging evidence of increasing seriousness of purpose and a growing commitment to quality in decision-making. This is what may make it possible to bridge the gap which has developed between administrative law and practice.

This is an urgent and important challenge because administrative agencies continue to have an immense impact on the lives of individual Canadians and on the social and economic environment of the country as a whole. As well, the courts have made it clear in recent years that they will not continually interfere but will to an ever greater degree leave it up to the agencies themselves to devise fair and effective ways of discharging their responsibilities. In this era of greater judicial deference to the competence of administrative agencies, it is essential that there be the means by which all who work at administrative agencies are able to appreciate, and then implement, the essential requirements of fair procedure and credible decision-making.

The general principles of administrative law are too important to be locked away in the inaccessible and arcane world of legal specialists. They need to be

FOREWORD

understood and applied by all who are called upon to administer the law. This volume will help to make this possible.

Hudson N. Janisch
Professor & Associate Dean
(Graduate Studies)
Faculty of Law
University of Toronto

December 4, 1995

INTRODUCTION

Practice and Procedure Before Administrative Tribunals was originally published in 1988. At the time it consisted of one volume. In the acknowledgements I explained that this book was not a law text. It was a book about administrative agencies and how they operate. I hoped to address, not only the "law" but the "how" of administrative action. In it I hoped that the reader would find a practical guide to dealing with the varied aspects of administrative agency operation in Canada.

It has become axiomatic that administrative agencies need not be, and should not be, dominated by lawyers (either on the agencies or as representatives before them). Administrative agencies are to be the home of individuals expert in the particular discipline in which the agency is to operate. Matters of procedure and process, however, are seldom, if ever, considered one of the needed areas of expertise. These are considered skills which can learned as need be, picked up along the way, so to speak.

The irony of this is that when I first set out to write this text there was no source in Canada of practical advice on the operations of administrative agencies. There were several excellent legal texts. But these texts addressed the legal concepts of administrative law and seldom, if ever, dealt with matters such as memorandums of understanding, the duties of hearing clerks, making arguments before administrative agencies or the writing of decisions. So what we had was a great pool of people carrying out diverse tasks, sometimes with vital consequences, with no real guide as to how to do it. If this was not bad enough, they were required to work under the vigilant eye of the courts who were quick to criticise what they perceived to be error. Compounding the irony was the fact that these courts, themselves, were struggling with unfamiliar concepts with little or no experience in the administrative reality in which agencies were required to work.

The hope of my text was to address the real world of administrative agency operation, shed some light on how it worked, and share some experience respecting the myriad details involved in making an administrative decision.

More than this, as I quite unabashedly admit, I hoped to share and proselytize my views on administrative law as a unique method of doing business separate from the courts and the departments from which they sprang. It has been a long struggle, and to a degree it still continues. But in my opinion, there is a growing perception amongst both the individuals who appear before administrative agen-

INTRODUCTION

cies and the courts which review their action that administrative agencies are not junior courts and are not expected to operate or be assessed by the standards developed for the judiciary. Whatever their failings, the modern concepts of institutional decision-making and curial deference are welcome signs of a growing recognition of this fact (although I can hardly claim credit for this).

Administrative law, by its nature, is not static. It grows and develops with the needs of the state and the people it serves. It adjusts and grows with the changing resources and technologies which surround it. The press of change in administrative law in the last number of years has been such that I was pleased in 1992 when James Sprague joined me as a co-author to assist in keeping this text abreast of the times.

To my surprise, my original single volume text has grown to three volumes covering every aspect of administrative agency practice from the appointment of members, to the demands of the electronic age. Realistically, though, three volumes of text, however insightful and invaluable, are, a bit much to carry about in one's brief case. Thus, I was pleased when Carswell proposed to publish an excerpt from the main work, consisting of what James and I hoped would be the most useful information for the core task of administrative agency operation, decision-making.

James and I have selected three chapters, 12 (the conduct of the hearing), 17 (an approach to evidence, and expert witnesses), and 22 (decision and reason writing) of *Practice and Procedure Before Administrative Agencies* for inclusion in this paperback. The appendices relating to those chapters have also been included. These chapters will take the reader through the basic elements of arguing and conducting an administrative hearing up through the decision-making process to the final writing and issuance of the decision and reasons. In preparing for this release James and I substantially rewrote and expanded chapter 12 to include, as much as possible, all of the various questions and procedures which arise in the conduct of hearing. It and chapters 17 and 22 have been completely updated.

It is our hope that both the individuals who preside over hearings and those who appear before them, counsel and agent, will find the material in this paperback a useful and practical guide to the sometimes complex, frequently confusing, and always challenging world of the administrative hearing.

R.W. Macaulay
October, 1995

TABLE OF CONTENTS

CHAPTER 12
A Hearing — Some Comments

TABLE OF CONTENTS

CHAPTER 17
Witnesses

CHAPTER 22
Tribunal Decisions

LEGISLATION

APPENDICES

ADMINISTRATIVE TRIBUNALS

TABLE OF CASES

All references are to paragraphs of the text.

TABLE OF CASES

TABLE OF CASES

TABLE OF CASES

TABLE OF CASES

TABLE OF CASES

TABLE OF CASES

TABLE OF CASES

TABLE OF CASES

12

A Hearing — Some Comments

12.1 INTRODUCTION

There are many forms of hearing. Some "hearings" need not even be oral. They may, depending on the statutory mandate being performed, be conducted solely through the filing of written documents.[1] In this chapter, however, I intend to take the reader through the various stages of an oral hearing.

There is no standard form of oral hearing. Indeed the courts have studiously refused to impose any standard form on agency hearings.[2] However, while the technical details may vary between the hearings conducted by agencies with different mandates, the overall purposes being served by the oral hearing process, the questions which arise and the principles underlying the process are generally very similar. This chapter will outline those common matters.

There is extensive case law on the procedural aspects of a hearing. Where appropriate, much of this law will be highlighted. However, this chapter should not be approached only as a summary of the law of natural justice. It is also intended to be a procedural guide for both decision-makers and practitioners which may be referred to as a checklist or as a source of practical commentary on what may or may not, should and should not be done at each stage of an oral hearing.

12.2 UNDERLYING PRINCIPLES

Before dealing with particular aspects of a hearing it will be useful to outline five basic principles underlying hearings:

---

1 See generally chapter 9 of this text. For a discussion of the meaning of a statutory requirement to hold a "hearing" see *Manitoba (Attorney-General) v. Canada (National Energy Board)*, [1974] 2 F.C. 502, 48 D.L.R. 73 (T.D.). Excellent discussions of this point are also found at pp. 49 to 54 of Reid and David's *Administrative Law and Practice* 2nd ed. (Butterworths, 1978) and pp. 543 to 547 of Sir William Wade's *Administrative Law* 6th edition (Oxford University Press, 1988).

2 See, for example, *Downing v. Graydon* (1978), 21 O.R. (2d) 292, 92 D.L.R. (3d) 355 (C.A.) where Mr. Justice Blair noted that "The appropriate procedure depends on the provisions of the statute and the circumstances in which it has to be applied."

i. hearings are a tool to collect necessary information;

ii. hearings require structure;

iii. hearings must be fair;

iv. the form of administrative agency hearings is dictated by the mandate to be accomplished; and

v. the role of an agency member is not the same as the role of a judge.

Whatever an agency's mandate may be, both the individual or individuals presiding over the hearing and the participants in that hearing would be well advised to remember these principles in approaching any procedural question respecting an oral hearing. Each of these principles is obviously related to the other and no single one is paramount. While it is common to look at the requirement that hearings be fair from the perspective of the parties and their ''right'' to fairness, an agency which ensures that a party is aware of the case against him and able to present his case will also ensure that it is securing all of the information necessary for a sound decision. A hearing which is unstructured and ad hoc stands a good chance of being unfair and of missing important information. Thus, it may be useful to discuss these five principles somewhat further before proceeding.

12.2(a) Hearings Are A Tool To Collect Necessary Information

The purpose of a hearing is to gather in evidence and argument that will allow the agency to fulfill its statutory mandate. A hearing which is conducted in a way that is not geared to this purpose is not being conducted properly. A hearing which is conducted in a way that obstructs the proper gathering of information by the agency is a waste of resources.

Hearings are not Hyde Park soap boxes for anyone with a view to espouse. As I have argued elsewhere, the frequently espoused comment that a hearing serves the useful social purpose of allowing the disenchanted the opportunity to ''let off steam'' is simply not correct and should not, for a number of reasons, be followed by the able practitioner.[3]

On the other side of the coin, one must keep in mind the ultimate hearing purpose of collecting relevant and useful evidence and argument. You hold a hearing in order to get access to individuals with information necessary or useful to the accomplishment of your mandate, and, equally, to give them access to you. It should not be treated as some formal procedural gesture that must be gotten through, nor as a hindrance to the effective control of an agency's backlog. Thus, the extra time which may be necessary to hear out the unsophisticated applicant,

---

3 These reasons are set out in c. 17.1(f).

to explain a process clearly, or to test the ability of a proffered expert, may be well compensated by the quality of the resulting decision. Equally, one should not adopt procedures or rules that are not geared to the ultimate mandate to be served by your agency and you should be ready to depart (always in a way that is fair) from the technicalities of any procedures which you do adopt which may in an individual case be counterproductive to the collection of relevant and useful information.[4]

12.2(b) Hearings Require Structure

Hearings require structure. A decision-maker must at all times be aware of the purpose of the hearing, where it is going and how it should get there.

An individual, or panel, presiding over a hearing must appear at all times to be aware and competent to direct the proceedings. The unstructured and undirected hearing will not serve its purpose as well as one which is. The parties will lack confidence in the rulings of the decision-maker. The unscrupulous or those with a special agenda will use it for their own ends. An unstructured hearing is an inefficient one and will delay the accomplishment of the agency's mandate and its ability to deal with other matters. This is not a task to be approached lightly by a decision-maker. It requires a in-depth knowledge of the substantive function of the agency, a good grasp of the law respecting procedure, and an ability to control, without suppressing, public meetings.

12.2(c) Hearings Must Be Fair

An agency which conducts a hearing in the exercise of statutory powers (other than legislative powers) to make decisions that affect the rights of individuals must conduct that hearing in a way that it is fair.[5]

---

4 See, for example, *ter Stege v. O.P.S.E.U.*, [1994] O.L.R.B. Rep. 1375. In that case a panel of the Ontario Labour Relations Board refused to place any weight on a petition which had been filed by fax. The panel took the position that the Board's Rules of Procedure were quite clear that the Board would not receive a petition filed in that way. The person who filed the petition advised the panel that she had phoned the Board and been advised that she could file the petition as she did, however, the panel disposed of this concern by stating that "[a]s the Board has noted previously, persons who rely on information from someone at the Board in situations such as this do so at their own peril." On the basis of the sparse information set out in the report of this case, this is an astonishing position to take, particularly if the panel actually believed that the person had been misled by someone at the Board. The case report fails to indicate the importance of the petition in question or what prejudice, if any, might have been suffered had the petition been admitted or the petitioner allowed to file the original of the petition after the fact or during an adjournment. There is no indication in the report that the panel considered its power in sections 19 and 22 of the Board's Rules to grant relief against the strict application of the Rules.

5 "All administrative bodies, no matter what their function, owe a duty of fairness to the regulated parties whose interest they must determine." (*Nfld. Telephone Co. v. Nfld. (Board of Commissioners of Public Utilities)*, [1992] 1 S.C.R. 632, 4 Admin. L.R. (2d) 121, 134 N.R. 241, 89 D.L.R.

As I have noted frequently in this text, to a great extent administrative law is composed of a tension between the effective and expeditious performance of public duties and the protection of the rights of the individual. In the context of oral hearings, this tension is reflected in determining the form and degree of participation to be permitted participants in the process.

It is generally considered that the more extensive the participation rights granted the longer, more expensive and less expeditious the hearing process becomes. However, while this statement has all the attractiveness of the platitude that it is, it should not be accepted as an absolute truth. The fact is that procedurally restricted hearings are not necessarily quicker or cheaper than more liberal ones. For example, in many cases, it is much easier and faster to solicit information from an individual through an oral hearing where he is available for direct questioning than through written communications. The former is better suited for clarifying uncertainties and for exploring unexpected possibilities.

In the short term, cutting corners on the rights of individuals may appear to be expeditious and efficient as it may permit an agency to issue more decisions faster. However, in the long term, cutting corners on fairness likely costs more, takes more time and results in an inferior product.

On the most practical level, a decision resulting from an unfair hearing will be quashed by the courts. When this happens, the "quick and dirty" decision often ends up just being "dirty" and time and expense is added to the process by the resulting court challenge and consequent re-hearing by the agency.

On a more abstract level, decisions which are not arrived at fairly will not likely accomplish their purpose. Decisions which are not respected will not be accepted by the public. An agency makes decisions in order to accomplish some mandate. If that mandate is to be accomplished, the agency's decisions must be accepted by the individuals to whom they are directed. No one will respect, or accept, decisions which are perceived to have been arrived at unfairly. In his book, *The Road to Justice*,[6] Lord Denning wrote:

> People will respect rules of law which are intrinsically right and just and will expect their neighbours to obey them, as well as obeying the rules themselves: but they will not feel the same about rules which are unrighteous or unjust. If people are to

---

(4th) 289 (S.C.C.), *Nicholson v. Haldimand-Norfolk (Regional Municipality) Commissioners of Police*, [1979] 1 S.C.R. 311, 88 D.L.R. (3d) 671, 23 N.R. 410). See also *Knight v. Indian Head School Division No. 19*, [1990] 1 S.C.R. 653, [1990] 3 W.W.R. 689, 83 Sask. R. 81, 69 D.L.R. (4th) 489 (S.C.C.) and *Cardinal v. Director of Kent Institution* (1985), 24 D.L.R. (4th) 44 where Justice LeDain states "there is, as a general common law principle, a duty of procedural fairness lying on every public authority making an administrative decision which is not of a legislative nature and which affects the rights, privileges or interests of an individual: (*Nicholson v. Haldimand-Norfolk Regional Board of Com'rs of Police*, [1979] 1 S.C.R. 311, 88 D.L.R. (3d) 671, 23 N.R. 410; *Martineau v. Matsqui Institution Disciplinary Board (No. 2)* (1979), [1980] 1 S.C.R. 602, 13 C.R. (3d) 1, 115 D.L.R. (3d) 1, 50 C.C.C. (2d) 353, 106 D.L.R. (3d) 385, 30 N.R. 119; *A.-G. Canada v. Inuit Tapirisat of Canada*, [1980] 2 S.C.R. 735, 33 N.R. 304."
6 Stevens and Sons, London, 1955.

feel a sense of obligation to the law, then the law must correspond with what, they consider to be right and just, or, at any rate, must not unduly diverge from it. In other words, it must correspond as near as may be, with justice.

On the other side of the coin, one should not fall into the trap of believing that the fairness of a hearing is directly proportionate to the degree of participation allowed its participants. What is fair is relative and is defined by the nature of the mandate being performed and the individual circumstances involved. If a particular procedure is not necessary to enable an individual to present his case adequately or to know the case against him, it is not unfair to deny that form of participation. Intervenors, for example, because they have a different role to perform in a proceeding, need not be given the same degree of rights as parties. The Federal Court of Appeal has even held in *Country Music Television Inc. v. Canada (Canadian Radio-Television & Telecommunications Commission)*[7] that all parties need not be given the same participation rights. In that case the fact that one party was given an opportunity to supplement through oral proceedings the case it had made to the Commission in writing did not automatically entitle an opposing party to the same supplemental oral hearing where the circumstances were such that the latter party was fully able to know the case against it and to present its side in its written presentation.

What then is "fair"? To a large extent the dictates of fairness have come to be expressed in the concept of natural justice and fairness of which there are two major principles: the right to be heard (audi alteram partem) and the right to be heard by someone who is listening, that is to say the right to be heard by an unbiased decision-maker.

Natural justice's guaranty of a right to be heard dictates that agencies must ensure that their hearings provide parties with ample opportunity

  i. to know the case made against them;

  ii. to dispute, correct or contradict anything which is prejudicial to their positions; and

  iii. to present arguments and evidence supporting their own case.

As Lord Denning stated in *Kanda v. Government of Malaya:*

> If the right to be heard is to be a real right which is worth anything, it must carry with it a right in the accused man to know the case which is made against him. He must know what evidence has been given and what statements have been made affecting him; and then he must be given a fair opportunity to correct or contradict them.[8]

---

7 (1994), 178 N.R. 386 (Fed. C.A.), leave to appeal to S.C.C. refused (January 26, 1995), Doc. 24477 (S.C.C.).
8 [1962] A.C. 322 (P.C.) at p. 337.

Within the confines of procedural fairness, the common law affords administrative tribunals significant autonomy in formulating the procedural content of their hearings. The procedures required for a hearing to be fair will vary from agency to agency and will differ according to the circumstances of each particular case (*Martineau v. Matsqui Institution Disciplinary Board (No. 2)*[9]). In *Homex Realty and Development Co. v. Wyoming (Village)*[10] Dickson J. (as he then was) stated (in dissenting reasons):

> Above all, flexibility is required in this analysis. There is, as it were, a spectrum. A purely ministerial decision, on broad grounds of public policy, will typically afford the individual little or no procedural protection. . . . On the other hand, a function that approaches the judicial end of the spectrum will entail substantial procedural safe-guards, particularly when personal or property rights are targeted, directly, adversely and specifically.[11]

Furthermore, the essence of administrative law is the balancing of the procedural rights to be accorded individuals in the protection of their rights with the need of society for efficiency in administrative decision-making. As Lord Pearson said in *Pearlberg v. Varty (Inspector of Taxes)*:

> If there were too much elaboration of procedural safeguards, nothing could be done simply and quickly and cheaply. Administrative or executive efficiency and economy should not be too readily sacrificed.[12]

An agency exists to accomplish some statutory purpose (its mandate). One cannot determine the fairness of a situation without taking into account that which the agency is supposed to accomplish and the practical constraints facing it in this task. As Justice Gonthier noted for the majority of the Supreme Court of Canada in *Consolidated Bathurst Packaging Ltd. v. International Woodworkers of America, Local 2-69*[13] (in discussing the practice of the Ontario Labour Relations Board of holding full board meetings to discuss policy matters in the absence of the parties):

---

9 [1980] 1 S.C.R. 602, 13 C.R. (3d) 1, 50 C.C.C. (2d) 353, 106 D.L.R. (3d) 385, 30 N.R. 119. To the same effect see *Chiarelli v. Canada (Minister of Employment & Immigration)*, [1992] 1 S.C.R. 711, 72 C.C.C. (3d) 214, 16 Imm. L.R. (2d) 1, 2 Admin. L.R. (2d) 125, 135 N.R. 161, 90 D.L.R. (4th) 289 (S.C.C.), *Syndicat des employés de production du Québec & de l'Acadie v. Canada (Canadian Human Rights Commission)*, [1989] 2 S.C.R. 879, 89 C.L.L.C. 17,022, 62 D.L.R. (4th) 385, 11 C.H.R.R. D/1, (*sub nom. Syndicat des employés de production du Québec & de l'Acadie v. Commission canadianne des droits de la personne*) 100 N.R. 241.
10 [1980] 2 S.C.R. 1011, 13 M.P.L.R. 234, 116 D.L.R. (3d) 1, 33 N.R. 475.
11 116 D.L.R. (3d) 1 at p. 10 (S.C.C.).
12 [1972] 1 W.L.R. 534 at p. 547.
13 [1990] 1 S.C.R. 282, 73 O.R. (2d) 676 (note), 42 Admin. L.R. 1, 105 N.R. 161, 38 O.A.C. 321, 68 D.L.R. (4th) 524.

... the rules of natural justice must take into account the institutional constraints faced by an administrative tribunal. These tribunals are created to increase the efficiency of the administration of justice and are often called upon to handle heavy caseloads. It is unrealistic to expect an administrative tribunal such as the Board to abide strictly by the rules applicable to courts of law. In fact, it has long been recognized that the rules of natural justice do not have a fixed content irrespective of the nature of the tribunal and the institutional constraints it faces. . . . The main issue is whether, given the importance of the policy issue at stake in this case and the necessity of maintaining a high degree of quality and coherence in Board decisions, the rules of natural justice allow a full board meeting to take place subject to the conditions outlined by the Court of Appeal and, if not, whether a procedure which allows the parties to be present, such as a full board hearing, is the only acceptable alternative. The advantages of the practice of holding full board meetings must be weighed against the disadvantages involved in holding discussions in the absence of the parties.[14]

The above comments address the concept of fairness in terms of the common law. Fairness is not, however, defined solely by these common law principles. To a large extent, "fair" is what Parliament or the Legislature says it is. The principles of natural justice and fairness were the invention of the courts, which simply assumed that when Parliament gave an agency the authority to do something Parliament intended that the agency would act in a fair manner. It has been said that in imposing the duty of fairness the courts are merely filling in the gaps left by Parliament.

The implication of this approach, however, is that where Parliament has established the procedure to be followed in any particular instance, then whatever procedure Parliament set out is the procedure to be followed. The application of the principles of natural justice and fairness are subject to statute and may, thus, be ousted by legislation.[15] A legislative direction (which can be in either statute, regulation or some other binding statement of law) respecting a particular procedure is paramount over any common law concepts which may be in conflict with it.[16] Nonetheless, the courts will generally require clear and unequivocal

---

14 At pp. 554-555 D.L.R.

15 This broad principle, however, is today subject to the Charter. The power of Parliament and the Legislature to establish procedure is subject to the rights guaranteed by the constitution (*Singh v. Canada (Minister of Employment & Immigration)* (1985), 17 D.L.R. (4th) 244 (S.C.C.)). In addition, Parliament or the Legislature may impose controls upon itself. For example, federal law is subject to the provisions of the Canadian Bill of Rights. Similarly, Quebec has adopted the Quebec Charter of Rights.

16 See, for example, *Innisfil (Township) v. Vespra (Township)*, [1981] 2 S.C.R. 145, 12 O.M.B.R. 129, 123 D.L.R. (3d) 530, 37 N.R. 43 at p. 547 where the Court noted that: "These principles [natural justice], of course, are of diminished impact in instances . . . where the constituting statutes themselves outline the necessity for a hearing and, by direction and indirection, establish the procedure to be followed in the conduct of such a hearing. In proceeding to examine some of the authorities, new and old, one must constantly be cautious that the overriding consideration is

language in order to find natural justice ousted by Parliament.[17] Furthermore, the principles of natural justice and fairness can still be relevant even in the face of a legislatively created procedure. One will often find gaps in legislative directions or discover that not all the questions respecting the matter in hand were dealt with.[18] In such cases, one looks to the common law requirements of natural justice and fairness to supplement the deficient legislative direction.[19]

Having said this, the power of Parliament and the Legislature to oust the principles of natural justice and fairness, is, today, subject to the guarantees of the constitution, and particularly the Charter of Rights and Freedoms.[20] In addition, Parliament or the Legislature may impose controls upon itself in the form of generic rights or procedures statutes such as, at the federal level, the Canadian Bill of Rights, and at the provincial level statutes such as the Quebec Charter of Rights, Ontario's Statutory Powers Procedure Act, Alberta's Administrative Procedures Act, or the various provincial human rights legislation. As these statutes contain paramountcy provisions, their procedural provisions or guarantees can displace the procedural provisions of a particular statute.

Consequently, in approaching any procedural question, one first looks to see whether there is a legislative provision dictating the procedure to be followed. To the extent that that procedure does not conflict with the Charter, or the Canadian Bill of Rights (for federal legislation) or any other paramount provincial statute, one follows that procedure.

Where the legislation is silent, or there is a gap to be filled, one looks to the common law principles of natural justice and fairness. One may also find oneself looking to those principles in the context of a conflict between a particular piece of legislation and a paramount generic statute such as the Statutory Powers Procedure Act as many of the concepts in those statutes are fed by the original

---

the statutes themselves." The authority of Parliament to oust natural justice was similarly recognized in *Re Bradley and Ottawa Professional Fire Fighters Association*, [1967], 2 O.R. 311 (C.A.) at p. 317.

17 *Innisfil (Township) v. Vespra (Township)*, [1981] 2 S.C.R. 145, 12 O.M.B.R. 129, 123 D.L.R. (3d) 530, 37 N.R. 43. In *Collins v. Pension Commission (Ont.)* (1986), 56 O.R. (2d) 274, 21 Admin. L.R. 186, 31 D.L.R. (4th) 86 (Div. Ct.), *Downing v. Graydon* (1978), 21 O.R. (2d) 292, 92 D.L.R. (3d) 355 (C.A.), and *Hryciuk v. Ontario (Lieutenant Governor)* (1994), 18 O.R. (3d) 695, 26 Admin. L.R. (2d) 271, (*sub nom. Commission of Inquiry into removal from office*) 115 D.L.R. 94th) 227 (Div. Ct.) express statutory exclusions of Ontario's Statutory Powers Procedure Act were found not to exclude the operation of the common law principles of natural justice and fairness notwithstanding that the SPPA is generally considered to be a codification of many of those principles.

18 For an example of a gap, one need only look to the direction in Ontario's SPPA that the notice given shall be "reasonable" with no indication as to what constitutes "reasonable". A similar difficulty arises in the case of Alberta's APA where it requires that the notice given shall be "adequate".

19 *Collins v. Estevan Roman Catholic Separate School Division No. 27*, [1988] 6 W.W.R. 97, 68 Sask. R. 86 (C.A.).

20 *Singh v. Canada (Minister of Employment & Immigration)* (1985), 17 D.L.R. (4th) 244 (S.C.C.).

common law principles.[21] In determining the appropriateness of a procedure under the common law one asks the following questions:

   i. What mandate is the agency supposed to be attempting to accomplish through the hearing?

  ii. Will the procedure contemplated contribute to the accomplishment of this mandate?

 iii. What interest do the participants have in the proceeding?

 iv. Will the procedure contemplated be adequate (or will it impede) their ability to sufficiently know the case to be met and to present their case in turn in order to protect that interest?

  v. If there is a conflict between the procedure required for accomplishment of the agency's mandate and the procedure required for an individual to protect his interest, which of the two, ultimately, is the more important and can a compromise procedure be arrived at which will contribute to the accomplishment of the more important while providing some protections to the latter?

Where one must develop one's own procedures, the key in evaluating the procedural content of a hearing is to determine whether or not the available procedures facilitate or frustrate the opportunity for an informed and effective presentation of a party's case to the tribunal involved.

The factors which will be of importance in determining the degree of "fairness" required in any process are:

1.   The nature of the interest of the individual, which may be affected by the exercise of the agency's powers. The more the interest likely to be affected by a proceeding is unique and personal to one individual the greater the package of procedural rights accorded to that individual. At one end of the spectrum one has a proceeding whose only subject is the interest of one person where he will, for example, be given the right to participate at every stage of the hearing, to test and argue each point as the matters progresses to its end. At the other end of the spectrum, the individual might be only one of thousands whose interest might be affected. Here his right to participate might be restricted to the right to come before the agency and make his views and the information he possess known to it. But he might not have the right to be advised of the views of every other person or to test each fact as it goes before the agency, or to argue each policy matter. This is partly a matter of

---

21 For example, the concept of "fundamental justice" in s. 7 of the Charter includes the procedural rights encompassed by natural justice. The determination of what constitutes "reasonable" notice under Ontario's Statutory Powers Procedure Act is also guided by the common law principles.

practicality, and partly a presumption that the more uniquely one's interest is to be affected, the more likely it is that you are the person who possesses the information necessary to decide it.

2. The consequences of the exercise of those powers upon those interests. The greater the impact of a decision on an individual, the more likely he is to be accorded greater procedural rights.

3. The nature of the tribunal and its powers. The concept of "fairness" is closely connected to the nature of whatever the agency must do. For example, it is not fair to deny an individual the right to extensively place or test facts before an administrative agency if the agency's decision, by its nature, cannot be made so much on facts but rather on broad theory or policy. Equally, the nature of the decision-maker itself guides the courts in determining the extent of what Parliament must have felt was fair. When Parliament selects a body such as the Governor-in-Council or a Minister to be the decision-maker, Parliament is assumed to have known that these bodies, by their nature, do not, and cannot operate as does a court. No one would seriously argue that someone, whose interests are to be affected by a decision of the Governor-in-Council, could or should expect to receive an oral hearing before the Governor General and cabinet. Ministers operate as the apex of a department and rely extensively upon the advice they receive from staff. They could not be expected to operate without relying extensively upon that assistance.

No one of these factors are determinative of a question. They are considered as a whole. The inherent fluidity in the common law's approach to the appropriate procedural content of administrative hearings is at once both its most appealing and confounding property. On the one hand, this flexibility takes into account the often significant differences which exist among administrative tribunals and the tasks entrusted to them. Yet, it also leads to a good deal of unpredictability, and hampers efforts to provide certainty in the law. The best guide is that quoted above in Dickson J.'s dissenting judgment in *Homex*. Thus, one must recognize that there is a "sliding scale" of procedural rights; in other words, if one takes the procedural content of a court as the ideal standard, the further removed from the judicial model a particular function is, the weaker will be the analogy between the procedure appropriate for its exercise and that followed in a court of law.[22] Looking at a scale with the courts at one end and the Legislature at the other, the more the proceeding in question approaches one of those two points, the more the procedural package of rights is fixed by reference to the procedure associated with it.

---

22 *de Smith, Judicial Review of Administrative Action*, J.N. Evans (ed.) (4th ed., 1980) p. 185.

12.2(d) The Form of Administrative Agency Hearings Is Dictated By The Mandate To Be Accomplished

As hearings exist to garner information necessary to perform a particular statutory mandate it is obvious that the particular mandate assigned to an agency will affect the form of the hearing. Different mandates can result in different procedural requirements.[23] A hearing called primarily to canvass community opinion should be conducted in a different fashion than disciplinary proceedings before a professional body.[24] Thus, it is important, in structuring one's hearing, that you adapt the process to the thing which is supposed to be accomplished by it.

One thing which must be noted, however, is that while an agency hearing and a court hearing may both be oral, an agency hearing is not a court hearing. It is not held for the same purpose and, consequently, it need not, and in some cases it should not, be conducted as if were a court hearing.

Generally, court hearings involve the resolution of a dispute between private individuals, or the resolution of a dispute between a private individual and the state, regarding private rights (a lis inter partes). Agency hearings are held under a large assortment of conditions, few of which could be said to involve a lis inter partes (that is, conflicting private claims between competing parties). Courts should not pretend, as they often do, that there is a lis in administrative agency matters where there is none simply because the courts are comfortable with lises. In fact, courts' allegations that lises exist when they do not exist confuse the real issue which is the public interest. Courts sometimes "shove square pegs into round holes" by saying "there is a sort of lis, between sort of parties". I have read court decisions that refer to a situation where there is no true lis inter partes a "quasi-lis between quasi-parties". In *Hurd v. Hewitt* [25] the Ontario Court of Appeal (in obiter-and incorrectly, in my opinion) stated that:

---

23 *Walters v. Essex County Board of Education*, [1974] S.C.R. 481, 38 D.L.R. (3d) 693 at p. 699 D.L.R.

24 This principle is reflected in decisions such as *Bortolotti v. Ministry of Housing* (1977), 15 O.R. (2d) 617, 76 D.L.R. (3d) 408 (C.A.) where the Ontario Court of Appeal, in discussing the applicability of the rules of evidence to a commission of inquiry, stated that: "The Commission of Inquiry is charged with the duty to consider, recommend and report. It has a very different function to perform from that of a court of law, or an administrative tribunal, or an arbitrator, all of which deal with rights between parties. . . . It is quite clear that a commission appointed under the Public Inquiries Act, 1971 is not bound by the rules of evidence as applied traditionally in the Court, with the exception of the exclusionary rule as to privilege (s. 11). . . . The approach of the Commission should not be technical or unduly legalistic one. A full and fair inquiry in the public interest is what is sought in order to elicit all relevant information pertaining to the subject-matter of the inquiry."

25 (1994), 20 O.R. (3d) 639 , 120 D.L.R. (4th) 105 (C.A.).

[c]ivil trials and purely administrative hearings,[26] be they public or private, are invariably disputes between parties or institutions. There is some lis between the participants presented for determination by the decision-maker. The driving force is the adversary system which assumes that each party will present the best possible evidence and argument in favour of that party's position and that the role of the tribunal or judge is to reach a decision based upon that evidence and argument.

With respect, the Court of Appeal is simply not correct in this assertion. While it is true that some administrative proceedings may be adversarial in nature, it is by far too broad a statement that all proceedings are driven by an adversarial engine. The Supreme Court of Canada recognized this in its decision in *Innisfil (Township) v. Vespra (Township)*:[27]

The procedural format adopted by the administrative tribunal must adhere to the provisions of the parent statute of the Board. The process of interpreting and applying statutory policy will be the dominant influence in the workings of such an administrative tribunal. Where the Board proceeds in the discharge of its mandate to determine the rights of the contending parties before it on the traditional basis wherein the onus falls upon the contender to introduce the facts and submissions upon which he will rely, the Board technique will take on something of the appearance of a traditional Court. Where, on the other hand, the Board, by its legislative mandate or the nature of the subject matter assigned to its administration, is more concerned with community interests at large, and with technical policy aspects of a specialized subject, one cannot expect the tribunal to function in the manner of the traditional Court. This is particularly so where Board membership is drawn partly or entirely from persons experienced or trained in the sector of activity consigned to the administrative supervision of the Board. Again where the Board in its statutory role takes on the complexion of a department of the executive branch of Government concerned with the execution of a policy laid down in broad concept by the Legislature, and where the Board has the delegated authority to issue regulations or has a broad discretionary power to license persons or activities, the trappings and habits of the traditional Courts have long ago been discarded.[28]

It is not possible to go through the many grounds upon which an agency is seized with jurisdiction. Fundamentally, the majority of hearings in Canada are brought about because:

---

26 The Court made an exception for investigations and public inquiries.

27 (1981), 123 D.L.R. (3d) 530 (S.C.C.) at pp. 546-47.

28 The Court had earlier, on the same page, noted that "That is not to say that because our Court system is founded upon these institutions and procedures [adversarial system] that administrative tribunals must apply the same techniques. Indeed, there are many tribunals in the modern community which do not follow the traditional adversarial road." The Court had made an earlier statement to the same effect, in *Kane v. University of British Columbia*, [1980] 1 S.C.R. 1105, 18 B.C.L.R. 124, [1980] 3 W.W.R. 125, 110 D.L.R. (3d) 311, 31 N.R. 214, respecting a university Board of Governors conducting a disciplinary hearing: "The Board need not assume the trappings of a Court. There is no *lis inter partes*, no prosecutor and no accused."

(1) an industry or person may not be able to proceed with a course of action without the consent and order of a specific agency; there is likely no lis there;

(2) a person may be appealing from a decision made by another agency or a minister. This may or may not involve a lis, but often not;

(3) an agency may have been asked to hold a hearing by the Royal Representative, or because a complaint has been lodged with it, or because as part of its function the agency requires or desires public input; there is likely no lis here;

(4) a utility or seller of services may need to have a tribunal establish a rate for its product; there is likely no lis here;

(5) many by-laws cannot come into force without certain administrative agency approvals (or when challenged require agency approval); there is likely no lis here;

(6) many certificates of public necessity can only issue after a public hearing; there is likely no lis here; and

(7) some agency proceedings involve requests by specified claimants upon public funds especially created for them (eg. social assistance claims, pensioners, veterans, victims of crime). In these proceedings there is only one party, the claimant who, often may not in the position to present the very best case to be made for him; there is likely no lis here.

There are literally dozens of other ways a matter can come before an agency. Many can only be resolved through a public hearing because the mandating legislation says so, yet there may not be any parties in the traditional sense. Even where there may be parties, there is often a third interest being represented, the public interest, which the agency is charged with defending. While it is, apparently, easy to be misled by the simple fact that an agency may be conducting an oral hearing in which argument and evidence is led, this superficial appearance should not blind one to the fact that the agency may be performing quite a different function than that being carried out in an oral hearing before a court. This was recognized by the Ontario Divisional Court when it held that the Ontario Municipal Board in considering an approval or modification of an official plan is performing an administrative function. The Court noted that although the Board must give the parties before it a full and fair hearing and consider their submissions, it is not bound by their views and it may choose to overrule them in light of the larger considerations of administrative policy. The fact that there is a hearing does not transform the matter into a lis between the parties. "A hearing means that the parties and the public be given an opportunity to be heard . . . the

Board...must exercise its independent judgment on the merits of the application. . . ."[29]

Agency hearings should be structured in a way which takes into account the mandate to be accomplished and the circumstances, including the number and type of participants, relevant to the performance of that mandate. Many agencies may choose to follow a structure very similar to that employed by the courts. The applicants are more or less given the carriage of the matter (ie. they decide when and how witnesses are called or information is presented) and the hearing proceeds generally as follows:

<u>Applicant Presents His Case</u>

Calls first witness examination-in-chief by applicant
cross-examination by respondents
re-examination by applicant
clarification questions by decision-maker

Calls second witness
examination-in-chief by applicant
cross-examination by respondents
re-examination by applicant
clarification questions by decision-maker

and so forth until the applicant has no further witnesses

<u>Respondent Presents His Case</u>

Calls first witness
examination-in-chief by respondent
cross-examination by applicant
re-examination by respondent
clarification questions by decision-maker

and so forth until respondent has no further witnesses

Summary of evidence and argument by applicant
Summary of evidence and argument by respondent

While in some cases this process may be very effective, there is no rule that an oral hearing must be structured this way.[30] A decision-maker should look at what it hopes to accomplish through its process, the nature of the matter which it

---

29 *Oro (Township) v. BAFMA Inc.* (1995), 21 O.R. (3d) 483, 31 O.M.B.R. 487, 121 D.L.R. (4th) 538 (Div. Ct.).

30 There is no rule that an agency must conduct its hearings in a prescribed sequence without exception (*Dilts v. University of Manitoba Faculty Association*, [1973] 5 W.W.R. 263, 41 D.L.R. (3d) 401 (Man. C.A.)).

will be dealing, and the types of participants involved, to structure a procedure that best suits these demands. Let me give the example here of the (now defunct) Ontario Residential Tenancy Commission which, among other things, had the mandate of controlling residential rents and of approving rent increases sought by landlords. This was a cost analysis process in which rent increases were based on increases in the operating costs of a residential complex. Landlords were as frequently not represented by legal counsel as they were represented by accountants, or other forms of rent review agents, or they represented themselves. Hearings also often involved large numbers of tenants (represented and unrepresented by counsel or agent). In order to facilitate the understanding of the extensive costing information submitted, the Commission created a pre-published form listing each likely expense on a line-by-line basis (heat, hydro, maintenance, etc.). Landlords, who were required by statute to file their documentary evidence in advance of a hearing, were asked by the Commission to arrange their filed documentary material according to the categories in which they had put a particular expense on this form. At some Commission hearings a landlord or his counsel was not simply asked to present his case. Rather, the parties were advised that the decision-maker would be using the pre-published form as a procedural guide and that they would work through each item as it appeared on the form. For each item, the landlord was permitted to explain his case and submit his evidence, the tenants were also permitted to present their case on that item as well. In this way the hearing proceeding on a logical basis that made it easy for everyone to follow (and made it easier for the decision-maker as well when it came to making its decision). Furthermore, some Commissioners never applied the restrictions imposed by the rules concerning examination-in-chief, cross-examination and re-examination in my proceedings as they felt that the value in getting all the information relevant to the matter, and the time saved in not having to deal with technical objections as to questions had to be asked, outweighed the possible delays to the proceedings arising from not requiring parties to follow the strict legal rules of presentation.

I suggest that you will be in trouble, if rather than identifying the needs of your system and the mandate which you are given, you simply adopt, rigidly, the system adopted by the courts, without considering whether that will operate fairly in the context of your mandate.

12.2(e) The Role of An Agency Member Is Not the Same As The Role of A Judge

Just as an agency hearing is not a court hearing, an agency member is not restricted to the same role at a hearing as is a judge in court. Agency proceedings often do not involve an equal contest between interests represented by trained representatives. Frequently parties will be unsophisticated and unrepresented. Even where the parties are ably represented the public interest which is represented by the agency often requires that an agency member play a more active role in a proceeding than would a judge in court. In some cases the government may be represented. But this does not, it itself, transform the proceedings into the traditional judicial, adversarial model.[31]

Unlike judges, agency members, as a rule, are permitted to ask questions to determine the truth of a matter. They are not restricted simply to determining a matter on the basis of the case, the issues or the information which the parties chose to present to them.[32]

However, as I have argued in ''Evidence Before Administrative Agencies'' (1995), 8 C.J.A.L.P. 263 at 285:

> Notwithstanding, agency members must still strive to maintain impartiality. They must avoid making enquiries in such an aggressive manner as to appear to be attempting to build a case for one side or the other. They must not act in a biased or unfair way. Decision-makers must not ask their questions in a bullying manner, or in an insensitive way which indicates a clear bias.[33] Nor, absent some legislative authority, do agencies have the authority (beyond asking questions of the parties

---

31 In *R. v. National Insurance Commissioner, Ex parte Viscusi*, [1974] 1 W.L.R. 646 (C.A.) Lord Denning M.R. illustrated this point in discussing proceedings before an industrial injuries board:
  At the outset I would like to say a word about the proceedings on an application for insurance benefit. The proceedings are not to be regarded as if they were a law suit between opposing parties. The insured person is not a plaintiff under a legal burden of proof. The proceedings are more in the nature of an inquiry before an investigating body charged with the task of finding out what happened and what are the consequences. The man tells about the accident and his injury. He describes his disablement. The Ministry are not there to oppose him. They are simply there to help the tribunal to come to a correct decision. It is very proper for the Ministry to make investigations, to get medical reports, and to put them before the tribunal. They do it not as trying to defeat the man's claim, but simply to see whether his case is a true one or not.

32 In *Kalina v. Directors of Chiropractic (Ontario)* (1981), 35 O.R. (2d) 626 (Div. Ct.), leave to appeal to C.A. refused (1982), 35 O.R. (2d) 626 (C.A.), Justice Steele wrote (at p. 628) ''A member of a Board has greater latitude than a judge because he has a public duty to inquire into the merits of an application. Short of apparent bias or oppressiveness, there is nothing wrong with a member asking questions.'' For other cases to the same effect see *Mahendran v. Minister of Employment & Immigration* (1991), 14 Imm. L.R. (2d) 38, 134 N.R. 316 (Fed. C.A.), leave to appeal to S.C.C. refused (1992), 138 N.R. 404 (note); and *W. (C.) v. Manitoba (Mental Health Review Board)* (1994), 26 C.P.C. (3d) 1, [1994] 8 W.W.R. 761, 95 Man. R. (2d) 153, 70 W.A.C. 153 (C.A.), leave to appeal to S.C.C. refused 36 C.P.C. (3d) 247 (note), [1995] 6 W.W.R. lxxii (note) (S.C.C.).

33 *Yusuf v. Canada (Minister of Employment & Immigration)*, [1992] 1 F.C. 629, 7 Admin. L.R. (2d) 86, *(sub nom. Yusuf v. Ministre de l'emploi et de l'immigration)* 133 N.R. 391 (C.A.), *Sivaguru v. Canada (Minister of Employment & Immigration)*, [1992] 2 F.C. 374, 11 Admin. L.R. (2d) 220, 16 Imm. L.R. (2d) 85, 139 N.R. 220 (C.A.), *Rajaratnam v. Canada (Minister of Employment & Immigration)* (1991), 135 N.R. 300 (C.A.). See also *Rusonik v. Law Society ed. of Upper Canada* (1988), 28 O.A.C. 57 (Div. Ct.) where the court concluded that in disciplinary proceedings, although the disciplinary committtee had a duty to act judicially, it should not be judged by precisely the same exacting standards required of a judge in court.

and witnesses in the proceedings) to investigate matters themselves.[34] Even with such authority, decision-makers should not, themselves, go out and investigate a matter before or after the hearing. Why? Because the perception is, having investigated the matter you will have come to some preliminary views or identify yourself with one position or another. Rather than asking questions in order to determine the truth, you may be asking questions to confirm the views you have already formed. Finally, the fruits of any investigation must be shared with the parties.[35]

Having outlined these overall guiding principles, let us now look at the specific components of a hearing, starting with the most important, notice.

12.3 NOTICE

12.3(a) What Is Notice?

Isn't it:

embarrassing to open your hearing in an empty room?

infuriating to be ordered to do something with no chance to say anything about it first?

frightening to face a secret agenda?

The purpose of notice is, among other things, to ensure that these things do not happen.

As the main purpose in holding a hearing is to help the agency get the information it needs to perform its mandate, a decision-maker will want the individuals with that knowledge to come to it. People who will be affected by an agency's decision will want to come to make certain that it has all the information they think is important. And both the agency and those who may be affected by its actions, will want to know what the agency is dealing with in the proceedings in order to decide what they have to do. Thus, before a hearing can be held notice must be given.

Notice Can Refer to Different Things

Notice takes many forms in a proceeding. The filing of an application with an agency can be considered to be giving notice to the agency that it is being

---

34 *Teneycke v. Matsqui Institution Disciplinary Court*, [1990] 2 F.C. 106, 43 Admin. L.R. 294, 33 F.T.R. 181.

35 *Lord v. Yukon Territory (Commissioner)* (1992), 6 Admin. L.R. (2d) 241 (Y.T. S.C.), *Pfizer Co. v. Deputy Minister of National Revenue (Customs & Excise)*, [1977] 1 S.C.R. 456, *New Brunswick (Minister of Health & Community Services) v. M. (R.-M.)* (1993), 141 N.B.R. (2d) 16, 361 A.P.R. 16 (C.A.).

called upon to do something and what that something is.[36] A party's keeping an agency advised of his changes of address can be considered an aspect of notice. Service of an application on a party is giving notice to him that a particular proceeding will be taking place that can affect his interests. The most obvious aspect of notice is the notice of hearing when an agency advises those concerned of when and where a specific proceeding may be held. Notice also extends to telling those concerned what the issues are in a proceeding and making known the evidence which is to be used so that the participants can familiarize themselves with it and ensure that their case is adequately documented while the weaknesses in the opposition's is fully identified. All these difference aspects of notice have one purpose: telling someone who needs to know the things he needs to know in order that the agency can properly perform its statutory mandate.

All aspects of notice have one thing in common — KNOWLEDGE. That is the essence of notice. Notice is given to individuals to ensure that they are sufficiently aware of the subject matter of the proceeding that they can decide if the matter affects them and, if it does, that they can prepare and fully present their cases. Notice is given to the agency so that it knows what it is being called upon to look into or decide. While most of the judicial decisions approach the question from the perspective of the protection of individual rights (i.e. being able to protect one's interests) an agency also has an interest in the provision of adequate notice. The agency needs information in order to best perform its mandate. The giving of adequate notice ensures that those who are likely to possess the best information respecting a matter are in the best position to produce it.[37] Thus, the requirement for notice is both a protection for individual interests and an insurance for the proper accomplishment of an agency's mandate.

The concept of good notice extends beyond the mere giving of a document setting out the time, date, and place of hearing. An individual's right to notice extends to the total package of information necessary for an individual to be able to know what is the subject of the proceedings and to be able to adequately present his case.

12.3(b) Statutory Requirement To Give Notice

If one is lucky, the statute under which the proceedings are being held, or a general procedures statute, such as Ontario's Statutory Powers Procedure Act or Alberta's Administrative Procedures Act, will set out the who, what, when, and how of notice.

---

36 *Mackin v. New Brunswick (Judicial Council)* (1987), 82 N.B.R. (2d) 203, 208 A.P.R. 203, 44 D.L.R. (4th) 730 (N.B.C.A.).

37 This aspect of proper notice was even cited by Justice Laskin in the Supreme Court's seminal decision on fairness *Nicholson v. Haldimand-Norfolk (Regional Municipality) Commissioners of Police*, [1979] 1 S.C.R. 311, 23 N.R. 410, 88 D.L.R. (3d) 671 at p. 682.

12.3(b)(i) Ontario

Ontario's SPPA contains several notice provisions. However, aside from one provision respecting allegations against character, these provisions only deal with the duty on the agency to tell a person the when, why, what and where of a proceeding. The SPPA contemplates three types of hearings: oral, written and electronic. (As noted elsewhere in this book, the idea of a hearing where all three forms of communication are used does not appear to have been contemplated by the legislation. Consequently, the notice provisions found in the statute are basically directed to proceedings which are conducted in their entirety in one form. It is uncertain what type of notice must be given for mixed hearings, or whether special notice must be given before an agency can switch between modes of communication in a proceeding. Presumably common sense will prevail and any questions which may arise as to the adequacy of the notice will be determined by looking to the principles established under natural justice and fairness.)

The relevant provisions are as follows:

6. (1) The parties to a proceeding shall be given reasonable notice of the hearing by the tribunal.

Parties are defined in section 5 as being the persons specified as parties by or under the statute under which the proceeding arises or, if not so specified, persons[38] entitled by law to be parties to the proceeding. As to who is entitled by law to be a party, see the discussion below respecting who must be given notice pursuant to the principles of natural justice and fairness.

(2) A notice of hearing shall include a reference to the statutory authority under which the hearing will be held.

(3) A notice of an oral hearing shall include,

(a) a statement of the time, place and purpose of the hearing; and

(b) a statement that if the party notified does not attend at the hearing, the tribunal may proceed in the party's absence and the party will not be entitled to any further notice in the proceeding.

(4) A notice of a written hearing shall include,

(a) a statement of the time and purpose of the hearing, and details about the manner in which the hearing will be held;

---

38 The Ontario Rent Review Hearings Board once added as parties to an appeal "All the Tenants" in a residential complex. The Divisional Court ruled this improper, noting that the statutory power of the Board was to add as a party any "person" who should have been included as a party. In the opinion of the Court, "All the Tenants" did not represent and was not a person. The Board should have used the actual names of the tenants ((1991), 81 D.L.R. (4th) 145 (Ont. Div. Ct.)).

Since the nature of a written hearing is that it does not start at a particular time but involves the filing, and reading, of written documents over an extended period, it is uncertain what is meant by this requirement that a notice set out the time of a written hearing. Presumably this is a slip in the drafting of the provision and what is likely meant is that the hearing notice set out when the written filings must be made. Note the extra requirement, which is not present in the provisions respecting oral and electronic hearings, that the notice must set out the details about the manner in which the hearing will be held. The statute is silent as to what amount of details must be given. Looking to the underlying principles of natural justice and fairness indicates that these details are likely those which are necessary for the individual concerned to be able to know and present his case. For example, filing deadlines, rights to review the file and comment on other material, etc.

 (b) a statement that the party notified may object to the hearing being held as a written hearing (in which case the tribunal is required to hold it as an electronic or oral hearing) and an indication of the procedure to be followed for that purpose;

 (c) a statement that if the party notified neither acts under clause (b) nor participates in the hearing in accordance with the notice, the tribunal may proceed without the party's participation and the party will not be entitled to any further notice in the proceeding.

(5) A notice of an electronic hearing shall include,

 (a) a statement of the time and purpose of the hearing, and details about the manner in which the hearing will be held;

 (b) a statement that the only purpose of the hearing is to deal with procedural matters, if that is the case;

 (c) if clause (b) does not apply, a statement that the party notified may, by satisfying the tribunal that holding the hearing as an electronic hearing is likely to cause the party significant prejudice, require the tribunal to hold the hearing as an oral hearing, and an indication of the procedure to be followed for that purpose; and

 (d) a statement that if the party notified neither acts under clause (c), if applicable, nor participates in the hearing in accordance with the notice, the tribunal may proceed without the party's participation and the party will not be entitled to any further notice in the proceeding.

8. Where the good character, propriety of conduct or competence of a party is an issue in a proceeding, the party is entitled to be furnished prior to the hearing with reasonable information of any allegations with respect thereto.

As I have written in issue 14 of *Administrative Agency Practice*, at page 97, section 8 "requires the person calling the good character, propriety of conduct or competence of another party into question to provide sufficient information with respect to those allegations in advance of the hearing in order that the person can identify the basis for those allegations and be able to defend himself or herself with respect thereto. It is not sufficient merely to accuse the person of a general type or class of failing (e.g. "X is generally incompetent"). One must identify with sufficient precession the alleged failing and note the grounds or bases on which this conclusion was reached. This information need not be included in the original application or in the notice of hearing provided that it is conveyed in some way to the subject person sufficiently in advance of a hearing to allow a proper defense to be developed. Section 8 does not require the disclosure of the actual evidence which a party intends to use to prove the allegations. The right does not appear to extend to witnesses or to intervenors. Section 8 has been triggered by allegations that a party discriminated against another, did not conduct himself or herself according to the general rules of his or her trade union, is not competent to perform his employment duties, and has committed professional misconduct.[39]

12.3(b)(ii) Alberta

Alberta's Administrative Procedures Act also contains a number of provisions respecting notice. The Alberta statute does not set out as much detail as

---

39 For the major decisions on s. 8, please see the following (all of which are summarized in my article on s. 8 in issue 4 of vol. 1 of *Administrative Agency Practice: DiNardo v. Ontario (Liquor Licence Board)* (1974) 5 O.R. (2d) 124, 49 D.L.R. (3d) 537 (H.C.), *Don Howson Chevrolet Oldsmobile Ltd. v. Registrar of Motor Vehicle Dealers* (1974), 6 O.R. (2d) 39 (Div. Ct.), *Kellar v. College of Physicians & Surgeons (Ontario)* (1977), 17 O.R. (2d) 516 (Div. Ct.), *All Ontario Transport Ltd. v. Ontario (Highway Transport Board)* (1979), 26 O.R. (2d) 202 (Div. Ct.), *Takahashi v. College of Physicians & Surgeons (Ontario)* (1979), 26 O.R. (2d) 353, 102 D.L.R. (3d) 695 (Div. Ct.), *Aamco Automatic Transmissions Inc. v. Simpson* (1980), 29 O.R. (2d) 565, 113 D.L.R. (3d) 650 (Div. Ct.), *Wilson v. College of Physicians & Surgeons (Ontario)* (1981), 24 C.P.C. 52 (Div. Ct.), *Cwinn v. Law Society of Upper Canada* (1980), 28 O.R. (2d) 61, 108 D.L.R. (3d) 381 (Div. Ct.), *Commodore Business Machines Ltd. v. Ontario (Minister of Labour)* (1984), 49 O.R. (2d) 17, 10 Admin. L.R. 130, 6 O.A.C. 176 (Div. Ct.), *Assn. of Professional Engineers (Ont.) v. Smith* (1989), 38 Admin. L.R. 212 (H.C.), *McColl v. Gravenhurst (Town)* (1991), 52 O.A.C. 398 (Div. Ct.). *Richmond Square Development Corp. v. Middlesex Condominium Corp.* (1993), 103 D.L.R. (4th) 437 (Div. Ct.), *Hryciuk v. Ontario (Lt. Governor)* (1994), 18 O.R. (3d) 695, (sub nom. *Hryciuk v. Commission of Inquiry Re Judge Hyrciuk* 71 O.A.C. 289, sub nom. *Hryciuk v. Ontario (Commission of Inquiry Into Removal From Office* 115 D.L.R. (4th) 227 (Div. Ct.), *Dubajic v. Walbar Machine Products of Canada* (1980), 1 C.H.R.R. D/228 (Bd. of Inquiry), *Bezeau v. Ontario Institute for Studies in Education* (1982) 3 C.H.R.R. D/177 (Bd. of Inquiry), *L.I.U.N.A., Local 183 v. Olympia Floor & Wall Tile*, [1987] O.L.R.B. Rep. 762 (Ont. Labour Relations Bd.), *Pebra Peterborough Employees Association v. Pebra Peterborough Inc.*, [1987] O.L.R.B. Rep. 421 (Ont. Labour Relations Bd.), *International Brotherhood of Painters and Allied Trade, Local 1590 v. Pedersen*, [1987] O.L.R.B. Rep. 367 (Ont. Labour Relations Bd.), *Bhadauria v. Toronto (City) Board of Education* (1988), 9 C.H.R.R. D/706 (Bd. of Inquiry), *Morin v. Noranda Inc. and I.G. Barrie, Hemlo Project* (1988), 9 C.H.R.R. D/813 (Bd. of Inquiry) *Re Coalition of Laid-off Workers*, [1990] O.L.R.B. Rep. 129 (Ont. Labour Relations Bd.).

Ontario's SPPA, but the thrust of the provisions are similar and clearly reflect the requirements of natural justice and fairness.

> 3. When
>
>> (a) an application is made to an authority, or
>>
>> (b) an authority on its own initiative proposes
>
> to exercise a statutory power, the authority shall give to all parties adequate notice of the application which it has before it or of the power which it intends to exercise.

Somewhat more guidance is given in Alberta's statute than in Ontario's as to who is a party. Section 1 defines ''party'' as meaning ''a person whose rights will be varied or affected by the exercise of a statutory power or by an act or thing done pursuant to that power''.

> 4. Before an authority, in the exercise of a statutory power, refuses the application of, or makes a decision or order adversely affecting the rights of a party, the authority
>
>> (b) shall inform the party of the facts in its possession or the allegations made to it contrary to the interests of the party in sufficient detail
>>
>>> (i) to permit him to understand the facts or allegations, and
>>>
>>> (ii) to afford him a reasonable opportunity to furnish relevant evidence to contradict or explain the facts or allegations.

The case law appears to view the requirements of section 4 as being essentially similar to those imposed by natural justice and fairness.[40]

12.3(c) Natural Justice and Fairness

Notice is also an essential component of the audi alteram partem aspect of natural justice.[41] Thus, even where a statute is silent respecting procedural matters, the principles of natural justice and fairness will likely impose some duty to give notice. However, just as the extent of all the rights encompassed by natural justice are shaped by the circumstances of the particular case, so to is the extent of the common law requirement to give notice. The necessity to give notice, what must

---

40 See for example, *Peacock v. Surface Rights Board (Alta.)* (1989), 94 A.R. 25 (Q.B.) and *Central Western Ry. Corp. v. Surface Rights Board* (1987), 56 Alta. L.R. 115 (Q.B.).

41 *Knight v. Indian Head School Division No. 19*, [1990] 1 S.C.R. 653, 43 Admin. L.R. 157, [1990] 3 W.W.R. 289, 69 D.L.R. (4th) 489, *Sinkovich v. Police Bd. of Commissioners (Strathroy)* (1988), 65 O.R. (2d) 292, 28 O.A.C. 326 (Div. Ct.), *Young v. Cape Breton County* (1987), 77 N.S.R. (2d) 389, 191 A.P.R. 389 (S.C.), *Rochon v. Spirit River School Division #47* (1994), 24 Admin. L.R. (2d) 115, 111 D.L.R. (4th) 452 (Alta. C.A.), *Gage v. Ontario (Attorney General)* (1992), 90 D.L.R. (4th) 537, 55 O.A.C. 47 (Div. Ct.).

be given and when is dictated by the circumstances.[42] The entitlement to notice, and the amount of notice which must be given, will be dependant on the nature of the interest to be protected, the seriousness of the consequences to the individual of the proceedings, the issues which must be canvassed, the type of evidence and argument involved. All these factors combine to determine the extent of the notice to be given. Notice, as an aspect of natural justice, is a balancing of the ability of an agency to accomplish its mandate with the requirement of an individual to know what is happening in order to protect his individual interest. In considering whether the Ontario Pension Commission was required to give employees notice of an application by an employer to withdraw surplus funds from their pension plan Justice Reid possed the question as follows:

> Is the requirement of notice imposed by common law? Does the doctrine of fairness require it? Those questions require consideration of the nature of the commission's mandate, and the nature of the interest that members of the plan, or their agent, the union had in the subject-matter of the commission's deliberations.[43]

What amounts to adequate notice is, thus, a combination of a number of factors such as the importance of the mandate of the agency, the importance of the interest of the individual at stake, the nature of the case (complex or simple), and the type of information or argument which must be prepared or reviewed in order to be able to adequately present one case.

---

42 *R. v. Ontario (Racing Commission)*, [1971] 1 O.R. 400 (C.A.), *Quebec (Attorney General) v. Canada (National Energy Board)*, [1994] 1 S.C.R. 159, 20 Admin. L.R. (2d) 79, 112 D.L.R. (4th) 129, 163 N.R. 241.

43 See, for example, *Skinner v. Canada (Minister of the Environment)* (1986), 10 F.T.R. 67 where the fact that the interest at stake was only the ability of a visitor to a national park to allow her dog to run loose in the park. The Federal Court Trial Division felt that only the basic requirements of procedural fairness were required. After being notified by park officials on several occasions of public complaints about the dog's conduct, including a warning that if that conduct was not immediately curbed the dog would be ordered to be removed, the visitor was finally served with such an order following her failure to do anything. Although the visitor was not given formal notice at the time of the final issuance of the order, the Court concluded that "upon considering the particular situation and the nature of this particular case" that no error had been made by the officials. In other words, small interest, small impact, small notice requirement. In *Shah v. Canada (Minister of Employment & Immigration)* (1994), 170 N.R. 238 (Fed. C.A.) the Federal Court of Appeal held that in an application for admission to Canada on compassionate and humanitarian grounds "the applicant does not have a "case to meet" of which he must be given notice; rather it is for him to persuade the decision-maker that he should be given exceptional treatment and exempted from the general requirements of the law. No hearing need be held and no reasons need be given. The officer is not required to put before the applicant any tentative conclusions she may be drawing from the material before her, not even as to apparent contradictions that concern her. Of course, if she is going to rely on extrinsic evidence, not brought forward by the applicant, she must give him a chance to respond to such evidence."

12.3(c)(i) Who Is To Get Notice

The superficial answer to who is to get notice is the parties to the proceeding. Of course, this begs the question of who are the parties. In the absence of a statutory definition of "party" one must have recourse to the common law for guidance.

The question of who is to get notice of a proceeding is an extremely vexing one. Subject to statute, the general rule as to who is to get notice of a proceeding is that expressed by Lord Denning in *Selvaragan v. Race Relations Board:*

> The fundamental rule is that, if a person may be subjected to pains or penalties, or be exposed to prosecution or proceedings, or deprived of remedies or redress, or in some such way adversely affected by the investigation and report, then he should be told the case against him and be afforded a fair opportunity of answering it.[44]

Of course, the world is an interconnected place and it is not every individual who is caught in the widening ripples resulting from administrative action who is entitled to notice. Only individuals whose interests will be *directly* affected by what the agency is doing must receive notice. The limits of Lord Denning's general rule were noted by Marceau J.A. in *Canadian Transit Co. v. Public Service Staff Relations Board (Can.):*

> It is clear to me that mere interest in the eventual outcome of a proceeding before a tribunal, whether financial or otherwise, is not in itself sufficient to give an individual a right to participate therein. The demands of natural justice and procedural fairness certainly do not require so much and in any event it would be impossible in practice to go that far. In my judgment, to be among the interested parties that a tribunal ought to involve in a proceeding before it to satisfy the requirements of the audi alteram partem principle, an individual must be directly and necessarily affected by the decision to be made. His interest must not be merely indirect or contingent, as it is when the decision may reach him only through an intermediate conduit alien to the preoccupation of the tribunal, such as a contractual relationship with one of the parties immediately involved.[45]

Unfortunately, making this determination is not always easy. Where an individual's particular interests will be singled out and extensively affected by the agency's actions it is clear that notice should be given to him.[46] However, the

---

44 [1976], 1 All. E.R. 13 as quoted with approval by the Supreme Court of Canada in *Nicholson v. Haldimand-Norfolk (Regional Municipality) Commissioners of Police*, [1979] 1 S.C.R. 311, 23 N.R. 410, 88 D.L.R. (3d) 671, 23 N.R. 410 (Laskin J.).

45 (1989), 99 N.R. 330 (Fed. C.A.).

46 See, for example, *Re Mannion (No. 2)* (1983), 44 O.R. (2d) 37 (H.C.) where the fact that a group may have an intellectual or philosophical interest in a question, or even have put in briefs and arguments to the Legislature in the creation of a statute, does not "determine that they, of necessity, have an "interest" in any subsequent litigation interpreting parts of such legislation."

interests being affected are not always self evident. For example, in rent control hearings in Ontario, tenants were able to bring applications to the Residential Tenancy Commission for a determination of the lawful rent chargeable for their units during their tenancies. It was not uncommon for individuals who were former tenants to bring such applications respecting the periods of their tenancy. In such cases it was clear that the landlord of the building to whom they paid the rent (and who would have to repay any overcharges) should receive notice of the application. However, since current rents were in many cases based on the lawful rents charged in the past, notice was also required to be given to the current landlord (if the building had changed hands since the tenancy in question) and the current tenants as their rents would be affected by any Commission's declaration of the legal rent on the application.[47] Thus, even though these latter individuals neither charged nor paid the rents which were the subject of the proceedings, the fact that their current rental structure would be affected by any declaration arising from the application meant that they also were entitled to notice of the proceedings. (Even though, in practice, they frequently had no information which could contribute to the determination to be made.)[48] To illustrate this further, one need only consider the *Canadian Transit* case noted earlier. There Justice Marceau noted that the determination of affected interest could be circuitous process and granted standing to a bridge owner in a labour dispute before the Public Service Staff Relations Board between the federal government and its employees concerning allegedly dangerous conditions relating to the bridge . Notwithstanding his earlier statement standing should not be given to an individual who would only be affected by proceedings through contractual relations, Justice Marceau noted that the bridge owner was required by statute to maintain its bridge to certain standards and that the Board would be required in the course of its proceedings to determine whether the bridge owner was maintaining these standards.[49] Where there is doubt, the safest approach may simply be to give notice

---

47 In such cases, where the names of the persons are not known, it is usually sufficient if the notice is given in such a way that the concerned person can identify himself. For example, notices sent to a particular municipal address addressed to "occupant" would likely be acceptable. The question at stake in the *Central Ontario Coalition* case (1984), 46 O.R. (2d) 715 (Div. Ct.) was whether an individual could know from the geographical description of the area to be affected whether the individual should be concerned with the proceedings. (The Court found that they could not.)

48 In *Foothills v. Alta. Assess. App. Bd.* (1986), 72 A.R. 370 (*sub nom. Foothills (Municipal District) v. Okotoks (Town)* (Q.B.) the Municipal District of Foothills was entitled to notice of an assessment appeal by one of the towns in the Municipal District respecting payments to the school district where any lowering in the town's assessment would automatically result in a proportionate increase in the assessment of the Municipal District.

49 For other cases where the notice requirement might not have seen self evident see *Manitoba (Egg Producers' Marketing Bd.) v. Siemens* (1989), 58 Man. R. (2d) 81 (Q.B.), affirmed (1989), 62 Man. R. (2d) 59 (C.A.) (changes to an existing quota policy which may adversely affect a quota holder cannot be made without notice to the holder) and *Cline v. New Brunswick (Board of Management)* (1994), 135 N.B.R. (2d) 35 (Q.B.) where the Court held that where a person may

to every person who may appear to be affected in some way. Given the costs of failing to give proper notice, it is probably better to be safe than sorry.

12.3(c)(ii) How Much Information Need Be Given

How much information must be given before one can be said to be able to present one's case? There are two types of information being conveyed by proper notice: information going to the procedure of the matter (when , where and how the matter is to proceed) and information going to the substance of the matter (what concern is actually being dealt with, what are the issues involved, etc.).

Procedural Information

The responsibility for procedural information usually falls on the agency. Procedural information would go to both that information which is necessary to identify where and when a proceeding is to take place and information as to the procedure to be followed leading up to and during that proceeding. With respect to this last point it is likely that the duty would be met by outlining the usual procedures in some form (pamphlets, guidelines, hearing guides and so forth) and making it publicly known that the documentation is available on request or for viewing at some office.[50] Its availability could be noted in any notices to the participants. The Alberta Court of Queen's Bench has stated that "some responsibility for determining the procedure of a particular forum must lie on those who wish to appear before it."[51] Another alternative is to issue procedural orders or notices outlining the procedure to be followed in a particular case.[52]

---

lose a position as a result of the adjudication of a grievance he was to be given adequate notice of the adjudication in order to appear and defend his own case. The analysis can sometimes approach the Byzantine. For example, see *Tovell v. Minister of Natural Resources* (1988), 64 O.R. (2d) 332, 49 D.L.R. (4th) 636 (Div. Ct.), local ratepayers living in proximity to a gravel pit were found not to be "directly affected" by an application for a renewal of the pit's licence as the licence renewal being sought was on identical terms and conditions to the original. Therefore, the court reasoned, the ratepayers were not affected in any way by the issuing of the new licence since there would be no change in the operation!

50 In setting down the usual procedures it may be prudent to attempt to avoid the creation of a "legitimate expectation" of the parties in that particular procedure being followed without exception (for a case of such a legitimate expectation see *Pulp, Paper & Woodworkers of Canada, Local 8 v. Canada (Minister of Agriculture)* (1994), 174 N.R. 37, 84 F.T.R. 80 (note) (C.A.). Thus, the documentation should note that procedures may differ depending on the circumstances of the particular case and inviting inquiries or reserving the discretion to change those procedures before or during a hearing to accommodate the unexpected or unusual.

51 *Robertson v. Edmonton (City)* (1990), 44 Admin. L.R. 27 (Alta. Q.B.). In this case the decision-maker, the city council, had established its procedure in its by-laws. The Court felt that this satisfied a statutory duty to "outline" its procedure. The Court did note that more specific notice would be logical if the city intended to deviate from its procedures.

52 For examples, see Appendix 11.2 and 19.2.

Substantive Information

The duty to give substantive information will generally fall on whoever is making an allegation, raising a claim or putting forward an argument to which someone else must respond. Thus, the duty is often shared by many different individuals in a proceeding, including the agency. Sufficient information as to the substance of a matter must be given such that an individual can know:

   i. whether he is the subject of the proceeding;[53]

   ii. the subject of the proceeding;[54]

   iii. the relevant issues;[55]

---

53 *Sinkovich v. Police Board of Commissioners (Strathroy)* (1988), 65 O.R. (2d) 292, 28 O.A.C. 326 (Div. Ct.). In *Central Ontario Coalition Concerning Hydro Transmission Systems v. Ontario Hydro* (1984), 46 O.R. (2d) 715 (Div. Ct.), a notice was found to be inadequate as, not only did not lead individuals to realize that they could be affected by the proceedings, it actually misled some into believing that they would not be affected.

54 In *Mackin v. New Brunswick (Judicial Council)* (1987), 82 N.B.R. (2d) 203, 208 A.P.R. 203, 44 D.L.R. (4th) 730 (N.B.C.A.) a letter requesting the New Brunswick Judicial Council to look into statements made by a judge in his court concerning the proper administration of justice did not constitute a proper complaint as it was far too vague. Details should have been given both as to what was said and when and where it was said. It matters not whether the person possessing the information is of the opinion that the individual seeking it is capable of understanding or properly using the information sought, if that information is reasonably necessary for the person to adequately meet the case against him and present his own case.

55 See, for example, *Ellis v. Ontario (Minister of Communications & Social Services)* (1980), 28 O.R. (2d) 385 (Div. Ct.). This is true whether the issue is one raised by the parties or the agency. In *Westfair Foods Ltd. v. R.W.D.S.U. , Local 454* (1993), 15 Admin. L.R. (2d) 260, 110 Sask. R. 139 (Q.B.) the court found that the Saskatchewan Labour Relations Board erred in finding an unfair labour practice respecting an issue which was neither requested nor expected by the parties and which the Board neither advised the parties it was considering or gave them an opportunity to make representations with respect thereto. See also *355 & 365 Grandravine Holdings Ltd. v. Pacini* (1991), 8 O.R. (3d) 29, 87 D.L.R. (4th) 718, 84 O.A.C. 380 (Div. Ct.), *Seymour v. Correctional Service Canada (Pacific Region)* (1987), 17 F.T.R. 15, *Mackin v. New Brunswick (Judicial Council)* (1987), 82 N.B.R. (2d) 203, 208 A.P.R. 203, 44 D.L.R. (4th) 730 (C.A.), *Danakas v. War Veterans Allowance Board* (1985), 59 N.R. 309 (Fed. C.A.), *McAllister v. New Brunswick Veterinary Medical Association* (1985), 62 N.B.R. (2d) 119, 161 A.P.R. 119 (C.A.) leave to appeal to Supreme Court of Canada refused (1985), 66 N.B.R. (2d) 270, 169 A.P.R. 270 (S.C.C.), *Chen v. Canada (Minister of Employment & Immigration)*, [1995] 1 S.C.R. 725, 27 Imm. L.R. (2d) 1, 123 D.L.R. (4th) 536 (S.C.C.). In *Canada (Attorney General) v. McKenna*, [1994] 1 F.C. 694, 22 C.H.R.R. D/512, 88 F.T.R. 202, it was argued that the opposing party should have known the issue being raised by the applicant as the applicant's questions on cross-examination could only have gone to that issue. The Court rejected this argument stating that a party should not be expected to discover the fundamental nature of the case from opposing party's cross-examination.

See Appendix 12.2 for an example of an agency notice of issues settled on following a conference which had been held for the purpose of identifying what the issues which might be relevant to the proceeding.

iv. the evidence which is before the agency;[56]

v. the consequences which may arise out of the proceeding;[57] and

vi. he must know this information sufficiently in advance of the hearing to properly prepare his case.[58]

The purpose is to avoid surprise.[59]

Exactly how much information must be given to meet this burden will be dependant on circumstances, for examaple what it is one is trying to convey and to whom one is attempting to convey it.[60] Simple concepts or issues may require

---

56 *Kane v. University of British Columbia*, [1980] 1 S.C.R. 1105, 18 B.C.L.R. 124, [1980] 3 W.W.R. 125, 110 D.L.R. (3d) 311, *R. v. Ontario (Racing Commission)* (1970), 13 D.L.R. (3d) 405 (H.C.), affirmed [1971] 1 O.R. 400 (C.A.). In *Barton v. Canada (Attorney General)* (1993), 17 Admin. L.R. (2d) 207, 66 F.T.R. 54 (T.D.) the Public Service Commission's Appeal Board would only grant access to confidential test data it possessed to persons with the need to know *and* the capacity (in its opinion) to make sense of it (in this case a person who was nationally or provincially registered, or a certified psychologist, expert in the field of testing- but not the agent's representative who was not even a lawyer). The Federal Court Trial Division held that the Appeal Board's ruling was tantamount to denying the applicants the right to a representative and a breach of procedural fairness.

57 *Lakeside Colony of Hutterian Brethren v. Hofer*, [1992] 3 S.C.R. 165, [1993] 1 W.W.R. 113, 142 N.R. 241, 97 D.L.R. (4th) 17, 81 Man. R. (2d) 1, 30 W.A.C. 1, *Michaud v. Institut des comptables agréés (Nouveau-Brunswick)* (1993), 137 N.B.R. (2d) 125, 351 A.P.R. 125 (Q.B.), affirmed (1994), 149 N.B.R. (2d) 328, 381 A.P.R. 328 (C.A.), *Ontario (A.G.) v. Grady* (1988), 34 C.R.R. 289 (Ont. S.C.), *Godfrey v Ontario (Police Commission)* (1991), 5 O.R. (3d) 163, 7 Admin. L.R. (2d) 9, 83 D.L.R. (4th) 501 (Div. Ct.), *DeSoto Developments Ltd. v. Ontario New Home Warranty Program* (1992), 8 O.R. (3d) 792, 57 O.A.C. 87 (Div. Ct.), affirmed (1994), 21 O.R. (3d) 738 (C.A.), *R. v. Ontario (Racing Commission)* (1970), 131 D.L.R. (3d) 405 (H.C.), affirmed [1971] 1 O.R. 400 (C.A.). A notice that regulatory action under a statute is being considered is sufficient, even if the notice does not precisely reflect the statutory provision in question, provided that the notice makes it clear what action is being contemplated and the recipient is not misled: *Yorkton Restaurant Venture Capital Corp. v. Saskatchewan (Minister of Economic Development)* (1994), 124 Sask. R. 8, 118 D.L.R. (4th) 735 (Q.B.).

58 All of which is summarized in *Canadian Radio-Television and Telecommunications Canada (Commission) v. London Cable TV Ltd.* (1976), 67 D.L.R. (3d) 267 (Fed. C.A.).

59 Thus, in *Okeynan v. Prince Albert Penitentiary and National Parole Board* (1988), 20 F.T.R. 270, a prisoner facing a parole hearing did not have to be given notice of the Board's intention to look at his previous convictions as an individual facing parole cannot credibly claim to have been taken by surprise in respect to those matters. Contrast this with *Cardinal v. Canada (National Parole Board)* (1990), 46 Admin. L.R. 445, 61 C.C.C. (3d) 185, 38 F.T.R. 315 (T.D.), affirmed (1991), 4 Admin. L.R. (2d) 29, 68 C.C.C. (3d) 384, 54 F.T.R. 321 (note), 140 N.R. 135 (C.A.) the National Parole was said to have erred when it suspended an individual's mandatory supervision on the grounds of his breach of a condition against alcohol when its notice and actions gave every indication that its concern was with allegations of new criminal activity.

60 *R. v. Ontario (Racing Commission)*, [1971] 1 O.R. 400, 15 D.L.R. (3d) 430 (C.A.), *Quebec (Attorney General) v. National Energy Board*, [1994] 1 S.C.R. 159, 20 Admin. L.R. (2d) 79, 14 C.E.L.R. (N.S.) 1, 163 N.R. 241. See for example, *Murnaghan v. Assn. of Nurses (Prince Edward*

very little information to clearly identify the subject at hand and the issues relating thereto, while very complex concepts, may require disclosure of much more information. This requirement is usually referred to in a manner similar to that used by Justice Reid in *Central Ontario Coalition Concerning Hydro Transmission Systems, Re* :

> [W]here the form or content of notice is not laid down it must be reasonable in the sense that it conveys the real intentions of the giver and enables the person to whom it is directed to know what he must meet.[61]

The Supreme Court of Canada expressed the concept in terms of giving sufficient information to allow ''meaningful participation''.[62]

Where everything is equal, the amount of information which must be disclosed is dependent on how much is necessary for an individual to be said to be able to be aware of the case against him and to be able to present his own case. As noted above, this goes beyond merely advising a person of the subject of the hearing. The duty to give notice of the relevant issues extends to any argument, including agency policy, to be considered.[63] For example, in *Dale Corporation v. Nova Scotia (Rent Review Commission)*[64] the Nova Scotia Court of Appeal held that the Rent Review Commission was obliged to disclose to a participant the policy guidelines which the Commission intended to consider on its application.

The obligation to disclose the relevant issues extends to the disclosure of any legal advice which agency counsel may have provided the agency which the

---

Island) (1994), 116 Nfld & P.E.I.R. 355, 363 A.P.R. 355 (P.E.I. T.D.) where complainants at the first stage of a discipline process were not required to advise a nurse of the particular discipline offence alleged but merely the facts which they felt would constitute some form of discipline offence. The P.E.I. Supreme Court held that the discipline process was intended to be a two stage proceeding. The first was a type of preliminary inquiry to provide an opportunity for members of the public to complain against what they considered to be improper conduct. At this stage it was only necessary to give notice of the incidents complained of rather than attempting to identify exactly what type of disciplinary offence was being alleged. At this stage the discipline committee would determine if there was sufficient evidence to warrant the holding of a formal hearing. It was only at that time, when the nature of the proceeding was more specific, that the requirement arose to advise the member of the specific breaches of the Nurses Act being alleged. Thus, the nature and purpose of the hearing dictated the extent of the notice given.

61 (1984), 46 O.R. (2d) 715 (Div. Ct.). In this decision Justice Reid sets out an extensive list of cases which explore what constitutes adequate notice.

62 *Quebec (Attorney General) v. National Energy Board*, [1994] 1 S.C.R. 159, 20 Admin. L.R. (2d) 79, 14 C.E.L.R. (N.S.), 1, 112 D.L.R. (4th) 129, 163 N.R. 241.

63 *Canada (Attorney General) v. Canada (Human Rights Tribunal)* (1994), 19 Admin. L.R. (2d) 69, 76 F.T.R. 1, *Transx Ltd. v. Reimer Express Lines Ltd., Re.* (1986), 39 Man. R. (2d) 48, 28 D.L.R. (4th) 392 (Man. C.A.), *Irving Oil Ltd. v. Public Utilities Commission* (1986), 34 D.L.R. (4th) 448 (N.B. C.A.), *Griffin v. Canada* (1989), 39 Admin. L.R. 215, 26 F.T.R. 185.

64 (1983) 2 Admin. L.R. 260 (N.S. C.A.).

agency wishes to consider, notwithstanding any solicitor-client privilege between the agency and its counsel.[65]

As noted above, the principle also extends to ensure that all the participants are aware of the evidence before the agency such that they can prepare their own case to meet it. In *Scott v. Rent Review Comm.*[66] the Nova Scotia Court of Appeal stated that:

> [T]he courts have uniformly held that an "opportunity to be heard" or an "opportunity to make representations", whether prescribed by statue or by common law, is afforded a person only if the tribunal lets him know the essentials of the evidence on the principal issue it has to decide, so that he may make representations on that issue, if he is able to do so.[67]

Notwithstanding the foregoing, the actual evidence, policy document itself, etc., need not always be disclosed. (Although, as a practical rule, unless there is a specific purpose in not disclosing, it is preferable to do so and thus avoid uncertainty and subsequent argument.)[68] The purpose of disclosure is to ensure

---

65 *Melanson v. New Brunswick (Workers' Compensation Board)* (1994), 114 D.L.R. (4th) 75, 146 N.B.R. (2d) 284, 374 A.P.R. 294 (C.A.), leave to appeal to S.C.C. refused (1994), 25 Admin. L.R. (2d) 219n, 116 D.L.R. (4th) vii (note) (S.C.C.). See also *League for Human Rights of B'Nai Brith Canada v. Commission of Inquiry on War Criminals* (1986), 28 D.L.R. (4th) 264, 69 N.R. 110 (Fed. C.A.) where the Federal Court of Appeal ordered the disclosure of legal opinions prepared for a Commission of Inquiry by a working groups of lawyers established by the Commission to advise on the issue of legal recourse to bring war criminals to justice. The Court stated, at p. 267 D.L.R.:
> In the particular circumstances of this commission, the reports of the working group will not play the peripheral or incidental role which legal opinions usually play in the result of an inquiry. Instead, they are directed precisely to matters which the commission is expressly required to address in its report. They are in the nature of expert evidence and to be dealt with accordingly.

66 (1977) 23 N.S.R. (2d) 504, 32 A.P.R. 504, 81 D.L.R. (3d) 530 (C.A.) at p. 521 N.S.R.

67 See also *Kane v. University of British Columbia*, [1980] 1 S.C.R. 1105, 18 B.C.L.R. 124, [1980] 3 W.W.R. 125, 110 D.L.R. (3d) 311. *R. v. Ontario (Racing Commission)* (1970), 13 D.L.R. (3d) 405 (H.C.) affirmed [1971] 1 O.R. 400 (C.A.), *Madison Dev. Corp. v. Alberta (Rent Regulations Appeal Bd.)* (1977), 4 Alta. L.R. (2d) 73, 7 A.R. 360 (T.D.), *Shah v. Minister of Employment & Immigration* (1994), 170 N.R. 238 (F.C.A.), *Sorkhabi v. Canada (Secretary of State)* (1994), 26 Imm. L.R. (2d) 287, 89 F.T.R. 224 (T.D.) and *Barton v. Canada (Attorney General)* (1993), 17 Admin. L.R. (2d) 207 (T.D.). The reader may also wish to review the cases of *Downing v. Graydon* (1978), 92 D.L.R. (3d) 355 (Ont. C.A.) and *Workers' Compensation Board of Nova Scotia v. Cape Breton Development Corp.* (1984), 62 N.S.R. (2d) 127, 136 A.P.R. 127 (C.A.) where the courts rejected the argument that common statutory provision that no member or staff of an agency shall divulge information obtain by him in making an inspection (except in the course of the performance of his duties) provide the authority for non-disclosure of evidence to parties involved in the proceeding.

68 See, for example, the comments of Justice Décary in *Mercier v. Canada (Human Rights Commission)*, [1994] 3 F.C. 3, 25 Admin. L.R. (2d) 161, (*sub nom. Mercier v. Commission canadienne des droits de la personne)* 167 N.R. 241 (Fed. C.A.):
> I am not saying that the rules of procedural fairness require that the Commission systematically

that the individual to whom it is given is aware of the case against him and can therefore present his own to the best advantage. Thus, in some cases, it may only be necessary to disclose the gist or substance of the matter requiring disclosure provided that that gist or the substance of the issue, argument, evidence, etc., is sufficient to identify with sufficient certainty the matters with which the individual will have to deal so that he will not be taken by surprise and he can adequately mount a reply.

Argument lends itself more easily to summarized or abbreviated disclosure than does evidence. It is usually not necessary to see the physical format in which argument is presented to the agency. As argument is concerned with concepts, summarizing, rephrasing or paraphrasing the argument will usually be sufficient to notify the other side of the logic of the case he must meet. For example, if an agency's solicitor has provided the agency with an interpretation of a statutory provision relevant to a particular proceeding, the agency would only have to ensure, if it wishes to consider that argument, that the parties are aware of its gist. It would not be necessary to disclose that the argument came from agency counsel, nor to provide them with an actual copy of the opinion. It would only be necessary to advise them of the substance of the argument itself so that they can deal with it. Thus, where the same argument is presented to the agency in different forms it is not necessary to advise the parties each time the argument resurfaces. It is sufficient that the party be aware of the argument itself. Equally, there is no obligation on an agency to advise a party of new case law it becomes aware of which was not raised at the hearing,[69] or of the internal policy discussions it might have,[70] provided that no new issues are raised by this case law[71] or policy discus-

---

disclose to one party the comments it receives from the other; I am saying that they require this when those comments contain facts that differ from the facts set out in the investigation report which the adverse party would have been entitled to try to rebut had it known about them at the stage of the investigation, properly speaking. I recognize that it will not always be easy to determine when comments cease to be "argument", to use the words of Sopinka J., and become new allegations that must be brought to the attention of the other party; if the Commission were to decide to continue its general practice of not disclosing comments, it will still have to examine each case individually and practise great vigilance so as to avoid a party in a particular case, such as the case at bar, not receiving disclosure of comments that are such as should have been brought to that party's attention. It would seem to me that it would be in the Commission's interest, if only to protect itself in advance from any criticism, to require that the parties exchange their respective comments.

69 *Canada (Attorney General) v. Levac (sub nom. Levac v. Canada (Armed Forces))*, [1992] 3 F.C. 463, 94 D.L.R. (4th) 266 (C.A.), *Liyanagamage v. Canada (Minister of Citizenship & Immigration)* (1994), 176 N.R. 4 (Fed. C.A.), *Theiventhiran v. Canada (Minister of Citizenship & Immigration)* (1994) 88 F.T.R. 94 (Fed. T.D.).

70 *Consolidated Bathurst Packaging Ltd. v. International Woodworkers of America, Local 2-69*, [1990] 1 S.C.R. 282, 73 O.R. (2d) 676 (note), 42 Admin. L.R. 1, 105 N.R. 161, 38 O.A.C. 321, 68 D.L.R . (4th) 524. See also the further discussion of this case later in s. 22.3.1(i)(v).

71 In *Theiventhiran v. Canada (Minister of Citizenship & Immigration)* (1994) 88 F.T.R. 94 (T.D.), the Court noted that if the new decision of the higher court results in a fundamental change in the law, practically speaking the decision-maker should take it into consideration to avoid being

sion that were not already canvassed at the hearing. The obligation is simply that a party be aware of the issues and the essence of the argument it must meet.

While the principle also applies to evidence,[72] failure to disclose the actual evidence before the agency appears to be a riskier proposition. It has frequently been found that, in the circumstances of the case, a person was not able to adequately prepare for his case without having examined the physical evidence itself. Merely advising him that it existed and its extent was not found sufficient in those cases. For example, in *Nrecaj v. Canada (Minister of Employment & Immigration)*,[73] the Court held that it was not sufficient to simply say that one had a number of documents and evidence of a prior inconsistent statement without giving sufficient particulars to identify the documents in question and the statement alleged to be inconsistent. In *Napoli v. British Columbia (Workers' Compensation Board)*[74] the British Columbia Court of Appeal ruled that providing summaries of the material on the file of a person seeking compensation was not adequate disclosure. The summaries referred to very damaging reports which the court felt that counsel would want to challenge. To challenge the reports effectively, the Court felt, would require production of the original reports.[75] Thus, to the degree possible it may be prudent to disclose the actual evidence in question, rather than relying on summaries or reports.

In determining the adequacy of a notice the nature of the recipient should be taken into account. For example, in judging the adequacy of a notice whose intended recipients are the ordinary residents of a particular region and whose purpose is to advise people that land in that area may be expropriated, Justice Reid indicated in the *Central Ontario Coalition* case, one must take into account what a reasonable person living in that area would have understood from it. Thus, a notice directed only to the local residents of a geographic region might properly refer to an area by its local name. The same notice dealing with the same geographic region but directed to individuals located outside of the region, who

---

overturned on appeal and in such cases, one could expect, out of fairness, that counsel for the parties would be allowed to make representations on their clients' behalf.

Having said this, however, it is a good practice to bring such case law to the attention of the participants where possible and to, at least, invite written submissions thereon. This will allow the agency to benefit from the expertise of the participants. The hearing may always be reconvened if the new submissions warrant it.

72 *Radulesco v. C.H.R.C.* , [1984] 2 S.C.R. 407, 55 N.R. 384 , *Labelle v. Canada (Treasury Board) v. Canada (Canadian Human Rights Commission)* (1987), 25 Admin. L.R. 10, 76 N.R. 222 (Fed. C.A.).

73 [1993] 3 F.C. 630, 14 Admin. L.R. (2d) 161, 20 Imm. L.R. (2d) 252 (T.D.).

74 (1981), 126 D.L.R. (3d) 179 (B.C.C.A.).

75 (The Court also noted that the summaries failed to note some facts.) For other cases where a summarized disclosure was found to be insufficient see *Gough v. Canada (National Parole Board)* (1990), [1991] 2 F.C. 117, 45 Admin. L.R. 304, 3 C.R. (4th) 325 (T.D.) affirmed (1991) 47 Admin. L.R. 226, 3 C.R. (4th) 346, 41 F.T.D. 240n, 122 N.R. 79 (C.A.), *Re Hornby* (1993), 63 F.T.R. 189 (T.D.), *Okeynan v. Prince Albert Penitentiary* (1988), 20 F.T.R. 270 (T.D.), *Wong v. Roberts* (1983), 147 D.L.R. (3d) 375 (B.C. S.C.).

would not reasonably be expected to be familiar with local place names, would likely have to refer to the areas formal geographic name. The test appears to be objective, rather than subjective, and is determined on the basis of what would a reasonable person think in those circumstances.[76] Evidence from individuals that they had or had not been misled is either unnecessary or inconclusive.[77]

Finally, one cannot determine how much information is necessary in order to present one's case without taking into account what "one's case" is. Disclosure obligations may be quite low as one approaches the legislative end of the spectrum, where the more "one's case" is restricted to simply bringing your views and information to the attention of the decision-maker the less one needs to know about the views and information being brought by others.[78] In a proceeding which approaches the judicial end of the spectrum, where an important and unique interest possessed by an individual may be seriously affected by an agency's proceeding, "one's case" may require full disclosure of the information before the agency. Where one's interest is similar to countless thousands of others a newspaper notice geared to reasonably reaching the attention of those thousands may be sufficient notice. Where one is the only individual likely to be affected by a decision, personal notice may be required to ensure that you, being the person who most likely possesses the information the agency is likely to need as well as being the person who will actually be affected by the proceeding, are aware of it. In other words, the degree of disclosure required is fixed by what it is one has to do, and what would a person with that task be reasonably expected to know in order to carry it out.

12.3(c)(iii) Content, Not Form, Important

Absent a legislative direction as to the form of notice, it is not the particular form which notice may take, but the information which is conveyed thereby which is important.[79] Thus, there are cases to the effect that oral notice is sufficient

---

76 Thus, in *R. v. Ontario (Racing Commission)*, [1971] 1 O.R. 400 (C.A.) the notice of a racing offence inquiry was found to be adequate by the court in light of the familiarity with the racing industry of the recipients of the notice. For a similar result see *Re Cardinal Insurance Company* (1982), 44 N.R. 428 (Fed. C.A.), leave to appeal to Supreme Court of Canada refused (1982) 45 N.R. 534 (S.C.C.). In *Nfld. Telephone Co. v. Canadian Radio-Television & Telecommunications Commission* (1995), 179 N.R. 388 (Fed. C.A.), leave to appeal to S.C.C. refused (September 21, 1995), Doc. 24705 (S.C.C.) the Newfoundland Telephone Co. claimed that it had not been given notice that a particular issue was to be considered on an application to the C.R.T.C. The Federal Court of Canada dismissed the allegation because, among other reasons, it held that the company knew the practice on such applications was to consider that specific issue, and that this was also the practice followed by the provincial regulator before whom the company used to apply.

77 *Wilson v. Secretary of State for the Environment*, [1973] 1 W.L.R. 1083, as approved in *Central Ontario Coalition Concerning Hydro Transmission Systems, Re* (1984), 46 O.R. (2d) 715 (Div. Ct.).

78 See, for example, *Temple v. Ontario (Liquor Licence Board)* (1982), 41 O.R. (2d) 214 (Div. Ct.).

79 Thus, the service of a subpoena on an individual requiring him to attend a hearing was not found

or that the actual knowledge of the individual in question of the proceedings may dispense with the necessity for formal notice,[80] or that a deficient original notice may be compensated for by the subsequent provision of the missing information.[81] In the same way, notices in the newspapers may be appropriate where the number of participants are uncertain or too large and unwieldy to make individual formal notice practical or possible.[82]

12.3(c)(iv) Non-Disclosure In Order To Protect Some Other Interest

As I have said, when everything is equal, everything before the decision-maker should be disclosed. Often, however, everything is not equal. There may be a conflict between the individual's right to know and someone else's interests (such as in cases involving informer's or other confidential sources of information), or the ability of the agency to function. In such cases a balancing of interests is required and a reasonable accommodation between them reached. Neither Parliament nor the courts are ignorant of the realities of the world and recognize that sometimes the complete disclosure of information as would ordinarily be

---

to be good notice of the hearing as a subpoena may not advise the person of the time the hearing actually commences (only when his attendance is necessary) and a subpoena does not give notice that the hearing concerns the individual other than as a witness (*Elson v. St. John's (City) Residential Tenancies* (1980), 33 Nfld. & P.E.I.R. 373, 93 A.P.R. 373 (Nfld. Div. Ct.).

80 *Re Cardinal Insurance Company* (1982), 44 N.R. 428 (Fed. C.A.), leave to appeal to Supreme Court of Canada refused (1982), 45 N.R. 534 (S.C.C.), *Newfoundland v. Canada (Solicitor General)* (1995), 179 N.R. 388 (Fed. C.A.) (disclosure of issues made clear in interrogatories at the pre-hearing stage), *Ontario (Liquor Control Board) v. Karumanchiri* (1988), 25 O.A.C. 161 (correcting reasons reported at 27 O.A.C. 246) (Div. Ct.). Thus, absent some statutory direction to the contrary, where there is insufficient time to finish a hearing at a session and the decision-maker announces to the participants its adjournment to a specific date, time and place, separate formal notice need not be given of the reconvened hearing (*Stuart v. Assiniboine Park-Fort Garry (Community Committee of Winnipeg (City)* (1992), 4 Admin. L.R. (2d) 3, 76 Man. R. (2d) 276 (Man. C.A.). However, where the proceeding is simply adjourned to some other, as a yet undetermined date, or a previously announced date of reconvening is changed, or all of the participants (with the consent of the agency) are not present at the adjournment, a separate notice must be given of the new date. The importance of actual knowledge over mere form is illustrated by the decision of the Quebec Court of Appeal in *Régie de l'assurance-maladie du Québec c. Chamberland* (1986), 24 Admin. L.R. 304 (Que. C.A.) where the effect of a perfectly proper written notice was undermined by the subsequent actions of the agency which lead the individual concerned to believe that a much narrower matter than indicated in the written notice was to be the subject of the proceedings.

81 *M. (A.B.) v. Manitoba (Director of Child and Family Services)* (1995), 10 R.F.L. (4th) 379 (*sub nom. M. (B.) v. Manitoba (Director of Child and Family Services)* 100 Man. R. (2d) 47, 122 D.L.R. (4th) 693 (Man. C.A.).

82 Normally, those papers read within the geographic area involved in the hearing are used. The newspapers selected by an agency for publication will usually have broad as well as local readership. Examples of notices published in a newspaper are set out in Appendix 12.1.

required would be naive and cause more harm than good.[83] Thus, legislation frequently provides for less than full disclosure (for example, where full disclosure of all details would threaten police sources, be injurious to the conduct of investigations, contrary to national security needs or some other public interest).[84] It is very common in proceedings regarding commercial interests for parties to claim confidentiality respecting matters of trade secrets. In fact, where proceedings are held precisely to determine the confidentiality of certain information full disclosure would obviously be anti-productive and destroy the very thing the proceedings are being held to determine.[85]

Where the harm resulting from disclosure may outweigh the harm resulting from non-disclosure, the individual's "right to know" may be subordinated to some extent to the greater interest at stake. Thus, in *Chiarelli v. Canada (Minister of Employment & Immigration)*[86] an individual facing an inquiry by the Security Intelligence Review Committee as to allegations of his being part of organized crime was given a report setting out the nature of the information received by the Review Committee, including that he had been involved in drug trafficking, and was involved in the murder of a named individual. He was also provided with an extensive summary of surveillance of his activities and a summary of intercepted private communications relating to the murder, and, although excluded from the first day of the Committee's hearing, he was provided with a summary of the

83 In *Bruce v. Canada (Attorney General)* (1992), 5 Admin. L.R. (2d) 258, 13 C.R. (4th) 384 (N.B. C.A.), the New Brunswick Court of Appeal, in approving the limits imposed by prison authorities upon the amount of information they were willing to disclose to a prisoner who was being transferred to a maximum security prison because of drug dealing, stated that "it would have been irresponsible for the decision-maker to have followed a course other than the one he did." In *Chiarelli v. Canada (Minister of Employment & Immigration)*, [1992] 1 S.C.R. 711, 72 C.C.C. (3d) 214, 16 Imm. L.R. (2d) 1, 2 Admin. L.R. (2d) 125, 135 N.R. 161, 90 D.L.R. (4th) 289, the Court discussed disclosure in light of the state's "considerable interest in conducting national security and criminal intelligence investigations and in protecting police sources." In *Demaria v. Regional Classification Board (Can.)*, [1987] 1 F.C. 74, 21 Admin. L.R. 227, 53 C.R. (3d) 88, 30 C.C.C. (3d) 55, 69 N.R. 135 (C.A.) Justice Hugessen stated that "There is, of course, no doubt that the authorities were entitled to protect confidential sources of information. A penitentiary is not a choir school and, if informers were involved . . . it is important that they not be put at risk."

84 For example, s. 17(5) of the federal Parole Regulations, SOR/78-428 provided that information should not be disclosed where disclosure could reasonably be expected to threaten the safety of the informants, or reasonably be expected to be injurious to the conduct of lawful investigations.

85 It is not uncommon, where agencies work in areas involving trade or economic secrets, for there to be an elaborate legislated confidentially process. For an example see Appendix 12.10. All confidentiality provisions are not so sophisticated, however. The federal Immigration Act, R.S.C. 1985, c. I-1 simply provides in s. 29. (2) that "Where an adjudicator is satisfied that there is a serious possibility that the life, liberty or security of any person would be endangered by reason of an inquiry being conducted in public, the adjudicator may, on application therefor, take such measures and make such order as the adjudicator considers necessary to ensure the confidentiality of the inquiry."

86 [1992] 1 S.C.R. 711, 2 Admin. L.R. (2d) 124, 72 C.C.C. (3d) 214, 16 Imm. L.R. (2d) 1, 135 N.R. 161, 90 D.L.R. (4th) 289.

evidence given. Finally, he had been offered, and rejected the right to call his own witnesses and to cross-examine the R.C.M.P. witness who had testified in the closed proceedings. Writing for the Court, Justice Sopinka concluded that:

> In my view these various documents gave the respondent sufficient information to know the substance of the allegations against him, and to be able to respond. It is not necessary, in order to comply with fundamental justice in this context, that the respondent also be given details of the criminal intelligence investigation techniques or police sources used to acquire that information.

He concluded that "[h]aving regard to the information that was disclosed to the respondent, the procedural opportunities that were available to him, and the competing interests at play in this area" the principles of fundamental justice were not violated.

The simple fact that somebody may not wish something disclosed or that the information may be confidential is not, in itself, sufficient grounds for non-disclosure.[87] There must be some serious concern to be protected by the non-disclosure.[88] The interest sought to be protected by the non-disclosure, and the harm to that interest resulting from the disclosure, must be sufficiently important to warrant the intrusion on the rights of the individual to protect his interests.

There is no clear test in determining whether some form of non-disclosure is appropriate and the degree which is appropriate. It is a balancing of the circumstances in light of:

   i. the importance of the individual's interest at stake;

   ii. the importance of the interest being attempted to be protected by non-disclosure;

---

87 *Downing v. Graydon* (1978), 92 D.L.R. (3d) 355 (Ont. C.A.). Justice Reed in *Cadieux v. Director of Mountain Institute* (1984), 13 C.C.C. (3d) 330 quoted Lord Diplock on this subject in *D. v. National Society for Prevention of Cruelty to Children*, [1978] A.C. 171 at p. 218:

> The fact that information has been communicated by one person to another in confidence, however, is not of itself a sufficient ground for protecting from disclosure in a court of law the nature of the information or the identity of the informant ... The private promise of confidentiality must yield to the general public interest that in the administration of justice truth will out, unless by reason of the character of the information or the relationship of the recipient of the information to the informant, a more important public interest is served by protecting the information or the identify of the informant from disclosure in a court of law.

88 In *Barton v. Canada (Attorney General)* (1993), 17 Admin. L.R. (2d) 207 (Fed. T.D.) the Public Service Appeal Board was found to be wrong in refusing to allow an individual's representative access to confidential test data. The Board wanted to restrict access only to those people it felt had a need to know it *and* the capacity to understand it. The Board was not attempting to protect some interest by non-disclosure. It merely wanted to control the characteristics of the individual to whom it was released. The Federal Court of Appeal felt that this was tantamount to denying the applicant the right to a representative.

iii. the impact on that protected interest by disclosure; and

iv. the need of the individual for the information in order to protect his interest.

Thus, where the individual's right at stake is of lesser importance, or the information at stake may be of lesser importance to his ability to present his case, non-disclosure may be appropriate where the information in question could cause serious harm to some other important interest.[89] Equally, where the information in question is very important for an individual to adequately present his case in order to protect an important right, greater disclosure may be required where the interest sought to be protected by non-disclosure is not of as much importance.[90]

Notwithstanding that non-disclosure is sometimes possible, the burden is always on the individual resisting disclosure to demonstrate that he has withheld only such information as is strictly necessary to ensure the purpose claimed for the non-disclosure[91] and the courts are reluctant to approve it. In *Cadieux and Director of Mountain Institution*[92] Justice Reed emphasized that there must be a nexus between the content of the information and the protection of the public interest said to be served by non-disclosure. That case involved the cancellation by the National Parole Board of a prisoner's unescorted temporary absence rights. Justice Reed thought that it would be rare that an inmate could not be told at least the gist of the reasons against him when the conduct in question took place outside of an institution. Although the learned Justice thought that it might be possible to envisage some situation where it might be necessary to refuse to disclose even the gist of the case when conduct in question took place within an institution where the content of the information was such that its disclosure would automatically lead to the identity of the informer becoming known (and thus undermine the ability of the Board to function), I am not aware of any decision in which an individual was denied *total* knowledge of the information in question. Some three years after *Cadieux* the British Columbia Court of Appeal, looking at a disclosure question respecting conduct within an institution, took an even stricter stance in ruling that, under section 7 of the Charter, "The principles of fundamental justice

---

89 It is important to note that in *Chiarelli* the applicant had only a lesser interest to be protected. The only effect of a negative ruling by SIRC was that the individual would not have the right to appeal a deportation order on compassionate grounds (his right to appeal on the merits would remain). The Court had already concluded that the individual had no right to an appeal on compassionate grounds. Thus, the Court was weighing the individual's interest in a privilege against the state's need for security and the importance of protecting police sources.

90 See *Gough v. Canada (National Parole Board)* (1990), [1994] 2 F.C. 117, 3 C.R. (4th) 325, 45 Admin. L.R. 304 , 40 F.T.R. 91 (T.D) at p. 312 Admin. L.R., affirmed (1991), 47 Admin. L.R. 226, 122 N.R. 79 (C.A.), 3 C.R. (4th), 346, 41 F.T.R. 240n.

91 *Demaria v. Regional Classification Bd. (Can.)*, [1986] 1 F.C. 74, 21 Admin. L.R. 227, 53 C.R. (3d) 88, 30 C.C.C. (3d) 55, 69 N.R. 135 (C.A.).

92 (1984), 13 C.C.C. (3d) 330 (Fed. T.D.).

require that [the inmate] know the substance of the information said to be against him. . . ."[93]

To my knowledge, a requirement has always be imposed for *some* disclosure, whether that disclosure takes the form of requiring at least the gist, or substance, of the information to be disclosed[94] or of requiring disclosure only to counsel. In any event, the Courts appear to demand that, be it through excising the names of confidential sources, providing an outline, a summary, or the gist of the information, information must be given such that the right to make an answer is not frustrated. It may well be that there will be a case where a extremely important interest requires total non-disclosure of some evidence which is not extremely important in a case where the individual seeking disclosure's interest was very small. However, I have seen no example of it yet.

Assuming that some non-disclosure is necessary, there appear to be any number of ways of accomplishing it. In some cases an expurgated version of the information is disclosed with suitable deletions of the material sought to be protected (usually the names of sources or informants).[95] In the prison cases noted above, summaries or reports of the substance of the allegations are used. In other cases the courts have permitted disclosure only to counsel on an undertaking not to disclose the information to his client.[96]

---

93 *Ross v. Kent Institution* (1987), 25 Admin. L.R. 67, 34 C.C.C. (3d) 452, 57 C.R. (3d) 79, 12 B.C.L.R. 145 (C.A.), leave to appeal to S.C.C. refused (1987), 59 C.R. (3d) xxxiv (note) (S.C.C.).

94 There are numerous prison or parole cases to this effect where authorities refused to disclose the names of informers, or details of the information in their possession which they felt would help to identify those sources. Some of the cases are decided under natural justice and fairness (*Ericson v. Canada (Deputy Director of Correctional Services)* (1991), 5 Admin. L.R. (2d) 206, 10 C.R. (4th) 235 (B.C. S.C.), *Demaria v. Regional Classification Bd. (Can.)* (1986), 21 Admin. L.R. 227 (C.A.)) and others under the fundamental justice right set out in s. 7 of the Charter (*Desjardins v. Canada (National Parole Board)* (1989), 39 Admin. L.R. 200 (Fed. T.D.), *Gough v. Canada (National Parole Board)* (1990), [1991] 2 F.C. 117, 45 Admin. L.R. 304 , 40 F.T.R. 91 at p. 312 Admin. L.R., affirmed (1991), 3 C.R. (4th), 346, 41 F.T.R. 240n, 47 Admin. L. R. 226, 122 N.R. 79 (C.A.), *Latham v. Solicitor-General of Canada* (1984), 12 C.C.C. (3d) 9, 9 D.L.R. (4th) 393, [1984] 1 F.C. 734, 39 C.R. (3d) 78 (T.D.), *Cadieux v. Director of Mountain Institution* (1984), 13 C.C.C. (3d) 330 (Fed. T.D.), *Ross v. Kent Institution* (1987), 34 C.C.C. (3d) 452, 57 C.R. (3d) 79, 12 B.C.L.R. (C.A.), leave to appeal to S.C.C. refused (1987), 59 C.R. (3d) xxxiv (note) (S.C.C.).

95 For an example, see *Ruiperez v. Lakehead University* (1981), 130 D.L.R. (3d) 427 (Ont. Div. Ct.), (1983), 41 O.R. (2d) 552 (C.A.).

96 *Abel v. Ontario (Advisory Review Board)* (1980), 119 D.L.R. (3d) 101 (Ont. C.A.), *Egglestone v. Ontario (Advisory Review Board)* (1983), 150 D.L.R. (3d) (Div. Ct.). In the latter decision the Court rejected the argument that the lawyer was under a duty to share the information with his client:

> While I am sympathetic to the fact that counsel receiving the information on the limited basis here is placed in a very awkward position so far as his client is concerned, it seems to me that this is the only reasonable order that could have been made by the chairman to achieve a balance between the right of the patient to disclosure of the relevant facts, as against the right, indeed duty, of the Board to preserve confidentiality of information in sensitive areas.

Disclosure to counsel, but not to his client, was also noted as a possibility in *Gough v. Canada*

12.3(c)(v) Duty to Disclose Information Which Is Not Before Decision-maker

Traditionally, the duty to disclose is couched in terms of revealing the information which is before a decision-maker[97] and sometimes even only that part of that information which is prejudicial or adverse to a party seeking disclosure[98] Since the 1991 decision of the Supreme Court of Canada in *R. v. Stinchcombe,*[99] a line of cases is emerging whose focus is on information in the hands of an opposing party who does not intend to put it before the decision-maker, or, where the agency has investigative functions, in the hands of the agency generally but not before the specific decision-maker hearing the matter. It is likely still too soon to draw any firm conclusions from these cases which do, however, appear to be moving towards some sort of right to discovery in administrative proceedings. To the extent that it is possible to draw conclusions from this mixed bag of lower court decisions the following principles appear to be emerging from them. The reader should note that this area of the law is developing and it may yet be too soon to determine the extent of its parameters.

1. Evidence in possession of an opposing party or the agency should be disclosed where it is relevant to evidence already before, or to be before, the decision-maker and is necessary to test or otherwise deal with that evidence.[100]

(National Parole Board) (1990), [1991] 2 F.C. 117, 45 Admin. L.R. 304 (T.D.) at p. 322, affirmed (1991), 47 Admin. L.R. 226 (Fed. C.A.). In *Barton v. Canada (Attorney General)* (1993), 17 Admin. L.R. (2d) 207 the Federal Court Trial Division also noted that where confidential information is at stake, unauthorized disclosure should be addressed by the conditions under which counsel or a representative receives it, such as the duty not to copy it, or perhaps the requirement to use it only at specified locations. It stated that conditions will be dependent on the degree of sensitivity of the information and counsel should be asked for submissions before the agency imposes them.

97 *R. v. Ontario (Racing Commission)* (1970), 13 D.L.R. (3d) 405 (H.C), affirmed [1971] O.R. 400 (C.A.).

98 See *Kane v. University of British Columbia*, [1980] 1 S.C.R. 1105, 18 B.C.L.R. 124, 110 D.L.R. (3d) 311 at p. 322 D.L.R., *Downing v. Graydon* (1978), 92 D.L.R. (3d) 355 (Ont. C.A.) at p. 374 D.L.R.

99 [1991] 3 S.C.R. 326.

100 *Nrecaj v. Canada (Minister of Employment & Immigration)*, [1993] 3 F.C. 630, 14 Admin. L.R. (2d) 161, 20 Imm. L.R. (2d) 252 (T.D.), *Siad v. Canada (Secretary of State)* (1994), 21 Imm. L.R. (2d) 6, 77 F.T.R. 49 (T.D.), and the dissent of Laskin J.A. in *Howe v. Institute of Chartered Accountants (Ontario)* (1994), 19 O.R. (3d) 483 (C.A.), leave to appeal to S.C.C. refused (1995), 119 D.L.R. (4th) vii (note) (S.C.C.). (The majority in *Howe* refused to deal with the issue as they felt the application was premature, however, in a simple obiter they opined that it was not clear that a refusal to order the production of documents was a denial of natural justice.) This principle can easily be seen as simply the extension of the principle that a party before an agency cannot withhold information material to the process or allow an agency to misdirect itself by withholding necessary or material information (see for example, *Ball v. Ontario Hydro* (1974),

2.   Evidence which is not relevant to the proceedings before the agency need
     not be disclosed.[101]

3.   Where an opposing party is responsible for an individual being unable to
     access relevant and material information the opposing party must disclosure
     that information if it is in his or her possession.[102]

4.   The closer the agency function appears to approach the judicial end of the
     spectrum the more important the decision's impact upon the individual be-
     comes in determining the duty to disclose. Where the decision is perceived
     as having a serious impact, the duty becomes the highest. Thus, the *Stinch-
     combe* disclosure principles were found applicable in the disciplinary pro-
     ceedings of the RCMP where the individual was exposed to a possible penalty
     of imprisonment of up to one year.[103]

5.   Conversely the closer the agency function approaches the administrative end
     of the spectrum the more important becomes the impact of full disclosure on
     the performance agency's mandate.[104]

6.   Disclosure under any of the above principles remains, nonetheless subject to
     exceptions for information whose disclosure would unduly harm some other
     important interest in much the same way as the traditional right of disclosure
     is subject.[105]

---

53 D.L.R. (3d) 519 (Ont. Div. Ct.) and *IMP Group Ltd. v. Dillman* (July 19, 1995) Doc. C.A.
111572 (N.S. C.A.) For a related decision see *Pathak v. Canada (Canadian Human Rights
Commission)* (1993), 63 F.T.R. 301 (T.D.). Strictly speaking, this is not a *Stinchcombe*-agency
decision as it involves disclosure on judicial review to the Federal Court and the judge does not
cite that case as support for his conclusions. The principles of disclosure enunciated therein is
similar to those that would be used at the agency level—note that the Trial level decision was
reversed on appeal on the basis of the interpretation of the Federal Court Rules ([1995] 2 F.C
455).

101 *R. v. Stinchcombe*, [1991] 3 S.C.R. 326, *Nuosci v. Royal Canadian Mounted Police* (1993),
[1994] 1 F.C. 353, 68 F.T.R. 200 (T.D.), affirmed (Feb. 22, 1995), Doc. A-552-93 (Fed. C.A.),
leave to appeal to S.C.C. refused (Aug. 17, 1995), 24689 (S.C.C.).

102 *Williams v. Canada (Regional Transfer Board, Prairie Region)* (1993), 15 Admin. L.R. (2d) 83
(Fed. C.A.).

103 *Nuosci v. Royal Canadian Mounted Police* (1993), [1994] 1 F.C. 353, 68 F.T.R. 208, affirmed
(February 22, 1995), Doc. A-552-93 (F.C.A.), leave to appeal to S.C.C. refused (August 17,
1995), Doc. 24689 (S.C.C.). See also *Human Rights Commission (Ont.) v. House* (1993), 67
O.A.C. 72 (Div. Ct.), *IMP Group Ltd. v. Dillman* (July 19, 1995), Court File 111572 (N.S. C.A.).
A similarly broad disclosure duty has been found in one case in Ontario in the context of
professional disciplinary proceedings: *Markandey v. Ontario (Board of Ophthalmic Dispensers)*,
(March 14, 1994) Court File RE 2661/93, (Ont. Gen. Div.). As will be discussed further below,
in my opinion, the approach used in these latter cases in determining the extent of disclosure
required left much to be desired.

104 *Re Ciba-Geigy Canada Ltd.*, [1994] 3 F.C. 425 (*sub nom. Ciba-Geigy Canada Ltd. v. Patented
Medicine Prices Review Bd.*) (T.D.), affirmed (1994), (*sub nom. CIBA-Geigy Canada Ltd. v.
Patented Medicine Prices Review Bd.*) 170 N.R. 560 (Fed. C.A.).

105 *Stinchcombe* expressly made an exception for information necessary to protect the identity of

7. In many of the cases where total disclosure has been made, the courts have made an analogy between the role of the person from whom disclosure is sought and the role of the Crown in criminal proceedings.[106]

Before discussing this emerging trend further, it should be noted that, legal requirements aside, disclosure is a good thing. It speeds proceedings up by avoiding surprise, it allows for the best case to be before the agency, and it generally contributes to a co-operative and productive atmosphere. Full disclosure should be practice *wherever it will not impede the proper functioning of the agency*.

For the most part, it would be incorrect to view the cases which have emerged since *Stinchcombe* as developing a expanded aspect of the fairness duty to disclose. The fact that an individual may require the disclosure of information which has not been, or will not, be placed in evidence before the agency in order to be adequately present his case was recognized before *Stinchcombe*.[107] It would perhaps be better to look at these cases as highlighting collateral principles to the traditional concept of disclosure as an aspect of fairness. Much of the above disclosure guidelines likely existed under the traditional concept of fairness even in the absence of *Stinchcombe*, notably those principles set out in points 1, 2 and 3.[108] There is, in fact, little to be concerned with in the imposition of the duties

---

informants. See also Laskin J.A.'s dissent in *Howe v. Institute of Chartered Accountants of Ontario* (1994), 19 O.R. (3d) 483 (C.A.) at p. 497, leave to appeal to S.C.C. refused 91995), 119 D.L.R. (4th) vii (note (S.C.C.).

106 I suggest that this last principle is not a useful exercise and warrants abandonment before it goes any further. To the extent that the duty to disclose is based on fairness the nature of the opposing side holding it (aside from questions of privilege) should be irrelevant. Disclosure is either required for fair play or it is not. The need for the information should not change with the nature of the person holding the information sought. The analogy is conceptually weak as well. As far as I know, the disclosure duties on a Crown arise from the concept and role of Crown counsel itself, not from any fairness principle. To say that fairness demands disclosure because somebody looks like a Crown is to mix unrelated concepts.

107 For example, in *Biscotti v. Ontario Securities Commission* (1990), 74 O.R. (2d) 119 (Div. Ct.), in addition to particulars of the allegations contained in the notice of hearing, summaries of the case against each respondent, and detailed statements of the evidence expected to be given by each witness, investigators of the Ontario Securities Commission agreed to disclose to the individuals facing disciplinary proceedings before the Commission everything of relevance which would support innocence or mitigate the offences alleged. (The Commission was challenged for even more disclosure of the transcripts of the interviews with witnesses as part of the duty of fairness, the Ontario Divisional Court concluded that the disclosure made was sufficient for the requirements of both fairness and s. 7 of the Charter, should it apply. On this point the Divisional Court was affirmed by the Court of Appeal (1991), 1 O.R. (3d) 409 (C.A.). A statutory power to disclose the evidence of witnesses given to investigators was, however, treated as a separate discretionary authority of the Commission (apparently beyond the duty of fairness) whose exercise the Commission was to consider on a witness by witness basis. The Court of Appeal, however, disagreed with the Divisional Court as to the guiding principles of the exercise of that discretion.)

108 Indeed, one of the decisions imposing a duty to disclose where the information in question was related to evidence already filed before the agency, *Pathak v. Canada (Canadian Human Rights*

set out in those points and, to the extent that those principles might not have been expressly recognized earlier their highlighting by the *Stinchcombe* case is likely a welcome development.

However, it may be useful to look for a moment at those cases where the courts have gone beyond what would be, perhaps, considered the traditional parameters of the disclosure required by fairness, and imposed a duty of disclosure on what they considered to be a duty arising out of *Stinchcombe*; a duty of full disclosure — something which approaches (if it is not actually) the discovery process in civil actions or Crown disclosure in criminal proceedings.

First, *R. v. Stinchcombe* itself. *Stinchcombe* involved a criminal proceeding where the Crown had interviewed a witness who had given evidence earlier in the proceeding which was was favourable to the accused. The Crown concluded that the evidence of this witness was undependable and decided not to call the witness in the trial. The defence sought disclosure of the interview thinking that there might be something favourable in it. The Crown refused. The case made its way to the Supreme Court where the Court ruled in favour of a general duty of disclosure (other than for irrelevant information or information which was privileged) on the Crown (but not the defence). Essentially the reasons for this ruling were:

1.   Disclosure eliminates surprise at trial and thus better ensures that justice is done in a proceeding.

2.   The duty of the Crown in a criminal proceeding is to lay before a jury all available legal proof of the facts; it is there to secure justice, not simply a conviction . Thus, the fruits of its investigation are the property of the public to be used to ensure that justice is done. (Defence counsel, on the other hand is there to secure an acquittal.)

Stinchcombe, itself, did not deal with administrative law. The Court was careful to state that in reaching its conclusions it was not to be taken as laying down principles for disclosure in circumstances other than criminal proceedings by indictment.[109] For this reason the Court did not look beyond the criminal law setting in its analysis.

Commission) (1993) 63 F.T.R. 301, reversed [1995] 2 F.C. 455 (C.A.) did not find it necessary to cite *Stinchcombe*.

109 Justice Sopinka, writing for the Court, stated that:

The general principles referred to herein arise in the context of indictable offences. While it may be argued that the duty of disclosure extends to all offences, many of the factors which I have canvassed may not apply at all or may apply with less impact in summary conviction offences. Moreover, the content of the right to make a full answer and defence entrenched in s. 7 of the Charter may be of a more limited nature.

In *Nuosci v. Royal Canadian Mounted Police*[110] it was argued that the *Stinchcombe* principles should not apply to a disciplinary proceeding by the RCMP insofar as disciplinary proceedings were administrative proceedings, not criminal. This was argued on the basis of the Supreme Court of Canada's decision in *Trimm v. Durham Regional Police Force*,[111] where the criminal protections under the Charter afforded by the Court's earlier decision in *R. v. Wigglesworth*[112] were found not to be applicable to administrative disciplinary proceedings. Justice Gibson, however, rejected this argument noting the fact that an individual before the RCMP disciplinary proceedings faced a possible penalty of up to one year's imprisonment. This elevated those proceedings to a different level than those in *Trimm* and put them into the *Wigglesworth* class of proceedings with true penal consequences. Thus, it was appropriate for the principles in *Stinchcombe*, a criminal case, to apply.[113] The analysis in *Nuosci* appears to be basically sound.

However, *Stinchcombe* has also been used in two Ontario cases to impose a general duty of full disclosure on the parties and the agency in administrative matters where the application of those principles is somewhat questionable *(Human Rights Commission (Ont.) v. House*[114] and *Markandey v. Ontario (Board of Ophthalmic Dispensers).*[115] *House* involved a inquiry before an Ontario Human Rights Board of Inquiry. The party who was the subject of the inquiry sought disclosure from the Ontario Human Rights Commission, which has the statutory carriage of the action in proceedings before the Board. The Board ordered the Commission to "provide the respondents, with all statements made by the complainants to the Commission and its investigators at the investigation stage, whether reduced to writing or copies by mechanical means." The Commission was also ordered to provide the respondents with the statement and identity of any witness interviewed by the Commission or its agents who the Commission did not intend to call as witnesses and whose statements might reasonably aid the respondents in answering the Commission's case. The Commission sought judicial review and lost. It argued that confidentiality of witnesses was necessary to

---

110 (1993), 68 F.T.R. 208, affirmed (February 22, 1995) Doc. A-552-93 (Fed. C.A.), leave to appeal to S.C.C. refused (August 17, 1995), Doc. 24689 (S.C.C.).

111 [1987] 2 S.C.R. 582, 29 Admin. L.R. 106, 81 N.R. 197.

112 [1987] 2 S.C.R. 541, 28 Admin. L.R. 294, 45 D.L.R. (3d) 235.

113 Disclosure was, however, refused as the information sought was irrelevant to the proceedings.

114 (1993), 115 D.L.R. (4th) 279, 67 O.A.C. 72 (Div. Ct.). *House* was approved of, in obiter, by the Nova Scotia Court of Appeal in *IMP Group Ltd. v. Dillman* (July 19, 1995), Doc. 111572 (N.S. C.A.).

115 (March 14, 1994), Doc. 2661/93 (Ont Gen. Div.). The disclosure which Laskin J.A. would have imposed on a professional society in his dissent in *Howe v. Institute of Chartered Accountants* (1994), 19 O.R. (3d) 483 (C.A.), leave to appeal to S.C.C. refused (1995), 119 D.L.R. (4th) vii (note (S.C.C.) related to the expert reports made by an investigator *when that investigator was to be a witness* in the proceedings. It therefore falls more into the first category of fairness where disclosure should be made of material necessary to test the evidence of witnesses before the agency.

foster an environment where witnesses feel comfortable about coming forward with relevant and sometimes sensitive information. Another reason was the Commission's desire to protect against the potential for intimidation of witnesses, who may have continuing involvement with the respondents and to guard against reprisals. The Court refused to recognize the claim for confidentiality on the grounds that it failed to meet the "Wigmore" criteria.[116] The Court then concluded, in just two paragraphs, essentially that the *Stinchcombe* rationale for disclosure applied in the context of human rights proceedings on the grounds that:

> "[J]ustice was better served when the element of surprise was eliminated from the trial and the parties were prepared to address issues *on the basis of complete information of the case to be met*". (Emphasis added.) It does not take a quantum leap to come to the conclusion that in the appropriate case, justice will be better served in proceedings under the Human Rights Code when there is complete information available to the respondents.

> *R. v. Stinchcombe* also recognized that the "fruits of the investigation" in the possession of the Crown "are not the property of the Crown for use in securing a conviction but the property of the public to be used to ensure that justice be done". We are of the opinion that this point applies with equal force to the proceedings before a Board of Inquiry and the fruits of the investigations are not the property of the Commission.[117]

These principles the Court then tied into natural justice by noting that the severe consequences and damage to an individual's reputation resulting from a negative finding by a Board of Inquiry made the *Stinchcombe* principles an aspect of natural justice. Finally, the Court disposed of the Commission's argument that such a severe disclosure obligation would discourage victims of racial discrimination from making legitimate complaints. The Court felt that it was of public importance that the complainants appreciate that allegations of racial discrimination are indeed serious and therefore should be made in a responsible and conscientious fashion.

---

116 Generally four criteria used in legal actions to determine whether a privilege against disclosure existed for material given in confidence. Originally formulated by the great British evidence scholar, Wigmore, these principles were endorsed in Canadian law by the Supreme Court of Canada in *R. Fosty*, [1991] 3 S.C.R. 263, 8 C.R. (4th) 368, [1991] 6 W.W.R. 673, 130 N.R. 161. There are actually few Canadian cases in which the Wigmore criteria have actually been considered to have been met.

117 The Court went on to exclude from the disclosure obligation material collected after the Board of Inquiry had been appointed and which had been prepared to assist counsel in the prosecution of the case. This distinction, which does not appear to be equivalent to the recognized solicitor-client privilege insofar as here it arises only after the appointment of the Board of Inquiry, escapes me. What is the difference between material collected to decide if an action should be brought and material collected to assist once it is brought? Both are amassed for the purposes of litigation.

The subsequent case of *Markandey v. Ontario (Board of Ophthalmic Dispensers)* amounts to little more, in my opinion, than a general assertion that full disclosure is a necessary element of fairness:

> The importance of full disclosure to the fairness of the disciplinary proceedings before the Board cannot be overstated. Although the standards of pre-trial disclosure in criminal matters would generally be higher than in administrative matters (See *Biscotti et. al. v. Ontario* (1990), 74 O.R. (2d) 119 (Div. Ct.) and (1991), 1 O.R. (3d) 409 (C.A.)), *tribunals should disclose all information relevant to the conduct of the case, whether it be damaging or supportive of a respondent's position, in a timely manner, unless it is privileged as a matter of law* [emphasis added] . . .[118] The Board has a positive obligation to ensure the fairness of its own process. The failure to make proper disclosure impacts significantly on the appearances of justice and the fairness of the hearing itself. Seldom will relief not be granted for a failure to make proper disclosure. For comparable principles in the context of criminal proceedings see *M.H.C. v. The Queen* (1991), 63 C.C.C. (3rd) 385 (S.C.C.); *R. v. Stinchcombe*. . . .

There are serious concerns with the approach of the Ontario courts in *House* and *Markandey* and the holus bolus adoption of the *Stinchcombe* principles by the Ontario courts in an administrative setting. If one wished to argue on technical grounds, one could fault the decisions for giving little more than lip service to the fact that the Supreme Court in *Stinchcombe* was expressly laying down guidelines in the context of criminal proceedings. The Ontario courts in *House* and *Markandy* made no attempt to reconcile those principles with the existing concepts of administrative law into which the criminal standards were roughly injected. For example, one must ask why, if the criminal indictment standards for disclosure in *Stichcombe* are necessary for fairness in the human rights context because of the seriousness of the result to the individual, are not the criminal standards for burden of proof, or the Charter protections relating to criminal matters, also not imported into those proceedings. Yet they are not. Those cases do not deal with, or even appear aware of, the extensive body of administrative law dealing with the non-disclosure of staff reports. Nor do the courts deal with the idea that , if natural justice and fairness contains a duty of total disclosure (similar to discovery in civil court actions) then natural justice and fairness would imply a power in the agencies whose functions are subject to natural justice and fairness to order pre-hearing disclosure or discovery of all material in the possession of a party. Yet the Supreme Court of Canada decision in *Canadian Pacific Air Lines Ltd. v. Canadian Air Line Pilots Assn.*[119] impliedly argues against any such power (by focusing on the express statutory grants as the source of such power which would

---

118 One can hardly imagine how requirements in criminal matters could be higher than the obligation imposed by the Court on this administrative proceeding.

119 [1993] 3 S.C.R. 724, 17 Admin. L.R. (2d) 141, 108 D.L.R. (4th) 1.

not have been necessary if such a power was implied simply by the duty to hold a fair hearing).[120]

More fundamentally, however, the principal fault that I see in the approach adopted by *House* and *Markandy* is that they are examples of the courts, again, failing to discern the differences between administrative agencies and the traditional judicial decision-makers. When they come to judge the requirements for fairness, they do it on the basis of what would be fair, for example, in a criminal process, not an administrative one. They determine fairness on the basis of what is necessary for the mandate being performed by a criminal court (or a civil court, to the extent that the disclosure duty can be likened to a full discovery right). In fact, it could be argued that to the extent that those decisions purport to find full disclosure an element of fairness they misunderstand the meaning of that term in administrative law.

Fairness in the context of administrative agencies has, firstly, never been directed to ensuring the best process for an individual facing an administrative proceeding . Its focus has always been on ensuring an *adequate* system. While no one would deny that full disclosure of all relevant material in the hands of an opposing party or before an agency would maximize the ability of an individual to defend itself, fairness (as illustrated earlier) has never required FULL disclosure — only such disclosure as will enable an individual to adequately prepare and present his case. Of course, one might validly ask why should such restraint be shown? To my mind it is because in imposing standards of procedure the courts recognize that they are intruding into an area in which they may not be able to judge the BEST procedures. As I have argued earlier, procedure is very much a matter of the mandate being performed. To be able to judge the best procedure one should be fully conversant with the complexities and special needs of the matter being dealt with. This expertise, the courts have always said, rests with the agencies who are expert in those matters. The role of the court is simply to ensure a type of basic procedural fairness. While they cannot gauge the best procedure to be followed, the courts have perceived their role as ensuring that procedures should not fall below specific minimums. The courts take this approach because generally they recognize that, in gauging procedural fairness, they, by their nature and own limitations, tend to look at questions from the perspective of their own expertise. This brings me to my second concern with the *House* and *Markandy* approaches.

In determining the requirements of fairness in administrative law, those courts looked at the question from the perspective of the needs of judicial processes, not the mandates assigned to the agencies under review. One of the main arguments in *Stinchombe* was that disclosure eliminates surprise and thus ensures justice. This simply may not be true in all administrative proceedings. In some proceedings, total disclosure may disrupt the overall mandate of the agency and

---

120 For the extent of an agency's implied powers please see the discussion in chapter 29 (Implied Powers of an Agency).

that cannot be considered the embodiment of justice. It looks to me that the courts in *House* and *Markandy* looked at the process, decided that it looked like a court process, and then imposed the values which have become associated with judicial process and which were geared to accomplishing judicial ends. The human rights process, however, much as it may look like a traditional court action, serves somewhat different purposes. The court in *House*, in asserting that the full disclosure requirement would ensure that complainants appreciate that allegations of racial discrimination are indeed serious and therefore should be made in a responsible and conscientious fashion, appears to completely fail to grasp the fact that Parliament may have wanted to encourage all complaints and concerns to be brought forward to the Human Rights Commission and that it is the role of the Commission to act as the filter to ensure that only responsible and conscientious complaints go forward. The nature of the problem at stake, the difficulties in determining what truly amounts to discrimination and the circumstances in which discrimination arises, are such that public concerns should be brought forward at that initial stage before the Commission. In this way Parliament has balanced the public need to identify and bring forward possible areas of human rights abuse with the right of an individual to protection from unwarranted actions. Truly, the court equated the Human Rights Commission as a Crown prosecutor to the exclusion of its policy and social roles.

To be fair, however, it is possible to view *House, Markandy*, and the obiter in *IMP v. Dillman* as being consistent with the concept still held by the courts in administrative law that the greater the impact of a decision on an individual, the greater the procedural protections he is entitled to have. The problem here, however, is that courts look to themselves as possessing the ultimate procedural protections. When the impact of proceedings approaches the high range of seriousness for an individual, the courts tend to look at the judicial package of procedures as being the best protection that individual can have for his rights REGARDLESS of whether that procedure is, from a functional perspective, actually the best method of accomplishing what is hoped to be accomplished.[121] Looking at disclosure then from this perspective likely inevitably leads one to a disclosure process based on the judicial model.

This is not to say that there should not be some circumstance in which total disclosure or some form of pre-hearing discovery may not be appropriate. *Nuosci*

---

121 For example, in *MacInnis v. Canada (Attorney General)*, [1995] 2 F.C. 215, 37 C.R. (4th) 152 (T.D.) the Court found that a lifer had a right to cross-examine the authors of conflicting psychological reports being considered on a parole application mainly because parole was the only chance a lifer in prison had for freedom. The question of whether an oral cross-examination was the best method to test the psychological reports was never considered. To me, it seems that oral cross-examination by a legal counsel of the authors of phycological reports would not be as certain an approach in determining which of the two reports were correct as would an approach based in writing where the expert details and implications could be logically and clearly explored without dramatics or the weakness in oral human expression. In questions such as this, one is dealing, not so much with credibility, as with knowledge and expertise.

appears to be a good example of such a case. What I am arguing for, however, is that the extent of disclosure rights should be determined in the context of the mandate of the agency in which the question arises. The parameters of fairness have always taken into account mandate and institutional constraints. This approach is illustrated by the decision of the Federal Court of Canada (both Trial and Appeal Divisions) in *Re Ciba-Geigy Canada Ltd.*[122]

In *Ciba-Geigy*, both the Trial and Appeal Divisions of the Federal Court rejected the application of the broad disclosure principles outlined in *R. v. Stinchcombe* to investigations and reports by staff of the Patented Medicines Prices Review Board. Both levels of Court declined to follow the earlier decision of the Ontario Divisional Court in *House*.

The Patented Medicines Prices Review Board is a regulatory agency responsible, among other things, for obtaining information with respect to the price being charged in Canada for patented medicines and ensuring that such prices are not excessive. In the case in point, staff of the Board had made substantial disclosure to the drug company and had disclosed (or would be disclosing prior to the hearing) all of the information in its possession which was prejudicial to it. Notwithstanding this broad disclosure, the drug company argued that it was entitled to all the evidence which the Board's staff had secured in its investigations leading up to a hearing, whether that evidence was favourable or prejudicial to the applicant.

In rejecting the application of the *Stinchcombe* principles the Trial Division noted that the Patented Medicines Prices Review Board was concerned with the economic regulation of medicine prices. In order to carry out its regulatory mandate the Board and its staff were required to receive a constant supply of information on prices (which the Court noted was similar to the statutory needs of other federal regulators such as the CRTC and the National Energy Board). The Court had earlier noted that much of this information was provided on a confidential basis but that, in the end, it might not be used by the staff. The Court held that information supplied to the Board pursuant to statutory authority for purposes of economic regulation was, prima facie, confidential. In its opinion, there was no point in the Legislature creating a regulatory tribunal if the tribunal was thereafter to be treated as a criminal court. The obligations concerning disclosure imposed by the doctrine of fairness and natural justice were met if the subject of the inquiry is advised of the case it has to meet and is provided with all the documents that will be relied on. ''Law and policy require that some leeway be given an administrative tribunal with economic regulatory functions, if, in pursuing it mandate, the tribunal is required by necessity to receive confidential information. It is not intended that proceedings before these tribunals be as

---

122 [1994] 3 F.C. 425 (*sub nom. Ciba-Geigy Canada Ltd. v. Patented Medicine Prices Review Board*) 77 F.T.R. 197, affirmed (*sub nom. Ciba-Geigy Canada Ltd. v. Canada (Patented Medicine Prices Review Board)*) (1994), 56 C.P.R. (3d) 377, 83 F.T.R. 2 (note), (*sub nom. CIBA-Geigy Canada Ltd. v. Patented Medicine Prices Review Board*) 170 N.R. 560 (C.A.).

adversarial as proceedings before a court. To require the Board to disclose all possibly relevant information gathered while fulfilling its regulatory obligations would unduly impede its work from an administrative viewpoint.'' Thus, the applicant was not entitled, in the words of the Court, to the ''fruits'' of the Board's investigations. The Federal Court of Appeal agreed with this assessment by the Trial Division. It agreed that the Board had properly balanced its duty of fairness to the drug company against its ability to discharge its public responsibilities on an ongoing basis. In the opinion of the Court of Appeal ''[a] trustful relationship with its investigative staff and proceeding 'as informally and expeditiously as the circumstances of fairness permits' are valid Board objectives.''[123]

I suggest that, in determining the extent of the duty to disclose information which is not actually before the decision-maker in an administrative proceeding, the contextually situated approach followed in *Ciba-Geigy* is more proper and more consistent with administrative law as a body than the approach to fairness adopted in either *House* or *Markandy*.

12.3(c)(vi) Forms of Notice

Given the extent of the information required for good notice it readily becomes evident that all of the various information required for adequate notice likely cannot be conveyed by a single document. Certainly, it would be rare for the traditional ''notice of hearing'' to contain sufficient particulars as to the

---

123 The Trial Division also rejected the applicant's request for disclosure of the staff report to the Chairperson of the Tribunal on which he had based his decision that a hearing was warranted in the circumstances. The Court held that the document only became relevant if the Board was going to rely on it. The Chairperson had stated that the Board's duty in law was to make its final decision on the basis of the evidence placed and tested before it during the hearing. Thus, there was no adverse effect to the applicant in the Board's refusal to disclose the report. It subsequently appeared that the Board was relying on evidence which had not been placed before it at the hearing the applicant could bring a further application at that time. This issue was not addressed before the Court of Appeal.

Nuosci v. Royal Canadian Mounted Police (1993), 68 F.T.R. 208, affirmed (February 22, 1995), Doc. A-552-93 (Fed. C.A.), leave to appeal to S.C.C. refused (August 17, 1995), Doc. 24689 (S.C.C.) is also another example of a contextually based approach to the application of *Stinchcombe*. Also, although it is strictly speaking not a fairness based disclosure case, the reader may wish to see the pre-*Stinchcombe* decision of the Ontario Court of Appeal in *Biscotti v. Ontario Securities Commission* (1991), 1 O.R. (3d) 409 (C.A.) where the Court of Appeal held that the Ontario Securities Commission was correct, in exercising its statutory discretion to reveal information given to its investigations, to take into consideration the fact that this was not simply information in the hands of the Commission, but was information secured by the Commission through an investigatory power to compel a witness to make statements under oath. The Court stated that, in these circumstances, the fact that a statement secured by such compulsion was relevant did not make it compellable. There was a public interest in this type of evidence remaining confidential unless the Commission, considering the matter on a witness by witness basis, considered it proper to do so. (The Court had already concluded that the very wide disclosure made by the Commission, which included any evidence which tended to exculpate the respondents, was adequate to ensure fairness.)

evidence and argument to be adduced at a hearing. Good notice is better thought of as a cumulative thing. Absent a legislative direction to the contrary, the fact that information may be given to the individual through a series of documents or disclosures is irrelevant provided that the cumulative effect is that the individual requiring notice ends up with sufficient information with respect to the proceeding to be able to prepare and present his case.[124] It is not uncommon, for example, to give summary notices of proceedings in a newspaper in which the principle information is set out sufficient to identify the matter in question but readers are referred to another source or location for fuller details. Where proceedings are commenced on the application by one of the parties, much of the required information may be set out in the application made by the applicant which is served on the other parties and filed with the agency (the nature of the claim, the particulars, the remedies being sought, etc.). In such cases the agency may easily incorporate the information set out in the application simply by identifying with sufficient particularity in its notice the application with which the proceeding is to be concerned.

12.3(c)(vii) The Notice of Hearing

At some point, however, an agency will likely have to notify the parties of the time, date and place of a hearing. Under the common law there is no particular format which a notice might take. (There may, however, be legislation which dictates the form the notice must take. The most common example can be found in those statutes which provide for the prescription of forms by regulation.)[125] The document need not even take the appearance of a form notice. It may, for example, simply be a letter.[126] Personally addressed notices are common where the participants are known. However, where the notice must be given to a very large or uncertain number of individuals, "to whom it might concern" notices in newspapers are commonly used. Like the overall requirement for notice, it is not the particular format of a notice, but the content which is important.

---

124 For example, in *Wood v. Nova Scotia (Board of Registration of Nursing Assistants)* (1988), 51 D.L.R. (4th) 625 (N.S.C.A.) the notice of hearing referred only superficially to the complaint to be considered in the proceedings. The particulars of the complaint were contained in a separate letter which was enclosed with the notice of hearing. See also *Collins v. Bd. of Educ. of Estevan R.C. Sep. Sch. Div. No. 27*, [1988] 6 W.W.R. 97 (Sask. C.A.), *R. v. Ontario (Racing Commission)*, [1971] 1 O.R. 400 (C.A.), *Herman Motor Sales Inc. v. Registrar of Motor Vehicle Dealers* (1980), 29 O.R. (2d) 431 (Div. Ct.).

125 On a side note, I have never understood the intent of the legislator who includes, as part of a prescribed form, the current address of the agency or other information likely to change rather than simply calling for the insertion of that information when the individual documents (e.g. "insert address of agency here") are completed for use. Including the current address in the prescription of the form will inevitably require the amendment of the regulation when the agency moves or the information in question changes.

126 As was done in *Wood v. Board of Registration of Nursing Assistants* (1988), 51 D.L.R. (4th) 625 (N.S. C.A.).

In practical terms, it is common for a notice of hearing given by an agency to contain the following information:

1. the name of the agency;

2. an identification of the matter which is to be the subject of the proceeding[127]

3. the legislative provision under which the proceeding is being held;[128]

4. the purpose of the proceeding;

5. time, date and place of proceeding;

6. any information required by statute to be included in a notice;[129] and

7. how to contact the agency for more information.

If possible, it is useful to include in the notice:

1. if the information has not already been included in one of the preceding steps, or been incorporated by reference to any form of application or statutory provisions, the issues to be considered in the proceeding and the possible consequences arising from the proceeding;

2. where any agency procedural rules or polices may be found;

3. where more information as to the application may be found, or the files may be reviewed; and

---

127 Where only a few parties are involved, it is common to name the parties. However, where the parties are very numerous or as of yet unascertained, some other reference is given to identify the proceeding—sometimes a reference to the thing to be done coupled with a geographical or municipal description.

128 This is actually an excellent short form way of conveying information. Just as a reference to an application will incorporate the information set out in that document, a reference to the statutory authority being relied on will incorporate the information included in the statutory provision referred to. Where legislation sets out the matters to be considered on an application or the consequences of a proceeding in separate legislative provisions it is also useful to include a reference to these legislative provisions to ensure that a party is aware of them. It may be imprudent for an agency simply to refer to the statutory provision referring to the commencement of a proceeding in the expectation that a party will be aware of all of the related legislative provisions. See, for example, *355 and 365 Grandravine Holdings Ltd. v. Pacini* (1991), 8 O.R. (3d) 29 (Div. Ct.). In that case, the Ontario Rent Review Hearings Board, sitting on appeal from the Minister of Housing, erred in failing to expressly advise the parties of its intention to deal with a particular issue or finding of the Minister. It appears, although it is not clear in the case report, that the Board's notice did not refer to the statutory provision that all appeals before the Board were to be by way of de novo proceedings.

129 Section 6 of Ontario's Statutory Powers Procedure Act, for example, sets out information that must be included in notices of hearing. This information differs depending on the type of hearing: oral, written or electronic.

4.   other information which would have the effect of forestalling delays of the hearing.[130]

As noted above, from a practical perspective, an agency will want to ensure that the participants in its proceedings are as fully informed as possible as this will result in their being in the best position to supply the agency with the information it needs to perform its mandate. From a legal perspective, failure to provide proper notice can result in the agency's decision being found to be void by the courts on judicial review.[131] If one takes the time to look at a decision of the Divisional Court of Ontario dealing with the inadequacy of the notice given by Ontario Hydro and approved, I judge, by the Environmental Assessment Board, one can sense the huge costs measured in millions of dollars that can be occasioned by an inadequate notice.[132] Thus, early on in its proceeding an agency should ensure that proper notice has been given. This can most easily be done at the opening of the proceeding where the presiding decision-maker should expressly ensure that there has been adequate service of the application (if any) and the notice of hearing.

12.3(c)(viii) Timing of Notice

All the information in the world will not allow one to adequately prepare for a proceeding if the information is given with too little time to adequately review it and prepare one's one case. Thus, notice must be given sufficiently in advance of a proceeding to permit one to present one's own case adequately.[133] Subject to

---

130 For example, I learned that, in order to avoid delays arising from the language requirements of the *Official Languages Act,* the Canada Labour Relations Board has a practice of advising participants of the language in which a hearing will proceed. This avoids surprise and allows necessary arrangements for interpretation to be made in advance of the hearing. Examples of forms of notices are set out in Appendix 12.1 (newspapers) and 12.1.1 (by mail). See also the very useful article by Gillian Burton "How to Prepare a Notice of Hearing" at pp. 16 to 26 of vol. 1 of *Administrative Agency Practice* (Carswell) which also contains examples of different types of notices.

131 *Supermarchés Jean Labrecque Inc. v. Trib. du Travail (Québec)* (1987), 28 Admin. L.R. 239 (S.C.C.), *McCarthy v. Nova Scotia (Provincial Medical Board, Discipline Committee)* 128 N.S.R. (2d) 322, 111 D.L.R. (4th) 273 (S.C.).

132 *Central Ontario Coalition Concerning Hydro Transmission Systems v. Ontario Hydro* (1984), 46 O.R. (2d) 715, 8 Admin. L.R. 88, 27 M.P.L.R. 165, 4 O.A.C. 249, 10 D.L.R. (4th) 341, 16 O.M.B.R. 172 (Div. Ct.). See also *Danakas v. War Veterans Allowance Board, Can.* (1985), 10 Admin. L.R. 110, 59 N.R. 309 (Fed. C.A.); *Forest v. La Caisse Populaire de St. Boniface Credit Union Society Ltd.* (1962), 41 W.W.R. 48, 37 D.L.R. (2d) 440 (Man. C.A.); and *Wiswell v. Metro Winnipeg,* [1965] S.C.R. 512, 51 W.W.R. 513, 51 D.L.R. (2d) 754.

133 *York Condominium Corporation No. 216 v. Dudnik* (1991), 3 O.R. (3d) 360, 45 O.A.C. 381, 79 D.L.R. (4th) 161 (Div. Ct.), *Godrey v Ontario Police Commission* (1991), 5 O.R. (3d) 163 (Div. Ct.), *Nrecaj v. Canada (Minister of Employment and Immigration),* [1993] 3 F.C. 630 (T.D.), *MacKinnon v. Saint John* (1984), 55 N.B.R. (2d) 340, 144 A.P.R. 340 (Q.B.), affirmed as appeal moot (1984) 58 N.B.R. (2d) 64, 151 A.P.R. 64 (C.A.). In *Namusa Enterprises Ltd. Etobicoke*

legislative direction, there is no specific amount of time required for good notice. The length of time required is a function of the purpose being served by giving the notice. A short notice period may be sufficient if that is all that is necessary for the individual to prepare adequately for whatever the notice is being given.[134] Failing disclosure in advance of a hearing, where a party is taken by surprise by the proffering of unexpected evidence at a hearing, an adjournment may be granted to permit a party to examine and meet the surprise evidence. Again, the length of adjournment will depend on the nature and importance of the evidence. Sometimes only a short adjournment may be necessary. In other cases the hearing may have to be adjourned to another day.[135]

This too, however, is not an absolute rule. In emergency situations, where there simply is not sufficient time to give proper notice, short or no notice at all may suffice *provided* that the individual is subsequently given a chance to defend his interests.[136]

12.3(c)(ix) Service of Notice

Subject to statutory direction, the general rule is that it is preferable that notice either be given personally or sent by registered mail.[137] It is not uncommon, however, for statutes to set out acceptable methods of service.[138] Frequently,

---

(City) (1984), 47 O.R. (2d) 769 (Div. Ct.) an individual was given only four days notice of which the Court stated that "The notice given . . . was so insufficient as to amount to no notice. The opportunity was insufficient in the circumstances of the case."

134 *Eldorado Seafoods Ltd. v. Director of Labour Standards* (1988), 76 Nfld. & P.E.I.R. 137 (Nfld. S.C.), *Rochon v. Spirit River School Division #47* (1994), 111 D.L.R. (4th) 452 (Alta. C.A.), *Yerxa v. Canada* (1993), 66 F.T.R. 59. See also *Richmond Square Development Corp. v. Middlesex Condominium Corp. No. 134* (1993), 103 D.L.R. (4th) 437 (Ont. Div. Ct.) where the Ontario Divisional Court agreed with an agency that five calendar days was sufficient opportunity for a party to review five volumes of documents when much of the information in question had been in the hands of the party earlier or was insignificant or merely expanded items which had been clearly identified to the party earlier in conciliation proceedings. (The agency had advised the party that it would be willing to consider objections to specific pieces of information when it was referred to in evidence at which time each objection would be considered in light of the importance and complexity of the document.)

135 See *Pleasant View Holdings Ltd. v. Liquor Control Commission (P.E.I.)* (1993), 104 Nfld. & P.E.I.R. 66, 329 A.P.R. 66 (P.E.I. C.A.) where the P.E.I. Court of Appeal held that merely showing evidence to a party during the course of a hearing will not meet the duty to disclose sufficient information that a party can know the case it has to meet.

136 *Tomko v. Nova Scotia (Labour Relations Board)* (1975), 69 D.L.R. (3d) 250 (S.C.C.), *Cardinal v. Kent Institution*, [1985] 2 S.C.R. 643, 24 D.L.R. (4th) 44, 63 N.R. 353, 16 Admin. L.R. 132.

137 *Bradley v. Ottawa Professional Fire Fighters Association*, [1967] 2 O.R. 311 (C.A.).

138 Some, such as s. 49 of Ontario's Rent Control Act, 1992, set out numerous ways in which service may be affected. Others are much more limited. Section 73 of British Columbia's Police Act, R.S.B.C. 1979, c. 53, merely provides that "Every notice required under this Act shall be in writing and shall be served personally or mailed by registered mail." Section 18 of Ontario's Statutory Powers Procedure Act, R.S.O. 1990, c. S.22, sets out the method of service for decisions and authorizes the use of regular mail, electronic transmission, telephone transmission by

however, difficulties may arise in locating a person who should get notice, or the person may be evading notice. Some statutes expressly deal with this problem and authorize the agency to give directions permitting service by alternate means (such as notice in a newspaper).[139] Absent such legislative provision, it cannot be said with certainty that an agency possesses an implied authority to issue such directions. There is a decision of the Ontario Court of Appeal respecting the authority of an arbitration board in which, in obiter, the Court stated that this power could be regarded as part of the board's initial arbitral authority.[140] On the whole, it seems likely that an agency does possess this authority.

An agency will only have such powers as are reasonably required for it to perform its mandate. Thus, the extent of an agency's implied authority to issue directions as to the form or service of notice would likely turn on the nature and demands of the mandate entrusted to it and the extent to which the agency is diminishing the right to notice. Notice is a matter of procedure and agencies are the masters of their procedure. Consequently, it would appear reasonable to assume that the determination of the type of notice required for a specific matter would turn on the type of matter or thing to be accomplished. A planning matter of broad implications for a very large geographic area would likely be satisfied with a very different form of notice (such as newspaper advertisements) than a small matter involving only two applicants (where one would expect personal notice to be more the rule). As the authority of agencies over their procedure springs from the recognition that different mandates require different procedures, it is reasonable to assume, that agencies do possess the implied authority to direct

---

facsimile, "or some other method that allows proof of receipt, in accordance with the tribunal's rules. . . ."

139 Section 49(4) of Ontario's Rent Control Act, 1992 for example, provides that a rent officer may in writing direct that a notice or document be given in a manner other than as provided in that section. Section 24(1) of Ontario's Statutory Powers Procedure Act, R.S.O. 1990, c. S.22 provides that:

24. (1) Where a tribunal is of the opinion that because the parties to any proceeding before it are so numerous or for any other reason, it is impracticable,

    (a) to give notice of the hearing; or

    (b) to send its decision and the material mentioned in section 18,

to all or any of the parties individually, the tribunal may, instead of doing so, cause reasonable notice to be given to such parties by public advertisement or otherwise as the tribunal may direct.

Alberta's Administrative Procedures Act contains no similar provision.

    By analogy to the decisions made under similar provisions of the Rules of Court, (*Clipper Ship Supply Inc. v. Samatour Shipping Co.* (1984), 19 F.T.R. 15, *Lower St. Lawrence Ocean Agencies Ltd. v. Samatour Shipping Co.* (1984), 47 C.P.C. 199 (Fed. T.D.), *Babineau v. Babineau* (1983), 32 C.P.C. 229 (Ont. Master)) it is likely that in determining the appropriate form of alternative service the decision-maker must be satisfied that there is at least a reasonable possibility that the information will come to the attention of the intended recipient if that method is chosen. Express statutory authority would likely be necessary to order a type of service where it was clear that it would not bring the matter to the attention of the intended recipient. Otherwise, the order would be tantamount, in practical terms, to dispensing with notice altogether.

140 *Bradley v. Ottawa Professional Fire Fighters Association*, [1967] 2 O.R. 311 (C.A.).

the form and service of notice. This would seem correct in light of the fact that the form of notice required by natural justice is a function of its circumstances. As differing circumstances may justify different forms of notice, and insofar as it is, at least on a preliminary basis, the agency which will have to determine the adequacy of notice, it seems reasonable to assume that the agency, as part of its duty to perform its mandate, possesses the authority to issue directions as to the form and service of notice.

It must be seriously doubted, however, that this implied authority would extend to dispensing with notice altogether (which would likely include directing a form of notice in which there was no reasonable likelihood of notice being given to the intended recipients). Notice of some sort is an integral part of natural justice and fairness and, as stated by the Supreme Court of Canada in *Innisfil (Township) v. Vespra (Township)*:

> [W]here the rights of a citizen are involved and the statute affords him the right to a full hearing, including a hearing of his demonstration of his rights, one would expect to find the clearest statutory curtailment of the citizen's right to meet the case against him. . . .[141]

It is clear, however, that where a participant provides an agency with an address for service the agency is entitled to rely on that address. Notice sent to that address by the agency will satisfy the requirement for service. The obligation is on the individual to keep the agency advised of any changes in address.[142]

Where a participant provides an agency with his address for service the agency is entitled to rely on the propriety of that address.[143] If there are any changes in that address prior to the end of the proceedings the participant must advise the agency of them.

---

141 (1981), 123 D.L.R. (3d) 530 (S.C.C.) at p. 546. This comment was made in the context of the right to cross-examination.

142 *Willis v. Canada (Minister of Employment & Immigration)* (1988), 87 N.R. 216 (Fed. C.A.), *Hall v. Canada (Minister of Employment & Immigration)* (1994), 25 Imm. L.R. (2d) (Fed. C.A.) (in this case the individual was under an express direction to keep the agency advised of his address).

143 *Bowen v. Minister of National Revenue*, [1992] 1 F.C. 311, 139 N.R. 167, [1991] 2 C.T.C. 266 (*sub nom. Canada (A.G.) v. Bowen*) (1991), 91 D.T.C. 5594 (C.A.). On the other side of the coin, the Immigration and Refugee Board was unable to rely on its ability to service a person by registered mail when it failed to include the full address for service given by the applicant. The applicant had asked that letters be sent to him at a particular address in care of his sister. The Board simply addressed the notices to the individual at the municipal address and omitted the ''in care of'' portion of the address. The letter was returned marked ''moved''. The Federal Court of Appeal held that the Board was not able to rely on its statutory authority for service by registered mail. In the opinion of the court, ''[w]here an address for service includes the name of a person as well as a street address, both are essential parts for the purposes of proving service by registered mail.'' *Singh (Manjit) v. Canada (Minister of Employment & Immigration)* (1989) 107 N.R. 83 (Fed. C.A.).

12.3(c)(x) Consequences of Failure to Give Proper Notice

As a general rule, if proper notice has not been given, a proceeding should not continue until proper notice has been given insofar as a decision which was arrived at without proper notice having been given may be a nullity.[144]

Whether or not a hearing must be recommenced from the beginning depends on the nature and effect of the failure. Usually if the failure goes to a party at a hearing being surprised by evidence or policy which he was not made aware of earlier an adjournment (for whatever period would reasonably allow the person who did not receive the notice to consider the evidence or policy) may compensate for the defective notice. Where the defective notice has resulted in the agency having heard matters of substance in the absence of a person entitled to notice of those matters, then the hearing will likely have to be recommenced. If the deficiency goes to the issues to be raised and it appears that some individuals may not have attended the proceeding as they did not think a particular issue was to be dealt with, the hearing will likely have to be done over again after proper notice has been given. Equally, if a proceeding has already proceeded to the stage where it has begun to deal with the substance of the matter when a failure to give notice of the hearing, or a failure to give notice of the bringing of the application is discovered the hearing will have likely have to begin again after proper notice has been given.

However, there are circumstances when a failure in notice will not require remedial action. If the requirement to give notice was statutory, the effect of the failure to comply with that statutory direction will depend on whether the direction was discretionary (e.g. "may give notice"), or imperative (e.g. "shall give notice"). If discretionary, notice is not a necessary precondition to the hearing and, provided that the discretion was exercised on proper principles, the decision not to give notice will not delay the conduct of the hearing. Failure to comply with an imperative statutory direction, however, may result in a void proceeding, depending on whether the imperative direction is mandatory or directory in nature.[145]

If the direction is mandatory, failure to give notice will mean the hearing cannot proceed until proper notice is given . Because the trend today is to treat all imperative statutory procedural commands as being directory unless it would be seriously inconvenient to do so,[146] the role of prejudice is somewhat circular. If the failure to follow a statutory procedural direction would cause no prejudice to *any* interest (including some public interest) that statutory direction will gen-

---

144 *Central Ontario Coalition Concerning Hydro Transmission Systems, Re* (1984), 46 O.R. (2d) 715 (Div. Ct.).

145 For a discussion on whether an imperative statutory provision is mandatory or directory see section 22.5.1.

146 *British Columbia (Attorney-General) v. Canada (Attorney-General)* (1994), 114 D.L.R. (4th) 193 (S.C.C.), *Bridgeland-Riverside Community Assn. v. Calgary (City)* (1982), 19 Alta. L.R. (2d) 361 (C.A.).

erally be considered to be directory in nature. If, however, some serious prejudice will arise, the direction will be considered mandatory.[147] Hence, technically, one will never be asking whether the absence of prejudice will mitigate against the failure to comply with a mandatory statutory procedural direction. By definition, the breach of a mandatory statutory procedural direction will always give rise to some prejudice.

Where there is a public interest being protected by a mandatory provision, failure to comply with it likely cannot be waived by any individual.[148] This is only logical. As the individual is not the only intended recipient of the procedural protection, he cannot waive its application. However, if the mandatory provision exists only for the interests of an individual who is willing to waive it, there seems little reason to insist on strict compliance.

Statutory time limits for the commencement of matters, or the service of documents which commence a matter, are, as a rule, mandatory in nature.[149]

If an imperative statutory notice provision is directory, however, the failure to give notice will not stop the hearing if the agency is satisfied that no prejudice to anyone results from the failure.[150] (On a technical point, establishing the absence of prejudice may be difficult to do if the persons who were entitled to notice are not present at the hearing.) A statutory direction to give notice which is imperative but only directory may likely be waived by the individual entitled to the notice.

It is not uncommon for statutes with provisions respecting service to contain an ameliorating legislative provision to the effect that failure to meet the technical legislative requirements will not invalidate the proceedings, sometimes with the added rider that the intended recipient actually receives the notice or is aware of its contents. These provisions are not always obvious. For example, in *Wolek v. Herzog*[151] the Ontario Divisional Court concluded that the statutory direction that "Every decision of the Commission shall be upon the real merits and justice of the case" was equivalent to the Rule of Court which provided that no proceeding shall be defeated by a mere formal objection. In the Court's opinion, the statute did not impose a rigid restriction on the ability to give notice. Thus, while it was clear that the tenants had not served the landlord with the notice of appeal in the

---

147 *Bay Village Shopping Centre Ltd. v. Victoria*, [1983] 1 W.W.R. 634, 31 D.L.R. (3d) 570 (B.C. C.A.), *Nisga's Tribal Council v. Environmental Appeal Board* (1988), 32 Admin. L.R. 319 (B.C. S.C.).

148 *Newton v. Tataryn* (1990), 65 Man. R. (2d) 175 (Q.B.).

149 See for example, *Costello v. Calgary (City)*, [1983] 1 S.C.R. 14, [1983] 2 W.W.R. 673, 23 Alta. L.R. (2d) 380, 43 D.L.R. (2d) 285, *Newton v. Tataryn* (1990), 65 Man. R. (2d) 175 (Q.B.), *Ans v. Paul* (1980), 41 N.S.R. (2d) 256 and 76 A.P.R. 256 (N.S. S.C.), *Gage v. Ontario* (1992), 90 D.L.R. (4th) 537 (Div. Ct.), *Vialoux v. Registered Psychiatric Nurses Association (Manitoba)* (1983), 2 D.L.R. (4th) 186 (Man. C.A.) and *Manitoba v. Manitoba (Human Rights Commission)* (1983), 2 D.L.R. (4th) 759 (Man. C.A.).

150 *Robertson v. Edmonton (City)* (1990), 44 Admin. L.R. 27 (Alta. Q.B.), *Tesky v. Law Society (British Columbia)* (1990), 45 Admin. L.R. 132 (B.C. S.C.) additional reasons at (1990) 49 B.C.L.R. (2d) 223, 74 D.L.R. (4th) 146 (S.C.).

151 (1984), 46 O.R. (2d) 513 (Div. Ct.).

manner directed by the statute, the landlord became aware of the existence of the appeals and the fact that the notices were available at the Commission's offices for viewing. The Court felt, in these circumstances, and in light of the "merits and justice of the case" provision, the Residential Tenancy Commission was wrong to hold that the service directions in the statute were mandatory. Instead, the Court held, the Commission should have determined if there had been some unfairness or underhanded conduct on the part of the tenants or if there was some reason why the landlord could not be protected from additional prejudice involved in granting him an adjournment to properly review the material.

If reliance is to be placed upon an ameliorating statutory provision of this type it is important to take careful note of the extent of the leeway granted by it. For example, the British Columbia Supreme Court in *Mack v. Yu* (1991), 7 Admin. L.R. (2d) 67 held that the alleviating provision found in section 51 of the B.C. Residential Tenancy Act only permitted that a notice be *given* in some way other than as specified in the Act. It did not provide any relief from the statutory requirements regarding the form, contents or timing of service of the notice.

A breach of a natural justice duty to disclose will, generally, invalidate a proceeding *where it results in the denial of a fair hearing*. The case law on this point, while clear as to the principle, is somewhat misleading to the extent that it gives the impression that the courts are not concerned with whether or not the breach gave rise to any prejudice. In *Supermarches Jean Labrecque Inc. v. Labour Court*[152] the Supreme Court of Canada held that "the absence of any real and present prejudice, which is not disputed by appellant, can in no way remedy [the failure to give the parties proper notice and an opportunity to be heard]". Thus, the courts will not speculate as to what would have happened had proper notice been given.[153] However, notwithstanding these comments, the existence or absence of prejudice does play a role. It is true that once a breach of natural justice is found, the courts will not be concerned with the question of prejudice. But prejudice is relevant in the determination of whether or not there was a breach of natural justice in the first place. For example, in *Université du Québec à Trois-Rivières v. Syndicat des employés professionnels de l'Université du Québec à Trois-Rivières*[154] the Supreme Court held that not every technical failure to admit relevant evidence amounted to a breach of the duty to be fair, but where the rejection of relevant evidence has such an impact on the fairness of the proceeding it may lead unavoidably to the conclusion that there has been a breach of natural justice.[155] Thus a court will generally not intervene by reason of a failure to give

---

152 (1987), 43 D.L.R. (4th) 1 (S.C.C.).

153 *Kane v. University of British Columbia* (1980), 110 D.L.R. (3d) 311 (S.C.C.), *Cardinal v. Institution*, [1985] 2 S.C.R. 643, 24 D.L.R. (4th) 44.

154 (1993), 148 N.R. 209 (S.C.C.).

155 See also *Nisbett v. Manitoba (Human Rights Commission)* (1993), 101 D.L.R. (4th) 744 (Man. C.A.) where the Manitoba Court of Appeal noted that delay may give rise to a breach of fairness

notice if it is clear that no harm resulted from the failure (for instance where the individual comes by the necessary information within adequate time despite the failure in service).[156] Essentially, the principles of natural justice and fairness exist to ensure a fair hearing. A technically flawed process, which in no way impairs the individual's right to a fair hearing, does not amount to a denial of natural justice.

In addition to determining whether there has been a breach of natural justice, lack of prejudice also appears to be considered by the courts on judicial review as a factor in determining whether their discretion to intervene should be exercised or not. There is some case law where the courts declined to exercise their discretion to intervene in order to remedy a breach of natural justice where there was no resulting prejudice.[157]

The bottom line appears to be that whether one approaches the question from the angle of determining whether the failure amounted to a breach of natural justice or from the angle of a court's discretion to grant judicial review, prejudice is relevant to determining the consequences of a failure to give notice.

---

where "there has been prejudice of such a kind and degree as to significantly impair the ability of a party to receive a fair hearing".

156 This is to be contrasted with a breach of the prohibition against bias, for which there is no cure (*Nfld. Telephone Co. v. Newfoundland (Board of Commissioners of Public Utilites)* (1992), 4 Admin. L.R. (2d) 121 (S.C.C.). Lack of notice was not held fatal to the proceedings in *Fong v. Canada (Minister of Employment & Immigration)* (1993) 67 F.T.R. 188 when the Court concluded that there would have been no difference to the outcome even had notice been given. See also *Toshiba Corporation v. Anti-Dumping Tribunal* (1984) 8 Admin. L.R. 173 (Fed. C.A.) where the Court concluded that although there had been a failure to disclose a preliminary staff report "everything contained in the preliminary staff report is either a matter of general or public knowledge or is based upon facts and sources which were, in due course, properly brought out at the hearing in such a manner that all the parties to that hearing had a full opportunity to test them. Thus, while . . . there might have been a technical breach of the rules of natural justice, it can be said with confidence at the end of the day that such breach was minor and inconsequential and that the result of the inquiry would not have been different had such breach not occurred." The Ontario Divisional Court, however, once held that prejudice was to be presumed where a disciplinary agency, in order to avoid a legal challenge to its jurisdiction, intentionally withheld proper notice from a serving police officer performing a public duty such that he was misled as to what was happening (thereby giving the other side a 10-month advantage in preparing its case against him) (*Gage v. Ontario (Attorney General)* (1992), 90 D.L.R. (4th) 537 (Div. Ct.)). For other cases where breaches of natural justice did not invalidate proceedings where there was no prejudice resulting from the breach, see *Hryciuk v. Ontario (Lieutenant Governor)* (1994), 18 O.R. (3d) 695 (Div. Ct.), *Schaaf v. Canada (Minister of Employment & Immigration)*, [1984] 3 W.W.R. 1 (Fed. C.A.), *Eaton v. Brant (County) Board of Education* (1994), 71 O.A.C. 69 (Div. Ct.) where the literature reviewed after the hearing in the absence of the applicant did nothing more than confirm the decision-makers independent assessment of the evidence before it and the various admissions of the applicants' experts with regard to that research.

157 See for example, *Samuel, Son & Co. v. Restrictive Trade Practices Commission (Can.)* (1987), 17 F.T.R. 267, *Schaaf v. Canada (Minister of Employment & Immigration)*, [1984] 3 W.W.R. 1 (Fed. C.A.), *Giroux v. Canada (National Parole Board)* (1994), 89 F.T.R. 307, and *Berg v. British Columbia (Attorney General)* (1991), 48 Admin. L.R. 82 (B.C. S.C.).

Legislation may also dispense with the common law duty to give notice.[158]
A failure to give notice as required by natural justice may be also be waived by
the individual affected.[159]

12.3(c)(xi) Practice Hints

1.   Where an agency holds hearings on a regular basis it may develop its own
     notice list.

2.   Where a specific type of hearing is infrequently held, the agency may instruct
     the applicant to submit a draft notice list to the agency for review. In addition,
     (and as noted earlier) an agency may, based upon its experience, order a
     party, or move itself, to place a notice in a number of daily or weekly
     newspapers.

3.   When faced with requests which require a preliminary decision on the part
     of the agency (e.g. a request to reopen a hearing) where it appears that a
     prima facie case has been raised warranting an oral hearing of the matter,
     the best practice is for the agency to combine the functions of the hearing so
     that the notice states that the first purpose of the hearing is to consider the
     request and the second is to consider the substance of the matter if the request
     is granted.[160]

4.   Some proof of the service of applications, or the sending of notices should
     always be placed on the agency's file (this applies equally to notice given
     by the agency staff and the participants):

     —   If notice was given personally, a statement or an affidavit of service by

---

158 *Manitoba v. Canada (National Transportation Agency)* (1994), [1995] 1 F.C. 603 (C.A.).
    Although this decision is sound in its reliance on the principle that statute can dispense with the
    requirement for notice, the length to which the Court was willing to go to find such a statutory
    intention is quite unusual and open to serious question. The authority to statutorily dispense
    with an aspect of natural justice and fairness would, of course, be subject to the dictates of s. 7
    of the Charter and s. 2(e) of the Canadian Bill of Rights (where applicable) (*Singh v. Canada
    (Minister of Employment & Immigration)* (1985), 17 D.L.R. (4th) 244 (S.C.C.)).

159 *Hryciuk v. Ontario (Lieutenant Governor)* (1994), 18 O.R. (3d) 695 (Div. Ct.), *Gal Cab Invest-
    ments Ltd. v. Liquor Licensing Board* (1986), 34 D.L.R. (4th) 363 (N.W.T. C.A.) Generally, the
    principles of natural justice may be waived: *Khakh v. Canada (Minister of Employment &
    Immigration*, [1994] 1 F.C. 548, 23 Imm. L.R. (2d) 38 (T.D.), *Balka v. McDonald* (1994), 120
    Nfld. & P.E.I.R. 7, 373 A.P.R. 7 (Nfld. T.D.). In *Eaton v. Brant (County) Board of Education*
    (1994), 71 O.A.C. 69 (Div. Ct.) the Ontario Divisional Court held that a decision-maker did not
    err in reviewing extra literature on the matter after the hearing without advising the applicant
    when the applicant had invited it to do so.

160 Notwithstanding this comment, there is case law to the effect that notice of the request itself
    need not be given provided that individuals opposing it are given an opportunity to challenge
    the agency's actions at the beginning of the hearing (*Canada (Canadian Transportation Accident
    Investigation & Safety Board, Re (sub nom. Parrish, Re.*, [1993] 2 F.C. 60, (*sub nom. Canadian
    Transportation Accident Investigation & Safety Board v. Parrish*) 60 F.T.R. 110.

the person who served (a copy of the notice given should be completed and filed (see Appendix 12.3 for an example).

— If notice was given by mail, a statement or affidavit should be placed on the file certifying the setting out to the names and addresses to which the notices were sent , the type of mail used (registered, regular or other), and the date notices were mailed. A copy of the text of the notice given — omitting the individual addresses — should be attached.

— If notice was given in some other form, the person who gave the notice should file a statement or affidavit certifying how (e.g. by newspaper) and (if known) to whom the notice was given, and the date it was given. A copy of the notice should be attached.[161]

5. Prior to the hearing, the decision-maker should review the file, or have the file reviewed to verify that all notices required to be given by the agency were given. The decision-maker should also verify the prima facie propriety of the application (if any) and the propriety of service of the notice of hearing by the agency (by referring to the proof on file).

6. Concerns respecting the adequacy of notice should be raised as early as possible in the proceedings (in order to avoid being found to have waived a possible objection). At the opening of the hearing the decision-maker should ask if there are any concerns respecting the adequacy of notice (and deal with any concerns raised). This should be done as early as possible in the proceedings in the event that a serious problem with notice exists which may necessitate redoing the hearing.

12.4 INTERVENTIONS

Intervenors are generally individuals or groups who do not meet the criteria to be a party but who still have a sufficient interest, or some expertise or view which the agency feels will benefit the proceeding to have represented. As the Supreme Court of Canada commented in the *Canadian Council of Churches v. Canada*[162] "[T]he views of the public litigant who cannot obtain standing need not be lost. Public interest organizations are, as they should be, frequently granted intervenor status. *The views and submissions of intervenors on issues of public importance frequently provide great assistance to the courts."* [emphasis added.]

If not expressly given by statute, an agency's authority to grant intervenor status flows implicitly from the power to conduct a hearing or to hold an inquiry.[163]

---

161 For an example where failure to take this simple precautionary measure resulted in an agency being unable to determine (and thus rely on) the fact that it had given proper notice by registered mail see *Singh (Sucha) v. Canada (Minister of Employment & Immigration)* (1989), 102 N.R. 304 (Fed. C.A.).

162 (1992), 132 N.R. 241 (S.C.C.).

163 *Nfld. Telephone Co. v. TAS Communications Systems Ltd.* (1987), 45 D.L.R. (4th) 570 (S.C.C.).

It appears that, at least in the case of a public officer, in order for an agency to grant such status the person seeking intervenor status must have the ability himself to receive the grant.[164]

There is no common law *right* to be an intervenor. Statute may, of course, grant such a right but in the absence of such a statutory provision, intervenors are added at the discretion of the agency. Furthermore, unlike a party, who is given certain rights by natural justice and fairness, the extent of an intervenor's participation is fixed by the agency (subject to statutory direction, of course). The degree of participation will be determined by the extent the agency feels the intervenor's participation will assist it in its mandate.[165] Sometimes two or more individuals or groups may bring before the agency essentially the same expertise or views. In that case the agency may require that they pool their resources and appear through a single spokesman. However, it must be remembered that an intervenor is there to bring a view or an expertise before the agency which will be useful in determining the matter which is before the agency. An intervenor should not be given leave to speak to questions which are not raised by the underlying proceeding.[166]

Once notice has been given of the hearing, those who want to take part will give notice of their wish to participate in the hearing by filing with the tribunal a notice of intervention: see Appendix 12.4.

The notice of intervention should be precise and should set out:

(1) the style of cause (to allow the agency to identify the proceeding in question);

(2) a description of the intervenor (to allow the agency to know who is seeking the intervention and what he can bring to the proceeding);

---

164 In *Nfld. Telephone Co. v. TAS Communications Systems Ltd.* (1987), 45 D.L.R. (4th) 570 (S.C.C.) the Supreme Court held that the Newfoundland Board of Commissioners of Public Utilities could not grant intervenor standing to the federal Director of Investigation and Research as the federal government had not given that officer the mandate to appear before provincial agencies. The Court held that "Whatever scope may be reasonably assigned to the implied power or discretion of the board to permit intervention, it cannot have been intended that the board should have authority to permit intervention by a public officer in his official capacity if the officer has been denied the necessary authority to intervene by his governing statute. . . . To permit intervention where a public officer is shown to lack the necessary authority to intervene would be to permit him to exceed his authority and thus would be contrary to a fundamental principle of public law." The Court had earlier held that the official required some statutory authority to intervene in the capacity of his office as that intervention would amount to "an assertion, in an adjudicative context, of the authority and expertise of a public official. In such a case, a public officer puts the weight of his opinion and knowledge acquired in the exercise of his official duties, on the adjudicative scales. He extends, on his own initiative, the effective reach and influence of his office and authority with potential direct legal effect."

165 See for example, the description of the role of intervenors before the National Energy Board in c. 5.5(d)(iv) and the Ontario Energy Board in c. 5.4.

166 *Rudolph v. Canada (Minister of Employment & Immigration)* (1992), 139 N.R. 233 (Fed. C.A.).

(3) a description of how the intervenor can be impacted or affected by the matters before the agency;

(4) a brief description of the positions being taken by the intervenor for or against; and

(5) the address for service upon the intervenor.

Few agencies have a procedure to strike out a notice of intervention if it fails to disclose any substantial interest of the intervenor. I believe that most agencies should allow standing to most intervenors.[167] In the end, the agency will have to decide what weight should be given to the submissions. This practice is in the public interest.

Where an agency has no requirement for the filing of any supporting material in advance by the applicant, there will obviously be no requirement that material be filed with a notice of intervention. Many agencies have no requirement that an intervenor file any material. He only has to appear the day the hearing commences, having given notice of his intent to intervene. Many agencies do not even require a notice of intervention to intervene. Most agencies fall somewhere between the extremes of substantial pre-filings and no filings at all.

12.5 INTERROGATORIES

Once a notice calling a hearing has been given and the notices of intervention have been received, the tribunal may issue a procedural order advising all parties of the procedure, in terms of interrogatories and other preliminary matters.

Interrogatories are written questions directed by parties to each other, copies of which are filed with the tribunal and sent to or served on all other parties. Usually the procedural order, where interrogatories are part of a tribunal's practice, will described how a party may intervene and put interrogatories to opposing parties. Such a procedural order is attached as Appendix 12.5.

Interrogatories were introduced many years ago by some agencies such as the NEB and the OEB as a substitute for examination-for-discovery. Most boards can authorize (order) discovery, but it is not common to do so. The concept of interrogatories is that if a party does not understand material that has been filed, it may address questions in writing to another party. The interrogatories shall be answered by the other party in writing on or before a certain date, unless a motion

---

167 For an interesting limitation on the authority of an agency to grant intervenor status see *Director of Investigations and Research Under the Combines Investigation Act v. Nfld. Telephone Co.*, [1987] 2 S.C.R. 466, 68 Nfld. & P.E.I.R. 1, 209 A.P.R. 1, where the Supreme Court of Canada held that an provincial agency could not grant a federal official intervenor status in its proceedings when Parliament had not given that office the mandate to intervene. The agency's provincially based power could not alter the mandate of the federal official.

is brought before the tribunal dispensing with a duty to answer the question. The practice, where there are interrogatories, is that the question and answers are numbered so that they can be easily associated with the party asking the question and the subject matter.

Needless to say, an interrogatory process, although common with regulatory tribunals is not common with other kinds of agencies. This is, perhaps, because the issues coming before regulatory boards are unusually complex. They involve, as a rule, a large volume of paper and statistics.

It is not possible to lay down any rule as to how, if at all, agencies should make use of the interrogatory process. However, there is something to be said for the use of more, rather than less, pre-filed material so that parties have a clearer advance knowledge of how parties' interests are affected or could be affected by the hearing. In addition, the parties can more usefully participate on behalf of the public interest and assist a tribunal if it knows more rather then less about the issues in advance. The pre-filed material becomes part of the record as soon as it is identified by the witness. The material is not read into the record. The tribunal must have read and understood the material, as filed, before the hearing commences. Thus, a traditional panel carries into a regulatory hearing a very substantial appreciation of the application, which comes to a large extent from the interrogatory process and the pre-filings, as well as the accumulated expertise and experience of the tribunal. A sample of an interrogatory with the answer is contained in Appendix 12.6.

12.6 PRE-FILING OF EVIDENCE

12.6(a) Authority to Require

As a creature of statute, if an agency is to have the authority to require the pre-hearing exchange of information between participants or pre-hearing filing of evidence with the agency, it must have been given it by Parliament or a Legislature, either expressly or impliedly.

For an example of an express (if indirect) grant see *Pasquale v. Vaughan (Township)*[168] the Ontario Court of Appeal held that the Ontario Municipal Board was granted the authority to order production and inspection of documents by virtue of the wide grant of authority found in section 37 of the Ontario Municipal Board Act, R.S.O. 1960, c. 274. This section provided that the Board "for the due exercise of its jurisdiction and power and other wise for carrying into effect the provisions of this or any other general or special Act, has all such powers . . . as are vested in the Supreme Court with respect to the amendment of proceedings, [other matters mentioned in the section] and all other matters necessary or proper therefor. The Court concluded that "the section . . . contemplates as a corollary

---

168 [1967] 1 O.R. 417 (C.A.).

to the production and inspection of documents, a situation where the Board, by its order, may if it sees fit order examination for discovery.''[169]

The power to order pre-hearing filing or exchange of documents can also exist by way of an implied grant of authority *to the extent that that authority is reasonably necessary for the performance of the agency's mandate.* Thus, an agency's authority over its procedure will authorize the agency to require the pre-hearing exchange or filing of information which the parties intend to file or rely on at the hearing.[170] The authority can also flow from the mandate to hold a hearing to the degree that the pre-hearing disclosure or exchange of information can be seen as being required by natural justice.[171] Otherwise, if the authority to order the pre-hearing exchange or filing cannot be seen as being reasonably necessary for the performance of the agency's mandate or as being required by natural justice and fairness an agency will not have the authority to do so.

12.6(b) Value of Pre-filing

The purposes of pre-filing generally is:

(1) to focus the hearing;

(2) to avoid waste of time and money;

(3) to prevent surprise; and

(4) to enable parties, intervenors and the tribunal to better prepare for the hearing.[172]

Some agencies have such pre-filing requirements.[173] Some agencies have none. I believe that most should have such a practice. As noted above, it is an

---

169 *Pasquale* was subsequently followed in *Lilly v. Gairdner* (1973), 42 D.L.R. (3d) 56 (Ont. Div. Ct.).

170 *Morista Developments Ltd. v. Ontario Municipal Board* (1990), 2 Admin. L.R. (2d) 113 (Ont. Div. Ct.).

171 *Markandey v. Ontario (Board of Ophthalmic Dispensers),* (March 14, 1994, Doc. 2661/93 (Ont Gen. Div.). The extent to which natural justice may require such disclosure is discussed earlier in c. 12.3(c)(v).

172 Pre-filing allows an agency to become more familiar with the documentary evidence and better able to understand explanatory argument respecting it and deal with any concerns which may be raised respecting it. For a related topic, see chapter 19 (Preparing a Case Before An Agency).

173 For example, in Broadcasting matters the CRTC has adopted the rule that ''No evidence may be introduced at a public hearing except in support to statements contained in an application, intervention or reply or in support of documents or material filed in support thereof.'' A similar rule was adopted by the Commission in Telecommunications matters: ''Where an intervenor intends to present evidence at a central hearing, memoranda consisting of the material intended to be presented as evidence shall be served on all other parties forty-eight hours before the calling of the witness in respect thereof or such longer period as the Commission may consider necessary under the circumstances.''

element of good notice that disclosure be made of evidence which a person will have to meet in a proceeding. Pre-filing will avoid claims of surprise and the resulting requests for adjournments. In addition, complex, detailed and lengthy evidence can be more quickly put on the record through pre-filings. Most regulatory tribunals have very elaborate pre-filing requirements because the hearings are complex and can impact on many people. If the evidence to be considered were to be put on the record viva voce, it could take months to do so even without the time taken in cross-examination.

In a typical Hydro rate reference before the Ontario Energy Board, the pre-filed evidence, including exhibits, runs to approximately 6,000 pages with about 400 exhibits and perhaps 1,000,000 or more figures. It would be a colossal waste of time and money to have that evidence read into the record. Thus, the evidence is pre-filed and adopted by witnesses. Witnesses are not taken through the evidence by counsel. If counsel tries to do so, he is stopped unless there is some special reason to do so. The practice is for counsel to ask that the witness to confirm the evidence, make any necessary corrections, highlight his curriculum vitae and then turn the witness over for cross examination. This is known as the "dump and run" process. Even additions to the evidence should be pre-filed.

Were this process not in effect, most regulatory tribunals would have to triple their size. Not only that, but one case could take up to a year to complete if typical court procedures were applied.

All the pre-filed material, the interrogatories, and the answers are read by all the parties, counsel and the panel members before the hearing commences. This is one of the reasons it may take those who are actively involved far longer to prepare for a hearing than it does to hear it. It is important, however, for agencies to realize that pre-filings are merely collections of paper. Absent consent, they do not become evidence until entered in evidence, explained or otherwise dealt with by an participant or witness at the hearing. One must also strive to keep an open mind in reviewing the material and avoid forming preliminary conclusions or views as to the merits of a matter. It is improper for an agency to start off a proceeding by noting that the "evidence" on file appears to support one case or another unless it can be shown otherwise. This amounts to a pre-judgement.

12.6(c) Practice Hint: The Document Book

Where there is likely to be extensive documentary evidence filed in a proceeding, and particularly where there is likely to be overlap between the evidence filed by different individuals, participants may find it very useful to use a "document book" to pre-file evidence before an agency. This is one or more bound volumes (either binders or cerlox binding may be used) containing all the documents that the parties (where agreement can be reached) or a party (where agreement cannot be reached) intends to use as evidence. The material should be arranged by tabs and an index provided with the book to enable the agency members to refer to a particular document quickly. Anita Lyon, in her article in

Administrative Agency Practice entitled "How to Make a Document Book: Persuasive Presentation of Documentary Evidence For Hearings Before Administrative Agencies", notes the following advantages in using document books:

> By presenting your documentary evidence in a bound chronological package you achieve the following:
>
> • Your presentation looks more professional.
>
> • The decision maker can quickly access the documents and follow along at the hearing.
>
> • Later the decision maker can easily access the documents during deliberation. Your case theory is reinforced with the chronological presentation of the documents.
>
> • You can quickly locate the documents you need. You have taken control of the paper. You prevent the noisy shuffling of papers and delay in shuffling through unbound documents that would otherwise impede a coherent and audible presentation of testimony and argument.
>
> • By making your presentation of documents organized and accessible you have enhanced your opportunity to persuade the decision maker of the merits of your case.[174]

12.7 THE HEARING SETTING

12.7(a) Hearing Room Set-up

Some agencies have their own hearing rooms and some do not. Some agencies hold hearings in many different places within the area of their jurisdiction. The hearings of some agencies last only an hour or so and some may last for months. The hearings of some agencies involve a large number of staff, consultants and a mountain of paper and reference material. Other agencies receive and review very little paper or reference material and use no staff or counsel of their own.

Some hearings will attract five to ten people whereas some will often attract over 150 participants, lawyers and observers. Royal Commissions, special public hearings and regular hearings of many agencies may attract up to 500 people in the audience.

The set-up of the hearing room will to a great degree depend on two factors: i. the type of hearing to be held, and ii. the resources available. The type of hearing

---

174 (1993) 1 A.A.P. 31 at p. 33. In this article Ms. Lyon sets out a number of practical suggestions on how to best put together and use document books. The reader should also noted the commentary by Jane Graham which immediately follows Ms. Lyon's article, "Commentary: The Use of Document Books Before the Competition Tribunal" by Jane Graham, (1993) 1 A.A.P. 35.

to be held will often dictate the hearing room set-up. Obviously a hearing room that can accommodate only 30 people will not be suitable for a large public hearing where hundreds of persons will attend and which will extend over several months. Having said this, the agency may be able to dream of the perfect hearing room to accommodate every need perfectly. Resources may be such, however, that it, and the public, will have to settle for what it can get.

Hearing rooms at the agency's offices are preferable to hearing rooms located elsewhere. There, if necessary, the members and the public can draw upon the agency's staff for assistance, have access to phones, photocopiers, fax machines, washrooms, etc. Internal hearing rooms can be designed to accommodate the type of hearing one usually holds. Depending on the number and size of hearings which an agency may hold an agency may wish to have two small hearing rooms for smaller proceedings and one large hearing room to accommodate the larger. If this is not possible, one large hearing room can accommodate both large and small hearings. (A large room can be equipped with a movable wall which can be used to expand or shrink the accommodation as needed.)

There are likely any number of different ways to set up hearing rooms. Appendix 12.7 sets out five basic designs and notes the advantages and disadvantages of each.

Here are some suggestions in setting up one's hearing room. Please note that the suggestions which follow do not concern hearing rooms used for video conferences or electronic hearings. The set up for these type of proceedings will be dealt with later in chapter 21A "The Electronic Age".

1. **Members tables:** In proceedings where the agency member(s) will be called upon to make binding decisions, he or they should be located at a separate table at the front of the room. The table must be large enough to accommodate the decision-maker(s) chair(s) (so that where there are several members they are not rubbing shoulders), his or their notes and papers, piles of exhibits (if these are not kept on a separate table), microphones (if any), and water. The table should be *slightly* raised if possible so that the member(s) can be easily seen and can see the participants. I have seen members tables that would make the red judges in London jealous at their height. I saw one such dias in a hearing which came equipped with an additional modesty panel at the top of the dias (in the event that the jolly green giant ever approached the bench) with the result that when a member sat at the dias he was completely hidden from view! If at all possible avoid very high, dias like, members tables. Aside from an unsuitably court-like appearance, these diases make it very difficult to easily exchange documents and otherwise communicate with the rest of the room.

    In the case of hearings where there will be a great deal of exhibits, documentary evidence or files, it may be prudent to provide a large table reserved for the storage of this material. Preferably it should be located for easy access by the members and the participants.

2. **Participants' tables:** Participants must be given large enough tables so that they can sit with their counsel, keep notes, manage their documentary exhibits etc. (If possible, modesty drapes are a welcome addition.) Sometimes there will be many, many participants, but the principle presentations will be made by only a few (with the remainder being content only to follow the proceedings and perhaps give evidence on one or two points. In such cases, the agency may be able to provide tables only for the principal participants and chairs in the public area for the other participants.

3. **Staff tables:** Tables should also be available for staff members who will be attending the hearing. Ideally a staff table should be placed in a position from which the staff have maximum access to the members and participants tables and the rest of the room as the staff will often be called upon to act as the arms and legs of the panel members (who are generally fixed at their tables) and to lend assistance to the participants (for example, in the making of photocopies, or in the circulation of exhibits or papers). It is very common for a staff table to be placed at the front of the room to the side and just below the members' table or, in very large hearings, directly in front of the members' tables. In the latter case, this will require that the members' table be sufficiently raised so as not to obscure the line of vision. A staff table may also be placed at the public door to the hearing room if staff is to be stationed there at the beginning of the hearing to assist people or material is to be made available for public distribution.

    The size of the staff table should be sufficient for the tasks being assigned to the staff. If the staff is being asked to run a sound system or keep the exhibits, the table(s) provided must be large enough to comfortably accommodate all of the equipment or material which the staff will be expected to run.[175]

    You may also require a separate table for an electronic control panel and the control technician needed to run it.

4. **Electrical outlets:** If you want to avoid the danger of long extension cords running every which way across the floor of the hearing room you must ensure that there are sufficient, and well placed, outlets. The biggest demand for outlets will be at the front of the room where participants may be using audio visual aids, and where the sound system is located.

5. **Clock:** This is a detail that is often forgotten but is very important. If possible, a clock should be placed on a wall to enable the agency members and all participants to check the time. If it is impossible to place a clock where all can see, then it should be placed where at least the agency members can see

---

175 The use of agency staff and counsel and the duties of a hearing clerk are discussed in chapters 14 and 15. Included in chapter 21A (The Electronic Age) are discussions of the historical development of transcription, the various methods of verbatim reporting methods, and hints in considering a reporting firm.

it and as many others as possible. The agency members, if the hearing is to be conducted efficiently and not go into overruns with no appropriate adjournments, must be in a position where they can keep track of the time passing.

6. **Chairs:** Chairs must be provided in the back half of the room for the public and any participants who do not wish to take a principal part in the proceedings.

7. **Doors:** In large proceedings, if possible, there should be two doors into the room. One leading to the middle or back half of the room for the staff, participants, and the public, and one opening to the front of the room for the members. This will allow the members to enter and leave the room quickly, avoid being caught up in the press of the crowd during adjournments (and thus perhaps being told extra evidence or comments by members of the public as they work their way out of the room). It will also allow the members to enter and leave the room with minimal disruption to the public. Where members are required to use a common public door to enter the hearing room it often opens to the main body of the public or participants, thus giving the members' entrance somewhat of a pomp and circumstances effect as they grandly stride through the waiting individuals to the front of the room.

8. **Witnesses:** If witnesses are going to be asked to come forward to a central location to give their evidence you will want to locate the witness stand at a central place where all, particularly the agency members, can hear and see them. Some agencies prefer to have their witnesses stand at a podium to give evidence. Others prefer to provide a small table where documents can be placed for easy access. If audio-visual material is to be used, the screens, etc. must be placed where both the agency members and the other participants can see them and the witness has easy access.

9. **Sound System:** In large hearings some sort of sound system is very useful to enable everyone to hear everyone else. In hearings where simultaneous translation or a transcript is being maintained it is a must. Simultaneous translation booths are usually located at the back or to the side of the hearing room (behind one way glass).

10. **Water:** Water should be provided at the members' table and all tables provided for the participants.

11. **The accoutrements:** Name plates for members can be very useful for the public to identify who they are. A name plate can be made for each member to keep and to take to each hearing. Bibles for oaths should be available. Some agencies provide their members (or the chair of a panel) with a gavel. I think this is unnecessary. If one has the money, flags may be set up at the front of the room behind the members' table (usually the Canadian and the respective provincial flag). In some hearings white boards, large poster

boards, or audio-visual aids will have to be provided (along with pointers), for the presentations by the participants. (A participant needing any auxiliary equipment MUST check with the agency involved to ensure that they have one and that it will be available.) Papers, pens, etc. may be provided. Whether or not they are, it is a good idea for the staff to bring extra for the emergency situation when somebody suddenly runs out. If possible a telephone should be located unobtrusively (but easily accessible to the staff) in the hearing room for emergency messages.

12. **Other facilities:** Ideally, the hearing room should be located with easy access to photocopiers, telephone, and washrooms.

13. **Video Conferences and Hearings:** The set up of hearing rooms for video conferences and hearings will be discussed in chapter 21A "The Electronic Age".

12.7(b) Obtaining Accommodations

When the hearing is not in the board's own hearing rooms, a few things are required. The checklist for accommodation, below, may be useful.

(1) Is the accommodation free for all the days that may be needed?

(2) Has a satisfactory arrangement to lease the hearing room been made? Are there funds and who will pay?

(3) Will it seat the anticipated audience?

(4) How do you handle a municipal council chamber that is only available part-time for certain days a week for a hearing that may last full days for four weeks?

(5) Has the lighting been tested under working conditions? Testing a few fuses is next to useless. Test it carefully with all tables, dias, etc., in place.

(6) Who will be there to fix the lights when they go out, as they unquestionably will?

(7) How do you control the furnace and the air conditioning? This must be written down and be in the charge of someone present at the hearing. Have the furnace and air conditioning been put into operation under the hearing conditions? "Sorry Sir, I didn't realize that the air conditioning machine would make it impossible to hear the witnesses," is not a helpful excuse.

(8) Where does the public part? Who will set up the tables, chairs, etc., when the bingo is over?

(9) Where are all the phones, especially the ones that ring on and on in the middle of a hearing and cannot be located and no one answers?

(10) Where are the public facilities and, when they operate, can one still hear the witness?

(11) Are there sufficient public notices near the building, in the newspaper, etc., of where and when the hearing is to be held?

(12) Have the acoustics been tested? Can a witness be heard? Can the board be heard? Are there microphones for the public to use? Are the counsel tables and chairs adequate? Some hearings can have 10 to 50 lawyers and an equal number of parties and consultants present.

(13) How will you handle the media? No one cares about a hearing as a rule in an urban centre, but in smaller centres the hearing may be big news. Is there a designated area for the media? Is it needed? Are there printed rules about tapping, photographs and T.V.?

(14) Is there a need for police or other protection?

(15) What do you do about privacy and lock up of documents, exhibits, etc., after each day of the hearing?

(16) The problems go on and on. Every board should have a checklist. What about:

— Coats, where does the audience put their coats in a winter hearing?
— Where are the exhibits to be displayed?
— How do you handle drunks?
— How do you deal with people who insist on smoking, drinking and chatting (or yelling) or breast feeding their children in the front row?
— How do you deal with picket lines?
— How do you get all the reference material usefully near the panel members?
— Does the accommodation enable overhead projectors, moveable boards with print-outs, computer simulators on the dias, computer memories to recall past or key word testimony?
— Is there reproduction equipment readily available for the public?
— Can the public inspect the public files?
— If fifty people want to see one file how do you handle it?
— Have you staff and a place to accommodate public inspection all day each day?
— Will you sit at night?
— Do you need extra insurance, etc.
— Who protects the exhibits at night?
— etc., etc., etc.

Judges don't realize how sheltered they are and what "a slice of life" they miss.

In Ontario, agency registrars may find the task of locating hearing rooms somewhat easier through the release by the provincial government of an electronic directory of all meeting rooms and hearing rooms in government owned or leased buildings to which ministries or government agencies may have access. The directory is available in both hardcopy and on diskette (WordPerfect 5.1). Included information in the director are the building address, the floor number or room location, the ministry or agency responsible for the room, the seating capacity, a contact person, telephone and any special facilities available. The directory can be obtained from the Property Support Services Branch, Ontario Realty Corporation.

12.8 MOTIONS DAY

Some tribunals provide for a ''motions day'' in their rules of procedure or in a specific procedural order. A motions day is a day that is set aside by the tribunal to hear motions in relation to a particular matter coming before it.

The kinds of motions include:

(1) a motion to expand the issues list;

(2) a motion to require an applicant or intervenor to answer an interrogatory;

(3) a motion to require an applicant or intervenor to give a better answer to an interrogatory than that given;

(4) a motion to require an applicant or intervenor to produce a document or a person;

(5) a motion to adjourn;

(6) a motion to issue a subpoena;

(7) a motion to order discovery; and

(8) a motion challenging jurisdiction, etc.

There are other types of motions that arise but the first six above can and should be provided for in a procedural order. There should be no need for both discovery and interrogatories. I believe that agencies should not use the discovery process.

Notices of motion, depending upon the applicable rules of procedure, can be oral or in writing. The advance timing of a notice of a motion may vary. Obviously, the notice should be given to all parties to the proceeding since they may all wish to take part.

Costs on motions may be awarded at the time, but are more often reserved to be dealt with in the final decision.

It is better practice for the presiding hearing panel to preside on motions that are brought *before* the hearing commences. Courts do not do this but agencies should.

The order following the motion can be oral or written with or without reasons. It is best if the decision is delivered as soon as possible with written reasons. Clear and full reasons should be given. The parties are entitled to this courtesy and the reasons may be essential to a court review of the proceedings: see Chapter 22 on Tribunal Writing.

12.9 DISCRETION

Throughout a proceeding an agency will be called upon to exercise the powers granted to it by Parliament or a Legislature. Sometimes an agency will have no choice in the exercise of a power. The legislators may have specified criteria which, if they exist, will require the agency to act. The exercise of such powers is considered a duty (and one can apply to court for an order of mandamus forcing the agency to exercise them if the agency fails to do so when it is required. Other times it is clear that the decision as to whether a power is to be exercised, or how that power is to be exercised, is to be left to the agency to determine. Those powers are discretionary. Discretionary powers are usually expressed by words such as ''as the agency may deem necessary'', ''the agency, where it is of the opinion that it is appropriate to do so, may . . .'', or ''where the agency feels it is in the public interest it may . . .''.

Frequently, a statute may appear to establish no restrictions on the discretion of the agency (e.g. ''Where the agency feels it is proper to do so, the agency may . . .''. This may give the impression that whether an agency should act or what form that action should take is totally in the discretion of the agency. The law, however, does not recognize the concept of absolute discretion. Even where Parliament sets down no express guidelines or parameters to the exercise of an agency's discretion the courts will imply the limitation that Parliament only intended the discretionary power to be exercised in accordance with the spirit and intent of the statute which grants it. There is an implicit restraint on the discretionary power that it can only be used for the purposes and in the manner Parliament or the Legislature intended it to be used when it gave the authority to the decision-maker. The leading case on this point in Canada is *Roncarelli v. Duplessis*,[176] where Justice Rand stated:

> In public regulation of this sort there is no such thing as absolute and untrammelled ''discretion'', that is that action can be taken on any ground or for any reason that can be suggested to the mind of the administrator; no legislative Act can, without express language, be taken to contemplate an unlimited arbitrary power exerciseable for any purpose, however capricious or irrelevant, regardless of the nature of purpose

---

176 [1959] S.C.R. 121, 16 D.L.R. (2d) 689.

of the statue. Fraud and corruption in the Commission may not be mentioned in such statues but they are always implied as exceptions. "Discretion" necessarily implies good faith in discharging public duty; there is alwyas a perspective within which a statute is intended to operate; and any clear departure from its lines or objects is just as objectionable as fraud or corruption.

A similar restriction on the exercise of discretionary powers was laid down by the British House of Lords in *Padfield v. Minister of Agriculture, Fisheries & Food.*[177] Here the Minister was refusing to exercise his authority to refer a matter to an inquiry. His refusal, however, was based on a consideration which did not appear to have anything to do with the purposes of the statute which granted him the referral power. The House of Lords intervened. Lord Reid explained:

> It is implicit in the argument for the Minister that there are only two possible interpretations of this provison — either he must refer every complaint or he has an unfettered discretion to refuse to refer in any case. I do not think that is right. Parlaiment must have conferred the discretion with th intention that it should be used to promote the policy and objects of the Act: the policy and objects of the Act must be determined by construing the Act as a whole and construction is always a matter of law for the court. In a matter of this kind it is not possible to draw a hard and fast line, but if the Minister, by reason of his having misconstrued the Act or for any other reason, so used his discretion as to thwart or run counter to the policy and objects of the Act, then our law would be very defective if persons aggrieved were not entitled to the protection of the courts. So it is necessary first to construe the Act.

When will the courts conclude that a decision-maker is exercising discretionary powers in a way not contemplated by Parliament or the Legislature in its grant of that authority? Generally, the courts will intervene where it appears that

i. any statutory conditions for the exercise of the power have not been met;

ii. the decision-maker is acting in bad faith;[178]

iii. the authority in question is being used for some purpose other than that for which it was given;[179]

---

177 [1968] A.C. 997 (H. of L.)

178 Included in this list in the sense of meaning malice. Bad faith is also simply acting for a purpose other than that contemplated by the statute (*Roncarelli*). That criteria, however, is noted separately in this list.

179 *Multi-Malls Inc. v. Ontario (Minister of Transportation & Communications)* (1977), 73 D.L.R. (3d) 18 (Ont. C.A.), *Teubner v. Ontario (Minister of Highways)*, [1965] 2 O.R. 221 (C.A.), *Re Doctors Hospital and Minister of Health* (1976), 12 O.R. (2d) 164, 1 C.P.C. 232, 68 D.L.R. (3d) 220 (Div. Ct.) (appendix 28.2 also sets out a list of decisions in which *Doctors Hospital* has been considered), *Congreve v. Home Office*, [1976] Q.B. 629 (C.A.), *Reference Re. Canada Business Corporations Act* (1991), 49 O.A.C. 67.

iv. the power was exercised for the purpose of discriminating against someone (in the absence of clear authority to do so);[180]

v. the decision-maker refuses to exercise his discretion (i.e. avoids making decision at all)[181];

vi. the decision-maker fetters his discretion (e.g. by adopting binding policy guidelines);[182]

vii. the decision-maker failed to take into account relevant and material evidence or considerations (or conversely, took into account irrelevant evidence);[183] or

viii. to the degree that natural justice and fairness applies, breached those principles were breached.[184]

Provided that a discretionary power is exercised within these wide parameters, the courts are reluctant to interfere with the merits of the exercise and will not do so unless it appears the agency has been acting on some improper principle

---

Frequently, the exercise of discretion is tied to "the public interest". See chapter 8 for a discussion of the concept of "the public interest".

180 *R. v. Coventry Council, Ex p. Phoenix Aviation*, [1995] 3 All E.R. 37 (Q.B.).

181 *Martinoff v. R.* (1993), 18 Admin. L.R. (2d) 191 (Fed. C.A.).

182 The proper, and improper, use of policy guidelines is discussed in more detail in chapter 6.

183 *Oakwood Development Ltd. v. St. François Xavier (Rural Municipality)*, [1985] 2 S.C.R. 164, *Apotex Inc. v. Quebec (Minister of Health & Social Services)* (19   ), 53 C.P.R. (3d) 479, 111 D.L.R. (4th) 622, (*sub nom. Apotex Inc. v. Coté*) [1994] R.J.Q. 795 (S.C.), *Apotex Inc. v. Canada (Attorney General)* (1993), 18 Admin. L.R. (2d) 122 (Fed. C.A.), affirmed [1994] 3 S.C.R. 1100 (Minister cannot take into account pending litigation), *Hirmann v. Toronto (City)* (1993), 13 O.R. (3d) 54 (Div. Ct.) (acknowledges that may be reasonable in some circumstances to consider impact of pending retroactive by-laws which have been passed by city council and only await Municipal Board approval), *Brown v. Alberta* (1991), 2 Admin. L.R. 116 (Alta. Q.B.), *Koenig v. Ontario (Minister of Municipal Affairs)* (1994), 77 O.A.C. 64 (Div. Ct.). In *Electric Power & Telephone Act (P.E.I.), Re* (1994), 116 Nfld. & P.E.I.R. 181, 363 A.P.R. 181 (P.E.I.C.A.) the Prince Edward Island Court of Appeal held that where the legislation is silent as to the factors an administrative agency must take into consideration, the agency has the discretion to determine the factors to be considered, however, those factors must be related to the purpose and object of the statute conferring the discretion. Failure to take account of relevant evidence which is not, however, material to a decision will not invalidate the resulting decision (*Université du Québec à Trois-Rivères v. Larocque* (1993) 101 D.L.R.(4th) 494 (S.C.C.)). Furthermore, the Federal Court of Appeal has held that the fact that a decision-maker may have taken into account irrelevant considerations in the exercise of a discretionary power will not invalidate that exercise provided that the decision-maker also took into account relevant considerations and the decision was not based predominately on the irrelevant factors (*Canadian Assn. of Regulated Importers v. Canada (Attorney General)* (1994), 17 Admin. L.R. (2d) 121 (Fed. C.A.)).

Acting on the basis of irrelevant considerations or evidence can also be seen as simply a form of acting for a purpose other than that for which the discretion is given.

184 Many of the principles of natural justice are discussed in this chapter. The interested reader will also find a discussion of bias in chapter 39.

or the decision is so wild as to amount to an injustice in the eyes of the court. The Supreme Court of Canada in *Pezim v. British Columbia (Superintendent of Brokers)*[185] approved the following discussion by the Ontario Court of Appeal in *Re Mitchell and Ontario Securities Commission*[186] of the authority of the Commission's discretionary power to suspend or cancel a broker's licence:

> Finally, the Commission may properly form its opinion to suspend or cancel any registration in the public interest without proof of actual injury to the public. . . . The Chairman and other members of the Commission are selected and appointed by the Lieutenant-Governor in Council for their high qualifications, ability and experience. It is the function and duty of the Commission under s. 8 of the Securities Act to form an opinion whether or not it is in the public interest to suspend or cancel the registration of any person. It is intended by the legislation that the Commission shall have extremely wide powers of discretion in forming its opinion.
>
> The opinion of the Commission should not be set aside or altered upon an appeal unless the Commission has erred in some principle of law or unless it appears clearly that the Commission has not proceeded to form its opinion in a judicial manner or unless it appears that the opinion is so clearly wrong as to amount to an injustice requiring a remedy on appeal.

This principle has been stated many times by various courts. See for example, *Hi-Fi Novelty Co. v. Nova Scotia (Attorney General):*[187]

> This court has said on several occasions that it will not interfere with a discretionary order, particularly an interlocutory one such as this, unless wrong principles of law have been applied or a patent injustice would result. Simply because we may possibly have reached a decision contrary to that of the judge on the facts is not sufficient. The burden on the appellant is heavy. See *Nova Scotia (Minister of Housing) v. Langilee and Roberts* (1992), 108 N.S.R. (2d) 348; 294 A.P.R. 348 (C.A.) and *Minkoff v. Poole and Lambert* (1991), 101 N.S. R. (2d) 143; 275 A.P.R. 143 (C.A.).[188]

---

185 [1994] 2 S.C.R. 557, 22 Admin. L.R. (2d) 1, [1994] 7 W.W.R. 1 (*sub nom. Pezim v. British Columbia (Securities Commission)*) 168 N.R. 321.

186 (1957), 12 D.L.R. (2d) 221 (Ont. C.A.).

187 (1993), 126 N.S.R. (2d) 70, 352 A.P.R. 70 (C.A.).

188 See also *R. v. Chaisson* (1995), 99 C.C.C. (3d) 289 (S.C.C.) (jurisdiction to review discretionary decisions of lower courts should only be exercised sparingly), *Bush v. Saskatchewan (Minister of Environment & Resource Management)*, [1994] 6 W.W.R. 622 (Sask. Q.B.), *Oro (Township) v. BAFMA Inc.* (1995), 21 O.R. (3d) 483, 121 D.L.R. (4th) 538 (Div. Ct.), *Ainsley Financial Corp. v. Ontario Securities Commission* (1993), 14 O.R. (3d) 280 (Ont. Gen. Div.) at p. 290, affirmed (1994), 21 O.R. (3d) 104 (C.A.), *Wrights' Canadian Ropes Ltd. v. Minister of National Revenue*, [1947] 1 D.L.R. 721 (P.C.) at 730-731. *Wiebe Property Corp. Ltd. v. Ontario (Minister of Transportation & Communications)* (1985), 50 O.R. (2d) 639 (Div. Ct.), *Vancouver (City) v. Simpson*, [1977] 1 S.C.R. 71. The reader may also wish to refer to the discussion of this point in Jones and de Villars *Principles of Administrative Law* (2d ed.). The authors list a number of discipline cases on p. 458 which they cite as being indicative of the reluctance of the courts to substitute their view of how a statutory delegate should exercise his discretion.

12.10 SUBPOENAS AND SUMMONSES-FOR PEOPLE AND DOCUMENTS

12.10(a) Use of Subpoenas and Summonses

In many cases individuals will possess information which is relevant to the performance of an agency's mandate. Sometimes these individuals may be willing to attend before the agency voluntarily, sometimes not. Sometimes the individuals may be willing to attend but require leave from the employer to do so in order not to lose pay. Other times, the individuals may be reluctant to appear to be voluntarily appearing before the agency should they give evidence which is embarrassing to their employer or some other important interest. And finally, some information is simply not available for the asking.[189] In such cases the common answer is to compel the attendance of the witness by means of a subpoena or a summons. From a practical perspective, it is often wise to secure a subpoena or a summons even for the voluntary witness to ensure that he does not have a last minute change of heart and not appear at the hearing.

It is important to note, however, that the purpose of the subpoena is to secure the attendance of the person at the hearing. There is authority for the proposition that where a potential witness is already present before a tribunal with the power to compel testimony that person can be required to testify there and then without a subpoena being issued to compel that testimony (*W. (C.) v. Mental Health Review Board (Man.).*[190] The advance notice requirements of natural justice do not apply to witnesses.[191] Where, as in Ontario, a witness has a right to counsel at a hearing, a potential witness who is present but did not know that he was likely to be called upon to give evidence would likely be able to secure a reasonable adjournment to secure counsel.

12.10(b) Meaning of Terms

Today, the terms "subpoena" and "summons" have come to be synonymous as an order by an agency or by a court for an individual to attend at a specific time, date and place to give oral evidence or to produce documents or both in a proceeding. As best as I can determine, the essential difference between these

---

189 See for example, s. 21 of Ontario Regulation 518/88 as amended which provided that "except as required by law, or, as provided in this section, no Board shall permit any person to remove, inspect, or receive information from medical records or from notes, charts and other material relating to a patient's care." The regulation continued on, however to provide that such information was available pursuant to a subpoena, summons or other requirement issued by a tribunal within the meaning of the Statutory Powers Procedure Act that was established under the Health Disciplines Act.

190 [1994] 8 W.W.R. 761, 26 C.P.C (3d) 1, 95 Man. R. (2d) 152 (C.A.), leave to appeal to S.C.C. refused (1995), 36 C.P.C. (3d) 247 (note) (S.C.C.).

191 *Hurd v. Hewitt* (1994), 20 O.R.(3d) 639, 120 D.L.R. (4th) 105 (C.A.).

documents is basically historical. In the past, a court could issue a summons to require an individual to appear in court. If that summons was backed with a penalty for not appearing it was known as a subpoena.[192] There were, technically speaking, two types of subpoenas: subpoenas ad testificandum which required a person to attend at the proceeding to give evidence, and subpoenas duces tecum which required him to attend and to bring specified documents with him. The terms ''summons'' and ''subpoena'' are today, at least in the common parlance of administrative law used interchangeably.[193] The Latin terms ''ad testificatum'' and ''duces tecum'' are still proper, however. They are not part of everyday usage, the tendency being simply to refer to a summons or a subpoena. Generally the terms appear only in introductory lectures on the law of evidence given by counsel to agency members (one hopes for some purpose other than to confuse the issue) and otherwise where a great deal of formality is being imposed. Certainly it is rare, if it happens at all, that a counsel will ask an agency for a compulsion order under either of these formal Latin titles. Generally speaking, today courts appear to issue ''subpoenas''. Where the authority of an agency to compel attendance is granted by way of a statutory reference to the agencies having the powers of a superior court (or some similar wording) ''subpoena'' also appears to be the accepted terminology for the compulsion document. Statutory provisions which grant agencies an express power to compel attendance usually use the term ''summons''.[194] There does not appear to be any substantive difference today

---

192 ''Sub poena'' meaning ''under penalty''. Thus, the essential historical difference between a subpoena and a summons is that the former was an order to attend for which a penalty was imposed for non-compliance. It appears that no penalty automatically flowed from the failure to comply with a summons which required the issuance of a second process to enforce it. (See *Blackstone's Commentaries*, book III, c. 19, John Indermaur's *Principles of the Common Law* (Stevens & Haynes, London, 1885) p. 475, J.H. Baker's *An Introduction to English Legal History* (Butterworth's, London, 1979) p. 88 , George Paton's *A Text-Book of Jurisprudence* 3rd ed. (Clarendon Press, Oxford, 1964) at p. 539, *Taswell-Langmead's Constitutional History, Phipson on Evidence* 14th ed. (Sweet and Maxwell, London, 1990), c. 8, and *Jowitt's Dictionary of English Law* (Sweet and Maxwell, London, 1977). This explanation is likely greatly oversimplified, as there appear to have been at different times in English history different court documents which went variously under the name of either subpoena or summons but served different purposes. Writs of summons for example, commenced actions in the High Court in the nineteenth century but this function was later carried out by subpoena; a subpoena was at one time a writ commencing an action in Chancery or in the Star Chamber, while a summons could at another time be used where the attendance of a witness was required before a Chancery master. A ''master's summons'' was used to wind-up proceedings under the Companies Act, 1985. There were also witness summons in criminal proceedings before the crown and magistrates courts, as well as witness orders and warrants.

193 Thus, s. 12 of the Ontario Statutory Powers Procedures Act grants agencies the authority to issue ''summons'' with which failure to comply can result in punishment by the Divisional Court under s. 13. In *United Association of Journeymen & Apprentices of the Plumbing & Pipe Filling Industry of the United States and Canada, Local 488 v. Foley* (1975), 60 D.L.R. (3d) 690 (Alta. T.D.), Justice Miller stated that in his view ''the terms subpoena, summons and notice to attend are synonymous and all refer to the same type of document and procedure.''

194 Thus, in *Quebec (Attorney-General) v. Canada (Attorney-General)* (1978), 90 D.L.R. (3d) 161

flowing from the particular terminology and, hereinafter, I shall refer to both these documents simply by the generic term "subpoena".

12.10(c) Authority of Agency to Issue

As creatures of statute an agency does not have the authority to issue a subpoena unless it is given that authority by Parliament or a Legislature.[195] Some agencies are given this authority directly by statute,[196] or indirectly through the grant of the powers of a superior or inferior court of record,[197] or by reference to them having the authority of a commissioner under the relevant Inquiries Act,[198] all of which amount to a grant of authority to compel the attendance of individuals with or without documents.[199]

In Ontario section 12 of the Statutory Powers Procedure Act, R.S.O. 1990, c. S.22 gives all agencies subject to that statute a broad power of compulsion:

12. (1) A tribunal may require any person, including a party, by summons,

    (a) to give evidence on oath or affirmation at an oral or electronic hearing; and

    (b) to produce in evidence at an oral or electronic hearing documents and things specified by the tribunal,

---

(S.C.C.) the document issued by the Commision of Inquiry, drawing upon the "powers of a superior court" was called a subpoena, while the express power to compel given to a coroner in Ontario's Coroners Act,1972, was the power to issue a "summons". However, to illustrate that this is more of a rule of thumb than anything else, the British Columbia Court of Appeal in *Canadian Fishing Co. v. Smith and Carignan* (1962) 35 D.L.R. (2d) 355 (B.C.C.A.) referred to an implied power of the Restrictive Trade Practices Commission to issue a "subpoena".

195 *Quebec (Attorney-General) v. Canada (Attorney-General)* (1978), 90 D.L.R. (3d) 161 (S.C.C.).

196 E.g. s. 92(2) of the Ontario Labour Relations Act, R.S.O. 1970:

    92. (2) Without limiting the generality of subsection (1), the Board has power,

        (a) to summon and enforce the attendance of witnesses, and compel them to give oral or written evidence on oath, and to produce such documents and things as the Board considered requisite to the full investigation and consideration of matters within its jurisdiction in the same manner as a court of record in civil cases.

197 E.g. s. 147(1) of Nova Scotia's Workers' Compensation Act, R.S.N.S. 1989, c. 508: "The Board shall have the like powers as the Supreme Court for compelling the attendance of witnesses and of examining them under oath, and compelling the production of books, papers, documents and things."

198 E.g. s. 87(1) of Alberta's Environmental Appeal Board Act, S.A. c. E-13.3: "The Board has all the powers of a commissioner under the Public Inquiries Act."

199 *Diamond v. Ontario (Municipal Board)*, [1962] O.R. 328, 32 D.L.R. (2d) 103, *Hawkins v. Halifax (County) Residential Tenancies Board* (1974), 47 D.L.R. (3d) 117, 2 C.C.C. (2d) 327 (N.S. S.C.). However, the right of a party in s. 10.1 of the Ontario Statutory Powers Procedure Act to conduct cross-examinations of witnesses at a hearing does not implicitly authorise an agency to compel the attendance of witnesses (*Ellis v. Ontario (Ministry of Community & Social Services)* (1980), 28 O.R. (2d) 385 (Div. Ct.).

relevant to the subject-matter of the proceeding and admissible at a hearing.

A compulsion power may also be implied in the mandate given an agency. For example, the British Columbia Court of Appeal, relying on the concept of a fair hearing, held that the authority of the Restrictive Trade Practices Commission to hold an inquiry implied such a power. Justice Davey stated that:

> I can conceive of circumstances in which a person will be denied a "full opportunity of being heard" on allegations made against him as provided by s. 18(4) unless he is allowed to call evidence, to compel the production of documents, or to obtain further cross-examination. It is in such cases, inter alia, that in my opinion the Commission is empowered by s. 18(3) to consider the "statement submitted by the Director . . . together with such further or other evidence or material as the Commission considers advisable".[200]

In *Kelly & Sons v. Mathers* (1915), 23 D.L.R. 225, 8 W.W.R. 1208, 25 Man. R. 580 (C.A.) the Manitoba Court of Appeal found an implied power of compulsion in the simple statutory grant of power to procure evidence.

In the event that an agency is without the authority itself to compel the attendance of a witness it can always appeal to a superior court for assistance. The superior courts have the inherent jurisdiction to issue subpoenas in aid of the inferior tribunals.[201] The agency may apply under the court's Rules, or if there is no specific rule, then "in any way consistent with the due administration of justice."[202]

12.10(d) Form of Subpoena

Aside from statutory direction, the form of a summons is not of great consequence. The form can be as gussy as one likes so long as it constitutes, in effect, an order or a direction of the tribunal.[203]

The form of summons to be used under section 12 of Ontario's Statutory Powers Procedure Act is prescribed by regulation.[204]

12.10(e) Limits on Use of Subpoena

There are limits on the authority of a subpoena. A subpoena should not be issued unless the agency is satisfied that the attendance and the documents sought

---

200 *Canadian Fishing Co. v. Smith* (1962), 35 D.L.R. (2d) 355 (B.C. C.A.).

201 *Canada Deposit Insurance Corp. v. Code* (1988), 49 D.L.R. (4th) 57 (Alta. C.A.).

202 *R. v. Monette* (1975), 10 O.R. (2d) 762, 28 C.C.C. (2d) 409, 64 D.L.R. (3d) 470 (H.C.).

203 One would not likely be able to impose any penalty for failure to obey a summons where it was unclear exactly what was being ordered. See the general discussion in c. 29A.9(b).

204 The regulated form is set out in the legislation tab in vol. 3 of this text.

fall within those limits. The agency may properly refuse to issue the subpoena if the person seeking it cannot, or will not, show that it would be proper to do so.[205]

The purpose of a subpoena is to secure information which is useful or necessary for the performance of an agency's mandate. Thus, any information sought thereby must be relevant. If it is not relevant the subpoena should not be issued.[206] Equally, a subpoena cannot be used to secure information which enjoys a privilege recognized by law.[207]

Some uses of a subpoena can amount to an abuse of the agency's process. In *Kotinopoulos v. Becker Milk Co.*[208] Chairman George Adams outlined many of the practices considered abusive:

> A subpoena duces tecum cannot be used as an instrument to harass or to annoy unreasonably an opponent; (see *René v. Carling Export Brewing Co.* (1927), 61 O.L.R. 495; *Clemens v. Crown Trust Co.*, [1953] O.R. 87 at p. 94, [1952] O.W.N. 434; and *Brittain Steel Fabricators Ltd. v. Amiable* (1967), 64 D.L.R. (2d) 663 (B.C.)). And a subpoena duces tecum should state with reasonable particularly the documents which are to be produced; (see *A.G. v. Wilson*, 9 Sim 526 at 529; *Earl of Powis v. Negus*, [1923] 1 Ch. 186 at 190; *The Commissioner for Railways v. Small,* [(1938), 38 N. So. Wales 564], and *Lee v. Angas* (1866), L.R. 2 Eq. 59). Furthermore, although the limits of this principle are vague, a subpoena duces tecum should not be used "for the purpose of fishing, i.e., endeavouring, not to obtain evidence to support [a] case, but to discover whether [one] has a case at all''; (see *The Commissioner for Railways v. Small*, supra, at p. 575; *Hennessy v. Wright* 24 O.B.D. 445 at 448; *Griebart v. Morris*, [1920] 1 K.B. 659 at 666). And finally, a subpoena to a party will be set aside as abusive if great numbers of documents are called for and it appears that they are not sufficiently relevant; (see *Steele v. Savory*, [1891] W.N. 195).[209]

---

205 In *Cotroni v. Quebec Police Commission* (1977), 80 D.L. R. (3d) 490 (S.C.C.) the Supreme Court held that an agency may refuse to issue a subpoena if it is not told what is to be proven thereby. See also *Reid v. Wigle* (1980), 114 D.L.R. (3d) 669 (Ont. Div. Ct.).

206 *Canadian Fishing Co. v. Smith* (1962), 35 D.L.R. (2d) 355 (B.C.C.A.), *Rahimpour v. University of Western Ontario* (February 28, 1992), (Ont. Gen. Div.)), *Re Koressis* (1968), 63 W.W.R. 566 (B.C.S.C.), *United Association of Journeymen & Apprentices of the Plumbing & Pipe Fitting Industry of the United States and Canada, Local 488 v. Foley* (1975), 60 D.L.R. (3d) 690 (Alta. T.D.), *Reid v. Wigle* (1980), 114 D.L.R. (3d) 669 (Ont. Div. Ct.).

207 E.g. solicitor-client privilege, privileges granted by ss. 37 to 39 of the Canada Evidence Act and similar provisions in the provincial evidence statutes (which include a public interest immunity for documents such as cabinet confidences), spousal communications, communications in furtherance of settlement, confidential material meeting the "Wigmore" criteria, etc. For a full discussion of the privileges provided at law see chapter 14 of *The Law of Evidence in Canada* by Justice John Sopinka, Sidney N. Lederman, and Alan Bryant.

208 [1974] O.L.R.B. Mon. Rep. 732.

209 See also the discussion of "Abuse of Process: Protection of Witness" found in the British text *Phipson on Evidence* 14th ed. (Sweet & Maxwell, London, 1990) from pp. 137 to 139. It also appears that a subpoena cannot be issued until the date and time of the proceeding, to which it relates, has been determined and notice given (*Mobilex Ltd. v. Hamilton*, [1950] O.W.N. 721 (H.C.)). One cannot, after all, command someone to appear without telling him when and where.

In *Kotinopoulos* the following provisions of a subpoena were challenged:

> . . . and to bring with you and produce at such time and place (1) employee records from January 1, 1971 to the present including the records of all employees dismissed during that period; (2) records of bank deposits made by all Becker Stores in Metropolitan Toronto, between March 30, 1972 and January 3, 1974; (3) copies of standard form Becker Store Manager Contracts used between January 1, 1970 and the present; [this item was not challenged] (4) all correspondence sent or received by Becker Milk Company to or from its employees concerning the formation of an employees' association and all internal memoranda, notes, documents and minutes of meetings related to the formation or existence of an employees' association.

The Board ruled that:

> item (1) (save for the records of those employees dismissed form January 1, 1971 until January 3, 1974) and item (2) are more in the nature of a fishing expedition, or at the very least, involve great numbers of documents that are not, at this time sufficiently relevant. In regard to item (4), while the request is somewhat vague, the lack of particularity is understandable. Moreover, the request, with some effort on the part of the respondent, is not so general to be incapable of being fulfilled. Thus the Board expects the "best efforts" of the respondent in this regard.

Finally, insofar as an agency only has such power to compel attendance as is given it, its powers are limited by the parameters of that grant.[210] Thus, a provincial agency cannot issue a subpoena to someone who is located outside of the province in which the agency operates as the agency's power is limited by the geographic boundaries which prescribe the boundaries of its Legislature.[211] A grant of power is equally limited by the legal limits on the authority of the Legislature under the constitution. Thus, while a provincial Legislature may grant a provincial body a general power of compulsion, that power will not permit the agency to subpoena a federal official as a provincial Legislature cannot confer such authority as against the Crown in right of Canada.[212]

---

210 Thus, in *Canadian Pacific Air Lines Ltd. v. Canadian Air Line Pilots Assn.* (1993), 108 D.L.R. (4th) 1 (S.C.C.) the Supreme Court held that the Canada Labour Relations Board could not use its compulsion powers to order disclosure for the purposes of an investigation by the Board when the statutory grant of power was restricted to the issuance of subpoenas only in the context of a formal hearing.

211 This fact is acknowledged in *Four Star Management Ltd. v. British Columbia Securities Commission* (1990), 71 D.L.R. (4th) 317 (B.C. C.A.). Most of the provinces have passed reciprocal legislation for the enforcement of subpoenas. See the discussion below respecting the various Interprovincial Subpoenas Acts.

212 *Quebec (Attorney-General) v. Canada (Attorney-General)* (1978), 90 D.L.R. (3d) 161 (S.C.C.). In that same case, the Supreme Court noted that while a Lt. Governor has the prerogative power to establish a commission of inquiry, the power to hold an inquiry in that case will not imply a power of compulsion, as such powers can only be granted by statute. Thus, an inquiry established by the prerogative lacks such authority. Natural justice cannot imply such a grant, as the

12.10(f) Can One Force An Agency To Issue A Subpoena?

Assuming that the information sought could properly be subpoenaed by an agency, what can be done to force an agency which will not issue a subpoena to do so? Unless there is a legislative provision which clearly provides to the contrary, the issuance of a subpoena is in the discretion of the agency.[213] There is no automatic right to subpoena anyone and anything a participant may wish. (This is consistent with the authority of an agency to control its proceedings by limiting the number of witnesses to be called.) Thus, provided that the agency is operating along proper principles in deciding whether or not a subpoena will issue, a court will not lightly interfere with that discretionary decision.[214]

Having said this, there are a number of decisions where the courts were prepared to, and did, interfere with an agency's refusal to issue a summons on the basis of protecting an individual's right to secure such information as is necessary to present his case. In each case mandamus was issued ordering the agency to issue the requested summons. In *Furniture Workers Union v. Alberta (Board of Industrial Relations)*[215] the Alberta Supreme Court appeared to liken the refusal to issue a subpoena to summon a relevant witness to a refusal to hear a relevant witness. Although the Court acknowledged that this decision lay within the jurisdiction of the agency whose decision should not lightly be interfered with, it nonetheless felt that the case in point was a proper case for such interference.[216] In the later case of *Carter v. Phillips*[217] the Ontario Divisional Court also based its decision on the ability of a party to prove his case. In this case the party seeking the summons alleged that the information need to do this rested in either the records maintained by the government or in the hands of the other side. The agency refused to issue a summons to either the appropriate government official or the other party allegedly possessing the information. The Court felt that the

---

principles of natural justice are simply an assumption by the courts of the authority and procedure which Parliament impliedly intended to give in the grant of statutory power. One cannot infer such a grant in the establishment of an inquiry by prerogative as prerogative has no ability to give such power, either expressly or impliedly.

213 *United Association of Journeymen & Apprentices of the Plumbing & Pipe Fitting Industry of the United States and Canada, Local 488 v. Foley* (1975), 60 D.L.R. (3d) 690 (Alta. T.D.).

214 *Cotroni v. Quebec Police Commission* (1977), 80 D.L.R. (3d) 490 (S.C.C.).

215 (1969), 69 W.W.R. 226, 6 D.L.R. (3d) 83 (Alta. S.C.).

216 As an alternative ground, the Court also held that the issuance of a subpoena was an administrative act and, therefore, subject to a prerogative writ of mandamus. The Court was not likely correct as to the nature of the act of compulsion. The Supreme Court of Canada has held that the issuance of a subpoena is a judical act, even when done by an administrative body (*Quebec (Attorney- General) v. Canada (Attorney-General)* (1978), 90 D.L.R. (3d) 161, [1979] 1 S.C.R. 218 and in the later case of *Canadian Pacific Air Lines Ltd. v. Canadian Air Line Pilots Assn.* (1993), 108 D.L.R. (4th) 1). In any event, it is difficult, however, to see the relevance of the nature of the beast where, administrative or judicial, it rests within the discretionary grant of the agency. The question is really to what extent will a court interfere with a discretionary decision made within an agency's jurisdiction.

217 (1987), 59 O.R. (2d) 289 (Div. Ct.).

party seeking the summons had effectively been locked out of her right to prove her case, thus in order to satisfy the dictates of natural justice and in order to ensure that the possibility exists for all relevant evidence to be placed before the agency the Court ordered the issuance of the summons.[218] Finally, the Prince Edward Island Supreme Court took a slightly different tack in *United Brotherhood of Carpenters and Joiners of America, Local 1338 v. Maclean Construction Limited Employees*[219] in holding that a refusal by the provincial Labour Relations Board to issue a subpoena amounted to a refusal to permit the exploration of an issue which appeared relevant to the proceedings. This, the Court felt, amounted to the Board failing to exercise its jurisdiction.[220]

Thus, the stronger the case one makes that the evidence sought is necessary for a fair hearing and the more clearly you can establish that there is no alternative way to secure it, the more likely one will be to convince a court to intervene to require the issuance of a subpoena. This will likely be an uphill battle in light of the courts strong disinclination to entertain judicial review applications on interim matters. As noted above, the Ontario Divisional Court's decision in *Carter v. Phillips* was reversed by the Ontario Court of Appeal[221] on the grounds that the application for judicial review to that Court had been premature. In order to avoid fragmenting the case the Court ruled that the tenant should have attempted to prove her case without the summons and then sought an appeal, if necessary, at the end of the case if the Commission ruled against her on the merits. A similar position was taken respecting disclosure by that court in *Howe v. Institute of Chartered Accountants of Ontario.*[222] Nonetheless, the prohibition against "fragmenting" a case, although strong, is not absolute. A court might be more willing to intervene if it can be established that the evidence sought was so vital that the denial was a clear breach of natural justice and proceeding in its absence would make the proceeding a waste of time.[223]

12.10(g) Challenging the Subpoena

A person subject to a subpoena may apply to the agency to have it vacated. Usually this is done at the commencement of the hearing (or at the time the

---

218 The Ontario Court of Appeal, at (1988), 66 O.R. (2d) 293 , subsequently reversed the Divisional Court on the grounds that the application for judicial review to that Court had been premature.

219 (1984), 52 Nfld. & P.E.I.R. 217, 153 A.P.R. 217 (P.E.I.S.C.).

220 For a similar decision see *Shepherd v. Canada (Minister of Employment & Immigration)* (1989), 9 Imm. L.R. (2d) 9 (Ont. H.C.).

221 (1988) 66 O.R. (2d) 293 (C.A.).

222 (1994), 19 O.R. (3d) 483 (C.A.), leave to appeal to S.C.C. refused (1995), 119 D.L.R. (4th) vii (note) (S.C.C.).

223 In *Carter* the Court noted that the commissioner had carefully considered the tenant's request, had decided that the evidence was not relevant to the proceedings, and had not breached any principle of natural justice while in *Howe* the Court recognized that the request for disclosure had only been refused on a interim basis by the Chair of the committee and that it could be renewed before the committee itself.

individual has been told to appear).[224] If the agency refuses to vacate the subpoena an application for judicial review (for certiorari) may be brought to the appropriate court to quash the order.[225] Given the reluctance of the courts to intervene in interlocutory matters before the agencies one would likely have to apply to the agency for relief first, however, it may be that in the exceptional case where great harm will result and the agency is unable to deal with the request sufficiently quickly one may be able to proceed directly to the courts.

12.10(h) Practice

In practical terms, a subpoena is the exercise of the power of the state to force an individual to disrupt their lives to attend and assist the state by providing evidence necessary for some mandate. People's lives should not be interfered with at whim. Thus, I do not believe in the practice of automatically providing on request blank, ready signed subpoena documents to parties.[226] The issuance of a subpoena is a judicial or quasi-judicial act.[227] Thus, it involves the exercise of discretion. Providing a pile of blank forms to be picked up at will amounts to (in the absence of clear legislative authority) an abandonment of that discretion.[228]

---

224 This procedure was followed in *Quebec (Attorney-General) v. Canada (Attorney-General)* (1978), 90 D.L.R. (3d) 161 (S.C.C.). If necessary that part of the hearing can be held in camera (*L. (Re)* (June 25, 1981) Ont. Cty Ct. [1981] O.J. No. 1).

225 *Quebec (Attorney-General) v. Canada (Attorney-General)* (1978), 90 D.L.R. (3d) 161 (S.C.C.), *Royal Com'n into Metropolitan Toronto Police Practices v. Ashton* (1975), 27 C.C.C. (2d) 31, 64 D.L.R. (3d) 477, 10 O.R. (2d) 113 (Div. Ct.).

226 See *Reid v. Wigle* (1980), 114 D.L.R. (3d) 669 (Ont. Div. Ct.).

227 *Canadian Pacific Air Lines Ltd. v. Canadian Air Line Pilots Assn.* (1993), 108 D.L.R. (4th) 1 (S.C.C.), *Quebec (Attorney-General) v. Canada (Attorney General)* (1978), 90 D.L.R. (3d) 161 (S.C.C.), *Quebec (Human Rights Commission) v. Canada (Solicitor General)* (1978), 93 D.L.R. (3d) 562 (Que. C.A.). In an earlier decision the Alberta Supreme Court (Trial Division) held that the issuance of a subpoena was "really nothing other than an administrative act". This view is not likely correct.

228 The role of discretion was discussed in some detail in the context of the Criminal Code power of a Justice of the Peace to issue a subpoena "where a person is likely to give material evidence in a proceeding" in *R. v. Laws* (1992), 8 O.R. (3d) 86 (Ont. Gen. Div.), affirmed (1992), 8 O.R. (3d) 94 (C.A.). Justice O'Driscoll quoted the following from the Sask. Court of Appeal in *Foley v. Gares* (1989), 53 C.C.C. (3d) 82, 74 C.R. (3d) 386 (Sask. C.A.):

> What type of inquiry is a justice acting under ss. 626 (now s. 698) and 627(2)(a) (now s. 699(2)(a)) required to make? It is safe to say that the standard of inquiry is not so high, for example, as that expected of a judge acting under s. 637(3) (now s. 699(3)), but the justice none the less should make some examination in the circumstances. He is given discretion in the matter of issuing the subpoena and he should exercise it judiciously if jot judicially. The justice may choose not to insist upon evidence on oath but he may want to conduct an oral examination, if only a cursory one, of some person who had knowledge of the circumstances. The extent of such an examination will depend on the circumstances of each situation. One thing however is certain. If he takes no steps whatever to satisfy himself that the person is likely to give material evidence, the justice is abusing his power and his discretion if he issues the subpoena. His decision to issue the subpoena may be set aside by a superior court on the

Individuals seeking a subpoena should make a request for it to the agency attaching a copy of the completed form for execution by the agency. This request may be made in writing, although in exceptional circumstances the agency may wish to hear from the individual personally (if it has questions for example). It is not necessary to advise the other side or to give notice to the person to whom the subpoena will be directed.

The request should indicate to whom the subpoena will be directed, what information is being sought and how it is relevant to the proceeding. It may also be prudent to explain why a subpoena is thought necessary to secure this information.

The subpoena itself should set out the name of the agency, the name of the proceeding, the name of the person to whom it is directed, a statement directing the person to attend before the agency at a specified date, time and place, in order to give evidence, any documents the person is to bring with them, and any other information required by legislation.[229] Care should be taken not to word requests for documents too broadly. Subpoenas which are worded so broadly as to make it impossible to know what to bring in response thereto or to judge if there has been compliance with the subpoena (e.g. ''everything in your possession relevant to this proceeding'') should be refused.

The answer as to who should sign the subpoena is found in the statute granting the subpoena power. As noted above, the issuance of a subpoena is a judicial or quasi-judicial act. Thus, it must be exercised by the individual or body to whom the power is given. If the compulsion power is given to ''the Board'' for example, it must be ''the Board'' which exercises it. In such cases quorum provisions or other legislative directions in the enabling statute become relevant in determining if the entire agency must consider a request or if it can be done by a single member of a panel.[230] However, once the decision has been made by the empowered decision-maker, it may be signed by an appropriate official of the agency (such as the Chair, the Vice-chair or the Board Secretary.[231]

In Ontario, section 12(2) of the Statutory Powers Procedure Act directs who shall sign a summons issued under that statute.

12. (2) A summons issued under subsection (1) shall be in the prescribed form (in English or French) and,

(a) where the tribunal consists of one person, shall be signed by him or her;

---

ground that without making any examination the justice had no jurisdiction to exercise his discretion to issue the subpoena. In short his decision is amenable to certiorari.

229 See the prescribed form of subpoena now required by Ontario's Statutory Powers Procedure Act which is located in the legislation tab.

230 *Cotroni v. Quebec (Police Commission)* (1977), 80 D.L.R. (3d) 490 (S.C.C.), *United Association of Journeymen & Apprentices of the Plumbing & Pipe Fitting Industry of the United States and Canada, Local 488 v. Foley* (1975), 60 D.L.R. (3d) 690 (Alta. T.D.).

231 *United Association of Journeymen & Apprentices of the Plumbing & Pipe Fitting Industry of the United States and Canada, Local 488 v. Foley* (1975), 60 D.L.R. (3d) 690 (Alta. T.D.).

(b) where the tribunal consists of more than one person, shall be signed by the chair of the tribunal or in such other manner as documents on behalf of the tribunal may be signed under the statute constituting the tribunal.

Presumably, an agency procedural regulation (or even a procedural policy) made under the authority granted by its enabling statute would serve to allow individual members of the agency, or one of the members sitting on proceeding to which a subpoena related, or the Chair of a panel of the agency sitting on that matter, or a particular staff member, to sign the subpoena. It appears, however, that section 12(2) goes only to the *signing* of the subpoena, not the decision to issue or not issue it in the first place. It would not, therefore, authorize the exercise of the agency's power to decide to issue a subpoena or not by someone who is not otherwise authorized to exercise the authority of the agency.

12.10(i) Service of the Subpoena

In the absence of a statutory direction to the contrary, a subpoena is generally requited to be served personally on the intended recipient. In Ontario section 12 (3) and (3.1) of the Statutory Powers Procedure Act requires personal service of a "summons". In the past the SPPA also required the payment of witness fees along with the subpoena. However, subsequent to the amendments to the SPPA by S.O. 1994, c. 27, it appears that, while the witness remains "entitled" to the payment of the same fees or allowance as are paid to a person summoned to attend before the Ontario Court (General Division) it is not necessary to pay those fees on service. Presumably, payment must be made on demand (SPPA subsection 12(3.1)).

12.10(j) Interprovincial Subpoenas

12.10(j)(i) Operation of Interprovincial Subpoenas Acts

It is not uncommon for an agency, particularly an agency holding a hearing near a provincial (or international) border to be asked for a subpoena directed to someone located outside of the province. A provincial agency cannot subpoena anyone located outside the geographic boundaries of its province insofar as a provincial Legislature cannot grant the agency power over individuals located outside the province. If it is clear that the individual will not be served within the province the agency should not issue the subpoena. It is an abuse of process for an agency to assert authority over an individual which it knows it does not have. (Such a subpoena could be issued where there is a chance that the individual might be properly served within the province.) The same difficulty arises with respect to the courts of the provinces operating under either under their inherent powers as a provincial superior court or under the grant of authority from a provincial statute. (The problem does not arise with federal agencies when their grant of authority comes from the federal Parliament.)

In order to compensate somewhat for this deficiency most of the provinces have passed reciprocal legislation providing a means for a subpena issued *by a court* in one province to be registered with a court in another.[232] In such cases it becomes a contempt of the receiving court not to obey the original subpoena.

Although the various statutes differ in some ways the registration and recognition process is essentially the same. The person in the province seeking to compel the attendance of someone located in another province first secures a subpoena in the ordinary way from the court in which the proceeding is being held. He then applies to the court specified in the statute of the province in which the witness whose attendance is desired is located[233] for a certificate, sealed with the court's seal, signifying that that judge, upon hearing and examining the applicant, is satisfied that the attendance in the issuing province of the person subpoenaed:

i. is necessary for the due adjudication of the proceeding in which the subpoena is issued, and

ii. in relation to the nature and importance of the cause of proceeding is reasonable and essential to the due administration of justice in that province.[234]

The subpoena, accompanied by the certificate, and the necessary witness fuss and travelling expenses[235] is taken to a court[236] in the receiving province (the province in which the person whose attendance is required. This court will receive and adopt the subpoena "as an order of the court"[237] if it is accompanied by the

---

232 Alberta: The Interprovincial Subpoena Act, S.A. 1981, c. 1-8.1; British Columbia: Subpoena (Interprovincial) Act, R.S.B.C. 1979, c. 396, Manitoba: The Interprovincial Subpoena Act, R.S.M. 1987 c. S212; New Brunswick: Interprovincial Subpoena Act, R.S.N.B. , 1973, c. I-13.1, Newfoundland: Interprovincial Subpoena Act, R.S.N. 1990, c. I-20; Ontario: Interprovincial Summons Act, R.S.O. 1990, c. I.12, Prince Edward Island: R.S.P.E.I. 1988, c. I-9; Saskatchewan: The Interprovincial Subpoena Act, R.S.S. 1978, c. I-12.1.

233 The particular court is specified in each of the respective provincial statutes, usually, but not necessarily, a superior court in that province.

234 The form of certificate is either prescribed by regulation or appended as a schedule to each statute. It is sufficient if the certificate issued is in "a form to the like effect" as the regulated or scheduled form.

235 As prescribed under the statute of the province in which the summons will be received. All of the provincial statutes also contain a provision permitting the person who is subject to the subpoena to request the court which issued the subpoena to order additional fees and expenses to be paid for attendance as a witness. Where that court is satisfied that the amount of fees and expenses originally paid is insufficient, it is authorized to order the party who obtained the subpoena to pay the person forthwith such additional fees and expenses as the court considers sufficient.

236 Some of the statutes expressly designate the receiving court, others simply refer to a "court" in the receiving province.

237 This phrase is similar to that used in the many statutory provisions dealing with the registering

certificate of the court of the issuing province and the necessary witness fess and travelling expenses and, upon hearing and examining the applicant the court is satisfied that the attendance in the issuing province of the person subpoenaed:

i. is necessary for the due adjudication of the proceeding in which the summons is issued, and

ii. in relation to the nature and importance of the cause or proceedings, is reasonable and essential to the due administration of justice in that province.

Once the subpoena is received by the receiving court, the person whose attendance is sought must be served with the adopted summons (along with the required witness fees and allowance). He then has 10 days, or such shorter period as the judge of the issuing province may indicate in his certificate, to attend in the issuing court. Failing this, the defaulting person is in contempt of the adopting court and subject to such penalty as that court may impose.

The operation of all of the provincial statutes is conditional on the receiving province having a law providing that a person in the province as a witness for the purposes for which the subpoena was issued shall be deemed, while within the issuing province, not to have submitted to the jurisdiction of the courts of that province other than as a witness in the proceedings which the person is subpoenaed and is absolutely immune from seizure of goods, service of process, execution of judgment, garnishment, imprisonment or molestation of any kind relating to a legal or judicial right, cause, action, proceeding or process within the jurisdiction of the legislature of the issuing province (but not with respect to proceedings arising from events occurring during or after the required attendance of the person in the issuing province). All of the interprovincial statutes have a provision granting such immunity.

12.10(j)(ii) Application To Agency Orders

All of the interprovincial subpoena statutes refer to the subpoena of a "court". However, in some provinces "court" is defined in a way that contemplates a subpoena issued by an agency. Thus, the ability to use the interprovincial subpoena statutes for agency orders depends on the individual statute and province. Unfortunately, it also appears clear that the wording of the statues is such that before the interprovincial scheme will work for agency orders the statutes of the provinces of both the issuing and receiving courts must provide for agency orders. The issuing province must provide for an agency order to be taken to the

---

of agency orders with courts for enforcement. On the basis of that case law it is likely that the filing of the order with the receiving court will not change its essential nature. It will remain an order of the issuing court. (See the discussion at c. 29A.7(b) respecting the registration of agency orders.) Thus, the receiving court would not have the jurisdiction to quash, vary or otherwise question the order beyond the criteria specified in the statute for its reception.

respective court of that province for the issuance of the interprovincial certificate *and* the statute of the receiving province must provide for the receipt of agency orders accompanied by such certificates.

In a situation, where either of the statutes does not apply to agency orders, an agency could always apply to a superior court in its province to come to its aid and issue the necessary subpoena for the attendance of the witness before the agency. One could then treat this subpoena as the originating subpoena, have the necessary certificate issued and attached to it and then attempt to have the court in the respective receiving province receive this subpoena. Given the wording of most of the provincial statutes (Saskatchewan is the only province which unreservedly treats agency subpoenas as "court" subpoenas) this is the process which is most likely going to have to be followed. To summarize it:

1. The person seeking the attendance of an out-of-province witness before an agency proceeding first applies to a superior court of the province in which the agency proceeding is to take place to "come to the aid of the agency" by issuing the necessary subpoena for the attendance of the witness.

2. This subpoena is then brought before the court designated in that province's interprovincial subpoena statute for the issuance of the necessary certificate.

3. The subpoena with the necessary certificate (and required fees) is brought before the court in the province where the witness is located in order to be received by that court.

4. The now "adopted" subpoena is served on the witness (along with the fees) who has 10 days (or less, depending on the certificate by the issuing court) to appear before the agency.

The actual treatment of agency orders by each provincial statute is set out below.

Alberta

The Alberta statute defines a "court outside of Alberta" as:

i.   a court in a province of Canada other than Alberta, or

ii. a board commission, tribunal or other body of a province that is designated by the Lt. Governor of Alberta, pursuant to section 9 of the statute, as a court outside Alberta for the purposes of the statute.

A "court in Alberta" includes a board, commission tribunal or other body in Alberta. Thus, for the purposes of the Alberta statute, the receiving Alberta court (Queen's Bench) can only receive orders issued by "courts" of other provinces and agencies of those other provinces which have been designated by the Lt. Governor.

Where another province is prepared to receive the orders of agencies, the Alberta statute does provide for the orders of Alberta agency orders to be taken to the Court of Queen's Bench to initiate the interprovincial process there by the issuance of the necessary certificate. Thus, Alberta agencies may take advantage of those other statutes which will receive agency orders.

British Columbia

The British Columbia statute does not provide for agency orders. The statute defines "court" as any court in a province of Canada. There is no mention made of agency orders. Although the term "subpoena" as used in the statute is broad enough to catch any form of compulsion order,[238] the Act is clear that it applies only to subpoenas issued by courts. There is no indication as to whether an agency is a "court". Since agencies are not generally considered to be so in the absence of some statutory indication[239] the British Columbia statute likely does not apply to agency subpoenas.

Manitoba

The Manitoba statute defines "court" "as any court in a province of Canada, and where a magistrate in a province of Canada has the power to issue a subpoena, includes a magistrate in that province." The French version of the statute uses the word "tribunal" as the equivalent of "court". While the French word "tribunal" is sufficiently broad in theory to catch an agency, the express reference in both the English and French versions of the statute to a magistrate (an inferior body) being a court in some circumstances likely indicates that the Legislature did not intend "court" or "tribunal" to include other types of inferior bodies, such as agencies. Thus, the Manitoba statute does not appear to be open to agency orders.

New Brunswick

"Court" in the New Brunswick statute is defined as "any court in a province of Canada, or such other boards, commissions, tribunals or other bodies of any other province [including a territory] as are designated by the Lieutenant-Governor in Council pursuant to section 9 as a court for the purposes of this Act."

---

238 Section 1 provides that "subpoena" means "a subpoena or other document requiring a person within a province, other than the province where the subpoena originates, to attend as a witness, to produce documents or other articles or to testify before that court."

239 The designation of an agency in its enabling statute as a "court of record" does not make that body a "court" in the legal or traditional sense (*Manitoba (Attorney-General) v. Canada (National Energy Board)*, [1974] 2 F.C. 502, 48 D.L.R. (3d) 73 (T.D.), *Committee for Justice and Liberty v. National Energy Board*, [1978] 1 S.C.R. 369, 9 N.R. 115, 68 D.L.R. (3d) 716).

It is clear that an agency outside of New Brunswick will not constitute a court of the purposes of the New Brunswick statute (i.e. will not be able to be received by the New Brunswick court) unless that body is designated as a court by the Lt. Governor in Council under section 9 of the statute. However, what is odd about the New Brunswick statute is that it does not make express provision for orders issued by agencies within New Brunswick. It would seem odd that, at least in some circumstances, that New Brunswick would be prepared to accept a subpoena issued by an agency outside of the province while not permitting its own agencies to take advantage of the reciprocal statute of another province. The definition of "court" as meaning "any court in a province" *OR* such other boards of any other province, etc. indicates that this is the case. Thus, New Brunswick agencies will not be able to secure the necessary certificate in that province (without first securing the necessary subpoena from a superior court).

The subpoenas of agencies outside of New Brunswick which are designated by the Lt. Governor of New Brunswick can be received by a New Brunswick. Outside agencies which are not so designated will first have to secure a subpoena from a superior court of their province compelling attendance which order will then have the necessary certificate attached in the issuing province and brought to New Brunswick for receipt there.

Newfoundland

"Court" in the Newfoundland statute is defined a "court in a province [including a territory] of Canada". Thus, the restrictions noted above in the case of British Columbia will apply in this province.

Ontario

In the English version of the Ontario statute the word "court" is defined as meaning "any court in a province". The French version of the statute uses the word "tribunal". As noted above in the case of Manitoba, the French term "tribunal" is capable of meaning both the traditional court and an agency. While it is not possible to say with certainty how this statute might be interpreted by the courts if the need arose, there is jurisprudence in a similar situation to the effect that the Quebec Human Rights Commission was a "court" for the purposes of section 41 of the Federal Court Act (*Quebec (Human Rights Commission v. Canada (Solicitor-General)* (1978), 93 D.L.R. (3d) 562 (Que. C.A.). In that case the English version of the statute referred to "court" and the French version to "tribunal". However, this jurisprudence is not likely to be successful in the case of the Ontario interprovincial subpoena statute by virtue of section 2 of that statute which provides for the receipt of another province's subpoena.

The term "court" is also used in section 2 of the Ontario legislation to refer to the body receiving a subpoena from another province. The use of that broad term here indicates that the term "court" is likely restricted to the traditional concept of a court, not an agency. It seems clear from all the reciprocal legislation that the receiving court in a province must be a traditional court, not an agency. This seems even more evident when one recognizes that failure to comply with a received subpoena amounts to a contempt of the receiving court. Many agencies in Ontario will not have a contempt power. If the term "court" as used in the receiving aspects of the Ontario statute does not likely contemplate an agency, it is likely that the term is similarly exclusive throughout the statute. Thus, it appear that the Ontario statute does not contemplate an agency orders constituting orders of a court. In order to access the Ontario interprovincial subpoena statute it appears that the individual seeking to compel the attendance of a witness before an agency would have to have recourse to the extra step of first securing the necessary original subpoena from a superior court in aid of the agency proceedings.

Prince Edward Island

"Court" in the Prince Edward Island statute is defined similarly to the British Columbia statute. The comments made above respecting that statute will also apply here.

Saskatchewan

Saskatchewan's statute provides that "court" means any court in a province and, where a board, commission, tribunal or other body or person in a province has the power to issue a subpoena, includes that board commission, tribunal, body or person". Thus, Saskatchewan appears to recognize agency subpoenas as subpoenas of a court.

Thus, the respective Saskatchewan courts could receive a subpoena from a foreign agency accompanied by the necessary certificate from the issuing province (and the necessary fees). Equally, its courts may issue the necessary certificate for its agencies to be taken to the foreign provincial courts for recognition. However, as noted at the beginning of this discussion, it is evident that before a foreign agency order could secure the necessary certificate from its own courts the statute of that province would have to recognize those agency subpoenas as the subpoena of a court. And before a foreign provincial court will be able to receive a Saskatchewan agency subpoena, even when accompanied by the necessary certificate from the Saskatchewan courts, that receiving province's statute must itself recognize agency subpoenas as being subpoenas of a court. In those cases where the other provincial statute does not recognize agencies as courts, recourse would have to be made to the superior court in the issuing province for a subpoena requiring the attendance of the individual in the agency proceedings.

12.10(k) Enforcement

The enforcement of subpoenas through the contempt power (of either agencies or the courts) is discussed in section 29A, which deals with contempt.

Subsections 12(4)-(7) of Ontario's Statutory Powers Procedure Act provides an alternative enforcement technique whereby an application is made to the courts for the issuance of a bench warrant to seize the defaulting individual and bring him before the agency.[240]

12.11 THE APPLICATION

Some proceedings before agencies must be commenced by an application brought to it by someone. In such cases, the ultimate responsibility to ensure that an application has been properly filed and that each and every requirement for doing so has been met rests with the person bringing the application. The agency may advise him but it is not the agency's responsibility to complete or otherwise ensure that it is properly served.[241] (The decision-maker would, however, have to satisfy himself that all preconditions to his having jurisdiction had been met before exercising that jurisdiction.)

There are times when an agency will discover that an application, which otherwise appears to be properly filed, has been made on behalf of one or more individuals by an agent or representative who, for some technical reason or other, lacked the status to act as an agent. An agency should be slow to dismiss an application for this cause, particularly where it may not be possible for the individuals to renew or make another application (where statutory time limits have expired, for example). If there is no prejudice to any other person (beyond the simple fact of allowing the application to continue) the agency, unless prohibited by statute, should give the parties the opportunity to take the application over personally or through another qualified individual. For the authority for this proposition see *Professional Sign Crafters (1988) Ltd. v. Wedekind.*[242] In that decision the Alberta Court of Queen's Bench held that it would not be proper to strike out a legal action as a nullity where that action was commenced on behalf of a corporation through the agency of a person who was not entitled to do so under the Legal Profession Act, S.A. 1990, c. L-9. (The Statement of Claim was drafted and issued by a director of the corporation who was not a member of the Law Society of Alberta.) The Court stated that the purpose of the Act was "to protect the public by preventing unqualified individuals from practising law.

---

240 The Statutory Powers Procedure Act, including s. 12, may be found in the legislation tab in vol. 3 of this text.

241 For a case to this effect in the context of a civil judicial proceeding see *North Hills Nursing Home Ltd. v. Roscoe Construction Ltd.* (1994), 25 C.P.C. (3d) 315, 130 N.S.R. (2d) 47, 367 A.P.R. 47 (S.C.).

242 [1994] 7 W.W.R. 136 (Alta. Q.B.).

Those who contravene the Act are subject to penalties. There is nothing express or implied in the statute imposing any sanctions on those for whom unqualified individuals purport to act. In many cases the "clients" will be ignorant of the lack of qualifications and it would be harsh to strike out their actions as nullities." In light of the fact that the defendants had suffered no prejudice and that the subject Statement of Claim was not defective in form and disclosed a cause of action, the Court felt that the proper disposition was to stay the proceedings until the plaintiffs were properly represented on the record.

Similar to that case was the decision of the Ontario Divisional Court in *van Beek & Associates v. Ontario Regional Assessment Commissioner, Region 14.*[243] That case involved an agent who had filed 758 appeals of 1992 property tax assessments to the Ontario Assessment Review Board. The agency agreement between the agent and the 758 tax payers was champertous. The Board dismissed the application as champertous arrangements are invalid under the Act Respecting Champerty, R.S.O. 1897, c. 327, sections 1 and 2. The dismissal resulted in the taxpayers' loss of their ability to appeal their 1992 tax assessments as the time limit for doing so had passed by the time of the Board's actions. On judicial review the Ontario Divisional Court quashed the Board's order. While the champertous nature of the arrangements rendered the agency agreements invalid between the taxpayers and the agent, it did not affect the right of the taxpayers to appeal their assessments to the Board. In the Court's view, the statute did not make agency authorizations a constituent element of any tax assessment appeal and the appeals had been brought in the names of the taxpayers, not the agent who was before the Board as a simple agent.

Finally, in the absence of a statutory direction to the contrary, where proceedings are contingent on the bringing of an application by an individual, the individual usually retains the authority to stop the proceedings by withdrawing the application. Once withdrawn, there is nothing before the agency to be heard. On this point see *Winnipeg (City) Assessor v. Winnipeg (City) Board of Revision.*[244] Here, taxpayers had filed review applications of their property assessments with the Winnipeg Board of Revision. Subsequently, due to a misunderstanding, the taxpayers withdrew their applications. The Board's administrative officer removed the applications from the Board's agenda. By the time the taxpayers discovered their error, the time for filing new applications with the Board had passed. The taxpayers asked the Board to continue with their original applications. The Board set dates for hearing. The city sought judicial review. The taxpayers argued that once an application is duly filed the applicant cannot unilaterally terminate the Board's mandate to adjudicate. Thus, the Board's administrative officer had no jurisdiction to withdraw the applications from consideration by the Board. There was no legislative provision granting the Board authority over the

---

243 (1994), 17 O.R. (3d) 114 (Div. Ct.).

244 (1993), 88 Man. R. (2d) 130, 110 D.L.R. (4th) 177 (C.A.), leave to appeal to S.C.C. refused (1994), 112 D.L.R. 94th) viii (note).

withdrawal of an application. The Manitoba Court of Appeal quashed the Board's decision to continue the applications. It held that the taxpayer's had the authority to unilaterally withdraw the appeals without the permission of the Board and once a matter was withdrawn it was out of the Board's jurisdiction. Admittedly, the Court took into account the fact that the legislation in question was taxing legislation. It stated that "Taxing legislation is to be construed strictly. Unless the Board is given the discretion to grant or to deny a party the right to withdraw, such a power cannot be inferred. A taxpayer who institutes a review application maintains the right to withdraw or abandon that application unless the legislature has seen fit to limit or otherwise curtail that right."

12.12 BACKGROUND BRIEFING MATERIAL

I believe that background briefing material given to a decision-maker should be put on the hearing record so that the parties and the public will have an opportunity to make submissions on the material given to the panel. It is a workable practice. This recommendation probably runs counter to much prevailing practice.

As to the law, while the requirements of natural justice generally provide that the parties are entitled to know the argument and evidence against them[245] there is a body of case law to the effect that the actual staff reports themselves need not be given to the participants provided that the information or argument conveyed therein comes out sometime in the proceedings so that the participants are aware of it and can adequately deal with it.[246]

This general principle is obviously part of the general rule respecting disclosure and thus will be subject to the over-arching principles noted above respecting natural justice and notice. Consequently, the duty to disclose staff reports will vary in degree with the nature and circumstances of the power being exercised. Thus, it may be that the interests of an individual cannot be adequately defended without the disclosure of the actual report rather than simply a summary of its substance.[247] The farther one gets away from decisions affecting individual rights

---

245 See the earlier discussions in this chapter under notice: "How Much Information Need Be Given", "Where Less Than Full Disclosure of Evidence May Be Sufficient" and "Duty to Disclose Information Which is Not Before Decision-maker".

246 For case law on this point see *Trans-Quebec & Maritime Pipeline Inc. v. Canada (National Energy Board)* (1984), 8 Admin. L.R. 177 (Fed. C.A.), *Toshiba Corp. v. Anti-Dumping Tribunal* (1984), 8 Admin. L.R. 173 (Fed. C.A.), *Radulesco v. Canada (Canadian Human Rights Commission)* (1984), 55 N.R. 384 (S.C.C.), *Magnasonic Canada Ltd. v. Anti-Dumping Tribunal*, [1972] F.C. 1239 (Fed. C.A.), *R. v. Ontario (Racing Commission)*, [1971] 1 O.R. 400, (C.A.), *Madison Dev. Corp. Ltd. v. Rent Regulation App. Board* (1977), 7 A.R. 360 (S.C.), *Knapman v. Saltfleet (Municipality) Board of Health*, [1954] 3 D.L.R. 760 (Ont. H.C.), affirmed [1955] 3 D.L.R. 248 (C.A.), affirmed (1956) 6 D.L.R. (2d) 81 (S.C.C.), *Lazarov v. Secretary of State of Canada*, [1973] F.C. 927 (C.A.) *Re Poffenroth Application* (1954), 13 W.W.R. 617 (Alta. T.D.).

247 See, for example, *Napoli v. British Columbia (Workers' Compensation Board)* (1981), 126 D.L.R. (3d) 179 (B.C. C.A.).

and approaches the legislative end of the spectrum and the more political in nature the decision-maker, the less the burden appears to be to disclose staff advice. See, for example, *Idziak v. Canada (Minister of Justice)*[248] in the Supreme Court of Canada which involved proceedings which the Court characterized as being legislative in nature. In this case the Minister of Justice was not required to disclose a memorandum prepared for the Minister by his staff counsel. The memorandum included a summary of the detained person's representations to the Minister and a recommendation. Insofar as the proceedings were legislative in nature, involving essentially policy considerations, the Supreme Court held that the Minister was not obliged to disclose the memorandum to the detained person prior to reaching his decision. Similarly, the British House of Lords in *Bushell v. Secretary of State for the Environment*[249] held that, in the making of a decision as to where major motorways where to be situated, a Minister was expected to consult with his staff and that the public, while they may have the right to ensure that their views and evidence are put before the Minister, do not have the right to demand that the Minister advise them of the advice he receives from staff in making his decision.[250]

Whether or not the parties should be able to cross-examine upon briefing reports which are made available to a board is a matter to be argued before a board. I believe that if the reports are relevant, cross-examination of briefing material prepared by a consultant may be permitted by the board depending on the circumstances.

12.13 TRANSCRIPTS AND OTHER RECORDS OF PROCEEDINGS

In *Kandiah v. Canada (Minister of Employment & Immigration)*[251] the Federal Court of Appeal held that neither section 7 of the Charter nor the principles of natural justice require an agency (in this case the Immigration and Refugee Board) to provide a verbatim transcript of its proceedings.[252] Some agencies do, of course, and this is a desirable practice. However, as noted in *Kandiah*, in the absence of a statutory duty to maintain such a record, the malfunctioning of a recording machine does not in itself constitute grounds for setting aside a decision.

Even when there is a legislative duty to keep a record of the proceedings it does not appear that an incomplete transcript resulting from some technological

---

248 (1992), 9 Admin. L.R. (2d) 1 (S.C.C.).

249 [1980] 2 All E.R. 608 (H.L.).

250 For a similar decision involving a municipal council see *Bourque v. Richmond (Township)* (1978), 87 D.L.R. (3d) 349 (B.C. C.A.).

251 (1992), 6 Admin. L.R. (2d) 42 (Fed. C.A.).

252 To the same effect see *Bauer v. Regina (Canadian) Immigration Commission*, [1984] 2 F.C. 455 (T.D.) which cites *Mindamar Metals (Corp.) v. Richmond County*, [1955] 2 D.L.R. 183 (N.S.S.C.) in support of the that conclusion. The Court in that case, however, did maintain the caveat that there may be circumstances where a shorthand record would have to be retained for the sake of fairness, but it gave no indication of what those circumstances would be.

defect in the recording will invalidate proceedings in the absence of any material harm arising from that defect. The Supreme Court of Canada has taken this position in the context of a criminal trial. In *R. v. Hayes*[253] Justice L'Heureux-Dubé made the following comments respecting a defective transcript:

> A new trial need not be ordered for every gap in a transcript. As a general rule, there must be a serious possibility that there was an error in the missing portion of the transcript, or that the omission deprived the appellant of a ground of appeal.

The Federal Court Trial Division reached the same conclusion in the context of defective machine recordings of proceedings of the National Parole Board. Despite a requirement in the regulations that the Board "shall" keep a voice or a written transcript of the hearing in neither *Okeynan v. Prince Albert Penitentiary*[254] nor *Desjardins v. Canada (National Parole Board)*[255] did the reviewing judge conclude that the defect was sufficient to warrant requiring a new proceeding. In *Okeynan* Justice Strayer commented that:

> It is unquestionably important that all the regulations be observed in the conduct of a detention hearing, including the making of a satisfactory recording. I do not believe, however, that failure to do so automatically nullifies the decision reached by the Board. But it might be quite relevant to the exercise of judicial review of such a decision and its absence here adds to the difficulty I have in satisfying myself that the applicant had a fair hearing.[256]

Some boards never have a reporter present; some boards sometimes have a reporter present; and some boards always have a reporter present.

The preferable choice is to have a reporter present. Reporters costs may be recovered by the tribunal in the hearing cost order at the end of the hearing. In some tribunals, the transcript of the day is available at suppertime that day; the earlier in the day, the better. In regulatory hearings, where the facts are very complex, daily transcripts are essential.

Corrections to transcripts should be made each morning in the transcript of the day before, by filing an errata sheet with the reporter who will include the sheet at the commencement of that day's transcript. If the correction requires confirmation by that witness, that should be done through counsel or the witness at the start of the day. Only errors and corrections which require explanation should be addressed.

Today, with the advance of technology, the transcript can be produced on a screen monitor instantly as the witness speaks. This monitor is connected to a computer. The computer enables the hearing panel to follow the evidence in

---

253 (1989), 89 N.R. 138 (S.C.C.).
254 (1988), 20 F.T.R. 270.
255 (1989), 29 F.T.R. 38.
256 To the same effect, see also *Giroux v. Canada (National Parole Board)* (1994), 89 F.T.R. 307.

written form on a screen as it is given and to review that the witness said an hour or a day ago on the same subject in that hearing. Testimony may be called up by inputting key words out of the computer's memory bank. It certainly keeps counsel, parties and witnesses on their toes, reduces elapsed time and settles many disputes instantly. The next improvement would be to move to large screens which the whole audience in the room can follow. The record is also simultaneously reduced to a written transcript.1 I believe that all courts and major tribunals will use this system before long.

It is important for the tribunal to carefully prepare its contract with the reporters to make sure that a number of points are covered. Attached, as Appendix 12.9, is a reporter contact. Note the issue of copyright and the problems created by in-camera hearings.

Sometimes a party will ask to keep a personal record of the proceedings. This personal record may run the spectrum from the individual keeping personal notes, to having an associate keep notes, to having a secretary keep shorthand notes, to having a privately retained court reporter keep notes, to running a tape recorder or to even video taping the proceedings.

Although the Ontario Divisional Court had concluded otherwise earlier (at least in respect of the personal note keeping by a party or his counsel)[257] it now seems clear that in the absence of any statutory direction, "a tribunal, whether it be a court of record or not, but which has been given control of its process, has complete discretion as to any mechanical or other recording of its proceedings, which means that the fact that it has adopted a general policy of refusing to permit such recording, provided that no discrimination is allowed to enter into the application of the policy, is legally unassailable".[258] The Federal Court of Appeal had reached the same conclusion earlier in 1983 in *Eastern Provincial Airways Ltd. v. Canada Labour Relations Board*,[259] where the Court held that the Canada Labour Relations Board's "refusal to permit EPA to make a verbatim record was not, per se, a denial of natural justice even though intended, inter alia, to make more difficult the pursuit of its remedy in this Court. Applicable as it was to both

---

257 In *Mroszkowski v. Ontario (Director of the Vocational Rehabilitation Services Branch of the Ministry of Community and Social Services)* the Ontario Divisional Court condemned the actions of a panel of the Social Assistance Review Board attempting to prohibit such personal note keeping:

At the hearing, the Board ordered a student assisting counsel to the appellant to refrain from taking what were described as "copious notes" of the proceedings. The Board then began to tape-record the balance of the hearing but refused to supply counsel with a transcript of the proceedings as taped.

In our view, the Board was wrong on both counts. The taking of notes by counsel or his assistant could, in no way, be considered disruptive of the proceedings or an abuse of the process. It was a fundamental right of counsel which ought not to have been interfered with.

258 *Rhéaume v. Canada* (1992), 11 Admin. L.R. (2d) 124, 153 N.R. 270 (Fed. C.A.), leave to appeal to Supreme Court of Canada refused (1993), 11 Admin. L.R. (2d) 126n (S.C.C.).

259 (1983), 6 Admin. L.R. 139 (Fed. C.A.).

parties in this dispute, indeed to all parties in all disputes generally, implementation of the policy cannot be found to have been procedurally unfair to EPA.[260]

An agency's power to restrict recording of its proceeding likely extends to prohibiting media access to its proceedings with video cameras. However, in the exercise of this power agencies should be aware that it is likely an infringement of section 2(b) of the Charter to indiscriminately prohibit media access to one's proceedings (at least those which are quasi-judicial in nature). Media access to judicial and quasi-judicial proceedings has been found to be guaranteed by s. 2(b) (freedom of expression).[261] However, at the moment, at least, it appears that a prohibition aimed at disruptions caused by video cameras with the aim of maintaining "a calm, quiet atmosphere which is essential for the proper administration of justice" would survive a challenge based on section 1 of the Charter.[262]

In my opinion, unless it can be established that the record keeping method selected by an individual is disruptive or somehow threatening to the proper progress of the hearing, it should be allowed. Some decision-makers feel pressured by record keeping. Some feel it imposes too restrained or "legal" a tone to the proceeding. As to the concern respecting the tone of a hearing, a tape or similar recording would likely not be proper at some form of mediation proceeding which by its nature is supposed to be informal and open to free, give and take, communication. Beyond this, when rights or privileges are being adjudicated, maintaining some record of the proceedings may be simply part of the game with which a decision-maker must come to grips. Some agencies appear to have a concern that an individual may attempt to use a record of the proceedings in some unscrupulous way. For example, in the *Eastern Provincial Airways Ltd. v. Canada (Labour Relations Board)* case noted above the court quoted the following reasons of the Canada Labour Relations Board explaining its prohibition on any personal stenographic or tape recording being made of a proceeding (the Board had also explained that it felt that these records would change the atmosphere of the proceeding and made them more judicial in tone):

> Although we see and our experience has shown us little advantage during the conduct of the hearing a recording may be of some advantage afterward. Otherwise why would a party want it? That advantage could be in written propaganda surrounding a dispute, or to play edited versions of the proceedings on radio or television, or to prepare future witnesses where there has been an exclusion of witnesses

---

260 To the same effect see *Bauer v. Regina (Canadian) Immigration Commission*, [1984] 2 F.C. 455 (T.D.).

261 *Edmonton Journal v. Alberta (Attorney General)*, [1989] 2 S.C.R. 1326, *Armdale Communications Ltd. v. Canada (Adjudicator appointed under the Immigration Act)*, [1979] 3 F.C. 242, 127 N.R. 342 (C.A.); *Pacific Press Ltd. v. Canada (Minister of Employment & Immigration)*, [1990] 1 F.C. 419 (C.A.).

262 *R. v. Squires* (1992), 11 O.R. (3d) 385, 18 C.R. (4th) 22, 78 C.C.C. (3d) 97 (C.A.), leave to appeal to S.C.C. refused (1993) 25 C.R. (4th) 103n, 83 C.C.C. (3d) viin (S.C.C.).

or adjournment, or for other reasons within the imagination of the parties. The Board will not allow its proceedings and mediative efforts to be open to this potential for compromise.

Personally, I am not particularly persuaded by such concerns. I think one must proceed on the basis that the citizenry will act lawfully. Besides, anyone willing to go to those lengths will likely find some other way to misconstrue the proceedings. An agency's own contempt powers and power over abuse of its process, or the contempt powers of a superior court where the agency has no such power, should be sufficient to control the unscrupulous.

Sometimes an agency will impose conditions on the more innovative forms of record keeping. For example, it may permit a party to retain its own court reporter on condition that any report is shared with the agency and the other parties.

The best method of avoiding all of these concerns, however, is simply for the agency to maintain its own comprehensive record which can then be made available to the participants or which may be made available for purchase by the participants.[263]

In closing the discussion on this aspect of hearings I will simply note the decision of the Alberta Supreme Court Trial Division in *Alberta Union of Provincial Employees v. R.*[264] in which the Court, in the context of a judicial review, held that its Rules of Court should not be interpreted so as to require the automatic transcription into writing of a taped proceeding of an agency. The tape itself should be permitted to be part of the record with the judge reserving the discretion to direct the written production of such portions of the tape as may be necessary.

12.14 OPENING OF THE HEARING

There is no legal obligation for an agency member, presiding over a hearing, to open the proceedings with an opening statement. Yet such statements are very useful tools in the successful conduct of a hearing.

A properly crafted opening statement serves many purposes. It is a practical way for the member to quickly and orderly get the preliminary information he or she will need from the parties and, in turn, to give the parties information which will make it easier for them to function. It can be a checklist to ensure that all

---

263 In *Mroszkowski v. Ontario (Director of the Vocational Rehabilitation Services Branch of the Ministry of Community and Social Services)* (1973), 20 O.R. (2d) 688 (Div. Ct.) the Divisional Court also held that once the Social Assistance Review Board had made a tape recording of the proceeding the transcript should have formed a part of the record and should have been made available to the parties. If there was a problem as to the costs of the transcript, the Court conceded, the tape should have been made available under some controlled circumstances.

264 (1978), 85 D.L.R. (3d) 387 (Alta. S.C.), affirmed on grounds that appeal was moot 42 D.L.R. (4th) 406n (Alta. C.A.).

preliminary procedural requirements have been met to vest the agency with jurisdiction. In my opinion, this is an easier way to do this than relying on the parties to bring the information out. It provides an opportunity to ensure that all the participants are aware of the process that will be followed, what they must do to make their case, and when and how they can do this. Making this clear in the opening statement may avoid later questions or attempts by parties to put in evidence or argument at inappropriate times or even to go off on matters unrelated to the application.

It is also useful to notify the parties who are more familiar with the process of proposed deviations from standard procedures. Objections or concerns could then be raised after the opening statement, at the beginning of the hearing rather than well into it.

Advising the participants as suggested above, increases the comfort level of individuals and diminishes the little insecurities (as to what to call someone, when and from where to speak, etc.). Anyone who has ever been a witness in judicial proceedings may know how out the of the picture the first time attendee can feel in the swirling court process that seems to just roll over them without explanation or understanding. The purpose of an administrative proceeding is to get information. I believe that this is easier to do with a comfortable, aware audience than a tense, confused one.

The time taken in making an opening statement is an opportunity for parties, observers and the agency members to settle down and get into the hearing mode. It eases them into the hearing so that everyone is settled and mentally ready to go when the substantive portion of the proceedings rolls around.

In my opinion, a opening statement by a presiding member or chair also serves the important psychological purpose of establishing that it is the agency that is in control of the proceedings, not one particular party or another. Having the agency member be the first person to speak, and to lay out the process, emphasizes that it is the agency which is in control.

Finally, I feel that using an opening statement to verify who the parties are and ensuring that preliminary procedural requirements have been met accustoms the participants to the inquiry powers and active role of the agency.

Generally, where a panel presides over a proceeding, it is the Chairman of the panel who delivers the opening statement as part of his or her responsibilities as Chairman. However, there is no rule requiring this and the Chairman may ask any member to do so if desired.

Opening statements can be made ad hoc or read from a prepared text. Obviously those gifted individuals who have the memory and elocution skills to speak ad hoc should do so. An opening statement is best delivered in a normal, conversational tone, with frequent eye contact with the participants. This is most easily done speaking ad hoc with a checklist.

It may be easier, however, to have a form of boiler plate/checklist written opening statement. Those parts which did not change from hearing to hearing may be written out completely. Other parts (such as the verification of preliminary procedural matters) may be set out in checklist form.

Whether you read, recite, or speak ad hoc it is important that this be done conversationally and professionally, Do not mumble or race over the opening statement. Do not sound bored. The idea is to convey and collect information and to establish a professional atmosphere. If you do not feel that your opening statement warrants the time to deliver it in a fashion that people can follow, you may wish to consider changing it or dropping it altogether.

The opening statement should be the statement that opens the hearing. It should be given as soon as the decision-maker (or panel) takes his seat and is prepared to commence the hearing (and it looks as if everyone else is also about ready). I believe that the agency member should be the first person to speak in administrative proceedings.

There is no set length for an opening statement. If you are going to have an opening statement it should be neither so short that it does not really serve any purpose nor so long that the room has long since drifted off into boredom and you into exhaustion. It is not practical to use an opening statement as a primer course in the substantive and procedural law of your agency. I suggest that you should decide why you are giving an opening statement and then make it only so long as to accomplish the goal you have set. An opening statement delivered in a proceeding where the participants are all experienced in the process may be shorter and geared towards securing the practical information which will assist the member in performing his or her duties (names of participants, satisfaction of jurisdiction pre-conditions, etc.) or announcing matters which might be different in this particular proceeding than in others. An opening statement which is delivered in a proceeding with a large number participants who are unfamiliar with the process might be longer and geared more to conveying sufficient basic information that will enable the participants to be comfortable and participate more fully. This is a judgment call that should become easier with experience.

An opening statement is a combination of personal preference and the nature of the application before the agency. In crafting an opening statement you may wish to consider doing some or all of the following:

1. Introduce yourself and any other panel members. Advise the participants how to address you.

2. Introduce the subject of the hearing.

3. Note the statutory authority under which you will be operating.

4. Set out in a summary form what the agency is trying to do.

5. Include any cautions or disclosures which the agency is required to make by law. This gets the task out of the way early in the proceeding. This may be an opportunity to advise the parties of the existence of policy guidelines

made public by my agency and caution them that I was aware of any agency guidelines.

6. Review the attendance, note the names of the parties and their representatives (verify spelling if necessary).

7. Include a checklist of the preliminary procedural requirements necessary to vest the agency with jurisdiction.

8. Caution participants of any statutory offence provisions relevant to your proceedings. This may serve as a reminder to individuals of the seriousness of the proceedings, notwithstanding any informal atmosphere.

9. Explain the general procedure to be followed in the proceeding. In cases where there is extensive pre-filed evidence one may wish to inform those attending that the members have read the evidence and that counsel are requested not to review or highlight the pre-filed evidence except with the approval of the board. If counsel wish to have the witnesses add to that which is pre-filed, such additions should normally be pre-filed as well.

10. Remind the participants of the days and hours of sitting. If certain days are not to be sitting days, this should be made known at this time. In large regulatory proceedings one may wish to set aside a day for public partici- pation. I have always felt that the practice of allowing public intervenors to put in their oral evidence before the applicant has finished its case is unfair, yet some agencies do so.

Separate days or hours are often set aside in advance to receive the evidence of certain witnesses. A tribunal should and must try to meet these commitments. Sometimes it is not possible. A tribunal should offer the same kind of thoughtful courtesy which it expects in return.

In many hearings before all sorts of tribunals, witnesses for parties may only be available on certain days because of many other commitments. Even if the witness will be called out of sequence or interrupt another witness, the tribunal should try to accommodate the witness' time constraints. Agency hearings are not court trials. The public interest can seriously suffer by inflexible formalism. What is important are the needs of the tribunal to get at the facts and in a way that conveniences the public input and participation. What a court, at any time, might do is totally irrelevant, so long as the tribunal procedure is fair. It is far better to change course frequently, if necessary, to hear a witness than to do without that evidence.

At the end of each day's hearing before adjourning, for the record, the chairman should review:

(1) which witnesses and panels are likely to be heard during the ensuing days;

(2) how long counsel plans to examine or cross-examine the expected witnesses. This gives the panel and the audience some warning of where the panel expects to end up over the immediate future. (Sweetheart cross-examinations are not really a serous problems in tribunal hearings because credibility is not usually a major issue. In fact, leading a witness can be helpful if carefully conducted.) and

(3) the exhibit numbers or other documents to which various counsel will refer the next day.

It is worthwhile having rules or policy to the effect that:

(4) each Counsel should make it known well ahead of time, to what documents or exhibits he will refer in his examination or cross-examination the next day. This saves hours of paper shuffling over an extended hearing. It also enables all participants to review the documents prior to the examination or cross-examination.

(5) if any counsel is going to question a witness on a document, the witness should be told at least a day ahead which document will be referred to and the pages thereof. There should be copies of the pages put before the panel, the witnesses and counsel at the time of the examination or cross-examination.

(6) if any counsel is going to take a witness through a lot of mathematical calculations, sheets of these calculations should be prepared and passed around well prior to the examination or cross-examination, such as the day before. Intelligent use should be made of overhead projectors, moving electric writing boards that reproduce the data written on them, etc.

(7) the procedure of many boards in Canada permits sitting at a desk to give evidence and sitting while examining. Many boards have done away with witness boxes. Many boards are so involved in referring to paper exhibits, that sitting at a table to give or examine on evidence is the only sensible route to follow in a modern age. The Canadian Radio-television and Telecommunications Commission ("CRTC") is a bit schizophrenic, depending on what function it is carrying out at a given moment, broadcasting as opposed to telecommunications, and does things differently in one function as opposed to another.

If the board has adopted or plans to adopt any special rules about the conduct of the hearing, they should be noted by the chairman at the commencement of the hearing. These kinds of announcements are not necessary in a court because of their consistent, historical and published procedural practices. Administrative agencies have not existed for a long period of time, their members are drawn from all walks of life and, accordingly, they tend to follow a much less rigid regime than the courts. Many boards sit in huge halls, skating arenas, church basements, the church proper, town council chambers, warehouses, libraries, etc., which environments are not easy to control and does not lend itself to formality.

The conduct of the opening day and the demeanour of the panel chairmen set the level of perception and audience expectation for the balance of the hearing.

12.15 REPRESENTATIONS AND WITNESSES AT THE HEARING

12.15(a) Introduction of Parties

At the opening of a hearing, or soon thereafter, the presiding member should ask the counsel and parties to identify themselves and the general position taken in relation to the matter before the tribunal.

The best practice is to call for representations *from all persons* in the room in the following order:

(1) from the *applicant(s)* or, in other generic proceedings, the *major parties* in alphabetical order. If there are no applicants, the tribunal should select the parties to be recognized and in what order;

(2) from *intervenors appearing through counsel*, in alphabetical order. The panel chairman should have before him a typed list of the names of those parties and counsel who are expected to attend in alphabetical order; and

(3) from *others generally* who are later arranged by the hearing clerk in alphabetical order.

Because most tribunals accept anyone who comes forward as an interested person to be a party there should be few issues involving standing.

However, the above comments regarding intervenor status are subject to the Supreme Court of Canada decision in *Director of Investigation and Research under the Combines Investigation Act v. Nfld. Telephone Co.*[265] In that case, the court held that the Director only had the status to be an intervenor if it could be found in the Combines Investigation Act. The provincial tribunal had no authority to give the Director intervenor status unless the Director could obtain that power directly or by implication from his legislation.

Boards should be careful whenever there is an intervenor whose existence is dependent upon a statute. In this situation, the board should require that the intervenor establish his or its legal right to intervene before that board. A copy of the statute should be filed and, in the event that a party in the hearing objects, a board order should carefully set out its grant of status and its reasons. A board

---

265 Supra, note 11.

should also be careful to note that the essence of its decision does not rest upon the intervention of the statutory intervenor, if that is the case. The point that is clear is that a board cannot grant legal status to someone who does not possess it under his mandating statute.

Where a tribunal has virtually no requirement for the filing of any supporting material in advance by the applicant, there will obviously be no requirement that material be filed with a notice of intervention. Many tribunals have no requirement that an intervenor file any material. He only has to appear the day the hearing commences, having given notice of his intent to intervene. Many agencies do not require a notice of intention to intervene.

Occasionally, parties to a hearing will deliver a petition to the tribunal members for their consideration, for example concerned residents before the OMB. My inclination/recommendation is that the petition should be admitted into evidence and given the weight it merits. At a minimum, the petition may reveal a part of the public sentiment spectrum. The proper procedure for admitting it would be to have its author sworn and explain to the tribunal what was presented or outlined to each of the signatories before the sign-up. Subsequently, the author should be cross-examined and proper weight accorded.

12.15(b) The Use of Panels of Witnesses

Panels of witnesses are not common in court proceedings, but are very common before many types of tribunals. Evidence is usually given verbally by individual witnesses, each of whom is sworn separately to tell the truth. Witnesses historically in the courts have been kept separated for the most part so that one could more easily test the credibility of a witness.

Panels of witnesses are used where a whole subject matter is to be spoken to and where there are a number of persons either sharing responsibility for the subject or where each of them has some expertise or knowledge, but each does not know or deal with the whole subject. There are many other occasions upon which the use of panels is appropriate. I believe that it should be left to the counsel calling evidence to decide if he wishes to use panels. If he wants to use panels, panels should be accepted by the tribunal whether the panel of tribunal members likes them or not.

Panels of witnesses are just as easy to examine and follow as individual witnesses. In addition, it takes less time to examine a panel of four witnesses than to examine four witnesses separately; the resulting evidence is also far clearer. An agency is concerned with the facts and the opinions of the witnesses. Credibility is often of little significance in most administrative hearings.

It is the exception rather than the rule that individual witnesses appear before many tribunals. Most regulatory boards have much the same experience. I once examined a panel of 25 witnesses. They were sworn together at one time, although they answered individually when asked. Panels of two to five witnesses are very common.

Questions are usually addressed to an individual witness but other panel members are welcome to add anything to the answer offered. In fact, often the questions are put to the panel as a whole and the most appropriate witness is invited to answer. What boards are looking for are the correct facts as quickly as possible. Patently, where there is only one witness to testify as to a limited subject, a panel would serve no purpose.

Most frequently, the panel may have subordinates sitting behind it who provide information to the panel in the event that the panel requires information that it does not readily have at hand.

Tribunals that do not have experience with panels should have no apprehension about using them.

12.15(c) Swearing of Witnesses

In some instances an agency may wish to receive the evidence of the witness before it under oath or affirmation. The value in this approach was noted by the Law Reform Commission of British Columbia in its *Report on Affidavits: Alternatives to Oaths*[266]

> Not all statements of fact may be taken at face value. A variety of circumstances exist in which it is appropriate to take some additional step to insure the honesty and accuracy of statements made. The most familiar way of insuring the veracity of a statement is to require that the statement be made under oath.
>
> The oath may be seen as operating at two levels. First, it is normally attended by elements of solemnity and ceremony. This is thought to impress upon the person taking the oath that the occasion is one of importance involving a special duty to tell the truth. A statement made in a context of solemnity and ceremony is less likely to be made thoughtlessly or carelessly.
>
> Second, where an oath truly binds the conscience of the person making the statement, the religious or moral implications of violating the oath makes it less likely that the person will tell an untruth. Even the individual who is unmoved by the religious or moral consequences of violating an oath will likely be deterred by the legal consequences it may attract. In most cases, giving false information under oath constitutes an offence under the Criminal Code. Depending on the circumstances, it may constitute perjury which can lead to imprisonment for up to 14 years.

If the authority to take evidence under oath is not found in the agency's enabling statute it can generally be found in the relevant Evidence Act for that jurisdiction. See for example, section 12 of the Manitoba Evidence Act, R.S.M. 1987, c. E150:

---

266 Ministry of the Attorney General, 1990.

12. (1) Every court may administer an oath or affirmation to every witness who is called to give evidence before it.

(2) Every officer of the court may administer an oath or affirmation to every witness who is called to give evidence before the court.

(The Act defines ''court'' in section 1 as ''the court, judge, arbitrator, commissioner, or person before whom a legal proceeding is held or taken.)

The actual form of oath is not important (although the various Evidence Acts specify the form in which an oath *may* be taken). Any manner or form or ceremony as the witness declares binding is sufficient.[267] Where a person objects to taking an oath, the evidence may be given under solemn affirmation instead.[268]

The taking of oaths presents difficulties to administrative agencies which are usually not faced by the courts. Firstly, some administrative agencies do not deal in information for which an oath is suitable. For example, where evidence is primarily opinion evidence, there may be little to be gained by taking that evidence under oath (other than the hope of impressing the witness with the solemnity of the occasion — which may be contrary to a desire of the agency to avoid having their proceedings appear too judicial). Secondly, not all agencies receive evidence from witnesses in an orderly and progressive manner from a witness box. Some agencies conduct very large public proceedings where there may be many witnesses present who give their information at irregular times at microphones from the audience without coming down to be sworn. Attempting to swear all of these witnesses would create logistical difficulties in attempting to keep track of who and who was not sworn and would also slow down the agency's proceedings substantially. Finally, as noted above, some agencies wish to keep their proceedings as non-threatening to the participants as possible, particularly when dealing with unrepresented individuals who may not be familiar with legal procedure. The use of the oath may not necessarily be suitable for them.

Whether an agency receives evidence under oath or not, the decision as to how evidence is to be received should be made, and made known, early in the proceeding. An agency should attempt to avoid the situation where it receives

---

267 Sopinka, Lederman, and Bryant, *The Law of Evidence in Canada* 2d ed. (Butterworths, 1992) at p. 587. To the same effect see *Phipson on Evidence* 14th ed. (Sweet & Maxwell 1990) at p. 158.

268 See, for example, ss. 14 and 15 of the Canada Evidence Act:
14. (1) Where a person called or desiring to give evidence objects, on grounds of conscientious scruples, to take an oath, that person may make the following solemn affirmation:
I do solemnly affirm that the evidence to be given by me shall be the truth, the whole truth and nothing but the truth.
(2) Where a person makes a solemn affirmation in accordance with subsection (1), his evidence shall be taken and have the same effect as if taken under oath.
15. (2) Any witness whose evidence is admitted or who makes a solemn affirmation under this section or section 14 is liable to indictment and punishment for perjury in all respects as if he had been sworn.

some evidence under oath and some evidence not under oath. Evidence under oath is considered to have more weight than unsworn evidence and one does not want to find oneself in the situation where earlier unsworn evidence is contradicted by later sworn testimony.

Generally, a witness will fall into one of four categories:

(1) a Jewish witness;
(2) a Scottish witness;
(3) a witness who wishes to affirm rather than swear; or
(4) all other witnesses.

The practice followed by most boards in Canada can be described as follows:

(1) A person legally qualified to administer oaths swears or affirms the witness. A tribunal should ensure that the administrator of the oath has the legal authority to do so.

(2) The witness will give his full name and, if it is complicated, he should spell the name for the record.

(3) The oath or affirmation is administered as follows:
     General Oath: The witness holds the Bible in his right hand, or places his right hand on it, and the administrator says:
     Do you swear that the evidence to be given by you to this Board in these proceedings shall be the truth, the whole truth, and nothing but the truth, so help you God.

And the witness replies: "I do".

Jewish Witness: The Bible shall be opened at Pentateuch, Exodus chapter 20. The witness shall hold the Bible, opened, with his head covered. The general oath shall be administered except that "so held you God" shall be "so held you Jehovah". A witness may take the oath with head uncovered if he declares himself bound by it under such circumstances.

Scottish Witness: The oath is:

You swear by Almighty God and as you shall answer to God at the great day of judgment that you will speak the truth, the whole truth and nothing but the truth.
In such case, the witness does not hold the Bible but merely holds up his right hand.

Affirming a Witness: The Bible is not used and the oath to be administered is:
You solemnly affirm that the evidence to be given by you to this Board in these proceedings shall be the truth, the whole truth, and nothing but the truth.

12.15(d) Natural Justice and Witnesses[269]

BIAS: There is no requirement that an individual must be impartial in a matter before he can give evidence. To the extent that a witness may be partial to one side or the other, or to one view or another, that partiality only goes to the weight to be placed on the evidence given by the witness.[270]
NOTICE: As to notice, the Ontario Court of Appeal has held that the principles of natural justice and fairness contain no absolute requirement that a decision-maker must give witnesses notice and an opportunity to be heard before making adverse findings against them (*Hurd v. Hewitt*[271]). The Ontario Court General Division had held that an arbitration panel had erred in finding that certain witnesses had conspired against a party where the witnesses had not been advised of these allegations or been given an opportunity to respond to them. Overturning that decision the Court of Appeal held that there were no absolute rules in Canada as to the questioning of witnesses. In concurring, separate reasons, Justice Griffiths noted that one would hope that where it is convenient and practical to do so (that is without unduly lengthening or complicating the process) that decision-makers generally would afford witnesses the opportunity to be heard before making findings reflecting on their character or integrity. The majority decision did not *preclude* a decision-maker from rejecting arguments based on incomplete evidence where the party making an allegation by-passed the opportunity to close out gaps. The cautious decision-maker, in order to ensure that he has the complete evidence before him should, therefore, adopt as a guiding principle that a party should not be able to challenge the evidence of a witness without, at some time, giving the witness an opportunity of knowing the weakness alleged and being able to respond to them. This is as much a protection to the party calling the witness as it is to the witness. As noted at the beginning of this chapter, a hearing is not a game of wits, it is a tool to gather the most and best information to enable an agency to carry out its mandate.

Right to Counsel: The Federal Court Trial Division has held that there is a common law right for a witness to have a counsel at a hearing:

> when a combination of some or all of the following elements are either found within the enabling legislation or implied from the practical application of the statute governing the tribunal; where an individual or a witness is subpoenaed, required to

---

269 For other topics related to witnesses, see chapter 17 (Witnesses), chapter 18 (Outside Consultants and Outside Evidence), and chapter 20 (Advice to Witnesses).

270 *Nassar v. College of Physicians and Surgeons (Man.)* (1994), 96 Man. R. (2d) 141 (Q.B.), affirmed (June 23, 1995), Doc. AI 94-30-01979 (Man. C.A.).

271 (1991), 13 Admin. L.R. (2d) 223 (Ont. Gen. Div.), reversed (1994), 20 O.R. (3d) 639, 120 D.L.R. (4th) 105 (C.A.). See the further discussion of this case in comment 13 in the *Cases and Comments* section of this text.

attend and testify under oath with a threat of penalty; where absolute privacy is not assured and the attendance of others is not prohibited; where reports are made public; where an individual can be deprived of his rights or his livelihood; or where some other irreparable harm can ensue.[272]

In Ontario, section 11 of the Ontario Statutory Powers Procedure Act provides that a witness at an electronic or oral hearing is entitled to be advised by counsel or an agent as to his rights, but such counsel or agent may take no other part in the hearing without the leave of the tribunal. Thus, unless the agency grants leave, counsel to a witness is there simply to advise the witness while that witness is giving evidence. He has no authority to ask the witnesses questions, even to clarify a matter, nor to call other witnesses, or cross-examine other witnesses, or present argument to the agency. The statute provides further, in subsection (2), that a counsel for a witness is entitled to be present during an *in camera* hearing only while the witness he represents is giving evidence. There is no similar provision respecting witnesses in the Alberta Administrative Procedures Act.

12.15(e) Exclusion of and Restriction on Calling Witnesses

It is common for counsel to request that witnesses be excluded from a proceeding other than when they are giving evidence. The purpose of such exclusion is simply to assist in ensuring that a witness will not tailor his evidence to the evidence which he has heard being given before him.

The power to exclude witnesses would appear to be included in the general mastery of an agency over its proceedings.[273] In *Homelite, a division of Textron Canada Ltd. v. Canadian Import Tribunal*[274] the Federal Court Trial Division was called upon to review the refusal of the Canadian Import Tribunal to exclude the witnesses of one company from the hearing while the witnesses of another were testifying. (The applicant was concerned that the two companies were allied in interest and that the witnesses would tailor their evidence to match if they were able to hear the testimony given by their allies.) The Tribunal had refused on the grounds that it was concerned that the exclusion order appeared to be too legalistic and unsuitable for the kind of economic inquiry it was conducting. Justice Strayer upheld the Tribunal's decision:

---

272 *Canada (Canadian Transportation Accident Investigation & Safety Board), Re (sub nom. Parrish, Re)*, [1993] 2 F.C. 60, *(sub nom. Canadian Transportation Accident Investigation & Safety Board v. Parrish)* 60 F.T.R. 110.

273 *Canada (Canadian Transportation Accident Investigation & Safety Board), Re (sub nom. Parrish, Re)*, [1993] 2 F.C. 60, *(sub nom. Canadian Transportation Accident Investigation & Safety Board v. Parrish)* 60 F.T.R. 110, *Homelite, a division of Textron Canada Ltd. v. Canadian Import Tribunal* (1987), 26 Admin. L.R. 126 (Fed. T.D.).

274 (1987), 26 Admin. L.R. 126 (Fed. T.D.).

> I am not satisfied that the requirements of fairness, or even those of natural justice, require that such a Tribunal order the exclusion of witnesses in these circumstances. Even if one imposes what is generally considered the highest standards, i.e. that applied by Courts, it is not possible to say that a refusal to exclude an adverse witness while evidence is received from another adverse witness amounts to a denial of a fair hearing. At best, the exclusion of witnesses is a matter for the exercise of discretion by the trial Judge. While an order for exclusion is normally given when requested, there are certainly situations where it is refused, if to grant the order will unduly impede the presentation of the case of the party who intends to call those witnesses. For example, normally a party who is to be a witness will not himself or herself be excluded while his or her witnesses are being heard, since the presence of the party in Court is necessary to assist in the instruction of counsel. Similarly, it is not usual to exclude expert witnesses in such circumstances because it is important for them to hear the evidence upon which their opinion is to be sought. In many trials no request is ever made for exclusion of witnesses and justice is not thereby impaired. So even applying the standard applicable to a Court, the decision of the Tribunal on this matter would be a matter of discretion and could be reviewed only if the discretion were exercised on some wrong principle. There is nothing in the transcript here to suggest that any wrong principle was applied.

The Court also concluded that the duty of the Tribunal, in conducting its essentially economic inquiry, was not simply to do justice among the various interested parties represented before it but to satisfy itself as to whether material injury was being suffered from the dumping of goods on the market. In that situation it may well be more informative and convenient to have all of the witnesses in the hearing room at one time — and that was a matter for the Tribunal to determine.

Subsequently, the Federal Court of Appeal held that, in an adversarial proceeding, where credibility is in issue, a decision-maker faced with a request for the exclusion of witnesses should ask itself whether there is any reason for the witness NOT to be excluded rather than whether there is any reason for the exclusion order to be made.[275] In other words, an exclusion order should be granted unless there is some reason not to do so.

Can an agency exclude a party, who may also be a witness, from its proceedings? Justice Strayer in *Homelite* (noted above) suggested that this was not normally done by the courts as the party's presence was necessary to instruct counsel. Some three years after *Homelite* the Federal Court Trial Division, in *Canadian Radio-Television and Telecommunications Commission v. Canada (Human Rights Tribunal)*,[276] held that the common law authority of an agency to control its procedure does not appear to contain any restrictions on the discretion of a tribunal to exclude witness, *including parties* who may be a witness. (Presumably, as with all discretionary powers, the agency would have to act on proper principles — as discussed earlier in c. 12.9 "Discretion".) However, in the same

---

275 *Wiebe v. R.* (1992), 5 Admin. L.R. (2d) 108 (Fed. C.A.).
276 (1990), 37 F.T.R. 50.

case, the Court acknowledged that statute law may impose such a restriction. Thus, the requirement in the Canadian Human Rights Act that the Tribunal ''shall give all Parties . . . a full and ample opportunity in person or through counsel, to appear before the Tribunal, present evidence and make representations to it'' prohibited a Human Rights Tribunal from making an exclusion order against a party to the proceeding who was also a potential witness. (The Court noted that a corporate party has the complete freedom to designate whomever it wishes as its delegate, even a potential witness, notwithstanding that there may be another person available who would not be likely to give evidence.)

Finally, an agency's mastery over its proceedings includes the authority to control or restrict the number of witnesses which may be called by a party. However, that authority cannot be exercised in such a way as to lead to unfairness. Thus, it is unlikely that an agency could refuse to hear a witness who had material and relevant information which was not otherwise already before the agency. However, agencies can stop the calling of witness who are to provide only repetitious evidence or irrelevant evidence. In exercising this authority, obviously, the agency must know the nature of the evidence to be proffered through the witnesses in question. Thus, in *Morin v. Port-Cartier Institution Disciplinary Tribunal*[277] the Federal Court Trial Division held that a prison disciplinary tribunal had erred in arbitrarily limiting the number of witnesses an applicant could call. The Tribunal should first have inquired as to who was to be called and why they were being called.

12.16 USE OF EXHIBITS

12.16(a) The Circulation of Exhibits

Depending upon the complexity of the case, exhibits should be circulated as follows:

(1) before a witness testifies, he must give advance notice, a reasonable estimate is three working days, of all papers, documents and charts to which he will refer. This should be a requirement of the tribunal and not depend upon counsel; there should be no trial by ambush; and

(2) there should be established a fair and open circulation system for exhibits. One of the easiest systems for long and complicated hearings is to have deposit boxes for each party outside the hearing room into which ''proper service'' is made when exhibits are deposited with a date stamp.

(3) see also the rules set out above under the heading Opening of the Hearing at 12.14.

---

277 (1991), 42 F.T.R. 155.

12.16(b) Exhibit Numbering

Exhibits should not be numbered from one to whatever because this tells one nothing about the exhibit. Exhibit numbers should have four or five digits.

(1) The first digit tells you that it is an exhibit and not an interrogatory or an undertaking, etc.;

(2) The second digit tells you the day of the hearing;

(3) The third digit corresponds to the person or witness who has presented the exhibit; and

(4) The fourth digit corresponds to the person or witness who has presented the exhibit; and

(5) The fifth digit is the sequence of that exhibit.

All exhibits should be recorded daily on an updated exhibit list, which is circulated daily by the clerk. As they are entered, exhibits should be recorded in the transcript, properly numbered and described, two, maybe three loose leaf binders should hold the exhibits; one for the hearing clerk and one or two for the public to inspect. The public should be able to inspect exhibits with/without a xerox machine in a public place on the hearing premises.

12.16(c) Board Members Filings

Some tribunals have a policy that if any member reads any material or hears of matters that could affect his decision, he will file what he reads as an exhibit on the record. This serves not as proof of anything, but merely to expose the matters to the parties so that they can address the matter by evidence or argument as they see fit. It is often done because one subscribes to many journals and papers dealing with administrative law, particularly dealing with the subject matter. One often reads something that may be material. It may have an impact on the panel. One cannot ignore what one reads and studies.

Perhaps too much can be put on the record, but that is better than knowing something that may be relevant, and failing to disclose it to parties who might be affected.

Board filings are given board prefixes and a day followed by the topic number, followed by the item number.

12.17 UNDERTAKINGS

A practice, developed by a number of boards that have lengthy hearings, is to develop a system for verbal or written undertakings.

Undertakings are commitments to produce later in the hearing a document, chart or material (often a calculation) or a witness. The undertaking is fully described, given a number by the clerk, recorded in the undertaking list and recorded in the transcript. Each undertaking given each day should be set out by number with a proper description on pages entitled "undertakings" so that one can quickly recover the information. An example is described below:

2.6.3.5.2: 2 Designates this as an undertaking (not an exhibit);
6 is for the sixth day of the hearing;
3 is for the subject matter, lets say "Rate of Return";
5 is for a named witness; and
2 is for the second such undertaking that day by that person.

Undertakings are then followed up by counsel acting for the board or the case manager.

Most information is sought by way of or through informal requests, interrogatories or formal board orders. If necessary, a witness may be recalled to speak to the material. This is often the best way to handle complicated calculations. Undertakings save time and allow the hearing to proceed with other matters.

12.18 CHALLENGES TO JURISDICTION

A challenge to jurisdiction should be raised by motion with proper notice. I would recommend a very carefully drafted written notice of motion as a good foundation for a review or appeal. The rules of procedure of a tribunal or an early procedural order may detail how motions should be brought and can therefore prevent early confusion. With a proper notice of motion, the parties and the tribunal can understand in advance what is being sought and the reasons therefore. The panel can more expeditiously deal with motions as a result.

Challenges can arise in many ways:

(1) inadequate or insufficient notice of the hearing;

(2) failure to comply with any applicable legislation;

(3) failure to comply with any procedural order;

(4) alleged bias;

(5) the application or matter before the tribunal is beyond the powers given to it;

(6) the reference is faulty or misunderstood by the tribunal; and

(7) a party has applied to a court to stop the proceedings.

The panel has the right to select the time at which it will hear the motion and not necessarily adopt the time selected by the mover. It is best to hear the motion as soon as possible lest the mover be prejudiced by delay. It may be best for the tribunal to reserve its decision and proceed. A decision can later be given in writing and read into the record with full and carefully drafted reasons.[278] Merely because a party has appealed or applied to a court, the hearing need not stop. What halts the hearing is an order of the court to stop the hearing.

Very few motions have to be resolved on the spot. If they do, then the board should rise to discuss the matter and carefully draft a decision to be read into the record. One should try to avoid giving a decision "with reason's to follow". A well-considered decision with adequate reasons is less likely to be challenged than "a shot from the hip".

Finally, the reader may wish to note that there is no obligation on agencies in the exercise of jurisdiction to expressly identify the source of their authority, however they must be able, not only to point to the jurisdiction, but support this source if challenged (*British Columbia (Milk Board) v. Clearview Dairy Farms Inc.*)[279]

12.19 QUORUM

Most agencies are composed of more than one individual. However, it is not usually necessary that the entire body of the agency's membership be gathered in order to exercise its powers. Exercise of an agency's authority by less than its

---

278 *Dilts v. University of Manitoba Faculty Association* (1973), 41 D.L.R. (3d) 401 (Man. C.A.), *Cedarvale Tree Services Ltd. v. Labourers' International Union of North America, Local 183*, [1971] 3 O.R. 832 (C.A.). In *New Brunswick Council of Hospital Unions New Brunswick* (1986), 35 D.L.R. (4th) 282 (N.B.C.A.) the New Brunswick Court of Appeal in holding that a jurisdictional question need not always be ruled on at the outset of a proceeding made the following comments:

> So, preferably, it [the jurisdictional question] should be decided at the outset. But that is not to say that it must always be decided at the outset. If rules of natural justice are offended or if one of the parties would be so put upon by being required to continue so as to create an abuse of discretion, a court could interfere and order the chairman to determine the matter initially. But where, as we were told occasionally happens, the parties, their witnesses and counsel are present in a distant town prepared for the hearing the greater hardship would be in not proceeding with the hearing. If . . . the taking of evidence was to last for three months it might be concluded that the chairman was abusing his discretion and a reviewing judge might well order the jurisdictional question to be decided at the outset. But where, as here, there is no such suggestion, there is no call to intervene. Whether the preliminary jurisdictional question will be considered initially is, in my view, a question for the chairman to decide in his properly exercised discretion.

279 (1995), 7 B.C.L.R. (3d) 1 (S.C.C.). Technically, this case dealt with whether an agency had to recite the source of its authority in the instruments whereby it exercised its authority to make regulations. The majority of the Court held that it did not. (The case did not resolve the question, however, as to what happens when an agency relies on the wrong source of authority and cites it as its source of authority (notwithstanding that it may, perhaps unknowingly possess the authority in question from some other, uncited source).

full membership can be authorized through the authorization of panels and through the concept of quorum.

It is common for legislation to provide that panels of members of the agency may exercise the powers of the agency and that the decision of the panel is the decision of the agency.

The concept of quorum deals with the minimum number of a collective who must be present for the exercise of authority which has been given to the collective as a body. Thus, quorum applies equally to the exercise of powers by an agency as a whole or by a panel of an agency. Quorum is the minimum number of that collective which is necessary for the collective to function. In *IBM Canada Ltd. v. Deputy M.N.R. (Customs & Excise)*[280] the Federal Court of Appeal stated that quorum was "the minimum number of members who must be present for [a] body to exercise its powers validly" and that "in the absence of a quorum no business can be transacted." The Court explained that in setting a quorum and requiring that a minimum number of persons participate in a decision, Parliament reposes its faith in collective wisdom, does so for the benefit of the public as well as for the benefit of those who might be affected by the decision, and expects those who participate in the decision either as members of the majority or as dissenting members to act together up to the very last moment which is the making of one united, though not necessarily unanimous decision.

The importance of the "collective" concept of action can be seen in *Zivkovic v. Canada (Minister of Employment & Immigration)*[281] where the Federal Court Trial Division struck down a decision of the Immigration and Refugee Board for denying an individual the quorum protection offered by the relevant statute. That case involved a challenge by a refugee claimant of the validity of a single member of a two-member panel issuing a decision on his refugee application after the other member had ceased to hold office. Technically, the remaining member of the panel had the authority to do this in these circumstances under section 63 of the Immigration Act, R.S.C. 1985, c. I-21. The Act provided that refugee claims were to be heard by a quorum of two members of the Refugee Division of the Board. It also provided that, if the applicant consented, one member of the Board could hear and determine a claim. Section 63(1) provided that a Refugee Board panel member who heard a case could, at the request of the Chairman, at any time within eight weeks after having resigned or otherwise ceased to hold office, make or take part in the disposition of the case. Where that member was unwilling or unable to take part in the disposition of the case, section 63(2) provided that the remaining members of the panel were to be deemed to constitute the panel. Earlier in *Weerasinge v. Canada (Minister of Employment & Immigration)*[282] the Federal Court of Appeal had held that "Recourse to s. 63(2) is a serious matter which

---

280 [1992] 1 F.C. 663 (C.A.).
281 (1994) 88 F.T.R. 192.
282 [1994] 1 F.C. 330, 161 N.R. 200 (C.A.).

denies a claimant a right accorded by the Act. A decision made by a single member is prima facie made without jurisdiction'' unless a claimant consented.

In *Zivkovic* the original two-member panel had adjourned the hearing to a date when it was known to both members of the panel that one of them was going to be a member of the Board for only a few days after the end of the hearing. The Court concluded that "It must have been known and anticipated by both members, at the time the applicant's claim was being heard, that only one of them would be rendering a decision.'' In striking down the decision, Justice Reed stated that:

> In my view, a decision by one member in these circumstances constitutes a breach of fundamental justice. I reiterate the statements of the Court of Appeal in *Weerasinge*: since Convention refugee hearing engages s. 7 of the Charter a claimant is entitled to a two-member panel and to the benefit of any disagreement between them. Recourse to s. 63(2) is a serious matter which denies a claimant a right accorded by the Act. I conclude, therefore, that purposeful action by a panel member which denies an individual that right, renders the decision which issues invalid.[283]

Where the quorum is met, those members of the agency forming the quorum may exercise the powers of the agency. Where a panel has been struck which consists of more than the quorum, the fact that some of its members may be unable to continue with a proceeding does not stop the remaining panel members from doing so long as the panel numbers do not fall below the minimum quorum.[284]

Quorum provisions are usually found in the statutes under which the proceeding takes place or in the agency's constituent statute. Failing that, the various Interpretation Acts contain quorum provisions which will usually be applicable to proceedings unless there is some contrary intent evident in the particular statues applicable to a proceeding.[285]

---

283 See also *Re B.C. Government Employees Union and Public Service Commission* (1979), 96 D.L.R. (3d) 89 (B.C.S.C.) (legislated quorum a matter of public interest which cannot be waived by parties).

284 See *Unicity Taxicab Ltd. v. Manitoba (Taxicab Board)* (1992), 80 Man. R. (2d) 241 (Q.B.), affirmed (1992), 83 Man. R. (2d) 305 (C.A.), *Mariano v. Mississauga (City)* (1992), 8 O.R. (3d) 657 (Div. Ct.).

285 In illustration, see s. 22 of the federal Interpretation Act which states:

22. (1) Where an enactment requires or authorizes more than two persons to do an act or thing, a majority of them may do it.

(2) Where an enactment establishes a board, court, commission or other body consisting of three or more members, in this section called an "association",

(a) at a meeting of the association, a number of members of the association equal to,

(i) if the number of members provided for by enactment is a fixed number, at least one-half of the number of members, and

(ii) if the number of members provided for by the enactment is not a fixed number but is within a range of having a maximum or minium, at least one-half of the number of members in office if that number is within the range,

constitutes a quorum;

(b) an act or thing done by a majority of the members of the association at a meeting, if

Absent a quorum the collective cannot function and cannot exercise the authority of the collective.[286] Thus, an agency panel presiding over an oral hearing which loses its quorum ceases to be able to proceed.[287] In such cases, unless there is some legislative authority providing for either a replacement member to be appointed to complete the proceeding, or for the parties to consent to the remaining members to complete it, the hearing must be recommenced before a newly constituted panel.[288] (This is because quorum provisions do not replace the "he who hears" principle. Maintaining a quorum in oral proceedings through the addition of replacement members who have not heard the evidence which preceded their joining the panel may alleviate concerns respecting quorum, but will likely lead to infringements of the requirement that "he who hears must decide".[289] In the case of written proceedings, where all the "he who hears" principle would require is that a member deciding a case have read the written material, it is likely a new panel member may simply step in to review the written material and then proceed to deliberate with the other members. "He who hears" is discussed in depth in chapter 22.)

---

the members present constitute a quorum, is deemed to have been done by the association; and

  (c) a vacancy in the membership of the association does not invalidate the constitution of the association or impair the right of the members in office to act, if the number of members in office is not less than a quorum.

The various Interpretation Acts are not worded identically. For example, the Ontario equivalent to section 22(2)(c) of the federal statute, section 28(c) of R.S.O. 1990, c. I.11 appears to be slightly broader in its application as it does not have the requirements for a maximum and minimum number of members to have been specified in the subject enactment:

  28. In every Act, unless the contrary intention appears,

    (c) where an act or thing is required to be done by more than two persons, a majority of them may do it.

286 *Inter-City Freightlines Ltd. and Highway Traffic & Motor Transport Board of Manitoba v. Swan River-The Pas Transfer Ltd.*, [1972] 2 W.W.R. 317 (Man. C.A.).

287 For an example, see *Sterling Crane v. B.S.O.I.W., Local 771* (1992), 8 Admin. L.R. (2d) 244 (Sask. Q.B.). In *Burroughs Employees Association v. Attorney General of Manitoba* (1983), 83 C.L.L.C. 14027 a three-member panel of the Manitoba Labour Board lost its quorum in the midst of a proceeding when the hearing was reconvened from a previous day in the absence of one of the members who was sick. The hearing proceeded, notwithstanding a statutory direction that the quorum be three: the chairman or a vice chair, one member representing the views of the employees and one member representing the views of the employer. The resulting decision was quashed and a rehearing ordered.

288 *Chromex Nickel Mines Ltd. v. British Columbia (Securities Commission)* (1992), 70 B.C.L.R. 186 (S.C.).

289 See *Sterling Crane v. B.S.O.I.W., Local 771* (1992), 8 Admin. L.R. (2d) 244 (Sask. Q.B.).

12.20 ADJOURNMENTS

12.20(a) Source and Nature of Authority

The power to adjourn is implicit in the power to hold a hearing. A party to a proceeding does not have an automatic right to an adjournment.[290] It is a discretionary power to be exercised in accordance with the principles of natural justice and fairness.[291] Like all implied powers, however, it is subject to express statutory direction.[292]

12.20(b) Considerations

Requests for adjournments are frequent. The best attitude to take in response to a request for an adjournment is "adjourn if necessary but not necessarily adjourn". Some requests for adjournment arise because of unanticipated events, happenings that no reasonably alert party or counsel could anticipate. Many adjournment requests arise because someone who should have known better did not.

What is usually involved is the balance of convenience between the interests of the parties, the board and the public.[293] To some agencies, an adjournment is nothing more than a modest inconvenience. To other boards an adjournment is a very serious matter. For example, adjournments should not be the order of the

---

290 *Flamboro Downs Holdings Ltd. v. Teamsters Local 879* (1979), 24 O.R. (2d) 400 (Div. Ct.).

291 "As a general rule [administrative] tribunals are considered to be masters in their own house. In the absence of specific rules laid down by statute or regulation, they control their own procedures subject to the proviso that they comply with the rules of fairness and, where the exercise judicial or quasi-judicial functions, the rules of natural justice. Adjournment of their proceedings is very much in their discretion." (*Prassad v. Canada (Minister of Employment & Immigration)* (1989), 57 D.L.R. (4th) 663 (S.C.C.).)

292 *Prassad v. Canada (Minister of Employment & Immigration)* (1989) 57 D.L.R. (4th) 663 (S.C.C.). See also *Canada (Minister of Employment & Immigration v. Jaouhari (sub nom. Ministre de l'emploi et de l'immigraton v. Jaouhari)* (1992), 59 F.T.R. 213. In this case the Federal Court Trial Division held that the discretionary authority of an Immigration Adjudicator to adjourn a proceeding was limited by the statutory direction to give his decision as soon as possible and to issue an deportation order once he determines that a person meets specified statutory criteria. The Adjudicator had determined that the applicant was a person who met the statutory criteria for the issuance of a deportation order. Nonetheless, he adjourned the proceedings pending the determination of claims by the applicants' children for refugee status. On judicial review the Court held that the statutory direction to issue the deportation order upon making the determination as to the applicants' status was paramount over the Adjudicator's adjournment power. The power to adjourn was set out in the regulations and was limited to situations where an adjournment would not impede or unreasonably delay the proceedings.

293 In *Richmond Square Development Corp. v. Middlesex Condominium Corp. No. 134* (1993), 103 D.L.R. (4th) 437 (Div. Ct.) the Ontario Divisional Court noted that an agency does not act arbitrarily if it balances the reasons for an adjournment request against the right of the parties to have a matter dealt with expeditiously.

day in large regulatory hearings involving 20 or 50 or more parties, all represented by legal counsel, and many with witnesses standing by, some of whom have travelled across the continent to attend. In attempting to strike the correct balance the agency must consider what is hoped to be accomplished by the adjournment, the reasons the adjournment has become necessary, the impact of refusing or granting the adjournment on the person requesting it and the other parties, and the impact upon the public interest. It is impossible when writing generally about a subject to identify each type of instance upon which an adjournment might be requested. The guiding principle should be how necessary is the adjournment for the proceeding to be considered fair. Thus, like so much else of administrative law, it is affected by the nature of proceedings in question, the purpose of the adjournment, the consequences of granting or refusing it, etc. And, as the power to adjourn is discretionary, the courts are prepared to grant at least a degree of deference to the expertise of the agency in determining whether the adjournment is necessary.[294] To the extent that the decision is discretionary in nature, the Courts should not intervene provided that the agency has applied the correct principles (i.e. the balancing of interests referred to above) in determining in which way its discretion should be exercised. Nonetheless, a court will intervene in the case of obvious unfairness.

Frequently a party will be in the position of having to seek an adjournment because of the actions of his counsel. In considering requests for adjournments an agency should not confuse the actions of the counsel, however undesirable, with the party, who may be quite blameless. One should not use the interests of parties as soapboxes to attempt to correct or discipline counsel.

On this point, the reader may wish to consult the decision of the Federal Court of Appeal in *Siloch v. Canada (Minister of Employment & Immigration)* (1993), 10 Admin. L.R. (2d) 285, 18 Imm. L.R. (2d) 239, 151 N.R. 76 (Fed. C.A.). In this case, a refugee claimant appeared at her "credible basis hearing" but her counsel failed to do so. He had allegedly been involved in a car accident that morning. The claimant requested that the hearing be adjourned. The hearing had already been adjourned once to permit the claimant to retain this counsel.

---

294 See, for example, *Flamboro Downs Holdings Ltd. v. Teamsters, Local 879* (1979), 24 O.R. (2d) 400 (Div. Ct.) where, in determining whether an adjournment should have been granted by the Ontario Labour Relations Board the Ontario Divisional Court stated:

Clearly, an administrative tribunal such as the Labour Relations Board is entitled to determine its own practices and procedures. Whether in a given case an adjournment should or should not be granted is a matter to be determined by the Board charged as it is with the responsibility of administering a comprehensive statue regulating labour relations. In the administration of that statute the Board is required to make many determinations of both fact and of law and to exercise its discretion in a variety of situations. In the case of a request for adjournment, it is manifestly in the best position to decide whether, having regard to the nature of the substantive application before it, the adjournment should be granted or whether the interests of the employer, the employees or the union who, as the case may be , oppose the adjournment should prevail over the party seeking it. As a matter of jurisdiction, it is for the Board to decide whether it should adjourn proceedings before it and in what circumstances.

The Adjudicator knew from past experience, and the fact that this counsel had failed to appear in another proceeding before the Adjudicator that very morning, that this particular counsel was unreliable and had a practice of "double-booking". The claimant had no knowledge of this alleged unreliability. The hearing proceeded and the claimant was ordered deported.

On judicial review the Adjudicator's order was quashed. The Federal Court of Appeal stated that:

> In the circumstances of this case, where the intention of the applicant to proceed was unquestionable, where the applicant had no reason to question the reliability of her counsel until the moment he did not show up, where the only adjournment granted in the case so far had been to allow the applicant to appoint counsel, where no fault or blame could be put on the applicant for not being ready, where the Adjudicator took into consideration a factor unknown to the applicant and therefore irrelevant as far as she was concerned, i.e. the actual experience of the Adjudicator that very same day in another case and the history of poor behaviour of counsel, where the Adjudicator did not enquire as to the length of the adjournment being sought nor offer the applicant a short adjournment to enable her to find new counsel and where there is absolutely no indication that a short adjournment would affect the immigration system or needlessly delay, impede or paralyse the conduct of this particular inquiry, the Adjudicator, in denying the adjournment on March 4, 1991, deprived the applicant of her right to a fair hearing.[295]

It is important to bear in mind that common sense as well as a sense of fairness lie basically at the root of whether an adjournment should or should not be granted. Where an adjournment is necessary to avoid a miscarriage of justice, one should adjourn. See, for example, *Grenier v. Region 1 Hospital Corp. (South-*

---

295 See also *Afrane v. Canada (Minister of Employment & Immigration)* (1993), 14 Admin. L.R. (2d) 201, 20 Imm. L.R. (2d) 312, 64 F.T.R. 1 where the Federal Court Trial Division held that, notwithstanding a counsel's failure to give advance notice of his inability to attend a hearing or any explanation for his unavailability, an Adjudicator should have granted a party a adjournment when the hearing in question was not preemptory and there was no evidence of a deliberate attempt to delay the process.

Contrast that case with the decision of the Federal Court of Appeal in *Canada (Minister of Employment & Immigration) v. Chung,* [1993] 2 F.C. 42, 18 Imm. L.R. (2d) 151, 100 D.L.R. (4th) 377, 149 N.R. 386 (C.A.). Here the Court upheld an Adjudicator's refusal of the Crown's request for an adjournment. Although the Crown had had the file regarding an upcoming hearing for three months it did not actually assign the file to a case presenting officer until the day before the hearing. The case presenting officer had therefore requested an adjournment as he had not had sufficient time to prepare for the hearing. The difference between these two cases is likely a perception by the Court that the case presentation officer was closer to a party than counsel for a party (which in this case would be the public interest). The decision can then be explained as being one of those where the party is "the author of his own misfortune". As well, the consequences of the refusal to adjourn were not likely felt to be as serious for the interest represented by the case presenting officer as would be the consequences for a person facing deportation.

east).[296] In that case, a hospital board, considering an appeal by a doctor regarding the refusal of privileges, received an inaccurate and unfair summary of the doctor's file. The Board refused to disclose this information to the doctor until hours before the hearing and then refused an adjournment which he requested in order to respond to the negative comments. The Board instead granted the doctor two weeks to make written submissions. The New Brunswick Court of Queen's Bench quashed the decision on the grounds of an appearance of bias.[297]

The circumstances giving rise to the need for an adjournment must also be considered. Sometimes an adjournment is required because of the foolishness or unreasonableness of a party. Such conduct can be considered a mark against the grant. Other times a party may have acted in all reasonableness and cannot be faulted for their actions. In such cases, fairness may require an adjournment.[298]

Nor can the duty on the decision-maker to carry out its mandate be ignored. In *Prassad v. Canada (Minister of Employment & Immigration)*[299] the Supreme Court made the following comments respecting a request to adjourn an administrative proceeding to allow another application to be pursued:

> In some circumstances, an adjournment may well be granted to enable such an application; in other circumstances, it may properly be refused. While the adjudicator must be cognizant that a "full and proper inquiry" be held, the adjudicator must also ensure that the statutory duty to hold an inquiry is fulfilled. As Wydrzynski, op cit., notes at p. 366: "Above all, there is a need to proceed expeditiously, and adjournments should not be viewed as a method to interminably delay the inquiry." The adjudicator might consider such factors as the number of adjournments already granted and the length of time for which an adjournment is sought in exercising his or her discretion to adjourn. Where an adjournment is requested in order that an application under s. 37 might be pursued, the adjudicator might also consider the opportunity available to the subject of the inquiry to apply to the Minister prior to the request for an adjournment.[300]

---

296 (1993), 133 N.B.R. (2d) 232 and 341 A.P.R. 232 (Q.B.).

297 Thus, the degree to which one may have a right to something (be it a right to counsel, or a right to disclosure and so forth) is relevant to whether one should be given an adjournment if that adjournment is necessary to secure or implement that right. See, for example, *Gasparetto v. Sault Ste. Marie (City)* (1973), 35 D.L.R. (3d) 507 (Ont. Div. Ct.). For examples of unfair adjournments see *De Oliveira v. Canada (Minister of Employment & Immigration)* (1988), 32 Admin. L.R. 138 (Fed. C.A.) where a new counsel was given only 45 minutes to review a transcript and to take instructions from his client, *De Sousa v. Canada (Minister of Employment & Immigration)* (1988), 32 Admin. L.R. 140 (Fed. T.D.) where the agency's refusal to adjourn to permit the individual to retain counsel was found to be tantamount to a denial of the right to counsel.

298 See, for example, *Gasparetto v. Sault Ste. Marie (City)* (1973), 35 D.L.R. (3d) 507 (Div. Ct.).

299 (1989), 57 D.L.R. (4th) 663 (S.C.C.).

300 See also *Howe v. Institute of Chartered Accountants (Ontario)* (1994), 21 O.R. (3d) 315 (Div. Ct.): "The public interest in expeditious disposition of disciplinary matters hangs heavily in the balance. The proper auditing of financial institutions is of immediate public concern."

In some cases, the consequences to a party of the refusal to grant an adjournment may be so serious that, unless there is something equally serious arguing against the adjournment, the adjournment should be granted.[301] Surprise, very often, is pleaded where, in fact, the real problem is that counsel or a party discover too late what should have been anticipated or was too lazy to get prepared. Very often, there is an alternative to an adjournment, such as going on with some other aspect of the case in the meantime.

An award of costs is no substitute for not going on with the proceeding.[302] The waste of time, money, space, preparation, etc., can be substantial. Inconvenience to or double bookings by counsel is not justification per se for an adjournment. Agencies should resist adjournments except where unavoidable. Even then, the adjournments should be as brief as possible, perhaps with costs (where there is a costs power in the agency) in favour of all those who ask for them.

12.20(c) Adjournments and Statutory Time Limits

An agency will often find itself faced with a request for an adjournment (which in itself may seem fair) on the one hand and a statutory time limitation to complete its work on the other. Frequently, these time limits are merely directory in nature.[303] In such cases the agency cannot refuse the adjournment on the basis of the restrictive time constraint. Such time as necessary must be taken for the adjournment and the time limit must give way.[304]

12.20(d) Adjournment for Concurrent Action

Sometimes an agency will find itself faced with a request to adjourn a proceedings pending the determination of some other matter taking place elsewhere which is already underway or to enable some other application to be brought. This is often a difficult decision to face. In such instances an adjournment may be appropriate where the two proceedings are closely linked. If continuing with the agency hearing can be perceived as in some way impacting on the fairness of the other proceeding or if the outcome of the other proceeding one way or another may be an important factor in the agency proceedings, an adjournment may be prudent (and sometimes necessary — see *Ramawad v. Canada (Minister of Manpower & Immigration)* (1977), 81 D.L.R (3d) 687, [1978] 2 S.C.R. 375, 18 N.R. 69.)

---

301 *Olech v. Royal College of Dental Surgeons (Ont.)* (1994), 70 O.A.C. 144 (Div. Ct.).

302 As for an ageny's authority to award costs see chapter 27 (Costs) and chapter 29 (Implied Powers of an Agency).

303 See the discussion of mandatory and directory time limits in chapter 22.5.1.

304 See *Sarco Canada Ltd. v. Anti-Dumping Tribunal*, [1979] 1 F.C. 247, 22 N.R. 225 (C.A.), and *Sandoz Ltd. v. Canada (Commissioner of Patents)* (1991), 42 F.T.R. 30.

The mere fact that another proceeding is underway does not in itself demand an adjournment. On this point contrast the following two decisions, one of the Nova Scotia Supreme Court and one of the Federal Court Trial Division, which came out at roughly the same time. In *Williams v. Superintendent of Insurance (N.S.)*[305] a Nova Scotian Advisory Board was considering suspending the licence of an insurance broker over his conduct in a particular matter. That same conduct was also the subject of concurrent criminal proceedings. The Nova Scotia Supreme Court issued an injunction against holding the inquiry. According to the Court the broker's right to practice his profession was protected by section 7 of the Charter. While it was improbable that the licence holder would be compelled to testify at the inquiry the Court felt that this would not avoid a potential violation of those Charter rights. The licence holder at the inquiry was to be provided with an opportunity to respond to the evidence in the possession of the Superintendent of Insurance. "The choice to attend the hearing and to either respond to the evidence and thereby waive the 'right to silence' or to maintain the 'right to silence' and thereby remain unresponsive to the evidence presented is, in fact, no choice at all. Where a statutory enactment provides an individual with an opportunity to respond to allegations it is only common sense that the opportunity offered be one that does not at the same time jeopardize his fundamental rights granted by the Canadian Charter of Rights and Freedoms."

An opposite conclusion, however, was reached by the Federal Court Trial Division in the similar case of *Canada (Minister of Employment & Immigration) v. Lundgren.*[306] Here an Adjudicator conducting an inquiry into the possible deportation of an applicant was held on judicial review to have erred in *granting* the applicant an adjournment pending the disposition of criminal proceedings regarding allegations that the applicant had illegally returned to Canada having already been the subject of a earlier deportation order. The Adjudicator had felt that an adjournment was necessary in order to avoid duplication of the criminal proceedings and to protect the applicant's right to remain silent. The Court held that the two proceedings should have been allowed to proceed concurrently as their purposes were different. The purpose of the criminal proceedings was to punish the applicant for disobeying an earlier deportation order while the immigration inquiry was to determine whether the applicant should be deported. In the Court's view there was no general principle in Canada that the existence of civil and criminal proceedings in court at the same time involving the same persona and the same facts is automatically a valid reason justifying the adjournment of the civil proceedings. Only extraordinary circumstances, in which the civil proceedings might cause some damage to the accused's defence to the criminal charge, would justify adjourning the civil action. In the case in point the applicant's right to silence was protected by section 11(c) of the Charter while section

---

305 (1993), 125 N.S.R. (2d) 323, 349 A.P.R. 323 (S.C.).
306 (1992), 13 Admin. L. R. (2d) 305 (Fed. T.D.).

5 of the Canada Evidence Act prohibited the admission in the criminal proceedings of any statement given in the civil proceedings which might incriminate the applicant.[307]

A similar result occurred in *Robinson v. Ontario (Securities Commission)*[308] where the Ontario Divisional Court stated that ''A regulatory proceeding should not be stayed except in extraordinary and exceptional circumstances In *Howe v. Institute of Chartered Accountants (Ontario)*[309] the Ontario Divisional Court affirmed that the test in considering a stay where there were concurrent proceedings underway was whether to proceed would give rise to a real risk of prejudice or injustice.

12.20(e) Adjournment for Judicial Review

A common type of adjournment request is likely the request for adjournment pending a judicial review of one of the many incidental decisions made by an agency leading up to its final conclusion. In most of the provinces of Canada an agency is not required by law to adjourn its proceedings because an application of judicial review has been brought (*Re Cedarvale Tree Services Ltd.*[310]). Such an adjournment may be appropriate where the agency feels there may be serious concerns as to one of its rulings which, if successfully challenged, would require a re-hearing of the entire matter. In such cases, prudence may dictate an adjournment. However, this is a discretionary call by the agency. The fact that a participant may disagree with a decision should not warrant an automatic adjournment for an application for judicial review.

Some years after the *Cedarvale Tree Services* case a decision of the Supreme Court of Canada, *R. v. Batchelor*,[311] introduced some confusion in this area. *Batchelor* is a ''technical'' decision, by which I mean its results were directed by the technicalities of rules, rather than conceptual analysis. In that case, the Supreme Court of Canada held that under the Ontario Criminal Rules the service on a lower court of an application for prohibition, coupled with an application to quash, resulted in an automatic suspension of the proceedings before the lower court. The majority decision by Ritchie J. reasoned that as the rules required the

---

307 The Ontario Court (General Division) reached a similar conclusion in the context of a request to stay a civil action in the courts pending the resolution of concurrent criminal proceedings. Although the defendant had raised concerns that the discovery process in the civil action might infringe the individual's right to silence in the criminal proceedings, the Court concluded that the protection given to the defendant by s. 11(c) and s. 13 of the Charter (including the derivative-use immunity now recognized by the Supreme Court of Canada) was adequate to make it unnecessary to halt the civil proceedings (*Belanger v. Caughell* (1995), 22 O.R. (3d) 741 (Gen. Div.).

308 (1993), 110 D.L.R. (4th) 166 (Ont. Div. Ct.).

309 (1994), 21 O.R. (3d) 315 (Div. Ct.).

310 [1971] 3 O.R. 832, 22 D.L.R. (3d) 40 (C.A.). To the same effect see *Daciuk v. Labour Board (Man.)* (1985), 34 Man. R. (2d) 265 (Q.B.).

311 (1977), 81 D.L.R. (3d) 241, 38 C.C.C. (2d) 113 (S.C.C.).

lower court to forthwith file its record (the conviction, order, warrant or inquisition, information, exhibits and any other papers or documents touching the matter) with the reviewing court the lower court was left with nothing on which to proceed. A concurring minority decision written by Justice Laskin concentrated on the aspect of the rule which provided that the return of the record by the lower court "shall have the same effect as a return to a writ of certiorari" which under the common law had the effect of suspending the lower court's proceedings (again because there was nothing left before the lower court).

Notwithstanding *Batchelor*, applications for prohibition where there was no express legislative direction for the filing of the agency's documents have been found not to automatically stay a lower court's proceedings (see *R. v. Turkiewicz*[312] and *Généreux v. Canada (General Court Martial)*.[313] However, there is still some question as to the effect of *Batchelor* in light of the specific provisions of some provincial judicial review legislation. For example, section 10 of Ontario's Judicial Review Procedure Act (which was passed after *Cedarvale Tree Services*) requires an agency served with an application for judicial review to "forthwith" file its record with the reviewing court (although the statute does not provide that this filing has the same effect as a return to a writ of certiorari). Section 17 of British Columbia's Judicial Review Procedure Act grants the reviewing court the discretion to order the filing of the agency's record or any part of it. (The Federal Court Act does not contain a similar requirement for an agency to file its record.)

In *U.F.C.W., Local 1252 v. Prince Edward Island (Labour Relations Board)*[314] the Prince Edward Island Supreme Court followed *Batchelor* and held that the service upon the P.E.I. Labour Relations Board of an application for certiorari to the P.E.I. Supreme Court *automatically* stayed the tribunal's proceedings until the certiorari is determined. The P.E.I. Court noted, but did not follow, *Cedarvale Tree Services.* The decision of the P.E.I. court was based on the wording of its rules which were similar to the *Batchelor* rules and which directed that upon service of the application for certiorari the body in question was to file its record with the court which filing was to have the "same effect as a return to a writ of certiorari".

The P.E.I. decision was rejected by the Newfoundland Court of Appeal in *Barry's Ltd. v. Fishermen, Food and Allied Workers' Union*[315] where the majority of the Court (Marshall and O'Neil, JJ.A.) held that the Supreme Court of Canada's decision in *Batchelor* dealt with criminal proceedings and had expressly left the question of civil proceedings open. The majority of the Court of Appeal held that, in civil proceedings, the question of whether an automatic stay should ensue from mere service of an application in the nature of certiorari upon the Newfoundland

---

312 (1979), 26 O.R. (2d) 570 (C.A.).

313 [1989] 3 F.C. 352 (T.D.).

314 (1987), 67 Nfld. & P.E.I.R. 148 (T.D.).

315 (1993), 198 D.L.R. (4th) 637 (Nfld. C.A.), leave to appeal to S.C.C. refused (1994), 112 D.L.R. (4th) vii (S.C.C.).

Labour Relations Board could not be determined in isolation from the legislative intent in creating the Board. The Board had been created in order to provide a speedy and final method for resolving labour disputes which could not effectively be dealt with in the traditional court structure. In recognition of this the Legislature had protected decisions of the Board with a privative clause. The majority felt that if proceedings before the Board were to be stayed it should only be at the order of a court after giving due consideration to the asserted grounds for the stay within the context of the competing statutory imperative of minimizing delays. Automatic stays would frustrate the legislative intent of the statute.

In separate concurring reasons, Goodridge C.J.N. also stated that the service of an application did not automatically stay proceedings before the Board. He noted that the decision in *Batchelor* had been based on rules made under the Criminal Code which required that on the filing of an application for judicial review was to have the same effect as a return of a writ of certiorari (which resulted in the inferior tribunal being required to transfer its file to the superior court thus leaving the inferior body with nothing to proceed with). In his opinion, any argument in favour of an automatic stay based on the Newfoundland Rules of Court had to fail as the rule-making power of the Rules Committee under the Judicature Act did not include the authority to make a rule requiring a statutory tribunal to surrender its file to the court.

Batchelor has also been found to be inapplicable to civil proceedings in earlier decisions of the Nova Scotia Supreme Court (*Aspen Properties Ltd. v. Nova Scotia (Rent Review Commission)*[316]) and Alberta Court of Queen's Bench (*U.A., Local 488 v. Fish International Canada Ltd.*[317]).

Thus, in Manitoba, Nova Scotia, and Alberta it is clear that the *Cedarvale Tree Service* position remains the law and an agency has the discretion to adjourn or not for judicial review proceedings (subject of course to any stay ordered by the reviewing court). Agencies in Prince Edward Island are likely bound by the decision in *U.F.C.W., Local 1252*. As for agencies in the other provinces, it is in the public interest that an agency maintain the discretion recognized in *Cedarvale Tree Services*. Given the overall body of case law on this topic, *Batchelor* should not be considered to have altered that law.

12.20(f) Adjournments for Pending Legislative Change

Should one adjourn one's proceedings to await the passage of pending legislation? As a discretionary power an adjournment can only be granted for some purpose which is relevant to the proceedings. Pending legislative changes are not, as a whole, considered relevant to proceedings which are underway. Thus, in *Canada Pacific Railway Co. v. Alberta*[318] the Supreme Court of Canada held

---

316 (1983), 56 N.S.R. (2d) 317, 117 A.P.R. 317 (N.S. S.C.).
317 (1985), 61 A.R. 9 (Q.B.).
318 [1950] 2 D.L.R. 405 (S.C.C.).

that the Board of Transport Commissioners erred in granting an adjournment of rate proceedings to await the findings of a Royal Commission and possible resulting changes in legislation. There is many a slip twixt the cup and the lip and, as the Federal Court of Appeal acknowledged in *Sethi v. Canada (Minister of Employment & Immigration)*[319] the mere fact that the executive may have announced a government intention does not mean that that that intention will necessarily become law. Furthermore, the presumption against retroactive application of law on substantive matters and the presumption against interference with vested rights makes it problematic (but not impossible) that legislative changes dealing with substantive rights would apply to applications already underway.[320]

12.20(g) Practice

The following practice hints may be useful respecting adjournments.

1. In order to avoid requests for adjournments, agencies (as much as possible) should attempt to co-ordinate their scheduling with the participants. A phone call to counsel to enquire as to open dates may avoid difficulties later. In proceedings with very large numbers of participants it may be only feasible to contact counsel for the major players.

2. If an agency adopts a policy of preemptory hearings (ie. once a hearing date is determined adjournments will be granted only in the rarest of situations) it must advise the participants of this fact. Notwithstanding that a hearing date may be preemptory, an agency must be prepared to at least consider requests for adjournments although the criteria may be stringent. It cannot unduly fetter its discretion by adopting an unbending policy of no adjourn-

---

319 (1988), 31 Admin. L.R. 123, 5 Imm. L. R. (2d) 161 (C.A.), leave to appeal to S.C.C. refused (1988), 36 Admin. L.R. xl (note) (S.C.C.).

320 However, for a case going the opposite way see *Yukon Utilities Board v. Commissioner in Executive Council* (1987), 26 Admin. L.R. 239 (Y.T.C.A.) where a statutory power to issue directives to the Yukon Utilities Board was found to include the power to issue a directive ordering the Board to adjourn its proceedings until the completion of negotiations for the transfer of a particular power commission were completed and a rates policy directive had been issued to the Board. The propriety of this decision may be somewhat doubtful insofar as it calls for the delay in the performance of a statutory duty in the expectation of some possible future change in circumstances coupled with the possibility of the issuance of policy directions. For a related, but not on all fours, case, see *Hirmann v. Toronto (City)* (1993), 13 O.R. (3d) 54 (Gen. Div.) where the Court stated that in some circumstances it might be reasonable for municipal planning authorities to refuse building permits on the basis of the more restrictive provisions of by-laws which were to be retroactive and which had been passed by city council but required approval by the Municipal Board. (However, it was not reasonable to do so, in the Court's opinion, where it was not possible to say whether the necessary approval of the Board might be given anytime in the near future.)

ments and must be prepared to accommodate circumstances where a failure to adjourn would give rise to a miscarriage of justice.

3.   Factors to consider on a request for adjournment are:

   i.   the purpose for the adjournment (is it relevant to the proceedings, is it necessary for a fair hearing);

   ii. has the participant seeking the adjournment acted in good faith and reasonably in attempting to avoid the necessity of adjourning;

   iii. the position of the other participants and the reasonableness of their actions;

   iv. the seriousness of the harm resulting if the adjournment is not granted;

   v.   the seriousness of the harm resulting if the adjournment is granted (to the other participants, to the agency, etc.) (this would include the length of adjournment required);[321]

   vi. is there any way to compensate for any harm identified;

   vii. how many adjournments has the participant seeking the adjournment been granted in the past;

   viii. was the hearing to be preemptory, and if so, were the parties consulted in selecting the date and were they advised of its preemptory nature;

4.   A party who may need an adjournment should advise the agency as soon as possible. If a notice of hearing has just been issued, a prompt call to the agency to advise them of a difficulty may allow the agency to simply reschedule the hearing by sending out new notices of hearing. Otherwise, it can only help one's cause if one has notified the other participants and perhaps even secured their consent to an adjournment. This reduces the ability of the other participants to claim prejudice. It also avoids the other participants

---

321 See, for example, *R. v. Ontario Labour Relations Board, Ex parte Nick Masney Hotels Ltd.,* [1970] 3 O.R. 461 (C.A.) where Laskin J.A. noted that the nature of the agency's mandate and the circumstances with which it is to deal constitute valid considerations on an adjournment request. He stated:

The Ontario Labour Relations Board deals in certification matters with fluid situations which cannot be judged by the more leisurely standards that operate in the prosecution of a claim for damages for a tort or fort a breach of contract where the situation is fairly well frozen when the tort or the breach of contract has occurred. Expedition is important to a union, to employees and to an employer since the certification is merely the first step in an often labourious collective bargaining process. When, as here, adequate notice has been given of a hearing date and an opportunity afforded to make representations, the failure of a party to secure an agreement for an adjournment, where it has not been misled by another party to that other's advantage and where the Board has stood above the negotiations and has properly followed its own rules, fashioned for the protection of all parties, there is no denial of natural justice to support a successful resort to certiorari against the Board.

showing up at a hearing with all of their evidence and witnesses and thus suffering prejudice if the adjournment is granted.

5.   An adjournment should not be granted without the other participants having been given notice and an opportunity to make submissions. (However, where the request is made almost immediately upon the issuance of a hearing notice being issued some agencies will reschedule without such notice.) It should not always be necessary to deal with requests for adjournments at a hearing. A party wishing to avoid having to attend at the hearing date should contact the other participants and secure their consent to the adjournment. Having secured this consent, the party should then contact the agency to determine if the hearing may be adjourned without the formality of a hearing or through an abbreviated proceeding in which the agency simply verifies the consent of the other parties.

6.   Before a particular member or panel of the agency has become seized with a matter, decisions respecting rescheduling can be made by the person assigned the scheduling duty by the agency. However, once a member or panel has commenced a hearing adjournment requests should be, and must be once the member has become seized with a matter (i.e. has embarked on hearing the substance of a matter), directed to that member or panel.

7.   In any event, the other participants and the agency should always receive as much notice as possible that one is seeking an adjournment. This enables them to prepare and reduces the likelihood of prejudice when the adjournment request is advanced.

8.   Where the other parties do not consent to an adjournment, one should appear ready to proceed with a case in the event that the agency refuses one's request for an adjournment. For some unknown reason, when requests for adjournment are denied, some counsel seem to think that they are scoring points to announce that they will not, or cannot, participate in "this sham", "travesty", "injustice" or whatever, and dramatically walk out of the hearing. This is equivalent to playing Russian roulette. It is very unlikely that the agency will be either impressed or intimidated by counsel's actions and it will likely simply continue the proceedings without the interest of the counsel's client being represented. On judicial review, unless the counsel is successful in convincing the court that the adjournment should have been granted as a point of natural justice or fairness, his withdrawal from the hearing will likely constitute a waiver of the right to have participated further in the hearing.[322] Thus, the risk is as a high as the drama in such a scenario. Generally, it does not serve one's client's interests.

---

322 See, for example, *Holoboff v. Alberta (Securities Commission)* (1991), 80 D.L.R. (4th) 603 (Alta. C.A.), *R. v. Ontario Labour Relations Board, Ex parte Nick Masney Hotels*, [1970] 3 O.R. 461 (C.A.).

12.21 STATING A CASE

Every agency should have the right in its statute to state a case to the court. This power, unless explicitly set forth in the mandating statute, does not exist. See Chapter 24 for more on this subject.

12.22 WAIVER

12.22(a) Substantive Law

Parties are often granted procedural rights under a statute of which, for one reason or another, they do not wish to take advantage. For example, suppose a party does not receive the specified period of notice directed by a statute. But the party, in fact, does not actually need that full statutory notice period and would rather proceed with the hearing right away rather than going through the formality of an adjournment he does not really require. Rather than taking the adjournment the party simply waives his right to object to the lack of notice.

Generally speaking, a party may waive any procedural right which exists for his own benefit.[323] In other words, private rights may be waived. Thus, a right of appeal may be waived[324] as can be the rights arising from natural justice and fairness, including bias.[325] (The ability to waive the protections afforded by natural justice and fairness is logical insofar as those rights are only implied to the extent necessary to ensure a fair hearing. If one is satisfied with one's hearing there is little to be gained by insisting on procedural protections which one does not wish.) In *MacHattie v. Veterinary Medical Association (N.S.)*[326] the Nova Scotia Supreme Court upheld the right of the participants to waive the statutory requirement that evidence be given under oath in circumstances when the agency was unable to administer the oath and the absence of the oath did not appear to lead to any unfairness.

However, where a procedural provision exists to protect some greater public purpose an individual cannot waive it.[327] He cannot waive it because it does not

---

323 *Korponay v. A.G. (Canada)*, [1982] 1 S.C.R. 41, *R. v. Heaslip* (1983), 9 C.C.C. (3d) 480 (Ont. C.A.).

324 *Smerchanski v. Minister of National Revenue* (1972), 72 DTC 6117 (Fed. T.D.).

325 See, for example, *Balka v. McDonald* (1994), 120 Nfld. & P.E.I.R. 7, 373 A.P.R. 7 (Nlfd. T.D.)(waiver of bias), *Ostrowski v. Saskatchewan (Beef Stabilization Board)* (1993), 115 Sask. R. 106 (Q.B.) (waiver of right to counsel). However, the British Columbia Supreme Court once held in *Devries v. Canada(National Parole Board)* (1993), 12 Admin. L.R. (2d) 309, 21 C.R. (4th) 36 (B.C.S.C.) that a statutory direction that a decision-maker is not to have previously participated in the decision under review could not be expressly or impliedly waived by the parties. Presumably underlying this decision was some public interest in the perception of an unbiased parole system.

326 (1991), 107 N.S.R. (2d) and 290 A.P.R. 361 (T.D.).

327 See, for example *Winnipeg School Division No. 1 v. Craton* (1986), 21 D.L.R. (4th) 1 (S.C.C.)

exist simply for him, but rather exists for the public generally. For an example of this principle in action see *Wassilyn v. Ontario (Racing Commission).*[328] That case involved a suspension of an individual's racing licence by the Ontario Racing Commission. In response, the individual commenced an application for judicial review challenging the suspension. Prior to the judicial review being heard the individual and the racing commission reached an agreement whereby the Commission agreed to reinstate the individual's licence in return for the individual withdrawing his application for judicial review. In accordance with the agreement the individual withdrew the judicial review application. The Commission, however, refused to reinstate the licence. It took the position that the most the individual was entitled to was a hearing as to the possibility of a renewal or reinstatement of the licence. The Ontario Court of Justice (General Division) reluctantly agreed with the Commission. It noted that Commission Rule 3.10 provided that "Any licensee suspended by virtue of the operation of this provision may make application to the Commission for a licence, and in such case, the Commission *shall* hold a hearing to determine such application" (emphasis added by Court). The Court held that as the rule in question was for the benefit of the public at large and not for the benefit of either the Commission or the applicant, it could only be waived through proper process by the Legislature on the public's behalf, but not by the Commission. The Commission had the authority to make, delete or change rules. But the power had to be exercised generally. It could not be exercised on an individual basis.[329]

Waiver cannot be ambiguous. Before a person will be found to have waived a right, the waiver must be clear and unequivocal.[330] Nonetheless a waiver is capable of being implied by one's actions. For example, knowingly refusing to attend at a hearing, or walking out of one on the failure of some objection which one has raised will be found to amount to a waiver of one's right to be present at the hearing. The agency will be permitted to continue without you.[331] Sitting in the bushes and failing to raise a procedural objection at the earliest opportunity can also constitute a waiver of one's right to object.[332] Thus, the Supreme Court

---

and *Ontario (Human Rights Commission) v. Etobicoke* (1982), 132 D.L.R. (3d) 14 (S.C.C.) (both of which state that one cannot contract out of the Human Rights Act which declares public policy).

328 (1993), 10 Admin. L.R. (2d) 157 (Ont. Gen. Div.).

329 To the same effect see *B.C. Government Employees Union v. Public Service Commission* (1979), 96 D.L.R. (3d) 86 (B.C.S.C.) (statutory provision for three member panel is a provision in the public interest, not merely a protective device for the parties).

330 *Rochon v. Spirit River School District No. 47* (1994), 24 Admin. L.R. (2d) 115, 149 A.R. 106, 111 D.L.R. (4th) 452 (C.A.).

331 *Holoboff v. Alberta (Securities Commission)* (1991), 80 D.L.R. (4th) 603 (Alta. C.A.).

332 See, for example, *Robertson v. MacDonald* (1994), 134 N.S.R. (2d) 380, 383 A.P.R. 380 (C.A.). In that case an appellant sought to appeal a decision on the grounds that he had been deprived of natural justice by the failure of the Nova Scotia Labour Standards Tribunal to provide him with a full opportunity to be heard and to examine the documents and notes to which a witness gave evidence. He also felt that he had suffered from the failure of the opposing side to call all

of Canada in *R. v. Whittle*[333] held that before one can waive the right to counsel in criminal proceedings one must have at least sufficient cognitive capacity to understand what one is saying and what is said. This includes the ability to understand a caution that the evidence can be used against the person. The person must be capable of communicating with counsel to order to instruct counsel and understand the function of counsel and that he or she can dispense with counsel even if this is not in the person's best interests. However, the Court did hold that the fact that a person waived the right to counsel because he did not care about the consequences or could not resist the urging of inner voices did not invalidate the waiver. Inner compulsion, due to conscience or otherwise, cannot displace the finding of an operating mind unless, in combination with conduct of a person in authority, a statement is found to be involuntary.[334]

However, one cannot bestow jurisdiction upon a statutory decision-maker by waiver or consent.[335]

---

the pertinent witnesses. The Nova Scotia Court of Appeal summarily dismissed the appeal on the grounds that the appellant had chosen not to ask for an adjournment which he could have had if he felt that his presentation was being rushed. Further, the Court concluded, if he felt that there were additional witnesses that the Tribunal should hear from, he could have simply asked for an adjournment to permit them to be called. See also *University of Saskatchewan Engineering Students Soc. v. Sask. Human Rights Commission* (1983), 24 Sask. R. 167 (Q.B.), *Khakh v. Canada (Minister of Employment & Immigration)*, [1994] 1 F.C. 548, 23 Imm. L.R. (2d) 38 (T.D.).

333 (1994), 170 N.R. 16, 73 O.A.C. 201 (S.C.C.).

334 In *Khakh v. Canada (Minister of Employment & Immigration)*, [1994] 1 F.C. 548, 23 Imm. L.R. (2d) 38 (T.D.) the Federal Court Trial Division held that waiver will not be implied unless the concerned person is aware of the facts giving rise to the right to object, has an opportunity to object, and is aware of his right to object. Thus, a refugee claimant was not found to have impliedly waived his right to object to the apparent bias of an Adjudicator when neither he nor his agent (who was not a lawyer) was aware of his right to raise an object at the time of the Adjudicator's actions which gave rise to the grounds for the objection. (The Court noted that this conclusion would likely have been different had the claimant been represented by legal counsel at the hearing before the Adjudicator. In *Mashinini v. Canada (Minister of Employment & Immigration)* (1990), 126 N.R. 391 (Fed. C.A.) no effective waiver of the right to counsel was found when the individual in question was surprised and unprepared when his counsel did not appear at a hearing as promised. When he was asked if he wished to proceed no explanation of the full nature of the inquiry or the consequences that could flow from it were given to him. See also *Clarkson v. R.*, [1986] 1 S.C.R. 3 where the Supreme Court considered the effect of intoxication on the ability of a person to be aware of the consequences of waiver.

335 *Scivitarro v. British Columbia (Minister of Human Resources)*, [1982] 4 W.W.R. 632, 134 D.L.R. (3d) 521 (B.C. S.C.), *Essex County Council v. Essex Inc. Congregational Church Union*, [1963] A.C. 808, 1 All E.R. 326 (H.L.), *Beauregard v. Comm. de la fonction publique (Qué)* (1987), 10 Q.A.C. 115 (C.A.), *Branigan v. Yukon Medical Council* (1986), 21 Admin. L.R. 149 (Y.T. S.C.), and *B.C. (A.G.) v. Mount Currie Indian Band* (1991), 54 B.C.L.R. (2d) 146, 64 C.C.C. (3d) 172 (S.C.). Decision-makers whose authority flows from the consent of the participants, however, (such as consensual arbitrators) can, logically enough, receive jurisdiction by further waiver or consent of the parties (see *Glace Bay Community Hospital v. Canadian Brotherhood of Railway, Transport and General Workers, Local 607* (1993), 120 N.S.R. (2d)

12.22(b) Practice Hints

1. A decision-maker who is assigned to a hearing from which it is undesirable that he step down unless required and who becomes aware of some ground that could give rise to a reasonable apprehension of bias should advise the parties of the circumstances at the earliest opportunity that arises after they become known and provide them with an opportunity to make representations thereon. In this way, if no person objects claims of bias relating to that disclosed ground of concern cannot be raised later to challenge the propriety of decisions.

2. Participants who become aware of a possible procedural objection should raise it at the earliest opportunity. If the ruling is against one, rather than storming out of the room in a huff, the recommended approach is simply to advise the agency that one maintains one's objection but will continue with the proceeding while reserving the right to seek judicial review if necessary subsequently. It is likely not necessary to formally note that one maintains one's objection. The mere raising of the objection at the earlier opportunity will likely preserve any subsequent review rights which one likely has.

12.23 RETROACTIVITY

12.23(a) Introduction

It is not unknown for changes to be made to statute law or regulations in the midst of a hearing. In such cases the agency is faced with the dilemma as to whether the old law or the new law should be applied. There is a presumption against retroactive application of statutes. There is also a separate (but related) presumption that Parliament does not intend to interfere with vested rights. Each of these concerns must be addressed in determining whether a legislative change applies to a proceeding in progress,[336] and in the discussion which follows I will canvass both, addressing first, the presumption against retroactive application, and then the presumption against vested rights.

This is not a text on statutory interpretation, however, and the reader interested in an in depth discussion of this topic may wish to consult either of the leading Canadian texts in this area: *Driedger on the Construction of Statutes* (either the second edition by Driedger or the third edition which is edited by Ruth

---

89, 332 A.P.R. 89 (C.A.), *Hunter Rose Co. Ltd. v. Graphic Arts International Union, Local 28B* (1979) 24 O.R. (2d) 608 (C.A.).

336 *Quebec (Attorney General) v. Quebec (Expropriation Tribunal)*, [1986] 1 S.C.R. 732; *Apotex Inc. v. Canada (Attorney General)* (1993), 18 Admin. L.R. (2d) 122 (Fed. C.A.), affirmed [1994] 3 S.C.R. 1100.

Sullivan — each of these editions have their strengths and weaknesses and one may wish to consult them both) (Butterworths), or Pierre-Andé Côté's *The Interpretation of Legislation in Canada* (Les éditions Yvon Blais Inc.).

12.23(b) What Is Retroactivity?

In her third edition to *Driedger on the Construction of Statutes* (Butterworths) Prof. Sullivan defines a retroactive provision as follows:

> A retroactive statute or provision is one that applies to facts that were already past when the legislation came into force. It changes the law applicable to past conduct or events; in effect it deems the law to have been different from what it actually was.

Notwithstanding the apparent simplicity of this rule, its application is, in fact, very difficult. In the second edition of his *Construction of Statutes* Prof. Driedger notes that there is a great deal of confusion in the case law as to when a statute should be considered to operative retroactively. Set out below are a number of excerpts from this text, at pages 185 to 203, which summarizes what constitutes a retrospective provision.

> When can it be said that a construction gives retrospective[337] effect to a statute? In all but the simplest enactments there is set out what may be called the fact-situation, namely, the facts that bring the rule of law into operation. This fact-situation can be set out by defining the subject of the enactment, by describing the circumstances that bring the rule into operation, or partly in the one way or partly in the other. The fact-situation may include a reference to past facts by employing clauses in the past or perfect tenses;[338] the question then arises whether the facts that arose before the

---

337 A retroactive provision is one which looks at a fact or event which is completed in the past, and attaches some new legal consequences to that event effective at some time in the past. A retrospective provision is one which also looks to a past fact or event and attaches new consequences to it, but those consequences attach only as of the date the new law is passed. The difference between "retroactive" and "retrospective" is complex. Prof. Sullivan in the 3rd edition of *Driedger's Construction of Statutes* writes that there has "been a growing confusion around the term "retrospective" in Canadian case law. The term is used in three different ways: (1) as a synonym for "retroactive" to describe legislation that applies to past facts; (2) in the special sense . . . to describe legislation that attaches new prejudicial consequences to closed transactions; and (3) most frequently, perhaps, to describe legislation that if applied immediately and generally would attach new prejudicial consequences to on going facts." Whether a provision is "retroactive" or "retrospective" the presumption works the same way. Thus, for the purposes of this text, I shall use the term "retroactive" to refer to both.

338 Prof. Driedger sets out a footnote here which reads: "E.g., every person who has done something or to whom something has been done; where a person has done something; whenever such and such has happened; where a person who had done something fails; whenever an accident has happened; where a person who has done something fails; whenever an accident has happened every person who was involved shall."

enactment bring it into operation, or only those that arose between the time of the enactment and the time of its application.

These past facts may describe a status or characteristic, or they may describe an event. It is submitted that where the fact-situation is a status or characteristic (the being something), the enactment is not given retrospective effect when it is applied to persons or things that acquired that status before the enactment, if they have it when the enactment comes into force; but where the fact-situation is an event (the happening or the becoming something), then the enactment would be given retrospective effect if it is applied so as to attach a new duty, penalty or disability to an event that took place before the enactment. . . .

In *West v. Gwynne*,[339] for example, the fact-situation was "leases containing a covenant against assignment", a description by characteristic, and accordingly the application of the statute to all leases coming within that description whether made before or after the enactment was not a retrospective operation. But if the statute had read "where a lease containing a covenant against assignment is entered into" the result might then have been different because that would be a description of an event, and the application of the enactment to an antecedent event would be a retrospective application. . . .

Thus, the position appears to be that whenever the operation of a statute depends upon the doing of something or the happening of some event, the statute will not operate in respect of something done or in respect of some event that took place before the commencement of the statute; but if the operation of the statute depends merely upon the existence of a certain state of affairs, the *being* rather than the *becoming*, the statute will operate with respect to a status which arose before the commencement of the statute, if it exists at that time. . . .

For retrospectivity the question is: Is there anything in the statute to indicate that the consequences of a prior event are changed, not for a time before its enactment, but henceforth from the time of enactment, or from the time of its commencement if that should be later?

Summarizing Prof. Driedger then, for a provision to be retrospective in nature it must

i. relate to a past *event*; and

ii. attach new consequences to that event as of some time after the enactment of the provision.[340]

---

339 [1911] 2 Ch. 1.

340 The reader should note that Prof. Sullivan in her 3rd edition of Prof. Driedger's classic work adopts a different approach in determining whether a legislative change is retroactive or prospective. Adopting the methodology introduced by Prof. Côté in his excellent text on statutory interpretation, Prof. Sullivan suggests that the determination be made by looking at whether the fact to which the law applies is in the past or not. The temporal location of the fact is determined on the basis of whether the fact is ephemeral, continuing or successive. I, personally, do not find this approach any easier that Prof. Driedger's original approach. However, neither is particularly

12.23(c) Presumption Against Retroactive Application

As a general rule, legislative provisions are not to be interpreted to operate retroactively. As noted by the Supreme Court of Canada in *Brosseau v. Alberta Securities Commission*[341] at page 19 (citing the decision of Mr. Justice Dickson for the majority in *Gustavson Drilling (1964) Ltd. v. Minister of National Revenue*:

> The general rule is that statutes are not to be construed as having retrospective operation unless such construction is expressly or by necessary implication required by the language of the Act. An amending enactment may provide that it shall be deemed to have come into force on a date prior to its enactment or it may provide that it is to be operative with respect to transactions occurring prior to its enactment. In those instances the statute operates retrospectively.[342]

Thus, a statute creating a public complaint process concerning the conduct of members of the R.C.M.P. was held not to apply to conduct occurring prior to the passage of the legislation.[343] Similarly, the Canadian Human Rights Act was found not to apply to discriminatory practices taking place prior to the passage of that statute (and not continuing thereafter).[344] In attempting to determine whether a provision is retroactive or not, it is important to take care to note what the triggering fact is. In *Kanerva v. Ontario Assn. of Architects*[345] it was argued that a statutory amendment giving a professional discipline committee the power to order costs against a member could not apply to disciplinary proceedings commenced (but not completed) before the statutory change. The Ontario Divisional Court disagreed, holding that the fact which attracted the imposition of costs was a finding of guilt by the committee. That finding had taken place after the change in the law. Thus, applying the costs provision to that case did not amount to giving the legislation a retroactive application.

In *Apotex Inc. v. Canada (Attorney General)*[346] the Federal Court of Appeal avoided a complicated analysis as to whether a change in regulations operated retroactively or not by simply noting that since the statute did not expressly or implicitly authorize the making of retroactive regulations the regulations in question could not apply retroactively.

---

easy to apply and it may simply be a question of which is most easily comprehensible to the individual. Thus, I recommend Prof. Sullivan's and Prof. Côté's work to those who find Driedger's original methodology unduly difficult.

341 (1989), 93 N.R. 1 (S.C.C.).

342 [1977] 1 S.C.R. 271.

343 *Re Royal Canadian Mounted Police Act* (1990), 123 N.R. 121 (Fed. C.A.).

344 *Latif v. Canada (Canadian Human Rights Commission)*, [1980], 1 F.C. 687 (C.A.).

345 (1986), 56 O.R. (2d) 518 (Div. Ct.).

346 (1993), 18 Admin. L.R. (2d) 122 (Fed. C.A.), affirmed [1994] 3 S.C.R. 1100.

12.23(d) Exceptions to Presumption Against Retroactivity

Notwithstanding the above, there are exceptions where the presumption against retroactive application will not apply. The presumption does not apply:

i. to procedural enactments;

ii. to enactments which bestow benefits, rather than prejudicial consequences;

iii. to enactments which impose a prejudicial consequence intended as protection for the public; and

iv. to enactments where the legislation in question expressly or by necessary implication, is intended to operate retrospectively.

(*Brosseau v. Alberta Securities Commission,*[347] *Bera v. Marr.*[348])

Procedural Enactments

In *Angus v. Hart*[349] the Supreme Court noted that the presumption against retroactive application does not apply to procedural enactments. It stated that: "A provision is substantive or procedural for the purposes of retrospective application . . . according to whether or not it affects substantive rights". Generally speaking, a procedural enactment deals with how one brings about or executes one's rights. Thus, a change in legislation respecting rate increase proceedings to the effect that in a proceeding an agency must grant adjournments on request would apply to proceedings already underway. A substantive enactment is one which gives one a right. A right of appeal is a substantive right[350] and thus a change in the law abolishing or creating an appeal right would not apply to a proceeding which is already underway unless the legislation in question expressly so provided.[351]

---

347 (1989), 93 N.R. 1 (S.C.C.).

348 (1986), 27 D.L.R. (4th) 161 (B.C. C.A.).

349 (1988), 52 D.L.R. 193 (S.C.C.).

350 *Upper Canada College v. Smith* (1920), 57 D.L.R. 648 (S.C.C.), *Colonial Sugar Refining Co. v. Irving,* [1905] A.C. 369.

351 There can be a twist, however, when an appeal provision is repealed and replaced with a new appeal provision. Section 14(2)(b) of Ontario's Interpretation Act provides that:

    14. (2) If other provisions are substituted for those so repealed or revoked

        (b) all proceedings taken under the Act, regulation or thing so repealed or revoked, shall be taken up and continued under an in conformity with the provision so substituted, so far as consistently may be.

There are a number of decisions in Ontario to the effect that where a statutory provision establishing a right of appeal to a particular appellate body is revoked and replaced with a new appeal right to another appellate body, s. 14(2)(b) operates to substitute the new appeal right for the old (*Re Rai* (1980), 27 O.R. (2d) 425 (C.A.), *Wilson v. Armitage* (1982), 37 O.R. (2d) 407

Beneficial Enactments

The exception for "beneficial" provisions appears to be limited to those provisions whose *only* effect is to grant some benefit.[352] A change in legislation extending the time to bring applications against insurance companies, for example, would not fall within this "beneficial" exception as the extension of time, while being beneficial to those seeking to bring the claims, would not be considered beneficial to those resisting them.

Protection of the Public

In decisions such as *Re a Solicitor's Clerk,* [1957] 3 All E.R. 617 (Q.B.) and *Brosseau* the courts have held that the presumption against retroactivity does not apply to a provision whose purpose is to protect the public in the future from individuals whose conduct in the past had demonstrated that they were not trustworthy. In *Re Royal Canadian Mounted Police Act*[353] the Federal Court of Appeal held that the exception as laid down in *Brosseau* was very limited and applied only to cases where there is:

1. a statutory disqualification,

2. based on past conduct,

3. which demonstrates a continuing unfitness for the privilege in question.

In the opinion of the Federal Court of Appeal this was the extent of this exception. If there were a wider connotation to that exception, which the Court found difficult to accept, the Court held that it could not be based simply on the fact that the purpose of the legislation was to protect the public.

> Whether there is a general category broader than the subcategory [discussed above], it must at least be recognized that there cannot be any public interest or public protection exception, writ large, to the presumption against retrospectivity, for the simple reason that every statute, whatever its content, can be said to be in the public interest or for the public protection. No Parliament ever deliberately legislates

---

(C.A.), *Stewart v. Davis* (1988), 37 M.P.L.R. 233, (*sub nom. Stewart v. Mississauga Fire Marshall*) 64 O.R. (2d) 403 (Div. Ct.)).

352 See *Royal Insurance Co. of Canada v. Ontario (Human Rights Commission)* (1985), 51 O.R. (2d) 797 (C.A.), and *Thiessen v. Manitoba Public Insurance Corp.* (1990), 66 D.L.R. (4th) 366 (Man. C.A.), leave to appeal to S.C.C. refused (1990), 68 Man. R. (2d) 380 (note) (S.C.C.).

353 (1990), 123 N.R. 121 (Fed. C.A.).

against the public interest but always visualizes its legislative innovations as being for the public good.[354]

Express or Implicit Statutory Exclusion of Presumption

The presumption against retroactivity can be displaced when "such construction is expressly or by necessary implication required by the language of the Act". The case law indicates that this is a heavy burden to discharge. As stated by Wright J. in *In re Athlumney; Ex parte Wilson*, [1898] 2 Q.B. 547 (cited with approval by the Federal Court of Appeal in *Re Royal Mounted Police Act* at page 138):

> Perhaps no rule of construction is more firmly established than this — that a retrospective operation is not to be given to a statute so as to impair an existing right or obligation, other than as regards matter of procedure, *unless that effect cannot be avoided without doing violence to the language of the enactment.* If the enactment is expressed in language which is fairly capable of either interpretation it ought to be construed as prospective only. [Emphasis added.]

An example of an express retroactive provision can be found in section 43 of the Ontario Succession Law Reform Act, S.O. 1977, c. 40, which the Ontario Court of Appeal found to displace the presumption in *Canada Trust Co. v. Sachs* (1993), 99 D.L.R. (4th) 209 (Ont. C.A.):

> 43. This Part applies to wills made before, on or after the 31st day of March , 1978 where the testator has not died before that date.

It is not unusual in the amendment or repeal and replacement of statutes today to include transition provisions which specify how proceedings already underway are to be dealt with. Such provisions can clarify the application of the new law to these proceedings. See, for example, *Huynh v. Canada*[355] for an example of a case where the transitional provision was found to expressly provide for the retroactive application of the new law to proceedings underway.

12.23(e) Concerns Re. Retroactivity Should Not Apply to Policy Guidelines

The concerns which arise respecting legislative changes should not arise in the context of changes of policy guidelines. Essentially, all a policy guideline is

---

354 Consequently, in that case, the Court held that the statutory authority of the R.C.M.P. Complaints Commission to investigate complaints by the public against members of the R.C.M.P. and make to recommendations with respect thereto to the Commissioner of the Force did not extend to complaints made prior to the establishment of the Commission.

355 [1995] 1 F.C. 633 (T.D.).

is notice of an approach which an agency believes is proper. It is not binding on the agency. The degree to which it is adopted by any particular decision-maker depends on how convinced that decision-maker is that it should be applied to the case before him. If an agency changes a policy position in the midst of a hearing, the decision-maker should advise the participants of the change and receive submissions as to the wisdom of the new policy or its applicability to the case before them in the same way that any policy guideline would be treated. (An adjournment may be necessary to permit the participants to consider the implications of the new policy.) To argue that a policy guideline should be treated in the same way as legislative change would be equivalent to arguing that an agency should not consider arguments against an existing policy in a proceeding.

12.23(f) The Presumption Against Interfering With Vested Rights

The Supreme Court has stated on several occasions that, regardless of whether a statutory provision is retrospective or prospective in application, there remains a presumption that Parliament does not intend to affect existing rights which have vested, or accrued or are accruing prior to the change in law.

> A legislative enactment is not to be read as prejudicially affecting accrued rights, or "an existing status" . . . unless the language in which it is expressed requires such a construction. The rule is described by Coke as "a law of Parliament" . . . meaning, no doubt that it is a rule based on the practice of Parliament, the underlying assumption being that, when Parliament intends to prejudicially affect such rights or such a status it declares its intention expressly, unless at all events, that intention is plainly manifested by unavoidable inference.[356]

This common law principle is reflected in provisions in all of the various Canadian Interpretation Acts similar to section 43(c) of the federal Act, R.S.C. 1985, c. I-21:

> 43. Where an enactment is repealed in whole or in part, the repeal does not
>
> > (c) affect any right, privilege, obligation or liability acquired, accrued, accruing or incurred under the enactment so repealed.

For administrative agencies, the presumption against interference with vested rights will likely arise most frequently in the context of agency proceedings when a provision permitting an individual to apply for some benefit, approval, or permission is repealed. The question then arises as to when the "right" to apply

---

356 *Spooner Oils Ltd. v. Turner Valley Gas Conservation Board*, [1933] S.C.R. 629. This presumption is now mirrored in the various Interpretation Acts. See for example, s. 44(c) of the Interpretation Act, R.S.C. 1985.

for that benefit, approval, or permission can be said to have "accrued" or "accruing"[357] to, or vested in an individual such that he can continue to apply for it notwithstanding the repeal of the provision in question.

The first point to note about the presumption is that it only applies where the legislation in question is ambiguous. No one is entitled to expect the law to remain unchanged. The Supreme Court has recognized that Parliament's laws reduce or remove rights all the time. "It is perfectly obvious that most statues in some way or other interfere with or encroach upon antecedent rights. . . ."[358] Thus, in the context of an application which is underway, but not yet determined, if legislation made it clear that the pending application was to be affected in the same way as all future ones that would be the end of the question. Frequently, however, legislative amendments leave some doubt as to the status of applications which are already under way. In such instances, where it is not certain if the application is to be governed by the law at the time of its being made or the law following the change, the presumption against interference with vested rights becomes relevant. If proceeding involves a right which has vested, or accrued or is accruing in the individual the changed legislation will not affect that right. It will be governed under the old law.

The relevant test in determining whether the courts will apply the presumption against vested rights appears to be a two fold one:

i. there must be a "right" at the time of the change of the law; and

ii. that right must be somehow personalized to the individual claiming it.

i. There Must Be a Right At the Time of the Change of the Law

"First, one must establish a tangible or particular legal right, the right cannot be abstract, it must be more than a possibility, more than a mere expectation."[359] Thus, if the thing being claimed is subject to statutory preconditions which must exist in order for it to exist, the absence of those statutory preconditions at the time of the change in the law will mean that there was no vested right. This can be illustrated by reference to *Hutchins v. Canada (National Parole Board)*.[360] In that case an individual who was in prison for a criminal offence was also in

---

357 The Saskatchewan Court of Appeal in *Scott v. College of Physicians & Surgeons (Saskatchewan)*, [1993] 1 W.W.R. 533 (Sask. C.A.) explained that "accrued" and "accruing" house the same basic idea with the difference being only of tense. Both refer to rights and obligations which are inevitable and arising in due course, as opposed to possible or even probable.

358 In *Gustavson Drilling (1964) v. Minister of National Revenue* (1975), 7 N.R. 401 (S.C.C.) the Supreme Court noted that the presumption against interference with vested rights applies only in the case of ambiguity or uncertainty as "It is perfectly obvious that most statutes in some way or other interfere with or encroach upon antecedent rights. . . ."

359 *Scott v. College of Physician and Surgeons (Saskatchewan)*, [1993] 1 W.W.R. 533 (Sask. C.A.).

360 (1993), 156 N.R. 205 (Fed. C.A.), leave to appeal to S.C.C. refused 91994), 16 Admin. L.R. (2d) 246 (note) (S.C.C.).

Canada illegally and was subject to deportation proceedings. The parole regulations at that time provided that early parole hearings could be granted if a person was subject to a deportation order. This meant that if the prisoner was ordered deported he would be granted early parole for the deportation to be carried out. The prisoner learned that the regulation in question was to be repealed. Anxious to secure his early parole, even if it meant being deported, he attempted to do everything in his power to have the deportation proceedings completed before the repeal of the regulations in question. However, he was unsuccessful. The deportation order was not issued until shortly after the repeal of the regulation in question. Nonetheless, the prisoner argued that his right to an early parole was "accruing" at the time of the change in the law and that he therefore retained the right to early parole once the deportation order was made.

The Federal Court of Appeal disagreed. It held that the right to an early parole hearing was dependent on there being a deportation order. (This was the statutory precondition.) There was no order at the time of the change in the law and therefore there was no right at that time. The fact that the prisoner had done everything in his power in order to secure the early parole hearing did not give him an accruing right to that hearing. "One cannot be accruing a nonexisting right" Justice Létourneau ruled. "To put it another way, a right cannot be accruing when its very existence is conditional on some other event which has not yet materialized. For example, if upon application a legislative provision confers a benefit to a person who is 40 years of age and if that provision is repealed, can it be seriously contended that a person who is 20 or 39 has an accruing right to that benefit because he applied for it before the provision was repealed?" The fact that the deportation order was inevitable was not relevant, in the opinion of the court, as aging was also inevitable in the example given.

The law recognizes a difference between a procedure used to *recognize or implement* an existing right and one which is used to *create* a right. It is only the former which is capable of attracting the presumption. The leading case cited in support of this proposition is that of the Privy Council in *Director of Public Prosecutions v. Sang*:

> It may be, therefore, that under some repealed enactment a right has been given but that in respect of it some investigation or legal proceeding is necessary. The right is then unaffected and preserved. It will be preserved even if a process of quantification is necessary. But there is a manifest distinction between an investigation in respect of a right and an investigation which is to decide whether some right should or should not be given. Upon a repeal the former is preserved by the Interpretation Act. The latter is not.[361]

Thus, the courts have held that an ability to make an application for something which rests completely in the discretion of the decision-maker cannot be a

---

361 [1961] A.C. 901.

right capable of vesting. The case of *Apotex Inc. v. Canada (Attorney General)*[362] is illustrative of this point. In this case the Federal Court of Appeal held that where a decision-maker has an absolute discretion in the exercise of a decision-making power, the passage of a new law restricting that discretion will apply to applications pending before the decision-maker but not yet determined at the time of the new law. Here there is no right in the individual to the relief claimed. It was always in the discretion of the decision-maker. However, if the decision-maker's discretion had been limited by some criteria prior to the new law, and the applicant met all of those criteria, then the individual may have an accrued right notwithstanding that the new law may come into effect prior to the decision in question being finalized.[363]

ii. The Right Must Be Somehow Personalized To The Individual Claiming It

Before an individual will be able to claim a vested right in some statutory provision, he must have had something more than the mere abstract possibility of taking advantage of that statute. The applicant must have done something which has transformed the abstract right which was available to anyone meeting the criteria of the statute into a tangible reality in respect of the applicant personally. An individual may have a right, but in order to be considered to have vested, the individual must have more than the mere right existing in the members of the community or any class of them at the date of the repeal of a statute to take advantage of a repealed statute. In other words, the applicant must have done something to indicate that he was exercising the abstract right[364] What exactly must be done will vary depending on the right in question. In *Esso Resources Canada Ltd. v. Minister of National Revenue*[365] and in *Re Falconbridge Nickel Mines Ltd. v. Ontario (Minister of Revenue)*[366] the public right was a legislative right to a refund of any excess taxes paid. That right was said to have particularized to the individual upon his payment of the excess taxes. In *Quebec (Attorney*

---

362 (1993), 18 Admin. L.R. (2d) 122 (Fed. C.A.), affirmed [1994] 3 S.C.R. 1100.

363 In *Falconbridge Nickel Mines Ltd. v. Ontario (Minister of Revenue)* (1981), 121 D.L.R. (3d) 403 (Ont. C.A.) the Ontario Court of Appeal considered the right of a company which had paid an excess of sales tax to claim a refund. The original law provided that the company could apply for a refund of excess tax payments. Whether or not the refund was to be granted was at the discretion of the Minister. The law changed and the right to a refund disappeared. The company nonetheless applied for a refund for excess taxes paid before the law was changed. The Court held that there was no right to the refund (as it had always been only a discretionary decision of the Minister.) However, the company retained the right to apply for the refund and have that application judged according to the old law (i.e. payable in the discretion of the Minister). The company's ability to make such an application prior to the change in law was a right which survived.

364 See, for example, *Quebec (Attorney General) v. Quebec (Expropriation Tribunal)*, [1986] 1 S.C.R. 732, and *Huynh v. Canada*, [1995] 1 F.C. 633 (T.D.).

365 (1990), 109 N.R. 272 (Fed. C.A.).

366 (1981), 121 D.L.R. (3d) 403 (Ont. C.A.).

General) v. Expropriation Tribunal[367] the general right was the Crown's right to unilaterally discontinue an expropriation. The fact that the Crown started a particular expropriation did not particularize the discontinuance right (respecting that instance), however. It appears that the Crown would have had to have done something to start its discontinuance (or indicate that they were exercising that right) before the Supreme Court was ready to see the right sufficiently crystallized in it.

I will note in closing, that one cannot have a vested right in procedure, only in substantive matters. Procedural changes come into effect as soon as they are made and apply to proceeding already underway.[368]

12.23(g) Authority of Retroactive Actions

An intra-jurisdictional error of law may be found by a court if the tribunal takes retroactive actions. There is a presumption that Parliament did not intend a tribunal to act retroactively. In *Canuk Holdings Western Ltd. v. Fort Nelson Improvement Dist.*[369] there is a discussion of this issue. See also *Consumers' Association of Can. v. A.G. of Canada.*[370]

The federal Statutory Instruments Act[371] places upon the regulation-making authority, the obligation to advise the Clerk of the Privy Council of the reasons why a regulation should come into force earlier than the day it is registered.

There is a presumption that a tribunal will not exercise its authority retroactively unless there is some clear statutory provision to the contrary. In the case of a regulatory tribunal, rates or provisions that reach backwards usually are not considered to be just and reasonable. But one should be careful to consider the applicable statute and the circumstances.

---

367 [1986] 1 S.C.R. 732.

368 *Wildman v. R.*, [1984] 2 S.C.R. 311, *Kanerva v. Assn. of Architects (Ontario)* (1986), 56 O.R. (2d) 518 (Div. Ct.). Sometimes, however, as acknowledged in *Wildman*, a provision which appears to be merely procedural, is in fact substantive. In *Wildman* the Court noted that rules or laws creating presumptions arising out of certain facts are substantive, not procedural, nor is solicitor client privilege. However, a spouse's confidentiality is procedural, as are the provisions respecting incompetence and compellability of s. 4 of the Canada Evidence Act. Costs were said in *Kanerva* (citing *Shea v. Miller*, [1971] 1 O.R. 199 (H.C.), affirmed [1971] 1 O.R. 203 (C.A.)) to be procedural in nature. The procedural/substantive question also arose in *Re Royal Canadian Mounted Police Act* (1990), 123 N.R. 120 (Fed. C.A.) where the Federal Court of Appeal had to determine if a statutory provision creating an public complaints process respecting conduct of the R.C.M.P. was procedural or substantive in nature. The Court held that it was substantive for "What is legislated is not just a *manner* of scrutiny, but the very *existence* of public scrutiny for the first time." See the discussion generally in Prof. Côté's *The Interpretation of Legislation in Canada* (2d ed.) at p. 159 ff.

369 *Canuk Holdings Western ltd. v. Fort Nelson Improvement Dist.* (1963), 42 D.L.R. (2d) 313 (B.C. S.C.).

370 *Consumer's Assn. v. A.G. Can.*, [1979] 1 F.C. 433, 887 D.L.R. (3d) 33 (Fed. T.D.).

371 Statutory Instruments Act, R.S.C. 1985, c. S-22, s. 9.

This short discussion is occasioned by the split decision of the Federal Court of Appeal, and is subsequent reversal by the Supreme Court of Canada, in *Bell Canada v. Canadian Radio-Television and Telecommunications Commission.*[372] As a regulator, I cannot agree with the Federal Court of Canada's decision in which I feel that the majority opinion misapplied or misunderstood long standing and highly regarded rate-making principles. The Supreme Court of Canada's reversal is must better founded on sound regulatory principles.

Before looking in some detail at the *Bell* case I would like to review some court decisions that regulators in Canada have long respected.

12.23(h) Court Decisions on Retroactivity in Rate Regulation

In *Re Northwestern Utilities Ltd. and the Public Utilities Bd. v. City of Edmonton*[373] the issue was whether future rates could recover a past deficiency. The court said no.

In saying so, the court laid down an honoured principle of rate regulation, practiced by regulators across North America, namely, that future rates could not be used to pick up accumulated losses in the past. There is a principle that times must match.

Mr. Justice Estey on behalf of the Supreme Court of Canada stated:

[T]he question is whether or not the interim rates prospectively applied will produce an amount in excess of the estimated total revenue requirements for the same period of the utility by reason of the inclusion in the computation of those future requirements of revenue shortfalls which have occurred prior to the date of the application in question, whether or not those "shortfalls" have been somehow incorporated into the rate base or have been included in the operating expenses forecast for the period in which the new interim rates will be applied.

This declaration, however, is subject, in my opinion, to two binding Supreme Court of Canada decisions which qualify and give flexibility in a vital way to that decision.

The *Edmonton (City) v. Northwestern Utilities Ltd.* case,[374] involved a "gas adjustment clause" often called a "variation account". Variation accounts are very common regulatory adjustment mechanisms. The Supreme Court of Canada held that a regulatory tribunal must estimate operating expenses as accurately as possible. But if the tribunal has concluded that, in the circumstances, it is not

---

372 (1987), [1988] 1 F.C. 296, 79 N.R. 58, 43 D.L.R. (4th) 30 (C.A.), reversed [1989] 1 S.C.R. 1722, 38 Admin. L.R. 1.

373 *Northwestern Utilities Ltd. and Public Utilities Bd. v. Edmonton (City)*, [1979] 1 S.C.R. 684, 7 Alta. L.R. (2d) 370, 12 A.R. 449, 89 D.L.R. (3d) 161, 23 N.R. 565 at S.C.R. p. 703, D.L.R. p. 173.

374 *Edmonton v. Northwestern Utilities Ltd. (No. 2)*, [1961] 1 S.C.R. 392, 34 W.W.R. 600, 82 C.R.T.C. 129, 28 D.L.R. (2d) 125 at S.C.R. p. 406, D.L.R. p. 139.

possible to estimate for the future it may, when it is in the best public interest for the consumers and the utility, establish a deferral account.

In the *City of Edmonton* case, the Court stated:

> [T]he proposed order would be made in an attempt to ensure that the utility should from year to year be enabled to realize, as nearly as may be, the fair return mentioned in the subsection and to comply with the Board's duty to permit this to be done. *How this should be accomplished, when the prospective outlay for gas purchases was impossible to determine in advance with reasonable certainty, was an administrative matter for the Board to determine, in my opinion.*
> [Italics are mine]

A second major case dealing with this issue before the Court of Appeal of Ontario in *Dow Chemical Canada Inc. v. Union Gas Ltd.*[375] The Court concluded that the statutes involved in the two *Edmonton* and *Northwestern* cases and the *Ontario* case were very close.

The Court of Appeal in the *Dow* case referred to the decision of Estey J. in the following terms:

> What Estey J. said as to the Alberta statute [in the 1979 *Northwestern Utilities Ltd.* case] is equally applicable to the *Ontario Energy Board Act*, but I do not believe that the prospective nature of the Act inflexibly circumscribes the power of the Board so as to limit it to the consideration only of future costs and expenses.

The Court concluded that the treatment of a premium in that case was prospective, that it was not possible to estimate the full cost of the premium yet, that an attempt to do so now would be unfair to the customers and that the tribunal had separated those funds at the time the expense first began to arise.

The essence of these decisions is that, in the absence of legislation to the contrary, future rates shall rely on future costs — the costs to serve the future customers. *However*, in setting those future rates, the tribunal has to consider the evidence and information available to it. If it cannot accurately estimate the cost of a known item it may set up deferral accounts or some similar concept. If the tribunal could not do that it would not be creating "just and reasonable rates".

The deferral period allows the tribunal time within which to determine the size of the cost and how the amounts should be allocated so as to create just and reasonable rates. The tribunal may establish deferral accounts or provide for future adjustments where, on the evidence, the tribunal cannot be sure of the extent of identified costs subjects or where not to make such a provision would be unjust to customers and the *utility alike*. A proviso, however, is that the tribunal must select a reasonable period over which to be able to make the adjustment.

---

375 *Dow Chemical Can. Inc. v. Union Gas Ltd.* (1983), 42 O.R. (2d) 731, 3 Admin. L.R. 314, 150 D.L.R. (3d) 267 (C.A.) at O.R. p. 736.

It is my view that an essential element of a deferral account or provision for a future adjustment is to give notice of it when setting the future rate. This removes the element of surprise and unfairness. Two questions are left open:

(1) How would a court deal with the matter had the item not been identified when the rate was struck? or

(2) Had the tribunal not been able, reasonably, to establish the need for the future adjustment? (Neither of which facts existed in the *Bell and CRTC* case).

In terms of past events, as opposed to future events, the court introduced another principal of flexibility in determining just and reasonable rates.

Second, in *Nova v. Amoco Canada*[376] the court held that a regulatory tribunal could vary rates and tolls retroactively based upon a complaint concept. Many rates in North America are set "as agreed" subject to complaint. The court held that the rates could be retroactively adjusted reaching back to the date of the complaint. If a tribunal did not have the implicit power to make that adjustment the rates would end up being unjust and unreasonable. This type of complaint based system was referred to as a "negative disallowance scheme" (as compared to the "positive approval schemes" in the *Northwestern* and *Edmonton* cases) by the Supreme Court of Canada in *Bell Canada v. Canadian Radio-Television and Telecommunications Commission.*[377] Referring to its earlier decision in *Nova v. Amoco Canada* the Supreme Court stated (at p. 55 N.R.) that "It has generally been found that negative disallowance schemes provide the power to make orders which are retroactive to the date of the application by the ratepayer who claims that the rates are not "just and reasonable". On the other hand, positive approval schemes have been found to be exclusively prospective in nature and not to allow orders applicable to periods prior to the final decision itself."

The difference between the *Northwestern* and the *Edmonton* cases, supra, and the *Nova* case, supra, was that the former dealt with prospective rates that would need to be adjusted in the future while the *Nova* case dealt with rates that were retrospective (existing rates) and were adjusted for the past. The *Nova* decision is important and much of its reasoning, in my opinion, is applicable whether one is talking of retrospective or prospective rate-making. The case deals with what would be unjust and unreasonable rates if the retrospective (retroactive) adjustments was not to be made.

Every day regulators across Canada are faced with applications to fix rate periods commencing before or after the date of application. The possibility of facing a period for which rates have not been adjusted upwards or downwards would lead to unjust determination and unfair rates, unless a tribunal could adjust for those everyday occurrences.

---

376 *Nova v. Amoco Can. Petroleum Co.*, [11981] 2 S.C.R. 437, [1991] 6 W.W.R. 391, 38 N.R. 381, 128 D.L.R. (3d) 1, 32 A.R. 613.
377 Supra note 32.

See also *Coseka Resources Ltd. v. Saratoga Processing Co.*[378] In that case, the court looked at whether the Alberta Public Utilities Board ("APUB") could readjust rates back to the date of an interim order, some three years earlier. The court found that the PUB had that authority. In that case, the PUB noted that it did not at that time have enough information and wanted a trial period.

The court found there would be a windfall gain and unjust losses to customers unless there was a retroactive final rate-fixing. The court also found that the authority to make interim decisions would be meaningless if it implied only the authority to issue a decision to be made final later.

See also the decision in *Re Eurocan Pulp and Paper Co. and British Columbia Energy Commission*[379] referred to by Justice Estey without distinction in the *Nova* decision where the British Columbia Court of Appeal approved the fixing retroactively of rates.

12.23(i) Interim Rate Approvals: The Bell Decision

In addition to the "deferral account" and the "negative disallowance scheme" discussed above, the ability to act retrospectively may also be found as implied in the authority to make interim rate orders. The authority of the CRTC to make a order having retrospective effect in order to adjust for an earlier interim order was challenged in *Bell Canada v. Canadian Radio-Television and Telecommunications Commission.*[380]

The Commission's authority to deal with rates was a "positive approval scheme" found in s. 335(1) of the Railway Act, R.S.C. 1985, c. R-3:

> 335.(1) Notwithstanding anything in any other Act, all telegraph and telephone tolls to be charged by a company . . . are subject to the approval of the Commission and may be reviewed from time to time.

In approving such rates the Commission was directed, by s. 340(1) of the Railway Act to ensure that "All tolls shall be just and reasonable. . . .".

The Commission also had the authority to make interim orders pursuant to s. 60(2) of the National Transportation Act, R.S.C. 1985, c. N-20:

> 60.(2) The Commission may, instead of making an order final in the first instance, make an interim order and reserve further directions either for an adjourned hearing of the matter or for further application.

---

378 *Coseka Resources Ltd. v. Saratoga Processing Co.* (1981), 16 Alta. L.R. (2d) 60, 126 D.L.R. (3d) 705, 31 A.R. 541. Leave to appeal to S.C.C. refused (1981), 40 N.R. 172, 34 A.R. 360 (S.C.C.). The Supreme Court of Canada expressly approved *Coseka Resources* in *Bell Canada v. Canadian Radio-Television Telecommunications Commission*, supra, note 32.

379 *Re Eurocan Pulp and Paper Co. and B.C. Energy Commn.* (1978), 87 D.L.R. (3d) 727 (B.C. C.A.).

380 Supra note 372.

In March 1984 Bell Canada applied to the CRTC for a general rate increase in its telephone rates. Rather than applying under the standard full inquiry procedures Bell made a special application under the summary process of the Commission's rules. It claimed that the extraordinary Canadian government's restraint program then in force restricting rate increases of federally regulated utilities to 5 and 6% provided sufficient justification to dispense with the normal procedure for general rate increases. (Presumably Bell argued that as it was likely to justify more than 5 or 6% the Commission could approve that lesser rate ceiling without carrying out the same degree of scrutiny it would ordinarily apply in approving rates.) The Commission, however, rejected this application and held that Bell had to apply under the normal procedure. The Commission went on to say that if Bell were to suffer financial prejudice as a result of the delays involved in preparing for the more complex procedure it could always apply for interim relief pending the hearing and a decision on the merits.

Subsequently, in September 1984 Bell applied for a general rate increase which would come into effect on January 1, 1986. This increase would be based on 1985 financial data. It also applied for an interim rate increase of 3.6%.

The Commission's policy with respect to rate increases was that they should only be granted following a full public process but that where special circumstances could be demonstrated, such as lengthy delays in dealing with an application that could result in a serious deterioration in the financial condition of an applicant, an interim increase could be granted. Bell argued that this was the situation in its case and on this basis the Commission granted it an interim rate increase of 2% in order to allow Bell to prepare for a hearing to be held in the fall of 1985 at which time the Commission would determine the final order which might be justified by looking at two test years 1985 and 1986. The Commission expressly calculated the 2% interim figure on the assumption that Bell's return on equity for 1985 should be 13.7% using that figure and further expressly stated that this would be subject to review in the final decision.

Before the full hearings commenced Bell's financial position improved substantially. This considerably diminished its desire for an early hearing. It asked the Commission to delay the full hearing until early 1986. In the meantime, it suggested, the 2% interim rate should be given final approval. The Commission permitted the postponement of the hearing but refused to make the interim order final. Further, it announced that it would monitor Bell's finances closely and required monthly statements to be filed with it in order to determine if any further rate action might be necessary. On the basis of these filings the Commission was alerted to Bell's improved financial situation and asked the company to provide reasons why it was necessary to continue the interim increase. After hearing from Bell the Commission determined that the interim increase was no longer necessary. In fact Bell's return on equity, which the interim increase was expected to maintain at 13.7%, had grown to 14.5%. Bell was ordered to return to its pre-interim increase rates. This was still pending the Commission's full review of the original 1984 application. Thus, even though these new lower rates were the same as the rates in effect prior to Bell's initial 1984 application they remained interim in nature.

Perhaps seeing the writing on the wall, Bell decided not to proceed further with its application for the general rate increase and sought to withdraw its application. The Commission refused to permit this and decided to conduct a review of the company's finances for the years 1985, 1986 and 1987 in the scheduled 1986 hearing.

In the final review in 1986 the Commission determined appropriate profit levels for Bell. In light of the greater financial detail now available to it the Commission calculated that a reasonable return on equity for 1985 was 13.75% and 13.25% for 1986. It then calculated the amount of excess revenue Bell had earned over this level in those two years ($206 million) by reason of the interim rate approvals. The Commission determined that Bell could not retain this excess revenue. It ordered Bell to repay the excess to its customers by a one time credit. Bell challenged the authority of the Commission to make this order and succeeded, in a split decision, before the Federal Court of Appeal. The majority of the court, Justices Marceau and Pratt, found against the Commission for separate reasons which concurred in the result. Mr. Justice Marceau held that the Commission had no statutory authority to deal with excess revenues of deficiencies in revenues arising as a result of a discrepancy between the rate of return yielded from the interim rates. In his opinion the relevant statutes made no mention of any retroactive powers and that the presumption against retroactivity therefore argued against any such power in the Commission. That power was not, in his opinion, implicit in the power to make interim decisions. Mr. Justice Pratt found that the order in question was not retroactive in nature since its effect was to force Bell to grant a credit in the future rather than change the rates charged in the past in a retroactive manner. However, in his opinion the only source for the power claimed by the Commission was its authority in section 60(2) of the National Transportation Act to reserve "further directions" respecting interim orders. However, he felt that any "further directions" which the Commission wished to make respecting an interim order had to be in the nature of an order which could be made initially under section 60(2). As section 60(2) did not authorize the making of one-time credit orders no "further direction" to that effect could be made.

The majority decision of the Federal Court of Appeal did not mention the *Northwestern Utilities* case, supra, or the *Dow* case, supra. The court also distinguished the *Nova* and *Coseka* decisions, supra.

With respect, the majority decision is hard to rationalize.

(1)   It fails to follow law which has been honoured for 25 years in Canada.

(2)   It wrongly distinguished several cases that are directly on point;

(3)   It failed to accept principles of regulation which have been in place across the continent for decades; and

(4)   It legislated a meaning to the power to grant interim orders that is, in my view, unsustainable.

The court's decision clearly demonstrates to me at least that it did not understand the basis of just and reasonable rates. (I think in addition the case was founded both in presentation and argument.)

The decision of Mr. Justice Hugessen in dissent is, in my opinion, the correct decision for the reasons set forth therein.

(1)   It is Bell who would get the windfall and it was Bell who caused the delay.

(2)   The CRTC at all times made it clear that the interim decision meant just that and that it might make a retroactive adjustment if the facts warranted;

(3)   An interim order imports, the authority to change the decision if there is sufficient reason to do so. For years regulators have been forced to make use of interim orders as costs have fluctuated quickly.

(4)   Surely, if we are truly living in an age of curial deference or administrative discretion, it would not have taken much imagination to have sided with the CRTC in protecting millions of Bell users rather than supporting the unjust enrichment of a number of Bell shareholders.

The last three of the above points were specifically noted by the Supreme Court of Canada in its subsequent reversal of the Federal Court of Appeal.

The Supreme Court held that although the one-time credit order was not retroactive in nature (because it did not purport to go back to 1985 and change the rates chargeable at that time) it was retrospective because its purpose was to remedy the imposition of rates approved in the past but found in the final analysis to be excessive. In other words the order was retrospective because it purported to give new consequences to a past event. In 1985 the rates charged were just and reasonable but as of the time of the Commission's new order in 1986 those rates were now unreasonable and monies collected had to be returned. (The subtle distinction here between retroactive and retrospective is that if the order had been retroactive the rates would have been declared to have been unreasonable as of 1985 when they were first charged.)

Before the Supreme Court Bell argued, as it had in the Federal Court of Appeal, that there was no authority in the Commission to make the one-time credit order. That its statutory authority was only to make prospective orders. In the absence of statutory ability, the Commission had no power to make retrospective orders. It argued that all rates, by reason of their approval by the Commission are presumed to be just and reasonable until they are modified by a subsequent order. The Commission had no authority to go back and alter a rate it had already approved. Its only authority respecting the interim rates was to change them for the future once it determined the proper rate at the final hearing. The Supreme Court, approving of the approach followed by the dissenting Justice Hugessen in the Federal Court of Appeal, rejected this argument noting that, given the ongoing rate regulation task of the Commission, all rate orders were "for the time being". All rate approvals were subject to adjustment in the future in order to reflect changing economic conditions. Thus, if the only adjustment which could be made respecting interim rate orders were to adjust the rates ordered up or down for the future it would be impossible to distinguish interim from final orders.

The Court found that in statutory scheme created by the Railway and National Transportation Acts one of the differences between interim and final decisions must be that interim decisions may be reviewed and modified in a retrospective manner by a final decision.

True, neither statute expressly gave the Commission this power. However, (at page 52 N.R.) the Court held that "The powers of any administrative tribunal must of course be stated in its enabling statute but they may also exist by necessary implication from the wording of the Act, its structure and its purpose. Although courts must refrain from unduly broadening the powers of such regulatory authorities through judicial lawmaking, they must also avoid sterilizing these powers through overly technical interpretations of enabling statutes."

In the case of rate regulation under the Railway and National Transportation Acts the Commission's authority to make a retrospective order came from the interim nature of the decisions under review. The Court reasoned that interim decisions were not final decisions and carried with them different consequences. It noted that the basis for the Commission's making the interim decision was quite different from the basis on which it would make a final decision. The interim rate increase had been awarded simply to relieve Bell from the deleterious effects caused by the length of the proceedings, in an expeditious manner, and on the basis of evidence which would have been insufficient for the purposes of the final decision. In its opinion the essential characteristics of an interim order was that it made no decision on the merits of the issues to be decided in the final decision and was intended to provide relief against the deleterious effects of the duration of the proceedings. In the case of the Commission, the power to make interim orders effectively implied the power to make orders effective from the date of the beginning of the proceedings. In turn, this power must comprise the power to make appropriate orders for the purpose of remedying any discrepancy between the rate of return yielded by the interim rates and the rate of return allowed in the final decision for the period during which they are in effect so as to achieve just and reasonable rates throughout that period.

Finally, Bell argued that the one-time credit ordered by the Commission would not necessarily benefit the customers who were actually billed excessive rates. On this point the Supreme Court felt that it owed curial deference to the decision of the Commission even though this was an *appeal* from that decision. The Court held that on appeals it was not appropriate to adopt the "reasonableness'' standard appropriate on judicial reviews of decisions protected by a privative clause. Nonetheless, the Court stated (at p. 40 N.R.) that ''within the context of a statutory appeal from an administrative tribunal, additional consideration must be given to the principle of specialization of duties . . . curial deference should be given to the opinion of the lower tribunal on issues which fall squarely within its area of expertise.'' The Court (at p. 60 N.R.) acknowledged the Commission's admission that the use of a one-time credit is not the perfect way of reimbursing excess revenues. ''However, in view of the cost and the complexity of finding who actually paid excessive rates, where these persons reside and of quantifying the amount of excessive payments made by each, and having regard to the appellant's broad jurisdiction in weighing the many factors involved in apportioning respondent's revenue requirement amongst its several classes of customers to determine just and reasonable rates, the appellant's decision was eminently reasonable . . . and should not be overturned.''

Thus, in the *Bell* decision, the Supreme Court corrected the faulty approach of the Federal Court of Appeal and affirmed the principle that in regulatory matters, depending on the particular statutory scheme, even in the absence of an express grant of authority, the power to approve interim rates pending final decisions, carries with it the implicit authority to retrospectively adjust for excesses (and likely shortages) in revenue collected pursuant to such interim approval notwithstanding that this may result in the making of a retrospective order.

12.24 PROSECUTIONS

Some legislation provides that before an event can take place, an order or certificate shall first be obtained from a tribunal or some other condition met. This provision in itself is not enforceable unless there is an offence provision in the legislation.

All agencies should review their legislation in terms of the adequacy of the enforcement and prosecution provisions. Most are lamentably inadequate. (Full of sound and fury but signifying nothing.)

Most prosecution sections require approval of a minister through which the tribunal reports. Some prosecutions proceed through the Attorney General. Once approved, if that is required, a prosecution proceeds in the normal fashion on behalf of the tribunal.

12.25 VIEWS

A ''view'' is when a decision-maker attends at some site outside the hearing room to note the physical and geographic conditions there. Views can be conducted for two purposes:

i. to better understand the evidence which has been given (eg. to better understand the description given by a witness of the site); or

ii. to gather evidence by the decision-maker's own observation.

The case law is somewhat divided on the propriety of the second purpose. Some cases hold that a view may only be used for the first purpose, to better understand the evidence which has been given, unless express (or "abundantly clear") legislative authority has been given for the second purpose. Some cases hold that a view may be used for both (without express authority). The Manitoba and Alberta courts hold to the wider view,[381] the Saskatchewan courts to the narrower one.[382] The Ontario Court of Appeal originally took the narrower position in its 1948 decision in *MacDonald v. Goderich (Town)*[383] Subsequently, in 1964 that view was rejected by the Court in favour of the broader view in its decision in *Allen v. Caledonia (Town)*[384] in which the Court noted that the earlier decision in *Goderich* had both relied on case law from England which had subsequently been displaced by later, more liberal decisions and had failed to note earlier decisions of the Supreme Court of Canada in favour of the broad view (*Calgary & Edmonton Railway Co. v. MacKinnon* (1910), 43 S.C.R. 379, *Toronto Suburban Railway Co. v. Everson* (1917), 34 D.L.R. 421, 54 S.C.R. 395). However, in the 1971 decision of *Phillips v. Ford Motor Co. of Canada Ltd.*,[385] the narrower view is again espoused (albeit in obiter). *Phillips* makes no mention of *Allen v. Caledonia (Town)* or the cases cited there. At the federal level, the Federal Court Trial Division in *Teneycke v. Matsqui Institution Disciplinary Court* (1990), 33 F.T.R. 181 has espoused the narrower view. In that case Mr. Justice Addy laid out what he considered to be the law with respect to views:

1)   In the absence of specific statutory provisions authorizing a view, views may only be conducted for the very restricted purpose of allowing the tribunal to better understand the evidence and never for the purpose of gathering evidence by the tribunal, except on the consent of the parties.

2)   Unless the right is waived, all parties must be present whenever a view is taken.

3)   In no event is a person presiding either at a trial or an administrative board

---

381 *G & J Parking Lot Maintenance Ltd. v. Oland Construction Co.* (1978), 16 A.R. 293 (S.C.) (which cites in support the earlier decision *Clarke v. Edmonton (City)* (1928), 2 D.L.R. 154 (Alta. C.A.), reversed on other grounds [1930] S.C.R. 137), *Meyers v. Manitoba* (1960), 26 D.L.R. (2d) 550 (Man. C.A.).

382 *Saskatchewan (Department of Labour) v. University of Regina* (1975), 62 D.L.R. (3d) 717 (Sask. Q.B.), *Sunnyside Nursing Home v. Builders Contract Management Ltd.* (1985), 40 Sask. R. 1 (Sask. Q.B.).

383 [1948] 1 D.L.R. 11, [1947] O.R. 908 (C.A.).

384 (1964), 48 D.L.R. (2d) 193 (Ont. C.A.).

385 [1971] 2 O.R. 637 (C.A.).

or tribunal charged with a decision-making responsibility involving the rights of others, entitled to actively gather evidence or to decide matters on the basis of his own observation of material facts which have not been established in evidence. One cannot be a judge, and a witness in the same cause.

There appear to be two primary concerns underlying the restricted concept of views. First, the difficulty which a party has in contesting an observation made by a decision-maker on a view. This is the concern summed up in the "cannot be a judge and a witness" in the same matter problem. To the degree that evidence rests on the physical perception of the decision-maker, a participant contesting that evidence is placed either in the position of being unable to cross-examine or test the evidence at all or of being in the uncomfortable (and likely hopeless) position of questioning the observations of the decision-maker. The second reason that I am aware of having been advanced against the broader purpose of views was that noted by the Sask. Court of Queen's Bench in *Sunnyside Nursing Home v. Builders Contract Management Ltd.*[386] (in the context of a view by a judge): "In a complex case, what is seen may be unclear, ambiguous and puzzling. Moreover, in a complex case, what is seen may be so much outside the ken of other than experts, as to be, or provide a danger of being, misleading and dangerous in the context of a judge taking into consideration his own observations."

On the other hand, the difficulty with the narrower perspective is that one cannot help but see things on a view. It is not logical, particularly in light of the wider role played in their proceedings by administrative decision-makers, for a decision-maker who is on a view, not to be able to take into account some matter which he observes and which is material and relevant to the proceeding simply because the participants, inadvertently or purposely, fail to draw to his attention.

Practice

1. Views can be time consuming and disruptive. As a general rule they should be avoided unless there is a real purpose to be served by them.

2. A participant requesting the conduct of a view should give the agency and the other participants advance notice of the request. This will assist the agency to ensure that there is sufficient time and opportunity to carry out the view if necessary, and avoid surprise on the part of the other participants and thus permit them to fairly address the request.

3. Participants requesting a view should be prepared to explain what is hoped to be gained by it. Conversely, participants opposing a request should be prepared to explain their opposition.

4. As to the use of a view, in my opinion, agencies would be best to guide

---

386 (1985), 40 Sask. R. 1 (Q.B.), reversed [1989] 3 W.W.R. 721 (C.A.), amended [1990] 5 W.W.R. 289 (C.A.).

themselves by the following principles (which are closely patterned on those enunciated by Justice Addy in *Teneycke*).

i.   Unless authorized by legislation, views should not be conducted without the consent of the parties and in their presence (unless waived). While an agency may question parties at a hearing, it cannot investigate matters on its own in the absence of legislative authority. The broader purpose of views appears to be a form of investigation and thus should not be undertaken without due authority.

      Even when authorized by legislation, views should be conducted in the presence of the participants or be conducted as investigations by staff who subsequently provide their observations (as witnesses, subject to the same testing as other witnesses) at the hearing. This is to avoid the appearance of a decision-maker attempting to "make the case" for one side or the other in doing solitary views. A solitary view also puts the decision-maker much more into a position of being a witness in his own hearing as he must recount his observations to the parties subsequently at the hearing where it is more difficult for them to address concerns raised than it would be if those concerns were drawn to their attention immediately on side.

ii.   When a decision-maker on a view observes some matter which he feels is material and relevant, but which the participants have not referred to, he should point this out at that time to allow the parties an adequate opportunity to explain or otherwise deal with the matter noted. If the parties chose to invite a decision-maker out to a site for their purposes they should have to take what arises from that visit. Just as a party cannot ask a decision-maker not to note the demeanour or evidence given by witnesses at a hearing unless they draw his attention to it, they should not be surprised that a decision-maker may observe something on a view which they did not intend or expect him to see. However, fairness, I think, should require that the decision-maker draw whatever this may be to the attention of the parties so that any concerns the decision-maker may have can be addressed.

iii. Observations not drawn to the attention of the parties at the time because they were not considered material or relevant but which become so subsequently in light of other evidence, should be drawn to the attention of the participants and an opportunity should be given to address them.

5.   If a view is to be taken, the decision-maker should simply adjourn to meet the participants at the chosen site at an agreed time. Where there is more than one participant, a decision-maker should not be taken by only one of the participants to the site. He should travel alone (or with staff) or with ALL of the parties (unless the parties consent otherwise).

6. If there is only one participant in a proceeding, a decision-maker should be accompanied by a member of staff on a view. In order to avoid possible problems in the future, a decision-maker should not be placed in a position of being alone with a party out of office.

7. Views of outdoor sites can be noisy and disorganized. It may be difficult for all the participants to hear all of the comments of the others. Thus, views should be restricted as much as possible to observations, and explanations as to what it is that a decision-maker is seeing, while leaving argument for the reconvened hearing.

12.26 RIGHT TO MAKE ARGUMENT

12.26(a) Common Law

Given that the audi alteram partem rule requires tribunals to provide parties with an adequate opportunity to present their case, it is obvious that tribunals caught by this rule must provide some mechanism to parties to offer proofs and arguments in support of the positions being maintained. In *R. v. Deputy Industrial Injuries Commissioner*[387], for instance, Diplock L.J. listed this obligation among the procedural requirements which he considered binding upon tribunals obliged to provide hearings. He stated that in this situation a tribunal must permit each person represented to address arguments to it on the whole of the case. In *Mayes v. Mayes*[388] a tribunal's refusal to allow a party to address it on the law and facts of the case resulted in a quashing of its decision as contrary to the rules of natural justice.

Of course, as there is nothing at common law necessarily obliging a tribunal to conduct oral hearings, the obligation to provide this right may be satisfied through the vehicle of written submissions. Furthermore, even in the context of oral hearings, there does not seem to be any one procedure pursuant to which the right to present arguments must be exercised. This is consistent with the general rule that a tribunal is empowered to determine its own procedure. Thus, there does not appear to be anything which requires tribunals to permit the presentation of argument in the presence of opposing counsel, assuming legal representation is allowed, or at the end of the proceedings, although this is probably the most efficient and convenient manner in which to proceed.

12.26(b) Administrative Procedures Act

Section 4 of Alberta's Administrative Procedures Act requires that before an authority (to which the statute applies), in the exercise of a statutory power,

---

387 [1965] 1 Q.B. 456 (C.A.).
388 [1971] 1 W.L.R. 679, cited in de Smith, supra, p. 212.

refuses an application or makes a decision or order adversely affecting the rights of a party, the authority shall give the party an adequate opportunity of making representations by way of argument to the authority. Thus, the duty imposed here is only to provide an opportunity to make argument when a negative decision is being considered. The statute does not appear to restrict the right of argument to oral proceedings only (which is sensible insofar as argument can sometimes be adequately conveyed in writing). This seems clear by virtue of section 6 (a) of the Act: "Where by this Act a party is entitled to make representations to an authority with respect to the exercise of a statutory power, the authority is not by this Act required to afford an opportunity to the party (a) to make oral representations . . . if the authority affords the party an opportunity to make representations adequately in writing, but nothing in this Act deprives a party of a right conferred by any other Act to make oral representations." It appears to me that the purpose of section 6 is simply to make it clear that that statute's imposition of a right to make argument does not require an agency to hold oral proceedings. It is doubtful that the section would operate to remove a right to an oral hearing where required by natural justice or fairness. In *Innisfil (Township) v. Vespra (Township)*[389] the Supreme Court of Canada stated that express words were required to remove a right required by natural justice. The wording of section 6 in the Alberta statute does not appear to me to be aimed at removing the right to oral proceedings where that right would be required by natural justice. Rather, it appears to be directed to clarifying the extent of the right granted *by the statute itself* and making it clear that section 6 was not intended to remove rights granted by other statutes.

The Ontario Statutory Powers Procedure Act (the "SPPA") establishes a procedural code for Ontario tribunals exercising a "statutory power of decision" conferred by or under an Act of the Ontario Legislature, where these tribunals are required, by statute or otherwise by law, to hold or to afford to the parties in proceedings before them an opportunity for a "hearing", before rendering a decision: see section 3. "Statutory power of decision" is defined in section 1 of the SPPA to mean ". . . a power or right, conferred by or under a statute, to make a decision deciding or prescribing,

(a)　the legal rights, powers, privileges, immunities, duties or liabilities of any person or party, or

(b)　the eligibility of any person or party to receive, or to the continuation of, a benefit or licence, whether the person is legally entitled thereto or not;"

Among the minimum procedural requirements imposed by the SPPA upon agencies falling within its purview is the obligation to provide parties with the right to present submissions. Specifically, section 10.1 of the Act provides in pertinent part as follows:

---

389 [1981] 2 S.C.R. 145, 123 D.L.R. (3d) 530, 37 N.R. 43.

10.1 A party to a proceeding may, at an oral or electronic hearing,

(a) call and examine witnesses and present evidence and submissions. . . .

Interesting enough, the statute, while recognizing the idea of written hearings, does not grant an express right to make argument in those proceedings. (I am not aware of any rule that says that argument or submissions can only be oral.) Nor does it bar that right. This appears to be an oversight of the drafters resulting from the 1994 amendments to the statute. In any event, as noted at the opening of this chapter, the common law rules of natural justice, and fairness will supplement the omissions of the SPPA unless it appears clear that they are not to do so. Insofar as argument has been recognized as an element of natural justice the failure of the SPPA to mention it in the context of written hearings likely does not mean that there is no such right in that form of hearing.

The SPPA does not elaborate as to how the right to make submissions should be exercised. Once again, it appears that this is left largely to the discretion of the agency itself. D.W. Mundell, Q.C., in his *Manual of Practice of Administrative Law and Procedure in Ontario*, states (at page 15) that it is most appropriate for arguments to be presented after all the evidence has been taken.

12.26(c) The Federal Court Act

There is, as yet, no federal counterpart to Alberta's or Ontario's general procedures statutes imposing minimum procedural requirements on federal tribunals. Thus, to the extent that there is a right to make argument before federal agencies, that right must be found in either the statute under which the matter in question is brought or in the common law. It should be noted, however, that the Law Reform Commission of Canada in its working paper *Independent Administrative Agencies* recommended that Parliament enact general legislation setting out minimum procedural safeguards which would be applicable to all independent federal administrative agencies. These would also serve as guidelines for tribunals in developing more elaborate rules of procedure for themselves.[390]

In May 1995 the Federal Department of Justice released a proposal for a broad and detailed Administrative Hearings Powers and Procedures Act. That proposal suggests that a party before agencies subject to the statute would have the right to call, and ask question of, witnesses, and present evidence, arguments and other submissions at an oral hearing. At time of writing (September 1995) the proposal was still undergoing public consultation. The entire proposal is set out later in chapter 38 of this text.

---

390 Working Paper, 25, 1980. See, e.g., p. 70.

12.27 RIGHT TO LEGAL COUNSEL AND OTHER REPRESENTATION

12.27(a) Common Law

12.27(a)(i) State of the Law

There is no absolute right to counsel at common law. However, as has been said earlier, the principles of natural justice and fairness require that an adequate opportunity be given for an affected individual to state his case and to know the case he has to meet. The degree to which ''an adequate opportunity'' will demand the recognition of a right to counsel will depend on the circumstances, including the scheme of the process in question. The right to counsel is a recognition that the nervous, inarticulate, uneducated or unfamiliar individual may require someone to speak or argue for him; that detailed and complex processes require individuals who are skilled in process and procedure to adequately represent a case; and that, when very serious matters are at stake an individual is entitled to skilled and expert assistance in the defence of his interests.

Thurlow C.J. once explained the right to counsel as follows:

> [W]hether or not the person has a right to representation by counsel will depend on the circumstances of the particular case, its nature, its gravity, its complexity and the capacity of the inmate to understand the case and present his defence. The list is not exhaustive. And from this, it seems to me, it follows that whether or not an inmate's request for representation by counsel can lawfully be refused is not properly referred to as a matter of discretion but is a matter of right where the circumstances are such that the opportunity to present the case adequately calls for representation by counsel. It may be that where the circumstances do not point to that conclusion a residual authority to permit counsel nevertheless is exercisable by the appropriate officials. . . .[391]

12.27(a)(ii) Where No Right To Counsel Found

There are many cases in which the circumstances were such that an individual was not found to have a right to counsel. For example, in *Dehghani v. Minister*

---

391 *Howard v. Stony Mountain Institute Inmate Disciplinary Court (Presiding Officer)* (1985), 45 C.R. (3d) 242, 57 N.R. 280 (Fed. C.A.), appeal quashed [1987] 2 S.C.R. 687 as being moot. In *Howard* the Court found that even s. 7 of the Charter does not create any absolute right to counsel. The right was still to be determined by the circumstances. The quotation noted in the main text was noted with approval in *Cramm v. Royal Canadian Mounted Police Commissioner* (1987), 80 N.R. 63 (Fed. C.A.). To the same effect see *Clark v. United Association of Journeymen and Apprentices of the Plumbing and Pipefitting Industry of the United States and Canada , Local 213* (1988), 89 N.B. R (2d) 426, 226 A.P.R. 426 (C.A.), leave to appeal to S.C.C. refused (1989), 91 N.B.R. (2d) 90, 232 A.P.R. 90 (note) (S.C.C.) *Irvine v. Canada (Restrictive Trade Practices Commission)*, [1987] 1 S.C.R. 181, 74 N.R. 33.

of Employment & Immigration[392] the Supreme Court of Canada found that a refugee claimant involved in the routine questioning of port of entry examination by immigration officials was not entitled to any right of counsel even though the claimant was under a statutory duty to answer questions and subject to criminal penalties for failure to answer or knowingly making a false or misleading statement. The Court felt that the fact that there was no expectation that people can freely cross international boundaries; that there was no stigma in being referred to this level of inquiry; and that the only consequences of a negative decision at this level was that there would be a full-scale formal inquiry where the claimant would have full representation rights was such that counsel was not required at this preliminary stage of the process. There has been found to be no right to counsel in the context of situations were authorities must act with speed or on an emergency basis and there is no time for counsel to be retained and properly instructed.[393] Where the issues are not complex such that the individual in question is felt perfectly capable of presenting his own cases, the right to counsel has also been dispensed with.[394]

12.27(a)(iii) Where Right to Counsel Found

However, a right to counsel has been found where there is a formal and somewhat complex procedure (particularly where the procedure is not unlike a court proceeding) where an agency is constituted to hear charges and receive evidence, where there is examination and cross-examination.[395] As I have noted

---

392 (1993), 101 D.L.R. (4th) 654 (S.C.C.).

393 *Latham v. Canada (Solicitor General)* (1984), 9 D.L.R. (4th) 393 (Fed. T.D.), *Williams v. Correctional Service of Canada* (1990), 38 F.T.R. 169, reversed [1993] 1 F.C. 710 (C.A.) on the grounds that there was no urgency.

394 *R. v. Board of Visitors* (1988), 115 N.R. 371 (H.L.) (prison disciplinary matter where there were no questions of law and individual was felt to be capable of presenting his own case), *Savard v. Morrison* (1986), 44 Alta. L.R. (2d) 353, 3 F.T.R. 1, *Walker v. Kingston Penitentiary Disciplinary Board* (1986), 52 C.R. (3d) 106, 3 F.T.R. 109. Most of these cases were considered, but not followed in *Tremblay v. Disciplinary Tribunal of Laval Institution* (1987), 25 Admin. L.R. 235 (Fed. T.D.) where the Court found that a prison inmate facing a disciplinary tribunal was entitled to counsel where serious penalties could flow from a conviction. The Court also considered the possible indirect penalties such as a later remission board taking the conviction into account to deny remission days. The Court also noted that it was possible that the legal issues of delay, double jeopardy, and autrefois acquit could be raised in the proceedings, and the individual would likely have had some difficulty in presenting his own case firstly because he was not a lawyer and secondly because his imprisonment would have left him with rather limited resources for communication and obtaining information. In *de la Sablonnière v. Sandhoff* (1993), 108 Saskatchewan R. 110 (Q.B.) the Sask. Court of Queen's Bench found that a party who was not represented by counsel, was not prejudiced by the fact that the other side was. The Court noted that the statute envisaged a forum where parties will often represent themselves.

395 See, for example, *Clark v. U.A., Local 213* (1988), 89 N.B.R. (2d) 426, 226 A.P.R. 426 (C.A.), leave to appeal refused 91989), 98 N.R. 280 (note) (S.C.C.). In *Joplin v. Vancouver (City) Chief Constable* (1982), 144 D.L.R. (3d) 285 (B.C. S.C.), affirmed (1985), 20 D.L.R. (4th) 314 (B.C.

several times in this text, the Courts take the position that proceedings involving very serious consequences for an individual require a high degree of fairness. In such cases there is a right to counsel.[396]

Readers should also be aware that, outside of the common law right to counsel embodied in section 7 of the Charter, section 10(b) of the Charter also protects the right to counsel on arrest or detention. Such arrest and detention can arise in the context of what would be considered administrative proceedings. See, for example, *R. v. Jacoy*[397] where the requirement by customs officials that an individual enter an interview room for interrogation was found to amount to a detention for the purposes of section 10.

12.27(a)(iv) Incompetent Counsel

As a general rule, the fact that one may have retained and been represented by an incompetent counsel does not, in itself, amount to a breach of natural justice or fairness. Justice Reed in *Williams v. Canada (Minister of Employment & Immigration)*[398] summed up the principle as follows:

> The general rule, in the courts, is that a client is considered to have authorized and be bound by the representations made on his or her behalf by counsel. The system cannot operate if this is not so. In my view, to grant a stay [of a deportation order] in circumstances where the only prejudice the applicant can demonstrate is that he may or may not have grounds for judicial review, but does not know because his former counsel did not properly prepare his case, would create an unworkable precedent. It is the professional accreditation bodies, such as the Law Society, not the courts, which have the mandate to regulate the professional performance of their members.

C.A.), Chief Justice McEachern stated that "a layman, even a policeman, cannot be expected properly to master the laws of evidence and criminal procedure in his own defence. It is powerful wisdom that a lawyer who acts for himself has a fool for a lawyer and a fool for a client." *Joplin* is a particularly interesting case as the Court found that a regulation which barred counsel at the type of proceeding in question was ultra vires. The Court held that Parliament, in granting the executive the authority to make regulations concerning the procedure of these proceedings, was deemed not to have intended to grant the power to make regulations that infringed natural justice.

396 In *Cramm v. Royal Canadian Mounted Police Commissioner* (1987), 80 N.R. 63 (Fed. C.A.) the Federal Court of Appeal looked at an internal disciplinary process where an individual could be found liable to pay damages in the hundreds of thousands of dollars. It stated that "Such serious potential results are visited upon the applicant by the recommendation of a board which had neither the benefit of advice as to the law of negligence from its own counsel or as a result of the cross-examination and submission by counsel for the person concerned, with knowledge of the law. Such a result is simply not fair''. See also *Joplin v. Vancouver (City) Chief Constable* (1982), 144 D.L.R. (3d) 285 (B.C.S.C.), affirmed (1985), 20 D.L.R. (4th) 314 (B.C.C.A.), *Howard v. Stony Mountain Institution Inmate Disciplinary Ct.* (1985), 45 C.R. (3d) 242, 57 N.R. 280 (Fed. C.A.), appeal quashed [1987] 2 S.C.R. 687 as being moot.

397 [1988] 2 S.C.R. 548.

398 (1994), 74 F.T.R. 34 (T.D.).

Nonetheless, the incompetence of a party's counsel can constitute grounds for review of a tribunal's decision on the basis of a breach of natural justice in *extreme* circumstances. In a situation where, through no fault of the applicant, the effect of counsel's misconduct is to completely deny the applicant the opportunity of a hearing, a reviewable breach of fundamental justice has occurred.[399]

Even in cases where it cannot be said that the effect of counsel's misconduct has been so egregious that there has been no hearing, where the incompetence or negligence of the counsel is sufficiently specific, and clearly supported by the evidence, such negligence or incompetence is inherently prejudicial to the applicant and will warrant overturning the tribunal's decision (notwithstanding the lack of bad faith or absence of a failure to do anything on the part of the tribunal). Such incompetence or negligence was found in *Shirwa v. Canada (Minister of Employment & Immigration)*[400] where an applicant for refugee status was misled by "counsel" to believe "counsel" was a lawyer, when in fact he was not, when the "counsel" put in no evidence at the hearing other than the personal information form respecting the applicant, when the "counsel" (as he personally had concluded that the applicant was not credible) failed to make further written representations (which he had undertook to make) respecting certain weakness in the applicant's case which were expressly drawn to his attention. (The Court also appeared to give some weight to the fact that there was no remedy which could be pursued before a Law Society as the "counsel" was not a licensed lawyer.)[401]

12.27(a)(v) Right to Counsel Not Absolute

Where there is a right to counsel, it is not absolute. An individual cannot insist that proceedings be suspended until a particular counsel is prepared and able to represent him. Also, an individual must be diligent in attempting to secure counsel.[402] There are cases where, after many adjournments had been given to permit counsel to be retained, it was found proper for a hearing to continue where

---

399 *Hathon v. Canada (Minister of Employment & Immigration)* (1988), 28 F.T.R. 217.

400 [1994] 2 F.C. 51, 22 Admin. L.R. (2d) 220, 23 Imm. L.R. (2d) 123, 71 F.T.R. 136.

401 Incompetent counsel was not found to be sufficient grounds for judicial intervention where a party fails to give any evidence of harm resulting from that incompetence. In *Sheikh v. Canada (Minister of Employment & Immigration)* (1990), 71 D.L.R. (4th) 604 (Fed. C.A.) a refuge claimant appearing before an Immigration adjudicator was burdened with a counsel who persistently fell asleep in the proceedings. The adjudicator was alert to the problem, however, and intervened regularly when necessary to either alert the counsel or to give an adjournment for counsel to gather his wits. The party failed to provide the Court on judicial review with any evidence as to harm resulting from the counsel's actions. The Court felt that the counsel's proclivity to sleep in the circumstances where there was no evidence of actual harm did not warrant intervention.

402 In the context of criminal proceedings, the Ontario Court of Appeal held in *R v. Richard* (1992), 55 O.A.C. 43 that the right to counsel cannot be used to dictate the date of trial so as to inconvenience other parties and prevent issues being dealt with fairly and efficiently.

the party did not appear to be seriously attempting to find a representative.[403] Nor can counsel expect an agency to shape its proceedings to his calendar. In *Gill Lumber Chipman (1973) Ltd. v. United Brotherhood of Carpenters & Joiners of America, Local Union 2142*[404] the New Brunswick Court of Appeal stated that:

> The Board must, of course, act fairly and give a reasonable opportunity to the parties to be present and to be represented by counsel if they so desire. On the other hand, counsel is not entitled to insist upon an adjournment merely to suit his own convenience and the Board must, in deciding whether to grant an adjournment or refuse it, take into consideration the reason for the request on the one hand and the right of other parties to have the matter dealt with expeditiously on the other.

12.27(b) Administrative Procedures Acts

Alberta's Administrative Procedures Act contains no express right for an individual to be represented by counsel. Nor does it expressly rule out that right. To the degree that the right to make argument or present evidence in section 4 is expressed in terms of the agency providing an "adequate opportunity" to do so, reference may be had to the common law in determining the extent to which it is necessary to have counsel in order for an opportunity to be adequate. Even then, however, section 6 appears to make it clear that *section 4* is not to be interpreted as requiring an adequate opportunity for any counsel to make representations *orally*, as long as an adequate opportunity is given for counsel to make representations in writing. As I stated earlier in the context of the right to argument, it is unlikely that the Administrative Procedures Act operates to oust the requirements of natural justice or fairness where counsel would be required under those principles given the absence of an express ousting of natural justice.

Section 10 of Ontario's Statutory Powers Procedure Act provides that *a party* to a proceeding may be represented by counsel *or agent*. Thus, the statute provides authority for individuals who are not licensed to practice law in Ontario to represent parties at hearings before Ontario agencies subject to the SPPA.

The SPPA, in section 11, also provides that a witness at an oral hearing or electronic hearing is entitled to be advised by counsel or an agent *as to his rights* but also states that such counsel or agent may take no other part in the hearing. Nor is the witness's counsel entitled to be present when an oral hearing is closed to the public except when the witness whom he represents is giving evidence.

---

403 See, for example, *Edumadze v. Canada (Minister of Employment & Immigration)* (1993), 59 F.T.R. 269.
404 (1973), 42 D.L.R. (3d) 271 (N.B.C.A.).

12.27(c) Practice

1. *Agency Attitude Towards Counsel*

Contrary to the views of some decision-makers, lawyers at a hearing are not by definition a hindrance and a burden. Properly instructed and competent counsel, the ones who win for their clients, do not bog down proceedings in endless debate on more or less irrelevant legal technical points. For the most part, in my opinion, competent counsel often facilitate the progress of a hearing. They help to ensure that the necessary evidence is gathered and properly ordered and presented logically to the hearing, are often most helpful in explaining the more difficult matters of law or policy to their clients, and aid in the presentation of ordered and logically convincing argument. It is often easier to convey the needs of the agency to experienced counsel who has appeared before it many times than to a nervous and unrepresented individual who is expected not only to be master of his own case but master of the policies and procedures which an agency has developed, sometimes over years of cases.

Lawyers are trained in the marshalling, testing and presentation of evidence and argument and such skills are often very useful in agency proceedings. The worst trap an agency member can fall into is the belief that he knows it all, that if he has not thought of it — it is not worth knowing. Perhaps surprising to some, in my experience counsel have often identified important points which had slipped by me, or come up with ideas that I had missed.

Do counsel make hearings longer? Who can say. Perhaps some hearings need to be longer. Remember the purpose of a hearing is to gather evidence and information. This includes argument. The presence of counsel is usually an insurance that all of a case will be examined, not simply that which appears most obvious or is most easily embraced by the current policies of an agency. Furthermore, trying to elicit all the relevant facts in any sort of ordered manner from the unrepresented, first appearance, individual who possess important information, and wants to convey it, but cannot identify exactly what is relevant and what is not, what is material and what is not, and when something should be put forward and when it cannot, can be time-consuming and exhausting as well. An agency faced with an unsophisticated and unrepresented individual may find itself having to take particular care to ensure that the individual is aware of his rights and is able to put his case forward. This dual role is not an easy one, particularly as one must be careful not to go over the line and appear to become the advocate of that individual's case.

Of course, there are difficult counsel. There are difficult agency members too. Perhaps the two deserve each other. For the most part, I have found counsel to be serious, concerned, knowledgeable and helpful individuals who have a job to do and who do it. Like any individual, counsel will react to circumstances and an ill-prepared, rude, or arrogant decision-maker may bring out the worst in less experienced counsel. (The more experienced counsel, of course, recognize that one catches more flies with honey.)

"Dealing with difficult counsel" is a popular seminar topic in the agency world. (The underlying premise sometimes seems to be that all counsel are "difficult". Like the silent "e" at the end of a word, we all know it is there, we just do not say it.) The "secret" to dealing with counsel (difficult or not) is in ourselves. Competence in the decision-making will bring out competence in the counsel. Properly structured and run hearings where the rules are known in advance and adhered to fairly (but not slavishly), where concerns of the parties are dealt with fairly and politely (and this does not mean fawningly or patronizingly) are the best way to deal with difficult counsel. It is a deeply set personal belief that many counsel, even the well meaning, do not understand the inherent differences between administrative and judicial proceedings. This lack of understanding often leads counsel to cast matters in terms of the judicial model with which he is most familiar. This can cause some delays, as the agency member must deal not only with the immediate suggestion of counsel, but more importantly with the underlying mind set. However, we are all, even counsel, capable of learning and we all, including the agency member, had to learn. Once the initial bump of "culture shock" is over, counsel, in my opinion, should be welcomed in most proceedings.

2. Dealing With The Truly Awful Counsel or Agent

Having said this, in some cases an agency will sometimes find itself faced with the truly awful legal counsel or agent, who displays such a complete lack of knowledge of the proceedings, basic courtesy, lack of control and common sense that the proceedings grind to a complete halt. In my opinion, the power of an agency over its own proceedings, which includes the power to control abuse of its process, extends to ordering such counsel off the proceedings.[405] In the case of legal counsel, consideration may also be given to complaining to the relevant law society. Contempt proceedings, either before the agency or the courts depending on whether the authority lies, is another option.[406]

3. Evidence From Counsel

Counsel are "officers of the court". They owe respect to the agency and a duty not to knowingly attempt to deceive it.[407] At the same time, I would not

---

405 In *Booth v. Ontario (Coroner) (sub nom. Booth v. Hunter)* (1994), 16 O.R. (3d) 528, *(sub nom. Donaldson Inquest, Re)* 111 D.L.R. (4th) 111, 69 O.A.C. 1 (Div. Ct.) the Ontario Divisional Court held that a coroner's power to control abuse of his process extended to ordering a counsel off the record where the counsel suffered from a conflict of interest.

406 For the law and practice respecting contempt see c. 29A of this text.

407 See, for example, Rule 10 of the Professional Conduct Handbook of the Law Society of Upper Canada which provides that counsel must treat the tribunal (which includes administrative

recommend the adoption of a practice whereby evidence is regularly tendered to the agency by counsel (rather than through someone who knows something about it). The most difficult aspect of such a practice is that it is a very effective tool for insulating the evidence from testing. Questions respecting the evidence will most often be met with the unfortunate response that counsel knows very little about it other than what he has said in presenting it. It also puts the counsel in the position of being a witness, and thus, technically, subject to all the procedures, such as cross-examination, applicable to witnesses. Does counsel really want his credibility to be up for comment in an administrative proceeding?

Minor, incidental or uncontentious items can quite properly be admitted through counsel, of course, but material evidence should be supported by individuals who know about it.

4. *The Team Approach*

On very technical or specialized matters counsel may wish to associate himself with an expert in the speciality area who may have a better grasp of the complexities of that topic. In this way, counsel will be responsible for the marshalling and presentation of evidence and argument and the associate expert will be responsible for identifying weaknesses in opposing evidence and guiding counsel through the technicalities.

5. *Legal Counsel or Other Agent?*

A party facing a choice between retaining legal counsel or a non-lawyer agent may wish to consider a number of factors.

i.   Cost. Before one assumes that lawyers cost more, inquire into the rates being levied by agents. Acting before administrative agencies is a booming business in some parts of the country and experienced and skilled agents who gets results often do not come cheap. Their fees can be comparable or greater than lawyers.

ii. What skills are you looking for. As a generality, lawyers are most valuable in legal interpretation and argument. Not all proceedings require these skills. Some proceedings turn principally on the facts. The law is well known and uncontentious. In such cases, knowing the area well such that the right evidence can be brought forward, organized in the right way may be more valuable than legal skills. Non-lawyer agents who specialize in one area may

---

agencies) with "candour, fairness, courtesy and respect" and provides, among other things, that counsel cannot knowingly attempt to deceive a tribunal by offering false evidence, misstating facts or law, or suppressing what ought to be disclosed. Nor can counsel knowingly misstate the contents of a document, the testimony of a witness, the substance of an argument or the provisions of a statute or like authority.

be the better choice here. Lawyers can specialize as well, of course, and may be as skilled in specific areas as well.

iii. Background training and skills. While not all lawyers are equal, and there are a number of duds out there, lawyers, at least, had to have undergone a training and testing period in the law before being called to the bar. Agents may not have had to do this. Although references and reputation are important in retaining lawyers and agents, it may be prudent to check more carefully into the abilities of non-lawyer agents.

iv. Differences resulting from legislative requirements. A lawyer could conceivably take one's case up through the administrative process and through to any final judicial proceedings. If one relies on an agent at a lower level of the proceeding one may have to switch for any reviews or appeals. Also, be aware that some legislation distinguishes between legal counsel and other agent. While both may be authorized to appear, the fact that the lawyer is subject to a governing council, and is considered to be an "officer of the court" often results in lawyers having a slight advantage in some schemes. Some regulatory processes, for example, will provide for disclosure of confidential information to legal counsel, but not to non-lawyer agents.

6. *Agency Authorizations*

Some legislative schemes require an agent who is not a lawyer to present proof that he acts as agent for an individual. In the absence of a legislative requirement some agencies adopt a similar policy through their power over their procedure. This may be a prudent course. I am aware of circumstances where parties who claimed to be acting on the part of others (as well as themselves) were in fact not doing so. Written agency authorization will avoid this problem. Lawyers, as "officers of the court" (and subject to profession discipline for misleading the agency) generally are not required to file such authorizations. While agency authorizations are generally required to be filed in advance, common sense dictates that an agent who has not come armed with such an authorization be permitted to participate on the direction that a proper authorization be filed by a specific date (failing which, in the absence of any extension by the agency, further participation will not be permitted, and any comments or argument made by the agent earlier will be disregarded).

In cases where large groups of individuals, including individuals grouped into loosely form ad hoc interest groups, are represented by counsel or agent it is prudent to have the agent or counsel be able to prove to the agency the names and addresses of those for whom they purport to act. This can be particularly important in the cases where technical standing rules will deny standing to unincorporated associations, or where orders for costs may be ordered against a party. In the latter case one must be able to identify who is required to pay the ordered costs.

12.28 CROSS-EXAMINATION

12.28(a) Common Law

At common law, there is no absolute obligation on agencies to allow cross-examination of witnesses in oral hearings or to allow cross-examination on the materials submitted or interlocutories when the hearing is conducted in writing.[408] The only right which the rules of procedural fairness guarantee to parties is the right to rebut opposing evidence and to correct or contradict prejudicial statements. If this can be achieved without recourse to cross-examination, then parties appearing before a tribunal are not entitled to it. The key is whether cross-examination is the only effective method open to a party to answer the case made against it.

As such, the availability of cross-examination as a matter of right, as with all other procedural requirements at common law, will largely depend upon the circumstances of the individual case and upon the nature of the particular tribunal involved. As Cory J. stated in *Tandy Electronics Ltd. v. United Steel Workers of America:*[409]

> The concept of natural justice is an elastic one, that can and should defy precise definition. The application of the principle must vary with the circumstances. How much or how little is encompassed by the term will depend on many factors; to name a few, the nature of the hearing, the nature of the tribunal presiding, the scope and effect of the ruling made.

> In some instances the denial of a right to cross-examine may well, in itself, constitute a denial of natural justice. In other situations a restricting or limiting of cross-examination on some aspect or topic could never offend the innate considerations of fairness which comprise the "natural justice" concept.

> . . . a denial of natural justice cannot be established in every case simply by demonstrating a refusal to permit cross-examination of a witness on one aspect of his testimony.[410]

One caveat must be added to my earlier statement that the extent to which cross-examination is required can be determined by the degree to which that procedure is the only *effective* method open to a party to answer the case against it. While it is logical, it is not necessarily correct, to assume that where one's case

---

408 *Four Star Management Ltd. v. British Columbia (Securities Commission)* (1990), 71 D.L.R (4th) 317 (B.C.C.A.), leave to appeal to S.C.C. refused (1991), 1 Admin. L.R. (2d) 264 (S.C.C.).

409 (1979), 26 O.R. (2d) 68, 102 D.L.R. (3) 126 at 132-133 (Div. Ct.).

410 Thus, the Supreme Court of Canada held that there was no right of cross-examination in a proceeding which was merely investigatory in nature and which could only give rise to a more formal inquiry where rights would actually be determined (*Irvine v. Canada (Restrictive Trade Practices Commission)* (1987), 41 D.L.R. (4th) 429 (S.C.C.)).

can be adequately presented by some means other than cross-examination, cross-examination will not be required by natural justice and fairness. In some instances where the proceedings in question are felt to have an extremely serious impact on an individual the courts, obviously, require that the proceedings be as fair as possible. To this one must add the gloss that the courts look upon *their* processes as being the *most* fair. Thus, in extremely serious proceedings one may simply have to assume that oral cross-examination may be required as of right, whether or not whatever is hoped to be achieved through the cross-examination can be adequately, or even better, accomplished in other ways.[411] In illustration of this point, see *MacInnis v. Canada (Attorney General)*.[412] That case dealt with parole proceedings for a person committed to prison for an indeterminate sentence. For such individuals the only hope of freedom is parole. Consequently, the Federal Court Trial Division held that, in light of such serious consequences, the National Parole Board had to grant the individual the right to orally cross-examine experts who had presented, in writing, conflicting expert testimony to the Board. The Court does not appear to have even considered whether oral cross-examination was the best method to test conflicts between expert views on technical issues. The decision is under appeal.

Accordingly, the closer a tribunal's procedures follow that of a court, the more likely it will be that refusal to permit cross-examination of a witness will constitute a breach of procedural fairness. As de Smith states in *Judicial Review of Administrative Action*, seldom can such a refusal be justified if a witness has testified orally and the party requests leave to confront and cross-examine him.''[413]

In *Innisfil (Township) v. Vespra (Township),*[414] for instance, the Supreme Court pointed to the similarities between Ontario Municipal Board hearings and court proceedings as one reason for holding that the board was obliged to permit cross-examination of witnesses tendering evidence thereat. Estey J., delivering the judgment of the court, stated that where a board determines ''the rights of the contending parties before it on the traditional basis wherein the onus falls upon the contender to introduce the facts and submissions upon which he will rely'', provision of a right to cross-examination is obligatory, unless there is the ''clearest statutory curtailment'' of this right.

---

411 Thus, in *Singh v. Canada (Minister of Employment & Immigration)*, [1985] 1 S.C.R. 177, in the context of determining the right to an oral hearing, Justice Beetz, writing for half the court, felt that ''The most important factors in determining the procedural content of fundamental justice in a given case are the nature of the legal rights at issue and the severity of the consequences to the individuals concerned.'' Justice Wilson, writing for the other half, appeared to accept, at least for the sake of argument, that in appropriate circumstances written proceedings may be an adequate substitute for an oral hearing even when matters of death, physical liberty and physical punishment are involved. However, this was a reluctant concession as she felt that on the surface matters of such fundamental importance would invariably require an oral hearing.

412 [1995] 2 F.C. 215 (T.D.).

413 4th ed. J.N. Evans ed. at p. 214.

414 [1981] 2 S.C.R. 145, 15 M.P.L.R. 250, 123 D.L.R. (3d) 530, 37 N.R. 43, 12 O.M.B.R. 129.

Courts will be particularly insistent that cross-examination be permitted when issues of credibility and veracity are at stake. In *Willette v. Royal Canadian Mounted Police (Commissioner)*,[415] for instance, it was held that the RCMP's Discharge and Demotion Board breached the rules of natural justice when it refused to make adverse witnesses available for cross-examination. The Federal Court of Appeal stated that while the attendance of adverse witnesses for the purposes of cross-examination is not always a requirement of the rules of natural justice, the conflicts of testimony and the issues of witnesses' credibility in this case made oral testimony and an opportunity for cross-examination of the witnesses an essential component of a fair hearing.

Reid and David, in *Administrative Law and Practice* submit that cross-examination should be permitted by administrative tribunals whenever a person's rights, reputation or status are, or are likely to be, in jeopardy. They add that cross-examination is particularly important when vital facts are contested. In this regard, they dismiss the concern that lawyers might exploit expanded opportunities to cross-examine "to indulge in an orgy of cross-examination" thereby interfering with the tribunal's proceedings. It is their view that a properly instructed tribunal is perfectly capable of imposing reasonable restraints on the availability of cross-examination. This to them is preferable to denying the right to cross-examination altogether.[416]

Some agencies are reluctant to allow strong cross-examination of a witness. There is a feeling that aggressive cross-examination is somehow improper and the agency will interpose itself, either by requiring cross-examination to be directed through the agency or by the agency interjects to restricting the cross-examination when the agency feels that it is becoming overly heated. The Society of Ontario Adjudicators and Regulators has published a pamphlet entitled *Principles of Administrative Justice: A Proposal* (June 1995). In the commentary on page 13 appears the statement "[Adjudicators] should consider the atmosphere of the hearing room and general comfort, and minimize use of legal or technical language. They should control excessive adversarial techniques of lawyers or agents, e.g. unnecessarily aggressive cross-examination." With respect, this statement is probably too broad insofar as it fails to take into account the variety of forums in which cross-examination may take place. Under some mandates most of the material being put forward to the agency will be opinion evidence. In such cases, as the pamphlet suggests, there may be little or no purpose to cross-examination and a more restrained level may be appropriate. However, in some proceedings where the honesty and credibility of the witness is in question and the evidence is something capable of direct observation (i.e. more of an adjudicative than legislative fact) it may be appropriate to allow cross-examination in its broadest, most destructive aspect. Ultimately, the purpose of cross-examination

---

415 (1984), 10 Admin. L.R. 149, 56 N.R. 161 (Fed. C.A.).
416 *Administrative Law and Practice*, 2d ed., (Butterworths 1978) pp. 81-82.

is to test the evidence. In some cases that testing may involve a rough ride for the witness. However, where such an examination can be fruitful and the interests at stake are serious it may be a denial of a fair hearing to the person who is adversely affected by the testimony not to allow that testimony to be subject to full and rigorous testing.

One further point should be noted. Notwithstanding all the arguments over whether cross-examination is required at common law, it is arguable that much of its overall effectiveness may be vitiated by the ability of administrative agencies to admit hearsay evidence. Indeed, in *Girvin v. Consumers' Gas Co.*,[417] this was cited as a reason for quashing an arbitrator's decision that an employee had been dismissed for just cause. The court held that since the arbitrator had based his findings of fact exclusively on hearsay evidence, he had deprived the employee of any real opportunity to test the evidence against him by cross-examination. The ability to admit hearsay evidence is, by its nature, at odds with a right to cross-examine. As a rule the courts attempt to balance the two concepts as required to achieve fairness in the context of the agency's mandate. The materiality of the hearsay evidence, the degree to which the decision is based on it alone, the ability of an individual to meet that evidence other than through cross-examination, are all factors considered by the courts in this analysis.

Thus, the B.C. Securities Commission was not found to have erred in receiving hearsay evidence which was not subject to cross-examination where the Commission expressly noted that the weight of that evidence would be affected by the lack of cross-examination and there was other evidence to support its findings. The reviewing court also stated that it was taking into account the Commission's obligation to protect the public.[418]

Contrast that case with decisions where courts have intervened when cross-examination was refused respecting hearsay evidence (which, of course, includes documentary evidence). These are all cases where the hearsay evidence played a very important role in the proceedings and the inability to test it through cross-examination worked to deny an individual a fair chance to defend himself. In *B. (J.) v. Catholic Children's Aid Society of Metropolitan Toronto*[419] the Ontario Divisional Court ruled that, notwithstanding the authority granted by section 15 of the Ontario Statutory Powers Procedure Act to receive hearsay evidence, receipt of that kind of evidence, coupled with a refusal to permit cross-examination on it, can give rise to a breach of natural justice. In this case the applicant was requesting the removal of his name from the child abuse registry. The hearing officer heard evidence only from a social worker as to out-of-court conversations she had had with the alleged victim. The victim herself was not called as a witness before the hearing officer. The Children's Aid Society, which was opposing the

---

417 (1973), 1 O.R. (2d) 421, 40 D.L.R. (3d) 509 (Div. Ct.).
418 *Four Star Management Ltd. v. British Columbia (Securities Commission)* (1990), 71 D.L.R. (4th) 317 (B.C.C.A.), leave to appeal to S.C.C. refused (1991), 1 Admin. L.R. (2d) 264 (S.C.C.).
419 (1987), 27 Admin. L.R. 295 (Ont. Div. Ct.).

removal of the name, refused to call the child as a witness as it felt that the child would deny that any molestation had taken place. Mr. Justice Craig noted that had the alleged victim been called it would have been almost impossible for the hearing officer to make a finding against the appellant. In the circumstances, the court ruled that where the appellant was denied the right to cross-examine the alleged victim the admission of the hearsay evidence amounted to a denial of natural justice.

In the case of *Kusi v. Canada (Minister of Employment & Immigration)*[420] a "credible basis" tribunal accepted and relied upon the notes of an immigration officer who recorded the answer given to the officer by a refugee claimant. The notes contained no conclusions reached by the officer. At the hearing the refugee claimant contested the accuracy of a number of the recorded answers. The claimant was unable to provide any reasonable explanation for those alleged inaccuracies. The claimant asked to have the officer produced and subjected to cross-examination on the matter of the accuracy of the notes. The tribunal refused. On judicial review the Federal Court Trial Division held that, in light of the importance of the interest involved, the rules of natural justice and fundamental justice required that cross-examination be allowed.[421]

12.28(b) Administrative Procedures Acts

Section 5 of Alberta's Administrative Procedures Act grants a right of cross-examination (at least with respect to the limited number of agencies to which the statute applies) which is similar to that found at common law. Pursuant to section 4, before an authority, in the exercise of a statutory power, refuses the application of or makes a decision or order that adversely affects the rights of a party, the authority is required to afford the party a reasonable opportunity to furnish relevant evidence to contradict or explain the facts or allegations made contrary to the interests of the party. Section 5 then provides when a party has a right under section 4 to contradict or explain facts adverse to his interests, and he will not otherwise have a fair opportunity of doing so without cross-examination of the person making the statements that constitute the facts or allegations, the authority shall afford the party an opportunity to cross-examine, in the presence of the authority or of a person authorized to hear or take evidence, the person who made the statements in question.

---

420 (1993), 19 Imm. L.R. (2d) 281 (Fed. T.D.).

421 For other cases where failure to permit cross-examination on hearsay evidence was found to give rise to a breach of natural justice see *Jackson v. Region 2 Hospital Corp.* (1994), 145 N.B.R. (2d) 51, 372 A.P.R. 51 (Q.B.), *841638 N.W.T. Ltd. v. Labour Standards Officer* (1988), 31 Admin. L.R. 70 (N.W.T. S.C.), and *Neves v. Canada (Minister of Employment & Immigration)* (1988), 97 N.R. 137 (Fed. C.A.) (where not only did the agency refuse the applicant the right to cross-examine on documentary evidence but also, peremptorily refused an adjournment to enable the applicant to attempt to rebut documentary evidence put in against him).

Section 10.1 of the Ontario Statutory Powers Procedure Act provides that a party to a proceeding may, at an oral or electronic hearing, conduct cross-examinations of witnesses at the hearing reasonably required for a full and fair disclosure of all matters relevant to the issues in the proceedings. The reader will note the limitation that the cross-examinations must be "required for a full and fair disclosure" of all matters "relevant to the issues in the proceedings". Thus the agency retains the discretion (implied in its mastery over its proceedings) to limit cross-examination where it is repetitious or irrelevant. Of course, before an agency can exercise that power to limit cross-examination, it must have some idea as to the nature of the cross-examination in question. Thus, it will generally have to ask what evidence is hoped to be adduced through the cross-examination. It cannot simply announce that it is limiting cross-examination without having any idea of the nature of the information which was to be adduced through that process.[422]

12.29 ABILITY TO REFUSE TO ANSWER QUESTIONS: SELF-INCRIMINATION

There are only two rights recognized in Canada which in common parlance would be considered protection against self-incrimination:

i)   the right of a person in criminal proceedings not to be compelled to be a witness against himself (which is today reflected in the protection offered by s. 11(c) of the Charter); and

ii)   the right of a witness not to have evidence given in a proceeding used against him in subsequent proceedings. This aspect of the matter is dealt with in the various federal and provincial Evidence Acts and s. 13 of the Charter.

These are the only protections respecting self-incrimination which are recognized in Canada.[423] There is also a related protection in the Charter against unreasonable search and seizure. This protection will be dealt with in the next section.

12.29(a) Protections for the Answers of a Witness in a Proceeding

As stated above it is now likely well known that in Canada there is no right in non-criminal matters for a witness to refuse to answer a question in a hearing

---

422 *Henderson v. Ontario (Securities Commission)* (1976), 14 O.R. (2d) 498 (H.C.).

423 *Thomson Newspapers Ltd. v. Canada (Director of Investigations & Research, Restrictive Trade Practices Commission)* (1990), 67 D.L.R. (4th) 160 (S.C.C.), *Stelco Inc. v. Canada (Attorney General)* (1987), 13 F.T.R. 128, affirmed (1987), 83 N.R. 193 (C.A.), affirmed [1990] 1 S.C.R. 617.

before an administrative agency on the basis that the answer will be against his interests. And there is no right for a party to resist being a witness simply because he is a party to the proceedings. All of the various provincial Evidence Acts contain a provision similar to s. 5 of the Canada Evidence Act which provides that all witnesses must answer the questions put to them.

> 5. (1) No witness shall be excused from answering any question upon the ground that the answer to such question may tend to criminate him, or may tend to establish his liability to a civil proceeding at the instance of the Crown or of any person.[424]

Section 5(2) of the Act, however, does provide a limited protection for the answers given by a witness in a non-criminal proceeding.

> 5. (2) Where with respect to any question a witness objects[425] to answer upon the ground that his answer may tend to criminate him, or may tend to establish his liability to a civil proceeding at the instance of the Crown or of any person, and if but for this Act, or the Act of any provincial legislature, the witness would therefore have been excused from answering such question, then although the witness is by reason of this Act, or by reason of such provincial Act compelled to answer, the answer so given shall not be used or receivable in evidence against him in any criminal trial, or other criminal proceeding against him thereafter taking place, other than a prosecution for perjury in the giving of such evidence.[426]

---

424 Some provincial examples are:

Ontario Evidence Act, R.S.O. 1990, c. E.23, s. 9(1): "A witness shall not be excused from answering any question upon the ground that the answer may tend to criminate the witness or may tend to establish his or her liability to a civil proceeding at the instance of the Crown or of any person or to a prosecution under any Act of the Legislature."

New Brunswick Evidence Act, R.S.N.B. 1973, c. E-11, s. 6: "A witness cannot by law refuse to answer a question relative to the matter in issue by reason only that the answering of the question may establish or tend to establish that he owes a debt or is otherwise subject to a civil suit, either at the instance of Her Majesty, or of any other person.

Alberta Evidence Act, R.S.A. 1980, c. A-21, s. 6: "A witness shall not be excused from answering any question on the ground that the answer may tend to incriminate him or may tend to establish his liability to prosecution to prosecution under an Act of the Legislature.

See also the B.C. Evidence Act, R.S.B.C. 1979, c. 116, s. 4; the Manitoba Evidence Act, R.S.M. 1987, c. E150, s. 6; the Newfoundland Evidence Act, R.S.N. 1990, c. E-16, s. 5; the Nova Scotia Evidence Act, R.S.N.S. 1989, c. 154, s. 59; the Prince Edward Island Evidence Act R.S.P.E.I. 1988, c. E-11, s. 6; and the Saskatchewan Evidence Act, R.S.S. 1978, c. S-16, s. 35.

425 The requirement that the witness object is not found in all of the provincial Acts. For example, s. 6(2) of Alberta's Act simply grants the protection outright and does not require a claim being advanced for its protection at the time of giving the original evidence. Ontario's Act, however, does require that the witness claim the protection first at the time of giving the evidence for which the protection is required.

426 The protection accorded by s. 9(2) of Ontario's Evidence Act is somewhat different. While s. 5(2) of the federal Act only provides that the protected evidence shall not be receivable in any

The fact that evidence may have been given in a proceeding under the protection of the Canada Evidence Act does not preclude any use of that evidence in a subsequent proceeding. It only operates to prohibit the use of that evidence to incriminate one in a subsequent proceeding. Thus, in *R. v. Kuldip*[427] the Supreme Court held that section 5 does not prohibit the Crown from using the testimony for the purposes of undermining the individual's credibility.

The protection offered by section 5(2) extends only to testimony. It does not extend to documents.[428]

Similar to the protections offered by the various Evidence Acts is the protection offered by section 13 of the Charter.

> A witness who testifies in any proceedings has the right not to have any incriminating evidence so given used to incriminate that witness in any other proceedings, except in a prosecution for perjury or for the giving of contradictory evidence.

The reader should note that, although the protection offered by section 13 of the Charter need not be expressly claimed, it only protects against the use of evidence to incriminate a witness in subsequent proceedings. Thus, the protection offered by the Charter does not extend to the use of evidence in subsequent non-criminal matters. Contrast this with the protection offered by section 9 of Ontario's Evidence Act which clearly does extend the protection to the use of the evidence in subsequent civil proceedings. The protection of section 9, however, must be expressly claimed at the time of the giving of the original evidence. Thus, witnesses in Ontario who may be concerned about subsequent civil suits should claim the protection of section 9 prior to giving their evidence.

What if the proceedings themselves are not criminal, but information secured in them could provide the grounds for laying a criminal charge? In *British Columbia (Securities Commission) v. Branch*[429] the Supreme Court considered whether individuals in proceedings before a regulatory body (in this case the British Columbia Securities Commission), who might subsequently be charged with a criminal or quasi-criminal offence, can be compelled to give evidence and produce documents which might be incriminating. The Court concluded that they could be. However, it laid down guidelines as to the extent of the protection offered by section 13 of the Charter with respect to the evidence given in the non-criminal proceedings.

With respect to oral testimony both the direct evidence given AND any derivative evidence which would not have been discovered but for that direct evidence, will not be permitted to be used to incriminate the witness in subsequent

---

criminal proceeding against the individual, s. 9(2) provides that the protected evidence shall not be used or receivable in evidence against him in any civil proceeding or in any proceeding under any Act of the Legislature.

427 (1990), 43 O.A.C. 340 (S.C.C.).
428 *R. v. Simpson*, [1943] 3 D.L.R. 355 (B.C.C.A.), affirmed [1943] 3 D.L.R. 367 (S.C.C.).
429 [1995] 5 W.W.R. 129 (S.C.C.).

criminal or quasi-criminal proceedings. Notwithstanding, the Court indicated that there were circumstances in which the courts could grant a witness an exemption from the compulsion to give oral evidence. As to documentary evidence, the Court held that there was no right against self-incrimination respecting documentary evidence created prior to the compulsion in question.

Branch arose out of an investigation by the British Columbia Securities Commission into the conduct of two directors of a corporation. The investigation was sparked by comments in the corporation's financial statements by its auditors that they were unable to express an opinion as to whether the statements were fairly presented and their references to serious deficiencies in the control, documentation and approval procedures of the corporation. The Commission has the statutory authority to conduct investigations it feels necessary for the administration of the Securities Act. Summonses were issued to the directors compelling their attendance for examination and requiring production of all information and records in their possession relating to the corporation and other named companies. The directors declined to answer or produce such evidence as they claimed that the investigation appeared to be preliminary to possible criminal or quasi-criminal charges. Ultimately the Commission sought and received an order from the B.C. Supreme Court for an order of contempt against the directors. The directors appealed, and lost, to the B.C. Court of Appeal and appealed again to the Supreme Court of Canada which dismissed the appeal. The directors had advanced arguments based on the right against self-incrimination under section 7 of the Charter and the freedom against unreasonable search and seizure under ssection 8. (I will discuss the search and seizure aspect of this case later in the context of that subject.)

On the question of the right against self-incrimination, the Court distinguished between the compulsion of oral testimony and the compulsion of documentary evidence. Writing for a majority of the Court, Justices Sopinka and Iacobucci noted that the Court had held in *R. v. S. (R.J.)*[430] that the principle against self-incrimination (one of the principles of fundamental justice protected by section 7 of the Charter) requires that persons compelled to give oral evidence, even in disciplinary or regulatory matters, be provided with subsequent "derivative-use" immunity in addition to the "use immunity" guaranteed by section 13 of the Charter (which provides that evidence given cannot be used to incriminate one in subsequent proceedings).

In order to invoke the derivative use immunity, the onus is on the accused (on a balance of probabilities) to show a plausible connection between the compelled testimony and the derivative evidence sought to be admitted. Once the connection is established, in order for the derivative evidence to be admitted, the Crown must satisfy (again on a balance of probabilities) that the authorities would have discovered the impugned derivative evidence without the compelled testimony.

---

430 [1995] 1 S.C.R. 451.

This restriction against the subsequent use of evidence applies only to later proceedings to which section 7 of the Charter applies.

Notwithstanding the general requirement that a witness must respond to questions in regulatory or disciplinary proceedings, the Court held that an exemption from this compulsion can be granted where the person claiming the exemption can show (on a balance of probabilities) that the predominant purpose of seeking to compel the evidence of the person is *not* to obtain relevant evidence for the purpose of that proceeding but rather to incriminate the witness. In such cases the party seeking to compel the testimony must justify the potential prejudice to the right of the witness against self-incrimination. If it is shown that the only prejudice which the person will suffer is the possible subsequent derivative use of the testimony then the compulsion to testify will occasion no prejudice for that witness as he will be protected against such use. If the witness can show any other significant prejudice that may arise from the testimony such that his right to a fair trail will be jeopardized, then the witness should not be compellable.

The purpose for the calling of the evidence is to be inferred from its overall effect in the proceedings. If the overall effect is that it is of slight importance to the proceeding in which it is compelled but of great importance in a subsequent criminal proceeding against the witness, then an inference may be drawn as to the real purpose of the compelled evidence. If the relationship is reversed, no such inference is to be drawn. The issue of compellability may arise either at the time the witness is called in the civil proceedings or later in a subsequent penal proceeding.

In the case in point, the Court determined that the predominant purpose of the investigation at which the witnesses were to testify was part of a larger framework regulating the securities industry throughout Canada with a paramount goal of protecting the economy. The predominant purpose of the inquiry was to obtain relevant evidence, in the regulation of the securities industry, for the purposes of the particular proceedings in question and not to incriminate either of the directors. Therefore, the testimony fell under the general rule whereby a witness is compelled to testify but receives in return evidentiary immunity respecting subsequent proceedings.

With respect to documentary evidence, the Court noted that there was no protection against self-incrimination respecting documentary evidence created prior to the compulsion.

12.29(b) The Right of an Accused Person to Refuse to Answer Questions in Criminal Proceedings

Unlike civil proceedings, there is a protection against self-incrimination in criminal matters. Section 11(c) of the Charter provides that any person who is charged with an *offence* has the right not to be compelled to be a witness in proceedings against that person in respect of the offence. In *Wigglesworth v. R.*[431] the Supreme Court had to decide if disciplinary proceedings under the Royal Canadian Mounted Police Act attracted the protection of section 11 so as to protect the officer in question from being required to answer questions. The Court concluded that the rights guaranteed by section 11 are "available to persons prosecuted by the state for public offences involving punitive sanctions, i.e. criminal, quasi-criminal and regulatory offences, either federally or provincially enacted. As to what these matters might be the Court held that they consisted of two types of matters: matters which are aimed at maintaining public order and thus criminal by their nature and matters which might not otherwise be considered criminal but which carry with them a "true penal consequence".

1. Matters Which Are "Criminal" By Their Nature

The Court distinguished between matters of a public nature which are intended to promote public order and welfare within a public sphere of activity (which would be caught by section 11) and private domestic or disciplinary matters which are regulatory, protective or corrective and which are primarily intended to maintain discipline, professional integrity and professional standards or to regulate conduct within a limited private sphere or activity (which would not be caught by section 11). "Proceedings of an administrative nature instituted for the protection of the public in accordance with the policy are also not the sort of "offence" proceedings to which s. 11 is applicable."

2. Matters Which Are "Criminal" Because They Involve a True Penal Consequence

Matters which might not be considered "criminal" may be so because they can result in the imposition of a "true penal consequence". As Wilson J. explained in *Wigglesworth*, "a true penal consequence which would attract the application of s. 11 is imprisonment or a fine which by its magnitude would appear to be imposed for the purpose of redressing the wrong done to society at large rather than to the maintenance of internal discipline within the omitted sphere of activity."[432]

The disciplinary proceedings in *Wigglesworth* were found by the Court not to be criminal by their nature, but criminal because an individual convicted in a

---

431 (1987), 28 Admin. L.R. 294 (S.C.C.).

432 Wilson J. stated that one indicium of the purpose of a particular fine is how the body is to dispose of the fines it collects. "If, as in the case of proceedings under the Royal Canadian Mounted Police Act, the fines are not to form part of the Consolidated Revenue Fund but are to be used for the benefit of the force, it is more likely that the fines are purely an internal or private matter of discipline."

disciplinary proceeding could be imprisoned for a year. This imprisonment penalty amounted to a "true penal consequence".

At the same time that the Supreme Court released its decision in *Wigglesworth*, it also released *Trimm v. Durham Regional Police Force*[433] in which it found that disciplinary proceedings under Ontario's Police Act did not constitute criminal proceedings insofar as they were neither criminal by their nature (they sought to enforce a duty which arose under the code of conduct in the Police Act), and there were no true penal consequences as there was no possibility of imprisonment.[434]

12.30 PROTECTION FROM UNREASONABLE SEARCH AND SEIZURE

Many agencies, particularly regulatory ones, have the statutory authority to investigate matters outside of, or preliminary to, a hearing and in the course of those investigations to require an individual under investigation to provide documents and other material for inspection. Are there any restrictions on the exercise of those powers? The answer which appears to be emerging from the case law is that such demands amount to an intrusion by the state into the affairs of the individual and thus comes under the protection afforded by section 8 of the Charter against unreasonable search and seizure.[435]

> 8. Everyone has the right to be secure from unreasonable search or seizure.

The purpose of section 8 is to protect the individual's reasonable expectations of privacy from unjustified state intrusion. Thus, the parameters imposed by section 8 on the procedures required to avoid infringing its protection will vary depending on the nature of the privacy interest at stake and the type of state intrusion in question.

---

433 (1987), 29 Admin. L.R. 106 (S.C.C.).

434 Since *Wigglesworth* none of the following have been found to be criminal proceedings subject to s. 11 of the Charter: "cease trading" proceedings before the Alberta Securities Commission (*Barry v. Alberta (Securities Commission)* (1986), 25 D.L.R. (4th) 730, 67 A.R. 222 (C.A.), affirmed [1987] 1 S.C.R. 301 and *Holoboff v. Alberta (Securities Commission)* (1991), 80 D.L.R. (4th) 603 (Alta. C.A.)), deportation proceedings under the Immigration Act (*Bowen v. Canada (Minister of Employment & Immigration)*, [1984] 2 F.C. 507, 58 N.R. 223 (C.A.) *Hurd v. Canada (Minister of Employment & Immigration)* (1988), 90 N.R. 31 (C.A.)), professional misconduct proceedings under the Alberta Medical Profession Act (*Fang v. College of Physicians and Surgeons (Alberta)* (1985), 25 D.L.R. (4th) 632, [1986] 2 W.W.R. 380 (Alta. C.A.)), and suspension of a licence under the Petroleum Products Act (*Petroleum Products Act (P.E.I.), Ref Re (sub nom. Petroleum Products Act, Re)* (1986), 33 D.L.R. (4th) 680 (P.E.I.C.A.)).

435 *Hunter v. Southam* (1984), 11 D.L.R. (4th) 641 (S.C.C.). *Comité paritaire de l'industrie de la chemise v. Potash*, [1994] 2 S.C.R. 406.

12.30(a) Investigations in Support of Criminal or Quasi-Criminal Offence Proceedings

In *Hunter v. Southam*[436] the Supreme Court of Canada considered the powers granted under the Combines Investigation Act (Can.) for the Director of Investigation and Research (or any representative), acting under a certificate from a member of the Restrictive Trade Practices Commission, to enter any premises on which the director believes there could be evidence respecting a possible offence under the Act, and to examine anything on the premises, and to take away for further examination any documents which could contain such evidence. The Court concluded that those powers infringed the protection against unreasonable search and seizure granted by section 8 of the Charter.

In *Hunter* the Director had exercised his authority to cause a search of the offices of the *Edmonton Journal* newspaper. The newspaper challenged the search. Ultimately the matter came before the Supreme Court of Canada where the powers were struck down. The Court felt that the absence of a requirement in the Combines Investigation Act for the Director (where feasible) to seek a prior authorization for the search from a neutral and unbiased judge or from a person acting judicially. This was to permit an opportunity for the balancing of the conflicting interests of the state and the individual so that the individual's right of privacy would be breached only where the appropriate standard had been met and the interests of the State have been demonstrated to be superior to the individual's expectation of privacy. The Court felt that a member of the Restrictive Trade Practices Commission could not provide such a prior review because the Combines Investigation Act gave the Commission significant powers of direction over the investigation under the statute. The Commission could not, therefore be considered sufficiently neutral. Furthermore, the standard established by the Act for the Commission to apply in granting the certificate was much too low. It merely required the member to satisfy himself as to the reasonableness of the Director's request. While the Court acknowledged that different tests might apply in different circumstances in the case in point the minimum test should have been reasonable and probable grounds, established on oath, to believe that an offence has been committed and that there is evidence to be found at the place of the search.

12.30(b) Investigations in Support of Ensuring Compliance with Regulatory Statute

In *Thomson Newspapers Ltd. v. Canada (Director of Investigation & Research)*[437] and *R. v. McKinley Transport Ltd. v. R.*[438] the Court held that the much

436 (1984), 11 D.L.R. (4th) 641 (S.C.C.).
437 (1990), 67 D.L.R. (4th) 161 (S.C.C.).
438 (1990), 68 D.L.R. (4th) 568 (S.C.C.).

lower expectations of individuals engaged in regulated industries for privacy in the matter of their operation of those industries warranted a much lower standard for what constituted a reasonable search or seizure than that adopted in *Hunter*. *Thomson* is one of those fragmented decisions of the Supreme Court where every judge issues separate reasons, sometimes concurring on this point, sometimes concurring on that point. *McKinley* suffers from the same difficulty insofar as, although it is much shorter, the judges noted that they retained their individual reservations as expressed in *Thomson*. However, a clearer picture is now emerging in the decisions of the Court which follow and interpret the two cases.

In *Comité paritaire de l'industrie de la chemise v. Potash*[439] the Supreme Court considered section 22(e) of Quebec's Act Respecting Collective Agreement Decrees, R.S.Q., c. D-2. That section empowered officials, at any reasonable time, to inspect a place of work, consult and copy documents relating to the regulated aspects of the business, verify certain work conditions (rates of pay, duration of work, apprentice system, etc.) and to require, even under oath and privately, from any employer or employee, all information deemed necessary. The Court concluded that such powers amounted to a "search" for the purposes of section 8 of the Charter given the purpose of that section to protect the individual's reasonable expectations of privacy from unjustified state intrusion. An inspection was "unquestionably" an intrusion. Nonetheless, the Court cautioned, the wording of section 8 did not prohibit all inspections without prior authorization. It simply imposes a requirement of "reasonableness".

As the Court had held earlier in *Thomson* and *McKinley* the scope of the protection offered by section 8 varies with the context. In an occupation which is extensively regulated by the state, the reasonable expectation of privacy which employers may have with respect to documents whose content is specifically provided for by the Act, or the premises where an activity subject to specific stands is conducted, is lower than that discussed in *Hunter*. *Hunter's* required prior authorization based on reasonable and probable grounds did not, the Court held, apply to administrative inspections respecting a regulated industrial sector. The purpose of the inspection is to ensure that a regulatory statute is being complied with.

In the opinion of the Court, an inspection for regulatory purposes does not carry with it the stigma normally associated with a criminal investigation and the consequences of an inspection are less draconian. While regulatory statutes incidentally provide for offences, they are enacted primarily to encourage compliance. In this case the penalties were restricted to very modest fines. Discovered breaches usually lead to a civil actions being launched to claim wages owing. Furthermore, reasonable constraints were placed on the power by the legislation. The inspectors were not authorized to make copies of documents other than those relating to the regulated aspects of the business, the powers had to be exercised

---

439 [1994] 2 S.C.R. 406.

in accordance with the purpose of the Act and the inspectors were required to act in good faith. Nor did the fact that an inspection could be instigated by a complaint change its nature as a complaint system is a practical means not only of checking whether contravention of the legislation have occurred but also of checking them. Thus, ''in view of the important purpose or regulatory legislation, the need for powers of inspection, and the lower expectations of privacy, a proper balance between the interests of society and the rights of individuals does not require, in addition to the legislative authority, a system of prior authorization''.

The Court returned to the consideration of section 8 in *British Columbia (Securities Commission) v. Branch*[440] Here the Court considered the B.C. Securities Commission's statutory authority to issue summons for compelling the attendance and examination of individuals in the course of investigations carried out as part of the regulation of that province's securities industry. In *Branch* questions had arisen from the inability of auditors to state that a corporation's financial statements were fairly presented. References had been made to serious deficiencies in the control, documentation and approval procedures of the corporation. The Commission issued summons requiring the attendance of two directors of the corporation for examination who were to bring along with them certain documents for review. The Commission's power was challenged and the matter worked its way up to the Supreme Court.

Following the lead of *Potash* the Court held that the Commission's demand for documents did not constitute an unreasonable search and seizure contrary to section 8 of the Charter. In determining the reasonableness of a seizure, the Court stated, one looks to both the privacy expectations of the individual and the nature of the seizure. With respect to the former, the Court held that persons involved in the business of trading securities do not have a high expectation of privacy with respect to regulatory needs that have been generally expressed in securities legislation. It was widely known and accepted that the industry was well regulated as a scheme of economic regulation designed to protect the economy.

With respect to the nature of the seizure, the Court referred to its decision in *R. v. Borden*[441] for the proposition that ''In the absence of prior judicial authorization, a search or seizure will be unreasonable unless it is authorized by law, the law itself is reasonable and the manner in which the search was carried out is reasonable.'' In the case in point, the demand for production by summons was one of the least intrusive of the possible methods which might be employed to obtain documentary evidence. The seizure was authorized by the statute and, as the Securities Act was found to have an important social purpose whose social utility justified the minimal intrusion, the Court found the law to be reasonable. The Court concluded that as the documents in question were business documents (personal documents might attract a higher expectation interest) relating to a

---

440 [1995] 5 W.W.R. 129 (S.C.C.).
441 [1994] 3 S.C.R. 145.

heavily regulated industry the individuals had a very low privacy expectation which was not infringed for the purposes of section 8 of the Charter by the summons requiring production.

12.31 IMPROPER USE OF INVESTIGATION POWERS

Before leaving the area of investigative powers, the reader should note that even a constitutionally lawful investigation power can be abused if it is used for a purpose other than that for which it was granted by the relevant statute.

See, for example, *R. v. Williams (G.F.J.)*,[442] which considered the use of the investigation powers granted the Nova Scotia Securities Commission to secure evidence for use in criminal proceedings. Section 27 of the Nova Scotia Securities Act gives the Securities Commission the authority to appoint a person to make an investigation and gives that person broad powers to investigate including the power to compel the attendance of witnesses, to compel them to give evidence and to compel the production of documents together with the power to apply to court for warrants for the entry and search of a premises and the seizure of applicable things. A breach of section 8 of the Charter resulted, however, when such an investigator used those powers to secure evidence against a broker in order to assist a criminal investigation. Although the broker was charged and convicted of an offence under the Securities Act as a result of this investigation, the Nova Scotia Supreme Court held that it was improper for the Securities investigator to turn the information over to police investigating Criminal Code offences. The investigator's "passing of the 'fruits of his investigation' obtained through his powers under the Securities Act, and for the purposes of that Act only, to [the police] without regard to the rightly stringent prerequisites of searches" violated the broker's right under section 8 to be free of unreasonable search and seizures. The broker's statements to the investigator given pursuant to the Securities Act investigation powers could also not be considered to be "voluntary" under section 7 of the Charter.

The Federal Court Trial Division reached a similar conclusion in *Samson v. Canada*.[443] In this case the Director of Investigation and Research was prohibited from using his power to compel the testimony of notaries in an administrative proceeding when the Director had, independent of this evidence, sufficient evidence for the purposes of the administrative proceeding and it appeared to the court that the sole purpose in attempting to compel the notaries to testify was to secure evidence against them for use in subsequent criminal proceedings. The Court acknowledged that such a procedure may be proper where the individuals were the only ones holding the information necessary about transactions which are the subject of the investigation and that information is sought without being

---

442 (1994), 130 N.S.R. (2d) 8, 367 A.P.R. 8 (S.C.).
443 [1994] 3 F.C. 113 (T.D.).

solely concerned with the self-incrimination of the suspects (*Morena (V.) v. M.N.R.*, [1991] 1 C.T.C. 78 (Fed. T.D.)). However, given the intended use of the information in the case at bar the Court held that the use of the Director's investigatory powers amounted to a breach of section 7 of the Charter.

12.32 COMBINING PROCEEDINGS AND SPLITTING ISSUES

An agency may sometimes find itself faced with multiple applications dealing with essentially the same circumstances and the same law. Is it necessary to hold separate proceedings for each of these applications or can an agency hear them together at the same time in one proceeding? Under the common law it appears that, where appropriate, the power to hear applications together fell under an agency's general mastery of its procedure.

This issue was considered by the Ontario Divisional Court in *Ontario (Minister of Transportation & Communication) v. Eat'N Putt Ltd.*[444] That case concerned a refusal of the Ontario Municipal Board to hear clearly related applications together in one proceeding. The Board felt that it had no jurisdiction to do so in the absence of consent from all the parties. It relied on a conclusion to that effect which it had reached in an earlier decision. The Divisional Court disagreed. Hearing the applications together was desirable in order to avoid inconsistent decisions. In its opinion, the procedure which the Board felt compelled to adopt "is one which will inevitably require duplication of proceedings with additional costs."

> No authority was cited in that decision for the conclusion quoted and no other authority to that effect has been cited to us. Respectfully we disagree with it as a proposition of law. No ground has been shown for the board denying itself such jurisdiction. In fact, s. 18 of the regulation in effect gives it that jurisdiction, *if any express authority is needed.* [Emphasis added.]

It was argued before the Court that each claim should be and appear to be decided on its own merits. The Court agreed, but stated that:

> the point surely is whether or not a joint hearing or some similar arrangement will reach the same objective. In our view, nothing has been shown to indicate that a hearing or some similar arrangement will reach the same objective. It does not advance the interests of any party, in any justifiable sense, to follow a procedure which carries the seeds of conflicting decisions by a tribunal such as the Ontario Municipal Board any more than it does with a court.

---

444 (1985), 59 O.R. (2d) (Div. Ct.). See also *Cape Breton Development Corp. v. Workers' Compensation Bd. (N.S.)* (1995), 139 N.S.R. (2d) 362, 397 A.P.R. 362 (N.S. C.A.).

As to the argument that there was no prejudice to the respondent who would have to defend all of the different claims in separate proceedings if the Board's view won the day, the Court agreed that there might be no prejudice:

> but it misses the point. It may be quite open to the respondent to advance evidence and argument but the problem, as we have already said, is the possibility or probability of inconsistent verdicts. At no point did the board consider the aspect of unfairness to the Minister who is the respondent in each of the claims.

Thus, it appears open to an agency to hear related applications in one proceeding. Such an approach is likely desirable in order to avoid unnecessary duplication of proceedings and the risk of conflicting decisions. In considering whether to make such a decision, the agency should consider the degree to which there is overlap between the applications, whether there would be any unfairness to any of the parties in proceeding with a joint hearing and the efficiencies and inefficiencies which would result from its adoption (or non-adoption).

Recent amendments to Ontario's Statutory Powers Procedure Act appear to mirror the common law authority of agencies in this regard. However, they have in fact reduced the power considerably by making the joinder conditional upon the consent of the parties and imposing conditions which even consent cannot dispense with.

> 9.1 (1) If two or more proceedings before a tribunal involve the same or similar questions of fact, law or policy, the tribunal may,
>
> > (a) combine the proceedings or any part of them, with the consent of the parties;
> >
> > (b) hear the proceedings at the same time, with the consent of the parties;
> >
> > (c) hear the proceedings one immediately at the other; or
> >
> > (d) stay one or more of the proceedings until after the determination of another one of them.
>
> (2) Subsection (1) does not apply to proceedings to which the Consolidated Hearings Act applies.
>
> (3) Clauses (1)(a) and (b) do not apply to a proceeding if,
>
> > (a) the Act under which the proceeding arises requires that it be heard in private; or
> >
> > (b) the tribunal is of the opinion that clause 9(1)(a) or (b) applies to the proceeding. [S. 9 (1) directs that proceedings shall be closed to the public where matters involving public security may be disclosed (para. a) or where there may be intimate financial or personal matters or other matters which the agency feels should not be public (para. b).]

The reverse side of the coin to hearing proceedings together is hearing the issues raised in a single proceeding separately. Again, this authority would appear to flow from an agency's authority over its procedure. The exercise of such a power may make perfect sense in circumstances, for example, where an application raises may complex issues but an answer is required quickly with respect to one of them. The agency may move to deal with that which can be dealt with quickly while reserving the other issues to a later date. The same considerations would likely be applicable here (except in reverse) as were applicable to joining proceedings — how closely interrelated are the various issues, what is the fairness of the situation, what efficiencies would result and what inefficiencies, etc.

12.33 JUDICIAL AND OFFICIAL NOTICE: MATTERS FOR WHICH EVIDENCE NEED NOT BE TENDERED

Not every matter relevant to a proceeding need be supported by evidence. Administrative agencies can take either ''judicial notice'' or ''official notice'' of some facts of which evidence has not been tendered.

Like the courts, agencies can take judicial notice of certain matters which, in a very general oversimplification, are so well known that they can be assumed. Sopinka, Lederman and Bryant in their excellent text on evidence law in Canada explain judicial notice as follows:

> Judicial notice is the acceptance by a court or judicial tribunal, in a civil or criminal proceeding, without the requirement of proof, of the truth of a particular fact or state of affairs. Facts which are (a) so notorious as not to be the subject of dispute among reasonable person, or (b) capable of immediate and accurate demonstration by resorting to readily accessible sources of indisputable accuracy, may be noticed by the court without proof of them by any party. The practice of taking judicial notice of facts is justified. It expedites the process of the courts, it creates uniformity in decision-making and it keeps the courts receptive to societal change. Furthermore, the tacit judicial notice that surely occurs in every hearing is indispensable to the normal reasoning process.[445]

The authority to take judicial notice is simply implied in the decision-making power. However, all of the various Evidence Acts contain a provision similar to the following provisions of the Canada Evidence Act.

> 17. Judicial notice shall be taken of all Acts of the Imperial Parliament, of all ordinances made by the Governor in Council or the lieutenant governor in council of any province or colony that, or some portion of which, now forms or hereafter may form part of Canada, and of all the Acts of the legislature of any such province or colony, whether enacted before or after the passing of the Constitution Act, 1867.

---

445 Sopinka, Lederman and Bryant, *The Law of Evidence in Canada*, 2d ed. (Butterworths 1992) at p. 976. The authors discuss the various subtleties and operation of judicial notice from pp. 976 to 988. This is an excellent text and I recommend it to any reader who wishes to pursue this topic further.

18. Judicial notice shall be taken of all Acts of Parliament, public or private, without being specially pleaded.

In Ontario, section 16 of the Statutory Powers Procedure Act also provides that a tribunal may take notice of facts that may be judicially noticed.

Official notice is knowledge or expertise which an agency possesses *because of its specialized knowledge in a certain field.* After hearing hundreds of cases involving galvanic erosion, for example, it is to be expected that an agency member will know something about it. Indeed, one of the reasons for creating administrative agencies is that the members will have a knowledge and insight into the specialized subject matter of the proceedings. An administrative agency decision-maker can take official notice of this knowledge. It does not have to be proven for him to note or rely on it.

It appears that before official notice can be taken of a matter, the knowledge must be in the general knowledge of the agency as a result of the expertise which it has developed. It is unlikely that official notice can be taken of knowledge which is only personal to an individual member and not shared by the agency as a whole. In *Huerto v. College of Physicians and Surgeons (Sask.)*[446] the Saskatchewan Court of Queen's Bench concluded that a disciplinary committee erred when it took into account its own personal knowledge in determining whether a physician had acted improperly.

A major difference between official notice and judicial notice is that, while one can assume that the parties are aware of matters which can be judicially noticed (given its definition), the same assumption cannot be made with respect to official notice. By its nature official notice is only information which the agency possesses because of its expertise. One cannot assume that everyone appearing before an agency possesses the same expertise. Furthermore, matters which may be officially noticed do not necessarily enjoy the same certainty as matters which may be judicially noticed. The agency's expertise may, in fact, be incorrect, or inapplicable to the special circumstances of the case before it. Thus, before an agency can take official notice of something it must give the participants notice of whatever is intended to be taken notice of and provide them with an opportunity to present evidence or submissions with respect to it if they wish.[447]

In addition to authorizing the judicial notice of information, section 16 of Ontario's Statutory Powers Procedure Act also grants agencies subject to the statute the authority to take notice "of any generally recognized scientific or

---

446 [1994] 9 W.W.R. 457, 26 Admin. L.R. (2d) 169, 124 Sask. R. 33, 117 D.L.R. (4th) 129 (Q.B.), affirmed (1995), 128 Sask. R. 208 (C.A.).

447 *Vance v. Harditt Corp.* (1985), 53 O.R. (2d) 183 (Div. Ct.), *Huerto v. College of Physicians and Surgeons (Sask.),* [1994] 9 W.W.R. 457, 26 Admin. L.R. (2d) 169, 124 Sask. R. 33, 117 D.L.R. (4th) 129 (Q.B.) (notice of appeal to Court of Appeal filed September 2, 1994, court file CA 1957), *Todorov c. Canada (Ministre de l'emploi et de limmigration)* (1993), 160 N.R. 158 (Fed. C.A.) (This last case involved a failure to comply with a statutory duty to disclose the information being "noticed".)

technical facts, information or opinions within its scientific or specialized knowl-edge.''

12.34 COMMUNICATING AT THE HEARING

12.34(a) The Right to Speak in the Official Languages

A number of statutes at the federal and provincial levels provide the right for a participant in a proceeding to use one of the two official languages of Canada, English and French.

At the federal level, the Official Languages Act directs that any person has the right to use either of the official languages in any federal court or in any pleading or process issuing from a federal court. A ''federal court'' is defined as any court, tribunal or other body that carries out adjudicative functions and which is established by or pursuant to an Act of Parliament. In his article ''The Use of the Official Languages Before Federal Administrative Agencies and Other Federal Courts''[448] Michel Francoeur explains the various directions respecting language contained in that statute including the right of the parties to have a decision-maker who understands the language being used, the right of the participants to chose the language of the proceeding (they may elect English, French or both), the right of witnesses to use either language, the requirement for decisions to be issued simultaneously in both languages (and the exceptions thereto — most notably where the decision-maker feels that the simultaneous availability of the decision in both official languages would cause a prejudicial delay to the public interest or any interest of a party, in which case the second language version can be issued later at the earliest possible time). Mr. Francoeur also notes the require-ments on federal courts and other federal institutions to serve the public in the official languages.

In Ontario the French Language Services Act, R.S.O. 1990, c. F.32 provides a right to services in French in sections 2 and 5:

2. The Government of Ontario shall ensure that services are provided in French in accordance with this Act.

5. (1) A person has the right in accordance with this Act to communicate in French with, and to receive available services[449] in French from, any head or central office of a government agency[450] or institution of the Legislature, and has the same right in respect of any other office of such agency or institution that is located in or serves

---

448 (1995), 1 *Administrative Agency Practice* 58 (Carswell).

449 ''Service'' is defined as meaning ''any service or procedure that is provided to the public by a government agency or institution of the Legislature and includes all communications for the purpose.''

450 ''Government agency'' is defined as including a board, commission or corporation the majority of whose members or directors are appointed by the Lieutenant Governor in Council.

an area designated in the Schedule. [The schedule to the statute lists specific regions in the province where, presumably the need for French language services was considered the highest.]

(2) When the same service is provided by more than one office in a designated area, the Lieutenant Governor in Council may designate one or more of those offices to provide the service in French if the Lieutenant Governor in Council is of the opinion that the public in the designated area will thereby have reasonable access to the service in French.

(3) If one or more offices are designated under subsection (2), subsection (1) does not apply in respect of the service provided by the other offices in the designated area.

The breadth of those rights is somewhat reduced by section 7 of the Act which provides that "the obligations of government agencies and institutions of the Legislature under this Act are subject to such limits as circumstances make reasonable and necessary, if all reasonable measures and plans for compliance with this Act have been taken or made."

Finally, section 6 makes it clear that the provision of the specific language rights by the Act "shall not be construed to limit the use of the English or French language outside of this Act."

In New Brunswick, English and French are declared the official languages of the province "for all purposes to which the authority of the Legislature of New Brunswick extends" by section 2 of the Official Languages of New Brunswick Act, R.S.N.B. 1973, c. O-1. The statute continues on to provide that, subject to section 15, all notices, documents, instruments required under the Act or any Act to be published in the province by the Province, any agency thereof, of any Crown corporation are to be printed in the official languages (section 8). Sections 10, and 13 then set out the rights of individuals before the courts and agencies to obtain services in either official language. (The reader may particularly wish to note the innovative substitute appointment power contained in section 13(1.3) whereby an appointing authority is given the authority to appoint a substitute for an appointee when it is necessary to do so in order to comply with the language requirements of the statute.)

10. Subject to section 15,[451] where requested to do so by any person, every public officer or employee of the Province, any agency thereof or any Crown corporation shall provide or make provision for such person

    (a) to obtain the available services for which such public officer or employee is responsible, and

    (b) to communicate regarding those services.

---

451 Section 15 provides a power to the Lieutenant Governor to make regulations determining the application of ss. 8,9, 10, and 13.

. . .

13. (1) Subject to section 15, in any proceeding before a court, any person appearing or giving evidence may be heard in the official language of his choice and such choice is not to place that person at any disadvantage.

(1.1) Subject to subsection (1), a person accused of an offence under an Act or a regulation of the Province, or a municipal by-law, has the right to have the proceedings conducted in the official language of his choice, and he shall be advised of the right by the presiding judge before his plea is taken.

(1.2) Subject to subsection (1), a person who is a party to proceedings before a court[452] has the right to be heard by a court than understands, without the need for translation, the official language in which the person intends to proceed.

(1.3) A power under an Act or regulation of the Province to appoint a person to or as a court includes, notwithstanding any provision of the Act or regulation, the power

   (a) to appoint for the purposes of the proceedings of that court, or such of them as may be specified in the appointment, another person to act in the place of the person appointed under the Act or regulation when it is necessary that another person so act in order to give effect to the right referred to in subsection (1.2), and

   (b) to fix the remuneration of the person so appointed.

(1.4) A person appointed in accordance with subsection (1.3) to act in the place of a person appointed under the Act or regulation of the Province has, for the purposes for which the appointment is made, all of the powers and duties of the person appointed under the Act or regulation.

12.34(b) Interpretation

The common law right of a party to a fair hearing includes the right to understand what is going on and to be understood.[453] In *MacDonald v. Montreal (City)*[454] Justice Beetz wrote:

It is axiomatic that everyone has a common law right to a fair hearing including the right to be informed of the case one has to meet and the right to make full answer and defence. Where the defendant cannot understand the proceedings because he is unable to understand the language in which they are being conducted, or because he is deaf, the effective exercise of these rights may well impose a consequential

---

452 "Court" is defined as including "judicial, quasi-judicial and administrative agencies."

453 *Societe des Acadiens du Nouveau Brunswick Inc. v. Assn. of Parents for Fairness in Education, Grand Falls District 50 Branch* (1986), 27 D.L.R. (4th) 406, [1986] 1 S.C.R. 549; *MacDonald v. Montreal (City)* (1986), 27 D.L.R. (4th) 321, [1986] 1 S.C.R. 460; *Roy v. Hackett* (1987), 45 D.L.R. (4th) 415, 62 O.R. (2d) 351 (C.A.).

454 (1986), 27 D.L.R. (4th) 321, [1986] 1 S.C.R. 460.

duty upon the court to provide adequate translation. But the right of the defendant to understand what is going on in court and to be understood is not a separate right, nor a language right, but an aspect of the right to a fair hearing.

It should be absolutely clear however that this common law right to a fair hearing, including the right of the defendant to understand what is going on in court and to be understood is a fundamental right deeply and firmly embedded in the very fabric of the Canadian legal system. That is why certain aspects of this right are entrenched in general as well as specific provisions of the Canadian Charter of Rights and Freedoms, such as s. 7, relating to life, liberty and security of the person and s. 14, relating to the assistance of an interpreter.

Thus, at a minimum, the right to a fair hearing includes the right to have a reasonable opportunity to secure an interpreter and is open to all those who have a difficulty communicating at a hearing.

Under the Official Languages Act a witness is not only entitled to speak in either official language but is also entitled to interpretation services and cannot be placed at a disadvantage for being heard in either official language. Furthermore, parties before federal courts are entitled to simultaneous interpretation at their request from one official language to the other (but not from other languages into French or English).[455]

Also at the federal level, subsection 2(g) of the Canadian Bill of Rights provides that no law of Canada shall be construed so as to deprive a person of the right to the assistance of an interpreter in any proceedings in which he is involved or in which he is a party or a witness, before a court, commission, board or other tribunal, if he does not understand or speak the language in which such proceedings are conducted.[456]

Section 14 of the Charter provides that "A party or witness in any proceedings who does not understand or speak the language in which the proceedings are conducted or who is deaf has the right to the assistance of an interpreter." In *Roy v. Hackett*[457] the Ontario Court of Appeal held that section 14 guaranteed the parties the right of an interpreter during proceedings before an arbitration board under the Canada Labour Code. In discussing the application of section 14 (in the context of criminal proceedings) the Supreme Court of Canada noted that "As part of their control over their own proceedings courts have an independent

---

455 Michele Francoeur, "The Use of the Official Languages Before Federal Administrative Agencies and Other Federal Courts" 1 *Administrative Agency Practice* 58 at p. 60.

456 In *Weber v. Canada (Minister of Manpower & Immigration)* (1976), 69 D.L.R. (3d) 473 (Fed. C.A.), the failure of an Immigration Adjudicator to ensure that a Portuguese individual was not provided with word-by-word translation as required by s. 2(g) and by regulations under the Immigration Act resulted in the quashing of the order arising from the proceedings and a re-hearing being ordered. Although an interpreter was present who attempted to interpret everything, on at least two occasions this was not done and the missed matters had to be interpreted to the person later in summary form. To the same effect see *Leiba v. Canada (Minister of Manpower & Immigration)* (1972), 23 D.L.R. (3d) 476 (S.C.C.).

457 (1987), 45 D.L.R. (4th) 415 (Ont. C.A.).

responsibility to ensure that those who are not conversant in the language being used in court understand and are understood."[458]

The right to an interpreter is not an absolute right to be granted regardless of need. In *Roy v. Hackett*[459] the Ontario Court of Appeal held that an opposing party has the right to challenge the basis for a request for the assistance of an interpreter by means of cross-examination at the time of the objection. The Court held that:

> In general, the judge or the chairman of the tribunal must come to a decision regarding the good faith of the witness or the person who has requested an interpreter before granting the request. In coming to his decision, however, he must take into account the legitimate desire of any witness to express himself in the language he knows best, usually his mother tongue. Therefore, he must avoid imputing an ulterior motive to a witness who asks for an interpreter, even if the witness has some familiarity with the language used and could, in a general way, understand the proceedings. The judge must certainly give s. 14 a broad and generous interpretation. That does not mean that the right to an interpreter is an absolute right and that cross-examination as to the linguistic competence of the person who requested such assistance is automatically oppressive and vexatious to the point of making the exercise of that right illusory.[460]

Nor is the right absolute as to the degree of interpretation. To the extent that the requirement flows from natural justice the extent of the right fluctuates according to the circumstances. In illustration, see the Federal Court Trial Division decision in *Brar v. Canada (Solicitor General)*[461] where the Court found that there was no right in a party to demand that the proceedings progress at a slow enough pace to permit an interpreter "to convey a verbatim translation of everything said, whether or not it was directed to the applicant or his counsel or was relevant directly for purposes of his testimony". The Court noted that the require-

---

458 *R. v. Tran* (1994), 117 D.L.R. (4th) 7 (S.C.C.).

459 (1987), 45 D.L.R. (4th) 415 (Ont. C.A.).

460 In *Khakh v. Canada (Minister of Employment & Immigration)*, [1994] 1 F.C. 548 (T.D.) the agent (who was not a legal counsel) for an applicant in an immigration inquiry requested that an interpreter be provided for the applicant as the applicant could not adequately communicate in English. The Adjudicator questioned the applicant to test his English and determined that no interpreter was necessary. The hearing was adjourned. When it was reconvened at a later date the applicant again requested access to an interpreter which the Adjudicator again denied. Subsequently, the applicant demonstrated great difficulty in communicating in English. The Adjudicator stated that he "wished to state for the record" that it appeared that the applicant's English skills had deteriorated since the earlier hearing. An interpreter was provided. Ultimately the Adjudicator decided against the applicant's claim. On judicial review the Federal Court Trial Division found that the Adjudicator's comment as to the applicant's deteriorating skill gave rise to a reasonable apprehension of bias! (This demonstrates the extreme care which decision-makers must take regarding their choice of words. It appears that the Court was concerned more with the apparent desire of the Adjudicator to make his statement "for the record" than with the statement that the skills had deteriorated.)

461 (1989), 43 Admin. L.R. 68 (Fed. T.D.).

ments for translation services in hearings before agencies will vary with the case and circumstances of the hearing. (The interests of an individual in proceedings before the Security Intelligence Review Committee were later found to be very low by the Supreme Court of Canada in *Chiarelli v. Canada (Minister of Employment & Immigration).*[462])

There is also a duty on the presiding decision-making to determine that a person has the competence and the impartiality to serve as an interpreter. In cases where there are opposing interests an interpreter should not be biased towards one side or the other.[463] In *Xie Wei Ming v. Canada (Minister of Employment & Immigration)*[464] the Federal Court of Appeal held, in the context of an immigration proceeding, that when an objection is taken to the competency of an interpreter, the tribunal is to stop the proceedings to determine the degree of competence of translation. This is to be done (with the participation of the participants who wish to do so) by asking the interpreter relevant questions, by the calling of evidence on the question of competence, and by the making of submissions in this regard. The decision-maker is not simply to rely on the assurances of the person requiring the translation as to the translator's competence. The decision-maker has a duty to satisfy himself of the matter.

Agencies must also note that the need for assistance in communication is not restricted simply to language. Physical contraints on individuals may also demand some form of assistance to aid communication. In *Matthews v. Board of Directors of Physiotherapy (Ontario)*[465] the Ontario Board of Directors of Physiotherapy was obliged to consider "independently and judicially" whether a blind physiotherapist required a braille or an audio taped form of notice and disclosure to understand the disciplinary proceedings being brought against him in order to fully defend himself. Not only did the Board fail to do this, it refused to permit the physiotherapist's family to assist him in a meaningful fashion. The resulting unfairness, the Divisional Court held, caused the Board to lose jurisdiction which could not be recovered. The provision of braille and audio material some months later by the Board, which might have been adequate if offered earlier, was found to be insufficient to cure the defect resulting from the Board's actions.[466]

If the agency wishes, it may require the interpreter to take an oath as to his competence and willingness to interpretate fully and freely. The following are examples of an interpreter's oath used in the courts in Ontario which may be adjusted for agency use as necessary.

<u>Where Oath Delivered By Clerk to Interpreter</u>

---

462 (1992), 2 Admin. L.R. (2d) 125 (S.C.C.).

463 *Unterreiner v. R.* (1980), 51 C.C.C. (2d) 373 (Ont. Co. Ct.).

464 [1990] 2 F.C. 336 (Fed. C.A.).

465 (1990), 40 O.A.C. 60 (Div. Ct.).

466 With respect to methods of ensuring access to agency proceedings for the deaf, see "Agency Access for Persons with Hearing Loss" by Carole Théberge in vol. 1 *Administrative Agency Practice*, at page 91.

Do you swear (or affirm) that you have a working knowledge of both the _____ and English languages, and that you will faithfully, and to the best of your knowledge and ability, interpret the oath(s) to the witness(es) and all the questions asked and answers given thereto (so help you God)?

(The interpreter replies, "I do so swear" or "I do so affirm" (in the case of a solemn affirmation.))

Where Interpreter Swears Himself In

I, (state your name) do solemnly swear (or affirm) that I have a working knowledge of both the _____ and English languages, and that I will faithfully, and to the best of my knowledge and ability, interpret the oath(s) to the witness(es) and all the questions asked and answers given thereto (so help me God).[467]

As to who pays for the interpreter's services, the British Columbia Supreme Court in *Wyllie v. Wyllie*[468] held that under section 14 of the Charter the initial responsibility to pay rests with the litigant requiring the service of the interpreter. However, the Court opined that there may be an obligation on the court or on the Crown in civil proceedings to pay an interpreter's fees upon the court being satisfied that the litigant is unable to pay the necessary fee.[469]

12.35 THE CHARTER[470]

Brief mention must be made of the impact of the Charter on the questions addressed in this addendum. That the charter can be invoked to require an administrative tribunal to grant an oral hearing, for instance, is clearly demonstrated in Wilson J.'s judgment in *Singh v. Minister of Employment and Immigration.*[471] In this case, Wilson J. (Dickson C.J.C. and Lamer J. concurring) held that the Convention refugee determination procedures of the Immigration Act violated notions of "fundamental justice", and, therefore, section 7 of the Charter. Although not basing her decision on the absence of the right to an oral hearing per se, Wilson J. clearly indicated that such a right is encompassed within the scope of "fundamental justice" in appropriate circumstances.

In discussing this issue in her judgment, Wilson J. began with the premise that the concept of "fundamental justice" includes the notion of "procedural

---

467 These examples of an interpreter's oath were kindly provided by the Court Interpretation and Translation Services, Ottawa, of the Ontario Ministry of the Attorney General. When looking for interpreters agencies may wish to contact the relevant court office in their jurisdiction which likely maintains a list of interpreters available.

468 (1987), 37 D.L.R. (4th) 376, 4 A.C.W.S. (3d) 183 (B.C.S.C.).

469 This view was concurred with by Justice Ruttan in *Marshall v. Gorge Vale Golf Club* (1987), 39 D.L.R. (4th) 472, 5 A.C.W.S. (3d) 382 (B.C. S.C.).

470 The jurisdiction of administrative agencies to consider Charter arguments is canvassed in chapter 23 (Tribunal and the Charter of Rights).

471 [1985] 1 S.C.R. 177, 12 Admin. L.R. 137, 14 C.R.R. 13, 17 D.L.R. (4th) 422.

fairness''. Accordingly, it was her view that "fundamental justice", at minimum, dictates that a tribunal which adjudicates upon rights must (a) act fairly, in good faith, without bias, and in a judicial temper, and (b) provide parties an adequate opportunity to state their case.[472]

Perhaps not surprisingly, Wilson J.'s analysis of the requirements of "fundamental justice" then closely tracked the approach courts have adopted to the non-constitutional questions of "natural justice" and "fairness". Thus, she acknowledged that "fundamental justice" may require different procedures in different contexts. As such, it was her view that section 7 does not always oblige decision-makers to grant oral hearings to the parties before them. By the same token, however, Madame Justice Wilson also warned that written submissions will not be satisfactory for all purposes either. In particular, she was of the view that where a serious issue of credibility is involved, fundamental justice requires that credibility be determined on the basis of an oral hearing. As she stated:

> I find it difficult to conceive of a situation in which compliance with fundamental justice could be achieved by a tribunal making significant findings of credibility solely on the basis of written submissions.[473]

Wilson J.'s major concern about the Immigration Act's procedural scheme for refugee determination, however, did not center upon its failure to provide applicants with an oral hearing. Rather, viewing the scheme as a whole, she considered it to be inadequate in providing a refugee claimant with the opportunity to know the case against him and to respond effectively to that case. In particular, she found that "fundamental justice" was violated because the Immigration Act denied the refugee applicant the opportunity to examine and probe the evidence and arguments contained in the minister's submissions to the Immigration Appeal Board, which would in large part form the basis of the board's decision. This effectively deprived the applicant of the ability to know what material would be relevant to his case, and, denied him any real chance to refute the minister's arguments against him.

R. v. Caddedu[474] is one instance in which the lack of an oral hearing *was* held to violate section 7 of the Charter. In this case, in which Caddedu's parole was revoked by prison authorities, the potential role of the Charter in expanding procedural rights is clearly evident. Caddedu challenged the revocation of his parole on the grounds that he was denied an oral hearing to present his case. Potts J. rejected the argument that Caddedu was guaranteed the right to an oral hearing by virtue of either the rule of "natural justice" or "fairness". He then held,

---

472 Supra, note 63, D.L.R. p. 464.

473 D.L.R. p. 465.

474 *R. v. Cadeddu*; *R. v. Nunery* (1982), 40 O.R. (2d) 128, 32 C.R. (3d) 355, 4 C.C.C. (3d) 97, 146 D.L.R. (3d) 629, 3 C.R.R. 312 (H.C.). Appeal abated (1983), 41 O.R. (2d) 481, 35 C.R. (3d) xxviii, 4 C.C.C. (3d) 112, 146 D.L.R. (3d) 653 (C.A.).

however, that the denial of this hearing *was* in violation of the principles of "fundamental justice" as enshrined in section 7 of the Charter. As he stated:

> Considering that the rights protected by s. 7 are the most important of all those enumerated in the Charter, that deprivation of those rights has the most severe consequences upon an individual, and that the Charter establishes a constitutionally mandated enclave for protection of rights, into which government intrudes at its peril, I am of the view that the appellant could not be lawfully deprived of his liberty without being given the opportunity for an in-person hearing before his parole was revoked.[475]

There are a number of other cases aside from *Caddedu* in which courts have accepted the argument that section 7 of the Charter has "enhanced" procedural rights by constitutionalizing them. In this connection, Mullan, in his article on natural justice cited above[476], points to the Federal Court of Appeal's decision in *Howard v. Presiding officer of Inmate Disciplinary Court of Stony Mountain Institution*[477] and *Re D & H Holdings Ltd. and Vancouver*[478], a decision of the British Columbia Supreme Court. In each of these cases, section 7 was held to guarantee procedural rights which had normally been denied under similar circumstances at common law. In *Howard*, for instance, the Federal Court of Appeal held that section 7 abrogated the long-standing rule at common law denying prison inmates legal representation at disciplinary hearings. Similarly, in *D & H* the court was of the opinion that fundamental justice was breached when a municipality refused to provide reasons for its revocation of a business licence, despite the fact that at common law the courts have been resolute in refusing to impose on tribunals a duty to give reasons for their decisions.[479]

Of course, appeals based on the Charter are not always successful. In *Re U.S. and Yue*[480], for instance, a claim that section 7 guarantees a right to cross-examination at an extradition hearing was rejected. White J. reasoned that as an extradition hearing is more in the nature of an interlocutory hearing than a final adjudication, fundamental justice did not mandate that cross-examination be permitted. As he stated:

> The concept of fundamental justice depends on the nature of the proceedings. At a trial in which the tribunal can make a binding decision determining issues of culpability, title in property, or any other final disposition of remedy, the right of cross-examination of material witnesses is inherent and part of fundamental justice. How-

---

475 Supra, D.L.R. pp. 641-642.
476 Supra, note 39, pp. 43-45.
477 [1984] 2 F.C. 642, 11 Admin. L.R. 63, 45 C.R. (3d) 242, 19 C.C.C. (3d) 195, 19 D.L.R. (4th) 502, 17 C.R.R. 5, 57 N.R. 280.
478 (1985), 15 Admin. L.R. 209, 64 B.C.L.R. 102.
479 See e.g. Megarry V.C.'s decision in *McInnes v. Onslow-Fane*, [1978] 1 W.L.R. 1520 (Ch.D.), another licensing case.
480 (1983), 42 O.R. (2d) 651, 7 Admin. L.R. 109, 6 C.C.C. (3d) 373, 150 D.L.R. (3d) 282 (H.C.).

ever, in a matter which is not a final adjudication by the tribunal such as an extradition hearing, the right to cross-examine is not inherent.[481]

Nonetheless, as Mullan points out, the danger inherent in section 7 is that the courts will employ it to impose uniform procedural requirements as a matter of course, thereby ignoring or dismissing considerations of administrative efficiency and curial deference. It is to be hoped, however, that the Charter will *not* lead courts to abandon the ungainly yet vital balancing process pursuant to which they have approached the question of procedural rights in the administrative sphere. This would be an unfortunate result.

[Note: Mr. Justice Beetz's judgment in *Singh* (*supra*) indicates that the Canadian Bill of Rights may yet have something to contribute to the area of procedural requirements as well.]

In any event, the impact of the Charter on administrative proceedings cannot be denied. Charter-protected interests are frequently the subject of, or related to, administrative proceedings, whether in the context of life, liberty and the security of the person (section 7), or the freedom from unreasonable search and seizure (section 8), or freedom of expression (subsection 2(b)). Here the effect of the Charter will be direct. However, even where a proceeding does not directly affect a Charter protected right, the impact of the Charter may be felt indirectly. The close relationship between the concepts of natural justice in administrative law and fundamental justice as guaranteed in section 7 of the Charter[482] likely means that developments in the latter will spill over to the former. Above all, however, natural justice and fairness are constructs of the common law and the Supreme Court has said, on more than one occasion that "It is clear . . . that the common law must be interpreted in a manner which is consistent with Charter principles. This obligation is simply a manifestation of the inherent jurisdiction of the courts to modify or extend the common law in order to comply with prevailing social conditions and values."[483]

---

481 Supra, note 72, Admin. L.R. p. 117.

482 The Supreme Court has acknowledged that fundamental justice includes at a minimum the notion of procedural fairness (*Reference re.: s. 94(2) of the Motor Vehicle Act* (1985), 24 D.L.R. (4th) 536, [1985] 2 S.C.R. 486, [1986] 1 W.W.R. 481, 63 N.R. 266).

483 Cory J. in *Hill v. Church of Scientology* (1995), 126 D.L.R. (4th) 129 (S.C.C.). Among the earlier Supreme Court decisions cited in support of this statement were *R.W.D.S.U., Loc. 580 v. Dolphin Delivery Ltd.*, [1986] 2 S.C.R. 573 and *B.C.G.E.U. v. British Columbia (Attorney General)*, [1988] 2 S.C.R. 214.

17

Witnesses

In this chapter I intend to canvass two related areas: i. a suggested approach to evidence before administrative agencies; and ii. a discussion of the qualification and testimony of expert witnesses.

17.1 EVIDENCE AND ADMINISTRATIVE TRIBUNALS[1]

17.1(a) An Approach to Evidence For Administrative Agencies

In this discussion, I will not be dealing with the technical rules of evidence in any detail. Rather, what follows is a suggested *approach* to evidence which administrative agency members should consider taking when faced with evidentiary problems.

17.1(b) Administrative Agencies Are Not Bound By the Rules of Evidence

For the most part, the traditional "rules of evidence" were developed for the courts, to help accomplish their mandates. These rules have not been developed to serve agency purposes. Thus, to a great extent, the technical rules of evidence do not apply, *and should not be applied*, to agency proceedings as they will not contribute to the tasks administrative agency decision-makers have to carry out.

Some members of administrative agencies believe that a basic familiarity with the technical rules of evidence would assist them in dealing with the objections made by legal counsel which were based on these technical rules. In my opinion, this is not true. It is self-deceiving to think so.

---

1 The discussion in c. 17.1 is based extensively on presentations which I have delivered in various administrative law seminars and a short paper I published in the Canadian Journal of Administrative Law and Practice.

Legal counsel spend several years in pre-bar training learning the rules and their exceptions. They practice them daily before the courts. There are massive texts arguing thousands of minutiae respecting these rules. This is the domain of trained and expert legal counsel. Members of administrative agencies who are not legally trained (and likely even many who are) cannot win, and likely cannot even compete, if they allow themselves to fight a battle on grounds not of their selection. A basic grasp of "rules of evidence" will not allow one to better deal with counsel's evidentiary objections. For one reason, it is impossible to limit the debate. Once one engages counsel in an evidentiary argument one will quickly be drawn out from the relatively safe shallows of the basics and into the dark and deep seas of the complex. Furthermore, you will have implicitly endorsed the correctness of counsel's approach that the "rule" in question is somehow determinative of the issue before you. Usually it is not, as I will explain.

A technical rule of evidence is usually not determinative of an issue before an agency simply because as a matter of common law the courts have said on many occasions that administrative agencies are not bound by the formal rules of evidence.[1.1]

Where did this bit of wisdom come from? Why shouldn't the rules of evidence apply equally to administrative agencies as to courts? To understand this, it helps to differentiate between matters of substantive rights and matters of procedure.

The law gives us certain rights and privileges. These are commonly known as substantive rights. The method by which you go about bringing these rights into effect is known as procedure. For example, the right of the winning lottery ticket holder to the jackpot is a substantive right. How the winner goes about proving that he holds that winning ticket would be considered a matter of procedure.

"Evidence" is considered, on the whole, to be a matter of procedure. It is an aspect of how one enforces or goes about bringing into effect one's rights rather than being a substantive right itself. [1.2]

As I have noted repeatedly in this text, administrative decision-makers are masters of their own procedure. They do not have to do things the way a court would do them. Subject to the dictates of statute law and natural justice, an agency

---

1.1 Lord Denning in *T.A. Miller Ltd. v. Minister of Housing and Local Government*, [1968] 1 W.L.R. 992 (C.A.) said at p. 995, "A tribunal of this kind is master of its own procedure, provided that the rules of natural justice are applied. Most of the evidence here was on oath, but that is no reason why hearsay should not be admitted where it can fairly be regarded as reliable. Tribunals are entitled to act on any material which is logically probative, even though it is not evidence in a court of law . . . ." There are many, many other decisions to the same effect. For example see *Canadian National Railways Co. v. Bell Telephone Co. of Canada and the Montreal Light, Heat and Power Consolidated*, [1939] S.C.R. 308, *Bortolotti v. Ontario (Ministry of Housing)* (1977), 76 D.L.R. (3d) 408 (Ont. C.A.), and the cases cited by Reid and David in *Administrative Law and Practice* (2d ed.) (Butterworths, Toronto, 1978) at pp. 72-74.

1.2 *Wildman v. R.* (1984), 14 C.C.C. (3d) 321 (S.C.C.); *R. v. Bickford* (1990) 51 C.C.C. (3d) 181 (C.A.).

has the authority to determine its own procedure. It follows, then, that because evidence is a matter of procedure an agency's mastery over its procedure means that it is not bound by the legal rules of evidence.

As is discussed in more detail in chapter 9 "Powers of An Agency to Control Its Own Procedure", for the main part, administrative agencies are not set up to do the same things as courts. Thus, the rules of procedure, and of evidence, which were developed by the courts, to do the things courts do, are not applied to agencies because they are not geared to the types of things agencies have to do.[4]

This freedom from the rules of evidence is a principle of common law. Even if an agency's statute does not expressly provide for this freedom, the agency will usually be considered not to be bound by the rules of evidence.

Notwithstanding this common law freedom, many agencies are, in addition, expressly freed by statute from the restrictions of the legal rules of evidence. The wording of these statutory releases vary. There are the direct, general and to the point, freedom clauses such as that found in section 19(1)(b) of the federal Status of the Artist Act, S.C. 1992, c. 33:

> 19. (1) In any proceeding before it, the Tribunal
> (b) is not bound by legal or technical rules of evidence.

Or, there is the slightly less direct, but equally broad, provision of which s. 17(c) of that same statute is an example:

> 17. The Tribunal may, in relation to any proceeding before it,
> (c) accept any evidence and information that it sees fit, on oath, by affidavit or otherwise, whether or not the evidence is admissible in a court of law.

Ontario's Statutory Powers Procedure Act contains another type of generic, although somewhat more limited, freedom from evidence for the agencies to which it applies:

> 15. (1) Subject to subsection (2) and (3), a tribunal may admit evidence at a hearing, whether or not given or proven under oath or affirmation or admissible as evidence in a court,
> (a) any oral testimony; and
> (b) any document or other thing,

---

4 In *Bortolotti v. Ontario (Ministry of Housing)* (1977), 76 D.L.R. (3d) 408 (Ont. C.A.) the Ontario Court of Appeal stated that: "The Commission of Inquiry is charged with the duty to consider, recommend and report. It has a very different function to perform from that of a court of law, or an administrative tribunal, or an arbitrator, all of which deal with rights between parties. . . It is quite clear that a commission appointed under the Public Inquiries Act, 1971 is not bound by the rules of evidence as applied traditionally in the Court, with the exception of the exclusionary rule as to privilege (s. 11) . . . The approach of the Commission should not be technical or unduly legalistic one. A full and fair inquiry in the public interest is what is sought in order to elicit all relevant information pertaining to the subject matter of the inquiry.

relevant to the subject matter of the proceeding and may act on such evidence, but the tribunal may exclude anything unduly repetitious.

>   (2) Nothing is admissible in evidence at a hearing,
>   (a) that would be inadmissible in a court by reason of any privilege under the law of evidence;[5] or
>   (b) that is inadmissible by the statute under which the proceeding arises or any other statute.

A more subtle, but likely equally broad form of statutory freedom clause is illustrated by section 5(4) of the Pension Act, R.S.C. 1985, c. P-6:

>   5. (4) Decisions of the Minister shall be made as informally and expeditiously as the circumstances of fairness permit.[6]

The freedom from the technical rules of evidence, however, may be a bit of a mixed blessing. While agencies may have greater freedom than the courts respecting evidence in that they need not be overly concerned with the technicalities of the legal rules of evidence, in some ways their task is harder than that facing the courts insofar as they cannot simply rely on such rules to determine whether something will be accepted or not as evidence in a proceeding. When an agency is faced with an evidentiary objection, the obligation on the agency is to determine what practical weakness is really being asserted as the basis for the rejection of the evidence and whether that weakness is sufficient to make the evidence sufficiently unreliable or unusable for the task it is intended to be put by the agency. This is not necessarily an easy task. What may be a weakness for some purposes, may not necessarily be a weakness for others. For example, the fact that some evidence may be pure opinion might not be a sufficient weakness justifying the CRTC's rejection of evidence in a broadcasting matter when it is attempting to gauge cultural values or needs. Thus, the agency must approach *each* evidentiary objection on the basis of the mandate facing that agency and the weaknesses and strengths of the particular evidence in question must be evaluated in light of that mandate.

---

5 In some ways, Ontario's Statutory Powers Procedure Act is not a "user friendly" statute. It does not, for example, indicate exactly what these privileges under the law of evidence might be. There are a number. Without attempting to be exhaustive or to explain the sometimes subtle operations of each, some of the better known privileges are the solicitor-client privilege, communications between husband and wife, and the privilege for disclosures made as part of settlement negotiations. There is also a limited form of privilege against self-incrimination as discussed in the context of regulatory proceedings in cases such as *British Columbia (Securities Commission) v. Branch*, [1995] 5 W.W.R. 129 (S.C.C.) and there is also a type of public interest immunity (for matters such as cabinet confidences).

6 For other examples, see the Canadian International Trade Tribunal Act, R.S.C. 1985, c. C-18.3, s. 34; the Aeronautics Act, R.S.C. 1985, c. A-2, ss. 37(1) and (5); the Canada Labour Code R.S.C. 1985, c. L-2, s. 16, the Cultural Property Export and Import Act, R.S.C. 1985, c. C-51, s. 25; and the Immigration Act, R.S.C. c. I-2, s. 68(3).

Hamilton v. Alberta (Labour Relations Board)[7] is an excellent illustration of this principle in operation. In that case the Alberta Labour Relations Board was considering a grievance by an individual against his union. When the individual had completed his case before the Board the union asked that his complaint be dismissed as he had not put in any evidence that could support it. There was evidence before the Board, but the union pointed out several weaknesses with it. In response the individual asked to be allowed to call further evidence which would rebut the weakness noted by the union. The Board refused on the ground that the individual was attempting to "split his case". The Board then proceeded to rule against the applicant on the basis of the weaknesses which the union had identified and which it had not allowed the individual to answer.

The Alberta Labour Relations Board's statute expressly stated that it was not bound by the rules of evidence relating to judicial proceedings.

On an application for judicial review, the Alberta Court of Queen's Bench overturned the decision of the Board because it had disregarded this freedom and bound itself by the legal rules of evidence. The Board had reasoned that its statutory provision gave it a discretion to use the common law rules of evidence and that in deciding whether to apply those rules the Board was to be guided by matters of logic and public policy. The Court disagreed. Justice Hutchinson wrote: "The effect of the section is not to give the Board a discretion to use common law rules of evidence, but liberates the Board from the strictures of the law relating to admissibility and evidence applicable to judicial proceedings."

The judge ruled that the task of the Labour Board panel was to ascertain all of the facts relating to the applicant's complaint. This it had not done. "Instead, the Asbell Panel seems to have been overly occupied with the question as to whether the applicant (or his solicitor) should have anticipated the evidence which was led by the Edmonton Police Association after the applicant had closed his case. In other words, the . . . panel became bogged down in a consideration of the rules of evidence and overlooked its fact finding mandate." In the Court's opinion:

> Section 13(5)(b) . . . says that the Board is not bound by the law of evidence applicable to judicial proceedings. Thus, the Board is permitted range beyond the restraints imposed in a court of law so as to adopt a more informal or flexible approach to its fact finding mission in order to permit the Board to exercise the powers given to it pursuant to the Code. The Board's primary duty in acting as a buffer between employers and employees is to act fairly and to be perceived at all times as acting fairly.

> I am persuaded that in this instance the Board has misconstrued the way in which the Code instructs it concerning the application of the rules of evidence. Rather than having been liberated from the common law rules of evidence as provided in s. 13(5)(b) of the Code, the Board has purported to apply its discretion so as to use common law rules of evidence to exclude evidence. The Board has adopted an

---

7 (1993), 19 Admin. L.R. (2d) 172 (Alta. Q.B.).

inflexible, formalistic approach to the acceptance of evidence which limits its ability to consider the facts presented by both sides. In doing so the Board has failed to take into account its mandate to be able to look beyond the evidence which is restricted in judicial proceedings and the Board has become enmeshed in the very rules of evidence from which it has been freed by s. 13(5)(b) of the Code. Rather than having placed itself in the position of hearing all of the evidence, its rigid adherence to rules of evidence leaves the impression that it has not acted fairly." (at pp. 183-184)

17.1(c) Despite Freedom From "Rules of Evidence" One Must Still Be Concerned With Evidence

Notwithstanding all the foregoing, however, individuals appearing before agencies and agency decision-makers cannot simply ignore the *concept* of evidence. The fact that an administrative decision-maker may not be bound by the legal "rules of evidence" does not mean that anything should go respecting the material which you receive in the course of a proceeding. The rules of evidence exist for a reason, and while, perhaps, one need not know the formal rules, one *must* know what the rules of evidence are trying to accomplish and one should try to guide one's approach to evidence according to those aims.

Failure to do so will usually result in judicial review by the courts. Most administrative decisions have to be made against the backdrop of some factual determination. Although the type of factual basis which may have to be established in an administrative proceeding may be different from that in a court, **some** factual underpinning usually has to be established. This can lead to judicial intervention from a number of approaches:

i. Generally the courts assume that Parliament intended agencies to operate fairly and according to the rules of natural justice or procedural fairness. While the degree of rights flowing from these principles will vary from circumstance to circumstance one can say that as a general rule natural justice and procedural fairness require:

    i)   that a party has an opportunity to know the case against him or her and to present his or case to the agency; and

    ii)   that the decision will be made by an unbiased adjudicator.

If an agency fails to operate with a concern to the underlying purposes of the rules of evidence it will likely find itself in breach of one or both of these principles. For example, a refusal to admit relevant and material evidence, which cannot be justified, will likely amount to a breach of a party's right to present his or her case.

ii. Secondly, agencies only have the authority to do such things as Parliament, either expressly or implicitly, authorized them to do. Failure by an agency to concern itself with the underlying purposes for which the rules of evidence were created will often lead the courts to find they have acted outside of the jurisdiction given to them by Parliament. For example,

a.   Parliament has not, to my knowledge, yet created an agency which it intended to act irrationally or at whim. Where an agency bases its decisions on facts for which there is no logical evidence whatsoever the decision may be considered to be irrational. The Court will intervene.

b.   Equally, if an agency takes into account facts which have no logical connection to the decision it has to make, or fails to take into account relevant and material facts, the courts will intervene on the grounds that Parliament never intended the agency to take into account irrelevant considerations or to make decisions without considering the relevant facts.[8]

c.   Some statutes provide for a right of appeal but only on a question of law. Whether material is capable of leading to a particular conclusion can be a question of law, thus, a nonchalant approach to evidence can give rise to such appeals.

d.   Another ground of judicial review by the courts is that a decision is patently unreasonable. A decision which is poorly supported by evidence might be seen as such. A decision which the evidence does not at all support *will* be viewed that way.

Beyond the question of judicial intervention, I assume that most agencies want their decisions to be as good as possible; where they are establishing social policy, that they will be capable of effecting the policy they are intended to accomplish; and where they are determining disputes between individuals that their decisions will be accepted by the concerned parties. A decision will only be as good as its underpinnings. Decisions which are not supported by good factual underpinnings, or which are perceived as having been arrived at unfairly, or which, indirectly cause more harm than any possible good the making of the decision can have, will not be good decisions. They will not serve their purpose.

---

8 The Federal Court Trial Division held in Puxley v. Canada (Treasury Board) (1994), 24 Admin. L.R. (2d) 43 (Fed. T.D.) that the statutory authority of an adjudicator under the Public Service Staff Relations Act to receive and accept such evidence and information as he or she sees fit, whether admissible in a court of law or not, and to refuse to accept any evidence that is not presented in the form and within the time prescribed, did not authorize the adjudicator to exclude relevant evidence, documentary or oral, or cross-examination on evidence offered where the line of questioning seeks to establish the case of one party or to weaken the case of the other by questions that are not clearly irrelevant to matters before the adjudicator. See also *Université du Québec à Trois-Rivières v. Larocque* (1993), 101 D.L.R. (4th) 494 (S.C.C.) for the proposition that the failure to admit relevant evidence which is not material to the decision made will not amount to a denial of natural justice.

Rules of evidence are geared to establishing sound factual underpinnings which do not create greater social harm in establishing those underpinnings than the social good those factual underpinnings are capable of producing.

17.1(d) What are the Underlying Concerns of the Rules of Evidence?

Underlying the rules of evidence are three basic purposes. And these should also be the heart of an agency's evidentiary concerns. The rules of evidence exist to:

    i.   establish a sound factual basis for decisions;

    ii.   ensure a proper balance between the harm in accepting evidence and the value in doing so; and

    iii.   maintain a fair and effective process.

I suggest that these concerns should also serve as an agency's guide. Whenever there is no statutory restriction on the admission of evidence and the agency is called upon to decide whether something should or should not be admitted in the proceeding before it, it should ask itself the following questions:

1.   Is this evidence capable, if believed, of creating a factual basis for the decision in question, and if so, how far can it logically be taken to do so?

2.   If it is capable of supporting the necessary factual base, is there some other reason why it should it be rejected? Will its receipt lead to some greater social harm than the good likely to be accomplished by accepting it?

3.   Assuming that the evidence meets the first two concerns, is there anything about the way the evidence is coming which threatens the fairness or the smooth operation of your hearing? And if so, is this threat of sufficient importance, in light of your mandate, to warrant its exclusion?

Let us now consider the operation of these concerns.

CONCERN 1:

Is this evidence capable, if believed, of creating a factual basis for the decision in question, and if so, how far can it logically be taken to do so?

Rules of evidence deal with what can be admitted in proceedings to ensure the creation of a good factual basis (i.e., that material submitted was capable of establishing the fact in question). Translated into the agency sphere, this means that the decision-maker has to be concerned with whether the material which it will be taking into consideration is sufficient to create the type of factual basis necessary for its proceedings.

One has to be concerned with two things in deciding whether a particular piece of evidence is capable of establishing a good factual base for a decision: its relevance and its weight.

a.   **Relevance**. The information which is offered must be capable, assuming
      that it were true, of logically establishing some fact which an agency needs
      in order to accomplish its mandate.

When evidence is admitted in a proceeding the agency is saying that it is
capable of logically proving the existence of some fact or matter which has to be
established in order for the agency to perform its statutory mandate.

Obviously, then, relevance is going to be affected by the mandate of the
agency. If an agency has been created by Parliament to determine if an aeronautics
licence holder flew an aircraft in a dangerous way that was not permitted by the
regulations it is a waste of everyone's time to tender reams of material that go to
establishing the economic effect of television shows produced in Canada. The
economic state of Canada is not a requirement of the Aeronautics Act or the
regulations made under it. However, the statement by a witness that he saw the
plane in question buzz bomb pedestrians may be relevant if there is something in
that legislation which prohibits such actions (and one hopes there is).

As a practical matter, then, it will obviously assist decision-makers if they
know the type of things which have to be proven for an application to be successful. This allows them to see where lines of questioning or the tendering of
evidence may be going and to gauge its relevance.

If a matter is not relevant it cannot be taken into account. It should not be
admitted into evidence.[9]

b.   **Weight**. In addition to determining its relevance, a decision-maker will
      have also to be concerned with how much weight the tendered evidence
      has. In other words, how much can the agency rely on it to establish the
      matter it is submitted to establish.

Weight should not be confused with relevance. Something could be relevant
to a question and yet actually have very little probative value. For example, an
unsigned, undated letter attesting to a fact in question is logically connected to
that question. It is relevant. However, because the truths of that letter cannot be
checked in anyway it may have very little probative weight. Weight can be very
important. For example, conflicting evidence may be resolved on the basis of
weight. Thus, evidence given under oath or affirmation is generally considered
to have more weight than evidence which is not given in that way.[10]

---

9 The converse of the rule is true too, that you should not reject relevant and material evidence.
   However, that fact that you admit irrelevant evidence, or reject relevant evidence, will not itself
   amount to a reversible error by the courts. It will come down to how important a role the evidence
   in question played (or failed to play) in your decision. If irrelevant evidence played a major role
   when admitted (or if the rejected relevant evidence would have played if admitted) then you likely
   have a reversible error on your hands. If, however, the impact was minimal, you do not. (*Université
   du Québec à Trois-Rivières v. Larocque* (1993), 101 D.L.R. (4th) 494 (S.C.C.)
10 This is why it is generally a good idea to try to decide at the beginning of a proceeding whether

Reliability plays a large role in determining weight. The more reliable evidence is, the greater the weight which is generally accorded to it.

Evidence which is relevant, but of little weight, may be admitted. Its lack of weight may be compensated for by the rest of the record, or, alternatively, the agency's mandate may be such to warrant taking into account matters of lesser weight than would a court.

Although weight can arise in a number of situations, one of the most common ways it will arise before one is in the context of hearsay evidence. It is also, I suggest, an excellent example of why one should not permit oneself to become bogged down in the discussion as to legal technicalities but instead be concerned with agency realities. I would like to illustrate this principle by looking, for a moment, at hearsay evidence.

Hearsay

Generally speaking, hearsay evidence is written or oral statements made by persons, otherwise than in testimony at the proceeding in which it is offered, which is offered in order to prove the truth of the matter asserted in the statement.[11] An easy example is a statement by a witness, Ms. Robinson, in a proceeding held to determine if Mr. Jones burnt down his barn, that Mrs. Smith had told the witness that she saw Mr. Jones light the fire. The purpose of the evidence is to prove that Mr. Jones lit the fire, yet the statement which is offered to prove this, ''I saw Mr. Jones light the fire'', was made by Mrs. Smith who is not present at the hearing. Hearsay can take many forms: witnesses recounting of oral conversations, newspaper reports, audited financial statements, etc. Documents are technically hearsay if offered as proof of their contents.

Hearsay is not, as a rule, admissible in judicial proceedings. (There are of course, numberless exceptions.) Consequently, it is very common for parties in an administrative proceeding to object to evidence being received on the grounds that it is hearsay.

I suggest that the prudent decision-maker will not become overly concerned with whether or not something is or is not hearsay. Practically speaking this exercise is not worth the effort and the determination as to what constitutes hearsay can be very complex.[12] Furthermore, there are many exceptions to the technical

---

testimony is to come to you under oath or affirmation or not. I suggest that it is prudent to attempt to avoid the situation where, in a proceeding where considerable evidence has gone in not under oath, a party requests particular testimony to be received in this way.

11 Sopinka, Lederman and Bryant *Law of Evidence in Canada* (Butterworths, 1992) at p. 156.

12 Something that may look like hearsay, yet not be so. Remember that hearsay is the repetition by a witness of something someone else said in order to establish the matter asserted in the statement was true. If the evidence is not tendered to prove the truth of the matter asserted in the second hand statement it is not hearsay. Here's an example: Mr. Brown is on trial for assaulting Mr. Jones. He claims in his defence that it was an act of self-defence as he believed Mr. Jones was a gangster who had been hired to get him for his unpaid gambling debts. When asked why he thought this Mr. Brown's response is that ''Mrs. Smith told me that Jones had been hired by a

rule against hearsay. Since an administrative agency can receive hearsay evidence in most cases anyway, the conjuring of that baleful term should have no power over it.

However, what is sauce for the goose is sauce for the gander, and I suggest that it is not a fully satisfactory response to a hearsay objection merely to say that you are not prohibited from receiving hearsay evidence because you are not bound by the rules of evidence. This amounts to a simple exchange of mystical formulae with very little actual communication.

The better approach, I suggest, is not to concentrate on whether something amounts to hearsay or not. Instead, concentrate on why the objection is being made. Why should the evidence, even if it were hearsay, be rejected? Have the objector identify and explain the weakness. This will also force the objector to clearly formulate the basis for the objection. Some objections may be based more on habit than on any real concern over the evidence.

More likely than not, the objection will go to the fact that, because the evidence cannot be tested, it is unreliable.

In the context of administrative proceedings, this type of objection really goes to the weight to be accorded the information rather than its acceptability. The issue before the decision-maker is not ''Is the information hearsay, and if so what can I do with it.'' The questions are really, ''What is the weakness with this evidence with respect to establishing a factual basis?'' and ''Given this weakness, to what degree can or should I rely on it in making my decision?''

Determine how reliable the evidence is. For example, is it supported by other evidence on the record? Is it reliable for some other reason? There are numerous exceptions to the hearsay based on the fact that the courts have determined that the evidence contained therein is actually reliable, notwithstanding that it comes to you in the form of hearsay. Dying declarations and admissions against interest, for example, are types of hearsay which the courts have found sufficiently reliable for judicial proceedings notwithstanding that they are hearsay.

Let us say that the decision-maker concludes that the tendered evidence is not completely reliable. It will then have to determine if the evidence is *sufficiently* reliable for the ageny's purposes. To answer this question, the decison-maker will have to look to the function which it is performing. Does it require the same degree of certainty as the courts do? Is the agency performing a function that goes to ensuring public safety? Is it merely making an advisory report on some aspect

---

loan shark to get me.''

Although Mr. Brown is repeating a statement made to him by another who is not present at the hearing to be tested, his evidence is not hearsay. It is being tendered to prove, not that Mr. Jones was a hired gangster, but that Mr. Brown had been told this fact and that it created a belief in his mind which led him to take defensive action. The statement is not tendered to prove the truth of the matter contained in the statement (Mr. Jones was a gangster) but to prove that something had happened (Mrs. Smith had told him something) and that this created a belief in his mind. In the defence raised by Mr. Brown, it does not matter if Mr. Jones was a gangster. It only matters that Mr. Brown thought he was. The statement is tendered as evidence supporting the fact of this belief and its reasonableness.

or other to another decision-maker? Is the agency deciding someone's career future? Given the task before it, does the decision-maker believe that it would be reasonable to rely on evidence suffering from this particular weakness?

I'll just give you two contrasting examples of how differences in task can affect the use of hearsay. In *Bond v. New Brunswick (Board of Management)* (1992), 8 Admin. L.R. (2d) 100 (N.B.C.A.) the New Brunswick Court of Appeal found that in an employment arbitration where someone's career hinged on the determination of sexual harassment charges, the gravity of the question indicated that the arbitrator should not base his decision almost wholly on hearsay evidence. In another case, however, after the employee's guilt had already been determined and the only thing left for the arbitrator was to determine the appropriate penalty, the Newfoundland Supreme Court held that it was perfectly acceptable for her to take into account hearsay evidence to establish facts in mitigation of the punishment *(Newfoundland (Treasury Board) v. Newfoundland Association of Public Employees* (1992), 99 Nfld. & P.E.I.R., 315 A.P.R. 232 (Nfld. S.C.)). In the latter case, the hearsay was being used in a less destructive or important way.

There is a continuing debate, which rises or falls in importance from time to time, as to whether hearsay should only be admitted as a fall back position where better evidence is not available or whether it should be admitted as a matter of course. In my opinion, this question should be determined in light of the importance of the evidence in question as well as the function which you are performing. Greater latitude should likely be extended to evidence which only goes to collateral, incidental or minor matters. Evidence which goes to the heart of a question may require a greater degree of reliability than hearsay is capable of.[13]

CONCERN II

If the evidence is capable of supporting the necessary factual base, is there some other reason why it should it be rejected? Will its receipt lead to some greater social harm than the good likely to be done by the agency's decision?

Sometimes a piece of evidence will be relevant and capable of proving an assertion, however, it may have been secured in such a way or it may have some characteristic that may lead one to reject it on the grounds of social harm. Under this concern one looks at whether the social good hoped to be accomplished through the process will be outweighed by some harm resulting from the admission and use of the evidence.

One illustration of the operation of this concern can be seen with respect to material which is subject to solicitor/client privilege. The courts have taken the position that the operation of the courts themselves, of the legal system, depends on the ability of individuals to seek legal advice. Thus, advice which is given by a solicitor, as a solicitor, to his client, is not admissible. It is open to you as an agency to take the same approach. You have to ask, what is the harm which will

---

13 For an example, see *J.B. v. Catholic Children's Aid Society of Metropolitan Toronto* (1987), 27 Admin. L.R. 295 (Ont. Div. Ct.).

result from my admitting and using this evidence and then balance it against the social good in doing so. (Technically speaking, solicitor/client privilege is a matter of substantive law, not procedure. Consequently, absent a statutory direction to the contrary, an agency's power over its procedure would not extend to receiving evidence subject to a solicitor/client privilege.)

This concern can also arise with respect to information which was disclosed as part of settlement negotiations or with respect to evidence which a party claims is confidential and should not be made public.

When faced with a social harm type of question ask yourself the following questions:

1.   How necessary is the information in order for you to accomplish your statutory mandate?

2.   How necessary is the evidence for one of the other parties to make his case? Can she do so by some other means?

3.   Is the disputed evidence really of the nature claimed by the party disputing its admission? For example, is it really confidential? I have heard Margo Priest give the example of where city road maps were claimed as confidential material in proceedings before the Ontario Telephone Services Commission.

4.   How much harm will result from its disclosure to the person opposing its use? Will there also be some harm to some public interest from its admission? if so, how does this harm compare to the value hoped to be achieved through your proceedings.

5.   Is there any way to minimize this harm? (disclosure only to counsel, in camera hearings, etc.)

I suggest that if one does this type of analysis (and assuming that there is no direct statutory compulsion on the agency to receive the evidence or statutory prohibition against doing so) the ageny's decision is likely to be upheld by the courts.

CONCERN III

Assuming that the evidence meets the first two concerns, is there anything about the way the evidence is coming in which threatens the fairness or the smooth operation of your hearing? And if so, is this threat of sufficient importance, in light of your mandate, to warrant its exclusion?

Many of the judicial rules of evidence are aimed at ensuring the fairness of a proceeding and its smooth operation. Advance disclosure requirements, for example, fall under this heading.

Administrative agencies have to be concerned with the underlying problem of ensuring a process which is both fair and efficient. It is very difficult to separate fairness from smooth operation. The two are often interrelated, and sometimes conflicting. For example, to be fair, a party has the right to present his or her case fully. However, the admission of some evidence, without notice to the other side may lead that side to request an adjournment to secure the necessary evidence to meet what has been entered. What should the agency do? To grant the adjournment can delay your proceeding. Justice delayed is justice denied! Yet, to refuse the adjournment may mean denying that party the right to fully present his case.

Under this third concern one must address yourself to adopting rules which lead to the smooth and efficient operation of a hearing and which ensure its fairness as well.

17.1(e) Likely Not Free From All "Rules"

Notwithstanding that an agency may be free from the rules of evidence under the common law there are likely some "rules" which are imposed on it by statute.

17.1(e)(i) Application of the Various Evidence Acts

The Evidence Acts of most of the provinces apply to the agencies within the sphere of that jurisdiction. In the federal sphere, all federal agencies are expressly made subject to the provisions of Part I of the Canada Evidence Act as section 2 of that statute provides that:

> This Part applies to all criminal proceedings and to all civil proceedings and other matters whatever respecting which Parliament has jurisdiction.

The Evidence Acts of Manitoba, British Columbia, and Saskatchewan contain a similar application clause (usually in s. 2 of the Act). Similar results occur respecting the Evidence Acts of Ontario, Nova Scotia, Alberta, Prince, Edward Island, and New Brunswick through either the definition of "court" or "action" which are defined sufficiently broadly to catch proceedings before an administrative agency. The application of the Newfoundland Evidence Act will depend on the wording of the particular provision of the Act in question. For example, section 18 of the statute refers to the evidence of a child in "any legal proceeding" while s. 20 applies to courts and to "persons having, by law or by consent of the parties, authority to hear, receive and examine evidence".

As a general principle (along with the Interpretation Act) the Evidence Act is a very useful tool in which one can find a lot of basic stuff that can be very valuable in the decision-making process. For example, the Canada Evidence Act provides that:

5. (1) No witness shall be excused from answering any question on the ground that the answer to the question may tend to criminate him, or may tend to establish his liability to a civil proceeding at the instance of the Crown or of any person.

. . . .

6. A witness who is unable to speak may give his evidence in any other manner in which he can make it intelligible.

. . . .

13. Every court and judge, and every person having, by law or consent of parties, authority to hear and receive evidence, has power to administer an oath to every witness who is legally called to give evidence before that court, judge, or person.

14. (1) Where a person called or desiring to give evidence objects, on grounds of conscientious scruples, to take an oath, that person may make the following solemn affirmation:

> I do solemnly affirm that the evidence to be given by me shall be the truth, the whole truth and nothing but the truth.

(2) Where a person makes a solemn affirmation in accordance with subsection (1), his evidence shall be taken and have the same effect as if taken under oath.

15. (2) Any witness whose evidence is admitted or who makes a solemn affirmation under this section or section 14 is liable to indictment and punishment for perjury in all respects as if he had been sworn.

. . .

17. Judicial notice shall be taken of all Acts of the Imperial Parliament, of all ordinances made by the Governor in Council or the lieutenant governor in council of any province or colony that, or some portion of which, now forms or hereafter may form part of Canada, and of all the Acts of the legislature of any such province or colony, whether enacted before or after the passing of the Constitution Act, 1867.

18. Judicial notice shall be taken of all Acts of Parliament, public or private, without being specially pleaded.

There are also restrictions on the receipt of evidence in the Act:

7. Where, in any trial or other proceeding, criminal or civil, it is intended by the prosecution or the defence, or by any party, to examine as witnesses professional or other experts entitled according to the law or practice to give opinion evidence, not more than five of such witnesses may be called on either side without the leave of the court or judge or person presiding. (Personally, I suspect that, even where applicable, this is one provision which is seldom applied in agency proceedings.)

There are also advance notice provisions before being able to submit certain types of books or records into evidence (ss. 28, s. 30(7)).

(Agencies which have an express statutory freedom from the legal and technical rules of evidence, are likely free from many of these restrictive provisions.)

17.1(e)(ii) Specific Statutory Provisions in the Agency's Enabling Act

Aside from the relevant Evidence Act, an agency's decision-making will likely also be affected by statutory directions in its own enabling statute.[14] An excellent example can be seen in section 5(3) of The Pension Act, R.S.C. 1985. This provision is illustrative of agencies' rules of evidence being adapted to the functions they are supposed to perform. The Pension Act (and the related veterans' legislation) are more than a simple income protection scheme for Canadian citizens. They are, as I understand, a recognition of the debt that the nation owes to those who serve in its armed forces and who fight in its defence. There is an obligation owed by the people and Government of Canada to those who served their country and to their dependents. The idea that veterans benefits are something more than a simple income protection plan but a repayment of an obligation owed to our veterans is reflected in the terms of section 5(3):

> 5. (3) In making a decision under this Act, the Minister shall
>
> (a)　draw from all the circumstances of the case and all the evidence presented to the Minister every reasonable inference in favour of the applicant or pensioner;
>
> (b)　accept any uncontradicted evidence presented to the Minister by the applicant or pensioner that the Minister considers to be credible in the circumstances; and
>
> (c)　resolve in favour of the applicant or pensioner any doubt, in the weighing of evidence, as to whether the applicant or pensioner has established a case.[15]

Section 5(3)(a) goes to the ability of something to prove a fact. It is directed at the situation where there is some missing piece in a puzzle. The ordinary civil burden of proof (which generally applies to administrative agencies) requires that he who is to benefit from some assertion be able to prove that its truth is more likely than not. Section 5(3)(a) appears to go to the situation where, although there is no actual disproof of a point, the applicant, while not quite being able to

---

14 It is likely unnecessary to remind decision-makers that these statutory provisions override the common law freedom of agencies from evidentiary rules. There is, for example, case law to the effect that the failure to follow a statutory evidentiary provision can lead to a loss of jurisdiction (*Hubbley v. Workers' Compensation Board (N.S.)* (1992), 111 N.S.R. (2d) 295, 303 A.P.R. 295 (N.S.C.A.); *Moore v. Workers' Compensation Board* (P.E.I.) (1992), 101 Nfld. & P.E.I.R. 119, 321 A.P.R. 119 (P.E.I. C.A.); *Burgess v. Workers' Compensation Board (N.S.)* (1994), 130 N.S.R. (2d) 32, 367 A.P.R. 32 (N.S. S.C.); *Paulson v. Canada (Canadian Pension Commission* (March 27, 1985) Doc. A-367-84 (Fed. C.A.)).

15 A similar provision exists in s. 39 respecting proceedings before the Veterans Review and Appeal Board. Both provisions are similar to the current s. 10(5) of the Pension Act.

prove something, has been able to bring sufficient evidence from which that something may be inferred.

For example, in *Moore v. Workers' Compensation Board* (1992), 101 Nfld. & P.E.I.R. 118, 321 A.P.R. 118 (P.E.I. C.A.), the Workers' Compensation had to determine if the applicant's medical problems had been brought about by his accident on the job. The Board had before it a medical report which indicated that the injury was "most likely" related to the accident in question and that it was not related to a previous existing medical condition. This report was not contradicted. Other medical reports considered the applicant's condition to be consistent with the accident. Even the Board's own medical consultant did not rule out the accident as the cause of the condition but merely said that it was difficult to say whether or not the medical condition would have developed without the accident. In that case, even though the applicant had not proven that his condition had resulted from the accident, the Prince Edward Island Court of Appeal held that the Board, taking into account all of the medical evidence to the effect that his injury *could* have been caused by the accident, and was not *inconsistent* with such a cause, and that there was no evidence that indicated otherwise, should have drawn the inference that it *was* the result of the accident. Taking a more simplistic example, if one sees a child crying in the street, with a burst balloon at his feet, and no other probable cause of his distress, section 5(3)(a) would direct that one draws the inference that the balloon belonged to the child and that it had burst (thereby entitling him to a new balloon) even though there may be other possible interpretations of the scene.

Section 5(3)(b) is aimed at alleviating technical concerns with evidence. It appears to be directed to the situation where the applicant has *uncontradicted* evidence which appears *believable* but which might have some technical inherent weakness which might make it inadmissible in a court of law. Hearsay evidence for example might be admitted under this rubric if it appeared believable that it was not contradicted. Another example might be an old document alleged to be from a World War I hospital unit, which could be accepted as being evidence of a some fact if it appears believable to the decision-maker (for example, because it looks to be about the right age and bears other signs that it is what it claims to be), be accepted as evidence notwithstanding that the document is undated or unsigned *provided* that there is no evidence contradicting it. Note the two criteria which must be met before section 5(3)(b) can be relied on. Firstly, the evidence tendered must, be uncontradicted. In other words, there cannot be other evidence refuting the fact it hopes to prove. Secondly, the evidence tendered has to be believable itself. Section 5(3)(b) does not appear to be a direction to accept anything, merely a direction to accept what is believable and uncontradicted even though, under the technical rules of evidence, it might be inadmissible. As a last point, it looks to me that section 5(3)(b) does not direct the decision-maker to accept the evidence as *proof* of a matter. It only, I think, directs the admission of the document as evidence. The decision-maker would still have to be satisfied on the appropriate balance of the proof of the particular fact in question. The decision-maker might admit the document, that it finds it capable of being evidence, but find that it has actually very little weight to sufficiently prove a point. That is where section 5(3)(c) comes in.

Section 5(3)(c) goes to the burden of proof. After the decision-maker has admitted all of an applicant's, somewhat questionable, but nonetheless believable and uncontradicted evidence and has drawn all the inferences that can be drawn from that evidence, he or she then has to decide whether the applicant has proven her eligibility for the benefit in question.

Generally, in civil proceedings before agencies whoever will take the benefit of establishing a fact or case must satisfy the decision-maker that the fact or the case exists on the balance of probabilities.[16] This means the person who is going to benefit must satisfy the decision-maker that a particular fact is more likely than not. He does not have to prove it absolutely. The reader is also likely already familiar with the principle that in criminal proceedings, the burden of proof on the Crown who asserts the criminality of the accused is to prove that criminality beyond a reasonable doubt. The Crown does not have to prove something as being absolutely certain. But it must take the decision-maker's comfort level with the likelihood of a fact or as assertion up to the point where the decision-maker has no doubts which could be considered reasonable.

Both of these burdens are displaced by section 5(3)(c). Section 5(3)(c) directs that in determining whether a claimant has proven a fact (or her case) the decision-maker must find in favour of the applicant if the applicant "has produced credible evidence that raises at least a reasonable doubt that the fact is true".[17] The claimant does not have to prove his assertion conclusively or even satisfy the decision-maker that it is more likely than not. If at the end of the day the decision-maker can say, "Although I am not convinced that the claimant has proven her case, I must concede that it is reasonably possible" then the claimant must win. Note that the section does not direct that the applicant wins if he brings in ANY evidence. The evidence must be sufficiently strong that it at least raises a reasonable doubt that the fact it is intended to proof is true.

The reader can see that section 5(3) is really a statutory reflection of the approach to evidence which I suggested at the beginning of this presentation; that agencies should approach evidentiary questions, not from the perspective of the legal rules of evidence, but from the perspective of ensuring a sufficiently reliable

16 *Nand v. Board of Education Public School District No. 7* (1995), 157 A.R. 123 (C.A.) *British Columbia (Superintendent of Brokers) v. Rak* (1990), 74 D.L.R. (4th) 725, 47 Admin. L.R. 243 (B.C. C.A.) *Flynn v. Nova Scotia (Criminal Inquires Compensation Board)* (1988), 49 D.L.R. (4th) 619 (N.S. C.A.) *Gillen v. College of Physicians & Surgeons of Ont.)* (1989), 68 O.R. 278 (Div. Ct.).

17 Teitelbaum J. in *Tonner v. Canada (Minister of Veterans Affairs)* (April 7, 1995), Doc. T-802-94 (Fed. T.D.). See to the same effect *Paulson v. Canada (Canadian Pension Commission)* (March 27, 1985), Doc. A-367-84 (Fed. C.A.), *Burgess v. Workers' Compensation Board (N.S.)* (1994), 130 N.S.R. (2d) 32, 367 A.P.R. 32 (S.C.).

factual base, which is fair and efficient as judged in the context of the mandate of the agency.

17.1(f) Dealing With the Irrelevant or Weightless Submission

Frequently in administrative proceedings attempts are made to enter evidence which is irrelevant or without any value to the mandate of the agency.

It is common, in agency discussions, for some to argue that one of the purposes of agency hearings is to allow the affected parties an opportunity to "blow off steam" and that in this case it is a useful exercise to allow individuals to put anything into the record rather than attempting to restrict the record to matters which are relevant to the proceedings.

Another common approach on evidentiary disputes is for an agency member to allow the disputed material in with the statement that they will give it due weight.

This latter approach can be very useful in circumstances when the weight of the matter is truly in dispute. It permits the weight or the relevance of the matter to be determined in light of all of the evidence and avoids premature rulings.

I do not really recommend either approach simply as a method of moving the hearing along.

Firstly, it will be rather rare, I suggest, for an agency to have been created with a mandate of simply providing a sounding board for the disgruntled or upset. Presumably, one has some purpose to accomplish through your hearing process. Time taken on irrelevant matters is time taken away from relevant ones.

Secondly, an agency hearing is not generally an emotionally cleansing experience. A party who is allowed to whip themselves up into deep concern over a matter which is irrelevant to the proceeding is not likely to be satisfied with one speech. He or she may wish to speak again and again. The indulgence in letting him or her "blow off steam" may in fact be simply creating more "steam" to let off. Also, allowing a party to put evidence in simply to let off steam will create the, not unreasonable, expectation that the decision-maker will also let others have an opportunity for others to let off steam. This will make it difficult for you to control the proceedings or have them proceed at a reasonable rate.

Thirdly, when one allows irrelevant material into one's proceedings, an uncertainty is created in the minds of other parties as to whether they should introduce evidence to counter the material which is being admitted. Furthermore, if the irrelevant remarks become intemperate or if they contain allegations against another party (however irrelevant to your proceedings) the other party may wish to respond, leading to further delays.

Fourthly, allowing great amounts of irrelevant evidence in will clutter agency proceedings and make it difficult for the decision-maker and the other parties to focus on the matter at hand. It increases the likelihood of some substantive error being made.

(A.T.) (1996 — Rel. 1)

Fifthly, by allowing the individual to put in irrelevant information you either build an expectation in that person's mind that you will be dealing with the matters he or she raises, an expectation which can lead to appeals or judicial reviews if you do not do so.

Lastly, if a decision-maker allows irrelevant evidence into its proceedings without making a ruling during the hearing it will likely have to expressly point out in its reasons that evidence which was found to be irrelevant lest a reviewing body assume that the decision-maker had based her its decision on irrelevant considerations.

On the other hand, it is also true that it is frequently easier and faster to allow some individuals to put irrelevant evidence than it is to attempt to stop them from doing so. Also, if you are too quick to leap in to cut someone off because it appears to you that the information is irrelevant you may fail to appreciate that in fact he or she is leading up to something that is very important.

Many decision-makers find it valuable when faced with what appear to be irrelevant evidence to allow the individual presenting it sufficient time to satisfy themselves that the material being put in is irrelevant (and to ensure that a reasonable person would believe that they have listened enough to be able to adequately judge its relevance). They then interject to attempt to control it. This usually involves explaining the purpose of the proceeding and an explanation as to why the evidence going in appears to be irrelevant. The person attempting to put the evidence in should then be allowed to argue why he or she thinks the material is relevant or sufficiently weighty. The ruling as to admissibility is then made and the hearing proceeds. Time taken up front in this exercise will save time in the long run as the decision-maker will have set the proper tone, be in control of the hearings (but fairly so), and be better positioned to control future diversions into irrelevancies.

17.2 WHAT COUNSEL NEEDS TO KNOW

My opening advice to counsel planning an introducing expert testimony is as follows:

(1)   know the qualifications of the presiding panel as soon as possible;

(2)   prepare a written curriculum vitae of your expert witness and file it as an exhibit;

(3)   lead your witness through the curriculum vitae by highlighting it;

(4)   any tribunal will want to hear the qualifications of the witness as quickly and efficiently as possible;

(5)   do not seek to destroy another expert immediately after he has given his qualifications, wait until it is your turn to cross-examine him. You must be alert however to keep him as close as you can to his expertise and do not make yourself into ''sand in the wheels of progress'' because the tribunal will likely hear, in any event, everything the witness has to say that is relevant. The weight to be attached to the testimony is something you can deal with in argument; and

(6)   understand (that means more than try to understand) how the tribunal, before which you are presenting evidence, operates. It has a published code, there are procedural orders. You might speak to other counsel who practice regularly before the tribunal or confer with the tribunal solicitor and look up transcripts to see how experts have been qualified before that tribunal in the past, etc.

If you are a trial lawyer be very careful. In my view, it is often a handicap to have been trained in court procedure if you come before an administrative tribunal, mostly because many trial lawyers make it clear from the start that they have been properly trained in law and know how things should be done.

17.3 THE EXPERT'S CURRICULUM VITAE (C.V.)

A typical c.v. may be found in Appendix 17.1. The c.v. should set out:

(1)   all degrees, the dates and the institutions;

(2)   postings year by year;

(*Continued on page 17-3*)

(3)   the professional experience;

(4)   boards, tribunals, courts in Canada and the U.S.A., or elsewhere, before which the witness has appeared, on behalf of whom and to what end;

(5)   the names of past major clients;

(6)   any government or government-sponsored organization with which he/she has been associated;

(7)   the practical field or operating experience other than the above;

(8)   positions held within his/her profession;

(9)   teaching experience;

(10) recognition and honours; and

(11) all publications, books, monographs, etc. to which he/she has contributed, the dates, the titles, and the names of the publishers.

The expert should be carefully led by counsel to highlight the c.v. This is not objectionable and is the most efficient way of dealing with the qualifications. If the tribunal members have a copy of the c.v. in hand and if it is filed in advance, which is recommended, it can be adopted and properly marked as an exhibit. Go through the c.v. even if the other counsel say you need not do so. Ensure that the c.v. is in writing, that it is filed and marked as an exhibit.

17.4 DISCRETION AND THE ADMISSIBILITY OF EVIDENCE

Over the past few decades, the responsibility for resolving many of the most significant controversies in numerous areas of modern Canadian society has shifted from the courts to administrative tribunals. Accordingly, the locus and nature of the decision-maker has changed. This change does not, however, suggest that administrative tribunals may ignore the traditional canons upon which decisions must be made. First and foremost, decisions must be made on reliable evidence. The soundness and the backbone, in short, the integrity of a decision is directly proportionate to the reliability of the evidence upon which it is made.[2]

Yet, while the rules relating to the inadmissibility of evidence in a court of law are generally fixed and formal, an administrative tribunal is seldom, if ever, required to apply those strict rules. Most legislation addressing the procedure and conduct before administrative tribunals is permissive. For

---

2   W.A. Kelly, Q.C., "Qualifying and Challenging Expert Witnesses", *Emerging Issues in Administrative Law and Administrative Law Practice*, Law Society of Upper Canada, Continuing Legal Education, September 10, 1983.

instance, in Ontario, section 15 of the SPPA[3] provides that "a tribunal may admit as evidence at a hearing, whether or not . . . admissible as evidence in a court", any oral testimony and any document or other thing "relevant to the subject matter of the proceedings". It is important to note that this legislation does not enjoin an administrative tribunal from applying the law of evidence.

Rather, it gives the tribunal the discretion to admit into the record of its proceedings evidence that would not otherwise satisfy the strict evidentiary tests as to admissibility.[4] Generally, discretion implies the reasonable exercise of a power or right and necessarily implies good faith in discharging public duty.[5] In the context of section 15 of the SPPA, the rationale behind the discretionary power of a tribunal to adopt evidence inadmissible in a court of law is expressed in the Manual of Practice which followed the passage of the Act in 1971 as follows:

> A tribunal has power to accept evidence inadmissible in court and evidence not proven by sworn testimony or to insist upon proof of any fact in accordance with the strict rules of evidence or by sworn testimony. The obvious purpose of the statute in conferring this power on the tribunal is to permit it to proceed informally, in so far as such informality is consistent with a just hearing to all parties, to save parties and other persons affected, such as witnesses, time and unnecessary expense and inconvenience. The power should be exercised by the tribunal in each case to achieve this purpose. The tribunal should not therefore issue ironclad blanket rulings that will apply in all proceedings before it. It may develop a practice or indicate a general course that it will follow but it should be prepared to apply its mind to the procedure to be followed in the circumstances of each particular case and having regard to the nature of the case.[6]

If one accepts the view that the law of evidence consists of arbitrary precepts designed to inhibit the introduction of material facts, this discretion is of little moment. On the other hand, if one accepts that it is a rational and articulate code which ensures the reliability and relevance of the facts tendered by the parties to the proceeding, the exercise of such a discretion by an administrative tribunal will have a considerable effect on the reliability of the evidence and a fortiori, the integrity of the decision that follows. Consequently, this discretion should be exercised with caution.

---

3   Supra, note 1. See also: Energy Resources Conservation Act, R.S.A. 1980, c. E-11, s. 30(2); and Utilities Commission Act, S.B.C. 1980, c. 60, s. 93.
4   See: Evidence Act, R.S.O. 1990, c. E.23; and Canada Evidence Act, R.S.C. 1985, c. C-5.
5   *Roncarelli v. Duplesis*, [1959] S.C.R. 122, 16 D.L.R. (2d) 689 at S.C.R. p. 140.
6   Prepared by D.W. Mundell, Department of Justice and Attorney General, February 1972.

17.5 OPINION EVIDENCE

17.5(a) Lay Persons

As a general principle, in a court of law, no witness may testify by means of expressing his or her opinion on any matter. Rather, witnesses are required to

(Continued on page 17-5)

express perceived facts, not inferences, value judgments or conclusions drawn from facts. The rationale behind the opinion rule is that, firstly, it reserves the critical function of drawing conclusions from objective facts to the judge or jury. Secondly, it underscores the cardinal precept of the law of evidence that only first-hand knowledge of a fact is reliable.

Realistically, however, the demarcation line between opinion and fact is often blurred, thus requiring the recognition of many exceptions to the opinion rule. For instance, lay witnesses may give opinion evidence where their testimony amounts to a concise summary of a sequence of inferences based upon perceived facts and the opinion is the only practicable vehicle by which to convey that evidence to the trier of fact. Where the opinion is merely a summary of a large, indistinct group of impressions within the normal realm of human experience, such as the identity or apparent age of an individual or the speed of a vehicle, it is admissible notwithstanding that, other than personal knowledge of the subject matter, the witness has no special qualifications to support the opinion. Of course, to be admissible, the lay witness must testify to those facts as well as to his or her opinion.[7]

17.5(b) Experts

The second and more broad exception to the opinion rule applies to expert witnesses. An expert witness is a person possessed of a special skill and knowledge acquired through study or experience that entitles him to give opinion evidence concerning his or her area of expertise.[8] To be allowed to give such evidence, the witness must be *qualified* to venture his or her opinion in the relevant field of expertise.

The principal restriction on expert opinion evidence in court is that it is only admissible where the judge or jury could not itself draw the necessary conclusions from the facts upon which the opinion is based. Expert opinion evidence is admissible because it is recognized that in areas of specialized knowledge, the court is not and a tribunal may not be competent to draw the necessary conclusions. Therefore, where it is established that the point in issue is of a specialized nature, it is incumbent upon counsel to establish that issue and the qualifications of the expert witness. If the opinion of the expert does not materially assist the court in a specific subject, it is generally not admissible. In a tribunal hearing, the evidence is likely admitted and weighed later.

As the strict rules of evidence do not generally apply to administrative proceedings, the opinion rule does not accordingly operate to exclude evidence. Strictly speaking, therefore, it *may not be necessary to qualify* an expert before an administrative tribunal to render opinion evidence admissible. Equally, however, the permissive nature of the legislation[9] suggests that a tribunal may exercise its dis-

---

7 *R. v. Davies*, [1962] 3 All E.R. 97, [1962] 1 W.L.R. 1111, 46 Cr. App. Rep. 292 (C.C.A.).

8 *Rice v. Sockett* (1912), 23 O.W.R. 602, 4 O.W.N. 397, 27 O.L.R. 410, 8 D.L.R. 84 (H.C.); and *R. v. Kuzmack* (1955), 20 C.R. 365 (Alta. C.A.).

9 Supra, note 1.

cretion and require the qualification of a witness. Since most hearings by an agency involve the public interest, some more than others, I would rather err on the side of letting in too much rather than too little information. Naturally, the exercise of a tribunal's discretion is not something that one can anticipate with accuracy. The granting of discretionary power does not imply that it is to be exercised universally, but rather in appropriate circumstances. Consequently, in the context of opinion evidence, it is the course of caution to qualify an expert appearing before an administrative tribunal because the mere presence of the witness suggests the specialized nature of the proceeding.

Most tribunals hear a witness' qualifications, including his evidence and later give whatever weight seems appropriate. Very few tribunals require an expert to be qualified and then cross-examined on his qualifications before hearing his evidence. The common practice is to file a c.v. as an exhibit, after which counsel usually highlights the expert's experience followed by the witness' examination. In cross-examination, those opposed in interest may attempt to attack the qualification. On the whole, the attack is a waste of time. What is far more effective is to attack the quality of the evidence directly rather than the qualifications of the donor.

The exercise of the tribunal's discretion whether or not to qualify a witness will depend entirely on the particular type of proceeding before it. For instance, a proceeding before a municipal board may involve the appearance of lay persons on their own behalf to resolve a simple minor variance or a major environmental concern. Alternatively, competent counsel and expert witnesses may appear before the same tribunal on behalf of parties who have a significant commercial conflict involving, for example, the construction of a shopping centre on agricultural land. In the former example, it may be proper for the board to exercise its discretion, informality being consistent with the context of the proceeding. On the other hand, the latter example may as easily lend itself to the same conclusion. While the tribunal has equal statutory discretion in each case, the exercise of such power must fit the rationale for its existence. Consequently, in a proceeding involving expert testimony, it is advisable for counsel to qualify the witness as we have discussed above.

Where an administrative tribunal commonly exercises jurisdiction over matters of a highly technical and complex nature, its members usually have, or are perceived to have, expertise in those areas. For example, a tribunal such as the Canadian Radio-television and Telecommunications Commission ("CTRC") or the Ontario Energy Board ("OEB") generally consists of members who possess knowledge of and who are experienced in matters related to the tribunal's activities. On the other hand, where a tribunal's jurisdiction is diversified over a broad range of subjects, the background of its members is likewise generally diverse.

The question, therefore, arises whether the expertise of the tribunal members ought to affect the approach to the application of the opinion evidence rule. Undoubtedly, where the expert testimony is on a subject unfamiliar to the tribunal, the members will expect to hear the qualifications of the witness. Equally, a tribunal consisting of members who have expertise in the subject matter under examination may be more eager to hear the qualifications of an expert witness, as it is in a better position to assess and weigh those qualifications at the outset. Although some tribunals are permitted to "take notice" within their own specialized knowledge or area of expertise, they may be more reluctant to do so where expert witnesses have been called.[10] Frankly, most tribunals composed of experts, while defferential to a witness, are not easily persuaded out of their convictions, as they may be drawn from 25 years of active involvement in a specific specialty.

The failure to qualify an expert will not normally cause the evidence to be inadmissible; it will, however, reduce its persuasiveness in the minds of the members of the tribunal. Where the tribunal lacks expertise in the subject of examination, persuasiveness is enhanced when the expert's qualifications are objectively reliable. Where the tribunal is comprised of members knowledgeable in the subject, it is important to establish qualifications that are both objectively and subjectively reliable so that the members will be persuaded to accept the expert's opinion and not simply substitute their own (a not-unheard-of event).

17.6 METHODS OF QUALIFYING AN EXPERT WITNESS

Traditionally, in judicial proceedings experts have been qualified orally by way of broad questions from counsel, followed by a cryptic monologue by the expert. The problem with this approach is that the critical task of qualifying a witness is assigned to that witness alone. Consequently, the witness may appear immodest or, for fear of appearing immodest, fail to state important qualifications. Furthermore, the witness proceeds at his or her own speed with his or her own emphasis.[11]

An alternative method of qualifying an expert has been adopted before administrative tribunals and is finding favour in some judicial proceedings as well. The current and better practice is to prepare a detailed c.v. for the expert as mentioned above.

At the outset of examination-in-chief, the witness should be asked to identify and examine his c.v. The witness should then be led through the highlights of his qualifications as an expert. It is considered generally proper and rarely objectionable to lead the witness in these circumstances. The identification and verification of the written c.v. is quick, snappy and to the point. The c.v. should be pre-filed as an exhibit and copies provided to the parties. The document may then be attested to in terms of its pre-eminent virtues rather than its protracted entirety. This approach obviates a great deal of writing on the part of the tribunal and permits the introduction to the record of a considerable amount of qualifying material without appearing to burden the tribunal. Nearly every tribunal in Canada engages in this practice and has for years.

Tribunals will often advise counsel that there is no need to go through the c.v. as the witness is well known to the tribunal. It is always wise to file the c.v. no matter who says that it is not necessary.

---

10 Supra, note 1, s. 16(b).
11 B. Pepper, "Scientific Proof", (1959) Special Lectures L.S.U.C., Jury Trials, 277 at p. 283.

17.7 CHALLENGING THE EXPERT WITNESS

In judicial proceedings, the rules respecting inadmissibility permit a party to challenge the expert witness immediately following his qualification by counsel. In administrative proceedings, however, the right to challenge the qualifications may not emerge since the tribunal has the discretion to dispense with the qualification process altogether. On the other hand, a party may prompt the opportunity by requesting the tribunal to exercise its discretion and require the witness to be qualified. Very seldom in administrative tribunal hearings is there a direct challenge to the qualifications before hearing the evidence and it is not recommended. This is particularly true if the tribunal has heard and accepted evidence from the expert on other occasions, which is frequently the case.

In seeking to conduct a frontal attack on the qualifications of a witness, counsel is required to establish that the witness is categorically unqualified to offer the proposed opinion evidence. As it is not common for opposing parties to call witnesses to give expert testimony who have no qualifications whatsoever, a party's case is unlikely to be advanced by seeking an opportunity to challenge the witness' expertise at a preliminary stage. It is generally more effective and appropriate to address the witness' qualifications based on the substance of the opinion evidence advanced by him at a later stage in the proceedings. If, however, cross-examination is to include an attack on the extent of the expert's qualifications, it should precede any intended attack on the substance of the opinion evidence once it has been put on the record.

The key is to listen attentively to the opinion elicited from the witness. As an expert is only entitled to offer opinions within the area of expertise in which he or she has been qualified, an objection is in order where the witness attempts to advance opinions outside that specific area.

Another common difficulty occurs when an expert witness offers opinions that are actually based on the knowledge and expertise of one or a number of other persons. Often, an expert will formulate an opinion that is based on works or publications of other experts in the field, making effective cross-examination virtually impossible. In such circumstances, it is clearly proper for counsel to take objection and indicate that the witness is not testifying as to personal knowledge and that, if he is permitted to proceed, the actual author or authors must also be called to facilitate a meaningful cross-examination. On the other hand, where the nature of the proceedings are such that the tribunal is required to consider a great deal of current scientific data which has been generated by a number of eminent international experts, it may be more practical and effective to ask that the material upon which the witness has based his opinion be filed in advance and marked as an exhibit. This would permit one's own witness to review that material and present his or her own interpretation of the data.

For instance, where the material issue involves the controversial calculation of separation zones which would protect the public from danger in the event of an explosion involving a novel, combustible substance, it may be more effective for the expert to underscore the extent of the difference of scientific opinion and for counsel to argue at the appropriate time that the tribunal should, in the circumstances, prefer the calculations of the more conservative expert.

One should keep in mind, however, that where the experts disagree in their interpretation of scientific data, cross-examination generally reveals only the depth of their disagreement rather than grounds for preferring one expert's interpretation over that of another. Cross-examination is significantly more helpful when the inferences and assumptions beneath the expert's interpretation are investigated. The validity of an expert's assumptions will obviously affect the accuracy of his or her inferences. The decision-maker is in a much better position to draw correct conclusions when he or she is made aware of the expert's assumptions through effective cross-examination.[12]

The importance of both qualifying and challenging experts before administrative tribunals is illustrated in *Re Denys and College of Nurses of Ontario*,[13] in which the Discipline Committee of the College of Nurses revoked a certificate of competence on the grounds that the appellant had forged signatures on narcotic control sheets in the course of her employment. At the hearing before the Committee, two experts gave conflicting testimony concerning the forged signatures. The Committee accepted the evidence of the expert who claimed that the appellant was the author of at least some of the forged entries. Upon reversing the Committee's decision, the Divisional Court held that the question to be determined was "the proper inferences to be drawn from conflicting professional opinions".[14] In preferring the evidence of the expert who testified on behalf of the appellant, the court cited the extent of that expert's qualifications as a factor in its decision. In addition, the court relied upon a number of points made by counsel for the appellant during cross-examination concerning the qualifications of the opposing expert witness. Clearly, this result would not have been possible had the witnesses not been qualified in the proceedings before the Committee. Moreover, the case illustrates that where "the matter in issue on the appeal is not one that falls within the expertise of the professional members"[15] of the tribunal, the court is less reluctant to interfere with its decision.

17.8 EXCHANGE EXPERTS' REPORTS BEFORE PROCEEDINGS COMMENCE

Expert evidence has caused frequent problems in traditional judicial proceedings. The adversarial process often limited access to an expert's opinion

---

12 J. McGarity, "Substantive and Procedural Discretion in Administrative Resolution of Science Policy Questions: Regulating Carcinogens in EPA and OSHA", (1979), 67 Georgetown L.J. 729 at pp. 776-778.
13 Ont. Div. Ct., Reid, Southey and Craig JJ., April 11, 1983.
14 Supra, note 13 at p. 8.
15 Supra, note 13 at p. 9.

evidence before an actual trial by virtue of solicitor-client privilege. Consequently, it was customary for counsel to withhold an expert's report until the very last permissible minute and to proceed to conduct a trial by ambush. Therefore, the opposing party would be put in a position in which it would be required to respond to very complex and persuasive expert testimony, usually quite unfavourable to its cause and for which it was quite unprepared. The problem was compounded by the hearsay rule which required experts to present their evidence through oral testimony in trial. The result was ineffective cross-examination. Alternatively, the opposing party would request an adjournment to prepare for cross-examination causing delays and incurring additional expense.[16]

To alleviate this deficiency, many Canadian jurisdictions have enacted provisions requiring the exchange of certain experts' reports before trial. In addition, provisions have been established permitting the admissibility of the reports in place of oral testimony at trial, unless a party requires otherwise. The pre-trial exchange of an expert's report as a pre-condition to its admissibility is not strictly a discovery device since it applies only to those reports that a party intends to rely upon at trial.[17] Nonetheless, it curtails unnecessary surprise and lawyers' "poker-playing habits of keeping the best cards up their sleeves".[18]

In Ontario, for instance, a party who intends to call an expert witness at trial must serve a copy of the expert's qualifications and report on all other parties at least ten days before the trial. If the party fails to comply with this provision, the expert may not testify on his behalf without leave of the trial judge.[19] These new guidelines allow an opposing counsel to prepare for cross-examination and each expert to prepare to testify concerning the opinion of the other. Consequently, it generates better cross-examination and rebuttal testimony and serves to define the controversy among the experts. In addition, it may also assist in the pre-trial settlement process.

By contrast, rules governing the practice and procedure before administrative tribunals have not usually been reduced to writing in advance of proceedings. Where written rules of practice do exist, they are often scant and enunciated primarily to ensure that the basic principles of natural justice, such as proper notice and the right to a public hearing, have been adequately addressed.[20]

The trend, however, is changing. Some progressive tribunals which conduct proceedings on a frequent basis have introduced formal rules of practice and procedure. Few have specifically addressed the issue of the form of expert testi-

---

16 Report of the Federal/Provincial Task Force on Uniform Rules of Evidence, Carswell, 1982 at p. 95.

17 *Yemen Salt Mining Corp. v. Rhodes — Vaughn Steel Ltd.* (1977) 5 B.C.L.R. 248, 7 C.P.C. 37, 82 D.L.R. (3d) 764 (S.C.); and *Haltech v. McCoy* (1974), 6 O.R. (2d) 512 (C.A.).

18 *Leithiser v. Pengo Hydra-Pull of Canada, Ltd.*, [1974] 2 F.C.R. 954 (C.A.) at p. 963, per Jackett, C.J.

19 Rules of Civil Procedure, R.R.O. 1990, Reg. 194, r. 53.03(1) and (2).

20 For instance, see R.R.O. 1990, Reg. 869, which sets out Rules of Procedure for proceedings before the Ontario Energy Board.

mony or the filing of qualifications and opinions in advance. Some, on the other hand, as common practice, generally operate on the basis that an exchange and filing of evidence in advance is fundamental to an efficient and fair proceeding. For instance, some tribunals issue a procedural order requiring an applicant and all parties intending to lead evidence, to pre-file their evidence with the board and all parties well in advance of a hearing.[21] Where the nature of the work performed by a tribunal involves complex, technical matters and its members possess a degree of expertise in the area, the evidence invariably includes the written testimony of many expert witnesses.

Consequently, while the exchange of expert testimony has only recently been made compulsory in court cases, this practice has been adopted through acquiesence and of necessity in complex administrative proceedings for many years. Where the issues before a tribunal are typically of a less complex nature, experts' opinions are by definition not normally contemplated. Nonetheless, it would advance the interests of all administrative tribunals if they were to establish and publish formal rules of practice and procedure subject to variation according to the needs of each case. These rules should require all evidence to be filed in advance of a hearing to permit the parties to prepare a complete response and to reduce to a minimum the time and money invested in the hearing itself. This remark is founded on the generally accepted philosophy that administrative justice must be fair, efficient and meaningful.

More to the point, however, where expert evidence is involved, specific provisions ought to be included requiring the qualifications and reports of the witnesses to be filed. These provisions would assist in ascertaining precisely the grounds upon which each expert is qualified to offer an opinion and to enable the experts to express their opinions in the most cogent language. In addition, it may obviate the calling of the actual expert witnesses if the reports are sufficiently comprehensive and detailed. If the parties have accepted the contents, the tribunal could decide the relevant issue(s) on the basis of the reports alone. To be effective in this context, the report should summarize the expert's opinion, qualifications and the facts upon which his or her opinion is based as well as the tests, investigations or other procedures carried out by the expert and the results obtained.

In my opinion, every tribunal should have as part of its mandate, the authority to hold ''paper'' hearings or consent hearings. These are part of the newest and most effective processes which administrative tribunals are pursuing in Canada today.

17.9 A TRIBUNAL'S POWER TO APPOINT EXPERTS

Modern civil disputes often require the assistance of scientific or technical expertise and the adversary system requires parties to retain expert witnesses to

---

21 Supra, note 20; the Ontario Energy Board usually directs an applicant to file material or evidence incidental to a proceeding; see s. 2(4).

support their positions at trial. The partisanship inherent in the adversarial system conflicts with the impartial methodology of scientific inquiry. The court hears expert opinions from witnesses who are paid for their services and instructed by the respective parties. Since the court, therefore, hears not necessarily the best expert opinions but rather those most favourable to each party, some bias is inevitable. Consequently, it is not surprising that there has been considerable debate over whether a court ought to be able to appoint an expert witness of its own.

In the United States, legislation or rules authorizing the use of impartial experts are permitted pursuant to the common law of power of a judge to call his own lay witness.[22] In Canada, however, the common law power of a judge to call witnesses without the consent of the parties no longer exists.[23] Although the rules of court throughout Canada empower a judge upon a motion, or in some cases on his own motion, to appoint masters, referees or assessors, their functions are very different from that of court-appointed expert witnesses.[24] Consequently, in *Phillips v. Ford Motor Company of Canada Ltd.*,[25] where a judge sought to call an expert witness in the interests of justice, the Court of Appeal held that the judge had exceeded his authority. The Phillips case is an instructive example of the unfairness, delay and undue intervention caused by the improvident appointment of a court expert. In that case, the trial judge interrupted the testimony of one of the plaintiff's experts to announce his intention to appoint his own expert. On appeal, the Court indicated that the conduct of the trial judge suggested that he was attempting to overcome his dissatisfaction with the theories advanced by the experts by introducing another theory preferable to himself, even before the initial theories were tested. The Court found that the judge had prejudiced the proceedings by virtue of the fact that he had, in effect, become himself an adversary in the conflict between the parties.

Recently, however, many Canadian jurisdictions have reconsidered the issue of court-appointed experts. In 1982, the Federal/Provincial Task Force on the Uniform Rules of Evidence recommended that "empowering a court to appoint an expert within a framework of procedural limitations and safeguards would improve civil trials without damaging the fabric of the adversary system."[26] American studies have shown that the appointment of experts by a court can have positive effects including increased likelihood of pre-trial settlements, reduced court congestion, improved fact-finding processes, and higher-quality expert tes-

---

22 M. McCormick, *Handbook of the Law of Evidence*, (2nd Ed., 1972) at p. 171.

23 See, *Re Enoch and Zaretsky Bock and Co.*, [1910] 1 K.B. 327 (C.A.); *Jones v. National Coal Board*, [1957] 2 Q.B. 55, [1957] 2 All E.R. 155 (C.A.) at Q.B. at p. 64, All E.R. p. 159; but see contra, *Re Fraser* (1912), 8 D.L.R. 955 (Ont. C.A.) at p. 962 per Moss, C.J.O.

24 J. Basten, "The Court-Appointed Expert in Civil Trials — A Comparative Appraisal", (1970) 110 Med. L. Rev. 1974.

25 *Phillips v. Ford Motor Company of Canada* (1971), 18 D.L.R. (3d) 641 (C.A.).

26 Supra, note 16 at p. 106.

timony.[27] Since 1952, New York has operated a system whereby lists of established experts in specialities most in demand as witnesses are prepared, updated and distributed to interested parties. A judge, in consultation with counsel for the parties, may order an expert of a particular type to be appointed and the registrar of the courts selects the particular specialist, usually next in rotation on the list.[28]

Ontario has recently adopted new rules which permit a judge to retain expert witnesses,[29] on a motion by a party or on his own initiative. The expert's report must be sent to all parties and filed as evidence to the proceeding and any party may cross-examine the expert at trial.[30] In addition, where a pre-trial conference is held, a judge may, at the request of a party, or of his own motion, direct the parties or their counsel to consider the advisability of having the court appoint an expert.[31] As a result, the long standing problems of bias and confusion which result from adversarial expert testimony can be curtailed in the proper circumstances.

In administrative proceedings, a tribunal is generally required to make a decision which determines not only the rights of the parties before it, but, even more important, the impact on the public at large. The public interest component of administrative decision-making makes it clear that it is very important for an administrative tribunal to have the power to appoint its own expert witnesses. All administrative tribunals are, however, creatures of statute. It is arguable, therefore, that the empowering legislation of each tribunal must stipulate if and when an expert may be appointed. On the other hand, since administrative tribunals are generally considered to be masters of their own practice and procedure, they may have an inherent power to appoint witnesses and experts to assist in resolving matters that affect the public interest.[32] While some tribunals are themselves empowered by statute to engage experts, technical consultants or advisors in the proper circumstances, others may require that the appointment of any expert be made by an order of the Cabinet.[33]

Curiously, in Ontario and British Columbia similar legislation provides that each respective tribunal has all such powers, rights and privileges as are vested in the Ontario Court (General Division) and the B.C. Supreme Court with respect to the attendance and examination of witnesses.[34] The OEB Act empowers the

---

27 P. Morgan, *Basic Problems of State Federal Evidence* (5th Ed., 1976).

28 Supra, note 27 at pp. 201-202.

29 Supra, note 19, r. 52.03.

30 Supra, note 19, rr. 52.03(7) and 52.03(8).

31 Supra, note 19, r. 50.01(g).

32 See for instance, Utilities Commission Act, supra, note 3, s. 9; and Public Utilities Board Act, R.S.A. 1980, c. P-37, s. 19.

33 Supra, note 2.

34 See Ontario Energy Board Act, R.S.O. 1990, c. O.13, s. 14; and Utilities Commission Act, supra, note 3, s. 89. Presumably, the Ontario Energy Board may now appoint experts in a manner consistent with that enunciated in the rules of court referred to in notes 29 and 30.

Board to engage consultants and others, which it does in almost every major case before it. Some consultants are active, some are passive, but no important case comes before that Board anymore in which at least one or two consultants have not been retained. Consultants are discussed in Chapter 18.

The issue is clearly most germane to proceedings involving complex technical matters which require the assistance of an expert. In such proceedings, it is not only common for the parties to have called expert witnesses to testify on their behalf, but also for the particular tribunal to possess a certain degree of expertise in the area. However, even where a board may take notice of opinions within its own specialized knowledge or experience, it is not uncommon to find issues and subjects that go beyond its own qualifications. As a result, all tribunals should claim access to an inherent right to call their own expert witnesses to ensure a complete and satisfactory record of their proceedings, especially where the matter impacts upon the public interest. This will curtail the bias and confusion that flows naturally from the adversarial process.

22

Tribunal Decisions

22.1 DECISION-MAKING

Many agencies use different techniques in arriving at decisions. The following are a few comments on the decision-making procedure that is followed at the Ontario Energy Board ("OEB").

Many, but not all hearings will cover a number of specific discreet subject matters. Most hearings are conducted by panels of three. After the panel has been selected, the expected subject matters of the case are divided up among the panel members. This is done by the panel chairman in co-operation with the panel. Each member will act as the leader within the panel discussing and addressing the specific subject matters assigned to him or her.

In the procedural order, outlining how the case will be heard, the subject matters, referred to above, are set out in the order in which they are to be dealt with during the hearing. Thus, the case will develop along predetermined subject lines. This makes it easy to break the case into parts, to organize evidence and witness time, to schedule the hearing and to write the decision quickly and well. We have taken the view that agency hearings, with some exceptions, are managed for the public interest, not for the parties' convenience. Therefore, a counsel for a party does not have the same freedom in organizing and presenting a case before an administrative tribunal that he would have before a court. This refers, of course, only to the order of presentation and not to the substance of the evidence.

The procedural order at the conclusion of the evidence sets out how and where argument will be presented. The order lists the subject matters to be addressed in the same order as above, subject to additions and deletions by order of the tribunal during the hearing. No counsel need argue all the issues, but if he does not wish to comment on an issue he must say that he has no comment. At the end of the list, there is a catch-all for counsel who wish to argue items that are not on the list. Thus, the case starts out to look at perhaps ten major subjects. It then proceeds to

(A.T.)(1988)

go through those subjects seriatim during the hearing. The argument follows that same order.

It is worth observing that by dealing with one subject at a time, all the evidence *of all of the parties* can be heard on one subject before moving to the next subject. This makes hearings shorter, easier to follow and far less expensive. Everyone is there to hear everyone else on one subject at a time. The opposition to this kind of an ordered hearing stems basically from those who have never tried it.

Thus by step 1 all subjects are allocated to separate panel members (each may end up with five or six subjects); by step 2 the case is conducted in accordance with those subjects and in that order; and by step 3 the argument, often in writing, is presented to the tribunal following the same order of subjects.

Each day after the hearing is completed, for that day, the hearing panel meets to:

(1) talk about what it thought of the day's evidence;

(2) hear from the panel member in charge of the discrete subject covered that day; and

(3) prepare the first outline of the expected issues arising from the subjects presented that particular day, i.e. the "Fact Sheet". See Appendix 14.1 for a sample Fact Sheet.

22.2 PREPARATION OF DECISION

22.2(a) Getting to the Final Draft

Once argument is over and all arguments are read by the panel members, one of three alternatives is usually followed by administrative agencies.

Alternative 1: The staff will commence drafting the decision with or without some direction by the panel. When the first draft is completed by the staff, the panel will review it and send it back to the staff with instructions for rewriting, etc.

The OEB does not follow this route but many boards do.

Alternative 2: The panel will meet and allocate the writing of the decision among the panel members. Some portion of the draft may be allocated to the staff, such as summaries of the evidence. Many boards follow this route.

Alternative 3: Is the preferred route at the OEB. This route is followed because members are of the view that they are appointed to decide. Deciding cannot be delegated. Writing with guidance and instructions can be delegated. This alternative permits members to decide first, assign the writing and then finalize the writing.

Under this alternative:

(1) each panel member reads all of the arguments;

(2) each panel member will prepare a Finding Sheet for each of his subjects;

(3) the panel will meet and go over all the Finding Sheets and agree (it should be remembered that the panel has been doing this each day of the hearing with these sheets);

(4) a final set of Finding Sheets is sent to the staff to prepare a draft decision in accordance with the Finding Sheets; and

(5) on occasion, a panel member may, if asked by the panel chairman, draft in full or part the text of a subject matter.

Once the first draft is complete, the panel goes over it and makes whatever readjustments are necessary until the panel is satisfied with the penultimate draft of the decision.

Once the decision is in its penultimate form, perhaps the fourth draft, it is sent back to the staff to proof it for errors or calculations, quotes from the transcripts, etc. The board solicitor will review the draft from the point of view of the law. The board secretary will review the draft as to form and to deal with the printer.

At the same time, the penultimate draft decision is circulated among other members of the board. Some tribunals do not take this step or so they say.

A board that has issued a decision naming a monument in Labrador may not need to circulate the draft decision for a number of obvious reasons. A board that has no members other than the panel will not need to circulate. A decision which adjudicates between A and B likely does not need to be circulated, although note that the Ontario Labour Relations Board ("OLRB") and the Immigration Appeal Board to different degrees, may circulate. There will be many other circumstances under which a tribunal will or will not need to circulate.

22.2(b) Circulating the Draft Decision

The OEB circulates draft decisions to other Board members for many reasons, among which are the following:

(1) The OEB regulates an industry with a plant investment in the billions of dollars which is a basic service to millions of Ontario residents. Any one of the decisions may have immensely broad public impact. Even a delay in a decision can have serious province-wide financial impacts.

(2) The decisions have to be accurate, consistent, clear, understandable and immediately implementable.

(3) Most of the decisions *immediately* affect essential services, thousands of jobs and hundreds of millions of dollars of revenue.

Decisions are circulated to all Board members and a limited number of technical staff to be on the look out for:

(1) *Factual errors*: If the panel has misstated the evidence or misquoted a witness or misunderstood an argument, it wants someone in the family to tell it so. Then, as a panel, it will review the matter and decide what, if any, corrections are needed.

(2) *Errors of law*: The board solicitor, *not* the case counsel, receives the drafts to check for statements of law, citations or legal quotes.

(3) *Mathematical errors*: In a case such as the Ontario Hydro Rate Review, the OEB panel will have to review thousands of pages of transcript, 400 exhibits running perhaps to 6,000 pages and it will have to evaluate perhaps millions of separate figures and thousands of calculations. The panel's problems are compounded by the fact that the April application of Hydro is based upon forecasts which are updated by May's, then June's, then July's before the case is over. It would be grossly negligent not to have a draft decision checked and double checked by the staff.

   The possibility of transposition and miscalculation is very high. The more often one reads and re-reads a decision, the tighter is the hold of one's stereotypes. One can read a patent error five times without seeing it, whereas someone new to the text may spot it instantly.

(4) *Grammatical indiscretions*: One should try to write well or at least as well as one can. Some write better than others; some shouldn't write at all. Circulating decisions can improve the quality of expression of the decision.

(5) *Clarity*: One of the cardinal rules of rate-making is to decide in simple, clear terms. Most statements can usually be made more clearly and briefly. Look for brevity and clarity. "Is that exactly what you mean?" Millions of dollars may rest on a single word. The difference between "used *or* useful" and "used *and* useful" may amount to significant dollar differences.

(6) *Consistency*: Decisions have to be consistent because they have an immense public impact and take effect immediately.

   Investment in any part of Canada depends in part upon the congeniality of the economic, social and political environment. If an investor cannot tell clearly how his proposed investment, reaching perhaps billions of dollars, will be treated, he won't make it. And he cannot sit around until a matter is exhausted through court procedure. In the meantime, the investment will go congenially to the U.S.A.

   In 1986, the OEB issued over 800 orders. The decisions are computerized, but the reasoning cannot be. No board member can read everything a board publishes no matter how hard he tries. Therefore, we circulate all important decisions. We are looking for consistency and predictability. If we are departing from a recent decision, are we aware of that fact? If we are not following a recent decisions have we clearly said why? It is very important to be clear about why a board acts as it does. Often others on the board are a better judge of clarity than the authors.

Our purpose in circulation is not to debate or change substantive conclusions, but rather to be sure that the conclusions are clear, consistent and well reasoned. It must also be borne in mind that the public interest is involved in every one of our decisions. The public interest is not a wobbling top to be viewed by separate board members, but is a firm point to be concurred in and upheld. Not only that, but while the "public" in the public interest will vary from tribunal to tribunal, it must be consensually understood within a single board.

(7) *Relationship to government policy*: Circulating a decision helps to ensure that, if there is government policy on the matter, everyone knows how that policy has been treated. It may be necessary for a board to re-open the hearing if some evidence or case law (except as to jurisdiction) is raised during circulations that could affect the substantive conclusion which was not fully argued during the hearing.

After the circulation is over, the panel reviews the decision taking into account any comments that have been made, comes to its own conclusions and issues its decision.

I want to add parenthetically that I know that many boards do not discuss decisions (so they say) and that some boards do not circulate decisions (so they say). I cannot resist relating a conversation which I had recently with a Chairman of one of the most important boards in Western Canada. We discussed that while the OEB did not arrive at decisions consensually, no decision emerged from our board until we all had had a look at it for the reasons I have set out above. The Chairman admitted to me that a panel of which he was not a member was about to decide perhaps its most important case in 25 years. Everyone who could hear thunder or see lightning knew that the provincial government had a strong policy on the matter before the Board. I asked the Chairman if he would review or be involved in the decision before it was released. He told me "No!" "Will you not even circulate the decision?" "No", was the answer! But he sheepishly added "Of course, you know the members pass each other in the hall!" So much for narrow halls.

22.3 HE WHO HEARS MUST DECIDE

22.3.1 Introduction

In this section I intend to discuss the following points:

It is a principle of natural justice that only the decision-maker who "heard" the evidence and argument in a matter may vote in the decision arising out of it.

2. In the context of oral proceedings, the decision-maker must have personally heard all of the evidence and argument presented by the parties.

3. Where the issues in oral proceedings are severable and in which each segment does not rely on the same evidence and argument the decision-maker need only have heard the evidence and argument relating to the segment he is deciding.

4. In the context of written proceedings, the decision-maker must have reviewed all of the written evidence and argument although that information may be collected and summarized for him by staff or other investigating officers.

5. Such investigating officers must pass that information on to the decision-maker. It is not sufficient for the investigating officers to collect the information and merely pass on their recommendations.

6. Generally, Ministers of the Crown, by virtue of the nature of their offices, are intended to work through officers of their department who may collect and consider the relevant information and pass their recommendations on to the Minister.

7. The "he who hears" principle of natural justice determines who is required to preside over re-hearings and reconsiderations.

8. The protection offered by the "he who hears" principle may be waived by the parties.

9. The "he who hears" principle may also be displaced by legislation.

10. Failure to comply with the requirements of the principle likely results in the decision in question being invalid where a disqualified member has voted in favour of the decision made. It is uncertain whether this is true where a disqualified member voted against the decision arrived at by the majority.

11. Prior to the decision of the Supreme Court of Canada in *Consolidated Bathurst Packaging Ltd. v. International Woodworkers of America, Local 2-69*[1] the rule was generally cited to preclude any participation in decision-making of any individuals who had not "heard" the evidence and argument. However, in *Consolidated Bathurst* the Supreme Court of Canada approved the practice of the Ontario Labour Relations Board whereby decision-makers were able to consult with other members of the agency in full board meetings in order to enhance consistency and quality in decision-making. Subsequently, in *Tremblay c. Québec (Commission des affaires sociales)*[1.1]

---

1 [1990] 1 S.C.R. 282, 73 O.R. (2d) 676n, 42 Admin. L.R. 1, 68 D.L.R. (4th) 524 (S.C.C.).

1.1 [1992] 1 S.C.R. 952, 3 Admin. L.R. (3d) 173, 135 N.R. 5, 90 D.L.R. (4th) 609, 47 Q.A.C. 169 (S.C.C.).

the Court indicated that the ability to "institutionalize" decision-making was not restricted only to agencies of the same characteristics as the Labour Relations Board but was open to any agency facing institutional constraints which made it difficult to promote consistency and quality in its decision-making.

12. Whatever process is adopted by an agency in pursuit of consistency and quality it must not intrude upon the independence of the decision-maker or the right of a fair hearing by the parties or give the impression of doing so. To this end, where full board meetings are initiated I believe that they must be voluntary and restricted to law and policy with the facts being taken as determined by the decision-makers. The parties must be advised of any new law or argument arising at such consultations and be given an opportunity to respond thereto.

13. To the degree that *Consolidated Bathurst* approves of after-hearing consultations with agency members similar consultations with staff are likely also permissible. After-hearing consultations should not be carried out with staff who have participated in the hearing unless that participation was restricted to areas of the neutral mechanics of the process or to the provision of legal advice to the agency at its request.

14. In reaching a decision in a matter the individual members of a hearing panel must be aware of each other's views. There need not be any formality to this communication which may be accomplished in any number of ways from oral discussions to circulation of draft decisions.

22.3.1(a) The Principle

The principle that "he who hears must decide" requires every decision-maker to (a) evaluate the relevant evidence placed before it, (b) consider the arguments of both sides, and finally, (c) direct his "mind" to the issues at hand so as to render his decision. Traditionally, the rule applied so as to insulate the decision-makers from the after-hearing influence of any non-agency member and any agency member who had not heard all of the evidence and argument in a matter. Only the agency members who had heard all the evidence and argument in a matter were permitted after a hearing to discuss how that case should be decided and to actually vote in the decision. However, in *Consolidated Bathurst Packaging Ltd. v. International Woodworkers of America, Local 2-69* (1990), 68 D.L.R. (4th) 524 (S.C.C.) the Supreme Court of Canada distinguished between participating in the consideration of the decision to be made and actually having a deciding vote in the matter. Following *Consolidated Bathurst*, where institutional constraints demand it, the consideration of a decision is now likely open to a much broader universe of participants than was formerly the case. Actual voting on a decision, however, remains limited to the agency members who personally heard all of the evidence and argument.

According to the principles of natural justice only the individuals who heard a matter may vote on the decision arising out of it.[1.2] The meaning of "heard", of course, is as flexible as the concept of the "hearing" required by natural justice (which is discussed in more detail in another section of this book). However, to the extent that natural justice requires a "hearing" it also requires that the persons who make the decision arising out of such a hearing must be the persons who "heard" the evidence and argument.[1.3] In other words, where oral hearings are required, the decision-maker must have taken part in the entire oral proceedings. Where written proceedings are contemplated, the decision-maker must have reviewed all of the written evidence and submissions.

22.3.1(b) Oral Hearings

Where the "hearing" right of an individual extends to an oral hearing only the board members who sat at that hearing and heard all of the evidence and argument can make the decision relating to it. Logic alone should dictate this result without recourse to the long line of judicial decisions in this area. It is a natural extension of the right to fully present one's case. The right to be heard would be illusory if the decision could be made by some one who to whom you have not made your case.

> [The maxim "he who hears must decide"] is a well-known rule according to which, where a tribunal is responsible for hearing and deciding a case, only those members of the tribunal who heard the case may take part in the decision. It has sometimes been said that this rule is a corollary of the *audi alteram partem* rule....This is true to the extent a litigant is not truly "heard" unless he is heard by the person who will be deciding his case. . . .[1.4]

It is not sufficient for the purposes of this rule that a decision-maker had heard some or most of the evidence or originally had been scheduled to preside at the hearing (but had not been able to attend some or all of it),[1.5] or had read

---

1.2 *Consolidated Bathurst v. International Woodworkers of America, Local 2-69* (1990), 68 D.L.R. (4th) 524 (S.C.C.) at p. 559.

1.3 However, where the ability of a decision-maker to make a decision is subject to the approval of another, the person giving that approval need not have "heard" the evidence. It is sufficient if the decision-maker himself has done so (*Precambrian Shield Resources Ltd. v. Alberta. (Provincial Treasurer)* (1989), 69 Alta. L.R. (2d) 344, 99 A.R. 76 (Q.B.)).

1.4 Pratte J. in *Doyle v. Restrictive Trade Practices Commission*, [1985] 1 F.C. 362, 60 N.R. 218, 7 C.P.R. (3d) 235, 21 D.L.R. (4th) 366 at p. 371, leave to appeal to S.C.C. (1985), 7 C.P.R. (3d) 235n.

1.5 *Bar of the Province of Quebec v. Ste-Marie and Tisseur*, [1977] 2 S.C.R. 414.

the transcript or report of the proceedings.[1.6] A member of an agency who has not attended throughout a hearing and heard all of the evidence and argument may not join in the final vote.

The rule has been applied in a number of instances. One of the more frequently cited cases is the decision of the Supreme Court of Canada in *Mehr v. Law Society of Upper Canada*, [1955] S.C.R. 344, [1955] 2 D.L.R. 289. That case involved a discipline hearing of a lawyer before the Discipline Committee of the Law Society of Upper Canada. The facts and the Court's view of the relevant law are found summarily in the decision delivered by Justice Cartwright at pages 294-295 D.L.R.:

> At the hearing before the Discipline Committee on September 18th, six members were present. At the hearing on October 2nd the same six members were present and two additional members were present. At the hearing on November 19th the eight members who had been present on October 2nd were present and one additional member was present. There is nothing to indicate that all nine of these members did not take part in deciding as to the report which the Committee should make to Convocation. While it is not necessary to express any final opinion as to whether such a course would render the report invalid[1.7] I am much impressed by the reasoning of Lord Hanworth M.R. and Romer J. in *R. Huntingdon Confirming Authority*, [1929] 1 K.B. 698. At p. 714 Lord Hanworth said: "One more point I must deal with, and that is the question of the justices who had not sat when evidence was taken on April 25, but who appeared at the meeting of May 16. We think that the confirming authority ought to be composed in the same way on both occasions: that new justices who have not heard the evidence given ought not to attend. It is quite possible that all the justices who heard the case and the evidence on April 25 may not be able to attend on any further hearing, but however that may be, those justices who did hear the case must not be joined by other justices who had not

---

1.6 *Doyle v. Restrictive Trade Practices Commission* (1985), 21 D.L.R. (4th) 366 (Fed. C.A.), leave to appeal to S.C.C. refused October 10, 1985 (two of three commissioners failed to attend throughout all the hearings); *R. v. Mason* (1983), 43 O.R. (2d) 321, 5 Admin. L.R. 16, 35 C.R. (3d) 393 (H.C.) (third member who was not present at hearings assigned to break tie between the two presiding members); *Hughes v. S.I.U.* (1961), 31 D.L.R. (2d) 441 (B.C.S.C.) (new replacement member appointed in mid-hearing); *Inter-City Freightlines Ltd. and Highway Traffic & Motor Transport Board of Manitoba v. Swan River-The Pas Transfer Ltd.*, [1972] 2 W.W.R. 317 (Man. C.A.) (where hearing panel lacks quorum by 1 member, subsequent informing of additional member of facts will not save quorum); *O'Brien v. Canada (National Parole Board)*, [1984] 2 F.C. 314, 12 Admin. L.R. 249, 43 C.R. (3d) 10, 17 C.C.C. (3d) 163 (T.D.) (Justice Strayer referred to the disqualified members' knowledge gleaned from the written record as "ignorance sufficient to preclude the exercise of any fair judgment upon the merits of the application"); *Hayes and Saskatchewan Government Employee's Union v. Saskatchewan Housing Corporation*, [1982] 3 W.W.R. 468 (Sask. Q.B.) (hearing commenced by first panel, completed by a second); *Singh v. Canada (Minister of Employment & Immigration)* (1994), 22 Admin. L.R. (2d) 299, 23 Imm. L.R. (2d) 117 (Fed. T.D.) (replacement member of panel using transcript to access evidence given prior to member joining panel).

1.7 The Court had already decided that the decision had to be quashed by reason of errors made by the Committee in the admission of evidence.

heard the case for the purpose of reaching a decision, on this question of confirmation.''[1.8]

Terminations of appointments, deaths and the sudden unavailability of members are all sources of problems in this regard. When a member's appointment is coming due it is important, in the absence of a statutory provision allowing a member to complete any outstanding duties,[1.9] to ensure that all outstanding decisions are completed prior to the expiry of the appointments of the members of a hearing panel or than an extension of the appointment be obtained. Retired members cannot be replaced in mid-hearing by new members who have not heard what has gone on before without necessitating the rehearing of the matter in its entirety.[1.10] In *Rosenfeld v. College of Physicians & Surgeons (Ontario)* (1969), [1970] 2 O.R. 438, 11 D.L.R. (3d) 148 (H.C.) a discipline committee held a hearing on December 12 and 13, 1966 regarding a complaint of professional misconduct against a doctor. The committee directed that the imposition of a penalty be postponed for one year subject to good professional conduct and that the appellant pay $1,500 as costs for the hearing. Before the matter was brought back on the original committee was replaced by a new discipline committee which was appointed in April, 1967. Two of the members of the new committee had not been members of the old committee. The new committee brought the matter back on before it at a hearing in March, 1969 to consider the penalty to be imposed.

1.8 Other fluctuating attendance cases with similar results are *Ramm v. Public Accountants Council (Ontario)*, [1957] O.R. 217, 7 D.L.R. (2d) 378 (C.A.); *R. v. Halifax (City) Committee on Works* (1962), 31 D.L.R. (2d) 45 (N.S.S.C.); and *Bailey v. Langley (Township) Local Board of Health*, [1982] 2 W.W.R. 76, 32 B.C.L.R. 298, 129 D.L.R. (3d) 448 (S.C.).

1.9 An example of such a provision is s. 104(7) of the Ontario *Labour Relations Act*, R.S.O. 1990:

(7) Where a member of the Board resigns, the member may carry out and complete any duties or responsibilities and exercise any powers that he or she would have had if he or she had not ceased to be a member, in connection with any matter in respect of which there was any proceeding in which he or she participated as a member of the Board.

An example of a statutory provision dealing with the death or unavailability of a member is s. 35(5) of the Immigration Regulations mentioned in *Virk v. Canada (Minister of Employment & Immigration)* (1992), 140 N.R. 290 (Fed. C.A.):

(5) Where the person concerned has made a claim to be a Convention refugee in accordance with subsection 43(1) of the Act, as amended by S.C. 1988, c. 35, section 14, and the inquiry is adjourned pursuant to the Act or these Regulations, the inquiry may be resumed by any other adjudicator and any other member of the Refugee Division where the consent of the claimant has been obtained or where no substantive evidence has been introduced.

A statutory provision dealing with expiry of appointments was also found to apply to cases of resignation in *Canada (Director of Investigation & Research) v. Air Canada* (1993), 50 C.P.R. (3d) 49 (Comp. Trib.)

1.10 *Faurot v. Horse Racing Commission (Man.)* (1984), 30 Man. R. (2d) 295 (C.A.).

Justice Fraser of the Ontario High Court quashed the decision of this new Committee and the penalty it had imposed saying (at page 164 D.L.R.):

> . . . I am of the opinion that the committee that sat on March 12th had no jurisdiction to hear evidence and to determine the penalty. It was a new and different committee.

(*Continued on page 22-10.1*)

I am also of the opinion that even if the Council had been properly constituted under the Act and By-law 26 that the participation of two persons in a total of five who had not heard a substantial part of the evidence was such a departure from natural justice that the recommendation of the committee was invalid.[1.11]

Care should also be taken in the signing of decisions in order not to run afoul of this principle. In *Chase Holdings Ltd. v. New Brunswick (Liquor Licensing Board)* (1988), 123 N.B.R. (2d) 384, 310 A.P.R. 384 (Q.B.) two members of the six member Liquor Licensing Board were absent throughout a hearing due to weather conditions. The written decision, however, was signed by all six members of the board, including the two members who had been absent from the hearing. The participation in the decision by the two members of the Board who were not present at the hearing was fatal and its decision was quashed.[1.12]

A *laissez-faire* attitude and blindness to the perceptions of the persons attending a hearing can also lead to trouble. In *Bourgoin v. New Brunswick (Liquor Licensing Board)* (1992), 123 N.B.R. (2d) 366, 310 A.P.R. 366 (N.B. Q.B.) a member of the Board came into a hearing very late in the proceedings. He sat with the panel. The member retired with the Board when it adjourned to consider its decision and returned with it where the Chairman announced the decision reached. Not surprisingly, the decision of the panel was challenged on judicial review for being tainted by the participation of someone who had not heard the full case. The New Brunswick Court of Queen's Bench upheld the decision but only on the grounds that the absent member had not taken part in the decision. He had not signed the decision and had sworn an affidavit that he had taken no part in the considerations leading up to it. (The member swore in an affidavit that to the best of his recollection he made phone calls in another office during the considerations of the rest of the panel.)[1.13]

The application of the rule is sometimes subtle. In *Grain Workers' Union, Local 333 v. Prince Rupert Grain Ltd.*, [1987] 3 F.C. 479, 38 D.L.R. (4th) 467

1.11 See also *Hughes v. S.I.U.* (1961), 31 D.L.R. (2d) 441 (B.C.S.C.) (member of a sailors' trial committee "shipping out" in mid-proceedings); *Beauregard v. Commission de la fonction publique (Qué.)*, [1987] R.J.Q. 2011, 10 Q.A.C. 115 (C.A.) (member replaced in mid-proceedings); *Virk v. Canada (Minister of Employment & Immigration)* (1992), 140 N.R. 290 (Fed. C.A.) (member of a "credible basis" panel under the Immigration Act dying).

1.12 The mere signing of an order in error by a member who had not taken part in the hearing will not invalidate it (*Canada (Attorney-General) v. Canada (Anti-Dumping Tribunal)*, [1973] F.C. 745, 39 D.L.R. (3d) 229 (C.A.)).

1.13 Another error of form, rather than substance, but on a much lesser scale, was discussed in *Ramsahoi v. Saskatchewan (Minister of Health)* (1990), 85 Sask. R. 42 (Q.B.). In that case the Chairman of a panel introduced the five members (including herself) present and presiding at the hearing and, in addition, a sixth member who was not present. The Chairman then advised the parties that "These are, including myself, the six people who will be making any decision to be made." The Saskatchewan Court of Queen's Bench refused to overturn the decision reached by the panel as there was no evidence that the missing person took part in deliberations. The Court found that the wording of the introduction was merely a "slip of the tongue".

(C.A.) a panel of the Canada Labour Relations Board had heard an application in 1984 and dealt with all of the issues except that of the potential exclusion of certain employees from the bargaining unit. The panel felt that the parties should attempt to resolve this issue before the Board intervened with respect to it. Consequently the panel declined to decide the exclusion issue and left it to the parties to attempt to resolve. It reserved jurisdiction over the issue, however, in the event that the parties could not agree. Subsequently, in 1986, when it was clear that the issue would have to be determined by the Board, the Board reconvened the matter. The hearing panel was not the same as that at the first hearing. One of the members of the original panel had been replaced by another.

In obiter, the Federal Court of Appeal stated that it was likely that the "he who hears" rule had not been offended in the particular circumstances of this case because the exclusions issue was completely separate and severable from the other issues decided at the first hearing and was based on totally unrelated evidence. Writing for the court, Justice Lacombe stated (at page 470 D.L.R.):

> The record clearly shows that the hearings conducted by the Board in 1984 and in 1986 are completely severable since, on these two occasions, it dealt with and disposed of two separate issues, on evidence and submissions which differed totally from one hearing to the other.

The Court noted that in the 1984 hearings the Board has exercised jurisdiction under section 151 of the Canada Labour Code while the 1986 hearings had turned on sections 118(p)(ii) and (v), 119 and 121. From the 1986 Board reasons the Court noted that that panel had not relied or even considered any evidence that was not adduced at the 1986 hearings and that the 1986 panel had not been influenced in any way by what was said in the earlier 1984 proceedings. "On the contrary, it appears from the record that the parties fought the issue of inclusions or exclusions from the bargaining unit strictly on fresh submissions and new evidence, which were complete and sufficient in themselves to lead the Board to its decision."[1.14] On this basis the Court felt that the conclusion was

> "inescapable that all three members of the quorum heard all the pertinent evidence and representations which were necessary to dispose of the issue they were called upon to decide. It follows that the requirements of the rule "he who decides must hear" have been observed in fact by the panel of the Board that conducted the 1986 hearing...."[1.15]

It is clear from the reasoning of the Court that the result would not have been the same had the issues in the 1986 hearings not been completely divorced from

---

1.14 p. 472 D.L.R.

1.15 p. 472 D.L.R. A similar result was also arrived at in *Civil Service Association of Alberta v. Farran (No. 2)* (1979), 98 D.L.R. (3d) 282 (Alta. C.A.) where the rating of individual applicants on interviews appears to have been viewed as separate issues unrelated to each other.

the earlier 1984 proceedings. In discussing section 120.1 of the Canada Labour Code (which permitted the Board to reserve jurisdiction on issues) Justice Lacombe stated (at page 473 D.L.R.):

> Counsel for the Board submitted that s. 120.1 of the *Canada Labour Code* confers on the Board statutory authority, in a case involving multiple issues, to have any of these issues decided by different quorums, subject only to being satisfied that the rights of the parties will not thereby be prejudiced. On its face, the subsection does not explicitly say that; it authorizes the Board to split the issues arising from an application or complaint for the purpose of separate adjudications thereon. In most, if not practically all cases contemplated by this provision, sheer common sense if not natural justice would dictate that there be no alteration of the quorum to hear the remaining issues on which the Board has reserved jurisdiction. This will obtain, for example, where all the issues arising from an application or complaint are inexplicably linked together or where the remaining issues stand to be decided on the same evidence as for the issue already disposed of or on additional evidence or upon further argument or supplementary investigation.

22.3.1(c) Paper Hearings, Investigations and "Delegated Hearings"

Where the agency is under no obligation to hold an oral hearing but may receive the evidence and representations of the parties in written form it is sufficient for the purposes of the rule that the deciding members have before them all the evidence which the parties have presented. The evidence need not have been directed specifically to each member and they may appoint one of their number or staff to investigate and secure the evidence for them.[1.16] Nor need they have the evidence and submissions in the exact form it was originally submitted; an accurate summary is likely sufficient.[1.17] This all seems apparent from the nature of the proceedings.

The fact that an agency (which otherwise need not have held an oral hearing) may have collected evidence through some form of oral investigation process does not mean that the ultimate decision-makers must have themselves presided over those proceedings. There are situations where an agency which need not hold oral hearings, nonetheless, wishes to use some type of oral proceeding. For example, some parties may be uncomfortable with written representations and be better able to express themselves orally. In these circumstances the agency may appoint an investigator or establish an investigating committee composed of members of the agency or its staff to meet with some or all of the parties, hear and record their evidence and representations and transmit that material back to

---

1.16 *Selvarajan v. Race Relations Board,* [1976] 1 All E.R. 12 (C.A.).

1.17 *Selvarajan v. Race Relations Board,* [1976] 1 All E.R. 12 (C.A.); *Jeffs v. New Zealand Dairy Production & Marketing Board,* [1967] 1 A.C. 551 (P.C.).

the deciding body. Such proceedings are sometimes referred to as "delegated hearings". Provided that there is no obligation on the agency to hold oral hearings the use of such "delegated hearings" or investigation committees does not offend the "he who decides" rule.[1.18]

The decision of the Federal Court of Appeal in *Trans Mountain Pipe Line Co. v. Canada (National Energy Board)*, [1979] 2 F.C. 118, 24 N.R. 44 (C.A.) is illustrative of these propositions. In that case the National Energy Board received an application for an order amending pipeline tolls charged by the applicant. Pursuant to section 14(1) of the *National Energy Board Act*, R.S.C. 1970, c. N-6, the Board authorized one of its members to take evidence and hear submissions respecting the application. The member conducted an oral hearing where the applicant and all other parties had an opportunity to lead evidence, cross examine witnesses and present argument. The member then made a report to the Board consisting of his findings and recommendations. The Board considered the report and adopted it as its own decision. The applicant attacked the adoption by the Board of the report on the grounds that the applicant had not had an opportunity to be heard before the Board on the contents of the report. The Federal Court of Appeal rejected this argument. Justice Pratte (with whom Justices Ryan and Kerr concurred) stated:

> It is the appellant's submission that natural justice required that it be given [an opportunity to be heard on the contents of the report]. I do not agree. The appellant, while not entitled to any particular form of hearing, was entitled to be heard on its application. It cannot, however, be contested that it was so heard since the record shows that both the evidence adduced and the submissions made by the appellant before the Presiding Member were communicated to the Board. Natural justice did not require, in my view, that the appellant be given the further right of being heard on the Presiding Member's report. The making of that report was part of the Board's decision process and I do not think that the appellant had the right to interpose itself in that process. The rights of an applicant, it seems to me are the same whether or not the decision is made pursuant to subsection 14(1); in both cases the applicant is entitled to be heard on its application. An applicant does not acquire a right to an

---

1.18 However, agencies should be aware of the decision of the Federal Court Trial Division in *O'Brien v. Canada (National Parole Board)*, [1984] 2 F.C. 314, 12 Admin. L.R. 249, 43 C.R. (3d) 10, 17 C.C.C. (3d) 163 (T.D.) where Justice Strayer held that the National Parole Board having held an oral hearing before three members (although it was under no obligation to do so) was bound by the rules of fairness such that only those three members (which was sufficient for a quorum) could make the final decision. This decision is likely incorrect in light of the principles discussed above. For the contrary, and likely more correct, view see *Callahan v. Newfoundland (Minister of Social Services)* (1993), 113 Nfld. & P.E.I.R. 1, 353 A.P.R. 1 (Nfld. S.C.) where Justice Puddester stated (at p. 55) that "..the fact that in this particular case the investigating arm has chosen to proceed in a manner more closely analogous to the purely judicial than the process inherently requires cannot, in itself, be used as a basis to them import some higher standard generally with respect to the process overall".

additional hearing when the Board chooses to resort to the procedure of subsection 14(1).[1.19]

In making their report, all the members of an investigation committee must have reviewed the evidence upon which it is based. However, where such evidence has been given to the investigating committee in oral form it is not likely necessary that all the members of the committee have heard the oral presentation. It will be sufficient if those members not present at the oral presentation review an accurate report of the evidence which was given.[1.20]

A similar conclusion was reached in *Armstrong v. Royal Canadian Mounted Police (Commissioner)* (1994), 73 F.T.R. 81, 24 Admin. L.R. (2d) 2. In that case Justice Rothstein had to consider a charge that the Commissioner of the R.C.M.P. had erred in having a staff member prepare a résumé of the materials to be considered by him in a decision. *Armstrong* dealt with the discharge of an R.C.M.P. officer under the Royal Canadian Mounted Police Act, R.S.C. 1985, c. R-10. The officer had had a hearing before a discharge and demotion board which had decided that she should be discharged. That decision was appealed to the Commissioner who, prior to making his decision was obliged by statute to refer the matter to the External Review Committee whose recommendations were not binding on the Commissioner (although he had to give reasons for not accepting them). The External Review Committee recommended that the officer not be discharged. That recommendation went back to the Commissioner who now had to decide the appeal. Under the statute the Commissioner was not required to hold an oral hearing to determine this appeal. The statute merely required him to review the decision of the discharge and demotion board and the recommendations of the External Review Committee before whom there were opportunities for oral hearings by the applicant.

Prior to reaching his decision the Commissioner had a staff member, a Sgt. Swann, (who had not previously participated in any of these proceedings) prepare a summary of the facts and material relating to the discharge question. This résumé summarized the facts relating to the applicant's employment with the R.C.M.P., the various procedures that had been followed, the evidence before the discharge and demotion board, the decision of the board and the findings and recommendations of the External Review Committee. It also contained the staff member's comments and recommendations including her opinions as to deficiencies in the External Review Committee's analysis. (The Court refused to characterise these opinions as new facts.) A great deal of this material was included *verbatim* in the Commissioner's decision as the factual background. However, the Commissioner personally considered and wrote the part of the decision in which he considered

---

1.19 The Newfoundland Supreme Court rejected a similar argument that the parties were entitled to review and make submissions regarding the report of the investigating committee in *Callahan v. Newfoundland (Minister of Social Services)* (1993), 113 Nfld. & P.E.I.R. 1, 353 A.P.R. 1 (Nfld. T.D.). The Court noted that no new argument or evidence had been raised in the report.

1.20 *Hawrish v. Cundall* (1989), 39 Admin. L.R. 255, 76 Sask. R. 208 (Q.B.).

the evidence and reached a conclusion. This portion of the decision was in different words from the staff member's résumé. Justice Rothstein saw nothing improper in this procedure. The Justice noted that the Commissioner was an appeal tribunal and did not hear or see witnesses and whose decision was to be made on the basis of the record, the decision of the External Review Committee and written reasons. Among other reasons cited for upholding the procedure in question,[1.21] the Justice stated that:

> . . . it is not realistic for the Commissioner to make appeal decisions in discharge matters without delegating to his subordinates some of the work involved in preparing the material in a manner to enable him to expeditiously perform his function. In this case, Sgt. Swann states . . . that she spent approximately 250 hours reviewing and preparing the résumé. It is to be expected that the Commissioner of the R.C.M.P. would require such assistance, it not being practical for him to expend that amount of time reviewing the material in discharge, grievance or disciplinary matters appealed to him. Such delegation does not, of itself, imply that the Commissioner did not put his mind, independently, to the decision-making process.

Later, Justice Rothstein concludes on this question that:

> It seems evident that the résumé was intended to provide the Commissioner with a summary of the proceedings, comments on differences between the discharge and demotion board decision and the External Review Committee findings, and alternatives open to the Commissioner. It does not purport to be a decision or to draw conclusions. That has clearly been left to the Commissioner.
> In these circumstances it appears that the Commissioner, while having received assistance from Sgt. Swann, was left to make his decision independently. There was not improper delegation and no breach of the rules of natural justice.[1.22]

The last part of the above quote indicates that care must be taken to ensure that the investigation body is charged only with the task of gathering evidence as opposed to making findings of fact which is the responsibility of the deciding members.[1.23] As a corollary principle, the investigating committee must actually transmit the material it has secured to the deciding agency rather than its conclu-

---

1.21 The Court also noted that, unlike other decision-making bodies, the Commissioner had many other functions beside considering appeals in discharge and discipline matters (which does not seem particularly relevant to anything) and that the staff officer in question had played no role in the preceeding processes.

1.22 For other instances where decision-makers validly delegated the investigation of facts see *Webb v. Ontario Housing Corp.* (1978), 22 O.R. (2d) 257, 93 D.L.R. (3d) 187 (C.A.) and *Callahan v. Newfoundland (Minister of Social Services)* (1993), 113 Nfld. & P.E.I.R. 1, 353 A.P.R. 1 (Nfld. T.D.).

1.23 *Saskatchewan (Labour Relations Board) v. Speers*, [1947] 2 W.W.R. 927, [1948] 1 D.L.R. 340 (Sask. C.A.).

sions or recommendations.[1.24] In *Jeffs v. New Zealand Dairy Production & Marketing Board*, [1967] 1 A.C. 551, [1966] 3 All E.R. 863 (P.C.) the Board established a committee to investigate and report on an issue before the Board. On its own initiative the committee decided to hold a public hearing and reported back to the Board.[1.25] The report did not reproduce, or even summarize, the evidence and submissions given to the committee. Instead the committee merely reported its conclusions on the evidence before it without setting out what that evidence was. When it came to make its decision the only evidence before the Board was the report of the committee. The Privy Council, while approving the use of investigating committees generally where agencies were not required to hold oral hearings,[1.26] held that the Board had reached its decision "without consideration of and in ignorance of the evidence". The Board's decision was struck down. There is, thus, a difference between a body delegating the gathering of evidence and the delegation of the duty to consider that evidence and reach conclusions as to the order to be made. The latter is an impermissible delegation

---

1.24 In *Selvarajan v. Race Relations Board*, [1976] 1 All E.R. 12 (C.A.) the secretary prepared a report for the members summarizing the evidence. She also included her comments that this was a "clearly predictable case" and made a recommendation as to the decision the committee should make. Of this Lord Denning commented (at p. 20 All E.R.):

It was, I think, unfortunate that the conciliation officer headed her report: 'Clearly predictable case'. But there was a good reason underlying it. In preparing the papers, it is very helpful for the staff to estimate the length of time needed to discuss the case and the amount of work to be done by the members to make a summary. But it was a mistake of the staff to prejudge the case by calling it 'clearly predictable' and by recommending to the board the opinion which it should form. That is undesirable because it might tempt the members of the board to take a short cut-and not read the papers-and merely rubber stamp the recommendation. The summary should outline the facts, the point in controversy and the issues. It should not tell the committee what the result should be.

1.25 In the course of its decision the Privy Council notes that the committee was not expressly charged with the duty of collecting evidence for consideration by the Board. Presumably, this observation would go to an argument that the committee acted outside of its mandate and thus its report was invalid. However, the Council never returned to this point. It seems to me that the question of the mandate of the committee and the fact that it held a public hearing are irrelevant. The mandate to "investigate and report" surely must include the ability to collect evidence. I fail to see anything improper in the collection of that evidence from all of the parties together in one forum rather than in individual interviews or communications, provided that the proceedings were not conducted for the purpose of reaching conclusions as to the ultimate decision to be made. This would surely be a simple matter of procedure and without the authority of the committee in the absence of any instructions to the contrary. See *Samuels v. College of Physicians & Surgeons of Saskatchewan* (1966), 57 W.W.R. 385, 58 D.L.R. (2d) 622 where Disbery J. stated that a committee formed to investigate suspected misconduct may take such steps as it deems proper.

1.26 The Council noted that where credibility was in issue an investigating committee was likely not appropriate.

of the judicial function.[1.27] I discuss this aspect of the restriction on delegated hearings in more detail later under the heading "delegatus non potest delegare".

22.3.1(d) Ministerial Decisions

An exception to the general rule may be found in the case of decisions entrusted to Ministers of the Crown. The application of the procedural protections of natural justice and fairness are imposed by the courts as the implicit intent of Parliament (as Parliament is deemed not to intend powers to be exercised "unfairly"). However, the courts have recognized that when Parliament grants a decision-making power to a Minister, generally, it does not expect the Minister to personally research or examine all of the material upon which a decision is to be made. A Minister, by the nature of his office, is intended to work through his department and thus is:

> expected to obtain his materials vicariously through his officials, and he has discharged his duty if he sees that they obtain these materials for him properly. To try to extend his duty beyond this and to insist that he...should do everything personally would be to impair his efficiency. Unlike a judge in Court he is not only at liberty but is compelled to rely on the assistance of his staff.[1.28]

This exception was considered by the Federal Court of Appeal in *Cyanamid Canada Inc. v. Canada (Minister of Health & Welfare)* (1992), 9 Admin. L.R. (2d) 161, 148 N.R. 147 (Fed. C.A.) concerning the authority of the Minister of Health to decide under where access must be granted to specific government documents under the *Access to Information Act*, R.S.C. 1985, c. A-1. Applications for access had been submitted to the Director of the Access to Information/Privacy Centre in the department who concurred with them. They were then passed on to the Deputy Minister who recommended them for approval by the Minister. The Minister accepted each recommendation and endorsed the requests with the words "I approve the recommendation". A party opposing the release of the information alleged that someone other than the Minister had exercised the approval power. This claim was rejected by the Associate Chief Justice of Federal Court Trial Division.[1.29] On appeal the Federal Court of Appeal upheld that decision and

---

1.27 *Ahmad v. College of Physicians & Surgeons (B.C.)*, [1971] 2 W.W.R. 60, 18 D.L.R. (3d) 197 (B.C.C.A.); *Lim v. Manitoba (Health Services Commission)* (1980), 117 D.L.R. (3d) 476 (Man. Q.B.). See also the dissent of Justice Robson in *R. v. Budnarski*, [1937] 1 W.W.R. 604, 68 C.C.C. 71, [1937] 2 D.L.R. 675 (Man. C.A.) at p. 608, disapproving of a decision made by the Government Liquor Control Commission which was made solely on the recommendation of the R.C.M.P.. "The Commission had no business to abdicate its duty to investigate to the police or to be influenced by the recommendation of the police without inquiry." The majority did not deal with this issue.

1.28 *Local Government Board v. Arlidge*, [1915] A.C. 120 (H.L.) at p. 133 per Viscount Haldane.

1.29 52 F.T.R. 22 (T.D.).

specifically approved the following words of the Associate Chief Justice (at page 157):

> In my opinion, the practice of departmental officials making recommendations to their Minister is entirely consistent with the requirements of the Act and of the delegating instruments. It is unthinkable that the Minister must personally conduct each and every investigation herself. In any event, common sense dictates that the Minister will be guided by her officials, particularly the Minister's most senior public servant, the Deputy Minister. The final determination must rest with the Minister. By signing, the Minister accepts the recommendation of her most senior officials and, accordingly, I reject any contention of impropriety in the delegating process or in the decision-making process at issue here.

22.3.1(e) Reconsiderations and Re-hearings

The application of the "he who hears" rule to reconsiderations and re-hearings will turn on the nature of the proceeding. In those instances where a decision is not yet finalized any return to the proceedings must be conducted by the same decision-makers where reliance is to be put on evidence given at the earlier hearing. Where, however, a final decision has been made, but the agency has the authority to reconsider the matter the decision-makers at the reconsideration need not have taken part in the original proceedings.

R. v. Huntingdon Confirming Authority, [1929] 1 K.B. 698 (C.A.) is the standard authority for the first proposition. That decision involved one continuing decision process extending over two tiers of decision-makers. An applicant for a licence first made his application to the licensing justices. They granted the licence. However, before such that licence became effective it had to be confirmed by the Confirming Authority. The Authority confirmed the licence but imposed two new conditions upon it. This necessitated the return of the application to the licensing justices to consider whether they also wished the two conditions attached to the licence. They did not. They approved the licence subject only to one of the conditions. The matter then had to go back up to the Confirming Authority which affirmed the licence subject to the one condition. Unfortunately, for the applicant, when the Confirming Authority met to consider, and ultimately to approve, the returned licence with the single condition attached two or three members took part in the meeting who had not taken part in the earlier meeting which had initially considered affirming the licence. The Authority's confirmation was upheld by a majority of the British Divisional Court but quashed by the Court of Appeal. In the Court of Appeal Lord Hanworth, M.R. held that the licence in question did not become effective and complete until it, and any terms to which it was subject, had been confirmed by both the licensing justices and the Confirming Authority. Thus, when the amended licence returned for confirmation to the Authority it remained part of the initial decision-making process and it was improper for new members of the Authority who had not sat on the first confirmation meeting to join in the decision at that time.

Where, however, a final decision has been rendered, but there remains an authority in the agency to reconsider that decision later in the light of different circumstances the re-consideration need not be conducted by the same decision-makers who made the first decision. Mr. Justice Strayer discussed this proposition in the context of the National Parole Board's authority to reconsider a day parole decision under section 14.2(1) of the Parole Regulations, SOR/78-428 (as enacted by SOR/86-951):[1.30]

> . . . counsel for the applicant argued that, because the hearing of September 10 was held by different board members from those involved in the May 15 hearing, there was a denial of the principle of natural justice that he who decides must hear. It was contended that the "new information" in the psychiatric report had to be related to the information already before the Board at the first hearing, but the personnel at the second hearing charged with this responsibility had not heard the evidence presented at the first hearing. In other words, there can only be a rehearing under subsection 14.2(1) if the same board members are involved. This would be a very restrictive interpretation of the Regulations and I would need to be firmly convinced that such an interpretation is necessary. Instead, I am inclined to think that counsel for the respondent presented the right analogy when he suggested that rehearings as to day parole should be viewed in the same way as a series of hearings with respect to matters such as bail, custody, or an interlocutory injunction. That is, it must be accepted that such hearings may be conducted by different personnel and that what they must focus on is the question of whether some factors have changed since the previous decision-maker head the matter so as to justify a change in the previous order. I believe that is the appropriate way to view the procedure under subsection 14.2(1).[1.31]

Thus, it is the "he who hears" rule which governs the proper re-hearing procedure when an agency's decision has been set aside by an appellate body and returned to the agency for reconsideration. Where the appellate body has not ordered that the re-hearing be done by a different panel the original decision-maker or panel which made the initial decision must conduct the re-hearing if the matter is not to be re-heard in its entirety but only on the matters with which the

---

1.30 14.2 (1) Where the Board grants an inmate a parole to be effective at a later date, the Board may, after a review based on new facts or information that was not available to the Board when parole was granted, reverse its decision and cancel parole before the inmate is released.

1.31 *Scott v. Canada (National Parole Board)*, [1988] 1 F.C. 473 at p. 480, 14 F.T.R. 154 (T.D.), aff'd (1987), 84 N.R. 230, 18 F.T.R. 80 (note) (C.A.). See also *Grillas v. Canada (Minister of Manpower & Immigration)*, [1972] S.C.R. 577, 23 D.L.R. (3d) 1 (S.C.C.) particularly the comments of Abbot J. at p. 6 D.L.R. and Pigeon J. at p. 14 D.L.R..

appellate court found error. If the matter is to be re-heard in its entirety, of course, it may be heard by a different panel.[1.32]

22.3.1(f) Waiver

Although the case law is uncertain on this point, I suggest that the right to have one's case decided in accordance with the "he who hears" rule may be waived. The rule is an aspect of the "audi alteram" principle and thus, like other aspects of that principle, such as bias, should be capable of waiver. Breaches of natural justice do not, borrowing from the words of Justice Dickson in *S.E.I.U., Local 333 v. Nipawin District Staff Nurses Assn.*[1.33] go to jurisdiction in the narrow sense of the ability of a body to enter upon an enquiry. Instead they are errors through which an agency, clothed with ostensible jurisdiction to deal with a matter, loses it through the manner in which it acts.[1.34] The dictates of natural

---

1.32 See *Webb v. Ont. Securities Commn.* (1987), 58 O.R. (2d) 704, 35 D.L.R. (4th) 733, 22 O.A.C. 390 (Div. Ct.). In that case the Ontario Securities Commission held a hearing, received argument and adjourned to consider its decision. Prior to the decision being issued the appointment of one member of the panel expired causing the panel to lose quorum. The Commission concluded that it could not render a decision and instead convened a second hearing before a newly constituted panel which started the matter afresh. The authority of the Commission to do this was contested on the grounds that the new hearing constituted a new proceeding which was barred by the two year limitation period set out in the *Securities Act*. The Ontario Divisional Court held that the earlier proceeding had never reached a decision nor had it been abandoned. It noted that the Ontario Court of Appeal in *Nicholson v. Haldimand-Norfolk (Regional Munic-ipality) Commissioners of Police* (1980), 31 O.R. (2d) 195, 117 D.L.R. (3d) 604 (C.A.), leave to appeal to Supreme Court of Canada refused, [1981] 1 S.C.R. 92, 31 O.R. (2d) 195n, 117 D.L.R. (3d) 750, had held that a re-hearing of a matter resulting from the quashing of an agency's decision was a continuation of the original proceedings and not a new proceeding. On this basis, even though the matter was being heard by a different panel of the Securities Commission than that which sat at the first hearing, the second hearing was equally merely a continuation of the first. The impact of the presence of a different hearing panel, however, was that the evidence and argument had to be presented again unless agreement could be reached otherwise between the parties.

1.33 [1975] 1 S.C.R. 382, [1974] 1 W.W.R. 653, 41 D.L.R. (3d) 6 (S.C.C.).

1.34 This point does not appear to have been realized in the discussion of the waiver question by Justice Legge in *Islands Protection Society v. British Columbia (Environmental Appeal Board)* (1988), 34 Admin. L.R. 51 (B.C. S.C.). Justice Legge, referring to the decision of Sir Jocelyn Simon P. in *Mayes v. Mayes*, [1971] 2 All E.R. 397, [1971] 1 W.L.R. 679 felt that a serious breach of a rule of natural justice which goes to the very basis of judicature cannot be waived. "One cannot by waiver convert a nullity into a validity." In *Island Protection Society* the disqualified member had only stepped out of the room for six minutes and the applicant in the full knowledge of this absence, continued to present evidence. Justice Legge found that this six-minute absence did not amount to a serious breach. However, while introducing the question of waiver, Justice Legge failed to deal with it, choosing instead to exercise his discretionary power to refuse relief where no serious breach of natural justice had been established. In the earlier decision of *Tameshwar v. R.*, [1957] 3 W.L.R. 157, [1957] A.C. 576, [1957] 2 All E.R. 683 (P.C.) the Privy Council, in striking down a conviction where the judge had absented himself during part of the evidence, did not give any effect to the failure of the accused to object. Waiver does not appear to have been specifically argued.

justice and fairness are based on a legal fiction adopted by the courts that, as Parliament does not intend its agents to act unfairly, it impliedly directs that the power it grants be exercised fairly. Fair play is a function of the circumstances in which it is found and a breach of the "he who hears" rule can hardly be seen to be unfair to a party who has waived its application. I fail to see any social policy objection to an applicant voluntarily and knowingly electing to have his case judged by someone who has not personally heard all of the evidence. One might agree, for example, to have the decision-maker review transcripts of past proceedings. This latter course may be socially laudable where the delays and expenses inherent in rehearings can be avoided in cases where they serve no practical purpose.

At the same time, the waiver of the "he who hears" rule must be explicit. The case law has been very reluctant to find implicit waivers of the rule. Pratte J. (concurred with by Ryan J.) in *Doyle v. Canada (Restrictive Trade Practices Commission)*[1.35] stated that:

> [The rule "he who hears must decide"] is a rule which actually affects the judge's jurisdiction. For that reason its violation may be invoked by a litigant who waived his right to be heard by the court which passed judgment on him. thus, a defendant who voluntarily declines to attend the hearing thereby waives the right to be heard; he does not, however, waive the right to be judged by a judge who has heard the evidence.

As I read it, *Doyle* stands for the proposition that waivers the right to be heard in a matter does not constitute a waiver of the necessity that the decision-maker must have himself reviewed all of the evidence and argument before him, even though a party has elected not to put any such evidence in himself.[1.36]

This was the approach taken by the Federal Court of Appeal in *Re Grain Workers' Union, Local 333 v. Prince Rupert Grain Ltd.*, [1987] 3 F.C. 479, 77 N.R. 310, 38 D.L.R. (4th) 467 (C.A.). In that case a panel of the Canada Labour Relations Board had heard an application and dealt with all of the issues except that of the potential exclusion of certain employees from the bargaining unit. The panel felt that the parties should attempt to resolve this issue before the Board intervened with respect to it. Consequently this issue was left in their hands to attempt to resolve, however, the panel reserved jurisdiction in the event that the parties could not agree. Subsequently, when it was clear that the issue would have to be determined by the Board it reconvened the matter. At that time it gave the parties notice that one of the original members of the panel would be replaced by

---

1.35 [1985] 1 F.C. 362, 21 D.L.R. (4th) 366 (C.A.) at p. 371, leave to appeal to S.C.C. refused (1985), 7 C.P.R. (3d) 235n (S.C.C.).

1.36 See also *Beauregard v. Comm. de la fonction publique (Qué.)* (1987), 10 Q.A.C. 115 (Que. C.A.) where Justice Kaufman, writing for the court, stated (at p. 117 Q.A.C.) that he was "not at all certain that simple failure to object would have conferred jurisdiction on the substitute commissioner".

another member at the new hearing. The union did not object to the change prior to or at the hearing. It only raised the issue after an, unfavourable, decision had been handed down. Citing the words of Justice Pratte in *Doyle* Justice Lacombe (for the Court) rejected the union's objection (at page 475 D.L.R.):

> Applying this principle to the case at bar, I would hold that the applicant, assuming but not deciding that it had such a right, waived its right to have its case decided by the same quorum of the Board that had reserved jurisdiction, by not objecting in a timely manner to the presence of Vice-Chairman Brault on the panel. It did not, of course, waive or lose its right to have its case decided in conformity with the rule "he who decides must hear". If one member of the quorum had been absent at any sitting of the Board where the case was being heard or considered or if the Board had rested its decision on evidence that was not adduced at the hearing but was tendered at the previous hearing, it is obvious that such a breach of the rule would have been amenable to judicial review in this court.

22.3.1(g) Statutory Suspension of Rule

As a principle of natural justice and fairness the "he who hears" rule may be displaced by statutory authority. The Supreme Court of Canada in *Consolidated Bathurst Packaging Ltd. and International Woodworkers of America, Local 2-69* (1990), 68 D.L.R. (4th) 524 approved Pratte J.'s words in *Doyle v. R.T.P. Comm.*, that:

> it must be realized that the rule "he who decides must hear", important though it may be, is based on the legislator's supposed intentions. It therefore does not apply where this is expressly stated to be the case; . . . nor does it apply where a review of all the provisions governing the activities of a tribunal leads to the conclusion that the legislator could not have intended them to apply. . . .

The Supreme Court itself had expressed a similar view in *CTV Television Network Ltd. v. Canada (Canadian Radio-Television & Telecommunications Commission)*, [1982] 1 S.C.R. 530, 134 D.L.R. (3d) 193 (S.C.C.). That decision turned on the express statutory role assigned to the CRTC's Executive Committee under the *Broadcasting Act*, R.S.C. 1970, c. B-11. The statutory scheme of the Act, as it existed at that time, was described by the Chief Justice Laskin, for the Court, as follows (at pages 199-200 (D.L.R.)):

> Pursuant to s. 19(4), the public hearing was put in charge of a panel of six, consisting for four full-time members and two part-time members. There is nothing in the *Broadcasting Act* that deals expressly with any powers of the hearing panel other than what is imported under s. 19(3) (respecting the holding of a public hearing in connection with the renewal of a broadcasting licence) and what is implicit in the relevant terms of s. 17(1). The hearing panel does not make the decision on licence renewal; rather it is the Executive Committee (or at least the prescribed quorum thereof): after consultation with the part-time members in attendance at a meeting

of the Commission''. Since not all members of the Executive Committee were part of the hearing panel nor all part-time members, it is obviously envisaged that those who did not participate in the hearing would have access to transcripts of the proceedings. It is further envisaged by s. 17(1) that the decision on renewal would be considered at a meeting of the C.R.T.C. at which part-time members who were present would be consulted.[1.37]

The case had come before the Supreme Court primarily on the grounds that members of the hearing panel were not consistent in their attendance during the hearing. One of the members missed part of one day's proceedings, on another occasion three of the six member panel were absent, another member retired early before the hearing had concluded for that day. The Supreme Court, declined to follow *Mehr*, and upheld the propriety of this process in light of the statute:

> Here the statute clearly envisages that members of the Executive Committee who were not on the hearing panel would participate in the decision on renewal. In fact, eight members so participated although only four were on the hearing panel. I can only read s. 17(1)(c), in respect of renewal or s. 17(1)(a) and (b) in respect of issue or amendment of a licence, as expressly authorizing all full-time members of the C.R.T.C., being the Executive Committee, to make the decision on renewal or issue or amendment of a licence, whether or not they heard the representations at the public hearing. Nor would I be justified in limiting or requiring participation to or of all members who were on the hearing panel, so long as there was a quorum of the Executive Committee involved int he decision on renewal. . . .
>
> What is implicit is that the hearing panel would, through transcripts or otherwise, bring the issues raised on the application for renewal to the members of the Executive Committee and would consult with the part-time members on a proposed decision. There was a transcript here. Moreover, C.R.T.C. and the Executive Committee was dealing with an experienced applicant which was aware of the provisions of the Act and appeared to understand that the absence of a member of two or even three from some parts of the hearing would not impair the power of the Executive Committee to make a decision. unusual as the decision-making authority may be when considered in relation to the composition of a hearing panel, the statue speaks clearly on the matter.[1.38]

1.37 See also *Virk v. Canada (Minister of Employment & Immigration)* (1992), 140 N.R. 290 (Fed. C.A.) (statutory provision that unavailable member may be replaced on consent); *Nova Scotia (Workers' Compensation Board) v. Cape Breton Development Corp.* (1984), 62 N.S.R. (2d) 127, 136 A.P.R. 127, 7 D.L.R. (4th) 514 (N.S.C.A.) (statute authorized fact finding inquiry).

1.38 At p. 208 D.L.R. See also *Lipkovits v. Canada (Cdn. Radio-Television & Telecommunications Commission)*, [1983] 2 F.C. 321, 45 N.R. 383 (C.A.), leave to appeal to S.C.C. refused (1983), 48 N.R. 80n (S.C.C.); *Virk v. Canada (Minister of Employment & Immigration)* (1992), 140 N.R. 290 (Fed. C.A.) (statutory provision that unavailable member may be replaced on consent); *Nova Scotia (Workers' Compensation Board) v. Cape Breton Development Corp.* (1984), 62 N.S.R. (2d) 127, 136 A.P.R. 127, 7 D.L.R. (4th) 514 (N.S.C.A.) (statute authorized fact finding inquiry); *Inter-City Freightlines v. Swan River-the Pas Transfer Ltd.*, [1972] 2 W.W.R. 317 (Man. C.A.) (court discusses statutory provision permitting single member hearing and subsequent recommendation to Board).

The application of the above decisions, however, must be considered in light of the Supreme Court of Canada's decision in *Singh v. Canada (Minister of Employment & Immigration)*, [1985] 1 S.C.R. 177, 12 Admin. L.R. 137, 17 D.L.R. (4th) 422 and the discussion therein by the judges of the impact of the *Charter*, notably section 7, (Wilson J.) and the *Canadian Bill of Rights*, notably section 2(e), (Beetz J.). In a case where the interest in question enjoys the protection of either of those constitutional documents the "he who hears" rule may not be subject to displacement by statute.

This was the fate of section 24(2)(b) of the federal *Parole Regulations*, SOR/78-428 in *R. v. Mason* (1983), 43 O.R. (2d) 321, 35 C.R. (3d) 393, 5 Admin. L.R. 16 (H.C.). That section made provision for a tie breaking vote to be cast by a Parole Board member who had not heard the case where a two member parole hearing panel was unable to agree on a decision. The section provided that:

> 24.(2) Where the minimum number of members prescribed by this section to vote on a review of a case of any inmate is two, the decision in that case shall require
> . . .
> (b) where there is no unanimity of votes, the assignment by the Chairman of the Board of a further member to case his vote and thereupon the decision shall be effected by majority vote.

In considering this provision Mr. Justice Ewaschuk stated (at page 321 D.L.R.):

> In the instant case, the critical third Board member did not see the inmate nor his assistant nor did he hear their submissions in person. Instead, he became a faceless and absent bureaucrat who cast his critical vote in some distant unknown place. And as important, the third member perforce decided against liberty on the basis of written materials and not personal pleas. In my respectful opinion, that procedure was fundamentally unjust.

Justice Ewaschuk set the Board's decision aside and directed that the matter be re-heard by a new panel of three members.

The constitutionality of a statutory delegated hearing process was recognized, however, in *Howard v. Architectural Institute (B.C.)* (1989), 39 Admin. L.R. 277, 40 B.C.L.R. (2d) 315 (S.C.). That decision considered the constitutionally validity of sections 44 and 48 of the British Columbia *Architects Act*, R.S.B.C. 1979, c. 19. These provisions essentially created a two-tier disciplinary process. Under section 48 an inquiry committee was to inquire into and determine the facts in allegations of professional misconduct. A member subject to discipline had the right to counsel, the right to call witnesses and the right to cross-examination in the inquiry process. The decision as to the existence of professional misconduct and the appropriate penalty to be imposed in the event of such a finding was given to another body, the council of the Architectural Institute of British Columbia. The committee had no authority to question or review the facts found by the inquiry committee. However, a member who it found guilty of professional misconduct was given an opportunity to make submissions as to penalty.

The constitutionality of this statutory scheme was challenged under section 7 of the Charter as a denial of a constitutionally protected right in a manner other than in accordance with the principles of fundamental justice. It was argued that it offended the "he who hears" rule.

Although Justice Huddart found that the right to practise a profession was a protected right under section 7 and could not be abridged except in accordance with the principles of fundamental justice, he felt that sections 44 and 48 did not offend the "he who hears" rule notwithstanding that the body determining guilt did not hear the evidence upon which that finding was based. In his opinion the statute established a two-tier process. The function of the inquiry committee was to determine the facts. The function of the council was to determine the verdict and the appropriate penalty on the basis of those facts. In both hearings Justice Huddart concluded that "he who decides" does "hear". In finding no breach of fundamental justice, Justice Huddart concluded (at pages 290-291) that:

> The basic tenets of our legal system do not require that there be only one "decision" or "decision-maker" in a proceeding. Whether the severance of issues with a proceeding such that they are heard by different persons or bodies is a breach of fundamental justice will depend on the particular scheme, not on the principle that no severance can occur. The scheme must be viewed in its entirety. . . .
>
> I consider the procedure prescribed by the *Architects Act* for disciplinary proceedings affecting an architect's right to practise to be a decent, fair procedure that accords with the basic tenets of our legal system. Most particularly, it does not offend the principle that "he who decides must hear". No member of the body which decided the facts is necessarily ignorant of the evidence on which he must make his findings. No member of the body which reaches a verdict and determines a penalty is necessarily ignorant of the facts on which he must base his decision.

22.3.1(h) Consequences of Breach of Rule

Does the participation of disqualified members in the vote automatically result in an invalid decision? The answer to this question is dependent on the extent to which the disqualified members' votes were a necessary component of the decision reached by the agency.

In every case where the disqualified members' votes are a necessary component of the agency's decision, the participation of the disqualified members has resulted in the agency's decision being found to be invalid. This is not the simple application of a formalistic rule. The necessity for personal knowledge of the evidence has been recognized by the Supreme Court of Canada in *Consolidated Bathurst Packaging Ltd. v. International Woodworkers of America, Local 2-69*, [1990] 1 S.C.R. 282, 73 O.R. (2d) 676 (note), 42 Admin. L.R. 1, 105 N.R. 161, 68 D.L.R. (4th) 524 (S.C.C.) at pp. 563-564. To the degree that a member has not "heard" the case in the manner required by natural justice or fairness he will not have sufficient knowledge of the matter in order to effectively (or fairly) make a decision as intended by Parliament.

It has been argued that decisions which are only tainted by, but not dependent on, the voting of disqualified members should not be struck down. That is to say, the decision should be upheld if it was supported by a sufficient number of members, constituting a quorum, who had properly heard the evidence. In most cases this argument has been rejected. Consequently, one can say with some confidence that the participation of disqualified members in the vote of a decision adopted by an agency will poison that decision beyond saving.[1.39]

However, there is at least one decision where this was not the case. In *Western Realty Projects Ltd. v. Edmonton (City)*, [1974] 5 W.W.R. 131 (Alta. Dist. Ct.), affirmed [1975] 1 W.W.R. 681 (Alta. C.A.), Judge Haddad had to determine the effect of the participation of a single disqualified councillor where, in a rezoning application, that member consistently found himself in the minority and outvoted by a substantial majority of qualified members who voted in favour of the application. The decision was attacked was the basis that the mere participation of the disqualified councillor rendered the decision invalid. Judge Haddad rejected this argument on the grounds that, in his opinion, it reduced the principles of natural justice to an overly rigid rule. He cited the views of Lord Morris in *Wiseman v. Borneman*, [1971] A.C. 297, [1969] 3 All E.R. 275 that:

> We do not search for prescriptions which will lay down exactly what must, in various divergent situations, be done. the principles and procedures are to be applied which, in any particular situation or set or circumstances, are right and just and fair. Natural justice, it has been said, is only "fair play in action."

In Judge Haddad's opinion, it would be unfair to invalidate a decision on the basis of a vote which had not been cast in its favour and had no effect on it.[1.40]

In *Western Realty Projects* the disqualified member obviously had no influence on the decision as he had voted against it. The Federal Court of Appeal in *Canada (Anti-Dumping Tribunal), Re (sub nom. Canada (Attorney General) v. Canada (Anti-Dumping Tribunal)*, [1973] F.C. 745, 39 D.L.R. (3d) 229 (C.A.), reversed [1976] 2 S.C.R. 739, 65 D.L.R. (3d) 354 considered the case where the disqualified member did not exercise any influence on the decision but still voted in favour of it. In that case the Chairman of the three member Anti-Dumping Tribunal had disqualified himself from participating in a particular application. He did not take part in the hearing nor in any of the deliberations leading up to

---

1.39 See *R. v. Committee on Works (Halifax)* (1962), 34 D.L.R. (2d) 45 (N.S. C.A.); *R. v. New Brunswick (Labour Relations Board)*, 102 C.C.C. 387, [1952] 2 D.L.R. 621 (N.B. C.A.); *Hughes v. Seafarers' International Union of North America, Canadian District and Heinekey* (1961), 31 D.L.R. (2d) 441 (B.C. S.C.).

1.40 Pp. 144-145 W.W.R. Judge Haddad's decision was affirmed on appeal by the Alberta Court of Appeal at [1975] 1 W.W.R. 681 although the court did not deal with this issue.

the final decision. Notwithstanding, prior to the formal decision being made the Chairman reached the (somewhat surprising) conclusion that it appeared to be a little known fact that while a member could withdraw from participation in the actual hearing he cannot withdraw from participation in the decision-making. This belief (apparently predicated upon the advice of a "Treasury solicitor" that, although two members of the Board could make a decision, it was safest to have all the members of the Board sign a decision)[1.41] led the Chairman to sign the final decision as "the more prudent thing to do".

Mr. Justice Cattanach of the Federal Court Trial Division upheld the decision on the grounds that the mere signature of the Chairman on the document did not mean that he had actually participated in the decision. The Federal Court of Appeal disagreed. It found that the Chairman had participated in the decision in that he knew the document in question was a decision, he intended to sign it, and that by that signature he meant to indicate that he had adopted that decision as his own. This was all that was needed. It was irrelevant that the Chairman may not have actually influenced the outcome of the decision. The decision was bad and the Court felt obliged to quash it.[1.42]

Much of the case law striking down decisions on the basis of the "he who decides" rule appears predicated on a concern that the presence and voting of the disqualified members could have, in some way have influenced the qualified members.[1.43] Mere influence by disqualified members, however, in the absence of any force or coercion, will itself no longer support such conclusions in light of the Supreme Court of Canada's decision in *Consolidated Bathurst Packaging Ltd. v. International Woodworkers of America, Local 2-69*, [1990] 1 S.C.R. 282, 73 O.R. (2d) 676 (note), 42 Admin. L.R. 1, 105 N.R. 161, 38 O.A.C. 321, 68 D.L.R. (4th) 524 (S.C.C.) that agency members may discuss proposed decisions with other members who had not heard the case, and be influenced by their argument. Thus, case law prior to *Consolidated Bathurst* relying upon the possibility of influence as an invalidating factor may no longer be good law. Whether or not, in the wake of *Consolidated Bathurst* the courts will continue to take the

---

1.41 There was no quorum provision in the Act.

1.42 The Court felt that, unlike applications for certiorari made by private applicants, it had no discretion to refuse a request for certiorari on the application of the Attorney-General on behalf of the Crown where a valid objection to the decision under attack had been demonstrated. On appeal the Supreme Court of Canada overturned the Court of Appeal and restored the decision of the Tribunal. The Supreme Court held that on the facts the Chairman had not participated in making the decision. His signature after the decision had been made did not amount to participation. Nor, in light of the explanation presented, did the signature raise a reasonable apprehension of such participation.

1.43 See the cases set out footnote 1.39 as well as *Ramm v. Public Accountants Council (Ontario)*, [1957] O.R. 217, 7 D.L.R. (2d) 378 (C.A.); the comments by Romer J. in *R. v. Huntingdon Confirming Authority*, [1929] 1 K.B. 698; *Western Realty Projects Ltd. v. Edmonton (City)*, [1974] 5 W.W.R. 131 (Alta. Dist. Ct.), aff'd [1975] 1 W.W.R. 681 (Alta. C.A.); *Bailey v. Langley (Township) Local Board of Health*, 32 B.C.L.R. 298, [1982] 2 W.W.R. 76, 129 D.L.R. (3d) 448 (S.C.).

position that *any* participation of disqualified members in voting will invalidate a resulting decision remains to be seen.

(*Continued on page 22-10.19*)

22.3.1(i) Consultations Between Agency Members

Prior to the decision of the Supreme Court of Canada in *Consolidated Bathurst Packaging Ltd. v. International Woodworkers of America, Local 2-69*, [1990] 1 S.C.R. 282, 73 O.R. (2d) 676 (note), 42 Admin. L.R. 1, 105 N.R. 161, 38 O.A.C. 321, 68 D.L.R. (4th) 524 (S.C.C.) there was considerable doubt as to the ability of the members of an agency who had heard the evidence and argument in a matter to consult with other members of the agency before reaching a decision. Certainly, the logic of the body of the case law noted above, with its insistence on the absence of influence upon decision-makers (even by other agency members), lined up squarely against the proposition that deciding members could access the insight and expertise of their fellow members who had not heard the evidence (at least without so notifying the parties and providing a further opportunity to make representations). The Ontario Court of Appeal, however, and then the Supreme Court of Canada, in *Consolidated Bathurst* would reconcile the protections offered for the interests of individual parties offered by the "he who hears" rule with the reality of institutionalized administrative decision-making and the obligation owed therein towards the community as a whole.

22.3.1(i)(i) Consolidated Bathurst: Brave New World

In *Consolidated Bathurst* the Supreme Court of Canada considered whether or not the Ontario Labour Relations Board breached the rules of natural justice in convening meetings attended by all the members of the board to discuss draft decisions of panels when major policy issues were involved.

The case arose out of a hearing before the Board where it was required to decide whether or not an employer had failed to bargain in good faith. The employer in *Consolidated Bathurst*, while in the midst of collective bargaining, had failed to advise the union of a decision the employer was considering to close a particular plant. In an earlier decision (the *Westinghouse* decision) the Board had decided that the obligation to bargain in good faith set out in section 14 of the Labour Relations Act included the obligation to reveal during the course of negotiations any decisions which may seriously affect members of the bargaining unit. However, *Westinghouse* did not extend to proposals that had not yet become hard decisions. In *Consolidated Bathurst* the union requested that the Board reconsider its holding in *Westinghouse*. The union argued that the test ought to be disclosure in any case where an employer is "seriously considering an action which if carried out will have a serious impact on employees". Such a change was later characterized by the Supreme Court as "a policy issue which had important implications from the point of view of labour law principles as well as of the effectiveness of collective bargaining in Ontario." The majority of the hearing panel decided that the *Westinghouse* case should be confirmed, one member dissented. Draft reasons to this effect were prepared. However, before the decision was finalized the panel elected to take advantage of the Board's "Full Board" meeting procedure. The "Full Board" meeting is explained in the affidavit prepared by the Chairman of the Board, George Adams for the subsequent judicial challenges:

> 8. After deliberating over a draft decision, any panel of the Board contemplating a major policy issue may, through the Chairman, cause a meeting of all Board members and vice-chairmen to be held to acquaint them with this issue and the decision the panel is inclined to make. These "Full Board" meetings have been institutionalized to facilitate a maximum understanding and appreciation throughout the Board of policy developments and to evaluate fully the practical consequences of proposed policy initiatives on labour relations and the economy in the Province. But this institutional purpose is subject to the clear understanding that it is for the panel hearing the case to make the ultimate decision and that discussion at a "Full Board" meeting is limited to the policy implications of a draft decision. The draft decision of a panel is placed before those attending the meeting by the panel and is explained by the panel members. The facts set out in the draft are taken as given and do not become the subject of discussion. No vote is taken at these meetings nor is any other procedure employed to identify a consensus. The meetings invariably conclude without he Chairman thanking the members of the panel for outlining their problem to the entire Board and indicating that all Board members look forward to that panel's final decision whatever it might be. No minutes are kept or such meetings nor is actual attendance recorded.

This procedure had actually been followed by the Board for approximately 25 or 30 years.

The draft decision was submitted to the full board meeting. Ultimately, the final conclusion reached by the panel remained unchanged. Three sets of reasons were issued with one member dissenting in part and the same member who had originally dissented remaining in dissent.

One of the parties became aware that a full board meeting had taken place concerning his case. He filed an application before the Board for a reconsideration of the decision reached by the Board on the grounds that the practice of holding full board meetings as described above were illegal. The Board held a hearing to decide the reconsideration but ultimately refused to do so.

The Board's decision was challenged before the courts. A majority of the Ontario Divisional Court found that the Board had breached the "he who hears" rule and quashed the decision ((1985), 51 O.R. (2d) 481). The Ontario Court of Appeal, however, rejected the reasoning of the Divisional Court and restored the decision of the Board. Writing for the court Mr. Justice Cory stated:

> The discussion by the full Board in this case did not amount to a denial of natural justice. Instead, it was an exercise of common sense whereby the significance and effect of a decision was discussed with other *experts in the field*. The discussion by other members of the Board did not amount to their participation in the final decision. It was no more than an amplification of the research of the hearing panel carried

out before they delivered their decision. It was a step taken pursuant to the statutory mandate of the Board to further harmonious relations between employers and employees. This goal was sought to be achieved by a careful consideration of the implications of their decision. Further, in the *interests of uniformity of their rulings*, it was helpful for all members of the Board to be aware of the problem and its eventual resolution by the hearing panel. (emphasis added)[1.44]

Notwithstanding its approval of this process the Court of Appeal noted that:

. . . if new evidence was considered by the entire Board, during its discussion, then both parties would have to be recalled, advised of the new evidence and given full opportunity to respond to it in whatever manner they deemed appropriate. In the absence of the introduction of fresh material, the evidence must be taken as found in the draft reasons for the purposes of the full Board discussion.
As in any judicial or quasi-judicial proceeding, the panel should not decide the matter upon a ground not raised at the hearing without giving the parties an opportunity for argument. It is also an inflexible rule that while the panel may receive advice there can be no participation by other members of the Board in the final decision.[1.45]

22.3.1(i)(ii) Consolidated Bathurst: Supreme Court of Canada

The majority of the Supreme Court of Canada upheld the decision of the Ontario Court of Appeal and the Board (Sopinka and Lamer, JJ. dissenting).[1.46]
Writing for the majority Justice Gonthier outlined the nature of the exercise to be undertaken in determining whether a practice breached the rules of natural justice.

. . . the rules of natural justice *must take into account the institutional constraints faced by an administrative tribunal.* These tribunals are created to increase the efficiency of the administration of justice and are often called upon to handle heavy caseloads. It is unrealistic to expect an administrative tribunal such as the Board to abide strictly by the rules applicable to courts of law. In fact, it has long been recognized that the rules of natural justice do not have a fixed content irrespective of the nature of the tribunal and of the institutional constraints it faces. . . . The main issue is whether, given the importance of the policy issue at stake in this case and the necessity of maintaining a high degree of quality and coherence in Board decisions, the rules of natural justice allow a full board meeting to take place subject to the conditions outlined by the Court of Appeal and, if not, whether a procedure which allows the parties to be present, such as a full board hearing, is the only

---

1.44 (1986), 56 O.R. (2d) 513 at p. 517, 86 C.L.L.C. 14,048, 15 O.A.C. 398, 31 D.L.R. (4th) 444, 21 Admin. L.R. 180 (C.A.).
1.45 At p. 517 O.R.
1.46 [1990] 1 S.C.R. 282, 42 Admin. L.R. 1, 73 O.R. (2d) 676 (note), 105 N.R. 161, 38 O.A.C. 321, 68 D.L.R. (4th) 524 (S.C.C.).

acceptable alternative. *The advantages of the practice of holding full board meetings must be weighed against the disadvantages involved in holding discussions in the absence of the parties.*[1.47] (emphasis added)

As the Justice noted later in his reasons:

. . . the rules of natural justice should in their application reconcile the characteristics and exigencies of decision-making by specialized tribunals with the procedural rights of parties.[1.48]

In the opinion of the majority, it was socially beneficial to maximize communication between the Board's decision-makers. Not only would members benefit from the acquired experience of their fellows (particularly important in the case of the Labour Board given the need to promote exchanges of opinions between management and union representatives), but such meetings would also help reduce inconsistency between individual panel decisions (also particulary important given that the Board's decisions were protected by a privative clause).[1.49] The traditional response to the achievement of these goals was to have important policy issues heard by the entire agency. However in the case of the Labour Board, its numerical make-up,[1.50] caseload[1.51] and the Board's tripartite nature (which demanded equal representation from labour and management on each panel) made it impractical, if not impossible, for every important policy issue to be heard in a formal hearing before the full board. The challenge which the Board faced was to develop a procedure through which the benefits of full communication could be achieved without compromising any panel member's capacity to decide a decision in accordance with his individual conscience and opinions. In the opinion of the majority, the Board's "full board" meeting did just this.

There was no doubt that the Board's procedure maximized communication. But did it not also compromise the protections afforded the parties by natural justice? The majority concluded that it did not. The "full board" meeting, AS PRACTISED BY THE LABOUR BOARD, did not interfere with the independ-

---

1.47 At pp. 554-555 D.L.R.

1.48 At p. 557 D.L.R.

1.49 Ironically, the increased ability of agencies to achieve consistency in decision-making arising out of *Consolidated Bathurst* would subsequently contribute to the Supreme Court of Canada's rejection of the argument that inconsistent agency decisions must be seen as being patently unreasonable for the purposes of judicial review. See *Domtar Inc. c. Québec (Commission d'appel en matière de lésions professionnelles)*, [1993] 2 S.C.R. 756, 15 Admin. L.R. (2d) 1, 105 D.L.R. (4th) 385, 154 N.R. 104 (S.C.C.).

1.50 In the 1982-83 term the Board had a caseload of 3189 cases, employed 12 full-time chairmen and vice-chairmen, 4 part-time vice-chairmen, 10 full-time Board members representing labour and management as well as another 22 part-time members.

1.51 The Board's full-time chairman and vice-chairmen have an average caseload of 266 cases per year.

ence of a member, nor did it breach the fair hearing rights of a party guaranteed by the *audi alteram* principle.

22.3.1(i)(iii) Independence

The majority quickly disposed of the appellant's big guns by distinguishing the traditional line of cases dealing with the "he who hears" rule. Those cases, Justice Gonthier stated, dealt with disqualified members who participated in the impugned decision. That was not the case here as only the three panel members who actually heard the evidence voted in the final decision. The case before the Court was only concerned with the possibility that other members of the Board, who had not heard the evidence, might have *influenced* the actual decision-makers and this (likely to the surprise of many administrative law traditionalists) did not compromise independence.[1.52] Justice Gonthier rejected the earlier case law to the extent that it indicated that the possible influence of disqualified members tainted a decision.

> I am unable to agree with the proposition that any discussion with a person who has not heard the evidence necessarily vitiates the resulting decision because this discussion might "influence" the decision-maker. In this respect I adopt Meredith C.J.C.P.'s words in *Re Toronto and Hamilton Highway Commission and Crabb* (1916), 32 D.L.R. 706 at pp. 707-8, 37 O.L.R. 656 (C.A.):
>
> > The Board is composed of persons occupying positions analogous to those of judges rather than of arbitrators merely; and it is not suggested that they heard any evidence behind the back of either party; the most that can be said is that they . . . allowed another member of the Board, who had not heard the evidence, or taken part in the inquiry before, to read the evidence and to express some of his views regarding the case to them. . . . *[B]ut it is only fair to add that if every Judge's judgment were vitiated because he discussed the case with some other Judge a good many judgments existing as valid and unimpeachable ought to fall; and that if such discussions were prohibited many more judgments might fall in an appellate Court because of a defect which must have been detected if the subject had been so discussed.*[1.53]

In coming to this conclusion Justice Gonthier noted that judicial independence was not only a long-standing principle of constitutional law it was also part of the rules of natural justice even in the absence of constitutional protection. However, the influence of other Board members, provided that it did not amount to compulsion or pressure upon a decision-maker, did not threaten independence.

1.52 Justice Sopinka (Lamer J. concurring), in dissent, did not accept this view. He held to the traditional view that the possible, and plausible, influence of disqualified members was bad.

1.53 At pp. 560-561 D.L.R. (emphasis added).

It is obvious that no outside interference may be used to compel or pressure a decision-maker to participate in discussions on policy issues raised by a case on which he must render a decision. it also goes without saying that a formalized consultation process could not be used to force or induce decision-makers to adopt positions with which they do not agree. Nevertheless, discussions with colleagues do not constitute, in and of themselves, infringements on the panel members' capacity to decide the issues at stake independently. A discussion does not prevent a decision-maker from adjudicating in accordance with his own conscience and opinions nor does it constitute an obstacle to this freedom. Whatever discussion may take place, the ultimate decision will be that of the decision-maker for which he assumes full responsibility.

The essential difference between full board meetings and informal discussions with colleagues is the possibility that moral suasion may be felt by the members of the panel if their opinions are not shared by other Board members, the chairman or vice-chairmen. However, decision-makers are entitled to change their minds whether this change of mind is the result of discussions with colleagues or the result of their own reflection on the matter. A decision-maker may also be swayed by the opinion of the majority of his colleagues in the interest of adjudicative coherence since this is a relevant criterion to be taken into consideration even when the decision maker is not bound by any *stare decisis* rule.[1.54]

The "full board" meeting procedure developed by the Ontario Labour Relations Board did not amount to compulsion. Meetings were not imposed on the panel members but were called only at its request or the request of one of its members. A meeting was carefully designed to foster discussion without trying to verify whether a consensus has been reached: no minutes were kept, no votes were taken, attendance was both voluntary and unrecorded and the decision was left entirely to the hearing panel. Nor was the practice meant to convey to panel members the message that the opinion of the majority of the Board members present had to be followed.

On the other hand, it is true that a consensus can be measured without a vote and that this institutionalization of the consultation process carries with it a potential for greater influence on the panel members. However, *the criteria for independence is not absence of influence* but rather the freedom to decide according to one's own conscience and opinions.[1.55] (emphasis added)

Of course, the majority acknowledged, even if the procedure did not amount to actual compulsion, it would still be bad if it appeared to do so. However, as established by *R. v. Valente*, [1985] 2 S.C.R. 673, 49 C.R. (3d) 97, 23 C.C.C. (3d) 193, 52 O.R. (2d) 779 (headnote only), 24 D.L.R. (4th) 161 (S.C.C.) at p. 169, the test for determining breaches of judicial independence was the same as that established for bias in *Committee for Justice & Liberty v. Canada (National*

1.54 At pp. 561-562.
1.55 At p. 563 D.L.R.

Energy Board), 68 D.L.R (3d) 716 at p. 735, [1978] 1 S.C.R. 369, 9 N.R. 115 in that:

> . . . the apprehension [of a breach] . . . must be a reasonable one, held by reasonable and right minded persons, applying themselves to the question and obtaining thereon the required information. In the words of the Court of Appeal, that test is 'what would an informed person, viewing the matter realistically and practically — and having thought the matter through — conclude. . . .'

In the opinion of the majority the Board's practice of holding ''full board'' meetings would not be perceived by an informed person viewing the matter realistically and practically — and having thought the matter through — as having breached his right to a decision reached by an independent tribunal thereby infringing this principle of natural justice.

Procedures, like the Labour Board's ''full board'' meetings, to the extent that they maximize access to the expertise of the agency for those members who wish to use them are not objectionable, they are highly desirable. However, they must remain as aids to decision-making and not become obstacles to be surmounted. To Justice Gonthier in *Consolidated Bathurst*:

> It is obvious that no outside interference may be used to compel or pressure a decision-maker to participate in discussions on policy issues raised by a case on which he must render a decision. It also goes without saying that a formalized consultation process could not be used to force or induce decision-makers to adopt positions with which they do not agree.[1.56]

22.3.1(i)(iv) Systemic Pressure

As suggested in *Consolidated Bathurst* decision-making independence can be threatened through more subtle means than direct orders by individuals in positions of authority. It can be threatened as well by the adoption of operational systems geared to making it difficult for members to deviate from ''accepted'' board practices. The establishment of systems which essentially make it easier for agency members to go with the flow rather than exercise their own powers of judgment[1.57] are a likely even greater threat to independence than more overt methods of interference. Very soon after *Consolidated Bathurst* the Supreme Court was called upon to consider just such a system.

Tremblay v. Québec (Commission des Affaires sociales), [1992] 1 S.C.R. 952, 3 Admin. L.R. (2d) 173, 90 D.L.R. (4th) 609 (S.C.C.) involved a much more

---

1.56 At p. 561 D.L.R.

1.57 Likely it is the ability of such systems to create a tendency to uphold the ''accepted'' position which led the Supreme Court in *Tremblay v. Québec (Commission des Affaires sociales)*, [1992] 1 S.C.R. 952, 3 Admin. L.R. (2d) 173, 90 D.L.R. (4th) 609 (S.C.C.) to state that they may also cause litigants to have an impression of bias.

formal consultation process than did *Consolidated Bathurst*. Furthermore, while in *Consolidated Bathurst* the consultation process was both voluntary and informal, *Tremblay* involved a process which essentially forced a consultation process upon decision-makers in the interests of consistency and quality. Although the Commission was careful that the final decision remained with the hearing members the Supreme Court found that the compulsory and formal nature of the Commission's process infringed the independence of the decision-makers and gave rise to a reasonable apprehension of bias.

When a hearing panel of the Commission des affaires sociales completed a draft of a decision it was to be sent to the Commission's legal counsel who reviewed it for drafting errors, the accuracy of legislative and caselaw citation, and consistency with other decisions of the Commission. In the event that the counsel had a concern with the draft it was sent back to the panel for reconsideration. At this point the panel could request that a given problem be discussed at a general meeting of the entire Commission. The President of the Commission could also request that the draft be put to a full board meeting where it dealt with a new principle, set out a new interpretation, or departed from a previous policy or precedent decided upon by the Commission even if the panel had no concerns regarding its decision or desire to undertake such a consultation. The evidence before the Court was that where the decision was contrary to earlier decisions of the Commission or contrary to its established policy the legal counsel would hold up the file and if the panel did not change its mind the file went either to the office of the President or the Vice-President and eventually to the consensus table.[1.58]

At such a general meeting formal minutes were kept and at the end of the discussion either a formal vote or a vote by show of hands was held on the issue which was the subject of the meeting the results of which was recorded in the minutes. Following the general meeting the decision passed back to the panel which was still free to decide the matter as it felt proper, regardless of any consensus at the general meeting.

In practice it was impossible for Commissioners to issue a decision without going through the above process.

Both the Ontario Labour Relations Board and the Commission des affaires sociales are comprised of a large number of members of diverse backgrounds. Both tribunals issue a large number of decisions each year. And both tribunals argued before the Supreme Court that their process was geared only to consistency of decision making. The Commission argued that the objective of consistency responded to the litigants' need for stability and the dictates of justice. As the Commission's orders were not subject to appeal the Commission argued that it had a duty to prevent inconsistent decision-making. Nonetheless, the Commission maintained, in each case the original panel members retained the full discretion to decide as they felt fit.

1.58 At pp. 623-624 D.L.R.

In making its decision in *Tremblay* the Court distinguished *Consolidated Bathurst* on the grounds of constraint or pressure on the decision-maker. In *Consolidated Bathurst* the consultation was purely optional. It took place only at the request of the concerned panel. The process was a purely voluntary consultation of views and could not be forced upon a panel. Its operation was extremely informal and its conclusions, if any, non-binding. This was not the case in *Tremblay*. The Court concentrated on the aspect of *pressure* present in the operation system adopted by the Commission. The panel, whether it wished to or not, was, on a *practical* basis, forced to consult. The formal record of the consultation meeting and the resulting vote clearly gave the impression of something much weighter and important than the casual consultation of the Labour Relations Board. The Court concluded that "[c]ertain aspects of the system established by the Commission create at the very least an appearance of 'systemic pressure'".[1.59] The deciding point in *Tremblay* was not that the decision-makers were forced to make a decision contrary to their will (for that was not the case) but that in order to make a decision outside of the norms generally accepted by the agency as an institution they had to undergo a process that could potentially exert "undue pressure on decision-makers. Such pressure may be an infringement of a litigant's right to a decision by an independent tribunal."[1.60]

There were a number of factors justifying the intervention of the courts in *Tremblay*. The first factor was constraint. As noted above, in practice the decision-maker had no option but to refer a draft to a full board meeting when legal counsel determined that the proposed decision was contrary to previous decisions. The agency member could not side step the legal counsel and direct that a decision be issued directly to the parties.[1.61] As the Court noted at page 624 (D.L.R.), while it was true that the agency members retained the right to decide a matter according to their consciences the system depicted was one "in which in actual fact constraint seems to have outweighed influence, regardless of any internal directive to the contrary." There were other factors as well, which "taken together could create an appearance of bias". The ability of the President to refer a draft to a consensus meeting constituted an outside interference compelling a decision-maker to participate in discussions on policy issues while the vote, attendance and minute keeping contributed to the impression of an attempt to establish prior consensus by individuals who were not responsible for deciding the case.

It is clear that there were a number of factors at work in *Tremblay* which individually might not taint a process. For example the keeping of minutes at an otherwise voluntary and informal meeting might not automatically give rise to concerns of bias or a lack of independence.[1.62] However, in my opinion, com-

---

1.59 At p. 625 D.L.R.
1.60 At p. 626 D.L.R.
1.61 At p. 623 D.L.R.
1.62 A recorded vote, however, might be perceived as a threat to reappointment in the event that the appointing authority was not pleased with the consequences of the vote.

pulsion was the primary destructive element of the process instituted by the Commission whose presence alone would have justified striking the process down. As noted by Justice Gonthier (at pages 624-625 D.L.R.):

> In my view, the mere fact that the President can of his own motion refer a matter for plenary discussion may in itself be a constraint on decision-makers. In such circumstances, they may not feel free to refuse to submit a question to the ''consensus table'' when the president suggests this. Further, the statute clearly provides that it is the decision-makers who must decide a matter. Accordingly, it is those decision-makers who must retain the right to initiate consultation; imposing it on them amounts to an act of compulsion towards them and a denial of the choice expressly made by the legislature.

There were other factors present in *Tremblay* which the Court noted justified its intervention such as the voting procedure, the keeping of attendance, and the recording of minutes. However, these were additional factors to the compulsion found by the Court. As Justice Gonthier stated (at page 626 D.L.R.):

> The present practice of the Commission to hold plenary meetings without members of a quorum having requested them, *as well as* the voting procedure and the keeping of minutes, may exert undue pressure on decision-makers. Such pressure may be an infringement of a litigant's right to a decision by an independent tribunal. (emphasis added)

Compulsion in *Tremblay* was found both in the requirement that the deciding-members could not issue a decision directly to the parties without undergoing the administrative review process and ultimate referral to the consensus table where it differed from previous decisions and in the ability of the President to similarly refer a draft. Either, I suggest, is fatal to a process.

I discuss the idea of mandatory controls on decision-making further later in this chapter in the context of mandatory reviews of draft decisions by agency counsel and other staff.

22.3.1(i)(v) Audi Alteram Partem

A major development in the Supreme Court's decision in *Consolidated Bathurst* was the majority of the Court's ability to distinguish between judicial and administrative decision-making and to recognize in the latter the public duty contained in policy development. One of the problems which the minority of the Court had with the ''full board'' meeting was the fact that the parties were not able to participate in all the discussions in which policy would be developed. The majority, however, distinguished between determinations of fact and policy. Facts are particular to the individual case and the full participation of the parties in determining those facts was not only their right but a necessity.

... the determination and assessment of facts are delicate tasks which turn on the credibility of the witnesses and an overall evaluation of the relevancy of all the information presented as evidence. As a general rule, these tasks cannot be properly performed by persons who have not heard all the evidence and the rules of natural justice do not allow such persons to vote on the result. Their participation in discussions dealing with such factual issues is less problematic when there is no participation in the final decision. However, I am of the view that generally such discussions constitute a breach of the rules of natural justice because they allow persons other than the parties to make representations on factual issues when they have not heard the evidence.[1.63]

Facts, therefore, had to be taken as found by the hearing panel. The development of policy, however, was not limited to the experience of the parties. Furthermore, the ramifications of whatever policy might be developed went beyond the interests of the parties to the public at large and must be based on that greater experience and need.

Policy issues must be approached in a different manner because they have, by definition, an impact which goes beyond the resolution of the dispute between the parties. While they are adopted in a factual context, they are an expression of principle or standards akin to law. Since these issues involve the consideration of statutes, past decisions and perceived social needs, the impact of a policy decision by the Board is, to a certain extent, independent from the immediate interests of the parties even though it has an effect on the outcome of the complaint.[1.64]

Insofar as policy development was concerned, the only right of the parties was to have an opportunity to be advised of the policy being considered and to make representations with respect thereto. Thus, to the extent that a new policy or argument might arise in after-hearing Board discussions the parties had a right to be advised of it and to make further representations. However, once the arguments of parties respecting a certain policy or argument was known the parties did not have a right to explore that policy in all its public ramifications. That was the mandate of the Board.

Since its earliest development, the essence of the *audi alteram partem* rule has been to give the parties a "fair opportunity of answering the case against [them]": Evans, *de Smith's Judicial Review of Administrative Action*, 4th ed. (1980), at p. 158. It is true that on factual matters the parties must be given a "fair opportunity ... for correcting or contradicting any relevant statement prejudicial to their view": *Board of Education v. Rice*, [1911] A.C. 179 (H.L.), at p. 182; see also *Local Government Board v. Arlidge*, [1915] A.C. 120 (H.L.), at pp. 133 and 141 and *Kane v. Board of Governors of the University of British Columbia*, supra, at p. 322. However, the rule with respect to legal or policy arguments not raising issues of fact is somewhat

---

1.63 At p. 564 D.L.R.
1.64 At p. 565 D.L.R.

more lenient because the parties only have the right to state their case adequately and to answer contrary arguments. This right does not encompass the right to repeat arguments every time the panel convenes to discuss the case. For obvious practical reasons, superior courts, in particular courts of appeal, do not have to call back the parties every time an argument is discredited by a member of the panel and it would be anomalous to require more of administrative tribunals through the rules of natural justice. Indeed a reason for their very existence is the specialized knowledge and expertise which they are expected to apply.[1.65]

Notwithstanding the foregoing, the Court was clear (in agreement with the Ontario Court of Appeal) ''that the parties must be informed of any new ground on which they have not made any representations. In such a case, the parties must be given a reasonable opportunity to respond and the calling of a supplementary hearing *may* be appropriate.''[1.66] (emphasis added)

Insofar as the Labour Board's ''full board'' meeting did not involve the discussions of new policies without those policies being brought back to the parties it did not, in the opinion of the majority offend the audi alteram rule.

The minority dissent by Justice Sopinka does raise one troubling, but not conclusive, concern with the majority's approach. Accepting for the moment the rules laid down by the majority, how is the ordinary party to *know* that the facts were taken as found by the hearing panel? How is he to *know* that no new policies were discussed.[1.67] In the abstract the answer to this is that, the courts having established the parameters for these procedures, one must simply assume, in the absence of any indication to the contrary, that agencies will operate, as would any citizen, within those rules.[1.68] We do not have a system in Canada where the assumption is that either its citizenry or its agencies will, given the chance, operate outside of the law.

On a practical level, I have doubts that this is a real problem. The fact that agencies may have been influenced by new facts or grounds of argument not

---

1.65 At p. 566 D.L.R.

1.66 At p. 566 D.L.R. Presumably, the Court was implying that there will be circumstances where an opportunity to make written submissions would be sufficient. The determinative factor would likely be whether the parties requested a further opportunity to make oral submissions.

1.67 Justice Sopinka writes at p. 540 D.L.R., ''While it cannot be determined with certainty from the record that a policy developed at the full Board hearing and not disclosed to the parties was a factor in the decision, it is fatal to the decision of the Board that this is what might very well have happened.''

1.68 See *Schabas v. University of Toronto* (1974), 6 O.R. (2d) 271, 52 D.L.R (3d) 495 (Div. Ct.) where Pennell J. said (at p. 505) that ''It is to be assumed that a body of men entrusted by the Legislature with large powers affecting the rights of others will act with good faith.''

made known to the parties will likely be capable of detection through the reasons (yet another argument for the issuance of reasons) or other means.[1.69]

Ultimately, the Supreme Court itself has responded to this practical problem. The recognition by the Court of the demands of what it calls "institutionalized decision-making" has (perhaps unexpectedly for agencies) led the Court to adopt a greater willingness to allow inquiries into the *processes* by which agencies make their decisions than would be allowed in the context of the courts themselves. As stated by Justice Gonthier in *Tremblay*:

> The institutionalization of the decisions of administrative tribunals creates a tension between on one hand the traditional concept of deliberative secrecy and on the other the fundamental right of a party to know that the decision was made in accordance with the rules of natural justice. . . .
>
> Accordingly, it seems to me that by the very nature of the control exercised over their decisions administrative tribunals cannot rely on deliberative secrecy to the same extent as judicial tribunals. Of course, secrecy remains the rule, but it may none the less be lifted *when the litigant can present valid reasons for believing that the process followed did not comply with the rules of natural justice.* (emphasis added)[1.70]

Accordingly, in *Tremblay* the Commission's secretary was permitted to give evidence, over the objections of the Commission, as to its process for dealing with draft decisions. Later in *Ellis-Don Ltd. and Ontario Labour Relations Board*, 6 Admin. L.R. (2d) 318, [1992] O.L.R.B. Rep. 885, 10 C.P.C. (3d) 186, 95 D.L.R. (4th) 56 (Gen. Div.), reversed (1994), 16 O.R. (3d) 698, 24 Admin. L.R. (2d) 122, [1994] O.L.R.B. Rep. 113, 110 D.L.R. (4th) 731 (Div. Ct.), leave to appeal to C.A. refused 24 Admin. L.R. (2d) 122n, [1994] O.L.R.B. Rep. 801 (C.A.), leave to appeal to S.C.C. refused January 12, 1995 and in *Glengarry Memorial Hospital v. Ontario (Pay Equity Hearings Tribunal)* (1992), 9 Admin. L.R. 61, 99 D.L.R. (4th) 682 (Ont. Gen. Div.), affirmed (1993), 99 D.L.R. (4th) 706 (Ont. Div. Ct.) subpoenas were issued in judicial review proceedings to members of agencies to explain apparent breaches of natural justice.[1.71]

The Supreme Court's approach to the *audi alteram* rule, at least in respect to policy decisions (as anticipated by the Ontario Court of Appeal) is a momentous

---

1.69 See for example *Ellis-Don Ltd. v. Ontario (Labour Relations Board)*, 6 Admin. L.R. (2d) 318, [1992] O.L.R.B. Rep. 885, 10 C.P.C. (3d) 186, 95 D.L.R. (4th) 56 (Gen. Div.) where the matter (characterized by the Board as a factual finding) set out in draft reasons circulated to the parties by the Ontario Labour Relations Board was changed in the final reasons following a "full board" meeting. (Subsequently, in reversing the Gen. Div's decision, the Divisional Ct. characterized the change as relating to a policy, rather than factual finding: (1994), 16 O.R. (3d) 698 (Div. Ct.). Leave to appeal the decision of the Divisional Ct. was denied by both the Ont. C.A. (June 13, 1994) and the S.C.C. (January 12, 1995).

1.70 At pp. 618-619 D.L.R.

1.71 See also *Montambeault c. Brazeau* (1992), 53 Q.A.C. 311 (C.A.). *Ellis-Don* was reversed by the Divisional Court at (1994), 16 O.R. (3d) 698.

step away from viewing agencies as junior or imitation courts to a recognition of the very different role of such agencies. In theory, there is nothing new in such a view. It is, after all one of the traditional explanations for the creation of agencies. However, there has frequently been a chasm between theory and application in the judicial approach to agency decision-making. In its discussion of the *audi alteram rule* the Supreme Court paid honest homage, and not just lip service, to a concept of natural justice as a balance between the need on the one hand for protection of the rights of parties and of society for efficiency and expertise in decision-making.

Consolidated Bathurst has since been followed to uphold the ability of a member of the Ontario Labour Relations Board to discuss a draft decision individually with other members of his agency (*Shaw Almex Industries Ltd. v. Labour Relations Board (Ont.)* (1988), 28 O.A.C. 71 (Div. Ct.)) and an immigration officer's ability to discuss a proposed decision with his superiors (*Virk v. Minister of Employment and Immigration* (1991), 46 F.T.R. 145 (T.D.)).

22.3.1(i)(vi) Application of Consolidated Bathurst to Other Agencies

Consolidated Bathurst, I suggest, does not stand for the proposition that the all administrative agencies, regardless of their mandate and structures, are free of the more restrictive aspects of the "he who hears" rule to the extent approved of in that case. It may well be that the majority of agencies will be so. However, in my opinion, the validity of any institutionalized decision-making process is dependent on the benefits of the particular process involved outweighing the costs to the protections of the rights of the parties offered by the rule.

In *Consolidated Bathurst* the Supreme Court was careful to note that the exercise before it was to determine the extent of the rules of natural justice in the context of the mandate and institutional constraints of the Ontario Labour Relations Board. That is to say, *Consolidated Bathurst* was predicated on an agency: 1. with a large number of members; 2. with an expertise in the matters being decided; 3. faced with a large caseload and statutory directions as to the composition of a hearing panel which made it impractical for the full board to consider all major policy questions but required that decisions be made by individual panels; and 4. whose mandate involved a high degree of policy development by the agency.

However, in *Tremblay v. Québec (Commission des Affaires sociales)*, [1992] 1 S.C.R. 952, 3 Admin. L.R. (2d) 173, 90 D.L.R. (4th) 609 (S.C.C.) the Supreme Court of Canada made it clear that the application of *Consolidated Bathurst* was not dependent on the existence of those same institutional factors. According to Justice Gonthier in *Tremblay* the primary justification for the consultation process approved of in *Consolidated Bathurst* was that it contributed to consistency and quality in decision-making. The Justice noted that the tripartite nature of the

Labour Board and the policy component of its work had played a role in *Consolidated Bathurst* but stated that they were "additional factors" to the Court's decision.

In *I.W.A.*, the court further noted at p. 556 the frequent policy nature of the O.L.R.B. and the tripartite make-up of the panels of that board as factors justifying an

(Continued on page 22-10.33)

institutionalized consultation procedure. These factors are not conclusive, but are additional indications. A plenary meeting may perhaps be the only practical means of gathering members from various backgrounds; clearly, it does not mean that only tripartite agencies may set up such consultation machinery. We have seen that the justification for institutionalizing decisions lies primarily in the need to ensure consistency in decisions rendered by administrative tribunals. Whether the latter make decisions with a high policy component or not, those decisions must be consistent with the requirements of justice. A consultation process by plenary meeting designed to promote adjudicative coherence may thus prove acceptable and even desirable for a body like the Commission [des affaires sociales], provided this process does not involve an interference with the freedom of decision-makers to decide according to their consciences and opinions. The process must also, even if it does not interfere with the actual freedom of the decision-makers, not be designed so as to create an appearance of bias or lack of independence.[1.72]

Thus, it appears that *Consolidated Bathurst* will be applicable to any agency facing institutional constraints which make it difficult to promote consistency and quality in their decision-making. This is likely a very large universe of agencies.

Nonetheless, notwithstanding the broad application indicated by *Tremblay*, I suggest that *Consolidated Bathurst*'s approval of an institutionalized decision-making process is not automatic. In approving the process discussed in that case the Supreme Court balanced the benefits sought to be achieved against the values of the protections afforded to the parties by natural justice. The benefits accruing in *Consolidated Bathurst* were found to be great while the institutionalized process, because of its voluntary nature and lack of constraint, was not found to intrude greatly on the requirements for independence and the provision of a fair hearing. In *Tremblay* the Court found that the serious intrusion upon natural justice resulting from the compulsory nature of the process established could not be balanced by the benefits sought to be achieved thereby. In other words, in *Consolidated Bathurst* the large benefits outweighed the small costs while in *Tremblay* the costs were too great to be balanced by the benefits. Agencies considering establishing a form of institutionalized decision-making process must do this mental exercise. They should determine exactly the benefits sought to be achieved by the process and balance them against the degree the rights of the parties are compromised. It may well be that in a case where only minimal benefits are sought to be achieved it may be improper for the agency to adopt even the institutionalized decision-making process approved of in *Consolidated Bathurst*.

22.3.1(j) Consultations With Staff

Where the mandate and institutional constraints of an agency will bring it under the principles established by the Supreme Court of Canada in *Consolidated Bathurst* there seems little reason not to extend the application of those principles

---

1.72 At pp. 622-623 D.L.R.

to at least the staff of that agency. Staff are often a vital element of the expertise of the agency, both as a source of knowledge and as a tool for analyzing and testing policy. Thus, after-hearing discussions with staff (provided that the methods adopted for such discussions do not threaten independence, raise new facts or grounds of argument not raised before the parties) should not invalidate a decision. However, in order to avoid a perception of bias after-hearing consultations should not be held with staff who have taken an active role in the hearing unless that participation was restricted to the neutral mechanics of the process or was restricted to providing the agency with legal advice at its request.

Consultations with staff, however, does not mean delegation to staff. The ultimate decision as to the decision to be made must remain with the agency members who heard the case. Even where the staff may be experts in their field, the decision rests with the members. The following comments were made by the Nova Scotia Court of Appeal as to the duty of lay members of an agency entrusted with overseeing the disciplinary process of a hospital:

> I cannot emphasize too strongly the heavy burden that falls upon a body entrusted with the responsibility of providing medical care to the public. True, the Board is composed almost wholly of lay persons. They must obviously rely on medical advice received through the credentials committee, the medical advisory committee and other staff physicians. However, the final responsibility is that of the Board members, and notwithstanding the professional advice given to them, the burden of decision is theirs. They must exercise a thoughtful, independent judgment and not act as a mere rubber stamp.[1.72A]

22.3.1(k) Necessity for Communication Between Panel Members

What happens when decision-makers not only do not consult their fellow agency members who have not heard the matter but do not even consult each other? There are a number of arbitration decisions involving tripartite panels which hold that members of a hearing panel must discuss the issues to be decided among themselves prior to making their decision. These arbitration cases hold that there need not necessarily be a face to face discussion, but the views of all of the members must be shared and the decision shaped therefrom.

> The proper discharge of the board's decision-making function required that the members of the board discuss amongst themselves the issues to be decided. That discussion should have included a consideration of the evidence and the arguments presented by each party. Such discussion, however, brief it may be, is essential if the board is to do its duty to the parties. Generally, that discussion should occur at

---

1.72A *Shephard v. Colchester Regional Hospital Commission* (1995), 29 Admin. L.R. (2d) 5, 137 N.S.R. (2d) 81, 391 A.P.R. 81, 121 D.L.R. (4th) 451 (C.A.), leave to appeal to S.C.C. refused (September 14, 1995), Doc. 24605 (S.C.C.).

a properly constituted session of the board, although particular circumstances might dictate some other form of communication amongst board members. But communication there must be.[1.73]

As illustrated in *U.N.A., Local 1 v. Calgary General Hospital* (1989), 39 Admin. L.R. 244, 70 Alta. L.R. (2d) 284, 63 D.L.R. (4th) 400 (Q.B.) the absence of such communication may result in an invalid decision. That case involved a three member Board of Arbitration consisting of a union nominee, a management nominee and a neutral chairman. Following the hearing the chairman declined the union nominee's request to meet immediately following the hearing to consider the board's decision. The chairman indicated that he would instead call a meeting at a later date. However, the chairman had difficulty in arranging the meeting. So instead he met and discussed the possible decision with the management nominee. As a result of this discussion the chairman prepared a draft decision. This he gave to the union nominee and met with her to discuss it. Following that meeting the chairman took away and reviewed the union nominee's notes. He then issued a decision, which was basically the original draft with a few modifications, as the award concurred in by the management nominee. The Alberta Court of Queen's Bench quashed the decision. In his decision Justice Virtue stated (at page 246):

> There are many ways in which deliberation by a tripartite board can be accomplished. What is essential is that the chairman arrange a means whereby each of the nominees has an opportunity to know, and respond to, the opinions of the other nominee, and for the chairman to know the nominees' final opinions and responses before he issues an award. Whether this is accomplished by the board meeting together, or by conference telephone calls, or by an exchange of correspondence, or by some other means, is not important so long as there is a opportunity for the board to deliberate before coming to a decision.
> The procedure employed by the chairman in this case did not, in my views, satisfy the conditions I have set out. While the chairman met with each nominee, he did so separately, so that there was no opportunity for either of them to know, or to influence, the opinions of the other.

In *Jasper v. Gallagher*, [1979] 6 W.W.R. 65, 106 D.L.R. (3d) 47, 17 A.R. 32 (C.A.) the Alberta Court of Appeal upheld an arbitration award where, in order to break a deadlock the party nominees withdrew from the decision-making process which was left up to the neutral members to decide. Relying on the doctrine of waiver the Court upheld the decision as the applicants could not have the best of both worlds; to accept the award if it is favourable or to attack it for irregularity if it is not. This decision cannot likely be extended to the decision-making process outside of the labour context as, while waiver can bestow juris-

---

1.73 Waite J. in *C.J.A., Locals 1779 & 2103 v. National Drywall (1975) Construction Ltd.* (1987), 29 Admin. L.R. 122 (Q.B.) at p. 124.

diction in the context of consensual arbitrations (*Hunter Rose Co. v. G.A.U., Local 28B* (1979), 24 O.R. (2d) 608, 79 C.L.L.C. 14,219, 99 D.L.R. (3d) 566 (C.A.); *Glace Bay Community Hospital v. C.B.R.T. & G.W., Local 607* (1993), 120 N.S.R. (2d) 89, 332 A.P.R. 89 (C.A.)) it cannot do so in other proceedings (*Scivitarro v. British Columbia (Minister of Human Resources)*, [1982] 4 W.W.R. 632, 134 D.L.R. (3d) 521 (B.C. S.C.); *Essex County Council v. Essex Inc. Congregational Church Union*, [1963] A.C. 808, 1 All E.R. 326 (H.L); *Beauregard v. Comm. de la fonction publique (Qué.)* (1987), 10 Q.A.C. 115 (C.A.); and *B.C. (A.G.) v. Mount Currie Indian Band* (1991), 54 B.C.L.R. (2d) 146, 64 C.C.C. (3d) 172 (S.C.)).

It is not certain to what degree these decisions would be followed outside of an arbitration process. In arbitration proceedings each party is represented by one of the members of the panel and it is therefore important that there be interaction between the members. The principle, however, was applied outside of that context in the British decision *R v. Army Board of the Defence Council, Ex parte Anderson*, [1991] 3 W.L.R. 42, [1991] 3 All E.R. 375 (D.C.) respecting a paper hearing. That case held that, notwithstanding that the written evidence and submissions may be read separately, there must be *some* communication of their particular views between the deciding panel members. It was not sufficient for each member to make his own decision independently. Lord Taylor stated (at page 55):

> There must be a proper hearing of the complaint in the sense that the board must consider, as a single adjudicating body, all the relevant evidence and contentions before reaching its conclusions. This means, in my view, that the members of the board must meet. It is unsatisfactory that the members should consider the papers and reach their individual conclusions in isolation and, perhaps as here, having received the concluded views of another member.

The application of this communication requirement to agencies outside of the arbitration context likely depends on the circumstances. The fact that members sit as a panel may not in itself automatically demand the application of the principle. However, the circumstances may be such to give rise to a presumption that communication is intended. One such circumstance can be found in statutory requirements for particular groups or expertize to be represented on a panel (similar to arbitration proceedings). Aside from this many statutory schemes refer to panels exercising the authority of the agency. This suggests to me that in those circumstances Parliament or the Legislature intended the dynamics of group decision-making to be the rule. One of the underlying reasons in mandating panel hearings, rather than individual decision-makers is to increase the expertize of the deciding body. It strikes me that this goal will not be achieved if panel members refuse to benefit from the insight of their fellows. In my opinion, communication between panel members should be the presumption from which there should be deviation only in circumstances where it is clear that Parliament of the Legislature intended some other approach to be taken. This was the approach adopted by the

Federal Court of Appeal in *IBM Canada Ltd. Deputy M.N.R., Customs and Excise* where Mr. Justice Décary, focusing on the statutory provision of a quorum, stated (at pages 673-74 (F.C.)):

> . . . in setting a quorum and requiring that a minimum number of persons participate in a decision, Parliament reposes its faith in collective wisdom, does so for the benefit of the public as well as for the benefit of those who might be affected by the decision, and expects those who participate in the decision either as members of the majority or as dissenting members to act together up to the very last moment which is the making of one united, though not necessarily unanimous decision. Having the proper quorum at all relevant times, from the beginning up to the very last moment is a question of principle, of public policy and of sound and fair administration of justice.
>
> The nature, degree and form of this ''acting together'' need not, cannot and should not be defined. Tribunals have their own ways and their own rules. Members of a panel have their own personality and habits and cannot be expected to hold hands from the time a case is heard until the time the case is decided. What must be done, however, is that, at some point in time, the panel must ''participate'' individually in that collective decision in agreeing with it or in dissenting from it. There has to be a meeting of the minds, each member being informed at least in a general way of the point of view of each of his colleagues. This, in my view, is what is meant by ''making the decision''.[1]

Certainly, where a single member purports to speak for a panel on interim matters (such as adjournments or evidentiary rulings) during a hearing there should be some communication between the panel members. Such rulings are to be those of the panel, not a single member or the chair of the panel. However, in *Liwiski v. Manitoba Pharmaceutical Assn.* (1990), 65 Man. R. (2d) 184 (Q.B.) the Court found that the failure of the chair to formally consult with his co-panellists on a request for a dismissal amounted to an irregularity but did not invalidate the proceedings. The Court held that as nothing precluded the co-panellists from taking a different position than the chair, their silence should be taken to indicate agreement with the chair's views. Failure to consult, however, on such interim matters exposes the person purporting to rule for the panel to the possible embarrassment of having his ruling publicly rejected by the other members of the panel.

Outside of the legal requirements, I suggest that discussions among co-panellists on the issues to be decided are invaluable and can only improve the decision ultimately reached as members' views are tested and refined in the consultation process.

---

1 [1992] 1 F.C. 663 (Fed. C.A.). The court went on to hold that issuance of a dissenting opinion after the issuance of the original decision did not, in the circumstances, indicate that the dissenter had not participated in the decision.

Panels should attempt to consider the various issues raised by a case as soon as possible after hearing it. This is particularly important in the case of panels who are on the road where the individual members may not have easy access to each other after the particular circuit is completed. In such cases, panels should consider meeting immediately after the conclusion of the hearing, or at the end of the day if there are a number of hearings scheduled together making it difficult to meet after each hearing. At such preliminary meetings, the issues can be identified and initial views expressed. The member designated to write the decision can subsequently write up a draft decision for circulation and comment among the other members. Care should be taken that any new views not raised at the preliminary meeting be communicated to all members of the panel.

A process similar to the foregoing resulted in the upholding of a decision of a Board of Arbitration by the Alberta Court of Appeal in *Crowsnest Pass (Municipality) v. Alberta (Bd. of Arbitration)* (1985), 65 A.R. 369 (C.A.). In that case the three members of a Board of Arbitration had met a few days after hearing a grievance to decide the issues. They discussed the matter but could not reach an agreement. The chairman undertook to write a draft and circulate it to the union and management nominees. The management nominee received the draft and advised the chairman that he did not agree with it. He sent the chairman a dissenting opinion. Shortly thereafter, the chairman and the union nominee issued an award which differed in content from what the chairman had sent earlier to the management nominee. It was not until sometime later that the management nominee was advised by one of the parties of the issuance of the award. Shortly thereafter, his dissent was returned to him by the chairman. The management nominee had never received any communication from the chairman or the union nominee as to the contents of the award which was ultimately made by the majority. The Alberta Court of Appeal found that the issues had been fully discussed at the first meeting of the panel members, and the reasonable inference from the facts was that the management and union nominees had expressed final opinions at the meeting. All that was left was the preparation of formal opinions and for the chairman to make up his mind. The Court held that following that first meeting the deliberations were over and there was nothing more to discuss.[2]

22.4 THE WRITING OF DECISIONS AND REASONS FOR DECISIONS

22.4.01 What Are Decisions and Reasons

Every question before an agency results in a decision, even if that decision is to do nothing. Although there is a tendency to use the terminology loosely and

---

2 The Court took care to state that it did not approve of the actions of the chair which were discourteous although not illegal in the circumstances.

interchangeably, technically, there is a difference between the decision and the reasons for a decision. Sometimes the decision and the reasons are in separate documents, sometimes they are mixed into one document. Absent some legislative direction to the contrary, what something may be is not affected by its form. It is the content which determines what the something is. Thus, a simple letter from a decision-maker which imposes some requirement, duty, or penalty upon someone can constitute a decision.[2.1] A letter from a staff member purporting to do the same may not be a decision (as it is not made by the decision-maker).[2.2] A simple standard form "check off the boxes" document may constitute reasons. A single document may be both the decision and the reasons.

The decision is what the agency has decided it will do with respect to a request or application, or as a result of an investigation. It deals with a claim, or a request, or imposes some duty, obligation, benefit, or penalty upon someone. Some legislative schemes distinguish between decisions and orders, the "decision" being what the agency decided to do, the "order" being the document in which the decision is set out. Other schemes envisage "orders" as being something which imposes some duty, benefit, obligation or penalty upon one, with decisions being more passive and covering things such as dismissals. For the purposes of this discussion, these are all considered decisions.

There may be many decisions made in the course of a hearing. Requests to add a party, or for an adjournment, or for a ruling on the admissibility of evidence, all result in decisions in which the agency gives its answer to the requests. These type of decisions, which go to matters which are ancillary to the main question before the agency, are known as interlocutory decisions. There are also interim decisions. These are decisions which are intended to be temporary and to be revisited and revised at the conclusion of the proceedings. Interim decisions are often related closely to the main question on the application (although they need not necessarily be so). For example, on a rate increase application an agency may approve an interim rate increase to tide matters over until the main decision is

---

2.1 *Civil Aviation Tribunal, Re* [1995] 1 F.C. 43, (1994), 116 D.L.R. (4th) 345, (T.D.). In *Osbourne v. Canada (Minister of Citizenship & Immigration)* (1994), 88 F.T.R. 238 (T.D.) the Federal Court Trial Division rejected the argument that the use of a form letter indicated that a decision-maker had not directed his mind to a question. The Court presumed that the use of form letters was necessitated by the volume of applications. In this case an incorrect form letter had originally been sent out followed by a correct form letter when the error had been discovered. The Court stated that "The wrong form letter had been used and its seems that when that came to the attention of the A/Area Manager the correct form letter was issued. While in a perfect world more personalized letters would be desirable, there is not anything legally incorrect about utilizing form letters."

2.2 Thus, a mere letter from an immigration official advising refugee claimants that their claims for refugee status were to be heard by the Immigration and Refugee Board, rather than under the backlog provisions of the Immigration Act, was not a decision and could not be challenged by means of judicial review. The proper course was for the claimants to challenge the Board's jurisdiction at the beginning of the hearing (*Demirtas v. Canada (Minister of Employment & Immigration)*, [1993] 2 F.C. 602, 149 N.R. 375, 59 F.T.R. 319n (C.A.).)

made. At that time the interim rate increase approved will be readjusted. Lastly, there are final decisions of an agency. These decisions decide the main question which was referred to it. (The reader should note, however, that the terminology is quite loose in this area. What I have termed an "interlocutory" decision also is sometimes referred to as an "interim" decision.)

Reasons are not decisions. Decisions are "what" the agency has decided to do, reasons are "why" the agency decided to do it. They are simply the explanation. Nonetheless, reasons are very important.

Narrowly speaking, there are reasons for every decision. It is impossible not to have some reason for a decision. The reason for a decision made on the flip of a coin is that heads or tails came up. However, for the purposes of this chapter, I am going to be using the term "reasons" in a more broad sense to refer not only to the "why" a decision was reached but also the communication of that why to others. In this sense, reasons (that is to say, good reasons) are

the MEANS by which the decision-maker communicates
IN AN UNDERSTANDABLE FASHION
HOW AND WHY
HE OR SHE
made a DECISION
to A PARTICULAR AUDIENCE.

Each of the words which I emphasised in my definition are a vital component in good reasons writing. If you address each of them in your reasons writing, you will do well.

22.4.02 Do You Have To Give Reasons?

The Law

From a legal perspective, unless there is a legislative requirement that an administrative decision-maker give reasons,[2.3] the common law imposes no obligation on a decision-maker to give reasons.[2.4]

2.3 S. 17(1) of Ontario's Statutory Powers Procedure Act provides that a tribunal shall give its final decision and order, if any, in any proceeding in writing and shall give reasons in writing therefore, if requested by a party. S. 7 of Alberta's Administrative Procedures Act imposes a duty on decision-makers who exercise a statutory power so as to adversely affect the rights of a party to furnish each party with a written statement of its decision setting out the findings of fact on which it based its decision and the reasons for the decision.

2.4 *Northwestern Utilities v. Edmonton (City)* (1978), 89 D.L.R. (3d) 161 (S.C.C.), *R. v. Morin*, [1992] 3 S.C.R. 286, 16 C.R. (4th) 291, 41 M.V.R. (2d) 161, 76 C.C.C. (3d) 193, 143 N.R. 141, 131 A.R. 81, 25 W.A.C. 81, *R. v. Richardson* (1992), 9 O.R. (3d) 194, 57 O.A.C. 54, 74 C.C.C. (3d) 15, *R. v. B. (C.B.)* (1993), 84 C.C.C. (3d) 429, 110 Nfld. & P.E.I.R. 59, 346 A.P.R. 59 (Nfld. C.A.), *Gill Lumber Chipman (1973) Ltd. v. United Brotherhood of Carpenters & Joiners of*

This traditional approach is under increasing erosion. There are now some cases which hold that in certain circumstances, reasons must be given by a decision-maker even in the absence of a legislative direction to do so. For example, in *Lee v. Canada (Correctional Service)*[2.5] the Trial Division of the Federal Court held that reasons are required by the Constitution where a decision affects an interest protected by section 7 of the Charter (right to life, liberty and security of the person)[2.6] and in *355 & 365 Grandravine Holdings Ltd. v. Pacini*[2.7] the Ontario Divisional Court held that where an agency had exercised discretion in making a decision it must give reasons explaining why it chose to exercise its direction in the way it did. This decision was echoed by the British Columbia Court of Appeal when it held that, where the law made a decision contingent on the opinion of the agency, the agency had to give reasons set out the grounds on which that opinion was based (*Orlowski v. British Columbia (Attorney General)*.[2.8] There are also cases requiring reasons where the failure to give them will frustrate a right of appeal.[2.9] All of these decisions, however, remain the exception to the rule. That rule may be slowly changing as it has been criticised severely by a number of academic writers, but as of this time, there is still no duty on a decision-maker to give reasons unless required to do so by legislation.

However, where there is legislation which requires that reasons be given, failure to do so can result in the decision in question being set aside[2.10].

The Reality

In reality, however, reasons can almost be assumed to be required. The bottom line is that for agency decisions to be accepted, they must be respected. To be respected, they must be understood and reasons are the means by which decisions are understood.

One also really has very little hope of avoiding appeals and judicial reviews if the parties cannot understand how a decision was reached. Now, while I do not offer this as a universal rule, it appears to me that well reasoned and explained decisions stand less of a chance of appeal (or reversal, if taken to appeal).

America Local Union 2142 (1973), 42 D.L.R. (3d) 271 (N.B. C.A.), *Alkali Lake Indian Band v. Westcoast Transmission Co.* (1984), 7 Admin. L.R. 64, 1 W.W.R. 766 (B.C. C.A.).

2.5 [1994] 1 F.C. 15, 17 Admin. L.R. (2d) 271, 67 F.T.R. 54 (T.D.).

2.6 The Nova Scotia Court of Appeal, however, took the contrary position in *Maritime Medical Care Inc. v. Khaliq-Kareemi* (1989), 35 Admin. L.R. 131, 57 D.L.R. (4th) 505 (*sub nom. Khaliq-Kareem v. Nova Scotia (Health Services & Insurance Comm.)*) 89 N.S.R. (2d) 388, 227 A.P.R. 388 (C.A.), leave to appeal to S.C.C. refused (1989), 93 N.S.R. (2d) 269n 242 A.P.R. 269n, 105 N.R. 158n (S.C.C.).

2.7 (1991), 8 O.R. (3d) 29, 87 D.L.R. (4th) 718, 54 O.A.C. 380 (Div. Ct.).

2.8 (1992), 94 D.L.R. (4th) 541 [1992] B.C. W.L.D. 1443 (B.C. C.A.).

2.9 See for example, *Cadillac Investments Ltd. v. Northwest Territories (Labour Standards Board)* (1993), 24 Admin. L.R. (2d) 81 (N.W.T. S.C.).

2.10 *Consumers' Assn. of Canada (Alberta & Edmonton) v. Public Utilities Board* (1985), 58 A.R. 72 (C.A.), *Northwestern Utilities Ltd. v. Edmonton (City)* (1978), 12 A.R. 449 (S.C.C.).

Reasons serve a number of important purposes. Christina Gauk, in her article "The Annotated Alberta Administrative Procedures Act — Section 7: The Duty to Give Reasons"[2.11] summarizes the purposes identified by various judicial decisions as follows:

1.   Written reasons are more likely to have been properly thought out and thus make for a better decision (ie. They reduce the likelihood of arbitrary or capricious decisions).

2.   Agencies benefit from having their decisions exposed to public scrutiny.

3.   Written reasons reinforce public confidence in administrative decisions.

4.   Written reasons allow the parties to assess whether there are grounds to appeal and to know the case to be met if there is an appeal.

5.   Written reasons allow the reviewing or appellate tribunal to know the basis of the decision.[2.12]

To this list, I would add another, practical, if not always necessary or desirable, use of reasons. Many agencies do not have transcripts of proceedings. Reasons are often used in the place of the transcript to set out the surrounding circumstances of the proceedings, who was then, what was said, what happened, etc. (Of course, this results in very long, very boring reasons which take a great deal of time to prepare and should not be considered a desirable necessity.)

Reasons can also be used as guides or precedents for the public. An agency may use the reasons as an educational tool to express its views and give direction on how it sees its statute or process working.

From the perspective of the appellate courts, there are now many cases where the appellate body has held that, notwithstanding that there may be no legal duty on the original decision-maker to give reasons, the absence of reasons will have a negative impact on the appeal court's determination of the correctness of the decision under appeal.[2.13] Where there is evidence capable of raising a reasonable doubt and the record, including the decision of the trial judge does not reveal directly or by implication that all of the evidence was considered, the appeal court may conclude that the trial judge failed to appreciate, or even consider, that

---

2.11 (1995) 1 *Administrative Agency Practice* 49.

2.12 The Supreme Court explained the requirement for reasons in essentially these terms in *North-western Utilities Ltd. v. Edmonton (City)* (1978), 12 A.R. 449 (S.C.C.).

2.13 See, for example, *R. v. Richardson* (1992), 9 O.R. (3d) 194, 57 O.A.C. 54, 74 C.C.C. (3d) 15, *Alkali Lake Indian Band v. Westcoast Transmission Co.* (1984), 7 Admin. L.R. 64, 1 W.W.R. 766 (B.C. C.A.). In the latter case the B.C. Court of Appeal, citing *Ross v. Toronto Police Commissioners*, [1953] O.R. 556, [1953] 3 D.L.R. 597 (H.C.) stated that "when the circumstances demand reasons, a tribunal that fails to state them must be prepared to accept adverse inferences."

evidence.[2.14] An appellate court may also refuse to grant deference to the decision of a specialised expert body if it cannot determine how, or if, the expertise of the body was in fact utilized.

Each tribunal will find its own solution as to how to prepare and present a decision. Some decisions appear to start at the end and work backwards. Some start at the beginning and work forward and some, like Stephen Leacock's lover, jump on the horse and ride off in all directions at the same time.

Decision-writing comes down to seven words: collect, collate, select, refine, rewrite, circulate and issue.

Good writing is an acquired art for most, acquired after experience and with hard work. The quality of tribunal writing in Canada is uneven. While much decision-writing in Canada is excellent, there is a great deal that is unreadable. Many decisions float on a sea of Latinisms, solipsisms (sentences only the author understands) and solecisms (sentences one cannot untangle with a crowbar). Tribunal members tend to be bilingual. They speak one language and write another.

It is said that former President Carter issued a proclamation that all legislation should be written so that common folk could understand it, particularly the common folk who would be affected by the legislation. Imagine actually being able to understand legislation!

There are no long-lasting rules of writing. What do exist are not carved in stone. They are at best local and temporary. The language which we speak in the eighties is not the language of 25 years ago much less 100 years ago. The words may be the same, but the presentation and mix produce a different meaning. Writing is a very personal exercise, poor writing is easier to detect in others.

Board decisions often don't mean what they say and frequently don't say what they mean. Board decisions should read as precisely and clearly as a cookbook. A reader should know at the beginning from where the tribunal is coming and the assumptions upon which the decision rests. Decision-reading should not be a scavenger hunt nor a test of a reader's deductive ingenuity.

In *Re Northwestern Utilities Ltd. and City of Edmonton*, [3] Mr. Justice Estey stated:

> The law reports are replete with cases affirming the desirability if not the legal obligation at common law of giving reasons for decisions . . . This obligation is a salutary one. It reduces to a considerable degree the chances of arbitrary or capricious decisions, reinforces public confidence in the judgment and fairness of ad-

---

2.14 *R. v. B. (C.B.)*, [1993] 1 S.C.R. 656, 29 C.R. (4th) 113, 84 C.C.C. (3d) 429, 110 Nfld. & P.E.I.R. 59, 346 A.P.R. 59 (Nfld. C.A.), *College of Nurses (Ontario) v. Quiogue* (1993), 31 O.R. (3d) 325, 104 D.L.R. (4th) 44; 63 O.A.C. 241 (Div. Ct.), *Salem v. Metropolitan Toronto (Municipality) Licensing Commission* (1993), 63 O.A.C. 198 (Div. Ct.)

3 *Re Northwestern Utilities Ltd.; City of Edmonton v. Public Utilities Bd.*, [1979] 1 S.C.R. 684, 7 Alta. L.R. (2d) 370, 12 A.R. 449, 89 D.L.R. (3d) 161, 23 N.R. 565, at D.L.R. pp. 175-176.

ministrative tribunals, and affords parties to administrative proceedings an opportunity to assess the question of appeal and if taken, the opportunity in the reviewing
or appellate tribunal of a full hearing which may well be denied where the basis of
the decision has not been disclosed. This is not to say, however, that absent a
requirement by statute or regulation a disposition by an administrative tribunal
would be reviewable solely by reason of a failure to disclose its reasons for such
disposition.

The Board in its decision allowing the interim rate increase which is challenged by
the City failed to meet the requirements of s. 8 of the *Administrative Procedures
Act*. It is not enough to assert, or more accurately, to recite, the fact that evidence
and arguments led by the parties have been considered. That much is expected in
any event. If those recitals are eliminated from the "reasons" of the Board all that
is left is that conclusion of the Board "that the forecast revenue deficiency in the
1975 future test year requested by the Company cannot be properly characterized

(*Continued on page 22-10.39*)

as 'past losses' ' '. The failure of the Board to perform its function under s. 8 included most seriously a failure to set out "the findings of fact upon which it based its decision" so that the parties and a reviewing tribunal are unable to determine whether or not, in discharging its functions, the Board has remained within or has transgressed the boundaries of its jurisdiction established by its parent statute. The obligation imposed under s. 8 of the *Act* is not met by the bald assertion that, as Keith, J., succinctly put it in *Re Canada Metal Co. Ltd. et al. and MacFarlane* (1973), 41 D.L.R. (3d) 161 at p. 171, 1 O.R. (2d) 577 at p. 587, when dealing with a similar statutory requirement, "my reasons are that I think so.

. . . the reasons must be proper, adequate and intelligible, and must enable the person concerned to assess whether he has grounds of appeal. Nor can the Board rely on the peculiar nature of the order in this case, being an interim order with the amounts payable thereunder perhaps refundable at some later date, to deny the obligation to give reasons. Brevity in this era of prolixity is commendable and might well be rewarded by a different result herein but for the fact that the order of the Board reveals only conclusions without any hint of the reasoning process which led thereto.

Many lawyers and, generally speaking, many boards engage in pretentious and dreadful prose. A well written decision can give pleasure while creating understanding.

In my view, the opening section of a decision is its most important segment because if one loses the reader at that point, one may never recapture him. There is something to be said for the rule of natural justice that directs "he who hears must decide" but there is nothing to commend the next assumption that "he who decides must write down what he has decided". There is much to be said for articulate clerks and proficient editors.

One is attracted to a sentence written by Ronald Goldfarb and James Raymond in a small book of legal writing entitled *Clear Understandings:* "[lawyers] may eventually become judges, and be spared the obligation of writing anything original, conspiring instead with Attorneys abetted by form books, to dispense justice in prepackaged language".[3.01]

One should approach decision-writing with boldness. Don't waffle around.

22.4.1 DELEGATION OF DECISION WRITING

In this section I intend to explore the degree to which agency counsel and other staff may assist administrative decision-makers with the task of writing the decision or reasons.

One cannot distinguish between the decision and the reasons for that decision. A proper decision is the result of the decision-makers having gone through a reasoning process from which the decision emerges. Thus, once a decision has

---

3.01 R. L. Goldfarb & J.C. Raymond, *Clear Understandings*, 1st ed. (New York: Random House, 1982).

been reached, the substance of the reasons, however rough in form, must also have been developed by the decision-makers. This is the core function of the agency which cannot be assigned to someone else to perform. However, having performed this task, there is little, I suggest, to *demand* that the decision-makers also be the ones who must, as a matter of principle, be the ones who physically record the decision or reasons or to the degree after-hearing consultations with other agency members are permitted, be prohibited from seeking similar consultations with staff. In fact, it should be readily apparent that the administrative process will be expedited by the recording of decisions and reasons, and possibly made more comprehensible to the reading public, by individuals who are hired precisely for that ability. The question, as in so many aspects of administrative law, is the degree to which this can be done in order to maximize efficiency and expedition (the public interest) without unduly compromising the rights of the individual parties.

22.4.1(a) Spring v. Law Society of Upper Canada

The decision in *Spring v. Law Society of Upper Canada*[3.1] raised again the issue of decision-writing by an administrative tribunal. Although the decision itself perhaps does not merit the space now given to it, the subject itself deserves some amplification.

22.4.1(a)(i) The Facts

Harold Spring, an Ontario lawyer, was disbarred by the Law Society of Upper Canada (the "Society") on the grounds that he had twice misapplied mortgage money and that he had lied to a client, a fellow lawyer and an auditor employed by the Society. A Society disciplinary committee (the "Committee") convened public hearings on October 16, 1986, December 15, 1986, December 16, 1986 and January 11, 1987 to hear evidence respecting the Society's allegations against Mr. Spring. The Society's formal Complaint against Mr. Spring detailed ten particulars of professional misconduct and two particulars of conduct unbecoming a solicitor. The hearing of evidence concluded on January 11, 1987. At that time, the proceedings were adjourned to February 27, 1987 to permit the Committee to make its determination as to whether or not the Complaint against Mr. Spring had been established. The members of the Committee met on the evening of February 26, 1987 and on the morning of February 27, 1987 to discuss the case and to make their decision.

According to the Affidavit of Roger Dennis Yachetti, Q.C., the Committee Chairman (the "Chairman"), at these two meetings the Committee had available to it:

3.1 (1988), 64 O.R. (2d) 719, 30 Admin. L.R. 151, 50 D.L.R. (4th) 523, 28 O.A.C. 375 (Div. Ct.).

(1)   the exhibits, including an Agreed Statement of Facts;

(2)   the hearings transcripts;

(3)   written submissions of both parties; and

(4)   the Committee members' own notes of the proceedings.

During these meetings, the Committee members weighed the evidence which had been presented and considered the submissions which had been made. They also made findings of fact and reached decisions respecting the credibility of the witnesses.

At the opening of the hearing on February 27, 1987, the Chairman announced that the Committee had found that all of the allegations in the Complaint, save for one, had been established. The Committee then heard submissions with respect to penalty. At the completion of the February 27th sitting, the Committee again met to consider this matter. At this meeting, the Committee decided to recommend to Convocation that Mr. Spring be disbarred.

Sometime before April 1, 1987, the Chairman telephoned Daniel P. Iggers, the Assistant Secretary of the Society at that time, to inform him of the Committee's decision. Mr. Iggers had acted as the Clerk to the Committee throughout the disciplinary proceedings against Mr. Spring. In that role, he took notes of the evidence, organized exhibits and swore witnesses. During the course of this telephone conversation, the Chairman also instructed Mr. Iggers (the "Clerk") to prepare a draft report containing the Committee's findings, the reasons for those findings and the evidence in support thereof, including the Agreed Statement of Facts. According to the Clerk's Affidavit, this discussion did not last much longer than five minutes or so; the Clerk admitted, however, that he had no specific recollection of this conversation's duration.

Pursuant to the Chairman's instructions, the Clerk prepared a draft report consisting of a review of the evidence, the reasons for the Committee's findings and the penalty recommendation. He forwarded copies of this draft report to each of the members of the Committee on or about April 1, 1987. According to the Chairman's own Affidavit, the Chairman carefully reviewed the portions of the Clerk's draft report which summarized the evidence. He also reviewed the portions of the report which dealt with the findings of fact and credibility, and the reasons for the findings of misconduct. The Chairman also stated that, where necessary, he made changes to the report in order to ensure that it fully and accurately reflected the Committee's reasonings. He also drafted and added the conclusion of the Committee regarding the recommendation on penalty. On April 30, 1987, the Clerk attended the Chairman's office in Hamilton to discuss the draft report. The Clerk states in his Affidavit that it was apparent that the Chairman had reviewed the draft thoroughly and that he was satisfied with its final form. The Clerk then prepared a final report incorporating the changes made by the Chairman and forwarded it to him. On May 14, 1987, the Chairman signed the report on behalf of the Committee. The Committee's recommendations were accepted by Convocation, which ordered that Mr. Spring be disbarred for professional misconduct and conduct unbecoming a solicitor.

22.4.1(a)(ii) The Issue

Mr. Spring appealed Convocation's decision to the Ontario Divisional Court. Mr. Spring claimed, inter alia, that the Committee had violated the common law rule that "he who hears must decide" in delegating to the Clerk the task of writing its report and reasons for decision. Mr. Spring argued that this procedure generated a reasonable apprehension of bias and raised doubts as to whether justice had in fact been done in his case, because it left open the distinct possibility that the reasons for decision contained in the Committee's report were actually those of the Clerk rather than of the Committee members themselves. The fundamental issue confronting the court, therefore, was whether, and to what extent, a Society disciplinary committee should be able to delegate the task of writing its reasons for decision to staff members.

22.4.1(a)(iii) The Decision

By a majority of two to one, the Divisional Court held that the procedures employed by the Committee in drafting its report were not so flawed as to create a reasonable apprehension of bias. As such, they held that there was no need to convene a new hearing. The two justices in the majority (Labrosse and Craig JJ.), however, differed in their evaluation of the appropriateness of the Committee's practice of delegating to the Clerk the duty of drafting its report.

In his Affidavit, the Clerk described the Committee's standard procedure as follows:

> The usual practice following the completion of the discipline hearing is for the Committee to request me to prepare a draft report for circulation among the Committee members. Some Benchers insist in writing the report themselves but this is an exception to the general pattern. Further, in a small number of cases . . . in addition to my draft, Benchers have prepared partial drafts of memoranda and I have amalgamated these in a final document. On some occasions, I am permitted to be present when the Committee members meet to discuss the evidence and their findings and recommendations; this is particularly useful in complex cases. However, in many cases the Committee members simply advise me of the result of their deliberations with little or no elaboration and I prepare a draft report based on my observations at the hearing. The elaboration may amount to several minutes of discussion. Once the draft report is submitted, I am often advised of typographical and stylistic changes; however, in most cases the draft report is signed without substantive changes being made; [at pages 2-3].

Mr. Justice Labrosse expressed rather strong disapproval for this procedure. As he stated (O.R. p. 722):

> It is highly desirable that a tribunal draft its own reasons and I deplore the practice of the committee in not drafting its own findings and the reasons for those findings. It is a responsibility of the office.

Notwithstanding these serious reservations, however, Labrosse J. would not accede to Mr. Spring's arguments that the Committee's procedures infringed his common law rights. In arriving at this conclusion, Labrosse J. relied very heavily on the Chairman's Affidavit. In particular, he emphasized the following facts as influencing his decision:

(1) The Clerk was not a member of the Society's Discipline Department which conducted Mr. Spring's prosecution. Consequently, the Clerk was not associated with the prosecution in any fashion.

(2) The Clerk had not attended the two meetings held by the Committee to deliberate on the allegations levelled against Mr. Spring. As such, it was clear that the Clerk had not influenced the Committee's findings of fact and its opinions regarding the credibility of the witnesses. Furthermore, it was equally true that the Clerk had exerted no impact on the Committee's decision that the allegations against Mr. Spring were well founded.

(3) The Clerk was not present when the Committee met to determine the appropriate penalty to mete against Mr. Spring. Therefore, he did not contribute in any way to this decision, nor to the reasons supporting this recommendation.

(4) After the Clerk prepared a draft report, the Chairman reviewed it and made changes to ensure that the report fully and accurately reflected the reasoning of the Committee. He also drafted and added a conclusion of the Committee regarding the recommendation on penalty. Upon completion of this review, the Chairman consulted with the Clerk and instructed him to prepare the final report to reflect these changes.

Based on these facts, Mr. Justice Labrosse concluded that the Committee's deliberations, findings and decisions were all made independently of, and without any input from, the Clerk. In his view, this was a major distinguishing point between this case and the two cases cited by Mr. Spring in support of his position, i.e., *Re Sawyer and Ontario Racing Commission*[3.2] and *Re Emerson and Law Society of Upper Canada*,[3.3] Labrosse J. asserted that in contrast to the situation here, in both *Sawyer* and *Emerson* the responsible tribunal's decision was tainted by improper outside influences. Thus, in neither of those cases could it have been said that the responsible tribunal arrived at its decision in an independent fashion. This, however, was clearly not the case here, at least in Labrosse J.'s opinion.

3.2 (1979), 24 O.R. (2d) 673, 99 D.L.R. (3d) 561 (C.A.).
3.3 (1983), 44 O.R. (2d) 729, 41 C.P.C. 7, 5 D.L.R. (4th) 294 (H.C.).

Furthermore, Labrosse J. could not see anything in the facts to justify a finding of reasonable apprehension of bias. [The *Sawyer* and *Emerson* cases are discussed in more detail following.]

Mr. Justice Craig agreed with Labrosse J. that the evidence did not justify a finding of apprehension of bias. He was, however, much more forgiving with respect to the Committee's practice of delegating the decision writing process to the Clerk. Thus, he did not view it as incumbent upon a tribunal in the Committee's position to actually draft its own reasons. As he stated (O.R. p. 725):

> . . . it is my view that the discipline committee should not be placed in a straitjacket. The reasons for the decision (including the findings of fact and any conclusions of law) as finalized must be those of the committee; those reasons are required by the *Law Society Act*, R.S.O. 1980, c. 233 [now R.S.O. 1990, c. L.8]. However, it is my view that the committee must be entitled to some journalistic and administrative assistance in articulating those reasons.

In other words, Craig J. held that while there is no doubt that a tribunal such as the Committee must arrive at its conclusions on its own, there is no reason to prevent it from utilizing staff members to reduce these conclusions to a formal written decision.

The dissenting justice in this case was Mr. Justice Trainor. To him, the Committee's procedures created considerable doubts as to whether the reasons for decisions as published were in fact the actual reasons of the Committee itself. In this regard, he cited a number of facts as being persuasive:

(1)   According to the Clerk's Affidavit, his only exposure to the Committee members' views prior to drafting the report took place in a very brief phone conversation with the Chairman lasting no longer than five minutes. Trainor J. could not see how this was sufficient time to adequately brief the Clerk, particularly given the complexity of this case.

(2)   Furthermore, Trainor J. could not find anything in either the Clerk's Affidavit or in that of the Chairman which conclusively indicated that the reasons for the Committee's findings and the evidence to support them were ever actually conveyed to the Clerk. In Trainor J.'s view, the only certainty was that the Clerk and the Chairman had held a "general discussion about the case" sometime prior to the commencement of the drafting process.

(3)   Finally, a comparison of the draft reasons with those ultimately signed by the Chairman on behalf of the Committee revealed that they were virtually identical in substance. Thus, it was clear that the Chairman's review process did not result in any significant alterations whatsoever.

In Trainor J.'s view, the end result of the Committee's drafting practices was to cloud with uncertainty the relative contributions made by committee members and the Clerk to the Committee's published decision. The Committee had not provided the Clerk with draft reasons or a preliminary outline of its opinion to assist him in his task. Nor was the Clerk merely commissioned to prepare a summary of the relevant case law for the Committee's benefit. Rather, the facts indicated that the Clerk had organized the evidence on his own, to reach essential findings of fact and to support conclusions with respect to credibility. The Clerk's activities, therefore, created a reasonable apprehension that he had improperly influenced the Committee's decision and reasons. It also denied Mr. Spring the right to conclusively know the reasonings and thought processes of the body which had condemned him. This effectively impeded his ability to mount an attack against the Committee's decision on appeal or review. In Trainor J.'s opinion, a tribunal is responsible for marshalling evidence, deciding facts, ruling on credibility and formulating its decisions without any outside assistance. Part of this process is the tribunal's obligation to write its own reasons, including all drafts. Nonetheless, Trainor J. was prepared to concede that some delegation in the writing process is permissible, provided that the staff members responsible for drafting these reasons is given an outline summarizing the tribunal's decision, its findings, and the evidence supporting its conclusions. Anything less would be insufficient to assure interested parties, along with outside observers, that the reasons appearing in the tribunals' final decision are actually those of the tribunal itself.

22.4.1(a)(iv) Analysis

The central issue arising from the *Spring* case, i.e. the extent to which tribunals may confer decision writing responsibilities upon staff members, implicates three broad principles of natural justice:

(1) the "he who hears must decide" rule;

(2) the "delegatus non potest delegare" rule; and

(3) the prohibition against bias in the decision-making process.

"He who hears must decide"
I have already noted earlier that much of the case law striking down decisions on the basis of the "he who decides" rule appears predicated on a concern that the presence and voting of the disqualified individuals could have, in some way, influenced the qualified members. Indeed, the mere presence of a non-tribunal member while a tribunal's deliberations were ongoing sometimes had the effect of vitiating that tribunal's decision. In *Middlesex County Valuation Committee v. West Middlesex Assessment Area Committee* Lord Wright M.R. said (in obiter) that:

It would be most improper on general principles of law that extraneous persons, who may or may not have independent interests of their own, should be present at the formulation of [a] decision.[3.4]

In the context of staff the principle was sometimes applied to invalidate decisions where the agency's deliberations were held in the presence of a prosecuting officer (which obviously also gives rise to apprehensions of bias) or other member of staff who pleads for a particular result.[3.5]

However, there is case law in Canada to the effect that the presence, and even assistance, of staff or agency counsel where they have not acted as prosecutor and otherwise appear to be free of some interest in the outcome, will not invalidate proceedings.

In *R. v. Public Accountants Council (Ontario)*[3.6] (the *Stoller* case) the Court held that there was nothing objectionable in the Public Accountants Council permitting its registrar and solicitor to attend its deliberations following the close of disciplinary hearings against accountants accused of professional misconduct. In fact, the court was seemingly prepared to accept some degree of participation by the registrar and the solicitor in the Council's decision-making process. Thus, Roach, J.A., speaking on behalf of the court, stated that the Council was legally entitled to have these individuals present during the course of its deliberations for such purposes as the Council might think necessary.[3.7]

The *Stoller* case was followed by another panel of the Court of Appeal in *Glassman v. College of Physicians & Surgeons (Ontario)*,[3.8] though not without certain misgivings. *Glassman* also involved disciplinary proceedings, this time before the Council of the College of Physicians and Surgeons of Ontario. The accused medical practitioner challenged the Council's decision against him on the grounds, inter alia, that the lawyer who had prosecuted his case had been present at the Council's deliberations.

Schroeder J.A., speaking for the majority, cited the *Stoller* case in rejecting the doctor's arguments that, as a matter of law, the mere presence of the prosecuting lawyer during the course of the Council's deliberations constituted a denial

---

3.4 [1937] Ch. 361 at p. 376. This case dealt with the right of an officer of the County Valuation Committee to attend hearings of the Assessment Area Committee to decide valuation lists. See also *R. v. East Kerrier Justices, Ex parte Mundy*, [1952] 2 All E.R. 144, [1952] 2 Q.B. 719 (Div. Ct.), where, again in obiter, it was stated to be irregular for a justice's clerk to retire with them as a matter of course. The proper course was for the clerk to remain in court until sent for to give advice.

3.5 *Kane v. University of British Columbia*, [1980] S.C.R. 1105, 18 B.C.L.R. 124, [1980] 3 W.W.R. 125, 110 D.L.R. (3d) 311; *Grenier v. Region 1 Hospital Corp. (Southeast)* (1993), 133 N.B.R. (2d) 232, 341 A.P.R. 232 (Q.B.).

3.6 [1960] O.R. 631, 25 D.L.R. (2d) 410 (C.A.).

3.7 D.L.R. 427. See also *Jackman v. Dental Board (Newfoundland)* (1990), 82 Nfld. & P.E.I.R. 91, 257 A.P.R. 91 (Nfld. T.D.) and *Liwiski v. Manitoba Pharmaceutical Assn.* (1990), 65 Man. R. (2d) 184 (Q.B.).

3.8 [1966] 2 O.R. 81, 55 D.L.R. (2d) 674 (C.A.).

of natural justice by creating a "real likelihood of bias" against him. Nonetheless, Schroeder J.A. admitted to having some reservations as to the propriety of this scheme. Accordingly, he suggested the appointment of an independent legal officer, as set out in the British Medical Act Rules to act as advisor to the Council on legal issues, thereby obviating the necessity of the prosecuting lawyer being closeted with the Council during its deliberations. Laskin J.A., dissenting in part, declined to comment on this issue. (The correctness of *Glassman* may be in some doubt, not because it involved the simple presence of agency counsel during the deliberations of the agency but because that counsel had acted as a prosecutor in the proceedings.)

Insofar, as I have noted above, that *Consolidated Bathurst* has, in my view, relaxed the application of the "influence" aspects of the "he who hears" rule case law that relaxation should also apply to questions of the presence of staff. To reiterate *Consolidated Bathurst*, the possibility that a person might have influenced the decision-maker is not sufficient to offend the "he who hears" rule. Thus, the mere presence or assistance of staff or agency counsel in the deliberations of the decision-makers will, in the absence of some other tainting factor, not itself invalidate a decision.

"Delegatus non potest delegare"

The "delegatus non potest delegare" rule establishes that a statutory body may not sub-delegate powers which have been conferred upon it in its enabling legislation; the general principle is that such powers must be exercised only by the authority to which they have been legislatively committed.[3.9] Of course, it is perfectly open to the legislature to expressly authorize a statutory body to delegate its powers to others. When that is the case, the only question will relate to the scope of permissible delegation, rather than the right of the tribunal to do so.

Examples of such express authorization to delegate can be found in, e.g., s. 7(8) of the Ontario Milk Act[3.10] and s. 7(7) of the Ontario Farm Products Marketing Act.[3.11] Pursuant to each of these provisions, the relevant statutory authority (the Ontario Milk Commission and the Ontario Farm Products Marketing Board respectively, which have now been joined together) is entitled to delegate certain of its regulatory powers to local marketing board: for a case considering the scope of the Ontario Farm Products Marketing Board's authority to delegate its statutory powers, see *Re Bedesky and Farm Products Marketing Board of Ontario*.[3.12]

According to Reid and David,[3.13] however, it is rare to find legislation containing such express authority to sub-delegate. Furthermore, even when such

---

3.9 See de Smith, *Judicial Review of Administrative Action* (4th ed., 1980), p. 268.

3.10 R.S.O. 1990, c. M.12.

3.11 R.S.O. 1990, c. F.9.

3.12 (1975), 8 O.R. (2d) 516, 58 D.L.R. (3d) 484 (Div. Ct.), affirmed, 10 O.R. (2d) 605, 62 D.L.R. (3d) 265 (C.A.), leave to appeal to Supreme Court of Canada refused 10 O.R. (2d) 106n, 62 D.L.R. (3d) 266n.

3.13 *Administrative Law*, 2nd ed. (Butterworths, 1978).

express authorization is inserted into legislation, it is likely to be narrowly construed by the courts. In support of this proposition, the learned authors cite *Re B.C. Hotel Employees Union and Labour Relations Board*,[3.14] in which it was held that the labour board's statutory authority to delegate to one of its members "any" of its functions or duties permitted delegation only of routine matters;[3.15] see also *R. v. College of Physicians and Surgeons of British Columbia, Ex parte Ahmad*,[3.16] in which the British Columbia Court of Appeal held that the Council of the College of Physicians could not delegate to a committee of three of its members the authority to investigate and conduct a hearing in to whether Dr. Ahmad possessed adequate surgical skills. This, notwithstanding s. 28 of the British Columbia Medical Act,[3.17] which provided that the Council could "appoint such committees of boards and delegate to them such powers as it from time to time sees fit."

Absent express statutory authorization to delegate, courts will only relax the "delegatus" rule if convinced that the legislature implicitly intended to permit such sub-delegation. According to Professor John Willis, in his seminal article on the matter, this will involve a careful analysis of the scope and object of the statute. The focus of the inquiry in this regard, then, will be to determine whether there is "anything in the nature of the authority to which the discretion is entrusted, in the situation in which the discretion is to be exercised, [and] in the object which its exercise is expected to achieve to suggest that the legislature did not intend to confine the authority to the personal exercise of its discretion". Professor Willis then proceeds to state that:

> This question is answered in practice by comparing the *prima facie* rule [i.e. that statutory powers cannot be delegated] with the known practices or the apprehended needs of the authority in doing its work; the court inquires whether the policy-scheme of the statute is such as could not easily be realized unless the policy which requires that a discretion be exercised by the authority named thereto be displaced; it weighs the presumed desire of the legislature for the judgment of the authority it has named against the presumed desire of the legislature that the process of government shall go on in its accustomed and most effective manner and where there is a conflict between the two policies it determines which, under all the circumstances, is the more important.[3.18]

In other words, in considering whether the legislation in question implicitly authorizes delegation, the following factors will be of interest to the courts:

3.14 (1956), 18 W.W.R. 101, 2 D.L.R. (2d) 460 (B.C.C.A.).
3.15 Note 3.13, supra, p. 289.
3.16 [1971] 2 W.W.R. 60, 18 D.L.R. (3d) 197 (B.C.C.A.).
3.17 R.S.B.C. 1960, c. 239.
3.18 "Delagatus Non Potest Delegare" (1943), 21 Can. Bar Rev. 257 at 260-261.

(1)   the nature of the authority on whom the statutory power was originally conferred;

(2)   the nature of the party to whom the delegation has been made;

(3)   the nature and extent of the power possessed by the original authority as well as the conditions upon which it can be exercised; and

(4)   the extent of the delegation in relation to the total power possessed by the original authority.[3.19]

For a case in which Professor Willis' formulation was cited with approval, see *Re London Board of Education and Fenn.*[3.20]

There is some case law which indicates that courts will be more prone to imply an authority to delegate when ''administrative'' functions are involved, as opposed to ''legislative'' or ''judicial'' ones: see e.g. *Ahmad*, supra, at page 202 where Branca J.A. stated that ''there is no doubt that judicial functions cannot be delegated unless by express authority or by necessary implication while on the other hand many administrative functions may be validly delegated''. On one level, this distinction has some merit, in that many merely administrative matters do not require the exercise and discretion of personal judgment, and, therefore, it is not really of any importance who exercises them in practice. On the other hand, the ''administrative''/''judicial'' dichotomy has for the most part been discredited in administrative law circles, largely because of the inherent difficulties in formulating workable distinctions between these two concepts. As such, it is submitted that implied delegation should not depend upon such amorphous categorizations; rather, one should analyze the types of factors outlined by Willis and Mullan above, and in that manner, determine whether delegation is permissible under the statutory authority's enabling statute or not: for a discussion of this point see Jones and de Villars, *Principles of Administrative Law* (1985), at page 106.

The correct approach to this matter is illustrated by the House of Lord's decision in *Vine v. National Dock Labour Board.*[3.21] In this case, a dock labourer challenged the decision of a discipline committee of the local Dock Labour Board to discharge him. He claimed that the action of the discipline committee was void, because the local board had no power to delegate its disciplinary powers to a committee. Though finding in the dock labourer's favour, the House of Lords rejected his argument that this disciplinary power could never be delegated, simply because it was ''judicial'' in nature. Lord Somervell, for instance, stated that, in his opinion, this distinction had no merit; thus, there are a number of ''judicial functions'' which can be delegated, while, on the other hand, many so-called ''administrative'' duties cannot be deputed to others. In his view, therefore, the determination of whether or not an implied power to delegate exists rests upon

---

3.19 D. Mullan, *Administrative Law* (2nd ed., 1979) at par. 11.

3.20 [1971] 2 O.R. 93, 17 D.L.R. (3d) 129 (H.C.) per Osler J.

3.21 [1957] A.C. 488.

an evaluation of the nature of the duty in question and the character of the authority purporting to delegate its powers. In this case, because the disciplinary power could be used to deprive a man of his livelihood, and because the Dock Labour Board had been constituted so as to effectively balance the interests of labour and management, Lord Somervell held that the disciplinary power could not be delegated to a committee, regardless of whether it was "judicial" in nature or not. Viscount Kilmuir L.C. agreed with Lord Somervell's view of the law. As he stated, in answering this question categorizations are beside the point; rather, it is necessary to consider the importance of the duty which is delegated and the nature of the people who delegate it.

Whatever approach is employed by a given court, however, it is fairly clear that any attempt by a tribunal to delegate its *decision-making functions* will be struck down; as Wade puts it, "the valid exercise of a discretion requires a genuine application of the mind and a conscious choice by the correct authority".[3.22] Thus, for instance, a tribunal cannot act solely on the basis of recommendations made by one of its own inspectors or investigators. In *Re Geddes and Metropolitan Toronto Board of Commissioners of Police*,[3.23] O'Driscoll J. quashed the dismissal of a police cadet because this dismissal was decided upon by the deputy chief of police, rather than the Metro Toronto Board of Commissioners of Police, as provided for in the Ontario Police Act.[3.24] O'Driscoll J. refused to imply into the Act a power of delegation because he rejected the argument that it was open to the Board to merely confirm and ratify decisions taken by the deputy chief of police. As he stated:

> Suffice it to say that the wording of s. 15 of the *Police Act* and the wording of s. 27(*a*) of the Regulations, make it abundantly clear that the authority and power of dismissal lies with the Board, a creature of statute which only has the power given to it by its creator, the Ontario Legislature; I have not been referred to any section of the Act or any section of any Regulation conferring power upon this Board to delegate the power of dismissal, nor have I found such authority *delegatus non potest delegare*.[3.25]

3.22 *Administrative Law* (5th ed., 1982), p. 321. *Volk v. Saskatchewan (Public Service Commission)* (1993), 12 Admin. L.R. (2d) 293, 109 Sask. R. 306 (C.A.).

3.23 [1973] 1 O.R. 199, 30 D.L.R. (3d) 547 (H.C.), affirmed 1 O.R. (2d) 591n, 41 D.L.R. (3d) 175 (C.A.).

3.24 R.S.O. 1940, c. 351.

3.25 Supra, note 3.23, O.R. p. 203. Delegation is not always obvious. It can result when a decision-maker builds a requirement for the consent of a third party into its order. See, for example, *Metropolitan Toronto Police Services Board v. Ontario Municipal Employees Retirement Board* (1994), 20 O.R. (3d) 210, 117 D.L.R. (4th) 243, 75 O.A.C. 227 (Div. Ct.), (application for leave to appeal to C.A. filed). That decision dealt with the authority of the Ontario Municipal Employees Retirement Board to approve the use of excess contributions to a pension plan in such "manner as the Board and the employer shall mutually agree". The Ontario Divisional Court held that the Board erred in making such approval conditional upon the approval of

See also *Re Carter and Metropolitan Board of Commissioners of Police*[3.26] for a similar decision.

This does not, however, mean that a tribunal must in every case conduct every aspect of the decision-making process itself. Where an oral hearing, for

(Continued on page 22-10.51)

---

bargaining units. ''Neither the power in s. 4(3) and (7) of the Retirement System Act . . . to appoint advisors nor the power in s. 22(5) of the Pension Benefits Act . . . to employ agents, gives OMERS the authority to subdelegate to a bargaining unit the statutory powers and duties of administration given to OMERS.''
3.26 [1971] 3 O.R. 559, 21 D.L.R. (3d) 155 (H.C.).

example, is not required by law, it is permissible for a tribunal to delegate to a group of its members, or to staff employed by it, the power to investigate and to hear evidence and submission. (See the discussion earlier in this chapter on Paper Hearings, Investigations and "Delegated Hearing"). However, it is still incumbent upon the tribunal as a whole to make itself genuinely familiar with the evidence presented, even if only in summary form, and to render an independent decision based upon its understanding of that evidence. In *Jeffs v. New Zealand Dairy Production and Marketing Board*,[3.27] the Privy Council struck down a decision of the New Zealand Dairy Production and Marketing Board because this decision was based solely upon the written report of a committee appointed by the Board to gather evidence. Viscount Dilhorne held that in following this procedure the Board had failed in its duty to act judicially and "hear" the interested parties. As he stated:

> In this case the board did not hear the persons interested orally nor did it see their written statements. It did not see the written statements produced by witnesses at the hearing. Its members, other than the members of the committee, were not informed of the evidence given. The report stated what submissions were made at the hearing but did not state what evidence was given nor did it contain a summary of the evidence. The members of the board other than the members of the committee did not see the written submissions sent in in response to the chairman of the committee's statement at the hearing.

> . . .

> In some circumstances it may suffice for the board to have before it and to consider an accurate summary of the relevant evidence and submissions if this summary adequately discloses the evidence and submissions to the board.

> Unfortunately no such procedure was followed in this case. . . . The committee's report did not state what the evidence was and the board reached its decision without consideration of and in ignorance of the evidence.

In sum, therefore, the "delegatus non potest delegare" rule requires that the decision taken must at all times be identifiable as that of the delegating authority; in other words, this authority must always retain effective decision-making power in its own hands.[3.28]

Bias

The other principle of administrative law which is implicated in the *Spring* case is the prohibition against bias in the decision-making process. It is a fundamental principle of natural justice that tribunals must determine the rights and interests of others in a disinterested and impartial manner. The rule is expressed in the legal maxim "nemo judex in causa sua debet esse"; i.e. no party shall be

---

3.27 [1967] 1 A.C. 551 at pp. 567-569.
3.28 See de Smith, supra, note 3.9, p. 270.

a judge in his own case. Bias comes in two forms: actual bias and apparent bias. Accordingly, a decision-maker will be disqualified if he has a material interest in the result, or, if circumstances are such that a reasonable person would think it likely or probable that the decision-maker would, or did, favour one side unfairly at the expense of the other.

The classic formulation of reasonable apprehension of bias can be found in the opinion of Lord Hewart C.J. in *R. v. Sussex Justices, Ex parte McCarthy*,[3.29] where he stated as follows:

> . . . a long line of cases shows that it is not merely of some importance but is of fundamental importance that justice should not only be done, but should manifestly and undoubtedly be seen to be done.

Thus, the appearance of injustice alone will often be enough to substantiate a finding of bias as a matter of law. It is not necessary to prove that the decision-maker is actually biased; rather, in this sort of case, it is the impression which outside observers would have of the process which is of importance.

Nonetheless, this appearance of bias must be "real". As Lord Denning stated in *Metropolitan Properties Co. (F.G.C.) Ltd. v. Lannon*,[3.30] "surmise or conjecture is not enough." Thus, even though Lord Hewart was of the opinion in the *Sussex Justices* case that "nothing is to be done which creates *even a suspicion* that there has been an improper interference with the course of justice", it is fairly clear that the law, as it now stands, requires something more substantial in nature. Some courts have demanded a "real likelihood" of bias: see e.g. Lord Denning's decision in the *Lannon* case, supra. In Canada, it appears that the test currently in favour is whether there exists "a reasonable apprehension" of bias: this has been the formulation employed by the Supreme Court in a number of cases, e.g. *Ghirardosi v. Minister of Highways for British Columbia*,[3.31] *Blanchette v. C.I.S. Ltd*,[3.32] and *Committee for Justice and Liberty v. National Energy Board*.[3.33]

The Case Law

An illustration of bias arising from the participation of outsiders can be seen in *Haight-Smith v. Kamloops School District 34*, 30 Admin. L.R. 298, 28 B.C.L.R. (2d) 391, [1988] 6 W.W.R. 744, 51 D.L.R. (4th) 608 (C.A.). In that decision the British Columbia Court of Appeal considered that the decision of a school board was tainted by the attendance, during its deliberations, by a person who had investigated and reported on facts in the hearing. The facts in that case were as follows. A school teacher was subject to disciplinary proceedings before her

---

3.29 [1924] 1 K.B. 256 at 259.
3.30 [1969] 1 Q.B. 577 (C.A.). . . . *Lannon* has been subsequently considered in Great Britain in *R. v. Gough* (1993), 155 N.R. 81, [1993] 2 All E.R. 724 (H.L.).
3.31 [1966] S.C.R. 367, 55 W.W.R. 750, 56 D.L.R. (2d) 469.
3.32 [1973] S.C.R. 833, [1973] 4 W.W.R. 547, 36 D.L.R. (3d) 561, [1973] I.L.R. 1-532.
3.33 [1978] 1 S.C.R. 369, 68 D.L.R (3d) 716, 9 N.R. 115.

school board arising out of allegations from some of her students. The superintendent of schools investigated the allegations and made a written report to the school board that he believed the allegations were true. The teacher was sus-

(Continued on page 22-10.53)

pended. As provided by statute, a meeting was subsequently convened to consider whether further penalty should be imposed or the teacher should be reinstated. The superintendent attended at this meeting and presented it with the results of his investigations and his recommendations, which included his belief, that the teacher was lying in her denial of the allegations. The board went *in camera* to deliberate. The superintendent, however, remained in the room with the board members during their deliberations. He took no part in these deliberations. The Court of Appeal felt that the fact that the superintendent had acted as an accusor and prosecutor barred his attendance during the board's deliberations. Justice Esson stated (at pages 752-753 W.W.R.):

> If the superintendent, at the point where the board retires to deliberate, has taken no position which disqualifies him from being present, it might well be appropriate for him to be present during deliberations. In this case, however, the superintendent's involvement in the proceedings clearly disqualified him from being present at that stage. The reason for his disqualification appears from the language of Spence J. speaking for the majority in *L.S.U.C. v. French.* [1975] 2 S.C.R. 678, 68 W.W.R. 745, 6 D.L.R. (3d) 120]. In that case, the issue was whether the decision of the law society had been vitiated by the participation in the final decision of two members of convocation who have been members of the disciplinary committee. . . .

> In this case, the superintendent had become an accuser or prosecutor. He had emphatically expressed to the board his view that the teacher's denials of wrong-doing were untrue. The members of the board, who had not had the advantage of seeing or hearing the complainants, had to decide whether to accept the teacher's denials. It is reasonable to apprehend that the board members' ability to impartially consider that question would be adversely affected by the mere presence of the superintendent during deliberations. The board's case is not assisted by the statement of the superintendent that he saw his role as being present to "make sure the board kept on track". But the result would be the same without that vaguely ominous description of his purpose in being present.

An unusual (one hopes) example of bias in the context of delegated decision writing can be found in *Misra v. College of Physicians & Surgeons (Sask.)*, 36 Admin. L.R. 298, [1988] 5 W.W.R. 333, 52 D.L.R. (4th) 477, 70 Sask. R. 116 (C.A.), leave to appeal to S.C.C. granted (1989), 79 Sask. R. 80 (note), 102 N.R. 156 (note) (S.C.C.), appeal to S.C.C. discontinued January 27, 1992. In 1982, a doctor was charged with drug offences under the Criminal Code. As a consequence his licence to practice was temporarily suspended by the Council of the Sasktchewan College of Physicians and Surgeons pending the resolution of the criminal charges. The doctor was ultimately acquitted of the criminal charges, but he was then charged by the College under the Medical Profession Act regarding the same incident which had given rise to the criminal charges. The doctor's licence was again suspended, this time pending the final hearing by the Council of these latest charges. Before the hearing (at which his licence was finally suspended) the doctor overheard the registrar of the Council dictating a draft resolution of suspension of his licence. Subsequently, the resolution of the Council suspending the licence was issued and was found to be identical to the wording of the draft which the doctor had overheard being dictated. The draft resolution had been prepared in advance of the hearing for reasons of efficiency because the members of the Council were busy and were meeting at some inconvenience. The Council was not aware of the draft until after the hearing. Nor did the registrar discuss the case with any Council member prior to the hearing.

The Saskatchewan Court of Appeal found that the actions of the registrar resulted in a reasonable apprehension of bias. The Court stated that while it was possible to understand an efficient administrator's desire to make things easy for the Council by having a draft motion ready it felt that, with respect to a body exercising a quasi-judicial function, the existence of the draft prior to the hearing, gave rise to a reasonable apprehension of bias. It stated that "any person, about to have his rights judged by a tribunal, who hears the chief administrative officer of that tribunal, prior to the hearing, dictating an order of the tribunal surely has a 'reasonable suspicion of biased appraisal and judgment, unintended though it may be'. The appearance that justice is being done is as important as justice being done."3.34

The question raised by the *Spring* case, then, is whether and to what extent a tribunal's practice of delegating to non-tribunal members or staff the responsibility for drafting its decisions violates the principles of administrative law considered above.

This issue has been dealt with in a number of Ontario cases prior to *Spring*. In *Re Bernstein and College of Physicians and Surgeons of Ontario*,3.35 for instance, the Divisional Court was clearly of the opinion that it was improper for counsel to a discipline committee to prepare its reasons for decision, when this counsel had been responsible for prosecuting the case against the accused. The *Bernstein* case concerned disciplinary proceedings against a doctor for professional misconduct. The Discipline Committee of the College of Physicians and Surgeons of Ontario conducted an inquiry into the allegation that this doctor had

---

3.34 An interesting application of the "reasonable appearance" test can be seen in the New Zealand case of *Potter v. New Zealand Milk Board*, [1983] N.Z.L.R. 620 (H.C.). In that case the Board's counsel had acted as the prosecutor in proceedings before the Vendor Review Committee of the New Zealand Milk Board. At the end of the hearing the Board's chair announced that the Board's counsel would not participate in the Board's decision. The hearing then ended and all left the hearing room except the three Committee members, the Secretary of the Board, the Board manager and the Board's counsel. The following day the Committee issued it decision revoking the licence in question. Judicial review was sought on the grounds of the improper participation of the Board's counsel in the deliberations of the Committee. There was no actual evidence that the counsel had taken part in those deliberations. The New Zealand High Court rejected the challenge partly because of the lack of evidence but principally in light of the chair's express statement at the hearing that the counsel would not be participating in the decision.

3.35 (1977), 15 O.R. (2d) 447, 76 D.L.R. (3d) 38, 1 L.M.Q. 56 (Div. Ct.).

been involved in an ''improper association'' with a female patient. At the conclusion of the hearing of evidence, the Discipline Committee found the doctor guilty as charged, and directed that he be suspended from practising for a year. Some time later, the Discipline Committee issued written reasons for its decision. The manner in which these reasons were drafted was set out in a letter from the Committee's counsel to the lawyer for the accused:

> As previously indicated, it has been the practice of the Discipline Committee in some cases after reaching its verdict, for the Chairman to prepare a rough outline of the Committee's reasons for judgment, after which I am directed by the Chairman to prepare a formal draft thereof for approval by him and the members of the Committee, and when such approval is obtained then the reasons are signed by the Chairman.

Notwithstanding that counsel to the Committee had the benefit of the Chairman's rough outline to assist him in preparing the draft reasons, the court did not hesitate to condemn the Committee's procedures in this area. As O'Leary J. stated:

> In my view it is an unusual and improper practice for counsel to write the reasons for the Discipline Committee even if the Chairman or some member of the Committee has drafted rough reasons to guide him. One who has stood trial before a disciplinary body is entitled to have that body's reasons for its decision and not the reasons the prosecutor composes for the decision. If the Committee has made an error in arriving at its conclusion the one who has stood trial, in fairness, should learn of it.[3.36]

Steele J. concurred with O'Leary J., while Mr. Justice Garrett, in an opinion delivered separately, agreed that the procedure followed by the Committee was ''seriously unsatisfactory''.[3.37]

A similar decision was rendered by the Ontario Court of Appeal in *Re Sawyer and Ontario Racing Commission*[3.38] In this case, the Ontario Racing Commission found the appellant Sawyer guilty of violating certain racing rules and suspended him from racing for ten years. It was subsequently learned that the Commission's formal reasons had been written by a lawyer from the Attorney General's Office who had prosecuted the case. This had been done at the request of the Commission itself.

The Ontario Court of Appeal overturned the Divisional Court's refusal to quash the Commission's ruling, and held that it was a denial of natural justice for the prosecuting counsel to draft the Commission's reasons for decision. This, even though (a) the counsel had played no part in the Commission's actual decision-making process, and (b) the Commission had adopted the draft reasons

---

3.36 O.R. p. 473.
3.37 O.R. p. 488.
3.38 (1979), O.R. (2d) 673, 99 D.L.R. (3d) 561 (C.A.).

for judgment only after careful consideration. In the court's opinion, it was far more persuasive that the Commission's counsel had drafted the reasons without any draft outline or summary from the Commission; indeed, it appeared as if the Commission had never *actually* communicated its reasons for decision to the counsel at all. As for the Commission reviewing the draft reasons, the importance to be accorded this factor was greatly reduced by the fact that the formal reasons issued by the Commission were identical to counsel's draft reasons; it was obvious that no changes whatsoever had been made to counsel's final draft.

Brooke J.A., speaking for the court, found the Commission's practice odious for a number of reasons. Firstly, he felt that it raised the spectre of a reasonable apprehension of bias:

> [Counsel's] role was to prosecute the case against the appellant [Sawyer] . . . He was counsel for the appellant's adversary in proceedings to determine the appellant's guilt or innocence on the charge against him. It is basic that persons entrusted to judge or determine the rights of others must, for reasons arrived at independently, make that decision whether it or the reasons be right or wrong. It was wrong for the Commission, who were the judges, to privately involve either party in the Commission's function once the case began and certainly after the case was left to them for ultimate disposition. To do so must amount to a denial of natural justice because it would not unreasonably raise a suspicion of bias in others, including the appellant, who were not present and later learned what transpired. In the circumstances justice does not appear to have been done and the decision cannot stand.[3.39]

In Brooke J.A.'s opinion, however, reasonable apprehension of bias was not the only problem with the procedure followed here. Brooke J.A. also agreed with O'Leary in *Bernstein* that the effect of the Commission's practice was to deprive parties appearing before it of the right to have the Commission's *own* reasons for its decision against them. He concluded that this rendered their right to appeal or judicial review illusory.[3.40] Furthermore, Brooke J.A. would not accept the argument that any failings in the Commission's procedures could be alleviated through the simple expedient of the Commission's counsel submitting an affidavit outlining how the reasons were actually drafted. As he explained:

> . . . justice cannot appear to have been done when the determination of how a case was decided depends, not upon the reasons over the signature of the real author, but rather upon the affidavit of a person who actually wrote the reasons and who now must explain how his thoughts were accepted after the decision of the tribunal. This is not good enough, for the appellant still has not been told by *the tribunal* why it found him guilty. (emphasis added)[3.41]

3.39 O.R. p. 676.
3.40 O.R. p. 677.
3.41 O.R. p. 678.

Another case involving the improper drafting of reasons by a staff member who had taken a position at the hearing is *Després c. Assn. des Arpenteurs-géomètres du Nouveau-Brunswick)* (1992), 8 Admin. L.R. (2d) 136, (*sub nom Després v. L'Association des arpenteurs-gèométres du Nouveau-Brunswick* 130 N.B.R. (2d) 210, 328 A.P.R. 210 (C.A.). In that case the New Brunswick Court of Appeal found that a reasonable apprehension of bias arose when the solicitor for the Association of New Brunswick Land Surveyors, who had acted as prosecutor for the Association in disciplinary proceedings against a surveyor before its complaints committee and then its discipline committee, assisted the discipline committee in writing its decision in the matter. Justice Hoyt, writing for the court, stated (at pages 140-141 Admin. L.R.) that:

> The failure of the committee to render its decision without the assistance of one of the lawyers that took part in the hearing would, in my opinion, lead a reasonable and well-informed person to conclude that the tribunal's decision was not reached fairly and impartially, thus creating the likelihood of a biassed decision. As in *Bernstein* and *Sawyer*, I do not impute any improper motive or activity by either Mr. Yerxa [the counsel] or the members of the discipline committee. One can understand the desire of a lay (in legal matters) committee, embarking on such a formal course, to have legal assistance. For better or worse, however, Mr. Després was entitled to have the reasons, however "rough" they may have been, of the committee that heard the complaint against him.

Bernstein and *Sawyer* were cited with approval and followed in *Re Emerson and Law Society of Upper Canada*.[3.42] In this case, a solicitor challenged the decision of a discipline committee of the Law Society of Upper Canada to recommend his disbarrment to Convocation. One ground for this challenge was that the committee's report to Convocation had been drafted by the Law Society's secretary. Henry J. upheld the solicitor's argument, and held that the committee had breached the rules of natural justice in delegating the drafting responsibility to that official. Henry J. was of the firm opinion that "it goes without saying that the written decision and reasons of the discipline committee, who are the judges in this process, must be prepared by them personally".[3.43]

In *Emerson*, however, the discipline committee had made no effort to "personally" draft a written decision with reasons. Rather, it had simply instructed the secretary, an employee of the prosecuting Law Society, to draft a "report" to Convocation, pursuant to s. 9(7) of the Law Society's regulations. This report, it seemed, was intended to form the actual written decision and reasons of the discipline committee itself. According to Henry J., however, in light of *Sawyer* this was "not good enough".[3.44] As he stated:

3.42 (1983), 44 O.R. (2d) 729, 41 C.P.C. 7, 5 D.L.R. (4th) 294 (H.C.).
3.43 O.R. p. 761.
3.44 O.R. p. 761.

> The drafting of this document by a third person (in this case, the prosecutor) is a fatal breach of the rules of natural justice; that function cannot be delegated.[3.45]

As for the argument that the discipline committee had been authorized to delegate the drafting responsibility to the secretary pursuant to the Law Society's regulations, Henry J. had this to say:

> It is my opinion that Convocation has not been empowered . . . to set aside by its own regulations a fundamental rule of natural justice . . . It would of course be otherwise if the Legislature itself had enacted s. 9. I hold therefore that s. 9 cannot extend to authorizing the secretary to prepare the written decision and reasons of the discipline committee . . .; they must be prepared by the committee.[3.46]

According to Henry J., therefore, the secretary's report was *not* to take the place of a written decision with reasons drafted by the committee itself. Rather, these were to be viewed as two separate functions. Firstly, the committee would write its own decision, independent of any outside influence or assistance. Then, the secretary would use this as the basis for the report to Convocation. The latter step was simply an administrative expedient designed for the Law Society's purposes alone; the first step, however, was required by the rules of natural justice. Therefore, only if the committee prepared its own independent reasons would the law be satisfied.

Application of the Case Law and Administrative Principles in Spring

As noted above, the majority and the minority in the *Spring* case diverged over the applicability of *Emerson* and *Sawyer* to the fact situation before them (*Bernstein* was not mentioned by any of the Divisional Court justices). Labrosse J., with whom Mr. Justice Craig agreed, held that these cases were distinguishable because they either involved prosecuting counsel, or officials tied to the prosecution, drafting the decisions. By contrast, the Clerk in *Spring* was not linked to the Society's Discipline Department at all. To these justices, therefore, this removed any problem of reasonable apprehension of bias.

Moreover, Labrosse and Craig JJ. asserted that in neither *Emerson* nor *Sawyer* did the tribunal in question provide the staff member involved with any background reasons to form a basis for the draft decision. Thus, it could not be demonstrated categorically that the tribunal members had arrived at their decisions without any outside influence. By contrast, in *Spring* the Chairman briefed the Clerk orally as to the Committee's reasons for finding the accused guilty. The Clerk used this to prepare his draft report. The Chairman then reviewed the draft to ensure that it complied with the Committee's thinking. Thus, it was clear to Labrosse J. and Craig J. that no part of the *decisional* process had been delegated,

---

3.45 O.R. p. 760.
3.46 O.R. p. 762.

even though the *writing* process had. In their opinion, however, it was the nature of the decisional process which was controlling.

Even though I am in general sympathy with the majority's ruling, I do not consider its reading of the case law to be without flaws. Firstly, Henry J.'s decision in *Emerson* does not appear to have been founded upon the Law Society secretary's function as a prosecutor. Henry J.'s language was much broader than that. He seemed to be saying that the drafting of a tribunal's reasons cannot be delegated to *any* third person, regardless of whether or not that person participated somehow in prosecuting the case in question.

Even in the *Sawyer* decision, where there was no doubt that counsel's role as prosecutor influenced the court's ruling, other reasons were raised for prohibiting the delegation of drafting responsibilities as well. Among them, as will be recalled, was Brooke J.A.'s opinion that this sort of practice deprived parties appearing before tribunals of the right to conclusively know the tribunals' reasons for deciding against them. In Brooke J.A.'s view, justice cannot appear to be done when the person signing a decision is not necessarily the author of that decision. Thus, both *Emerson* and *Sawyer* can be read as prescribing a much broader limitation on the delegation of decision-writing responsibilities than either Labrosse or Craig JJ. were prepared to acknowledge in *Spring*. This prohibition would extend to all tribunal staff members, not only to those engaged in prosecutorial functions.

In addition, it is not entirely clear that the case law unequivocally holds that delegation is permissible so long as the tribunal in question provides its delegate with draft reasons. It is true that this was *not* done in either *Sawyer* or *Emerson*. However, Henry J.'s interpretation of s. 9(7) of the Law Society's regulations can be taken as indicating that even if this *had been done*, the rules of natural justice would not have been satisfied. Thus, Mr. Justice Henry continuously emphasized that the committee was required to draft its own reasons *personally* and *independently*. That this decision could then be used as the basis for the secretary's report, was regarded by Henry J. as entirely ancillary to the central question. In his view, the key was to ensure that there existed an independent decision with reasons drafted by the committee itself. He did not seem to envision the possibility of any delegation in that process.

Furthermore, the *Bernstein* case is some authority for the proposition that a tribunal may not delegate its writing responsibilities *notwithstanding* that it provides a summary outline of its reasons to act as a guide. Of course, the *Bernstein* case involved the additional element of prosecuting counsel drafting the tribunal's reasons; it could be argued, therefore, that this factor outweighed everything else in the court's opinion. Nonetheless, as with Henry J. in *Emerson*, O'Leary J.'s decision can be interpreted so as to extend his prohibition against this sort of delegation beyond instances in which prosecuting counsel are involved. Thus, O'Leary J. did not appear to be concerned with issues of bias at all in his decision. Rather, O'Leary J. seemed to object to the discipline committee's practice on an alternative ground, namely that it deprived persons standing before the committee of the reasons of that body itself. This indicates that his misgivings were more broadly based and went beyond the participation of the prosecuting counsel in the writing process. It is arguable that he objected to the act of delegation altogether and, therefore, the fact that the committee provided an outline of its reasons was largely immaterial.

In sum, then, it appears that the basic principle enunciated in *Bernstein*, *Sawyer* and *Emerson* is not as Labrosse and Craig JJ. would have it; rather, these cases seem to hold that decision-writing responsibilities cannot be divorced from decision-making responsibilities, and therefore, just as administrative law principles for the most part prohibit delegation of the latter, the same must hold true for the former.[3.47]

The above interpretation of *Bernstein, Sawyer* and *Emerson* is consistent with that offered by the Ontario Court of Appeal in *Re Del Core and Ontario College of Pharmacists*.[3.48] In *Del Core*, Finalyson J.A. cited this trilogy of cases as standing for the following proposition:

> The courts have consistently held that the reasons given by discipline committees of self-governing bodies must be the reasons of the committees and cannot be written by counsel *or professional staff*.[3.49]

This uncompromising view of the case law is, of course, not in accord with the majority's interpretation in *Spring*. It is, however, the interpretation adopted by Trainor J., the dissenting justice in that case. According to Trainor J., *Sawyer* and *Emerson* establish that a tribunal must draft its reasons independently of all outside influence. The true issue in these cases, therefore, was whether or not it was clear beyond serious peradventure that the reasons issued by the tribunals were in all actuality the product of the thought processes of their members. As delegation of the responsibility to write decisions placed this in doubt, it was to be discouraged. That the writing task was delegated to a party fulfilling a prosecutorial function was one factor for consideration, but it did not go to the heart of the matter.

Notwithstanding his understanding of the relevant precedents, and despite the fact that he felt that the facts before him were undistinguishable from this case law, Trainor J. was not prepared to take the position that tribunals should be banned entirely from delegating the decision-writing process to others. Instead, he was willing to permit tribunals to do so, so long as the tribunal in question drafted summaries or outlines of its reasonings to serve as guidelines for use by the third parties in preparing more formal drafts. In Trainor J.'s opinion, this would be the minimum necessary to ensure that the tribunal remained the effective author of its own decision. It would also provide some evidence to counter possible

---

3.47 See McCormick, ''The Role of the Board's Counsel'' in *Speakers' Remarks from Seminar for Members of Administrative Tribunals* (1980).
3.48 (1985), 51 O.R. (2d) 1, 15 Admin. L.R. 227, 19 D.L.R. (4th) 68, 10 O.A.C. 57.
3.49 O.R. p. 8.

accusations that the tribunal had abandoned its decision-making responsibilities. Because no such written guidelines were provided by the Chairman to the Clerk in the *Spring* case, Trainor J. was unwilling to uphold the Committee's decision here.

Interestingly enough, Trainor J.'s position on this issue may be more lenient than that of Labrosse J., even though Labrosse J. was willing to uphold the Committee's procedure in this case while Trainor J. was not. As noted above, Labrosse J. "deplored" the Committee's practice of not drafting its own reasons. In Labrosse J.'s opinion, composing written reasons for decision is an unavoidable "responsibility of office" for tribunal members and should not be delegated to others. His decision not to strike down the Committee's disbarrment of Mr. Spring was made very reluctantly, and only because he believed that the Committee had indeed arrived at its decision independently.

Of the three justices, Mr. Justice Craig was the most amenable to accepting delegation of drafting responsibilities. In his view, so long as it is clear that the tribunal has arrived at its decision independently, the tribunal is entitled to some journalistic and administrative assistance in articulating its reasons. He did not elaborate on the correct procedures to be followed, though it is obvious from his decision that the system used by the Committee did not strike him as unreasonable.

Assessment

Thus, in *Spring* the Divisional Court failed to definitively resolve the issue as to the extent to which tribunals may delegate the task of drafting decisions. That issue would be resolved by the Ontario Court of Appeal in *Khan v. College of Physicians & Surgeons (Ontario)* (1992), 9 O.R. (3d) 641, 11 Admin. L.R. (2d) 147, 76 C.C.C. (3d) 10, 94 D.L.R. (4th) 193 (C.A.) (discussed below). However, it may be stated with some confidence that the *Spring* decision represents a noticeable shift away from the positions enunciated by previous Ontario courts in *Bernstein, Sawyer, Emerson* and *Del Core*. These cases seemed to indicate that delegation of decision-writing responsibilities would rarely if ever be accepted by the courts. The *Spring* case still evidences a certain distaste for this practice, but by upholding the Committee's decision it illustrates that some delegation *is* possible. Even Trainor J. did not object to this procedure in principle; he dissented here because he did not believe, based on the facts, that the Committee had done everything in its power to give the appearance that justice had been done. If the Chairman had provided the Clerk with a written summary of the Committee's reasons, it is more than likely that Trainor J. would not have resisted the Clerk producing the final version of the decision either. The same could not be said with certainty with respect to the courts in *Emerson, Del Core, Sawyer* and even *Bernstein*. It is submitted, therefore, that the *Spring* case represents a step forward, albeit a shaky one. Thus, all three opinions evidenced an increased willingness to countenance more liberal delegation by tribunals of their writing responsibilities. This is to be encouraged.

In particular, both Labrosse and Craig JJ. take care to distinguish between decision-making and decision-writing powers; this is no doubt a positive development (Trainor J. seems to balk at this distinction, but he is willing to accept some form of delegation nonetheless). There is little gain saying the proposition that the decision-making powers conferred upon tribunals must be exercised by tribunal members themselves in an independent fashion and cannot be delegated to others; decision-making is the precise reason for which tribunals are created, and their members are appointed to perform that very function. But decision-writing is another matter entirely. Given the average tribunal's heavy caseload, and taking into account the difficulties which lay tribunal members face in writing judicial or quasi-judicial decisions, delegation seems to be the ideal way to expedite the process and at the same time to obtain better reasoned and more cogently argued decisions.[3.50] It is submitted, therefore, that the "delegatus non potest delegare" rule should be relaxed in this situation. Certainly, however, this cannot be done in such a manner that tribunal members effectively abdicate their decision-*making* responsibilities. The concerns of the case law are well-founded in this regard. Yet these concerns should not serve to foreclose tribunals from exploiting very useful administrative mechanisms.

The key is to impose sufficient safeguards on the delegation process so as to ensure that the tribunal's final reasons are in fact its own. This would serve to satisfy the "he who hears must decide" rule and remove any taint of bias or appearance of injustice as well. It would also provide an additional reason for a less rigorous application of the "delegatus non potest delegare" rule, for as de Smith writes:

> The more significant the effective powers of control retained by the delegating authority, the more readily will the courts uphold the validity of the delegation; and they may choose to uphold its validity by denying that there has been any delegation at all, on the ground that in substance the authority in which the discretion has been vested by statute continues to address its own mind to the exercise of the powers.[3.51]

I believe that these principles are recognized in the decision of the Ontario Court of Appeal in *Khan v. College of Physicians & Surgeons (Ontario)* (1992), 9 O.R. (3d) 641, 11 Admin. L.R. (2d) 147, 76 C.C.C. (3d) 10, 94 D.L.R. (4th) 193 (C.A.). That case involved discipline hearings by the discipline committee of the Ontario College of Physicians and Surgeons against a Dr. Khan. The committee had retained a private law firm to act as counsel to assist it in these hearings. There were no allegations relating to any impropriety on the part of this counsel at the hearing. The committee found Dr. Khan to be guilty of the charges. It was not suggested that the counsel played any role in the committee's deliberations or its decision. Some three months after making its decision the committee

---

3.50 McCormick, note 3.46, supra, p. 116.
3.51 Supra, note 3.9, p. 302.

released its reasons. At that time it became known that the counsel to the committee had, at the request of the committee, reviewed the draft of the committee's reasons and provided "journalistic and administrative assistance", but not legal advice with respect thereto. In a letter to Dr. Khan's lawyer, committee counsel, R.W. Cosman, outlined the role he and his partners played as counsel to the committee, including their role in the hearing process, and the subsequent preparation of the reasons. It is important to note that counsel in *Khan* did not prosecute the case against Dr. Khan. He appeared to take a much more neutral stance as legal advisor to the committee:

> First, where the Discipline Committee requires legal advice in the course of the hearing, we provide it, fully disclosing the nature of such advice to the parties and ensuring that the parties have the opportunity to make submissions to the Committee regarding that advice as they consider appropriate. Where I gave such advice in this case, I put that advice on the record in open hearing. The transcript discloses the advice I gave on all occasions when I gave it.
>
> Secondly, where the Discipline Committee invites us to join them and asks for legal advice in the course of its deliberations, after the completion of evidence and argument, it is our practice to provide that advice and then to inform the parties as to the nature of the advice given, and that if they wish to make submissions with respect to such advice they may do so before a decision is made by the Committee. In this case no legal advice was sought or provided in the course of the deliberations of the Committee. We take no part in the deliberations of the Committee, and the Decision of the Committee is that of the Committee alone.
>
> Thirdly, we provide no legal advice to the Committee in their preparation of written reasons for their decision. The Committee understands that they are obligated to provide the reasons for their decision. The written Decision and Reasons for Decision is in every case drafted in the first instance by the Chairman of the panel or a member of the panel designated by the Chairman for that purpose. In the ordinary course we are provided with a copy of the draft, review it with the Chairman and assist the Chairman to express the reasons of the Committee. The draft Decision and Reasons for Decision in this case went through this process, and through subsequent review and revision by members of the Committee in conference, and was ultimately approved and signed by each Committee member.
>
> In the Khan case, as in all others, the Decision and Reasons for Decision are those of the Committee. We are satisfied that the journalistic and administrative assistance that we provide in the above respect is not "legal advice" within the meaning of Section 12(3) of the Act. Our role here is to assist the Committee to express their decision and their reasons for that decision. We regard that practice as falling squarely within the practice approved by the Divisional Court in *Spring and the Law Society of Upper Canada* (1988), 50 DLR (4th) 523.

On judicial review a majority of the Ontario Divisional Court found this practice to be objectionable. Justice O'Driscoll (writing for himself and Justice Rosenberg) felt that it was impossible for lawyers to review draft decisions and not give "legal advice" thereon:

> . . . it is difficult to see how a lawyer trained as he is and whose role is counsel for the committee can distinguish between changes that are made for journalistic and administrative reasons and those that are made for legal reasons. If a sentence is left out, does it change the meaning of what is being said and might it not affect the court's view of the reasons? Lawyers are not retained for their journalistic or administrative abilities and it is unlikely that a lawyer with the best of intentions can confine his advice to be only of journalistic and administrative assistance.[3.52]

Justice O'Driscoll had already noted that section 23(3) of the *Health Disciplines Act*, R.S.O. 1980, c. 196 [now R.S.O. 1990, c. H.4] permitted the committee to retain independent legal advice, but required that it be made known to the parties any such advice it received. Consequently, the failure to disclose the "legal advice" received during the review of the draft reasons invalidated the decision. Mr. Justice Holland in dissent, could not accept that section 23(3) applied to advice of a mere journalistic or administrative nature nor that lawyers were incapable of providing anything but legal advice. In his opinion, it "would be ridiculous if this committee of lay persons was to be deprived of this type of assistance when, under the Law Society Act, R.S.O. 1980, c. 233 [now R.S.O. 1990, c. L.8], a discipline committee of lawyers may obtain such assistance."[3.53]

On appeal, the Ontario Court of Appeal rejected the somewhat black and white view of the majority of the Divisional Court, and laid down the parameters in which delegation of decision-writing may take place.

The Court of Appeal quickly disposed of the section 12(3) Health Disciplines Act argument by noting that it applied only to legal advice received during the hearing itself. In its opinion, the hearing phase of a discipline process encompasses the taking of evidence, the hearing of argument and the rendering of the decision. It did not include the preparation of reasons for that decision. (The Health Disciplines Act did not require the provisions of reasons for its decisions).

However, even if section 12(3) extended to the preparation of reasons it would not have caught the type of assistance rendered by committee counsel in *Khan*. The Court rejected the narrow view of Justice O'Driscoll that any advice given by lawyers has to be "legal advice". In determining whether advice constitutes legal advice, the Court held that it is the *nature* of the advice, not its effect on the final product which must be considered:

> Advice intended to improve the quality of the Committee's reasons by, for example, deleting erroneous references to the evidence or adding additional relevant references to the evidence, is not advice on a matter of law but is rather advice as to how the Committee should frame its reasons in support of its decision. If the Committee accepts such advice, it may improve the quality of the reasons ultimately provided

---

3.52 *Khan v. College of Physicians & Surgeons (Ontario)* (1990), 76 D.L.R. (4th) 179, 48 Admin. L.R. 118 (Ont. Div. Ct.) at p. 200, reversed (1992), 9 O.R. (3d) 641, 11 Admin. L.R. (2d) 147, 76 C.C.C. (3d) 10, 94 D.L.R. (4th) 193 (C.A.).
3.53 at p. 206 D.L.R.

by the Committee and render the decision of the Committee less susceptible to reversal on appeal. This does not, however, transform advice as to the content and formulation of reasons into advice on a matter of law.[3.54]

Thus, ''journalistic and administrative assistance'', as approved in *Spring* and *Khan*, is not restricted to spelling and grammar. It would appear to extend to pointing out how the agency's reasons might be improved through the addition or deletion of references to evidence (and presumably argument). The reviewing counsel is not determining the reasons of the agency. He is merely assisting to better express the argument already determined by the decision-maker.

Aside from the legal requirements of section 12(3), the Court of Appeal also felt that the assistance provided by the legal counsel in *Khan* did not raise any questions as to fairness or integrity.

As in the earlier case law, the Court made it clear that it was not endorsing the concept of staff writing reasons to explain decisions:

> The reasons for a decision made by the Committee must be those of the Committee. . . . The rationale underlying this principle is self-evident. In discipline proceedings the parties are entitled to know, and if so inclined challenge on appeal the Committee's decision. Someone else's explanation for or rationalization of that decision is no substitute for the Committee's reasons. With the reasons of the Committee, a party cannot know why the decision was made , or who made the decision. The right of appeal also becomes illusory.[3.55]

However, the ''ultimate responsibility'' of the committee for the authorship of the reasons did not preclude its availing itself of counsel's assistance during the drafting process provided. Following the lead of the Supreme Court in *Consolidated Bathurst* the Court felt that the task before it was to reconcile the characteristics and exigencies of decision-making by specialized tribunals with the procedural rights of the parties:

> The ultimate aim of the drafting process is a set of reasons which accurately and fully reflects the thought processes of the Committee. To the extent that consultation with counsel promotes that aim, it is to be encouraged. The debate must fix, not on the Committee's entitlement to assistance in the drafting of reasons, but on the acceptable limits of that assistance.[3.56]

According to the Court of Appeal in *Khan* assistance is permissible provided that it compromises neither the fairness of the proceedings nor the integrity of the process:

3.54 At pp. 670-671 D.L.R.
3.55 At p. 671 D.L.R.
3.56 p. 672 O.R.

Without attempting an exhaustive description of these concepts, **fairness** includes considerations of bias, real or apprehended, independence, and each party's right to know the case made against them and to present their own case. **Integrity** concerns encompass those fairness concerns, but include the broader need to ensure that the body charged with the responsibility of making the particular decision in fact makes that decision after a proper consideration of the merits. If the reasons presented for the decision are not those of the decision-maker, or do not appear to be so, it raises real concerns about the validity of the decision and the genuineness of the entire inquiry.[3.57] (emphasis added)

The determination as to whether either of these concepts had been breached in any given case is to be determined in the context of the institutional constraints of the agency in much the same way as the Supreme Court of Canada had approached full board meetings in *Consolidated Bathurst*:

The nature of the proceedings, the issues raised in those proceedings, the composition of the tribunal, the terms of the enabling legislation, the support structure available to the tribunal, the tribunal's workload and other factors will impact on the assessment of the propriety of procedures used in the preparation of reasons. Certainly, the judicial paradigm of reason writing cannot be imposed on all boards and tribunals. . . .[3.58]

Like the Supreme Court in *Consolidated Bathurst*, the Ontario Court of Appeal in *Khan* rejected the idea that reviewing counsel could not influence the decision-maker. Influence alone was not improper. It would only become improper where it resulted in a breach of one of the fairness or integrity of the proceedings (for example by introducing new argument on which the parties would have no opportunity to make submissions.[3.59]

3.57 p. 672 O.R.

3.58 p. 673 O.R.

3.59 At p. 673 O.R. Influence was also considered by the Federal Court in *Bovbel v. Canada (Minister of Employment and Immigration)* (1993), 70 F.T.R. 66, reversed [1994] 2 F.C. 563, 18 Admin. L.R. (2d) 169, 113 D.L.R. (4th) 415, 167 N.R. 10 (F.C.A.), leave to appeal to S.C.C. refused (1994), 23 Admin. L.R. (2d) 320n, 115 D.L.R. (4th) vii (note). The Trial Division felt that the policy of the Immigration and Refugee Board requiring that any draft reasons reviewed and commented on by agency counsel as part of a voluntary review process were to be left on file and accessible to the other panel members was a "blatant attempt to influence" and a breach of the rules of natural justice. The Court of Appeal, however, disagreed saying that "if there is nothing wrong in the author of the reasons receiving the comments of a legal advisor, there cannot be any wrong in making those comments known to the other member of the Board who is asked to concur in the reasons". In my opinion, the Court of Appeal must be correct in its conclusions. However, I suggest it is a preferable practice for members drafting a decision to first consult with their fellow members on the draft before sending it to review by staff. This also ensures that the staff's time is not taken up with the necessity of reviewing progressive revisions of a draft as the different views of members are accommodated therein.

In the case of Dr. Khan, nothing in the record suggested that the reviewing counsel's involvement in the writing of reasons compromised either the independence or the impartiality of the committee. As to fairness, counsel was independent of all the parties, his involvement in the writing process was not mandatory and was totally under the control of the committee and his assistance could not have had any coercive effect on its members. Nor did the involvement undermine Dr. Khan's ability to know the case against him or to present his own case. There was no evidence that counsel had advanced one position over the other during the drafting process, nor was there any evidence of new facts or arguments having been advanced.

On this last point (of no new facts or arguments being raised) readers may wish to take note of two decisions arising out of the Federal Court of Canada. In *Armstrong v. Royal Cdn. Mounted Police Commissioner* (1994), 73 F.T.R. 81, 24 Admin. L.R. (2d) 2. Justice Rothstein stated that the opinions and views of a staff officer preparing a summary of a matter for the decision-maker did not constitute "facts".[3.60] Subsequently, in *Bovbel v. Canada (Minister of Employment and Immigration)*, [1994] 2 F.C. 563, 18 Admin. L.R. (2d) 169, 113 D.L.R. (4th) 415, 167 N.R. 10 (F.C.A.), leave to appeal to S.C.C. refused (1994), 23 Admin. L.R. (2d) 328n, 115 D.L.R. (4th) vii (note) the Court of Appeal overturned the Trial Division's rejection of the policy of the Immigration and Refugee Board to provide agency counsel on a review of a draft set of reasons with the full file. Justice Rouleau at the Trial Division had felt that the review of the file by the counsel might taint counsel's comments with his own perception of the facts (which might differ from the agency member's). The Court of Appeal felt that pursuant to the Board's policy "the legal advisors were not expected to discuss the findings of facts made by the members but merely, if there was a factual inconsistency in the reasons, to look at the file in order to determine, if possible, how the inconsistency could be resolved." Sending the entire file to a reviewer is, in my opinion, consistent with the views of the Ontario Court of Appeal in *Khan*. In *Khan* the Court had stated that such things as "deleting erroneous references to the evidence or adding additional relevant references to the evi-

---

3.60 This is consistent with the case law regarding the disclosure of staff reports. Staff reports must be disclosed to parties if new evidence or issues are raised therein which do not come out at hearing or, in other words, are necessary for the person to know the full case being made against him.(*Radulesco v. Cdn. Human Rights Comm.*, [1984] 2 S.C.R. 407, 9 Admin. L.R. 261, 14 D.L.R. (4th) 78, 55 N.R. 384 (S.C.C.); *Madison Dev. Corp. v. Alberta (Rent Regulation App. Bd.)* (1977), 4 Alta. L.R. (2d) 73, 7 A.R. 360 (Alta S.C.)). However, an agency is not required to disclose reports where merely a summary of general or public knowlege, or facts and sources which are properly brought out at the hearing in such a manner that all the parties to that hearing have a full opportunity to test them, or which contain the summary and comments of staff on the evidence and submissions made at the inquiry. (*Trans Quebec & Maritime Pipeline Inc. v. Canada (National Energy Board)*, [1984] 2 F.C. 432, 8 Admin. L.R. 177 (C.A.); *British Columbia (Workmen's Compensation Board) v. Rammell*, [1962] S.C.R. 85, 37 W.W.R. 49, 31 D.L.R. (2d) 94. *Toshiba Corp. v. A.D.T.* (1984), 8 Admin. L.R. 173 (Fed. C.A.)).

dence'' did not constitute legal advice and thus allowable as per *Spring*. How one could do such things in the absence of the file is beyond me.

Before leaving the fairness aspect of *Khan* I feel that it is important to take further note of the fact that in that case the court felt that the agency counsel had not assumed the role of advocate, advancing one position over the other. I have already noted that a number of cases found error in the participation of counsel in the preparation of reasons when that counsel acted as prosecutor in the hearing (*Bernstein*, *Sawyer*, *Dépres*). The participation of a prosecutor in the drafting of the decision relating to the matter he prosecuted easily gives rise to a reasonable apprehension.

The Court of Appeal in *Khan* also demanded that the integrity of the process be maintained. It concluded however this integrity had not been compromised. The Committee had remained firmly in control of the drafting process as:

i) A committee member prepared the first draft of the reasons;

ii) Counsel, with the chairman of the Committee, revised and clarified the first draft but did not write independently of that draft;

iii) The Committee met to consider and revise the draft as amended by counsel and the chairman. Counsel played no role in this review and revision; and

iv) The final product which emerged from the drafting process was signed by each member of the Committee.

Considered as a whole this procedure effectively counteracted any legitimate concerns as to the authorship of the reasons.

The Court of Appeal in *Khan* did not state that the procedure approved of, in that case, was the only appropriate procedure. Whatever the procedures adopted, however, provided that the participation of the responsible official does not breach the fairness of the process and he is otherwise adequately briefed as to the tribunal's conclusion, the evidence upon which it is relying, and the manner in which it has reached that conclusion, there would seem little reason to fear that his participation will be found to breach the integrity of the proceedings.

In this connection, an agency must also take care not to simply rubber stamp its staff's comments on a decision. It should review this draft carefully, making all the changes that its sees fit. It must at all times be clear that the tribunal turned its collective mind to the issues at hand and that it considered them carefully, and that the decision and the reasons therefore were those of the agency.

22.4.1(b) Mandatory Review of Reasons By Agency Counsel

Can an agency go further than *Khan* and establish a *mandatory* system of review of draft decisions by agency counsel and other staff?

Certainly, I would argue that there is nothing wrong in encouraging a board member to voluntarily access a review system made available by an agency. In fact, it is highly desirable to do so. It would be illogical for a court to recognize the benefits which can flow from such a review system and allow agencies to

(*Continued on page 22-10.69*)

create review systems which members can access while, at the same time, hold that the agency cannot encourage the members to do so (provided that that encouragement does not amount to pressure). In *Bovbel v. Canada (Minister of Employment & Immigration)*, [1994] 2 F.C. 563, 18 Admin. L.R. (2d) 169, 113 D.L.R. (4th) 415, 167 N.R. 10 (C.A.), leave to appeal to S.C.C. refused (1994), 23 Admin. L.R. (2d) 328n, 115 D.L.R. (4th) vii (note), the Federal Court of Appeal came to the same conclusion. That case concerned a policy in the Immigration and Refugee Board's *Convention Refugee Determination Division's Members' Handbook* which expressly provided that draft reasons for negative decisions *may be voluntarily* submitted to the board's legal services for review. However, other references dealing with the administrative processing of decisions in the same manual and in the *IRB Case Processing Manual* implied that draft decisions were automatically forwarded for review. When the case was before the Trial Division Justice Rouleau concluded that, while the policy was optional in theory, in practice most if not all draft decisions were submitted for review. This policy, Justice Rouleau gave rise to the perception that draft reasons were to be reviewed as a general rule which gave rise to a reasonable apprehension of a lack of independence. The Court of Appeal disagreed. Pratte J., for the Court, stated that:

> [The trial judge's] first reason was that the Board's Reasons Review Policy, although not mandatory, was formulated so as to give the impression that draft reasons were to be reviewed as a general rule. Assuming the correctness of that finding, we fail to understand how, if the Board's policy was otherwise unobjectionable, the fact that it was generally applied could make it bad.[3.60A]

It would be difficult to disagree with the Court of Appeal on this. Otherwise the mere fact that all, or a majority of board members recognized a review system as a valuable tool and voluntarily followed it would (illogically) result in the practice becoming improper.

But can an agency go beyond encouragement and adopt a *mandatory* review policy? In their article "Advising the Board: The Scope of Counsel's Role in Advising Administrative Tribunals"[3.61] Murray Rankin and Leah Greathead set out an interesting argument in favour of a compulsory policy requiring board members to submit their draft reasons to review by agency counsel. This article is recommended to readers for its exploration of this very important question. The authors suggest (at p. 40) that:

3.60A In reaching this decision the Court relied on its earlier decision in *Weerasinge v. Canada (Minister of Employment & Immigration)* [1994] 1 F.C. 330, 17 Admin. L.R. (2d) 214, 22 Imm. L.R. (2d) 1 (C.A.) in which the Court held that no breach of any tenet of natural justice arises in circumstances where a panel, which may not be legally trained, seeks the advice of its counsel with respect to legal matters in its reasons when considering complex legal issues in serious proceedings affecting the liberty of parties where the parties may also not be legally trained.

3.61 7 C.J.A.L.P. 29.

So long as it is made clear that the purpose of mandatory review of a board's reasons by legal counsel is not to try to persuade board members to change their minds on decisions they have reached, but rather to provide information to board members so that they might produce consistent and well-reasoned justifications for their decisions, it seems that the courts would not object. Board counsel should be permitted to bring to members' attention all law that runs contrary to the view expressed by the board. They should likewise be permitted to inform members of all law that supports the board's position. In cases where the law is contradictory, counsel should provide the board with the law on each side of the issue. Further, they should be permitted to explain the relevant value of the law: for example, the higher the court, the more important value the decision; and the more recent the case, the more weight it should have, and the like. They should be able to present arguments for distinguishing or applying certain cases.

Applying the "institutional constraints" approach suggested in *Consolidated Bathurst* the authors concluded that:

The size and complexity of certain large administrative tribunals, combined with the need for internal coherence and consistency, and the incredible volume of cases facing such board, provide a strong basis for an argument that it is not contrary to natural justice for the board to mandate the review of members' reasons by board counsel. Nevertheless, care must be taken to ensure that in practice as well as on paper, the review policy remains advisory [as to whether the comments should be accepted] and in no way can be seen as exerting pressure.[3.62]

In my opinion, the *usefulness* of such a policy in ensuring that decisions meet the highest standards cannot be doubted. Through it a chair, and the public, can be confident that the agency members are fully aware of the law and other agency and court decisions in the area of the decision being considered. Review by counsel, and other staff, is also invaluable in catching clerical omissions or accidental slips as well in providing suggestions for improvements to logical and legal arguments as set out in *Khan*.[3.63]

However, I believe that there are serious concerns with the adoption of a mandatory review policy by counsel and staff. It would, in my opinion, be an unacceptable interference with the independence of decision-makers.

In my opinion, *Tremblay* rejects the notion of any sort of "compulsory" system being proper. Even if this is a misleading of that decision (and I do not think that it is) I suggest that making any review process mandatory gives rise to the same concerns felt by the Supreme Court in *Tremblay* relating to the formalized record keeping and voting of the consensus table process discussed in that case. The Court had earlier noted in *Consolidated Bathurst* that the informality of the full board meeting employed by the Ontario Labour Relations Board was such that "It cannot be said that this practice is meant to convey to panel members

---

3.62 At pp. 42-43.
3.63 The value of such reviews is discussed further later in this book in c. 35.20.

the message that the opinion of the majority of the Board members present has to be followed.''[3.64] To my mind the very opposite is conveyed by the implementation of something as a mandatory process. The very fact that it is mandatory suggests that its result must be important and perhaps adopted.

(Continued on page 22-10.71)

3.64 *Consolidated Bathurst* at p. 563 D.L.R.

In my opinion, the voluntary nature of the review policies in question played a much stronger role in *Consolidate Bathurst, Tremblay,* and *Khan* than the Mr. Rankin and Ms. Greathead suggest. In *Khan* the Court of Appeal noted that:

> Nothing in this record suggests that counsel's involvement in the writing of the reasons compromised the independence or impartiality of the Committee. Counsel for the Committee *was the servant of the Committee* and was totally independent from the College or Dr. Khan. His involvement in the writing of the reasons was not mandatory, *and was entirely under the control of the Committee.* Counsel's assistance could not have had any coercive effect on the Committee.[3.65] (emphasis added)

I have my doubts that a mandatory review policy would be characterized in the same way by the Court. Forced assistance may not be perceived as assistance. It may be seen as coming perilously close to an approval process whereby the quality of the member's draft is submitted for scrutiny to staff. Obviously, unlike the case in *Khan*, the review would not be "entirely under the control" of the decision-makers. A mandatory policy would, by its nature, determine the extent and nature of the review and impose it upon the individual decision-makers. As I have noted earlier, the thrust of *Consolidated Bathurst, Tremblay* and *Khan* is that the independence of an agency decision-member can be threatened by the adoption of operational systems geared to making it difficult for members to deviate from "accepted" board practices. To this extent, a *mandatory* review process may not stand up to judicial scrutiny.

I do not believe that the nature of the office of the person with whom one is compelled to consult is relevant. To imply that agency legal counsel or other staff may be less influential than board members is to underestimate the expertise of such officers and the esteem in which they are held in their agencies.

It is clear, following *Consolidate Bathurst* and *Tremblay*, that an agency cannot adopt any sort of institutionalized decision-making process which forces a decision-maker to consult with respect to the facts or the policy issues raised by a case on which he must render a decision. This likely extends to questions of law as well given Justice Gonthier's express statement in *Consolidated Bathurst* that policy was akin to law.[3.66] There is little difference to me in *requiring* a decision-maker to consider the views of others with respect to the proper under-standing of policy and their views with respect to the proper understanding of the law.[3.67] Furthermore, I suggest that any policy which directs that a decision-maker is unable to issue his decision until it has been reviewed by staff (be it legal

---

3.65 (1992), 9 O.R. (3d) 641 at p. 674.

3.66 At p. 565 D.L.R.

3.67 It would even extend, I suggest, to reviews geared simply to bringing conflicting decisions of the agency to the attention of the decision-maker. What is the purpose of bringing such cases to the attention of the decision-maker if not to have him consider the conflicting policy or legal decisions reached therein.

counsel or other staff) even where that review is for matters which do not go to the essence of his decision (such as spelling and grammar) also infringes upon the required independence of the decision-maker. This would be so even if the policy provided that some administrative officer or the chair of the agency could, at his discretion, exempt individual decisions from the policy at the request of the decision-maker. It may be wise to have staff reviews but not wise to force them.

In *Valente v. R.*, [1985] 2 S.C.R. 673, 52 O.R. (2d) 779 (headnote only), 49 C.R. (3d) 97, 23 C.C.C. (3d) 193, 24 D.L.R. (4th) 161 (S.C.C.), the Supreme Court recognized that there was more to independence than merely the ability to decide an issue in a particular way. In discussing the independence of the courts from the state, McLachlin J. in *MacKeigan v. Hickman*, [1989] 2 S.C.R. 796, 41 Admin. L.R. 236, 72 C.R. (3d) 129, 50 C.C.C. (3d) 449, 61 D.L.R. (4th) 688 (S.C.C.) noted that control over the essential administrative aspects of the decision was an equally important aspect of that independence. Decision-makers must retain control over "matters directly affecting adjudication — 'assignment of judges, sittings of the courts, and court lists — as well as the related matters of allocation of courtrooms and the direction of the administrative staff engaged in carrying out these functions' ".[3.68] Later, in *Lippé et autres v. Québec (Procureur général)*, [1991] 2 S.C.R. 114, 61 C.C.C. (3d) 127, with written reasons at (1991), 64 C.C.C. (3d) 513, 128 N.R. 1 (S.C.C.) Justice Lamer noted (at page 29 N.R.) that the requirement for independence extended not only to independence from the state per se but from:

> any person or body, which can exert pressure on the judiciary through authority under the state. This expansive definition encompasses, for example, the Canadian Judicial Council or any Bar Society. I would also include any person or body within the judiciary which has been granted some authority over other judges; for example members of the court must enjoy judicial independence *and be able to exercise their judgment free from pressure or influence from the Chief Justice.* (emphasis added)

Clearly, an individual decision-maker has no jurisdiction to determine the hearing logistics of a matter prior to his being seized of it. However, once the decision-maker has embarked on the hearing no one would argue that a Chair or other administrative officer of the agency has any authority to control the progress of that hearing, for example, by restricting the adjournments which a decision-maker might be requested to make. To reduce or deny the ability of a decision-maker to accede to the requests of a party for the immediate issuance of a decision without awaiting some review by some administrative officer would be an equal interference with an essential aspect of decision-making; the issuance of the decision.

3.68 At p. 722 D.L.R.

Aside from legal constraints, there are also a number of practical disadvantages relating to a mandatory review process by staff. A mandatory review policy has the potential of sowing dissention in an agency. This potential is even greater if the suspicion arises that the staff are expected to use these reviews to "warn" the Chair of decisions which might in their opinion be incorrect or controversial. There is, I suggest, a very real different human reaction to being told that one *must*, as opposed to may, take advantage of assistance. The latter has the potential of poisoning the relations between board members and staff. Regardless of actual ability, the board member or panel of members is the person or body entrusted with the ultimate responsibility for making a decision. He must be allowed to judge whether he requires the assistance of staff in that task. A compulsory system of review can give rise to a perception that staff are more capable than agency members to write the decision and reasons. (In fact, what they really have is the advantage of distance from the writing. As readers, rather than writers, they are better able to detect errors.)

Furthermore, one has to question the practical value of a *compulsory* written review system. Rankin and Greathead suggest that the "pressure" resulting from a system of written comments may be less dangerous than the "consensus table" in *Tremblay* as those comments may simply be disregarded by the decision-maker. What value is there in forcing a decision-maker to seek such written comments (thereby delaying the issuance of reasons as well as consuming the valuable time and labour of staff) if the decision-maker is likely to simply discard the comments when received?

It is true that a mandatory review process will at least ensure that the best advice is placed before a decision-maker leaving it "on his head" if he chooses not to look at it. But the same result can be achieved by a voluntary review policy. Any "blame" that may attach to a decision-maker for failing to consider the review of his legal counsel might just as easily be seen as arising where a board member fecklessly decides not to voluntarily avail himself of the best tools open to him in making his decision.

Finally, it is not all decisions, surely, that demand review by counsel. Non-contentious, simple matters may not value much from such reviews, nor may decisions written by experienced and expert board members. To impose a universal review system would undoubtedly impose a heavy burden on the time of agency counsel which have other functions to perform in those agencies which have a large caseload. Yet a system requiring the review of only certain types of decisions is much more vulnerable to attacks of bias than is a universal system. (It could be argued that one is essentially creating a system in which board members wishing to speed up the issuance of their decisions or avoid the bureaucratic requirements of review might be tempted to do so by avoiding dealing with the particular issues or decisions triggering the review, thus giving the appearance that the system is biased towards certain types of decisions. The most extreme example would be a system requiring review and comment where a decision-maker considered deviating from board policy. Such a system would thus make it easier to issue a decision following board policy than one differing from it.)

What advantage does a mandatory review system have over a voluntary one? The greatest advantage I can see is that it will ensure that decision-makers will avail themselves of the benefits of staff review (which I have argued are many). However, I believe one really must question the underlying philosophy here. The adoption of a *mandatory* policy must be predicated on a belief that individual decision-makers will not themselves be anxious to achieve the best decisions or that they are incapable of determining what is needed to reach that goal. In the final analysis one cannot, in the real world, force quality upon one's fellow board members. Such attempts are more likely to lead to rancour and dissention. One has to approach the question from the principle that agency members are responsible and competent individuals who, when presented with the tools and arguments for quality will be anxious to partake of them. One should also assume that decision-makers, having been given the responsibility to make important social and economic decisions impacting on the lives of others are capable of judging the degree to which they require assistance in doing so. It is beyond me how one can ask the public, the courts or Parliament to respect an agency at the same time the agency or its Chair adopts a system which implies that its members must be forced to act professionally and responsibly.

So where does this leave us? At the moment I believe that there is a strong argument that the imposition of mandatory quality controls upon decision-makers will be perceived as an intrusion upon independence. Thus, insofar as a voluntary system of review is capable of accomplishing the same results as a mandatory one with fewer negative implications for the agency I believe that the adoption and encouragement of a voluntary review process is preferable over a mandatory one.

22.4.1(c) Conclusion

The overriding consideration here, as with so many other issues in administrative law, is to avoid applying legal maxims so rigidly that the result is to strangle the efficient functioning of the administrative process. The importance of decisions like *Consolidated Bathurst* and *Khan* is that they recognize that the principles of administrative law cannot be applied so as to ignore the realities of the administrative setting. Thus, so long as the irreducible minimum of the fairness and integrity of the system is maintained tribunals should be given the freedom to tailor their proceedings to their own peculiar needs.

While this liberal approach by the Courts should make it easier for agencies to perform the specialized tasks assigned to them, in some ways it also puts new burdens on them. It appears that, for the moment at any rate (and sadly one cannot say how long it will last) the Courts are restraining the urge to dictate the procedures for agencies. This has the advantage of allowing the agencies to tailor make procedures to meet their needs. However, the corollary of this freedom is the responsibility to do so in a manner which balances effectiveness with fairness. This is a burden which can be difficult. Agencies must, using only the general parameters laid down in cases such as *Consolidated Bathurst* and *Khan*, themselves lay down procedures which in their context are fair both to the parties and the public in whose interest the agency acts. The greater freedom given decision-makers to utilize their staff in after hearing deliberations, for example, means that decision-makers must constantly be on guard not to become overly reliant upon this valuable tool. Independence of judgment must be maintained. The agency must never fall into the trap of valuing the advice of staff over that of parties simply because of the close working relationship of staff, nor should they defer to the professional expertise of staff or look upon themselves as incapable of making valuable decisions without the assistance of staff. No doubt, as in *Tremblay*, agencies will, with the best of intentions, stumble from time to time. However, the liberal approach of the courts is, in my opinion, forcing an increasing degree of professionalism upon agencies as a whole and upon their individual members. This development, in turn, will assist agencies in meeting the challenges of the brave new world following *Consolidated Bathurst*.

22.4.2 RECOMMENDED GUIDELINES

1.   The deciding agency-members themselves must decide the matter and select the reasons for that decision. However, they can be assisted by staff in the formalization of how the decision and reasons are expressed.
2.   The decision to seek the assistance of staff or counsel must be voluntary on the part of the member's charged with the decision-making responsibility. As a matter of courtesy (and practicality) the member charged with drafting a decision should consult with his co-panellists prior to seeking the assistance of staff.
3.   To the extent that the agency's work may involve a large element of public policy it may consult with its counsel and staff in the analyzing and testing of policy proposals provided that no facts or arguments are considered on which the parties have not had an opportunity to make representations.
4.   Opinions or conclusions on the material by the staff do not constitute new facts.
5.   No assistance should be sought from counsel or staff who participated in the hearing process unless that participation was restricted to areas of the neutral mechanics of the process or to the provision of legal advice to the agency at its request as was the case in *Khan*. Staff charged with either a prosecutorial role or with the discovery or presentation of facts during the hearing should not be consulted or play a role in the drafting of the decision or reasons.
6.   At a minimum, in seeking assistance in the drafting of reasons the agency should provide counsel or staff with a written summary or preliminary draft indicating the decision of the agency and the underlying reasons it had in

reaching that decision. It is best, I suggest, that the members provide the
first draft and then consult with staff.

7. It may be best that counsel and staff restrict themselves to commenting
upon the written summary or drafts of the agency members. However,
provided that sufficient detail is set out in the instructions from the agency
it may be acceptable that counsel or staff "flesh" out the expressed thoughts
of the decision-makers. The principle is that the decision and reasons are to
reflect the thought processes of the decision-makers. Thus, a general direction to "write up a decision concluding in such a way" would not be
supportable while a more specific direction indicating the grounds on which
the conclusion was reached and directing staff to locate the exact references
to evidence and argument would likely be acceptable.

8. Counsel or staff's participation in the review of draft reasons may extend
to:
    i)   reviewing the reasons for clerical, spelling or grammatical errors or
         accidental omissions;
    ii) comments regarding the framing of the reasons such as noting internal
         contradictions in the reasons, deleting erroneous references to the
         evidence or adding relevant references to the evidence; and
    iii) advising the agency as to the relevant law, and the existence of judicial
         and agency decisions relevant to the matter.

9. Parties must be given an opportunity to make representations with respect
to any new fact or argument arising in this process.

10. All comments or drafts by counsel or staff must go back for detailed consideration and approval by the deciding agency-members. The agency
should not simply adopt the exact comments of the staff.[3.69] However, it
may be permissible to adopt the wording of staff regarding the recital of
uncontentious matters provided that where decisions have been required,
the wording of those decisions is that of the decision-maker.

11. The final decision should be signed by each of the members endorsing it.

22.5 TIMING

22.5.1 LEGISLATIVE TIME LIMITS

Many statutes contain procedural provisions stating that an agency "may"
or "shall" act in a certain way. The obligation to comply with such provisions
will vary depending on whether Parliament or the Legislature intended the proviso
to be discretionary or imperative. In the case of the former compliance is not
required and is, as suggested by its characterization, in the discretion of the agency.

3.69 See *Adair v. Health Disciplines Board (Ontario)* (1993), 15 O.R. (3d) 705 (Div. Ct.).

Imperative provisions, on the other hand, must be complied with. The consequence of failing to comply, however, will vary depending on whether the imperative direction is mandatory or directory.[4] Failing to comply with a mandatory direction will render any subsequent proceedings void while failing to comply with a directory command will not result in such invalidation (although the person to whom the command was directed will not be relieved from the duty of complying with it — i.e. he may be subject to an order of mandamus or to internal discipline[4.1]).

The determination of whether an imperative command is mandatory or directory, however, turns on the intent of the statute.[4.2] The courts will determine if Parliament in drafting the legislation intended that failure to comply with an imperative procedural direction will render void an action which was predicated on that procedure. Thus, in determining whether an imperative provision is likely to be mandatory or directory one looks to the particular procedural function in question, the person to whom it is directed, the purpose the procedure is to serve and the overall object of the statute.

Some statutes provide that the agency "shall" issue its decision or reasons within a specified period of time. Section 11 of the federal Interpretation Act, as do similar sections in the provincial Acts, provides that the word "shall" indicates that the provision is imperative (absent some indication to the contrary in the statute). The various Interpretation Acts, however, do not provide much guidance as to whether as "shall do" provision is mandatory-imperative or directory-imperative.

Maxwell on the Interpretation of Statutes provides the following guidance on this question:

> It is impossible to lay down any general rule for determining whether a provision is imperative [mandatory] or directory. "No universal rule," said Lord Campbell L.C., "can be laid down for the construction of statutes, as to whether mandatory enactments shall be considered directory only or obligatory with an implied nullification for disobedience. It is the duty of Courts of Justice to try to get at the real intention of the Legislature by carefully attending to the whole scope of the statute to be construed." [*Liverpool Borough Bank v. Turner* (1860) 2 De G.F. & J. 502, at pp. 507, 508.] And Lord Penzance said: "I believe, as far as any rule is concerned, you cannot safely go further than that in each case you must look to the subject-matter; consider the importance of the provision that has been disregarded, and the relation of that provision to the general object intended to be secured by the Act; and upon a review of the case in that aspect decide whether the matter is what is called imperative [mandatory] or only directory." [*Howard v. Bodington* (1877) 2 P.D. 203, at p. 211.][4.3]

---

4   *Teskey v. Law Society (British Columbia)* (1990), 45 Admin. L.R. 132 (B.C. S.C.), additional reasons at (1990), 49 B.C.L.R. (2d) 223, 74 D.L.R. (4th) 146 (S.C.).

4.1 *Montreal Street Railway v. Normandin* (1917), 33 D.L.R. 195 (P.C.) at p. 198.

4.2 *Montreal Street Railway v. Normandin* (1917), 33 D.L.R. 195 (P.C.).

4.3 *Maxwell on the Interpretation of Statutes* 12th edition by P. St. J. Langan, at pp. 314-315. See

The operation of this approach can be seen in the analysis of the court in *Gage v. Ontario* (1992), 90 D.L.R. (4th) 537, (Div. Ct.) in attempting to determine whether the time limits imposed by statute for the giving of notice of an application were mandatory or directory:

> Applying the test in cases such as *Re Carfrae Estates Ltd. and Stavert*, 13 O.R. (2d) 537 (Div. Ct.), and *Howard v. Bodington* (1877), 2 P.D. 203, we are inclined to the view that the word "shall" in s. 19(4) is mandatory. The extremely time-sensitive nature of this particular provision in the overall structure of the Act, its critical nature as the trigger for a hearing with potentially drastic consequences for the reputation and career of the officer, its crucial importance as the officer's first notice of his potential jeopardy and first notice of the exact charge he is required to meet, its central relevance as the first opportunity to prepare to meet the actual case set up against him, its vital significance to the officer's counsel as the first legal crystallization of all the previous steps and the legal root of the entire case against the officer, all suggest that the word "shall" is mandatory and that it must, as suggested by the *Interpretation Act*, R.S.O. 1980, c. 219, s. 30(34) be construed as imperative.

Statutorily imposed time limits for the performance of public duties generally are not strictly applied such that the failure to meet those time limits will not result in the invalidation of the action in question. This logic seems sound insofar as the body entrusted with the performance of the duty is not usually the intended beneficiary of that performance. As noted by the Privy Council in *Montreal Street Railway v. Normandin* (1917), 33 D.L.R. 195 (P.C.) at page 198:

> When the provisions of a statute relate to the performance of a public duty and the case is such that to hold null and void acts done in neglect of this duty would work serious general inconvenience or injustice to persons who have no control over those entrusted with the duty, and at the same time would not promote the main object of the legislature, it has been the practice to hold such provisions to be directory only. . . .[4.4]

Following *Normandin* the courts have come to look to three indicia in determining whether a statutory duty falls within the "public duty" umbrella:

> 1. Will the strict application of the provision result in the failure to perform a public duty which would seriously inconvenience those who had no control over those entrusted with the performance of the duty and thus not promote the main objective of the enactment?
> 2. Has the statute failed to impose any penalty or sanction for non-compliance?

---

also P.-A. Côté, *The Interpretation of Legislation in Canada 2d ed.* (Yvon Blais, Cowansville 1991) at pp. 196-207.

4.4 *Montreal Street Railway v. Normandin* (1917), 33 D.L.R. 195 (P.C.) at p. 198.

3. Will little or no prejudice be caused to any party in the event that the duty is not performed as required?[4.5]

In the event that all three of these questions can be answered affirmatively, the procedural direction will be found to be directory only.

In 1982, in *Bridgeland-Riverside Community Assn. v. Council of Calgary (City)*[4.5A] the Alberta Court of Appeal took a swing at the Gordian knot in laying down the following simplified approach to mandatory/directory provisions:

> I would put aside the debate over void or voidable, irregularity or nullity, mandatory or directory, preliminary or collateral. These are only ways to express the question: Shall or shall not a procedural defect (whether mandated by statute or common law) vitiate a proceeding? In my view, absent an express statutory statement of effect, no defect should vitiate a proceeding unless, as a result of it, some real possibility of prejudice to the attacking party is shown, or unless the procedure was so dramatically devoid of the appearance of fairness that the administration of justice is brought into disrepute.[4.5B]

Although *Bridgeland-Riverside Community Association* was not cited in the Supreme Court of Canada's decision in *British Columbia (Attorney-General) v. Canada (Attorney General)*[4.5C] the Court appears to have expressed a very similar view. It stated that the *Normindin* approach had come to be capable of being expressed in a single sentence "Would it be seriously inconvenient to regard the performance of some statutory direction as an imperative?"[4.5D]

4.5   See *Sarco Canada Ltd. v. Anti-Dumping Tribunal* (1978), [1979] 1 F.C. 247, 22 N.R. 225 (C.A.), *Sandoz Ltd. v. Canada (Commissioner of Patents)* (1991), 42 F.T.R. 30 (T.D.), *Robertson v. Edmonton (City)* 44 Admin L.R. 27, 72 Alta. L.R. (2d) 352, [1990] 4 W.W.R. 232 (Q.B.), *Teskey v. Law Society (British Columbia)* (1990), 45 Admin L.R. 132, 71 D.L.R. (4th) 531 (B.C. S.C.), additional reasons at (1990), 49 B.C.L.R. (2d) 223, 74 D.L.R. (4th) 146 (S.C.); *Melville v. Canada (Attorney General)* (1981), [1982] 2 F.C. 3, 129 D.L.R. (3d) 488 (T.D.), reversed [1983] 2 F.C. 123, 141 D.L.R. (3d) 191 (C.A.); and *St. John's School Tax Authority v. Luby* (1993), 111 Nfld. & P.E.I.R. 23, 348 A.P.R. 23 (Nfld. T.D.).

4.5A (1982), 19 Alta. L.R. (2d) 361 (C.A.).

4.5B This approach has not been disavowed by any court, to my knowledge, and has been followed in a number of cases such as *Jackson v. Vancouver Reg. Transit Comm.* (1986), 4 B.C.L.R. (2d) 321 (B.C.S.C.) (failure to comply with statutory direction to consult prior to decision), *Geusebroek v. Alberta (Labour Relations Board)* (1983), 48 A.R. 144 (Q.B.) (failure to give proper notice); and *Shah v. Christiansen* (1992), 96 D.L.R. (4th) 644 (Alta. C.A.) (failure to renew writ within specified time). In *Sparvier v. Cowessess Indian Band No. 73*, [1993] 3 F.C. 142, 13 Admin. L.R. (2d) 266, 63 F.T.R. 242 (T.D.) additional reasons at [1993] 3 F.C. 175, 13 Admin. L.R. (2d) 293, 66 F.T.R. 266 (T.D.) failure to comply with a statutory timing provision respecting the election of an Indian Appeal Tribunal did not invalidate a proceeding as the timing requirement was not felt to be of sufficient importance that noncompliance with it should result in the actions of the Tribunal being considered void.

4.5C [1994] 2 S.C.R. 41, 21 Admin. L.R. (2d) 1, 6 W.W.R. 1, 91 B.C.L.R. (2d) 1, 166 N.R. 81, 44 B.C.A.C. 1, 71 W.A.C. 1, 114 D.L.R (4th) 193.

4.5D Although constitutional directions are to be considered an exception to this liberal approach

Statutory directions that an agency "shall" issue decisions or orders within a set period of time have generally been characterized as duties imposed upon the agency. On the basis of the *Normandin* reasoning they have been found to be directory only and a decision or set of reason issued outside of the specified time will not be invalid.[4.6] The reasoning behind this principle is obvious. Invalidating a decision sought by the parties by reason of an agency (over whom the parties have no control) failing to issue it on time will generally require the re-hearing of the entire matter, something which hardly benefits either the parties or the public. This was noted by the Newfoundland Court of Appeal in *Stephenville Minor Hockey Assn. v. N.A.P.E.*[4.7] when it considered the failure of an arbitrator to render his decision either 30 days (as specified by the collective agreement) or 35 days (as specified by statute. The Court found that the issuance of the decision approximately four months late did not affect its validity. Among other judicial precedents, the Court quoted the words of the Supreme Court of Canada in *Air Care Ltd. v. U.S.W.A., Local 7010*, [1976] 1 S.C.R. 2 at 8,49 D.L.R. (3d) 467 that "The right of a party should not be lost or in any way prejudiced as the result of dilatory conduct on the part of a Board over which it has little or no control." In upholding the arbitrator's decision the Court felt that to "nullify the arbitration proceedings because of the dilatory conduct on the part of a Board would not only be manifestly unjust to the parties affected, who had no control over the events, but would also be inconsistent with the purpose and intent of the Act" which was to maintain a harmonious industrial relationship between the parties and provide the means for a final resolution of disputes.

Sometimes, however, the wording of the relevant statute will indicate that a specific time limit is intended to be mandatory. See for example, *Newfoundland (Treasury Board) v. N.A.P.E.*[4.8] That case was triggered was the setting aside and remitting back of an arbitration award. The relevant statute required the arbitration

---

(*Ref re. Language Rights Under s. 23 Manitoba Act, 1870 and s. 133 of Constitution Act, 1867*, [1985], 2 S.C.R. 347, [1986] 1 W.W.R. 289, 19 D.L.R (4th) 1.

4.6 In *Sandoz Ltd. v. Canada (Commissioner of Patents)* (1991), 42 F.T.R. 30, the Federal Court Trial Division held that the statutory direction that the Commissioner of Patents dispose of a compulsory licence application not later than eighteen months after the service of the application was directory only. Consequently, the Commissioner did not lose jurisdiction by failing to comply with this time requirement. See also *Sarco Canada Ltd. v. Anti-Dumping Tribunal* (1978), [1979] 1 F.C. 247, 22 N.R. 225 (C.A.); *Teskey v. Law Society of British Columbia* (1990), 45 Admin. L.R. 132, 71 D.L.R. (4th) 531 (B.C. S.C.), additional reasons at (1990), 49 B.C.L.R. (2d) 223, 74 D.L.R. (4th) 146 (S.C.); *Morton v. Versatile Cornat Corp.* (1981), 17 Man. R. (2d) 139, 126 D.L.R. (3d) 734 (C.A.); *Fleischhacker v. Saskatchewan (Minister of Environment)* (1985), 40 Sask. R. 283 (Q.B.); *McCain Foods Ltd. v. Canada (National Transportation Agency)* (1992), 8 Admin. L.R. (2d) 184, [1993] 1 F.C. 583 (C.A.), leave to appeal to S.C.C. refused (1994), Admin. L.R. (2d) 193 (note), 174 N.R. 223 (note) (S.C.C.); *Metropolitan Toronto Board of Police Commissioners and Metropolitan Toronto Police Association*, [1973] 3 O.R. 563, 37 D.L.R. (3d) 487 (H.C.); and *Air Care Ltd. v. U.S.W.A.*, [1976] 1 S.C.R. 2, 49 D.L.R. (3d) 467.

4.7 (1993), 12 Admin. L.R. (2d) 281, 106 Nfld. & P.E.I.R. 257, 334 A.P.R. 257, 104 D.L.R. (4th) 239 (Nfld. C.A.).

4.8 (1994), 116 Nfld. & P.E.I.R. 206, 363 A.P.R. 206 (Nfld. T.D.).

board to issue an order within 90-days following its remission to the board by a court. The board, however, did not convene to consider the matter for two years following the remission and, therefore, was unable to comply with the 90-day time limit. The board held that the time limit did not apply. On judicial review, the reviewing court held that the 90-day time limit did apply and the board's decision was set aside. The court noted that while the legislation expressly provided for the extension of the time limits in making awards in other situations it was silent as to any such ability with respect to matters remitted to the board.

22.5.2 WHEN TO WRITE

A decision should be written as soon as possible after the hearing is completed for at least two reasons.

The parties and the public are entitled to be informed of the result of the hearing as soon as possible after the close of the hearing. Rights, investments and public policy may be affected by the decision. Regulatory or tribunal delay is explainable, but not well regarded.

The sooner a decision is put down on paper after the evidence and argument have been completed, the faster and easier it is to write. Even if the tribunal has a daily or other transcript, and particularly if it does not, the authors will save time if they start writing sooner rather than later; the memory fades. As the memory fades, the time taken to review the evidence increases. Not only is the transcript important, but so are the notes of the tribunal members. Transcripts do not remind the members of the tone, weaknesses and strengths of the evidence as clearly as the notes of the tribunal members. All members of all tribunals should take extensive notes as the evidence and argument are presented.

22.6 MECHANICS

In drafting a decision, it is useful to have a dictionary, a thesaurus and a book on common grammatical usage readily at hand. Some boards find it useful in drafting a decision to take two initial steps.

Write one short paragraph to describe the major issues underlying the decision and the way in which the board has disposed of those issues. To do so focuses the mind and the central thrust of the decision. This single paragraph will likely be written and rewritten five or ten times over the course of writing the decision.

An early step to be taken after the evidence and argument are complete is for the panel to sit together and brainstrom. The purpose of the brainstorm is to compose the question list. This may take a few minutes, a few hours or a few days. Just keep writing down questions on a chalkboard. Don't try to editorialize the writing; the art is to keep jotting down key thoughts. This is followed by the panel formalizing the questions. Properly phrase the questions so that they are unambiguous and ask what you really want answered. Having made up the list of questions, the questions should be shuffled so that they are placed in a logical sequence. Having a list of questions presented in a logical sequence, the panel can now brainstorm ideas that:

(1)   answer;

(2)   flesh out resolution(s) to each question; and

(3)   allocate reasons for each answer.

The next step is to create chapter headings into which the questions and answers can most easily be grouped. Having skeletonized the first chapter, proceed to skeletonize the second chapter. Once each chapter has been skeletonized, each chapter can quite easily be fleshed out. End each chapter with your findings. Create a summary at the commencement or end of the decision containing all of the findings.

A chapter list should correspond generally with the issues list that was laid down by the board in one of its early procedural orders and as also laid down in the board's order to counsel in presenting argument. A sound structure is the backbone of a well presented decision. The dullest, least read and most insignificant decisions are those that start at the Garden of Eden and grow moss with every page.

Once the question and answer procedure has taken place, a first draft of the decision can be produced quickly and with some confidence that the whole panel will concur.

The decision envisaged above is a reserved decision, dealing with all of the issues in the case before the board. There are instances, however, where a board may give an oral decision covering all of the issues or only part of the issues before the board. Experience suggests that, except in simple cases or procedural matters, it is better practice to reserve a decision and give written reasons that can be read into the record or subsequently presented in writing.

Many boards have the power to review or rehear a decision even after rendering it. Nevertheless, the parties and the public deserve to have in the first instance the best written decision possible. Oral decisions, if resorted to, should state that upon reading the transcript the board may decide to supplement the oral decision. This, then, raises the caveat that a board should be careful that the oral decision and the supplementary written decision are not in conflict. If they are in conflict, the better opinion is that the oral decision having been first given will prevail, if challenged. It may be convenient on occasion to issue separate written decisions on separate issues.

Just as a decision should be written as soon as possible after the evidence is in and argument is completed, the decision should be released as soon as possible after it is written. Decisions should be circulated to all parties. In addition, the circulation should include libraries, the responsible ministry, a limited number of like-positioned boards, the media and other interested parties. As I explain elsewhere, I always offer to brief the Ministry to which the OEB reports on all but the simplest cases.

Some boards hold a press conference to answer media or other questions at the time a decision is released. If these conferences are carefully orchestrated, they can be of invaluable assistance to the board in getting its message across. Sometimes a press release simply stating the issues and the disposition can keep the publication of a decision in perspective. Often it is essential to do this. Many boards are timid about their image, relying entirely on the decision to express the board intent. Experience advises that often the plainest words of a decision are not understood and a conference may be useful.

It is often wise to send a copy of a decision with an explanatory note to various journals and reporting services for better dissemination and understanding by the public. Decisions are written to be read and understood. It is useful, therefore, to:

(1)   Stop and ask yourself, "Who is our audience?"

(2)   Try to think the way our reader will think rather than to write as a writer.

(3)   Try to persuade and win over your reader to your point of view. In doing so, induce him to proceed with his reading rather than frustrating him with your obfuscations.

There is no requirement that in writing a set of reasons a decision-maker must always start afresh with a perfectly blank paper. It is acceptable for checklists or precedents, or boiler plates to be used as memory aids to ensure that the decision-maker covers all of the issues, or sources of quotes or approaches.[4.9] Some types of applications particularly lend themselves very easily to a standard form of reason. These are applications in which the same issues arise on a regular basis. A common approach is the creation of a "boiler plate" decision which sets out each of the standard issues to be addressed while leaving blanks for the decision-making to set out and explain his decision on each issue. Another practical approach, made even easier with the expanding use of computers, is the reference and quotation of earlier decisions. For example, to explain in his reasons a point which he has explained earlier in a different set of reasons, or which has been addressed by another decision-maker in his reasons, the decision-maker is not required to express himself afresh on that point. Provided that he has considered the matter and has not changed his view he can merely cite the other decision, or cite the other decision and lift the appropriate quotation from it. I suggest that

---

4.9 In *Komanov v. Canada (Minister of Employment & Immigration) (1992), 7 Admin. L.R. 135, 17 Imm. L.R. (2d) 15, 143 N.R. 233 (Fed. C.A.)* the Federal Court of Appeal rejected the contention that the use of a standardized "pattern" decision rejecting refugee status to claimants from Bulgaria gave rise to a reasonable appearance of bias. In the view of the Court, the document went only to form, not to substance. It was clear that the form was only to be used by members who have heard a particular case, and have made up their minds to reject the claim.

when one is lifting text verbatim from another decision that one makes this clear in one's reasons, noting that your views have remain unchanged after hearing the argument in the case before you, or words to that effect. This avoids the possibility of giving the appearance that one has not considered the matter afresh but are merely repeating earlier decisions.

22.7 CONSIDERING YOUR AUDIENCE

When it comes time to write one's reasons, one should not be concerned that one's writing emulates that of the great jurists of legal writing. The purpose of your reasons is to explain your decision in terms that your audience will understand. Thus, you need not be overly concerned if you are expressing yourself in perfect legal terminology. It is, again, the substance, not the form, which is important. The courts have long taken the position that administrative agencies are lay bodies which are not expected to use exact legal language and that a reasonable and liberal interpretation of reasons should be adopted.[4.10]

Your audience may be far broader than the audience for a court decision. Your decision should, therefore, be broadly based. You should not assume that your audience is sophisticated or well informed. It does not take many well chosen words to bridge the gap between ignorance and knowledge. Nor does it take beautiful language to transform reader indifference into reader concern.

Tribunals have a duty to communicate. No matter how sophisticated or experienced your audience may be no reader should have to reread to understand what you are saying. Rather, you should rewrite. Any statement not clearly understandable with one pass through or about which there could be any debate should be rewritten. Rewrite ten times, if necessary, until what you have written is unequivocable. Tribunals do not need their own language.

Although there are those who believe that the audience of tribunal decisions is limited in number, one should not forget that most tribunal decisions are read by a very broad cross-section of our population. Consequently, decisions should be written so that they can be understood by every legitimate audience.

Above all, remember that your decision becomes a public document with your name on it. Those public documents shape practice, procedure, policy and law.

The following compose your potential audience:

(1)   *The parties to the hearing.* One ought to realize that each decision will be

---

4.10 See, for example, *Kalina v. Directors of Chiropractic (Ontario)* (1981), 35 O.R. (2d) 626 (Div. Ct.), leave to appeal to C.A. refused (1982), 35 O.R. (2d) 626 (C.A.), *Mackey v. Chiropractors' Assn. of Saskatchewan* (1990), 47 Admin. L.R. 36, 88 Sask. R. 274, 24 A.C.W.S. (3d) 1019 (Q.B.), *Huerto v. College of Physicians & Surgeons (Saskatchewan)* (1994), 26 Admin. L.R. (2d) 169, 117 D.L.R. (4th) 129, 124 Sask. R. 274, [1994] 9 W.W.R. 457, (Q.B.), notice of appeal filed on Sept. 2, 1994, court file CA 1957.

reviewed with varying intensity by different readers. However, the decision should be very clear to the parties, whether an applicant, respondent or intervenor.

(2) *The media.* The media is particularly interested in regulatory and policy-making decisions. Because of the large volume of material which must be reviewed on a day-by-day basis by the media, a tribunal owes it to itself to make its decisions brief, clear and to the point. Where the decision cannot be brief, it should be summarized at its end or beginning and perhaps accompanied by a media release. It should be remembered that the very timing of the release of a decision will affect the quality of the media treatment of the decision.

(3) *The legislature or Parliament.* Many decisions do and should comment upon existing or proposed legislation. Therefore, the tribunal must always count the legislative members among its audience.

In addition, members of the legislative body may be affected in different ways by the decision. One should not assume otherwise. In fact, one should assume legislative involvement. Therefore, write with the legislature members in mind. If you recommend for or against legislation, clearly outline what and why.

(4) *The involved ministry.* Virtually every tribunal reports to a ministry. A few tribunals report directly to a legislature or Parliament. The body to whom the tribunal reports should be in the minds of the tribunal as being among the audience. The ministry should clearly understand what the decision is intended to achieve. As well, it should be briefed ahead of time.

(5) *The industry involved.* Many federal and provincial tribunals have a significant role in the regulation and management of a substantial number of industries in Canada. The role of the tribunal is one of constant presence and influence. That being so, it is of cardinal importance that every decision be written with the involved industry clearly in mind. Individual corporations may invest or may not invest hundreds of millions of dollars, in the face of the known regulatory climate. A tribunal must be clear and precise in its language.

(6) *Trade journals.* There are trade journals in many major areas of commerce and society which report each administrative decision of importance in Canada. These trade journals represent one of the chief ways in which tribunals can communicate with the industry and others. Every decision can and should be written with one eye cast upon the trade journal editor.

The trade journal may require a different dept of detail than some other members of the audience. Trade journal editors have more time to read, compare and digest than the news media. That difference in time should be borne in mind.

(7) *Teaching institutions and libraries.* Both these institutions collect and distribute tribunal decisions. University courses are increasingly taught in the field of administrative law. In that its decision will be on view for a wide slice of the population to hold up to critical analysis, from a broad perspective, it behooves every tribunal to write and think clearly. This means writing four or five drafts, all handwritten or composed on a computer terminal.

(8) *Other tribunals.* It is very important that every tribunal realize that other tribunals research and review the outpourings of like tribunals in Canada. This is particularly important to remember for a regulatory or administrative tribunal involved in the more dynamic aspects of the economy and society. It used to be good enough for a tribunal member to know how to get to the office and back. It is vital now to know not only how the courts deal with administrative substance and procedure but, as well, how other tribunals deal with the many changing and emerging trends.

 The regulation of a distribution industry in any one province is part of a national regime. Every tribunal must be up-to-date on a daily basis as to what is going on in the industry. Therefore, every tribunal owes it to every other tribunal to write clearly and well.

 In addition, it is the duty of every tribunal, through its decisions, to add to its own stature and reputation as well as to that of administrative tribunals as a whole.

(9) *The courts.* The courts are or may be a vital member of the audience. Every tribunal should write every decision with the courts in mind because decisions of tribunals may be reviewed by the courts. The decisions of a tribunal may be challenged in the courts in relation to the tribunal's exercise of its jurisdiction or its understanding and application of the facts. One should remember several facts in relation to the courts:

(a) Administrative law is a relatively new field of law in Canada only recognized as such since the sixties. Being recent, it is not yet well known to the courts.

(b) Very few judges or commentators have ever been members of administrative tribunals and, therefore, their concepts are likely court oriented.

(c) Administrative tribunals cannot and should not be conducted as if they were courts. We are quickly reaching the day in Canada where the role and practice of such tribunals are clearly distinguishable from that of courts.

 These facts require that a board clearly set out in its decision a full discussion of its jurisdiction, where it is in issue, and the facts upon which it bases its decision. The courts should not have to guess the basis upon which a board has acted. The general case law makes it clear that the courts will likely uphold the decision of a tribunal if the tribunal will only give the court a fair chance to do so.

The more I consider court decisions which review tribunal decisions, the more I realize how important it is to outline the jurisdiction, the procedure and the facts and reasons which support the findings of the tribunal. Not only does a court need to know the basis of the tribunal's decision in order to support the decision, but the parties to it are entitled to know as well.

(10) *Other professions.* High on the list of the audience is the legal, accounting, engineering and financial community. Decisions affecting practice and procedure of tribunals are of importance to anyone appearing before a particular tribunal. Decisions dealing with forecasting, accounting procedure, rates of return, cost allocation, rate design, environmental impact, design and safety of equipment, economic planning, etc. affect a number of professions and disciplines other than the direct parties involved. Therefore, decisions must be of the highest quality.

(11) *The cabinet.* The Governor or Lieutenant Governor in Council often has authority to reject, amend or substitute his/her own decision. If a cabinet is given a reasonable chance to support a tribunal decision, it will likely do so. But no cabinet will gladly sustain a poorly presented and written decision.

(12) *The general public.* The public in general is affected by most administrative agency decisions. They constitute, with the others named above, the public interest. The basic duty in matters before most courts is to decide upon the rights and wrongs between parties. The basic duty, in most administrative hearings, is not to determine a winner or loser, but, rather, to select a course that serves the "public interest". All represented parties may end up being "losers" in a court sense.

Thus, a large segment of the audience is the general public, which must be addressed and which must be a prime consideration in the decision of the tribunal.

22.8 SUGGESTED WRITING TIPS

Now that the audience has been identified, here are some suggestions for the actual writing process:

(1) Do not try to write memorable literature. It is a high enough reward to produce a well written and straight-forward structured decision. Leave the Pulitzer Prize for literature to those who have more time and are better paid.

(2) Use plain English. The plainer the better. The best words are the shortest and the most common. Avoid confusing words.

(3) The fact that substance should come before literary style is not to say that literary style is of no importance. Style is one's own fingerprint.

(4) Good writing becomes at one time, both the substance and the vehicle by which it is conveyed.

(5) Every reader should be able to move effortlessly from one paragraph to the next. The message of the decision can be destroyed by bad structure, too many footnotes, case references, Latin phrases, etc.

(6) The easier a decision is to read, the easier it is to accept its conclusion. Some writers believe that the conclusion is the most important part of the decision. On the contrary, the opening is the most important part because if you lose the reader here, he won't be around at the end.

(7) Decisions should be as short as possible, but long enough to be self-contained. Studies conducted in the U.S.A. indicate that legal writing can easily be reduced by 30 per cent.

(8) Rules of grammar and good writing are in a state of constant change. The rules are not carved in stone. Break them whenever it enhances your presentation.

(9) Once you state what the decision is all about, give enough background to enable the reader to understand from where the board is coming.

(10) There is no requirement to give reasons for a decision unless a statute requires it. However, as I explain elsewhere, reasons, in my opinion, should always be given. The Alberta Public Utilities Act, for example, requires that the facts upon which a decision is based be stated. A board may be forced to give reasons where it fails to do so in the event that the statute requires that reasons be given.

(11) It takes a lot of time to write a well-designed decision. It takes more time to write a short decision. Don't underestimate the time involved.

(12) Draft, draft and re-draft — and do it by hand. Dictaphones do not enable you to keep eye contact or close management of your writing.

(13) Undoing bad writing habits is far more time consuming than creating new ones.

(14) The effective implementation of your decision depends more upon its straight-line reasoning and less upon its adornments.

(15) The most complicated subject can be dealt with in a simple form. Sequence and structure dictates whether your form will be complicated and hard to follow or simple and a pleasure to read.

(16) You have everything to gain and nothing to lose by clarity.

Lord MacMillan, whose legal decisions and writings elevate the art of communication, wrote some years ago:

> A judgment may be defined as a reasoned pronouncement by a judge on a disputed legal question which has been argued before him. It is a literary composition, but a composition subject to certain conventions. It possesses its own characteristics and its own standards of merit. The art of composing judgments is not taught; it is acquired by practice and by study of the models provided in the innumerable volumes of the law reports in which are recorded the achievements of past masters of the art.[5]

(17) If you are quoting the evidence or summarizing it, do so correctly. A court upon review can correct your error of law but it is hard to have confidence in a board that misstates the evidence. If the board prefers one version of the facts to another, it should say why.

(18) Avoid criticisms of other boards, counsel or parties unless essential to a conclusion. Even then, be to the point, and as thoughtful as possible. Unsupported criticism of the courts, other boards, governments and persons can reduce the level of public confidence in the administration of justice and in government administration generally.

Don't reject an argument of a counsel. Find a way, instead, to prefer an argument of another. It is best to avoid commenting upon the honest and probity of any witness unless the witness' evidence is central to any issue.

(19) Reduce the use of modifiers to a minimum. Avoid colloquialisms but, if unavoidable, place them in quotation marks. Avoid Latin phrases but, where unavoidable and well understood, you may wish to underline them.

(20) If an issue of jurisdiction has arisen, deal with it at the beginning of the decision. Some boards appear to be hesitant to raise matters of their own jurisdiction as if to do so implies that they lack confidence. Stride into the decision and deal in full with the jurisdictional issue. In so doing, the board may face a court review or appeal; but, if a challenge is made, the court will be assisted by the board's full explanation. Courts are not as familiar with a board's public duty concern as are the boards themselves. A board decision is the selling document. It should be self-contained and persuasive. How will a court know the basis of a board's jurisdiction if the board fails to outline it? Less may not be better.

(21) Use short sentences and short paragraphs. Employ one main thought to a paragraph. Let every sentence in that paragraph bear directly upon the point of the paragraph. Some boards number paragraphs in a decision. This is a matter of preference and convenience for reference. By using numbers, one

---

5 MacMillan, L., "The Writing of Judgments", (1948), 26 Can. Bar Rev. 491 at p. 491.

is sometimes helped in the realization that it is time to start a new paragraph. A paragraph is a unit of thought. A paragraph is not a basket of ideas.

After one has written a paragraph, one should review it and treat it like a classified ad for which there is a cost for each word. Cut out everything you do not need and make sure each unit of thought is stated as clearly as possible. Rewriting a paragraph five times is not out of the ordinary.

(22) Watch to see that a plural verb is used with a plural noun. Try to end a sentence correctly. Punctuate for your own presentation, not for Emily Post. Never use a comma where you can use a period. Write for eye appeal and mental stimulation. Do not forget that presentation is at least half of the taste of a good meal. The rules and usage of grammar as evolving. Language is alive. Don't be a slave to tradition.

(23) Do not repeat. Remember, anytime you feel inclined to use the words "in other words" you know you have committed an error already and are about to commit another.

(24) Use strong vigourous verbs, not passive, weak-wristed verbs. One can cut more meat with short, sharp chops.

(25) Avoid committing future panels under differing circumstances.

(26) Spell words as they are spelled in the governing statute.

(27) The use of footnotes is arguable. Some authors love them. Some hat them. Some footnotes are patently used to give the illusion of sound support where the basic premise is weak. Develop a non-obtrusive way of using footnotes and case references. The fewer, the better.

Some authors insist that citations be given in a certain way. Citations should, in my view, show one source and not a string of hieroglyphics which destroy the eye appeal of what is written.

Lord Dunedin, who has been described as one of the greatest judges of his generation, stated to the American Bar Association in Chicago on August 21, 1930:

> I confess I am not one of those who attach an enormous value to the mere question of precedents. I think reported cases are only valuable when, in what is said by a judge, they give you in a crystallized form some of those great principles on which law depends.[6]

(28) Keep transcript quotes to a minimum. Use page references and paraphrase rather than quote long transcript passages.

(29) Once you refer to a party by a name or an acronym keep to that reference. It is much easier to follow.

---

6 Supra, note 5, at 497.

(30) The spacing on the page is of foremost importance. Don't try to save paper with single spacing and lose your audience.

(31) Use frequent headings of a different ink intensity and type size.

(32) All decisions should be self-contained. If you must refer to a source, include it in an appendix. Nothing is more infuriating than to be told to look to other reports or decisions before you can follow this one.

(33) Underlining is distracting and is often unnecessary.

(34) If you insist on using a dictaphone, do it only after you have handwritten the chapter skeletons. People who can economize with words and control continuity through a dictaphone are fewer than they think.

(35) Draft, draft and re-draft. Whittle away a bit at a time. Rewrite, don't cosmeticize.

(36) Don't be put off by a lot of doctrine about referring only to dead authors. In the new field of administrative law, the last written material may be the most valuable as being the most up-to-date.

22.9 HOW DETAILED MUST DECISIONS AND REASONS BE

Any decision issued by an agency must be clear as to exactly what the agency has decided. If anyone is required to act on the basis of that decision, it must be sufficiently clear and unambiguous that the person can know exactly what it is he is to do. An ambiguous decision likely cannot be enforced.[7]

A decision document should indicate the agency from which it issues, the names of the particular decision-makers if the decision was made by a panel or a single member, identify the proceedings, say exactly what the decision made was, clearly set out any terms or conditions (if any), be dated and signed by either the decision-makers or an individual authorized by the decision-makers to sign on their behalf. When a great deal of information is required to be set out in the decision form (for example when the rents are being set for each unit in a large complex) this information can be set out in an appendix and attached to the decision form. In those cases the appendix should be incorporated into the decision form by stating something like "and the rents are hereby ordered to be as set out in the attached Appendix A to this order.

As to reasons, the reader may refer to the comments of the Nova Scotia Supreme Court in *Thomas v. Dartmouth (City) (sub nom. Thomas v. Social*

---

7 *Vidéotron Ltée v. Industries Microlec Produits électroniques Inc.*, [1992] 2 S.C.R. 1065, 76 C.C.C. (3d) 289, 45 C.P.R. (3d) 1, 50 Q.A.C. 161, 96 D.L.R. (4th) 377, *Skybound Development Ltd. v. Hughes Properties Ltd.* 24 B.C.L.R. (2d) 1, [1988] 5 W.W.R. 355 (C.A.).

Assistance Appeal Board (Nova Scotia)).[8] In that case reasons were necessitated by the relevant regulations.

> [T]he purpose of the regulations is to enable a person who has applied for such redress and social assistance, to be able to understand the outcome without having to make further inquiries through lawyers or otherwise, as to how an Appeal Board came to a particular decision. This is not to suggest that the people who comprise the Appeal Board (and who do not happen to be legally trained) are obliged to go to great lengths or considerable detail to explain their reasons. But it does mean they are duty bound to express their reasons in such a way that they are unambiguous and clear to the person who has been turned down.

> Here all Mr. Thomas would have seen was "M.S.A. Policy 1.3.5". That does not meet the requirements. Mr. Thomas was entitled to know how it was that the Social Assistance Appeal Board came to its decision, and be given sufficient details on the form, or on an attached piece of paper, explaining to a reasonable informed reader how the Board related the facts to the issues in arriving at its conclusion.

Earlier in this chapter I referred to the "transcript" form of reasons in which every detail of the proceeding is carefully recorded in chronological order, every piece of evidence noted, every argument canvassed, and every comment, ruling, and conclusion of the decision-maker is dutifully set out. Frankly, if at all possible, I believe these types of decisions should be avoided. I recognize, however, that in proceedings where no form of record or tape recording, or transcript is kept these type of decisions may be necessary to serve as that record. Often, where an agency fails to maintain some sort of record of the proceedings, the reasons are the only way to ensure that important details of the proceeding are recorded. However, these types of reasons take a long time to write, are usually tedious to read, and sometimes end in obscuring the important with mountains of ancillary detail.

Reasons should be just that, the explanation for the important decisions which the agency made. Good reasons do at least two things:

1. They explain how the agency reached the decision it did. To do this, as a minimum, the reasons should set out the facts, law and reasoning which formed the basis for the decision reached.[9]

2. They show that due regard was had to the balance of the evidence and arguments advanced by the parties. This serves to avoid claims that the agency failed to consider some relevant evidence or argument which should have been considered.

---

8 (1992), 119 N.S.R. (2d) 159, 330 A.P.R. 159 (T.D.).

9 The British Columbia Court of Appeal, in the context of the reasons of a review board under the Criminal Code, once stated that "decision-makers, whether they be judges of first instance or

There is no clear rule indicating how much time should be spent on either of these elements. Sometimes the time spent dealing extensively with an argument which is ultimately rejected will serve to convince the parties of the propriety of the agency's position. Some people can never be convinced about anything and time spent elaborating on a point will be just wasted. Sometimes, clearly setting out the basis of one's decision, explaining the practical and legal ramifications and subtleties will result in a reviewing body according deference to one's expertise. Other times, Solomon himself could not wring deference out of the reviewing court. As a general rule, the time spent on a matter in one's reasons should be proportionate to the importance of the matter to the decision which one reached. The time spent on reasons overall should be determined in light of one's workload. If time simply will not permit the crafting of the perfect set of reasons, one should strive for the best that time will permit. In order to ensure that the overall mandate of the agency does not become lost in the slow and meticulous crafting of reasons one may have to develop priorities with more time spent on the more important decisions, and less time spent on those of less importance. Decisions with limited impact may warrant less time than decisions with far reaching and serious impact. Decisions intended to serve precedential value in numerous other instances may warrant greater care than decisions aimed squarely at one particular instance.

Summary reasons can be acceptable, provided that the essential matters are dealt with. Even where reasons are required by law, a decision-maker is not required to give reasons on each and every element of an argument presented to him (although he is required to consider them).[10]

In *R. v. B. (R.H.)*[11] the Supreme Court of Canada made the following comments respecting the duty on reasons given by a trial judge:

> [A] trial judge does not err merely because he or she does not give reasons for deciding one way or the other on problematic points: see *R. v. Smith*, [1990] 1 S.C.R. 991, affirming (1989), 95 A.R. 304 and *Macdonald v. The Queen*, [1977] 2 S.C.R. 665. The judge is not required to demonstrate that he or she knows the law and has considered all aspects of the evidence. Nor is the judge required to explain

---

tribunals such as the review board, cannot be expected to articulate every subsidiary decision leading to a final decision or disposition *unless it is foundational to that final decision.*'' (*Orlowski v. British Columbia (Attorney General)* (1992), 94 D.L.R. (4th) 541, 75 C.C.C. (2d) 138, 10 C.R.R. (2d) 301, [1992] B.C. W.L.D. 1443 (C.A.)).

10 *S.E.I.U., Local 333 v. Nipawin District Staff Nurses Assn.*, [1975] 1 S.C.R. 382, [1974] 1 W.W.R. 653, 41 D.L.R. (3d) 6. See also *Canada Post Corp. v. C.U.P.E.* (1993), 123 N.S.R. (2d) 128, 340 A.P.R. 128 (S.C.) where an arbitrator, in a summary manner, rejected an estoppel argument. The Nova Scotia Supreme Court noted that the arbitrator had referred to the argument and therefore concluded that he was aware of it and had chosen not to accept it. Given that the necessary elements to support an argument of estoppel did not exist in the evidence before the arbitrator he did not need to elaborate on his rejection of the argument.

11 [1994] 1 S.C.R. 656, 29 C.R. (4th) 113.

why he or she does not entertain a reasonable doubt as to the accused's guilt. Failure to do any of these things does not in itself, permit a court of appeal to set aside the verdict.

This rule make good sense. To require trial judges charged with heavy caseloads of criminal cases to deal in their reasons with every aspect of every case would slow the system of justice immeasurably. Trial judges are presumed to know the law with which they work day in and day out. If they state their conclusions in brief compass, and these conclusions are supported by the evidence, the verdict should not be overturned merely because they fail to discuss collateral aspects of the case.[12]

The most minimal reasons should include:

1. the question or matter decided by the decision to which the reasons relate;

2. the material facts relied upon in reaching the decision;

3. the law relied upon in reaching that decision;

4. the conclusions giving rise to the decision; and

5. the reasoning upon which those conclusions were based.

Beyond this, the agency should note any challenges made to its jurisdiction, and its conclusions with respect to them, set out any ancillary decisions which were made in the course of the hearing and the reasons for them, recite or summarize any evidence filed or argument made during the proceedings which were not relied upon and explain (however briefly) why they were not relied upon. This last suggestion will serve to avoid claims that the agency ignore or missed the evidence or argument in question.[13] Also, if time and space permit, it

---

12 See also *Hazarat v. Canada (Secretary of State)* (1994), 88 F.T.R. 128 (T.D.) where the Federal Court Trial Division expressed surprise that a decision-maker failed to expressly refer to some evidence which were in favour of the applicant. However, it concluded that there was no obligation in law to do so, expressly, as it appeared that the agency had reviewed it.

13 See, for example the decision of the Newfoundland Court of Appeal in *R. v. B. (C.B.)* (1993), 84 C.C.C. (3d) 429, 110 Nlfd. & P.E.I.R. 59, 346 A.P.R. 59 (Nfld. C.A.). That decision involved the reasons given by a trial judge in judicial proceedings. The Court of Appeal noted that there was not duty on a trial judge to give reasons for decisions. In the absence of evidence to the contrary, there is a presumption that the trial judge applied proper principles in reaching his or her decision (*R. v. MacDonald*, [1977] 2 S.C.R. 665, 29 C.C.C. (2d) 257; *R. v. Harper*, [1982] 1 S.C.R. 2, 40 N.R. 255, 133 D.L.R. (3d) 546, 65 C.C.C. (2d) 193)). However, "Where there is evidence capable of raising a reasonable doubt and the record, including the decision of the trial judge, does not reveal directly or by implication, that all of the evidence was considered, the appeal court may conclude there was a lack of appreciation or disregarding of such evidence. What the trial judge must do, or risk the appellate court finding an error, is ensure, through the decision, that the record reveals all of the evidence was considered." In *College of Nurses (Ontario) v. Quioque* (1993), 31 O.R. (3d) 325, 63 O.A.C. 241, 104 D.L.R. (4th) 44 (Div. Ct.) the Ontario Divisional Court concluded that the failure of the Discipline Committee of the College to make a specific finding in its reasons on an important issue forced the Court to conclude that the relative credibility of

is helpful to set out in full somewhere in one's reasons any statutory authority on which one relies in making one's decisions. This enables a reader to reference those authorities. He may not necessarily have the required legislation at hand when your reasons are reviewed.

Where a witness' evidence has been rejected as not being credible, the prudent agency may wish to give some indication why that finding of credibility was made (*Duriancik v. Ontario (Attorney General))*.[14] However, this may not always be necessary. In *Nassar v. College of Physicians & Surgeons (Manitoba)*[15] the Manitoba Court of Queen's Bench considered reasons in which a Discipline Committee stated "The committee has not placed any weight upon the evidence of Dr. Sunohara with respect to any patient about whom he testified. The committee has found his evidence to be of no assistance." The Court stated that "While there were no specific reasons given for attaching no weight to Dr. Sunohara's testimony, it is clear that the inquiry committee did in fact consider his evidence and found his testimony of no assistance. The committee need not ... provide an elaborate dissertation to support every conclusion of fact. Findings of fact based upon weight and credibility are within the province of the committee, and these findings must be respected by an appellate court." Ultimately, of course, the better one explains one's conclusions, the more likely they are to withstand a challenge.

The courts have also held that where a harsher penalty may be imposed only when a lesser one is not appropriate, some indication must be given as to why the lesser penalty was not appropriate (*Orlowski v. British Columbia (Attorney General))*.[16] The Ontario Court of Appeal has held that reasons must be given for findings of fact made upon disputed and contradicted evidence upon which the

---

the complainant and the respondent has not been fairly considered on the basis of all of the evidence. In *Canada (Minister of Citizenship & Immigration) v. Sahin* (1994), 87 F.T.R. 19 (T.D.) Justice Rothstein noted that "The authorities are clear that it is not necessary for a panel to advert to every piece of documentary evidence in its decision. However, where a document that may be adverse to his interest is produced by a person claiming Convention refugee status, which document may contradict one of the main reasons fro the panel's decision, making no reference to the document raised the question of whether the panel's decision would have been different had it taken the document into account."

14 (1994), 114 D.L.R. (4th) 504, 75 O.A.C. 27 (Div. Ct.), leave to appeal granted (1994), 114 D.L.R. (4th) 504n (Ont. C.A.). The Court cited as its authority for this proposition the decision of the Divisional Court in *Brisson v. Assn. of Architects (Ontario)* (1992), 6 C.L.R. (2d) 150, (*sub nom. Brisson v. Ontario Assn. of Architects*) 57 O.A.C. 232 (Div. Ct.). See also *College of Nurses (Ontario) v. Quioque* (1993), 31 O.R. (3d) 325, 63 O.A.C. 241, 104 D.L.R. (4th) 44 (Div. Ct.). See also *Karunatilleka v. Canada (Minister of Employment & Immigration)* (1994), 87 F.T.R. 89 (T.D.) where a panel of the Immigration and Refugee Board erred in finding that the claimant's testimony was a fabrication without making some specific findings on such matters as inconsistencies, demeanour and implausible incidents. The reviewing court held that to simply make a general statement that a claim was unreasonable and implausible was both unreasonable and unfair.

15 (1994), 96 Man. R. (2d) 141 (Q.B.) affirmed (June 23, 1995) Doc. AI 94-30-01979 (Man. C.A.).

16 (1992), 75 C.C.C. (3d) 138, 10 C.R.R. (2d) 301, 94 D.L.R. (4th) 541 (B.C. C.A.).

outcome of a case is largely dependent.[17] Finally, the reader may wish to note that the Alberta Court of Queen's Bench has held that it is not sufficient for an agency in considering the application of one of its policy guidelines, to simply advise an applicant that nothing in his case convinced the agency not to apply its general policy. The Court felt that, in order to avoid being found to have fettered its discretion, the agency must go on to explain why it had not been persuaded to make an exception (*Brown v. Alberta*).[18]

22.10 RELEASE OF DECISIONS

Decisions that could affect the finances of an industry or party whose shares are listed on a stock exchange should not be released until after the stock market is closed. It should be known upon which exchanges securities are listed.

It is a matter of choice whether the board releases its decision with an executive summary and/or a press release. Where a decision is of concern to the media and because the media may not be able to read and digest a 200 to 500 page decision quickly, it is usually preferable to issue a summary and overview to the media in the form of a press release.

In the event that a hearing involves a major issue, a lock-up for the media can be held prior to the issuance of a decision or report. By the time the report or decision is released, the media has had an hour or so with a staff briefing to understand the report or decision. Communication is very important for administrative agencies particularly when decisions that can affect three or four million people all at once are released.

---

17 *R. v. Richardson* (1992), 9 O.R. (3d) 194, 57 O.A.C. 54, 74 C.C.C. (3d) 15 (C.A.).
18 (1991), 2 Admin. L.R. (2d) 116, 81 Alta. L.R. (2d) 143, 82 D.L.R. (4th) 96 (Q.B.).

Administrative Procedures Act
R.S.A. 1980, c. A-2

HER MAJESTY, by and with the advice and consent of the Legislative Assembly of Alberta, enacts as follows:

Definitions

1. In this Act,

    (a) "authority" means a person authorized to exercise a statutory power;

    (b) "party" means a person whose rights will be varied or affected by the exercise of a statutory power or by an act or thing done pursuant to that power;

    (c) "statutory power" means an administrative, quasi-judicial or judicial power conferred by statute, other than a power conferred on a court of record of civil or criminal jurisdiction or a power to make regulations, and for greater certainty, but without restricting the generality of the foregoing, includes a power

        (i) to grant, suspend or revoke a charter or letters patent,

        (ii) to grant, renew, refuse, suspend or revoke a permission to do an act or thing which, but for the permission, would be unlawful, whether the permission is called a licence or permit or certificate or is in any other form,

        (iii) to declare or establish a status provided for under a statute for a person and to suspend or revoke that status,

        (iv) to approve or authorize the doing or omission by a person of an act or thing that, but for the approval or authorization, would be unlawful or unauthorized,

        (v) to declare or establish a right or duty of a person under a statute, whether in a dispute with another person or otherwise, or

        (vi) to make an order, decision, direction or finding prohibiting a person from doing an act or thing that, but for the order, decision, direction or finding, it would be lawful for him to do, or any combination of those powers.

Application of Act

2. The Lieutenant Governor in Council may, by order,

    (a) designate any authority as an authority to which this Act applies in whole or in part.

    (b) designate the statutory power of the authority in respect of which this Act applies in whole or in part, and

    (c) designate the provisions of this Act which are applicable to the authority in the exercise of that statutory power, and the extent to which they apply.

and this Act only applies to an authority to the extent ordered under this section.

Notice to parties

3. When

    (a) an application is made to an authority, or

    (b) an authority on its own initiative proposes

to exercise a statutory power, the authority shall give to all parties adequate notice of the application which it has before it or of the power which it intends to exercise.

Evidence and representations

4. Before an authority, in the exercise of a statutory power, refuses the application of or makes a decision or order adversely affecting the rights of a party, the authority

    (a) shall give the party a reasonable opportunity of furnishing relevant evidence to the authority,

    (b) shall inform the party of the facts in its possession or the allegations made to it contrary to the interests of the party in sufficient detail

        (i) to permit him to understand the facts or allegations, and

        (ii) to afford him a reasonable opportunity to furnish relevant evidence to contradict or explain the facts or allegations,

    and

    (c) shall give the party an adequate opportunity of making representations by way of argument to the authority.

Cross-examination

5. When an authority has informed a party of facts or allegations and that party

(a) is entitled under section 4 to contradict or explain them, but

(b) will not have a fair opportunity of doing so without cross-examination of the person making the statements that constitute the facts or allegations,

the authority shall afford the party an opportunity of cross-examination in the presence of the authority or of a person authorized to hear or take evidence for the authority.

When certain representations not permitted

6. Where by this Act a party is entitled to make representations to an authority with respect to the exercise of a statutory power, the authority is not by this Act required to afford an opportunity to the party

(a) to make oral representations, or

(b) to be represented by counsel,

if the authority affords the party an opportunity to make representations adequately in writing, but nothing in this Act deprives a party of a right conferred by any other Act to make oral representations or to be represented by counsel.

Written decision with reasons

7. When an authority exercises a statutory power so as to adversely affect the rights of a party, the authority shall furnish to each party a written statement of its decision setting out

(a) the findings of fact on which it based its decision, and

(b) the reasons for the decision.

Requirements of other Acts

8. Nothing in this Act relieves an authority from complying with any procedure to be followed by it under any other Act relating to the exercise of its statutory power.

Rules of evidence

9. Nothing in this Act

(a) requires that any evidence or allegations of fact made to an authority be made under oath, or

(b) requires any authority to adhere to the rules of evidence applicable to courts of civil or criminal jurisdiction.

Regulations

10. The Lieutenant Governor in Council may make regulations

(a) to prescribe the length of time that is reasonable for the giving of a notice in accordance with this Act, with respect to authorities generally or with respect to a specified authority;

(b) to prescribe forms of notices for the purposes of this Act;

(c) to carry into effect the purposes of this Act.

AGENCIES SUBJECT TO THE ALBERTA ADMINISTRATIVE PROCEDURES ACT
(as of January, 1994)

Agency	Legislation Subjecting Agency to Act
Appeal Board under the Assured Income for the Severely Handicapped Act	Assured Income for the Severely Handicapped Act, R.S.A. 1980, c. A-48, s. 11
Appeal Board under the Child Welfare Act	Child Welfare Act, R.S.A. 1980, c. C-8.1, s. 85
Appeal Board under the Windows' Pension Act	Widows' Pension Act, R.S.A. 1980, c. W-7.5, s. 9
Appeal Panel under the Social Development Act	Social Development Act, R.S.A. 1980, c. S-16, s. 28
Alberta Agricultural Products Marketing Council when acting under s. 35 of the Marketing of Agricultural Products Act	Alta. Reg. 135/80 as amended by Alta. Reg. 57/86
Alberta Assessment Appeal Board (s. 7 of the Procedures Act does not apply unless a party to an appeal before the Board requests that it apply)	Alta. Reg. 135/80 as amended by Alta. Reg. 57/86
Albert Motor Transport Board	Alta. Reg. 135/80
Alberta Planning Board when it is acting under sections 106,108 and 109 of the Planning Act, 1977	Alta. Reg. 135/80 as amended by Alta. Reg. 57/86
Board of Inquiry under the Individual Rights Protection Act	Individual Rights Protection Act, R.S.A. 1980, c. I-2, s. 29
Energy Resources Conservation Board	Alta. Reg. 135/80
Irrigation Council	Alta. Reg. 135/80
Local Authorities Board	Alta. Reg. 135/80
Members of the Legislative Assembly Pension Plan Board	Members of the Legislative Assembly Pension Plan Act, R.S.A. 1980, c. M-12.5
Natural Resources Conservation Board	Alta. Reg. 135/80 as amended by Alta. Reg. 192/91
Public Utilities Board except when it is imposing assessments, interest, penalties or costs under s. 20.1, 20.3, 20.4 or 60(1.1) of the Public Utilities Board Act	Alta. Reg. 135/80 as amended by Alta. Reg. 264/90

Review Panel under the Medical Profession Act	Medical Profession Act, R.S.A. 1980, c. M-12, s. 29
Surface Rights Board	Alta. Reg. 135/80

Statutory Powers Procedure Act
R.S.O. 1990, c. S.22

INDEXED

Definitions

1. (1) In this Act,

"electronic hearing" means a hearing held by conference telephone or some other form of electronic technology allowing persons to hear one another; S.O. 1994, c. 27, s. 56(3).

"hearing" means a hearing in any proceeding; S.O. 1994, c. 27, s. 56(2).

"licence" includes any permit, certificate, approval, registration or similar form of permission required by law;

"municipality" has the same meaning as in the *Municipal Affairs Act*, and includes a district, metropolitan and regional municipality, and their local boards;

"oral hearing" means a hearing at which the parties or their counsel or agents attend before the tribunal in person; S.O. 1994, c. 27, s. 56(3).

"proceeding" means a proceeding to which this Act applies; S.O. 1994, c. 27, s. 56(2).

"statutory power of decision" means a power or right, conferred by or under a statute, to make a decision deciding or prescribing,

  (a) the legal rights, powers, privileges, immunities, duties or liabilities of any person or party, or

  (b) the eligibility of any person or party to receive, or to the continuation of, a benefit or licence, whether the person is legally entitled thereto or not;

"tribunal" means one or more persons whether or not incorporated and however described, upon which a statutory power of decision is conferred by or under a statute;

"written hearing" means a hearing held by means of the exchange of documents, whether in written form or by electronic means. S.O. 1994, c. 27, s. 56(3).

Meaning of "person" extended

(2) A municipality, an unincorporated association of employers, a trade union or council of trade unions who may be a party to a proceeding in the exercise of a statutory power of decision under the statute conferring the power shall be deemed to be a person for the purpose of any provision of this Act or of any rule made under this Act that applies to parties. R.S.O. 1980, c. 484, s.1.

2. [Repealed, S.O. 1994, c. 27, s. 56(4).]

Application of Act

3. (1) Subject to subsection (2), this Act applies to a proceeding by a tribunal in the exercise of a statutory power of decision conferred by or under an Act of the Legislature, where the tribunal is required by or under such Act or otherwise by law to hold or to afford to the parties to the proceeding an opportunity for a hearing before making a decision. R.S.O. 1980, c. 484, s. 3(1), S.O. 1994, c. 27, s. 56(5).

(2) This Act does not apply to a proceeding,

(a) before the Assembly or any committee of the Assembly;

(b) in or before

(i) the Court of Appeal,

(ii) the Ontario Court (General Division),

(iii) the Ontario Court (Provincial Division),

(iv) the Unified Family Court,

(v) the Small Claims Court, or

(vi) a justice of the peace;

(c) to which the Rules of Civil Procedure apply;

(d) before an arbitrator to which the *Arbitrations Act* or the *Labour Relations Act* applies;

(e) at a coroner's inquest;

(f) of a commission appointed under the *Public Inquiries Act*;

(g) of one or more persons required to make an investigation and to make a report, with or without recommendations, where the report is for the information or advice of the person to whom it is made and does not in any way legally bind or limit that person in any decision he or she may have power to make; or

(h) of a tribunal empowered to make regulations, rules or by-laws in so far as its power to make regulations, rules or by-laws is concerned. R.S.O. 1980, c. 484, s. 3(2), *revised*, S.O. 1994, c. 27, s. 56(6).

Waiver of procedural requirement

4. (1) Any procedural requirement of this Act or of the Act under which a proceeding arises may be waived with the consent of the parties and the tribunal. S.O. 1994, c. 27, s. 56(7).

Same, rules

(2) Any provision of a tribunal's rules made under s. 25.1 may be waived in accordance with the rules. S.O. 1994, c. 27, s. 56(7).

Disposition of proceeding without hearing

4.1 If the parties consent, the proceeding may be disposed of by a decision of the tribunal given without a hearing, unless the Act under which the proceeding arises provides otherwise. S.O. 1994, c. 27, s. 56(7).

Panels, certain matters

4.2 (1) A procedural or interlocutory matter in a proceeding may be heard and determined by a panel consisting of one or more members of the tribunal, as assigned by the chair of the tribunal. S.O. 1994, c. 27, s. 56(8).

Assignment

(2) In assigning members of the tribunal to a panel, the chair shall take into consideration any requirement imposed by the Act under which the proceeding arises that the tribunal be representative of specific interests. S.O. 1994, c. 27, s. 56(8).

Decision of panel

(3) The decision of a majority of the members of a panel, or their unanimous decision in the case of a two-member panel, is the tribunal's decision. S.O. 1994, c. 27, s. 56(8).

Expiry of Term

4.3 If the term of office of a member of a tribunal who has participated in a hearing expires before a decision is given, the term shall be deemed to continue for the purpose of participating in the decision. S.O. 1994, c. 27, s. 56(9).

Incapacity of member

4.4 (1) If a member of a tribunal who has participated in a hearing becomes unable, for any reason, to complete the hearing or to participate in the decision, the remaining member or members may complete the hearing and give a decision. S.O. 1994, c. 27, s. 56(9).

Other Acts

(2) Subsection (1) does not apply if the Act under which the proceeding arises specifically deals with the issue of what takes place in the circumstances described in subsection (1). S.O. 1994, c. 27, s. 56(9).

Parties

5. The parties to a proceeding shall be the persons specified as parties by or under the statue under which the proceeding arises or, if not so specified, persons entitled by law to be parties to the proceeding. R.S.O. 1980, c. 484, s. 5.

Written hearings

5.1 (1) A tribunal may hold a written hearing in a proceeding, in accordance with its rules made under s. 25.1. S.O. 1994, c. 27, s. 56(10).

Exception

(2) The tribunal shall not hold a written hearing if a party objects. S.O. 1994, c. 27, s. 56(10).

Documents

(3) In a written hearing, all the parties are entitled to receive every document that the tribunal receives in the proceeding. S.O. 1994, c. 27, s. 56(10).

Electronic hearings

5.2 (1) A tribunal may hold an electronic hearing in a proceeding, in accordance with its rules made under section 25.1. S.O. 1994, c. 27, s. 56(10).

Exception

(2) The tribunal shall not hold an electronic hearing if a party satisfies the tribunal that holding an electronic rather than an oral hearing is likely to cause the party significant prejudice. S.O. 1994, c. 27, s. 56(10).

Same

(3) Subsection (2) does not apply if the only purpose of the hearing is to deal with procedural matters. S.O. 1994, c. 27, s. 56(10).

Participants to be able to hear one another

(4) In an electronic hearing, all the parties and the members of the tribunal participating in the hearing must be able to hear one another and any witnesses throughout the hearing. S.O. 1994, c. 27, s. 56(10).

Pre-hearing Conferences

5.3 (1) The tribunal may, in accordance with its rules made under s. 25.1, and subject to the Act under which the proceeding arises, direct the parties to participate in a pre-hearing conference to consider,

    (a) the settlement of any or all of the issues;

    (b) the simplification of the issues;

    (c) facts or evidence that may be agreed upon;

    (d) the dates by which any steps in the proceeding are to be taken or begun;

    (e) the estimated duration of the hearing; and

    (f) any other matter that may assist in the just and most expeditious disposition of the proceeding. S.O. 1994, c. 27, s. 56(11).

Who presides

(2) The chair of the tribunal may designate a member of the tribunal or any other person to preside at the pre-hearing conference. S.O. 1994, c. 27, s. 56(11).

Orders

(3) A member who presides at a pre-hearing conference may make such orders as he or she considers necessary or advisable with respect to the conduct of the proceeding, including adding parties. S.O. 1994, c. 27, s. 56(11).

Disqualification

(4) A member who presides at a pre-hearing conference at which the parties attempt to settle issues shall not preside at the hearing of the proceeding unless the parties consent. S.O. 1994, c. 27, s. 56(11).

Disclosure

5.4 (1) At any stage of the proceeding before completion of the hearing, the tribunal may, if its rules made under s. 25.1 deal with the matter, and subject to the Act under which the proceeding arises, make orders for,

(a) the exchange of documents;

(b) the oral or written examination of a party;

(c) the exchange of witness statements and reports of expert witnesses;

(d) the provision of particulars;

(e) any other form of disclosure. S.O. 1994, c. 27, s. 56(12).

Exception, privileged information

(2) Subsection (1) does not authorize the making of an order requiring disclosure of privileged information. S.O. 1994, c. 27, s. 56(12).

Notice of hearing

6. (1) The parties to a proceeding shall be given reasonable notice of the hearing by the tribunal.

Statutory authority

(2) A notice of hearing shall include a reference to the statutory authority under which the hearing will be held. S.O. 1994, c. 27, s. 56(13).

Oral hearing

(3) A notice of an oral hearing shall include,

(a) a statement of the time, place and purpose of the hearing; and

(b) a statement that if the party notified does not attend at the hearing, the tribunal may proceed in the party's absence and the party will not be entitled to any further notice in the proceeding. S.O. 1994, c. 27, s. 56(13).

Written hearing

(4) A notice of a written hearing shall include,

(a) a statement of the time and purpose of the hearing, and details about the manner in which the hearing will be held;

(b) a statement that the party notified may object to the hearing being held as a written hearing (in which case the tribunal is required to hold it as an electronic or oral hearing) and an indication of the procedure to be followed for that purpose;

(c) a statement that if the party notified neither acts under clause (b) nor participates in the hearing in accordance with the notice, the tribunal may proceed without the party's participation and the party will not be entitled to any further notice in the proceeding. S.O. 1994, c. 27, s. 56(13).

Electronic hearing

(5) A notice of an electronic hearing shall include,

(a) a statement of the time and purpose of the hearing, and details about the manner in which the hearing will be held;

(b) a statement that the only purpose of the hearing is to deal with procedural matters, if that is the case;

(c) if clause (b) does not apply, a statement that the party notified may, by satisfying the tribunal that holding the hearing as an electronic hearing is likely to cause the party significant prejudice, require the tribunal to hold the hearing as an oral hearing, and an indication of the procedure to be followed for that purpose; and

(d) a statement that if the party notified neither acts under clause (c), if applicable, nor participates in the hearing in accordance with the notice, the tribunal may proceed without the party's participation and the party will not be entitled to any further notice in the proceeding. S.O. 1994, c. 27, s. 56(13).

Effect of non-attendance at hearing after due notice

7. (1) Where notice of an oral hearing has been given to a party to a proceeding in accordance with this Act and the party does not attend at the hearing, the tribunal may proceed in the absence of the party and the party is not entitled to any further notice in the proceeding. R.S.O. 1980, c. 484, s. 7, S.O. 1994, c. 27, s. 56(14).

Same, written hearings

(2) Where notice of a written hearing has been given to a party to a proceeding in accordance with this Act and the party neither acts under clause 6(4)(b) nor participates in the hearing in accordance with the notice, the tribunal may proceed without the party's participation and the party is not entitled to any further notice in the proceeding. S.O. 1994, c. 27, s. 56(15).

Same, electronic hearings

(3) Where notice of an electronic hearing has been given to a party to a proceeding in accordance with this Act and the party neither acts under clause 6(5)(c), if applicable, nor participates in the hearing in accordance with the notice, the tribunal may proceed without the party's participation and the party is not entitled to any further notice in the proceeding. S.O. 1994, c. 27, s. 56(15).

Where character, etc. of a party is in issue

8. Where the good character, propriety of conduct or competence of a party is an issue in a proceeding, the party is entitled to be furnished prior to the hearing with reasonable information of any allegations with respect thereto. R.S.O. 1980, c. 484, s. 8.

Hearings to be public, exceptions

9. (1) An oral hearing shall be open to the public except where the tribunal is of the opinion that,

 (a) matters involving public security may be disclosed; or

 (b) intimate financial or personal matters or other matters may be disclosed at the hearing of such a nature, having regard to the circumstances, that the desirability of avoiding disclosure thereof in the interests of any person affected or in the public interest outweighs the desirability of adhering to the principle that hearings be open to the public,

in which case the tribunal may hold the hearing in the absence of the public. S.O. 1994, c. 27, s. 56(16).

Written hearings

(1.1) In a written hearing, members of the public are entitled to reasonable access to the documents submitted, unless the tribunal is of the opinion that clause 1(a) or (b) applies. S.O. 1994, c. 27, s. 56(17).

Electronic hearings

(1.2) An electronic hearing need not be open to the public. S.O. 1994, c. 27, s. 56(17).

Maintenance of order at hearings

(2) A tribunal may make such orders or give such directions at an oral or electronic hearing as it considers necessary for the maintenance of order at the hearing, and, if any person disobeys or fails to comply with any such order or direction, the tribunal or a member thereof may call of the assistance of any peace officer to enforce the order or direction, and every peace officer so called upon shall take such action as is necessary to enforce the order or direction and may use such force as it reasonably required for that purpose. R.S.O. 1980, c. 484, s. 9, S.O. 1994, c. 27, s. 56(18).

Proceedings involving similar questions

9.1 (1) If two or more proceedings before a tribunal involve the same or similar questions of fact, law or policy, the tribunal may,

(a) combine the proceedings or any part of them, with the consent of the parties;

(b) hear the proceedings at the same time, with the consent of the parties;

(c) hear the proceedings one immediately after the other; or

(d) stay one or more of the proceedings until after the determination of another one of them. S.O. 1994, c. 27, s. 56(19).

Exception

(2) Subsection (1) does not apply to proceedings to which the *Consolidated Hearings Act* applies. S.O. 1994, c. 27, s. 56(19).

Same

(3) Clauses (1)(a) and (b) do not apply to a proceeding if,

(a) the Act under which the proceeding arises requires that it be heard in private; or

(b) the tribunal is of the opinion that clause 9(1)(a) or (b) applies to the proceeding. S.O. 1994, c. 27, s. 56(19).

Conflict, consent requirements

(4) The consent requirements of clauses (1)(a) and (b) do not apply if the Act under which the proceeding arises allows the tribunal to combine the proceedings or hear them at the same time without the consent of the parties. S.O. 1994, c. 27, s. 55 (19).

Use of same evidence

(5) If the parties to the second-named proceeding consent, the tribunal may treat evidence that is admitted in a proceeding as if it were also admitted in another proceeding that is heard at the same time under clause (1)(b). S.O. 1994, c. 27, s. 56(19).

Right to counsel

10. A party to a proceeding may be represented by counsel or agent. S.O. 1994, c. 27, s. 56(20).

Examination of witnesses

10.1 A party to a proceeding may, at an oral or electronic hearing,

(a) call and examine witnesses and present evidence and submissions; and

(b) conduct cross-examinations of witnesses at the hearing reasonably required for a full and fair disclosure of all matters relevant to the issues in the proceeding. S.O. 1994, c. 27, s. 56(20).

Rights of witnesses to counsel

11. (1) A witness at an oral or electronic hearing is entitled to be advised by counsel or an agent as to his or her rights but such counsel or agent may take no other part in the hearing without leave of the tribunal. S.O. 1994, c. 27, s. 56(21).

Idem

(2) Where an oral hearing is closed to the public, the counsel or agent for a witness is not entitled to be present except when that witness is giving evidence. R.S.O. 1980, c. 484, s. 11, S.O. 1994, c. 27, s. 56(22).

Summonses

12. (1) A tribunal may require any person, including a party, by summons,

(a) to give evidence on oath or affirmation at an oral or electronic hearing; and

(b) to produce in evidence at an oral or electronic hearing documents and things specified by the tribunal,

relevant to the subject-matter of the proceeding and admissible at a hearing. R.S.O. 1980, c. 484, s. 12(1), S.O. 1994, c. 27, s. 56(23).

Form and service of summons

(2) A summons issued under subsection (1) shall be in the prescribed form (in English or French) and,

(a) where the tribunal consists of one person, shall be signed by him or her;

(b) where the tribunal consists of more than one person, shall be signed by the chair of the tribunal or in such other manner as documents on behalf of the tribunal may be signed under the statue constituting the tribunal. S.O. 1994, c. 27, s. 56(24).

Same

(3) The summons shall be served personally on the person summoned. S.O. 1994, c. 27, s. 56(24).

Fees and allowances

(3.1) The person summoned is entitled to receive the same fees or allowance for attending at or otherwise participating in the hearing as are paid to a person summoned to attend before the Ontario Court (General Division). S.O. 1994, c. 27, s. 56(24).

Bench warrant

(4) A judge of the Ontario Court (General Division) may issue a warrant against a person if the judge is satisfied that,

(a) a summons was served on the person under this section;

(b) the person has failed to attend or to remain in attendance at the hearing (in the case of an oral hearing) or has failed otherwise to participate in the hearing (in the case of an electronic hearing) in accordance with the summons; and

(c) the person's attendance or participation is material to the ends of justice. S.O. 1994, c. 27, s. 56(25).

Same

(4.1) The warrant shall in the prescribed form (in English or French), directed to any police officer, and shall require the person to be apprehended anywhere within Ontario, brought before the tribunal forthwith and,

(a) detained in custody as the judge may order until the person's presence as a witness is no longer required; or

(b) in the judge's discretion, released on a recognizance, with or without sureties, conditioned for attendance or participation to give evidence. S.O. 1994, c. 27, s. 56(25).

Proof of service

(5) Service of a summons may be proved by affidavit in an application to have a warrant issued under subsection (4). S.O. 1994, c. 27, s. 56(26).

Certificate of facts

(6) Where an application to have a warrant issued is made on behalf of a tribunal, the person constituting the tribunal, or, if the tribunal consists of more than one person, the chair of the tribunal may certify to the judge the facts relied on to establish that the attendance or other participation of the person summoned is material to the ends of justice, and the judge may accept the certificate as proof of the facts. S.O. 1994, c. 27, s. 56(26).

Same

(7) Where the application is made by a party to the proceeding, the facts relied on to establish that the attendance or other participation of the person is material to the ends of justice may be proved by the party's affidavit. S.O. 1994, c. 27, s. 56(26).

Contempt proceedings

13. Where any person without lawful excuse,

(a) on being duly summoned under section 12 as a witness at a hearing make default in attending at the hearing; or

(b) being in attendance as a witness at an oral hearing or otherwise participating as a witness at an electronic hearing, refuses to take an oath or
to make an affirmation legally required by the tribunal to be taken or
made, or to produce any document or thing in his or her power or control
legally required by the tribunal to be produced by him or her or to
answer any question in which the tribunal may legally require an answer; or

(c) does any other thing that would, if the tribunal had been a court of law
having power to commit for contempt, have been contempt of that court,

the tribunal may, of its own motion or on the motion of a party to the proceeding,
state a case to the Divisional Court setting out the facts and that court may inquire
into the matter and, after hearing any witnesses who may be produced against or
on behalf of that person and after hearing any statement that may be offered in
defence, punish or take steps for the punishment of that person in like manner as
if he or she had been guilty of contempt of the court. R.S.O. 1980, c. 484, s. 13,
revised, S.O. 1994, c. 27, s. 56(27).

Protection for witnesses

14. (1) A witness at an oral or electronic hearing shall be deemed to have
objected to answer any question asked him or her upon the ground that the answer
may tend to establish his or her liability to civil proceedings at the instance of the
Crown, or of any person, and no answer given by a witness at a hearing shall be
used or be receivable in evidence against the witness in any trial or other proceeding against him or her thereafter taking place, other than a prosecution for
perjury in giving such evidence. S.O. 1994, c. 27, s. 56(28).

(2) [Repealed, S.O. 1994, c. 27, s. 56(29).]

What is admissible in evidence at a hearing

15. (1) Subject to subsection (2) and (3), a tribunal may admit as evidence
at a hearing, whether or not given or proven under oath or affirmation or admissible
as evidence in a court,

(a) any oral testimony; and

(b) any document or other thing,

relevant to the subject-matter of the proceeding and may act on such evidence,
but the tribunal may exclude anything unduly repetitious.

What is inadmissible in evidence at a hearing

(2) Nothing is admissible in evidence at a hearing,

(a) that would be inadmissible in a court by reason of any privilege under the law of evidence; or

(b) that is inadmissible by the statute under which the proceeding arises or any other statute.

Conflicts

(3) Nothing in subsection (1) overrides the provisions of any Act expressly limiting the extent to or purposes for which any oral testimony, documents or things may be admitted or used in evidence in any proceeding.

Copies

(4) Where a tribunal is satisfied as to its authenticity, a copy of a document or other thing may be admitted as evidence at a hearing.

Photocopies

(5) Where a document has been filed in evidence at a hearing, the tribunal may, or the person producing it or entitled to it may with the leave of the tribunal, cause the document to be photocopied and the tribunal may authorize the photocopy to be filed in evidence in the place of the document filed and release the document filed, or may furnish to the person producing it or the person entitled to it a photocopy of the document filed certified by a member of the tribunal.

Certified copy admissible in evidence

(6) A document purporting to be a copy of a document filed in evidence at a hearing, certified to be a copy thereof by a member of the tribunal, is admissible in evidence in proceedings in which the document is admissible as evidence of the document. R.S.O. 1980, c. 484, s. 15.

Use of previously admitted evidence

15.1 (1) The tribunal may treat previously admitted evidence as if it had been admitted in a proceeding before the tribunal, if the parties to the proceeding consent. S.O. 1994, c. 27, s. 56(30).

Definition

(2) In subsection (1), ''previously admitted evidence'' means evidence that was admitted, before the hearing of the proceeding referred to in that subsection,

(a) in another proceeding to which this Act applies;

(b) in a proceeding to which this Act does not apply that is before an Ontario court or a court or other tribunal outside Ontario. S.O. 1994, c. 27, s. 56(30).

Witness panels

15.2 A tribunal may receive evidence from panels of witnesses composed of two or more persons, if the parties have first had an opportunity to make submissions in that regard. S.O. 1994, c. 27, s. 56(31).

Notice of facts and opinions

16. A tribunal may, in making its decision in any proceeding,

(a) take notice of facts that may be judicially noticed; and

(b) take notice of any generally recognized scientific or technical facts, information or opinions within its scientific or specialized knowledge. R.S.O. 1980, c. 484, s. 16.

Interim decisions and orders

16.1 (1) A tribunal may make interim decisions and orders. S.O. 1994, c. 27, s. 56(32).

Conditions

(2) A tribunal may impose conditions on an interim decision or order. S.O. 1994, c. 27, s. 56(32).

Reasons

(3) An interim decision or order need not be accompanied by reasons. S.O. 1994, c. 27, s. 56(32).

Decision

17. (1) A tribunal shall give its final decision and order, if any, in any proceeding in writing and shall give reasons in writing therefor, if requested by a party. R.S.O. 1980, c. 484, s. 17, *revised*, 1993, c. 27, Sch., S.O. 1994.

Interest

(2) A tribunal that makes an order for the payment of money shall set out in the order the principal sum, and if interest is payable, the rate of interest and the date from which it is to be calculated. S.O. 1994, c. 27, s. 56(33).

Notice of decision

18. (1) The tribunal shall send each party who participated in the proceeding, or the party's counsel or agent, a copy of its final decision or order, including the reasons if any have been given,

    (a) by regular lettermail;

    (b) by electronic transmission;

    (c) by telephone transmission of a facsimile; or

    (d) by some other method that allows proof of receipt, in accordance with the tribunal's rules made under s. 25.1. S.O. 1994, c. 27, s. 56(34).

Use of mail

(2) If the copy is sent by regular lettermail, it shall be sent to the most recent addresses known to the tribunal and shall be deemed to be received by the party on the fifth day after the day it is mailed. S.O. 1994, c. 27, s. 56(34).

Use of electronic or telephone transmissions

(3) If the copy is sent by electronic transmission or by telephone transmission of a facsimile, it shall be deemed to be received on the day after it was sent, unless that day is a holiday, in which case the copy shall be deemed to be received on the next day that is not a holiday. S.O. 1994, c. 27, s. 56(34).

Use of other method

(4) If the copy is sent by a method referred to in clause (1)(d), the tribunal's rules made under section 25.1 govern its deemed day of receipt. S.O. 1994, c. 27, s. 56(34).

Failure to receive copy

(5) If a party that acts in good faith does not, through absence, accident, illness or other cause beyond the party's control, receive the copy until a later date than the deemed day of receipt, subsection (2), (3) or (4), as the case may be, does not apply. S.O. 1994, c. 27, s. 56(34).

Enforcement of orders

19. (1) A certified copy of a tribunal's decision or order in a proceeding may be filed in the Ontario Court (General Division) by the tribunal or by a party and on filing shall be deemed to be an order of that court and is enforceable as such. S.O. 1994, c. 27, s. 56(35).

Notice of filing

(2) A party who files an order under subsection (1) shall notify the tribunal within 10 days after the filing. S.O. 1994, c. 27, s. 56(35).

Order for payment of money

(3) On receiving a certified copy of a tribunal's order for the payment of money, the sheriff shall enforce the order as if it were an execution issued by the Ontario Court (General Division). S.O. 1994, c. 27, s. 56(35).

Record of proceeding

20. A tribunal shall compile a record of any proceeding in which a hearing has been held which shall include,

(a) any application, complaint, reference or other document, if any, by which the proceeding was commenced;

(b) the notice of any hearing;

(c) any interlocutory orders made by the tribunal;

(d) all documentary evidence filed with the tribunal, subject to any limitation expressly imposed by any other Act on the extent to or the purposes for which any such documents may be used in evidence in any proceeding;

(e) the transcript, if any, of the oral evidence given at the hearing; and

(f) the decision of the tribunal and the reasons therefor, where reasons have been given. R.S.O. 1980, c. 484, s. 20.

Adjournments

21. A hearing may be adjourned from time to time by a tribunal of its own motion or where it is shown to the satisfaction of the tribunal that the adjournment is required to permit an adequate hearing to be held. R.S.O. 1980, c. 484, s. 21.

Correction of errors

21.1 A tribunal may at any time correct a typographical error, error of calculation or similar error made in its decision or order. S.O. 1994, c. 27, s. 56(36).

Power to review

21.2 (1) A tribunal may, if it considers it advisable, review all or part of its own decision or order, in accordance with its rules made under section 25.1, and may confirm, vary, suspend or cancel the decision or order. S.O. 1994, c. 27, s. 56(36).

Time for review

(2) The review shall take palce within a reasonable time after the decision or order is made.

Conflict

(3) In the event of a conflict between this section and any other Act, the other Act prevails. S.O. 1994, c. 27, s. 56(36).

Administration of Oaths

22. A member of a tribunal has power to administer oaths and affirmations for the purpose of any of its proceedings and the tribunal may require evidence before it to be given under oath or affirmation. R.S.O. 1980, c. 484, s. 22.

Abuse of Process

23. (1) A tribunal may make such orders or give it such directions in proceedings before it as it considers proper to prevent abuse of its process.

Limitation on cross-examination

(2) A tribunal may reasonably limit further examination or cross-examination of a witness where it is satisfied that the examination or cross-examination has been sufficient to disclose fully and fairly all matters relevant to the issues in the proceeding. S.O. 1994, c. 27, s. 56(37).

Exclusion of Agents

(3) A tribunal may exclude from a hearing anyone, other than a barrister and solicitor qualified to practise in Ontario, appearing as an agent on behalf of a party or as an adviser to a witness if it finds that such person is not competent properly to represent or to advise the party or witness or does not understand and comply at the hearing with the duties and responsibilities of an advocate or adviser. R.S.O. 1980, c. 484, s. 23.

Notice, etc.

24. (1) Where a tribunal is of opinion that because the parties to any proceeding before it are so numerous or for any other reason, it is impracticable,

(a) to give notice of the hearing; or

(b) to send its decision and the material mentioned in section 18,

to all or any of the parties individually, the tribunal may, instead of doing so, cause reasonable notice to be given to such parties by public advertisement or otherwise as the tribunal may direct.

Contents of notice

(2) A notice of a decision given by a tribunal under clause (1)(b) shall inform the parties of the place where copies of the decision and the reasons therefor, if reasons were given, may be obtained. R.S.O. 1980, c. 484, s. 24.

Appeal operates as stay, exception

25. (1) Unless it is expressly provided to the contrary in the Act under which the proceeding arises, an appeal from a decision of a tribunal to a court or other appellate tribunal operates as a stay in the mater except where the tribunal or the court or other body to which the appeal is taken otherwise orders.

Idem

(2) An application for judicial review under the *Judicial Review Procedure Act*, or the bringing of proceedings specified in the subsection 2 (1) of that Act is not an appeal within the meaning of subsection (1). R.S.O. 1980, c. 484, s. 25.

Rules

25.1 (1) A tribunal may make rules governing the practice and procedure before it. S.O. 1994, c. 27, s. 56(38).

Application

(2) The rules may be of general or particular application. S.O. 1994, c. 27, s. 56(38).

Consistency with Acts

(3) The rules shall be consistent with this Act and with other Acts to which they relate. S.O. 1994, c. 27, s. 56(38).

Public access

(4) The tribunal shall make the rules available to the public in English and in French. S.O. 1994, c. 27, s. 56(38).

Regulations Act

(5) Rules adopted under this section are not regulations as defined in the *Regulations Act.* S.O. 1994, c. 27, s. 56(38).

Additional power

(6) The power conferred by this section is in addition to any power to adopt rules that the tribunal may have under another Act. S.O. 1994, c. 27, s. 56(38).

Regulations

26. The Lieutenant Governor in Council may make regulations prescribing forms for the purpose of section 12. S.O. 1994, c. 27, s. 56(41).

27. to 31. [Repealed, S.O. 1994, c. 27, s. 56(40).]

Conflict

32. Unless it is expressly provided in any other Act that its provisions and regulations, rules or by-laws made under it apply despite anything in this Act, the provisions of this Act prevail over the provisions of such other Act and over regulations, rules or by-laws made under such other Act which conflict therewith. R.S.O. 1980, c. 484, s. 32, S.O. 1994, c. 27, s. 56(42).

33. to 34. [Repealed, S.O. 1994, c. 27, s. 56(43).]

Form 1 [Repealed, S.O. 1994, c. 27, s. 56(44).]

Form 2 [Repealed, S.O. 1994, c. 27, s. 56(44).]

O. Reg. 116/95

REGULATION MADE UNDER THE
STATUTORY POWERS PROCEDURE ACT

Forms

1. A summons issued under subsection 12(1) of the Act shall be in Form 1.

2. A warrant issued under subsection 12 (4) of the Act shall be in Form 2.

3. This Regulation comes into force on April 1, 1995.

FORM 1

SUMMONS

(Name of Act under which proceeding arises)

SUMMONS TO A WITNESS BEFORE *(name of tribunal)*

TO: *(name and address of witness)*

(For oral hearing)

YOU ARE REQUIRED TO ATTEND TO GIVE EVIDENCE at the hearing of this proceeding on *(day)*, *(date)*, at *(time)*, at *(place)*, and to remain until your attendance is no longer required.

YOU ARE REQUIRED TO BRING WITH YOU and produce at the hearing the following documents and things: *(Set out the nature and date of each document and give sufficient particulars to identify each document and thing.)*

IF YOU FAIL TO ATTEND OR TO REMAIN IN ATTENDANCE AS THIS SUMMONS REQUIRED, THE ONTARIO COURT (GENERAL DIVISION) MAY ORDER THAT A WARRANT FOR YOUR ARREST BE ISSUED, OR THAT YOU BE PUNISHED IN THE SAME WAY AS FOR CONTEMPT OF THAT COURT.

(For electronic hearing)

YOU ARE REQUIRED TO PARTICPATE IN AN ELECTRONIC HEARING on *(day)*, *(date)*, at *(time)*, in the following manner: *(Give sufficient particulars to enable witness to participate.)*

IF YOU FAIL TO PARTICIPATE IN THE HEARING IN ACCORDANCE WITH THE SUMMONS, THE ONTARIO COURT (GENERAL DIVISION) MAY ORDER THAT A WARRANT FOR YOUR ARREST BE ISSUED, OR THAT YOU BE PUNISHED IN THE SAME WAY AS FOR CONTEMPT OF THAT COURT.

Date _____   *(name of tribunal)*

_____
(Signature by or on behalf of tribunal)

NOTE: You are entitled to be paid the same fees or allowances for attending at or otherwise participating in the hearing as are paid to a person summoned to attend before the Ontario Court (General Division).

FORM 2

WARRANT FOR ARREST (DEFAULTING WITNESS)

Ontario Court (General Division)

(Name of judge)   *(Day and date)*

(Court seal)   *(Title of proceeding)*

WARRANT FOR ARREST

TO ALL police officers in Ontario
AND TO the officers of all correctional institutions in Ontario

WHEREAS the witness *(name)*, of *(address)*, was served under section 12 of the *Statutory Powers Procedure Act* with a summons to witness to give evidence at the hearing of *(title of proceeding)* before *(name of tribunal)* on *(day)*, *(date)* at *(time)*.

AND WHEREAS the witness failed to attend or to remain in attendance at the hearing *(or in the case of an electroinic hearing* to participate in the hearing in accordance with the summons),

AND WHEREAS I am satisfied that the witness' attendance or participation is material to the ends of justice,

YOU ARE ORDERED TO ARREST and bring the witness *(name)* before *(name of tribunal)* to give evidence in the proceeding, and if the tribunal is not then sitting or if the witness cannot be brought forthwith before the tribunal, to deliver the witness to a provincial correctional institution or other secure facility to be admitted and detained there until his or her presence as a witness is no longer required, or until otherwise ordered.

_____

(Signature of judge)

Index to Ontario's Statutory Powers Procedure Act

[References are to sections of the Act]

APPENDICE 12

APPENDIX 12.1

EXAMPLES OF NOTICES GIVEN BY NEWSPAPER

| Canadian Artists and Producers Professional Relations Tribunal | CANADA | Tribunal canadien des relations professionnelles artistes-producteurs |

PUBLIC NOTICE 1995-2

Application for Certification:
"Union des écrivaines et écrivains québécois"

In accordance with subsection 25(3) of the *Status of the Artist Act*, the Canadian Artists and Producers Professional Relations Tribunal hereby gives notice that it has received an application for certification from "l'Union des écrivaines et écrivains québécois" (UNEQ) to represent, throughout Canada, a sector composed of:

a) authors of original French-language literary or dramatic works intended for publication; and

b) authors of French-language literary or dramatic works originally intended for the stage, radio, television, cinema or audio-visual media at the time of publication of the work in any medium and for that purpose only.

Any artists' association that wishes to make a competing application for certification in respect of the same sector or any part of the same sector must file its application for certification no later than October 20, 1995. Competing applications for certification should be sent by mail to the address below.

Any artists, artists' associations or producers affected by this application wishing to make representations to the Tribunal regarding the proposed sector must notify the Tribunal in writing of their interest no later than October 20, 1995.

Any artists or artists' associations affected by this application wishing to make representations to the Tribunal regarding the representativeness of the applicant must notify the Tribunal in writing of their interest no later than October 20, 1995.

Affected parties should make their interest known by fax or mail to the address below.

Elizabeth MacPherson
Secretary General

The Canadian Artists and Producers Professional Relations Tribunal is the federal agency that administers labour relations between self-employed workers in the cultural sector and federal producers, as prescribed by the *Status of the Artist Act.*

For more information on this application or the
Canadian Artists and Producers Professional Relations Tribunal:

1-800-263-ARTS (2787)	Postal Address:
(613) 996-4052	240 Sparks Street
Fax: (613) 947-4125	8th Floor West
Internet Address:	Ottawa, Ontario
tribunal.artists@ic.gc.ca	K1A 1A1

Canadä

Example 2

Notice of Application and Directions on Procedure
The _____ Corporation.
Application to Export Electricity to the United States

By an application dated 30 March 1995, The _____ Corp. (the "Applicant") has applied to the National Energy Board under Division II of Part VI of the National Energy Board Act for authorization to export excess electrical power on a firm or interruptible basis to various utilities and/or industrial end-users in the United States. Annual exports of not more than 3000 gigawatt-hours may originate from the provinces of British Columbia, Alberta, Saskatchewan, Manitoba and Ontario.

The Board wishes to obtain the views of interested persons on this application before issuing a permit or recommending to the Governor in Council that public hearing be held. The Directions on Procedure that follow explain in detail the procedure that will be used.

1.   The Applicant shall deposit and keep on file, for public inspection during normal business hours, copies of the application at its offices located at Suite ____, _____ Ave. S.W., Calgary, Alberta and provide a copy of the application to any person who requests a copy. A copy of the application is also available for viewing during normal business hours in the Board's library, Room 100, 311-6 Ave. S.W., Calgary, Alberta, T2P 3H2.

2.   Written submissions in respect of the application shall be filed with the Secretary, National Energy Board, 311-6 Ave. S.W., Calgary, Alberta, T2P 3H2, facsimile: (403) 292-5503, and the Applicant, Suite ____, _____Ave. S.W., Calgary, Alberta, _____facsimile _____ by July 30, 1995.

3.   Pursuant to Section 119.06(2) of the Act, the Board shall have regard to all considerations that appear to it to be relevant. In Particular, the Board is interested in the views of submittors with respect to:

    a)   the effect of the exportation of the electricity on provinces other than that from which the electricity is to be exported.

    b)   the impact of the exportation on the environment; and

    c)   whether the applicant has

        i)   informed those who have declared an interest in buying electricity for consumption in Canada of the quantities and classes of service available for sale, and

        ii)   given an opportunity to purchase electricity on terms and conditions specified in the application to those who, within a reasonable time of being so informed, demonstrate an intention to buy electricity for consumption in Canada.

4.   Any answer to submission that the Applicant wishes to present in response to items 2 and 3 of this Notice of Application and Directions on Procedure shall be filed with the Secretary of the Board and served on the party that filed the submission by 14 August, 1995.

5.   Any reply that submittors wish to present in response to item 4 of this Notice of Application and Directions on Procedure shall be filed with the Secretary of the Board and served on the Applicant by 24 August, 1995.

6.   For further information on the procedures governing the Board's review, contact J.S. Richardson, Secretary (403) 299-2711, facsimile (403) 292-5503.

Example 3   E.B.R.O. 487

THE COMSUMERS' GAS COMPANY LTD.
RATES
<u>NOTICE OF APPLICATION</u>

The attached application dated January 14, 1994 (''the Application'') has been filed by
The Consumers' Gas Company Ltd. (''Consumers Gas'') with the Ontario Energy board
(''the Board'') under section 19 of the Ontario Energy Board Act, R.S.O. 1990, c. O.13.
Any customer of Consumers Gas may be affected by the Board's decision regarding the
Application.

Paticulars of the Application

Consumers Gas has applied for an order or orders approving or fixing just and reasonable
rates and other charges for the sale, distribution, transmission, and storage of gas. The
rates and other charges for which approval is requested would be effective October 1,
1994, and would be based upon projected results for a test year commencing October 1,
1994, and ending September 30, 1995 (''the fiscal 1995 year'').

Under current rates, Consumers Gas projects a revenue shortfall of approximately $30.1
million in 1995, based on a 10.23 percent overall rate of return, which includes a return
on common equity of 12.375 percent, on a proposed rate base of $2,461 million. The
estimates of the 1995 rate base, rate of return, revenue shortfall and customer bill impacts
may be updated and amended.

The level and pattern of consumption of each customer will determine the change in each
individual customer's bill if new rates are approved to cover this forecast 1995 shortfall.
For example, the impact on a typical residential customer using 3755 cubic meters of gas
per year (for space and water heating) would be an increase of $22.00 or 2.5 percent.

Consumers Gas anticipates that changes in the amount paid by it for its supply of gas will
result from price changes and from variations in the energy content of gas purchased for
resale. Furthermore, Consumers Gas anticipates that changes in the costs of transporting
gas may result from orders of the National Energy Board after hearings into matters before
that Board related to the tolls and toll structure of TransCanada PipeLines Limited.

The Application will be supported by written and oral evidence. The written evidence will
be pre-filed and may be amended before the hearing is completed. Pre-hearing meetings
with Board Staff and other intervenors may be held to clarify the pre-filed evidence and
attempt to identify and resolve some of the issue. Any agreement reached on any issue
will be submitted to the Board for its consideration during the hearing.

Consumers Gas has also applied to the Board for such final and interim orders as may be
necessary in relation to the Application, including the disposition of the outstanding
deferral accounts and the creation of additional deferral accounts or other accounts as may
be necessary.

How to See Applicant's Pre-filed Evidence

Copies of schedules supporting the Application will be available for public inspection at the Board's offices, and at Consumers Gas' head office in North York and at Consumers Gas's regional and divisional offices in Barrie, Mississauga, North York, Ottawa, Richmond Hill, Thorold, Whitby and Peterborough (addresses below). Copies of the complete pre-filed evidence supporting the Application, when it is filed, will be available for public inspection at the same locations.

How to Intervene

If you wish to intervene (i.e. actively participate) in the proceedings relating to this Application, you must file a written notice of intervention within 14 days after this notice of application is delivered. Your notice of intervention must be delivered or mailed by registered mail to the Board Secretary and to Consumers Gas at the addresses below. The notice of intervention must state:

- your name, address, and telephone and fax numbers;
- your intention to appear and participate at the hearing;
- your interest in the Application; and
- the issues you intend to address during the proceeding.

If you wish to participate in the proceeding in the French language, your answer must state this. All intervenors granted party status by the Board will receive notice of the time and place of any pre-hearing meetings and of the hearing.

The Board Secretary will distribute a list of intervenors to all intervenors and to Consumers Gas.

Intervenor Funding

You have the right as an intervenor to apply to the Board for advance intervenor funding to assist you or your group to participate in the proceeding. Intervenor funding may be awarded only in relation to issues which affect a significant segment of the public, and affect the public interest and not just private interests.

A person seeking advance intervenor funding shall file with the Board a written notice containing a clear statement indicating that the person requires intervenor funding, and how the funds, if awarded, will be applied. This notice must be delivered to the Board Secretary together with the notice of intervention. Following the Board's determination of intervenor status, application forms for intervenor funding will be distributed, by the Board Secretary, to intervenors seeking such funding. All applications for intervenor funding must be sent to the Board Secretary and to Consumers Gas by the due date.

How To Comment

If you wish to comment on the Application without becoming an intervenor, you may write a letter of comment to the Board Secretary stating your views and any relevant information. All letters of comment will become part of the public record in the proceeding and copies will be provided to Consumers Gas. Alternatively, you may write to the Board Secretary to state that you prefer to make your comments orally at the hearing, in which case you will be notified of the time and place of the hearing, and of your presentation. If you wish to comment in the French language at the hearing, your letter must state this.

IMPORTANT

IF YOU DO NOT RESPOND TO THIS NOTICE OR INDICATE TO THE BOARD SECRETARY THAT YOU WISH TO COMMENT AT THE HEARING, THE BOARD MAY PROCEED IN YOUR ABSENCE AND YOU WILL NOT BE ENTITLED TO ANY FURTHER NOTICE OF THESE PROCEEDINGS.

Procedural Orders

The Board may issue Procedural Orders as to how the Application will proceed, and copies will be sent to all intervenors. A copy of the Board's Draft Rules of Practice and Procedure is available from the Board Secretary.

Ce document est disponible en français.

Addresses

Ontario Energy Board
P.O. Box 2319
2300 Yonge Street
26th Floor
Toronto, Ontario
M4P 1E4
Attn: Mr. Paul B. Pudge
      Board Secretary

The Board accepts collect
calls at (416) 481-1967

Head Office of Consumers Gas:

Atria III, Suite 1100
2225 Sheppard Ave. East
North York, Ontario
M2J 5C2

All documents related to this Application should be directed to the following addresses.

If sent by mail:

The Consumers' Gas Company Ltd.
P.O. Box 650
Scarborough, Ontario
M1K 5E3

Attn: Mr. Keith A. Walker
      (416) 495-5221
      (416) 495-6072 (Fax)

If delivered:

The Consumers' Gas Company Ltd.
500 Consumers Road, Willowdale, Ontario

Attn: Mr. Keith A. Walker

Regional and Divisional Offices of Consumers Gas:

North York	Mississauga
500 Consumers Road	950 Burnhamthorpe Rd. West
Ottawa	Whitby
400 Coventry Road	101 Consumers Drive
Thorold	Richmond Hill
3401 Schmon Parkway	500 Elgin Mills Road East
Barrie	Peterborough
165 Ferris Lane	1 Consumers Place

Counsel for Consumers Gas:

Aird & Berlis
BCE Place
Suite 1800, Box 754
181 Bay Street
Toronto, Ontario
M5J 2T9

Attn: Mr. P.Y. Atkinson, and
      Mr. R.J. Howe
      (416) 364-1241
      (416) 364-4916 (Fax)

    DATED at Toronto January   , 1994.

                                    ONTARIO   ENERGY
                                    BOARD

                                    _____

                                    Paul B. Pudge
                                    Board Secretary

Example 3

CRTC   **PUBLIC NOTICE**   **Canada**

Public Notice CRTC 1995 - 129   The CRTC has received a request from Television Northern Canada incorporated (TVNC) to have its network signal added to Section "A:" of the list of "Part II Eligible Satellite Services" and to the list of "Part III Eligible Canadian Satellite Services". The CRTC considers it appropriate to provide an opportunity for public comment on the proposed amendment to the lists and on whether cable distribution of TVNC should be subject to the Distant Canadian Signal (P.N. 1993-74)   Written comments should be addressed to Allan J. Darling. Secretary General, CRTC, Ottawa, Ont. K1A ON2 **by 31 August, 1995**. Complete text of this notice may be obtained by contacting the Public Examination Room at (819) 997-2429 or through the offices in Montréal (514) 283-6607, Vancouver (604) 666-2111, Winnipeg (204) 983-6306, Halifax (902) 426-7997.

[Cdn Flag] Canadian Radio-television and   Conseil de la radiodiffusion et des
           Telecommunications Commission   télécommunications canadiennes

---

Example 4

ALBERTA ENERGY AND UTILITIES BOARD
NOTICE OF A PUBLIC HEARING OF AN APPLICATION BY NOVA GAS TRANSMISSION LTD. FOR APPROVAL OF NEW RATES, TOLLS AND CHARGES
NOTICE OF PUBLIC HEARING

Nova Gas Transmission Ltd. (NGTL) has applied to the Alberta Energy and Utilities Board (the Board) by way of a general rate application (GRA) for approval of new rates, tolls and charges and changes in existing rates, tolls and charges or schedules thereof for the services performed by NGTL in relation to the gathering, treating, transporting, storing, distributing, commingling, exchanging, handling, or delivery of gas carried by its pipelines or other facilities or any parts thereof, based on the test year 1995.

NGTL became subject to the **GAS Utilities Act** and to the jurisdiction of the Board effective January 1, 1995 pursuant to the **NOVA Corporation of Alberta Act Repeal Act** as amended. A public hearing with respect to Phase I of this GRA proceeding was held commencing August 1, 1995. A Decision establishing NGTL's revenue requirement for the test year 1995 is pending.

Phase 2 of the proceedings will deal with issues such as rate design, terms and conditions of service and quality of service. A public hearing with respect to Phase 2 will be held in Govier Hall, located in the Alberta Energy and Utilities Board Offices at 640 - 5th Avenue S.W., Calgary, Alberta, commencing January 8, 1996 at 8:30 a.m. A timetable for Phase 2 of the proceedings is available from either NGTL or the Board at the addresses below.

TO SEE THE APPLICATION

Complete copies of the application are available for inspection at the Board's offices in either Edmonton or Calgary. Interested parties may arrange to examine or obtain the filed information by contacting NGTL at the addresses indicated below.

TO INTERVENE IN THE HEARING

Interested parties who have not registered in Phase I and who wish to be registered an intervenors in the Phase 2 proceeding should set out, in a written notice of intervention, their name, address and the way in which these proceedings affect them. The notice of intervention is to be delivered or mailed, prior to the hearing, to the Board and NGTL at the addresses below before September 29, 1995. All parties who are registered as intervenors will be entitled to receive from NGTL and other participants copies of all evidence and material that may be filed with respect to the matter of the GRA. Registered intervenors may submit evidence and will also be entitled to cross-examine witnesses.

Any party who does not register as an intervenor will not be entitled to further notice of these proceedings and the Board may proceed without further notice.

If you require further information regarding the hearing process, contact the Energy and Utilities Board or NGTL at the addresses listed below.

Ms. Sheila Kerr	Alberta Energy and Utilities Board
NOVA Gas Transmission	Utilities Office
P.O. Box 2535, Station "M"	3rd Floor, 640 - 5 Avenue S.W.
Calgary, Alberta, T2P 2N6	Calgary, Alberta T2P 3G4
Telephone: (403) 261-8360	Telephone: (403) 297-6306
	or
	11th Floor
	10055 - 106 Street
	Edmonton, Alberta T5J 2Y2
	Telephone (403) 427-4901

Dated at the City of Calgary in the Province of Alberta, this 30th day of August, 1995

ALBERTA ENERGY AND UTILITIES BOARD
Original signed "M. Bruni"
M. BRUNI
COUNSEL

APPENDIX 12.1.1

Sample Notices of Hearing Given By Mail

Example 1

E.B.L.O. 250
E.B.A. 689/690
E.B.C. 214/215/216

IN THE MATTER OF the Municipal Franchises Act, R.S.O. 1990, c. M.55;

AND IN THE MATTER OF an Application by The Consumers' Gas Company Ltd. for a certificate of public convenience and necessity to construct works to supply gas and to supply gas to the inhabitants of the Corporation of the Township of Russell, the Corporation of the Township of Cambridge and the Corporation of the Village of Casselman, in the United Counties of Prescott and Russell;

AND IN THE MATTER OF an Application by The Consumers' Gas Company Ltd. for an order approving the terms and conditions upon which and the period for which the Corporation of the Village of Casselman and the Corporation of the Township of Cambridge are, by-laws, to grant to The Consumers' Gas Company Limited rights to construct and to operate works for the distribution of gas and to supply gas to the inhabitants of the said municipalities;

AND IN THE MATTER OF an Application by The Consumers' Gas Company Ltd. for an order dispensing with the assent of the municipal electors of the Corporation of the Village of Casselman and the Corporation of the Township of Cambridge regarding the said by-laws;

AND IN THE MATTER OF the Ontario Energy Board Act, R.S.O. 1990, c. O.13;

AND IN THE MATTER OF an Application by The Consumers' Gas Company Ltd. for an order granting leave to construct NPS 6 and NPS 4 pipelines and ancillary facilities from the Village of Metcalfe, Township of Osgoode, Regional Municipality of Ottawa-Carleton through the Townships of Russell and Cambridge to the Village of Casselman, in the United Counties of Prescott and Russell.

NOTICE OF HEARING

TAKE NOTICE THAT the hearing of the above matters will commence at 9:00 a.m. on April 24, 1995, in the Board's hearing room, 25th floor, 2300 Yonge Street, Toronto, Ontario.

IMPORTANT

IF YOU DO NOT ATTEND AT THE COMMENCEMENT OF THE HEARING, THE BOARD MAY PROCEED IN YOUR ABSENCE AND YOU WILL NOT BE ENTITLED TO FURTHER NOTICE OF THESE PROCEEDINGS.

DATED at Toronto, March 31, 1995

ONTARIO ENERGY BOARD

_____

Paul B. Pudge
Board Secretary

Example 2 (For the Purposes of s. 6(4) of the Ontario SPPA)

File 95-09-15-5

ONTARIO _____BOARD

IN THE MATTER OF Apartment 3B, 15 Little Hill Road, Anywhere, Ontario.

AND IN THE MATTER of an application under section _____ of the Ontario _____Act, R.S.O. 1990, c. _____.

BETWEEN

X

(landlord)

-and-

Y

(tenant)

NOTICE OF WRITTEN HEARING

The Ontario _____Board has received a application under s. _____of the Ontario _____Act, R.S.O., 1990, c. _____by Y in which Y requests a declaration of the lawful rent for the above unit and an order requiring X to repay any rents paid to him by Y over the lawful rent.

Pursuant to s. _____of the Ontario _____Act, R.S.O. 1990, c. _____, and ss. 5.1 and 6(2) of the Ontario Statutory Powers Procedure Act, R.S.O. 1990, c. S.22 and in accordance with rule _____of the Rules of the Board, the Board has decided to hold a written hearing and decide this matter on the basis of the written evidence and argument made by the parties.

Any evidence or submissions which you wish to make to the Board should be filed with the Board on or before November 16th, 1995. A copy of any material filed with the Board should also be given to each of the other parties in this matter. All parties will then have until November 30th, 1995 to examine the material on file with the Board and to make any comments thereon in writing. No further information may be filed respecting this matter after that date without the leave of the Board. In the event that the Board requires further information the parties will be notified in writing.

Parties should notify the Board, at the time of filing, of any information which they believe involves matters of public security; or of any information which should not be disclosed to the public on the grounds that it contains intimate financial or personal matters or other matters in which, having regard to the circumstances, the interests of the person affected or the public interest outweigh the desirability of adhering to the principle that hearings being open to the public.

After considering the material filed by all parties the Board will issue its decision in writing, a copy of which will be mailed to all participants. In the event that the decision is not accompanied by written reasons explaining it, written reasons will be issued following the decision if requested by any party.

TAKE NOTE THAT no oral hearing will be held for this matter unless a party objects to this hearing being held as a written hearing (in which case the Board shall decide the matter through an electronic or oral hearing).

AND TAKE NOTE THAT the Board is entitled to proceed with this matter without the participation of any party who fails to either notify the Board of any objection to the hearing being held as a written hearing or to file any information with the Board respecting this matter as set out above. That party will not be entitled to any further notice in the proceeding.

A copy of the application and the material filed in support of it are available for examination at the offices of the Board.

Copies of the Board's procedural rules, and Board policies may be also obtained at the offices of the Board.

For more information please contact the Ontario _____Board, Suite 107, 33 Somewhere Street, Toronto, Ontario, M45 8P6, (416) 444-5656, facsimile (416) 444-6565

Dated at Toronto, October _____, 1995.

_____
Joan Everywoman
Board Secretary

une version française de ce document est disponible
veuillez communiquer avec la Tribunal au (416) 444-5656

Example 3

	Rent Control Programs	Programmes de contrôle de loyers
[crest] **Ontario**	255 Albert Street, 4th Fl. Ottawa, Ontario, K1P 6A9 Tel: (613) 230-5114 Fax: (613) 787-4024	255, rue Albert, 4e étage Ottawa (Ontario) K1P 6A9 Tél: (613) 230-5114 Télécopieur: (613) 787-4024

Ministry of Municipal Affairs and Housing   Ministère des Affaires municipales et du Logement

NOTICE OF HEARING
Rent Control Act, 1992

Application Number: OT-1689-TT
IN THE MATTER OF: 228 Somestreet Rd, Ottawa, Ontario
BETWEEN: John Doe   Tenant
                      -and-   Landlord
                      Jane Doe
AND IN THE MATTER OF and application by the tenant on August 14, 1995 for a rent reduction.

Pursuant to section 65 of the Rent Control Act, 1992 a hearing before a Rent Officer will be held at:
Place: 255 Albert Street, 4th Floor, Hearing Room 2, Ottawa, Ontario
Date: Thursday, October 19, 1995   **Time:**   9:00 a.m.
Purpose: To consider the issues related to the application made under section 23 of the **Rent Control Act, 1992**.

If you can't come to the hearing, you can ask someone to represent you. If you do, you must give them your authorization in writing. If you haven't already done this, you may use the Agency Authorization form below.

If you don't come to the hearing and you don't authorize someone to represent you, the Rent Officer can proceed without you. In this case you will not be entitled to any further notice about the application. You will, however, be mailed a copy of the final decision respecting the application. Please keep us informed of any changes to your mailing address.

If you have any questions please call me at the Ottawa Rent Control office at (613) 230-5114, or if calling long distance dial 1-800-263-8957.

September 8, 1995

                                         _____
                                         Mary Someone
                                         Application Analyst

(Tear off this form, fill it in and give it to your authorized agent to bring to the hearing.)

AGENCY AUTHORIZATION

Application Number: OT-1689-TT
Address of Application: 228 Somestreet Rd, Ottawa, Ontario
Agent's Name: _____
Agent's Address: _____
Telephone Number(s)   Daytime: _____Evening: _____
I,_____ (your   name,   include   unit   number   if   tenant),   authorize
_____(agent's name) to represent me at the hearing for the application shown above.

_____   _____
Date   Signature

Example 4 (Simple Letter Notice)

Dear Mrs. _____

Re: Notice of Hearing of Assessment Appeal - Parcel Number 52498

Please take notice that your assessment appeal made on the above property for the year 1992 will be heard in the Hearing Room of the Island Regulatory and Appeals Commission on October 14, 1993 at 9:00 a.m.

The appeal hearing will be conducted in accordance with the rules of natural justice. You are entitled to invite any interested parties to speak on your behalf, and to cross-examine any witnesses who may appear on behalf of the Department of Provincial Affairs.

If you have any questions, please do not hesitate to contact me.

Yours sincerely,

Chris K. Jones
Director
Land and Property

Example 5

[crest]
THE ISLAND REGULATORY AND APPEALS COMMISSION

CANADA

PROVINCE OF PRINCE EDWARD ISLAND

BEFORE THE ISLAND REGULATORY AND APPEALS COMMISSION

IN THE MATTER of Section 46 of the Petroleum Products Act, R.S.P.E.I., Chap. P-5.1

-and-

IN THE MATTER of alleged non-compliance by _____with Section 30(b) of the Petroleum Products Act, supra, and Regulation No. 4(2) made thereunder in respect of _____, located at _____, supplied by _____, owned by _____, and leased to _____ and operated by _____under Petroleum Products License No. D __

NOTICE OF HEARING

TAKE NOTICE that the attendance of _____is required at a hearing to be held before the Island Regulatory and Appeals Commission commencing at _____ o'clock in the forenoon (_____a.m.) on _____, the _____st day of _____, A.D., 199___, at the Hearing Room of the Commission, 5th Floor, 134 Kent Street, Charlottetown, Queens County, Prince Edward Island.

AND TAKE NOTICE that the purpose of this hearing is to provide an opportunity to the above-noted party to show cause why Petroleum Products License No D. _____ issued in respect of _____located at _____, P.E.I. imposed pursuant to Section 41 of the Petroleum Products Act, supra, for non-compliance with Section 30(b) of the Petroleum Products Act, supra, and Regulation No. 4(2) made pursuant thereto. It is alleged that on _____, 199___, the prices of both regular and premium grades of gasoline were in non-compliance with the Commission's Decision and Order No. P.910424 (both products were priced at _____ths of a cent per litre above the maximum allowable prices for these _____gasolines). In addition, the produce grade was not identified on either side of the premium unleaded dispensing unit. This outlet is supplied by _____owned by _____, and leased to and operated by _____

AND TAKE NOTICE that in default of an appearance of the above-noted party at the time and date set forth above, an Order under Sections 23(1) and/or 41 of the Petroleum Products Act, supra, may be made with respect to this alleged non-compliance.

AND TAKE FURTHER NOTICE that in lieu of attending at the above-noted hearing, the Commission will accept payment of _____DOLLARS ($ ___.00) in acknowledgment of these instance of non-compliance, providing payment is made to the Commission within fifteen days from the date of receipt of this Notice.

DATED at CHARLOTTETOWN, P.E.I., this ___day of _____, A.D., 199_

H. Doris Pursey, Director
Petroleum Division
Island Regulatory and Appeals Commission

TO:

COPIES:

APPENDIX 12.2

E.B.R.O. 488

IN THE MATTER OF the Ontario Energy Board Act, R.S.O. 1990, c. O.13;

AND IN THE MATTER OF an Application by Natural Resource Gas Limited to the Ontario Energy Board for an order or orders approving or fixing just and reasonable rates for the sale, distribution and transmission of gas commencing October 1, 1994.

PROCEDURAL ORDER NO. 2

Natural Resource Gas Limited (''NRG'') filed an application with the Ontario Energy Board (''the Board'') dated July 22, 1994 (''the Application''), for an order or orders approving or fixing just and reasonable rates and other charges for the sale, distribution and transmission of gas for its 1995 fiscal year commencing October 1, 1994.

The Board issued a Notice of Application dated September 2, 1994.

On September 30, 1994, the Board issued an Order declaring NRG's current rates interim effective October 1, 1994 pending the Board's final decision and order in E.B.R.O. 488.

On October 11, 1994 a Technical Conference was held for the purpose of reviewing NRG's prefiled evidence and defining the issues relevant to the hearing of the Application. All parties presented a proposed list of issues to the Board by letter dated October 26, 1994.

The Board now considers it expedient to set out the list of issues for the hearing of the Application.

THE BOARD THEREFORE ORDERS THAT:

1. The Issues List for the hearing is finalized and is set out in Appendix ''A'' to this Procedural Order.

Dated at Toronto, October 31, 1994

ONTARIO ENERGY BOARD

_____

Paul B. Pudge
Board Secretary

Appendix ''A'' to
Procedural Order No.2 in

E.B.R.O. 488
dated October 31, 1994

Paul B. Pudge
Board Secretary

E.B.R.O. 488
NATURAL RESOURCE GAS LIMITED

ISSUES LIST

A. RATE BASE

1. Economic Feasibility
2. 1995 Capital Budget
3. 1994 and 1995 Franchise Costs
4. Continuity of Property, Plant and Equipment
5. Appropriateness of Accumulated Depreciation
6. Allowance for Working Capital
7. Variance in 1994 Capital Budget to E.B.R.O. 480 Approved

B. OPERATING REVENUE

1. Customer Attachments Forecast
2. Volumes Forecast
3. Normalization Methodology
4. Forecast Methodology
5. Other Operation Revenue (Net)

C. COST OF SERVICE

1. Gas Costs
2. Operations and Maintenance Expense
   a) Wages and Benefits
   b) Regulatory
   c) Travel and Entertainment
   d) Management Fees and Office Rent
   e) Insurance Costs
   f) Automotive
   g) Advertising and Promotional
3. Depreciation Expense
4. Property and Capital Tax
5. Income Taxes
6. Deferral Accounts

D. COST OF CAPITAL

1. Capital Structure
2. Cost of Debt

3.   Cost of Equity

E. COST ALLOCATION

1.   Proposed Methodology

F. RATE DESIGN

1.   Proposed Rates
2.   T-service Rate
3.   Monthly Customer Charge
4.   Long-term Rate Proposals
5.   Retroactivity — Revenue Deficiency or Excess

APPENDIX 12.3

Affidavit of Service

IN THE MATTER OF the Ontario Energy Board Act, R.S.O. 1990, Chapter O.13;

AND IN THE MATTER OF an application by Haldimand Gas and Oil Wells Limited to discontinue service to its customers;

I, Angela Kaija of the Municipality of Metropolitan Toronto in the Judicial District of York, make oath and say as follows:

A.   I am a Records Management Clerk employed by the Ontario Energy Board and as such have knowledge of the matters hereinafter set forth.

B.   I did no Friday, November 1, 1985 personally serve:

   1) Mr. Harold Nichol with a copy of the Notice of Application and Hearing attached hereto as Appendix "A", by leaving the same with the said Harold Nichol at his residence on R.R. #5, Hagersville, Ontario.

   2) Mr. James Nichol with a copy of the said Notice by leaving the same with the said James Nichol at his residence on R.R. #5, Hagersville, Ontario.

   3) Mr. Ken Link with a copy of the said Notice by leaving the same with the said Ken Link as his residence on R.R. #2, Cayuga, Ontario.

   4) Mr. Earl Link with a copy of the said Notice by leaving the same with the said Earl Link at his residence on R.R. #2, Cayuga, Ontario.

   5) Mr. Harold Bacher with a copy of the said Notice by leaving the same with the said Harold Bacher at his residence on R.R. #3, Cayuga, Ontario.

   6) Mr. John Hanenburg with a copy of the said Notice by leaving the same with the said John Hanenburg at his residence on R.R. #3, Cayuga, Ontario.

   7) Mr. Harry Kline with a copy of the said Notice by leaving the same with the said Harry Kline at his residence on R.R. #3, Cayuga, Ontario.

   8) Ms. Rena Richert with a copy of the said Notice by leaving the same with the said Rena Richert at her residence on R.R. #3, Cayuga, Ontario.

   9) Mr. Richard Schweyer with a copy of the said Notice by leaving the same with the said Richard Schweyer at his residence on R.R. #3, Cayuga, Ontario.

   10) Mr. Paul Cavanagh with a copy of the said Notice by leaving the same with the said Paul Cavanagh at his place of business, Cavanagh's IDA Pharmacy in Hagersville, Ontario.

   11) Walter Armstrong with a copy of the said Notice by leaving the same with Neale Armstrong, an adult person identified to me as the son of Waler Armstrong at the residence of Walter Armstrong on R.R. #2, Cayuga, Ontario.

APP-74.3   (A.T.) (1996 — Rel. 1)

12) Mr. Michael Gale with a copy of the said Notice by leaving the same with Patricia Gale, identified to me as the spouse of Michael Gale at the residence of Michael Gale on R.R. #3, Fisherville, Ontario.

13) Mr. William Waldbrook with a copy of the said Notice by leaving the same with Ms. Mary Jepson, identified to me as the spouse of William Waldbrook at the residence of William Waldbrook on R.R. #5, Hagersville, Ontario.

14) Mr. Keith Winger with a copy of the said Notice by leaving the same with Mrs. Keith Winger, identified to me as the spouse of Keith Winger at the residence of Keith Winger on R.R. #3, Cayuga, Ontario.

15) Mr. Frank Bakker with a copy of the said Notice by leaving the same with Edward Bakker, an adult person identified to me as the son of Frank Bakker at the residence of Frank Bakker on R.R. #3, Cayuga, Ontario.

16) Mr. Andrew Pollman with a copy of the said Notice by leaving the same with Mrs. A. Pollman, identified to me as the spouse of Andrew Pollman at the residence of Andrew Pollman on R.R. #3, Cayuga, Ontario.

17) Mr. Allan Bothwright with a copy of the said Notice by leaving the same with Mrs. A. Bothwright, identified to me as the spouse of Allan Bothwright at the residence of Allan Bothwright on R.R. #2, Cayuga, Ontario.

18) Mr. Carl Schweyer with a copy of the said Notice by leaving the same with Richard Schweyer, an adult person identified to me as the brother of Carl Schweyer at the residence of Richard and Carl Schweyer on R.R. #3, Cayuga, Ontario.

19) Mr. Bruce Mehlenbacher with a copy of the said Notice by leaving the same with Mrs. B. Mehlenbacher, identified to me as the spouse of Bruce Mehlenbacher at the residence of Bruch Mehlenbacher on R.R. #3, Cayuga, Ontario.

20) The Fire Hall with a copy of the said Notice by leaving the same with Dan Burgener, identified to me as the Secretary of the Fire Hall at the Municipal Affairs Building in Cayuga, Ontario.

21) The Town of Clerk of Haldimand with a copy of the said Notice by leaving the same with the said Town Clerk, Shirley Troubridge at her place of business, the Municipal Affairs Building on Cayuga, Ontario.

22) Mr. Faith Nablo with a copy of the said Notice by leaving the same with Mrs. A. Bothwright, identified to me as the daughter of Faith Nablo at the residence of Mrs. Bothwright on R.R. #2, Cayuga, Ontario. On Saturday, November 2, 1985, I spoke personally with Faith Nablo and confirmed that she did, in fact, receive the said Notice.

23) Mr. Clarence Bacher with a copy of the said Notice by leaving the same with Rena Richert, an adult person identified to me as a friend of Clarence Bacher with whom he was dining that evening, at the residence of Rena Richert, I subsequently telephoned Clarence Bacher to confirm that he had, in fact, received a copy of the said Notice.

24) Mr. Hugh Slimon with a copy of the said Notice by leaving the same with Laura Jane Slimon, an adult person identified to me as a secretary employed by Gallagher & Slimon at their place of business in Cayuga, Ontario.

C. I did on Saturday, November 2, 1985 personally serve:

1) Mr. Peter Paine with a copy of the said Notice by leaving the same with the said Peter Pain at his residence on Regional Road, Fisherville, Ontario.

2) Mr. Glen Helka with a copy of the said Notice by leaving the same with the said Glen Helka at his residence in Murphy's Harbour.

3) Mr. Murray Kruger with a copy of the said Notice by leaving the same with the said Murray Kruger at his residence on R.R. #1, Fisherville, Ontario.

4) Mr. Ian Bell with a copy of the said Notice by leaving the same with the said Ian Bell at his residence on R.R. #3, Cayuga, Ontario.

5) Kohler Gas with a copy of the said Notice by leaving the same with Faith Nablo, an adult person identified to me as the Secretary of Kohler Gas at the residence of Faith Nablo on R.R. #3, Cayuga, Ontario.

6) Mr. Joseph Curtis with a copy of the said Notice by leaving the same with Mrs. J. Curtis, identified to me as the spouse of Joseph Curtis at the residence of Joseph Curtis on R.R. #1, Fisherville, Ontario

7) Mr. Medric Legault with a copy of the said Notice by leaving the same with Joseph Legault, an adult person identified to me as the son of Medric Legault at the residence of Medric Legault on R.R. #1, Fisherville, Ontario.

8) Mr. Andrew Mehlenbacher with a copy of the said Notice by leaving the same with Mrs. A. Mehlenbacher, identified to me as the spouse of Andrew Mehlenbacher at the residence of Andrew Mehlenbacker on R.R. #3, Cayuga, Ontario.

9) Mr. Gerald Swent with a copy of the said Notice by leaving the same with the said Gerald Swent at his residence in Binbrook, Ontario

10) Mr. Henry VanMerkerk with a copy of the said Notice by leaving the same with the said Henry VanMerkerk at a neighbour's residence on R.R. #3, Cayuga, Ontario. The person with whom I left the said Notice identified himself to me as Henry VanMerkerk, a customer of Haldimand Gas and Oil Wells Limited.

Sworn before me in the Municipality of Metropolitan Toronto, in the Judicial District of York, this 7th day of November, 1985.

S.A.C. Thomas
A Commissioner
for Oaths in Ontario.

Angela Kaija

APPENDIX 12.4

NOTICE OF INTERVENTION

IN THE MATTER OF sections 46 and 48 of the _____
Act, R.S.O. 1990, c. _____;

AND IN THE MATTER OF the application by "Y" Gas
Limited to the Ontario _____ Board dated _____
to combine and amend E.B.L.O. # _____, and for an
Order or Orders granting leave to construct natural gas pipelines
and ancillary facilities affecting:

a) the City of Hamilton, the Towns of Ancaster and Dundas and
   the Township of Flamborough and Glanbrook, all in the Regional Municipality of Hamilton Wentworth;

b) the Township of North Dumfries, in the Regional Municipality of Waterloo and the Township of Flamborough, in the
   Regional Municipality of Hamilton-Wentworth.

INTERVENTION OF ECONOMICAL SAVERS OF ONTARIO INC.

TAKE NOTICE that Economical Savers of Ontario Inc. ("Economical Savers")
wishes to intervene in these proceedings.

1. Economical Savers is a non-profit corporation dedicated to promoting the economic
operation of public utilities in Ontario and maintaining the present level of economic
security enjoyed by the people of Ontario. Its headquarters is located in the city of Hamilton
and it comprises a membership of over 6,000 of the citizens living in the city of Hamilton
and surrounding environs.

2. Many of Economical Savers members are customers of "Y" Gas Limited ("Y").
Economical Savers is concerned that the construction of new pipeline facilities by Y may
not be economically feasibility at this time and will not promote sound economic operation
of public utilities. It is also concerned that this construction may affect the rates paid by
the members of Economical Savers who are clients of Y.

3. Economical Savers wishes to intervene in this matter in order to test the operating
hypothesis and data of Y to ensure the economic feasibility of the construction and to
make argument as to whether the application made by Y should be granted.

4. Economical Savers wishes to receive the pre-filed evidence and all other material made available to intervenors.

5. The address of Economical Savers is _____, Attention Robert J.L. Browne.

Dated _____, 1987.

Economical Savers Inc.

by its solicitors

Smith, Jones and Jones
P.O. Box 45
34 Anystreet
Toronto, Ontario
M8P 4L7

(416) 999-9999

Attn: Andrew P.B. Smith

APPENDIX 12.5

Procedural Order

Re: Interrogatories — How a Party May Intervene and Put Interrogatories
to Opposing Parties

IN THE MATTER OF the _____
Act, R.S.O. 1990, Chapter O.13 as
amended;

AND IN THE MATTER OF an application by ICG Utilities (Ontario) Ltd. to
the Ontario Energy Board, under the
provisions of Section 19 of the said Act
for an Order or Orders approving or fixing just and reasonable rates and other
charges for the sale of gas.

BEFORE:	R.W. Macaulay, Q.C.	)	
	Chairman and	)	
	Presiding Member	)	September 23, 1987
		)	
	O.J. Cook	)	
	Member	)	

Procedural Order

UPON ICG Utilities (Ontario) Ltd. ("ICG") having applied to the Ontario Energy
Board (the "Board") pursuant to section 19 of the Ontario Energy Act (the "Act") for
an Order or Orders approving or fixing just and reasonable rates and other charges for its
sale of gas for the 1988 fiscal year commencing January 1, 1988, as set out in its application
dated September 9, 1987 (the "Application");

AND WHEREAS it is expedient to make provisions for and related to the hearing of
this Application;

THE BOARD ORDERS THAT:

1. Intervenors who file answers in accordance with the Board's Notice of Application
   and Hearing dated September 11, 1987, and who wish information and material from
   ICG that is in addition to the evidence filed with the Board and that is relevant to the
   hearing, shall request the same by written interrogatories filed with the Board and
   delivered to ICG on or before 4:00 p.m. on Friday, October 9, 1987.

2. ICG shall deliver to intervenors and file with the Board responses to intervenors'
   interrogatories on or before 4:00 p.m. Wednesday, October 21, 1987.

3. Intervenors who wish to present evidence to the Board shall file that evidence with the Board and deliver that evidence to ICG and all other intervenors on or before Friday, October 23, 1987.

4. Filing, in this Order, means having the relevant document(s) in the hands of the Board Secretary no later than the dates and times specified herein.

ISSUED at Toronto this 23th day of September, 1987.

_____Board

_____

S.A.C. Thomas
Board Secretary

APPENDIX 12.6

Interrogatory with Answer

Ontario Energy Board
E.B.L.O. 218/219

TransCanada's Responses to Consumers Interrogatories

Question 1: In TransCanada's 1988 and 1989 Facilities Application at Tab Financial, Table 5, revised 87/09/25 TCPL presents its expected Eastern Zone 100% load Factor Toll.

(a) Please confirm that tolls presented in this table under column "With Proposed Facilities" include an NPS 36 Kirkwall Pipeline constructed by TCPL.

(b) Assuming Union Gas constructs the Kirkwall Pipeline, what would the corresponding Eastern Zone 100% load factor tolls be for:

(i) NPS 24 Kirkwall pipeline
(ii) NPS 36 Kirkwall pipeline

Response: (a) Yes, the tolls presented in Tab Financial, Table 5, for the "With Proposed Facilities" case were derived assuming that an NPS 36 Kirkwall Line would be constructed by TransCanada for November 1, 1989 in service.

(b) TransCanada is not in agreement with the capital cost estimates for the NPS 24 and NPS 36 Kirkwall Pipeline provided by Union. In order to provide a fair comparison, all tolls provided below are based on capital costs estimated by Union in their response to O.E.B. Staff Interrogatory, Question 12 for service in contract year 1988/89.

As M12 rates provided by Union were available only for fiscal 1990, tolls for contract year 1988/90 are provided below.

Eastern Zone 100% L.F. Toll, $/GJ
Operating Year Ending October 31, 1990

	NPS 36	NPS 24
Union Builds Kirkwall Line	0.978	0.978
TransCanada Builds Kirkwall Line	0.980	0.979

For information purposes, a projected cost summary is also provided to indicate the annual savings to Ontario distributors in contract year 1989/90 if TransCanada constructs the Kirkwall Line for service commencing 1988/89.

	Savings on Union ($ 000)	Increased Costs on TransCanada ($ 000)	Net Savings ($ 000)
NPS 35			
Consumers'	2915	695	2220
Union	967	532	435
Ontario, all	3972	1313	2659
NPS 24			
Consumers'	1981	407	1574
Union	657	312	345
Ontario, all	2700	769	1931

In addition to the Ontario customers, Gas Metro would have the following savings in contract year 1989/90.

	Savings on Union ($ 000)	Increased Costs on TransCanada ($ 000)	Net Savings ($ 000)
NPS 36	367	239	128
NPS 24	249	140	109

Question 2: If Consumers' Gas were to contract with TCPL to supply Consumers' Gas Niagara Region using storage gas what demand and commodity tolls would be applicable if:

(a) TCPL built the Kirkwall pipeline? or
(b) Union Gas built the Kirkwall pipeline?

Response: (a) While at the present time TransCanada's STS tolls are calculated using 1975 system average costs, for the purpose of this response, estimated 1990 system average cost of transmission calculated on the same basis as TransCanada's response to Question ' have been used to calculate the tolls.

If TCPL built ain NPS 36 Kirkwall Line, then for service from Kirkwall to Blackhorse (a distance of 93.2 km) the toll would be as follows:

Demand Toll	$= \$36.150/10^3 m^3/mo$
Commodity Toll	$= \$0.882/10^3 m^3$
CD Toll at 100% LF	$= \$2.071/10^3 m^3$

For an NPS 24 line, the toll would be as follows:

Demand Toll $= \$36.105/10^3 m^3/mo$

Commodity Toll $= \$ 0.882/10^3 m^3$

CD Toll at 100% LF $= \$2.070/10^3 m^3$

(b) If Union Gas built an NPS 36 Kirkwall Line, then for service from MLV 208A + 2.8 km to Blackhorse (a distance of 6.23) km) the toll would be as follows:

Demand Toll $= \$27,028/10^3 m^3/mo$
Commodity Toll $= \$ 0.882/10^3 m^3$
CD Toll at 100% LF $= \$ 1.771.10^3 m^3$

For an NPS 24 line, the toll would be as follows:

Demand Toll $= \$27,019/10^3 m^3/mo$
Commodity Toll $= \$ 0.882/10^3 m^3$
CD Toll at 100% LF $= \$ 1.771.10^3 m^3$

Question 3: At paragraph 16 of Union's evidence, Union stated that compression is to be added at the Greenbelt to accommodate increased requirements by S&T customers. Did Union approach TCPL on the possibility of using exchange volumes through either TCPL or Union's proposed Kirkwall pipeline to supply these incremental markets? Would an exchange agreement be an effective way of accommodating volumes?

Response: Yes, in our view, an exchange agreement, as contemplated above, would be an effective way of accommodating volumes.

TransCanada PipeLines Limited

TABLE 5

EASTERN ZONE 100% L.F. TOLL
($/GJ)

CONTRACT YEAR	WITH PROPOSED FACILITIES	WITHOUT PROPOSED FACILITIES	DIFFERENCE
1988-89	0.988	1.011	(0.023)
1989-90	0.981	0.988	(0.007)
1990-91	1.005	1.026	(0.021)
1991-92	1.024	1.040	(0.016)
1992-93	1.048	1.061	(0.013)
1993-94	1.072	1.080	(0.008)
1994-95	1.097	1.099	(0.002)
1995-96	1.122	1.119	(0.003)
1996-97	1.146	1.136	(0.010)
1997-98	1.173	1.157	(0.016)

1998-99	1.211	1.191	(0.020)
1999-2000	1.248	1.222	(0.026)
2000-01	1.288	1.256	(0.032)
2001-02	1.331	1.292	(0.039)
2002-03	1.357	1.333	(0.024)
2003-04	1.403	1.373	(0.030)
2004-05	1.448	1.417	(0.031)

APPENDIX 12.7

Tribunal Subpoena[1]

IN THE MATTER OF THE (*title and citation of statute under which proceedings take place*)

SUMMONS TO A WITNESS BEFORE (*name of agency*)

RE: (*the title of the proceedings to which the summons relates*)

TO: (*name and address of person to be summoned*)

YOU ARE HEREBY SUMMONED AND REQUIRED TO ATTEND BEFORE THE (*name of agency issuing summons*) at a hearing to be held (*detailed information respecting place of hearing: municipal address, relevant room number, if any, city and province*) on _____day, the _____day of _____, 19__ at the hour of _____o'clock in the (*morning or afternoon*) and so forth from day to day until the hearing is concluded or the (*name of agency*) otherwise orders, to give evidence on oath touching the matters in question in the proceedings and to bring with you and produce at such time and place

_____

_____

Dated at _____, this _____day of _____, 19__.

(*Name of Agency*)

_____
(*Signature of issuing officer*)
(*Title of issuing officer*)

NOTE:
You are entitled to be paid the same personal allowance for your attendance at the hearings as are paid for the attendance of a witness summoned to attend before the _____ Court.

If you fail to attend and give evidence at the hearing, or to produce the documents of things specified, at the time and place specified, without lawful excuse, you are liable to punishment by the _____ Court in the same manner as if for contempt of that court for disobedience to a subpoena (adjust if the agency possess the appropriate contempt power and would hold the contempt proceedings itself)

_____

1 This is an example of a generic subpoena. Some legislation, such as Ontario's Statutory Powers Procedure Act, prescribes a specific form of subpoena which must be used. For the form of subpoena prescribed under the SPPA see the Legislation tab.

APPENDIX 12.7.1

Hearing Room Set-ups

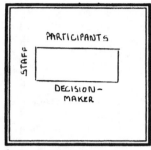

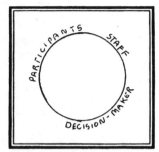

1. The Single Table: Rectangle   **2.** The Single Table: Round

Suitable: For only single decision-maker proceedings (with little documentary evidence) which is expected to proceed on an informal basis (eg. ADR or pre-hearing conferences) over a relatively short period of time. Note that this arrangement can accommodate only small numbers of people, does not really allow for testimony by non-party witnesses. There is little privacy available to the participants as everyone's notes and papers can easily be read by the other attendees. Only a single door need be provided for participants, staff and member.

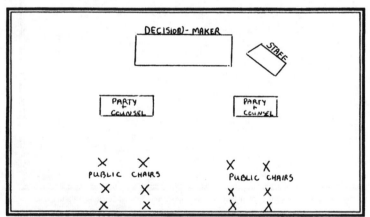

3. The Small Formal Hearing Room

Suitable: For smaller, formal hearings usually involving only one decision-maker, two parties, no intervenors and with no, or very few non-party witnesses. Any non-party witnesses that there are should give evidence from their seats. (They may come to the front to be sworn if necessary.) Only a single door for parties, staff and decision-maker is required.

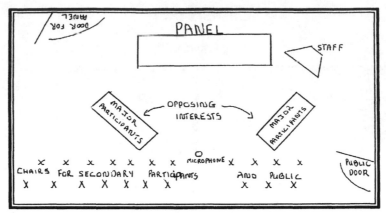

4. The Large Hearing Room For Two Primary and Several Secondary Participants

Suitable: For larger formal hearings where there will be a panel presiding or where there will be many participants but where one expects most of the particpantation will come from two primary participants with only periodic or lesser particpation from others. Note that the primary participants tables should be at an angle to allow the secondary particpants to see and hear them easily.

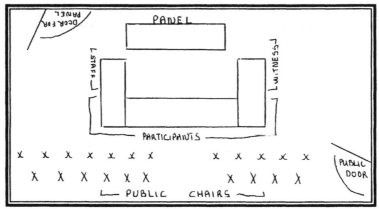

5. The Large Hearing Room For Greater Number of Primary and Several Secondary Participants

Suitable: For larger formal hearings where there will be a panel presiding or where there will be many participants but where one expects most of the particpantation will come from four primary participants with only periodic or lesser particpation from others. (Note that individuals sitting outside the square may find it more difficult to hear the participants at the squate who sit with their backs to the public.) In both examples 4 and 5 microphones will be useful in ensuring that everyone can hear. (They may be placed before each panel member, at the particpant tables, the witness stand, and centrally located in the public seating area if one expects evidence to be given from there rather than from a witnesses stand.)

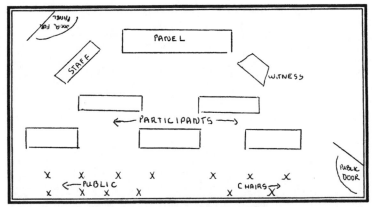

6. The Large Hearing Room For Greater Number of Active Participants

Suitable: Examples 6 (above) and 7 (below) are for larger formal hearings where there will be a panel presiding or where there will be many active participants or where the participants are expected to have to take notes or otherwise manipute documents. (Note the same hearing problem will exist for individuals sitting behind the speaker if there is no sound system.) The agency and participants tables must be large enough to accommodate up to four indiviudals with papers and files.

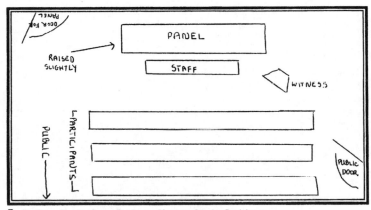

7. The Large Hearing Room For Greater Number of Active Participants

(*Continued on page APP-75*)

APPENDIX 12.8

Draft Rules of Practice and Procedure for OEB

1. These Rules may be cited as the Ontario Energy Board Rules of Practice and Procedure.

INTERPRETATION

2. In these Rules,

"Act" means the Ontario Energy Board Act;

"affidavit" includes a written affirmation;

"applicant", when used in connection with proceedings commenced by an application to the Board, means a person who makes an application, and, when used in connection with proceedings commenced by the Board on its own motion or by reference from the Lieutenant Governor in Council, the Minister of Energy or the Minister of Natural Resources, means the person deemed by the Board to be the applicant;

"application" means any application to the Board under the Act or any other Act;

"Board" means the Ontario Energy Board;

"document" includes any notice, application, notice of motion, intervention, reply or response to any interrogatory and, in addition to any other written documentation, includes graphs, maps, surveys, films, tapes, photographs and other materials;

"file" means file with the Board;

"interrogatory" means request in writing for information or particulars made from a party in a proceeding to any other party in the proceeding;

"intervenor" means a person, other than the applicant and the Board Staff, who files a written intervention pursuant to rule 29;

"motion" means a request for relief made in a proceeding or in an intended proceeding;

"party" means the applicant, Board staff and any person given status by the Board to be a party in the proceeding;

"proceeding" means any proceeding before the Board under the Act or any other Act;

"reference" means any reference made to the Board under the Act or any other Act;

"regulations" means any regulations made under the Act;

"written evidence" means information and material,

(a) in written form with consecutively numbered paragraphs;
(b) in written question and answer form with lines numbered; or
(c) in a form approved by the Board,

intended to be presented by a party as evidence and prepared by or under the direction of the person who will be available for questioning at any ensuing hearing and shall include a statement of the author's qualifications.

(A.T.)(1988)

Application of Rules

3.　Subject to rules 4 and 5, these Rules apply to all proceedings except where the context otherwise requires.

PART I — GENERAL

Orders on Procedure

4.　(1)　In any proceeding, the Board may issue orders on procedure which shall govern the conduct of the proceeding.

(2)　The Board may, at any time during a proceeding, amend any orders on procedure.

5.　In any proceeding, where the Board is satisfied that the special circumstances of the proceeding so require, the Board may by order dispense with, vary or supplement any of the provisions of these Rules.

Extending or Abridging Time

6.　The Board may, upon motion by any party or on its own motion, and upon such terms as it considers proper, extend or abridge the time prescribed by these Rules or otherwise directed by the Board, and may exercise this power although the application therefor is not made until after the expiry of the time prescribed.

Service

7.　(1)　Subject to subrule (3), service of any document, including a document originated by the Board, may be effected by personal service, in which case service shall be deemed to have been made on the date of delivery, or by registered mail, in which case service shall be deemed to have been made on the fifth day after the date of mailing, or otherwise as the Board may direct.

(2)　Service of any document may be on a party to the proceeding or on the authorized representative of the party where named in the application or intervention.

(3)　Where a public hearing is in progress, service of any document may be effected:

(a)　by making copies of the document available to the parties present at the public hearing;

(b)　by serving a copy on any other party who is not present and requests a copy; and,

(c)　as directed by the Board.

(4)　The Board may direct service of any document by public advertisement and any such service shall be deemed to be effected on the last day of publication.

(5)　An affidavit of proof of service and the means used to effect service shall, on the direction of the Board, be filed in respect of any document required to be served.

Filing

8. (1) Filing of any document may be personal or by registered mail or otherwise as the Board may direct.

    (2) Filing by registered mail is deemed to be effected on the fifth day after the date of mailing.

    (3) Subject to subrule (2), where any document is required to be filed, the date of filing shall be the date of actual receipt by the Board Secretary or anyone authorized by the Board to receive such document and where the document is received after the Board's business hours, it shall be deemed to have been filed on the next day that the Board's offices are open.

Affidavits

9. (1) Affidavits in a proceeding shall be filed as directed by the Board.

    (2) Where an affidavit is made as to information or belief, the source of the information or the grounds on which the belief is based shall be set out in the affidavit.

Verification

10. The Board may, at any time, require the whole or any part of any document filed to be verified by affidavit by issuing an order to that effect to the person from whom such verification is required.

Failure to Comply

11. (1) Where a party to a proceeding has not complied with any requirements of these Rules or any orders on procedure issued by the Board, the Board may,

    (a) stay the proceeding until satisfied that such requirements or orders have been complied with;

    (b) set aside the application, notice of motion, intervention, reply, or an interrogatory or response thereto, or strike out any part thereof; or

    (c) take such other steps as it considers just and reasonable.

    (2) No proceeding is invalid by reason only of a defect or other irregularity in form.

Formulation of Issues

12. In any proceeding the Board may direct the parties to make submissions in writing or may designate the first day of the proceeding as a pre-hearing conference, for the purpose of:

    (a) formulating or simplifying issues;

    (b) amending an application, intervention or reply for the purposes of clarification, amplification or limitation;

(c) admitting certain facts or proof of them by affidavit, or the use by any party of documents of a public nature;

(d) settling matters connected with interrogatories;

(e) deciding the procedure to be adopted in the proceeding;

(f) exchanging documents among the parties;

(g) setting the date and place for commencement of the hearing;

(h) deciding any other matters that may aid in the simplification or most just disposition of the proceeding.

Questions of Law

13. If it appears to the Board at any time that there is a question or issue of law or of jurisdiction or of practice or procedure that should be decided before a proceeding continues, the Board may,

(a) direct the question or issue to be raised for determination by the Board, or

(b) may state a case on a question of law as provided in the Act,

and the Board may, pending the determination of such question or issue, order the whole or any part of the proceeding to be stayed.

Production of Documents

14. (1) Where in any document filed by a party in connection with an application or a reference, a party refers to another document upon which the party intends to rely, any other party may, before the hearing, serve notice in writing, which shall be filed, upon the party from whom the document is requested, to produce that document for inspection and copying.

    (2) Any party who fails to comply with the notice given pursuant to subrule (1), before the earlier of ten days or the hearing of the proceeding and within 10 days of the receipt thereof, shall not thereafter put the requested document in evidence in the proceeding unless the Board is satisfied that there is sufficient excuse for the failure to file the document or the public interest otherwise requires.

Additional Information

15. At any time in a proceeding, the Board may order any party to provide such further information, particulars or documents as the Board deems necessary to enable the Board to obtain a full and satisfactory understanding of the subject of the proceeding.

Interrogatories

16. (1) Where a public hearing is to be held, the Board may permit interrogatories necessary to,

(a) simplify the issues;

(b) permit a full and satisfactory understanding of the matters to be considered; or

(c) expedite the proceeding,

to be directed by a party to any other party.

(2) Interrogatories shall be:

(a) addressed to the party from whom the response is sought;

(b) numbered consecutively in respect of each item of information requested, or as directed by the Board; and

(c) filed and served as directed by the Board.

Responses to Interrogatories

17. (1) Subject to subrule (2), where interrogatories have been directed to a party and served on that party within the time limit set by the Board, the party shall:

(a) provide a full and adequate response to each interrogatory on a separate page or pages; and

(b) file and serve a copy of the responses as directed by the Board.

(2) A party who is unable or unwilling to provide a full and adequate response to an interrogatory shall:

(a) (i) where the party contends that the interrogatory is not relevant, provide a response that sets out reasons in support of that contention;

(ii) where the party contends that the information necessary to provide an answer is not available or cannot with reasonable effort be provided, provide a response that sets out the reasons for the unavailability of such information and provide any alterantive available information that the party considers would be of assistance to the person directing the interrogatory;

(iii) where the party contends that the information sought is of a confidential nature, provide a response that sets out the reasons why it is considered confidential; or

(iv) otherwise explain why such an answer cannot be given; and

(b) file and serve a copy of the response provided as directed by the Board.

Summons

18. (1) A party who requires the attendance of a person in Ontario as a witness at a hearing may obtain a summons on request from the Board and the summons may also require the person to produce at the hearing documents and items specified in the summons.

(2) A summons shall be served personally on the person to whom it is directed at least 48 hours before the time fixed for the attendance of the person unless otherwise directed by the Board and, at the same time, that person shall be paid the same fees and allowances as are paid for the attendance of a witness summoned to attend before the Supreme Court.

(A.T.)(1988)

(3) A summons shall be in Form I and signed by an authorized representative of the Board and may be issued in blank and completed by the party or authorized representative of the party on whose behalf it is issued and may contain the names of any number of persons required to appear before the Board.

(4) A person seeking to challenge a summons must first make that challenge before the Board.

Evidence in Other Proceedings

19. Subject to section 63 of the Act, information or evidence received in any other proceeding before the Board or any other tribunal or any report, decision, finding or order made in respect thereof may, by leave of the Board, be received in the proceeding.

Form of Documents

20. (1) Every document made or submitted by any party in a proceeding shall be on either letter or metric size paper and the text shall be printed, typed, written or reproduced legibly (where practicable on both sides of each page) with double spaces between the lines.

(2) Every document filed in connection with any proceedcing shall be marked with the Board file number.

(3) Notwithstanding subrules (1) and (2), a letter under rule 28 may be in any form.

Amendments

21. (1) In a proceeding, the Board may, on condition or otherwise:
    (a) allow an amendment to any document;
    (b) order to be amended or struck out any document or any part thereof that may tend to prejudice, embarrass or delay a fair hearing of an application on the merits; or
    (c) order any other amendments that may be necessary for the purpose of hearing and determining the real question in issue in the proceeding.

(2) Where a document, or part thereof, made or submitted by any party in connection with a proceeding, is revised or amended:
    (a) each revised or amended page shall clearly indicate:
        (i) the date of revision or amendment, and
        (ii) the portion of the page revised or amended with a vertical line in the right hand margin opposite to the revision or amendment, with an asterisk or with other similar markings; and
    (b) each revision or amendment shall be accompanied with a statement explaining the nature of the amendment or revision.

Notice of Motion

22. (1) Any matter which arises in the course of a proceeding and which requires a decision or order of the Board shall be brought before the Board by notice of motion.

(2) A notice of motion shall be in writing and may be in any form provided that it contains a clear and concise statement of the facts, the order or the decision sought and the grounds therefor.

(3) A notice of motion shall be filed and served on all parties at least two days before the motion is heard.

(4) Any party who wishes to answer the motion may file and serve on all parties a written answer not later than 4:00 p.m. on the day before the motion is heard.

(5) Any document which a party may wish to submit in support of a notice of motion or answer shall accompany the notice or answer in question and shall be filed and served on all parties.

(6) Notwithstanding subrules (2) to (5), a notice of motion given during the course of a public hearing may be given orally at the public hearing and shall be disposed of in accordance with such procedures as the Board conducting the public hearing may direct.

PART II: PROCEEDINGS

Commencement of Proceedings

23. (1) Subject to this rule, a proceeding, other than a reference by the Lieutenant Governor in Council or the Minister of Energy or the Minister of Natural Resources, shall be commenced by filing an application.

(2) A proceeding initiated by the Board may be commenced by notice issued by the Board to the party affected and to such other persons as the Board considers appropriate or otherwise as the Board may direct.

(3) A proceeding initiated by a reference or an order in council may be commenced by notice issued by the Board or otherwise as the Board may direct.

(4) Where a party seeks to obtain,

   (a) an exemption from the requirements of subsection 46(1) of the Act; or

   (b) an approval, consent or determination provided for in a system of accounts prescribed under the Act and the regulations,

a proceeding may be commenced by the party by mailing or delivering a letter to the Board, signed in the case of a corporation by an officer thereof, setting forth the exemption, approval, consent or determination requested, and in such case the provisions with respect to applications and interventions do not apply.

Applications

24. An application shall be in writing and be signed by the applicant or authorized representative of the applicant.

25. (1) Every application shall,

   (a) contain a clear and concise statement of the facts, the grounds for the application, the statutory provision under which it is made, the nature of the order or decision applied for;

(b) be divided into paragraphs, numbered consecutively, each of which is confined as nearly as possible to a distinct portion of the subject of the application;

(c) where the applicant is of the opinion that the application affects any person other than the applicant,

    (i) set out the name and address of that other person, or

    (ii) in the case of any application where it is impractical to set out the names and addresses of all persons affected by the application because they are too numerous or for any other reason, set out

    (A) the reason that it is impractical to set out the names and addresses,

    (B) a general description of the persons affected by the application, and

    (C) a brief statement as to the effect on those affected;

(d) be endorsed with the full name, and telephone number of the applicant and of the authorized representative of the applicant upon whom documents may be served; and

(e) be filed in triplicate.

(2) The style of proceeding of an application shall:

(a) state the name of the applicant;

(b) describe the general nature of the application and the relief sought; and

(c) contain a reference to the statutory provision under which the application is made.

(3) Upon the filing of an application, the Board:

(a) shall give directions as to the form and service of notice of application; and

(b) shall give directions as to the form and service of notice of hearing; and

(c) may direct service of a combined notice of application and hearing, where, at the time it gives directions for service of notice of application, it sets a date for hearing the application.

Other Proceedings

26. Where the proceeding is initiated by the Board or by a reference or order in council, the Board may give directions as to the form and service of the notice of hearing.

Written Evidence

27. (1) Where the Board requires the preparation of written evidence as evidence incidental to a proceeding, such evidence shall be filed and served as directed by the Board.

(2) Where a party is unable to submit such written evidence as directed by the Board, the party shall:

(a) submit such evidence as is available at that time;

(b) identify the balance of the written evidence to be submitted; and

(c) state when the balance of the required written evidence will be submitted.

(3) Where a party is unwilling to submit any written evidence required, the party shall submit a statement setting out the objection and the grounds therefor for the written evidence not submitted.

(4) Where the Board does not sustain an objection taken pursuant to subrule (3), the Board shall so inform the party and the party shall submit the written evidence within the time set out by the Board.

(5) Where any written evidence required to be submitted to the Board is already in the possession of the Board, the written evidence may be omitted, but the party shall, in a statement, identify the written evidence and the circumstances under which it came into the possession of the Board.

Letters of Comment

28. (1) Where notice has been given of a proceeding, any interested person, who does not wish to intervene in respect of the proceeding but who wishes to communicate views to the Board regarding the matter, may file a letter commenting on the matter which describes the nature of the person's interest in the matter and states clearly the person's views regarding the matter together with any relevant information that may be useful in explaining or supporting those views.

(2) A person who files a letter pursuant to subrule (1) does not thereby acquire status as a party.

(3) The Board shall provide a copy of any letter filed pursuant to subrule (1) to the applicant.

(4) The applicant and any other party to the proceeding may file a reply to the letter and serve it on the person who filed the letter and such other person as the Board may direct.

(5) The letters of comment and the replies filed shall be on the public record.

Intervention

29. (1) Any person may intervene in respect of a proceeding by filing and serving the applicant, if any, a written intervention signed by the intervenor or authorized representative of the intervenor before the date prescribed by the Board.

(2) Every intervention:

(a) shall be divided into paragraphs, numbered consecutively;

(b) subject to subrule (3), shall state clearly the intervenor's intention to appear and participate at the hearing;

(c) shall describe the intervenor's interest in the proceeding;

(d) subject to subrule (3), shall state clearly the issues which the intervenor intends to address at the hearing;

(e) may be accompanied by any documents that may be useful in explaining or supporting the intervention;

    (f)   shall request the written evidence;

    (g)   shall set out the full name, address and telephone number of the intervenor and the authorized representative of the intervenor upon whom documents may be served; and

    (h)   shall be served on such other persons as the Board may direct.

(3)   Where, by reason of an inability or insufficient time to study an application or reference, an intervenor is unable to include in the written intervention the information required by subrules (1)(b) and (d), the intervenor shall state this fact in the written intervention and shall, within 15 days of receipt of a copy of the application and written evidence, if any, or 15 days of the filing of the written intervention, whichever is later, file and serve on the applicant a supplement to the written intervention containing the information required by paragraphs (1)(b) and (d).

(4)   A person shall not be allowed to participate in any proceeding without leave of the Board unless the person has filed an intervention pursuant to this Rule.

30.   Unless the Board otherwise directs, the applicant shall serve each intervenor with:

    (a)   a copy of the application or reference;

    (b)   any information and material submitted to the Board as written evidence if requested to do so by the intervenor;

    (c)   a copy of any information not submitted to the Board pursuant to subrule 27(5), if requested to do so by the intervenor; and,

    (d)   any orders on procedure issued by the Board.

Reply

31. (1)   An applicant may reply to an intervention.

    (2)   A reply shall be filed and served by the applicant as directed by the Board.

    (3)   A reply shall:

        (a)   contain a clear and concise statement of the allegations upon which it is based;

        (b)   be accompanied by any documents that may be useful in explaining or supporting the reply;

        (c)   be divided into paragraphs, numbered consecutively;

        (d)   be signed by the applicant or the authorized representative of the applicant;

        (e)   be addressed to the intervenor; and

        (f)   be served on the intervenor and such other persons as the Board may direct.

Public Record

32.   All documents shall be filed on the public record unless the Board orders otherwise.

PART III — PUBLIC HEARINGS

Witnesses and Evidence

33. (1) Subject to subrule (2), witnesses at a public hearing shall be examined *viva voce* under oath or affirmation unless otherwise directed by the Board.

    (2) The Board may at any time order that:

    (a) any particular facts be proved by affidavits;

    (b) the affidavit of any witness be read at a public hearing on such conditions as the Board considers reasonable; and

    (c) any witness be examined before a Commissioner or other person authorized to administer oaths appointed by the Board for that purpose.

    (3) Subject to subrules (4) and (5), any party who wishes to present evidence at a public hearing shall, prior to the appearance of any witness and as directed by the Board, file and serve its written evidence as directed by the Board.

    (4) The written evidence of the applicant shall be deemed to include the application or reference; the information identified pursuant to subrule 27(5); any information provided by the applicant in any response by the applicant to an interrogatory, and any written evidence filed and served pursuant to subrule (3).

    (5) The written evidence of an intervenor shall be deemed to include any information provided in its intervention and in any response by the intervenor to an interrogatory, and written evidence filed and served pursuant to subrule (3).

    (6) The Board may permit the introduction of written evidence at a public hearing as the evidence in chief of a witness who

    (a) testifies as to his qualifications; and

    (b) confirms under oath or affirmation that the written evidence was prepared by the witness or under the direction or control of the witness and is accurate to the best of the knowledge or belief of the witness.

    (7) Subject to rule 27, written evidence supplementing the written evidence referred to in subrule (3) may be filed after the date prescribed only with the leave of the Board and shall be served as directed by the Board.

Sittings

34. Where a public hearing has commenced, the hearing shall proceed, as far as may be practicable in the opinion of the Board, from day to day, but may be adjourned by the Board from time to time.

Argument

35. All argument shall be written unless otherwise ordered by the Board.

Hearings in Camera

36. (1) Where in any proceeding the Board directs a hearing or a portion thereof to be held in camera, the hearing may be attended only by:

    (a) the person who is to present confidential information at the hearing;

    (b) Board staff;

    (c) the authorized representative for the witness or for a party to the proceeding who has filed a Declaration and Undertaking in Form II, unless the Board considers, in its opinon, that there is good reason why such authorized representative should not be permitted to attend the in camera hearing;

    (d) a consultant to assist an authorized representative who has filed a Declaration and Undertaking in Form II, should the Board consider the matter in issue sufficiently complex to warrant assistance, and

    (e) such other persons that the Board considers should be present who have filed a Declaration and Undertaking in Form II.

(2) Exhibits, transcripts and arguments with respect to the hearing and all other confidential information filed with the Board under this rule shall be marked "Confidential" and shall be kept separate from the public record and access to this material shall only be by order of the Board.

(3) Where an expert witness is to testify at the hearing, confidential information may be made available to that witness at the discretion of the Board and on any conditions as directed by the Board.

(4) Transcripts of the in camera hearing may be made available to the authorized representatives who have filed a Declaration and Undertaking in Form II at the discretion of the Board.

(5) If argument requires more detail than through a general reference to a named witness or a numbered exhibit,

    (a) oral argument may be given in camera, or

    (b) the relevant portion of the written argument may be separately submitted and shall be marked "confidential" and shall be kept separate from the public record and access to this material shall only be by order of the Board.

(6) All authorized representatives and any expert witness testifying at the in-camera hearing shall return their transcripts, notes, and any other confidential documents to the Board Secretary at the end of the argument phase of the hearing.

Hearings in French

37. (1) The Board may conduct a hearing or a portion of it in the French language if requested to do so by a party who speaks the French language at the time of making an application or filing an intervention.

(2) Where a hearing or a portion of it is to be conducted in the French language, the notice of such hearing shall specify in English and French that the hearing is to be so conducted, and shall further specify that English may also be used.

(3) Subject to subrule (4), nothing herein shall preclude the presentation of submissions or evidence in either the French or English language.

(4) Where evidence is to be presented or submissions are to be made in French, notice shall be given to the Board.

(5) Where a written submission or written evidence is provided in either French or English, the Board may order any person presenting such written submission or written evidence to provide it in the other language if the Board considers it necessary for the fair disposition of the matter.

PART IV

Procedures Where Public Hearing Not Required

38. (1) Where the Board does not proceed by way of a public hearing, the Board may,

   (a) dispose of the matter on the basis of the written documentation before it;

   (b) require further information to be furnished; or

   (c) invite submissions from any person who may have an interest in the proceeding and issue orders on procedure.

(2) Where the Board invites submissions from any person having an interest, the Board may give or direct such notice of the matter as the Board considers reasonable.

(3) Notwithstanding that the Board has invited submissions pursuant to subrule (1)(c), the Board may determine that the matter shall be disposed of by means of a public hearing, in which case the procedures described in Part III shall apply.

PART V

Costs

39. In any proceeding, in addition to the costs of the Board, the Board may,

   (a) award costs to any intervenor who
      i) has or represents a substantial interest in the outcome of the proceeding of such a nature that the intervenor will receive a benefit or suffer a detriment as a result of the order or decision resulting from the proceeding;
      ii) has participated in the proceeding in a responsible way; and
      iii) has contributed to a better understanding of the issues by the Board;

   (b) award costs against an intervenor where the intervention is, in the opinion of the Board, frivolous or vexatious.

40. (1) A party applying for costs shall address its eligibility for costs and the proportion to be awarded, setting forth the reasons why costs should be awarded having

regard to the circumstances of the proceeding and the factors set forth in rule 39, in its final argument.

(2) A party objecting to a cost award shall set forth its objections in its final argument or reply.

41. The Board shall determine the eligibility for an award of cost and shall indicate,

    (a) whether a party is entitled to costs, or whether, having regard to the circumstances of the case and the factors set out in rule 39, no costs or only a proportion of costs should be awarded,

    (b) by whom the costs shall be paid, and

    (c) any other matters the Board considers appropriate.

42. (1) Within ten (10) working days of the release of the Board's Decision or Report, the party awarded costs shall file a Statement of Costs, verified by Affidavit, and all supporting documentation and shall serve a copy thereof on the party against whom costs were awarded.

    (2) The party against whom costs were awarded shall file any objections to the Statement of Costs within ten (10) working days of the receipt of the Statement of Costs and shall serve a copy thereof on the party awarded costs.

43. (1) The Board's solicitor, or such other officer as may be appointed by the Board, shall be the Assessment Officer.

    (2) The Assessment Officer:

    (a) shall consider the Statement of Costs and any objections filed;

    (b) may require further supporting documentation and/or reply from the party awarded costs;

    (c) may invite oral representations from the parties;

    (d) shall ensure that the costs claimed are,
        i) reasonable in the circumstances;
        ii) incurred directly and necessarily for the purposes of the proceeding, and
        iii) in accordance with actual expenditures;

    (e) shall make a recommendation to the Board as to the quantum of costs;

    (f) shall prepare written reasons where an objection has been filed and may do so where no objection has been filed; and

    (g) shall provide copies of the recommendation, and written reasons, if any, to the parties.

    (3) A party affected may object to the recommendation of the Assessment Officer by filing an objection and serving a copy thereof on the other affected party within ten (10) working days of the date of the recommendation.

44. (1) After the time prescribed in subrule 43(3) has passed, the Board:

(a) shall consider the recommendation and reasons, if any, of the Assessment Officer;

(b) shall consider any objections to the recommendation of the Assessment Officer;

(c) may, on its own motion or upon the request of a party, hold a hearing as to the quantum of costs to be allowed; and

(d) shall fix the quantum of costs to be awarded.

(2) The Board shall issue a cost order fixing the amount of costs.

PART VI

Applications for Rehearing or Review

45. (1) In this Part,

(a) "application" means an application for a rehearing or an application for a review as provided in the Act;

(b) "original proceeding" means the proceeding giving rise to the application for a rehearing or review.

(2) Subject to subrule (3), a rehearing or review shall be commenced by filing an application.

(3) A rehearing or review may be commenced by the Board by notice issued by the Board to the parties in the original proceeding and to such other parties as the Board considers appropriate.

(4) An application shall be in writing and be signed by,

(a) a party in the original proceeding, or

(b) any other person to whom the Board has granted leave to file an application.

(5) Every application shall:

(a) contain a clear and concise statement of the facts and the nature of the order or decision applied for;

(b) set out the grounds upon which the application is made, sufficient to justify a rehearing or raise a question as to the correctness of the order or decision, including,

(i) error of law or jurisdiction;

(ii) error in fact;

(iii) change in circumstances arising since the original proceeding;

(iv) new facts that have arisen since the original proceeding;

(v) facts that were not placed in evidence in the original proceeding and could not have been discovered by reasonable diligence at the time;

(vi) an important matter of principle, or a breach of natural justice that has been raised by the order or decision;

(c) be accompanied by any documents that may be useful in explaining or supporting the application;

    (d) be endorsed with the full name and address of the applicant and the authorized representative of the applicant upon whom documents may be served;

    (e) be filed in triplicate; and

    (f) be served on all parties in the original proceeding.

  (6) A person who was not a party in the original proceeding shall apply for leave to file an application and shall serve every party in the original proceeding with a copy of the application for leave and the provisions dealing with the application for rehearing or review apply *mutatis mutandis* to an application for leave.

46. (1) A party served with an application may file an answer within ten (10) days of service of the application.

  (2) An answer shall be served on all parties in the original proceeding.

47. An applicant may file a reply to an answer received pursuant to subrule 46(1) within ten (10) days of service of the answer.

48. Documents supporting an answer or reply shall be filed and served with the answer or reply.

49. (1) Subject to subrule (4), the Board may determine an application for leave to file an application with or without a hearing, and if it grants leave, it shall issue orders on procedure with respect to the application.

  (2) Subject to subrule (4), the Board shall determine in respect of any application for a rehearing whether the matter should be reheard and, if it finds that the matter should be reheard, it shall issue orders on procedure with respect to the rehearing.

  (3) Subject to subrule (4), the Board shall determine in respect of any application for review of an order or decision, whether that order or decision should be reviewed and, if it finds that the order or decision should be reviewed, it may then, in its discretion, either dispose of the application or issue orders on procedure with respect to the conduct of the review.

  (4) The Board shall not make any determinations under this Part until the times prescribed in rules 46 and 47 have expired.

Motion to Stay

50. (1) A motion to stay the order or decision pending the rehearing or review shall be made concurrently with the filing of the application for leave or the application for rehearing or review.

  (2) The provisions dealing with the application for rehearing or review apply *mutatis mutandis* to a motion to stay.

  (3) The Board may grant a stay subject to such terms and conditions as it considers just and reasonable in the circumstances.

51. Notwithstanding anything in Part VI, an application to reconsider an order or decision of a procedural nature made in the course of a proceeding, may be made pursuant to rule 22.

FORM I

Ontario Energy Board Act

SUMMONS TO A WITNESS BEFORE the Ontario Energy Board

RE:

TO:

You are hereby summoned and required to attend before the Ontario Energy Board at a hearing to be held at _____ in the _____ of _____ on _____ day, the _____ day of _____ 19____, at the hour of _____ o'clock in the _____ noon, and so from day to day until the hearing is concluded or the tribunal otherwise orders, to give evidence on oath touching the matters in question in the proceedings and to bring with you and produce at such time and place

_____

_____

_____

Dated this _____ day of _____, 19___.

ONTARIO ENERGY BOARD

_____

NOTE:

You are entitled to be paid the same personal allowances for your attendance at the hearing as are paid for the attendance of a witness summoned to attend before the Supreme Court.

If you fail to attend and give evidence at the hearing, or to produce the documents or things specified, at the time and place specified, without lawful excuse, you are liable to punishment by the Supreme Court of Ontario in the same manner as if for contempt of that Court for disobedience to a subpoena.

FORM II

(Style of Proceeding)
Declaration and Undertaking

I appear as counsel/agent in the above captioned matter for _____

I hereby declare:

1.   THAT I am ordinarily resident in Canada and am not an employee, officer, director or major shareholder of the party for which I act or of any other person known by me to be a participant in this hearing;

2.   THAT I have read the Ontario Energy Board Rules of Practice and Procedure and all Orders of the Ontario Energy Board that relate to this hearing and I understand that these Orders may be filed with the Supreme Court of Ontario. I further understand that any breach of the terms of the Orders could be the subject of contempt proceedings in the Supreme Court of Ontario.

I hereby undertake:

1.   THAT I will maintain the confidentiality of any information or evidence that I receive during the course of the hearing held in camera and will not disclose any information or evidence that I receive during the course of that hearing;

2.   THAT I will not reproduce in any manner, without the prior written approval of the Board, any information, notes, evidence, transcripts or written submissions dealing with the evidence taken and submissions made in the hearing held in camera;

3.   THAT at the end of the hearing, I will personally return to the Board Secretary all information provided to me by the Board during the hearing held in camera, and any notes taken by me with respect to evidence or information that I received during the course of that hearing.

   DATED AT TORONTO, ONTARIO, this ____ day of _____, 19___.

Signature: _____

Name: _____ _____

Firm: _____

APPENDIX 12.9

Reporter's Contract

This **AGREEMENT** made this 1ˢᵗ day of April, 1994

B E T W E E N :

Her Majesty the Queen in Right of Ontario, as represented by
—Ontario Energy Board
P.O. Box 2319
26 Floor
Toronto, Ontario
M4P 1E4

(hereinafter called the "Board")

- **and** -

Name of Contractor:

(hereinafter called the "Contractor")

Requisition Number:
Purchase Order Number:
Organization Unit Number:
Contract Number:
Work Title: Verbatim Reporting Services
Designated Board Representatives: Paul B. Pudge
                                                   Board Secretary
                                                   (416) 440-7607

                                                   Peter O'Dell,
                                                   Asst. Board Secretary
                                                   (416) 440-7605

The parties agree as follows:

1.0 DESCRIPTION OF THE WORK

1.1   The Contractor shall perform for the Board, as required by the Board from time to time, certain work and services as described in Appendix 'A' attached hereto, herein referred to as "services", upon the terms and conditions set out hereinafter.

1.2   The services shall be provided on a per hearing, per conference, or per meeting basis, as the case may be.

1.3   The Contractor agrees to perform services within the Metropolitan Toronto area and at such other locations in Ontario as required by the Board.

1.4   The Board will provide suitable office space and furniture required to provide the services for hearings held at the Board's offices. The Board will make reasonable efforts to provide suitable space and furniture required for hearings held elsewhere in Ontario.

2.0 CONTRACTOR'S WARRANTIES

2.1   The Contractor is duly qualified to conduct business wherever necessary to carry out its present business and operations and the terms of this Agreement.

2.2   The Contractor shall perform all services in a business-like manner and according to the best standards of the reporting profession, and the Contractor shall at all times promptly provide as many competent reporters and maintain such staff, equipment and supplies as are reasonably required to produce transcripts satisfactory to the Board, additional copies of transcripts within the time specified, exact electronic copies of transcripts in a form acceptable to the Board, and audio tapes of the event transcribed.

2.3   Acceptance or approval of any work or services by Board officials, whether express or implied, shall not alter the Contractor's responsibilities under this Agreement.

3.0 OPERATIONAL NOTICE

3.1   The Board shall provide reasonable notice of an assignment, generally not less than 48 hours notice for assignments within the Metropolitan Toronto area and not less than 72 hours notice for assignments outside the Metropolitan Toronto area. From time to time, the Board may require services to be provided on 24 hours notice.

3.2   The Board will provide the following information:
     3.2.1   starting date and location of an assignment,
     3.2.2   an estimate of the duration in days of the assignment,
     3.2.3   the expected session length in hours for each day,
     3.2.4   an estimate of the number of transcript copies required by the Board,
     3.2.5   the format and "Service Level" required, and
     3.2.6   the party responsible for the payment of services received by the Board.

3.3   The Board will promptly notify the Contractor of any changes to the information provided described in paragraph 3.2.

3.4   The Board agrees to give timely notice of cancellation of an assignment, not less than 24 hours prior to the commencement of an assignment within the Metropolitan Toronto area and not less than 48 hours prior to the commencement of an assignment outside the Metropolitan Toronto area. Where the Board provides notice of cancellation within the timeframes set out above, no "Cancellation Fee" shall be charged by the Contractor. Where the Board cancels an assignment upon shorter notice, the Contractor may charge the Board a "Cancellation Fee" as set out in the Applicable Pricing/Limits Grid.

3.5   Where the Board cancels a session upon less than 24 hours notice, and where the Contractor incurs staffing costs in respect of this assignment, the Contractor may charge the Board the "Cancellation Fee" as set out in the Applicable Pricing/Limits Grid.

3.6 Where any session concludes within one hour of commencing, the Contractor may charge the Board the "Minimum Fee" as set out in the Applicable Pricing/Limits Grid.

3.7 Despite Section 19 of this Agreement, notification under this section (3.0 Operational Notice) may be effected by the most expedient means, including facsimile transmission or telephone.

4.0 FEE SCHEDULE

4.1 Before any services are provided under this Agreement, the Board shall elect a single Pricing/Limits Grid from the four options for Year 1 contained in Appendix 'B'. This Pricing/Limits Grid shall be referred to as the "Applicable Pricing/Limits Grid" for the first year of this Agreement.

4.2 At each anniversary date of this Agreement, the Board shall elect a single Pricing/Limits Grid from the four options for Years 2 and 3 contained in Appendix 'B'. That Pricing/Limits Grid shall then be referred to as the "Applicable Pricing/Limits Grid", and shall replace the Grid previously in effect.

4.3 The Contractor shall notify the Board of the election options not less than six weeks prior to the anniversary date of the Agreement.

4.4 The elections referred to in paragraphs 4.1 and 4.2 of this Agreement shall be in the form provided in Appendix 'D'.

4.5 Unless otherwise agreed to by the Board and the Contractor, assignments in progress at the time of an election, shall be invoiced in accordance with the Applicable Pricing/Limits Grid in effect at the start of the assignment.

4.6 The Contractor agrees to charge the fees set out in the Applicable Pricing/Limits Grid, herein referred to as the "charges", for all services provided under this Agreement.

4.7 The charges for "Basic Service" as set out in the Applicable Pricing/Limits Grid shall include the Contractor's overhead and profit margin.

4.8 The Contractor agrees to sell "Additional Copies" of printed or electronic transcript, or portions thereof, at the prices set out in the Applicable Pricing/Limits Grid. The charges for additional transcript copies shall be based on the actual cost of duplication and shall not include overhead and profit margin.

4.9 The charges set out in the Applicable Pricing/Limits Grid, shall without exception apply to all parties.

4.10 The Contractor may, with the prior approval of the Board, provide value added services related to Board transcripts that are not covered in this Agreement. The Board may withhold its approval in respect of any proposed value added service, or may impose terms and conditions upon the provision of any value added service related to Board transcripts.

4.11 Transcript copies that are not delivered by the Contractor within the period of time established for the kind of delivery ordered, shall be charged for at the rates applicable to the time of delivery actually achieved; except that, if the Contractor, regardless of the type of delivery ordered, fails to deliver transcript, or electronic files within the applicable period prescribed for next day service, a further reduction in price shall be made as follows: 10% of the price for the transcript computed at the rate ordered for each Board business day or fraction thereof that delivery is delayed up to a total of 50% of the next day transcript price.

4.12 The total amount payable to the Contractor by the Board during the term of the Agreement shall not exceed $500,000.00.

4.13 With respect to any proceeding, the Board may make arrangements for another person to pay for the provision of services provided to the Board, termed herein as ''the designated payor''.

4.14 Where the Board has notified the Contractor that the designated payor will be responsible for the payment of said services, the Board will obtain a written undertaking from the designated payor that it will assume responsibility for the payment of said services and for disbursements made in accordance with this Agreement.

5.0 INVOICE FOR BASIC SERVICE

5.1 After each hearing is completed, or on a monthly basis, the Contractor shall invoice the person who has assumed responsibility for the payment of services provided to the Board, and deliver the invoice to the Board.

5.2 The Board shall verify all invoices for said service and, where applicable, shall send the invoice to the designated payor.

6.0 INVOICE FOR TRANSCRIPT COPIES

6.1 The Contractor agrees to invoice all persons other than the Board directly for transcript copies provided, and delivery charges.

7.0 INVOICE FORMAT

7.1 Every invoice and accompanying supporting documentation shall indicate (where applicable):

7.1.1 the name and address of the Contractor;

7.1.2 the invoice date;

7.1.3 the date and work title of this Agreement;

7.1.4 the Board File number;

7.1.5 the date(s) services were provided covered by the invoice;

7.1.6 the amount for which the invoice is rendered;

7.1.7 the total amount invoiced to date under the Board File number;

7.1.8 the number of transcript pages with the price per page;

7.1.9   the number of copies of each volume ordered on a daily basis, and the "Service Level" ordered;

7.1.10   details of expenses connected with services performed outside Toronto;

7.2 Failure to provide the information required in paragraph 7.1 may result in delay of payment or rejection of the invoice.

7.3 The Contractor shall certify that each invoice is true and complete.

8.0 MONTHLY REPORT

8.1 The Contractor shall provide the Board with a monthly report summarizing all invoices rendered to the Board and all other persons, for services provided under this Agreement and any value added services provided related to Board transcripts. The report shall be in a format acceptable to the Board.

9.0 PAYMENT

9.1 The Board, or the designated payor, shall pay the Contractor in accordance with this Agreement, subject to:

9.1.1   receipt and approval by the Board of a complete and certified invoice;

9.1.2   completion of the services referred to in the invoice to the satisfaction of the Board;

9.1.3   acceptance by the Board of the amounts for expenses claimed.

9.2 Travel expenses connected with services performed outside Toronto shall be reimbursed in accordance with Management Board of Cabinet Directives and Guidelines, and Board policies, procedures and guidelines. Any travel must be in the most economical way available.

10.0 SUBSTITUTE REPORTER

10.1 If the Contractor does not appear at the time and place specified for an assignment after being notified, or, if for any reason the Contractor is unable to provide competent personnel and equipment to report at any stage of any assignment, the Board representative may call in a substitute reporter and the Contractor shall reimburse the Board, or the designated payor, for any extra expenses incurred thereby. The Board may deduct, or the designated payor shall at the direction of the Board deduct, such expenses from any amounts otherwise due or that may become due to the Contractor.

11.0 TERM

11.1 Subject to paragraph 11.2, this Agreement is for a term of three years, commencing on the 1st day of April, 1994 and concluding on the 31st day of March, 1997.

11.2 For the purposes of section 4 of this Agreement, April 1st, 1995 and April 1st, 1996 are the applicable Anniversary dates.

11.3 If on the expiry date of this Agreement, the Contractor is providing services in a hearing or meeting, the term is deemed to be extended until all services have been provided for that hearing or meeting.

11.4 The terms of this Agreement do not prohibit the Board from temporarily assigning the verbatim reporting service for any assignment or session to an alternate supplier where the Board is of the opinion that the contractor cannot adequately provide services required for that assignment or session.

12.0 TERMINATION

12.1 Notwithstanding the term of this Agreement, the Board reserves the right to terminate this Agreement at any time prior to its expiration for any reason the Board considers sufficient upon the Board giving three (3) days notice of termination to the Contractor.

12.2 If the Board terminates the Agreement prior to its expiration, the Board shall only be responsible for the payment of expenditures incurred in connection with this Agreement up to and including the date of any such termination.

12.3 Upon receipt of payment from the Board under paragraph 12.2, the Contractor shall immediately turn over to the Board all material generated during the Agreement, and further the Contractor shall return all confidential information furnished to the Contractor by the Board under this Agreement.

12.4 The Contractor may terminate this Agreement at any time upon 45 days notice in writing to the Board.

12.5 If there is any dispute between the Contractor and the Board as to the amount to which the Contractor is entitled under Paragraph 12.2, the amount shall be determined by a single arbiter chosen in writing by the Contractor and the Board, and the decision of the arbiter shall be final and binding. In the absence of an Agreement as to the choice of an arbiter, the *Arbitration Act* shall apply.

13.0 CONTRACTOR COOPERATION DURING TRANSITION

13.1 The Contractor agrees that when this Agreement is about to be terminated or has been terminated, the Contractor, upon request by the Board, shall fully furnish all information as to current proceedings necessary to enable the proper continuation of, transcript and completion of orders begun under this Agreement, to the new Contractor.

14.0 PERSONS PERFORMING WORK

14.1 All work shall be performed by qualified employees or agents of the Contractor.

14.2 The Contractor, its employees and agents shall be and are deemed to be an independent contractor and shall not be, or deemed to be an agent, employee or servant of the Board, or to make any statement or representation that it has such authority.

14.3 The Contractor shall not be entitled to assign this Agreement or any portion thereof without the prior written consent of the Board. No assignment or sub-contract shall relieve the Contractor from any obligation under this Agreement or impose any liability upon Her Majesty or the Board to any assignee or sub-contractor.

15.0 LIMITATION OF LIABILITY, INDEMNIFICATION AND INSURANCE

15.1 In no event shall the Board be liable for any bodily injury, death or property damage to the Contractor, its employees, agents or sub-contractors or for any claim, demand or action by any third party against the Contractor, its employees, agents or sub-contractors arising out of or in any way related to this Agreement or the work, unless the same is caused by the negligence of an employee or agent of the Board while acting within the scope of his/her employment.

15.2 In no event shall the Board be liable for any incidental, indirect, special or consequential damages or any loss of use, revenue or profit of the Contractor, its employees, agents or sub-contractors, arising out of or in any way related to this Agreement.

15.3 The Contractor shall at all times indemnify, save and keep harmless the Board, its employees and agents, from and against all suits, judgments, claims, demands and losses (including, without limitation, reasonable legal expenses) incurred as a result of any claim, demand or action arising out of or in any way related to this Agreement or the work, unless the same is caused by the negligence of an employee or agent of the Board while acting within the scope of his/her employment.

15.4 The Contractor warrants that the work will not infringe upon or violate any patent, copyright, trade secret or any proprietary right of any third party.

15.5 The Contractor shall maintain and shall cause any sub-contractor to maintain comprehensive general liability insurance and automobile liability insurance (owned and non-owned or hired units) each subject to limits of not less than $1,000,000 inclusive per occurrence.

15.6 The Contractor agrees that all court reporting notes taken, audio tape recordings made and electronic files produced in connection with the services rendered under this Agreement, and master copies prepared therefrom, shall be filed and securely held by the Contractor, and adequately protected from loss or damage during the time that such materials are in the custody of the Contractor.

16.0 INTELLECTUAL PROPERTY

16.1 All materials, documents, findings, electronic data, data processes, technology, programs and inventions conceived, developed or produced by Contractor or jointly by the Contractor and the Board, arising out of this Agreement or the work, and the intellectual property (including without limitation copyrights, patents, trademarks, industrial designs, know-how and trade secrets) therein, shall be the property of the Board, and shall be delivered to the Board at the termination of this Agreement.

16.2 Copyright in the transcripts shall vest in and remain the property of the Board.

16.3 Without limiting the application of paragraph 16.2, the Contractor may sell copies of the transcripts for up to six (6) months after the end of the hearing, at the rates and terms prescribed in this Agreement. The six month period mentioned in this paragraph may extend beyond the term of the contract set out in paragraph 11.1.

16.4 The Contractor agrees to provide, without charge, reasonable access to any collection, compilation or database of the Board's transcripts that may be constructed or maintained by the Contractor.

16.5 The Contractor agrees that any sale of transcript copies shall be made on condition that the purchaser agrees not to resell or otherwise use the transcripts in a manner that may infringe any copyright or other proprietary interest of the Board.

17.0 CONFIDENTIALITY

17.1 The Contractor, its employees, agents or sub-Contractors shall not, without the prior written consent of the Board, disclose to any person, firm or corporation any information concerning the affairs of the Board or any information concerning or derived from this Agreement which they may have acquired in the course of or incidental to their performance of this Agreement or otherwise. The provisions of this paragraph apply equally to the negotiation period prior to signing of this Agreement, the term of this Agreement and any time thereafter.

18.0 CONFLICT OF INTEREST

18.1 The Contractor shall ensure that the work can be undertaken and completed without a conflict of interest. During the term of this Agreement the Contractor shall not undertake or engage in any work for another client that could reasonably result in a conflict of interest. In the event of any doubt as to whether there is or could be a conflict, the decision of the Board is final.

19.0 NOTICES

19.1 Any notice required to be given by this Agreement shall be given to the party to whom it is addressed,

19.1.1 By personal delivery to that party, in which case the notice shall be deemed to have been given on the day of the delivery; or

19.1.2 By prepaid post to the postal address shown for that party on the cover page of this Agreement, in which case the notice shall be deemed to have been given on the fifth day after the date of mailing.

20.0 DESIGNATED BOARD REPRESENTATIVE

20.1 The Designated Board Representative shall be the person(s) shown on the cover page of this Agreement, but the Board may substitute different representatives by notice in writing to the Contractor.

21.0 MANAGEMENT BOARD

21.1 This Agreement may be subject to approval of the Management Board of Cabinet of the Government of Ontario.

22.0 REPRESENTATIONS AND WARRANTIES

22.1 All representations and warranties, covenants and limitations of liability contained herein shall survive any termination or cancellation of this Agreement.

23.0 PUBLICITY

23.1 Any report, announcement, brochure, audio visual material or other public communication or publication relating to this Agreement or the work, must be approved in advance by the Board and will reflect the participation of each party in the work.

24.0 INDEPENDENT CONTRACTOR

24.1 The Contractor shall conduct its own business and maintain its status as an independent Contractor. This Agreement does not create an employer-employee relationship or any agency, joint venture or partner relationship. The Contractor hereby agrees not to hold itself out as an agent, employee or partner of the Board or to make any statement or representation that it has any such authority.

25.0 INSPECTION

25.1 The Board and its authorized representatives shall be entitled to review, during normal business hours, all results of the work and all records, documents, reports, accounts, or other materials of the Contractor relating to the work.

26.0 COMPLIANCE WITH APPLICABLE LAWS

26.1 The Contractor represents and warrants that the work will be carried out in compliance with the laws of Canada and the provinces, as applicable.

27.0 NO WAIVER

27.1 The failure of any party to enforce at anytime or for any period of time the provisions of this Agreement shall not be construed to be a waiver of such provisions or the right of such party thereafter to enforce each and every such provision. Waiver of any breach shall not be deemed a waiver of any other breach, even if similar in nature.

28.0 CANADIAN PREFERENCE

28.1 When utilizing services, supplies or equipment for the purpose of this Agreement, the Contractor agrees to give preference to Canadian suppliers where all other factors are equal.

29.0 TIME

29.1 Time shall be of the essence.

30.0 CONFIDENTIALITY OF TRANSCRIPTS

30.1 In the event of hearings held in the absence of the public (*in-camera* proceedings), the Contractor and its staff will be strictly bound to secrecy respecting those proceedings. The Contractor agrees not to provide transcript copies in respect of these proceedings to any person without the prior approval of the Board.

31.0 BOARD SECURITY REQUIREMENTS

31.1 The Contractor undertakes to abide by all appropriate Board guidelines pertaining to office and/or computer systems security.

32.0 GOODS AND SERVICES TAX

32.1 The Ontario Government is not required to pay the Goods and Services Tax (G.S.T.) for supplies or services. This is to certify that the property and/or services ordered/purchased hereby are purchased by the Board for the use of the Crown in Right of Ontario, and are not subject to the G.S.T.

32.2 Registered suppliers making taxable supplies to the Government of Ontario are entitled to claim input tax credits for the tax paid on purchases used in making such supplies to the Government of Ontario. Supplies made to the Government of Ontario that would otherwise be taxable at 7% are treated, for input tax credit purposes, in the same manner as zero-rated supplies.

32.3 Despite paragraph 32.1 above, where any person named as the ''designated payor'', as provided in paragraph 4.13, has assumed responsibility for the payment of services and disbursements under paragraph 4.14, then the G.S.T. may apply to invoices rendered for those services and disbursements.

33.0 SUCCESSOR RIGHTS

33.1 If the Contractor experiences an escalation of labour costs because of a successful claim against it arising out of application of the *Successor Rights (Crown Transfers) Act, R.S.O. 1990 c. S.27*, to the services provided to the Board by the Contractor under this Agreement, then the Contractor may apply to the Board for additional funds to offset such cost escalation due solely to the application of that Act to those services.

34.0 ENTIRE CONTRACT

34.1 This Agreement, including Appendices 'A', 'B', 'C' and 'D' as listed below, constitutes the entire Agreement between the parties. There are no prior or collateral agreements or representations.

34.1.1   Appendix A — Description of Services

34.1.2   Appendix B — Pricing/Limits Grid

34.1.3   Appendix C — The Ontario Government Purchase Order issued by the Ministry of Environment & Energy

34.1.4   Appendix D — Election of Pricing/Limits Grid

34.2 This Agreement shall not be varied except by a document in writing, dated, signed and sealed on behalf of the Board and by the Contractor. The original executed letter(s) of variation shall be attached to and form part of the original of this Agreement. A copy of any executed letter(s) of variation shall be supplied to the Contractor.

Date _____   _____

                                                            Marie C. Rounding
                                                            Chair, Ontario Energy Board

Date _____   _____

APPENDIX A

Attached to and forming part of Agreement between   and Her Majesty the Queen
dated April 1, 1994.

Terms of Reference

1.0 BACKGROUND

1.1 Hearings
    1.1.1   **Location:** Hearings are usually held at the Board's hearing rooms at 2300 Yonge Street, but may be held elsewhere in Metropolitan Toronto and at various locations throughout the province. The Contractor is expected to have the resources available to provide the necessary services for multiple, simultaneous hearings to be held at different locations within Ontario. The Board may also assign the Contractor to transcribe certain meetings, conferences or other proceedings from time to time, all termed as "Hearings" or "Assignments" for the purposes of this document.

    1.1.2   **Duration:** Sitting days, or Sessions, typically begin at 9:00a.m., and vary from one to ten hours in length, including some evenings. The Board may sit for longer hours than scheduled at any time, on short notice.

    1.1.3   **Notice:** While the Board is generally able to give reasonable notice of when hearings are to be held, it is the OEB's experience that **hearing schedules change on short notice**.

    1.1.4   **Content:** The subject matter of the hearings is often quite complex in terms of the financial, legal and technical language used (usually related to energy, economic and environmental matters).

1.1.5   **Language:** To date, all Board hearings since 1960 have been conducted entirely in English. Nevertheless, the *French Language Services Act* requires that the Board must be prepared to hear parties or witnesses who speak French. The Board will provide advance notice of this requirement to the Contractor.

1.1.6   **Parties:** For the purposes of this tender and accompanying contract, the active participants (or Parties) in the OEB's Hearings process can be summarized as follows:

1.1.6.1   **OEB Board Secretary personnel:** Group within the OEB that arranges and supervises the Hearing process. Normal contact for Contractor and daily operations. The contract's Designated Board Representative (DBR) is a member of this group.

1.1.6.2   **OEB Hearing Panel:** One to nine Board Members who listen to evidence and eventually prepare the official Decision or Report.

1.1.6.3   **OEB Technical Staff:** Group within the OEB that presents and tests evidence in the Hearing; also acts as a representative of the public interest.

1.1.6.4   **Applicant:** Typically a utility corporation, this organization prepares evidence and/or arguments to support its Application which is then tested in a Hearing. The Applicant typically bears the majority of Hearing related costs, including transcript costs.

1.1.6.5   **Intervenors:** Individuals or organizations that present evidence and/or arguments typically related to area(s) of particular special interest. Intervenor costs are generally paid by the Applicant at the Board's direction, including transcript costs.

1.1.6.6   **Public:** General public interested in Board activities, but generally assumed to not be active participants in the actual Hearings.

1.1.6.7   Note that in this document the first three groups are often collectively referred to as "the Board" while the Applicant and Intervenors are often referred to as "other parties".

1.2   Transcript Services/Products

1.2.1   **Official Copy:** The Board always requires a single printed and bound copy of the transcript, as specified herein, and referred to in this document and the accompanying contract as the Official Printed Copy. The Board also requires a corresponding Official Electronic Copy. These items will always, unless otherwise specified by the DBR, be **required within 2½ hours of the conclusion of each day's proceedings**.

1.2.2   **Additional Copies:** In addition to the above, multiple printed and bound copies are usually required by the Board and other parties to the proceeding (i.e., Applicant, Intervenors).

1.2.2.1   **Quantities:** The number of copies required varies significantly from case to case, often with many being required within 2½ hours of the conclusion of each day's proceedings.

1.2.2.2   **Print Format:** The print format required may vary. Note that the "Standard" format shall be the basis for defining pages for billing purposes.

1.2.3   **Electronic Data:** In addition to the above, the other parties to the proceeding require numerous electronic copies of the transcript, in ASCII text format, typically on 3½'' diskette. Other formats and delivery methods may be required from time to time (e.g. files via modem transfer, etc). Again, these are usually required within 2½ hours of the conclusion of each day's proceedings.

1.2.4   **Review Copy:** On occasion, the Board may require a portion of the transcript to be printed immediately (i.e., during the hearing) for review purposes.

1.2.4   **Audio Cassette:** The Contractor will be required to create an audio recording of the proceedings which is of sufficient quality to enable a full recreation of the transcript, if deemed necessary. The recording must be kept by the Contractor for a period of at least six months. A copy (i.e., an audio cassette) must be supplied in a timely fashion to any party requesting it.

1.2.6   **Quality:** The quality of transcript materials (i.e., accuracy, clarity, etc.) is of the highest importance to the Board. The Board is always the final arbiter of transcript quality issues.

1.2.7   **Format:** The format of transcript materials, both printed and electronic, is outlined herein. The Board reserves the right to make adjustments from time to time to the format, appearance and binding of the transcript documents, in consultation with the Contractor.

1.3 Timing/Service Levels

1.3.1   The timing of the delivery of the various transcript products is **critical** to Board operations. For example, all parties may use the transcript from today's proceeding to prepare for the next day's proceeding. This Agreement therefore defines the delivery times or **Service Levels** that may be requested by the Board or other parties as follows:

1.3.2   **Priority Copy:** Where requested by any party, the Contractor will deliver all Additional Copies ordered at this Service Level, both printed and electronic, to that party **within 2½ hours** of the close of the day's proceedings.

1.3.3   **Normal Copy:** Where requested by any party, the Contractor will deliver all Additional Copies ordered at this Service Level, both printed and electronic, to that party **within four hours** of the close of the day's proceedings.

1.3.4   **Next Day Copy:** Where requested by any party, the Contractor will deliver all Additional Copies ordered at this Service Level, both printed and electronic, to that party **at or before 9:00 a.m. on the day following** the close of the day's proceedings (including Saturdays).

1.3.5   **Historic Copy:** Where transcript copies from a previous proceeding are ordered by any party, the Contractor will prepare and deliver the copies ordered, in either printed or electronic format, within three business days of receipt of the order.

1.3.6   **Audio Cassette:** Where requested by any party, the Contractor will deliver an audio recording (i.e., an audio cassette tape) of the appropriate hearing to that party within three business days of receipt of the order.

1.4   Fee Structure

     1.4.1   **Overview:** For many reasons, and having regard to future directions, the Board intends to use the following "service oriented" fee and billing structure, as opposed to the "product oriented" pricing prevalent in the industry:

           1.4.1.1   A fee for *Basic Service* will cover all aspects of providing Verbatim Reporting Services to the Board. It will be charged to only one organization for each Hearing as directed by the Board.

           1.4.1.2   A fee for *Additional Copies* will be charged to each party requiring them, solely on an incremental cost basis; that is, this fee will represent the variable cost of copy production.

           1.4.1.3   *Other Fees and Charges* may be incurred in accordance with the Applicable Pricing/Limits Grid in the circumstances provided in this Agreement.

     1.4.2   **Basic Service:** This Agreement establishes a per page fee for the provision of a basic verbatim reporting service, that is, transcribing the proceeding, providing to the Board the Official Printed Copy and one equivalent Official Electronic Copy of the transcript within $2\frac{1}{2}$ hours of the close of that day's proceeding. This Basic Service Fee is expected to cover such costs as:

           1.4.2.1   verbatim reporting and transcription;

           1.4.2.2   editing and quality control;

           1.4.2.3   required production facilities;

           1.4.2.4   maintaining required audio recordings; and,

           1.4.2.5   **all of the Contractor's overhead costs and profit margins involved in doing business with the Board.**

     1.4.3   **Additional Copies:** This Agreement establishes fees for the timely provision of multiple transcript copies, both electronic and bound paper, to all parties. This fee for additional copies of transcript in either paper or electronic format is expected to recover the Contractor's incremental cost of reproducing these copies in the required timeframe, including materials and labour. These fees will be tiered according to the delivery time in which the copies are requested and received.

     1.4.4   **Other Fees:** This Agreement also establishes other fees as follows:

           1.4.4.1   A **Minimum Fee** which allows the Contractor to charge a set fee for Sessions of less than one hour;

           1.4.4.2   A **Cancellation Fee** which allows the Contractor to establish a fee to be charged for those occasions when a Session is scheduled to start, and is subsequently cancelled on less than 24 hours notice.

           1.4.4.3   An **Audio Cassette Fee** will determine what the Contractor will charge those parties asking for a copy of the audio recording of the proceeding.

     1.4.5   **Disbursements for Out of Town Hearings** enable the Contractor to recover reasonably incurred travel costs for those hearings held outside of Metropolitan Toronto. The rates and related procedures for disbursements will be set by the Board in accordance with applicable Government directives.

2.0   BIDDER & CONTRACT REQUIREMENTS The Contractor will meet the following requirements and qualifications:

2.1 General Requirements & Qualifications

    2.1.1   The Contractor shall diligently and with care provide all services stated in the contract;

    2.1.2   The Contractor must be a qualified CAT service provider;

    2.1.3   The Contractor must provide all equipment and operators reasonably necessary to meet the requirements of the contract;

    2.1.4   The Contractor shall ensure that reporters in attendance at hearings shall provide themselves with all supplies reasonably necessary to meet the requirements of the contract;

    2.1.5   The Contractor shall have the capability of accepting the scheduling of assignments via facsimile machine, and will promptly acknowledge all orders received to the DBR;

    2.1.6   The Contractor shall provide all services strictly in compliance with the contract.

2.2 Basic Service Requirements

    2.2.1   The Contractor must attend all Board Hearings, Meetings, etc. as assigned by the DBR;

    2.2.2   The Contractor must accurately transcribe all proceedings in their entirety using CAT equipment;

    2.2.3   All spoken words and significant events or gestures, shall be reported in the transcript, as directed by the Presiding Member;

    2.2.4   The Contractor shall produce a complete Printed and Electronic transcript, as specified herein;

    2.2.5   Provide the Official Printed and Electronic Transcripts, as described in Appendix 'B', to the Board within the required timeframe (generally within 2½ hours of the close of each day's proceedings);

    2.2.6   Create a quality audio recording of the proceedings to enable re-creation of the transcript, if deemed necessary;

    2.2.7   Adhere to the operating, billing and reporting procedures as described above or further detailed by the DBR.

2.3 Additional Transcript Copy Requirements

    2.3.1   Provide printed copies of the Transcript **at cost** to various parties in the desired format and within the required timeframe as specified herein.

    2.3.2   Provide electronic copies of the Transcript **at cost** to various parties within the required timeframe as specified herein.

3.0 FORMAT OF TRANSCRIPT PRODUCTS

3.1 Summary

    3.1.1   This section will describe the various formats for transcript, in various media, via various delivery methods, etc. While some portions of this section may be negotiated with the Contractor, it is strongly recommended that any major changes or assumptions be outlined in the RFP response.

3.1.2　　As discussed briefly in the preceding portions of this RFP document, it is the intent of the Board to minimize the amount of paper consumed in the course of Board proceedings. This has led to the requirement for not only electronic transcript, but also two forms of printed transcript. Based upon samples received, the Board hopes to achieve at least a 4:1 reduction in paper usage on a per transcript basis using the "Condensed" print format.

3.1.3　　It is absolutely essential that all formats, print and electronic, be completely identical with respect to their content and structure. The Board cannot allow transcript readers to ever be in doubt as to whether "this" format has the same information as "that" format. Also, that information must be found on the same page and line number. Obviously, how the page and line number appear may be different (i.e., compressed print or online electronic), but the relationship between the formats must be intuitively clear.

3.2　Print Format #1 ("Official", "Standard" or "Traditional" Format)

3.2.1　　The "Traditional" format shall be the basis for defining standard pages for billing purposes. Therefore, based upon previous experience, one "Official" page for billing purposes is expected to be approximately 250 words.

3.2.2　　Each page of the transcript volumes shall be 8½"×11" in size, and shall be printed on both sides unless the Board otherwise directs.

3.2.3　　The first page of the transcript will be a title page designed to be compatible with the outside transcript cover (see below).

3.2.4　　Each page (except the title page) shall start with a header including the page number, witness panel (if any) and examiner (if any). The layout of the header will be detailed with the Contractor.

3.2.5　　There are various pages of introductory information at the beginning of each transcript, outlining the case or hearing, witness appearances, index to proceedings, errata, etc. The layout of these pages will be detailed with the Contractor.

3.2.6　　Each page shall contain up to 25 lines of double-spaced transcript text, printed legibly in, or in a font equivalent to, Courier 12 point. Each line of transcript text will contain a line number.

3.2.7　　There are various "flags" that may be inserted into the text at various points to facilitate use of the transcripts. Final definitions of these flags will be detailed with the Contractor, but would include:

3.2.7.1　"start/stop" codes showing that the Hearing has begun, paused, finished, etc.;

3.2.7.2　"panel change" codes showing changes in the witness panel (i.e., "sworn", etc.);

3.2.7.3　"examiner change" codes showing changes as to the examiner (i.e., "direct", "cross", etc.);

3.2.7.4　"exhibit" codes showing formal tabling of exhibits;

3.2.7.5　"time stamp" codes showing the current time at that point in the proceeding.

3.2.8　　Details relating to the final format will be established by the Board in consultation with the Contractor.

3.3 Print Format #2 ("Condensed" or "Compressed" Format)

    3.3.1   Content must be absolutely identical to "Traditional" format. This includes all "flags", page & line numbers, etc. The relationship between the two formats must be obvious and clear. To that end, logical "Traditional" pages must be clearly visible in their smaller print format.

    3.3.2   The "Condensed" Format will use narrower margins; a smaller, proportionally spaced font; and in-line line numbers to enable more logical pages per actual physical printed page.

    3.3.3   Details relating to the final format will be established by the Board in consultation with the Contractor.

3.4 Form of Binding & Cover

    3.4.1   Each printed copy of a transcript produced by the Contractor shall be bound in a form to be determined by the Board in consultation with the Contractor. Acceptable binding methods include cerlox and "uni-bind", but others may be acceptable. The proposed binding method must be clearly stated in bid documents.

    3.4.2   Covers for bound copies shall be printed on a paper of suitable weight, and in a form to be determined by the Board in consultation with the Contractor, similar to that found in Attachment #3.

    3.4.3   In future, the Board will consider only having non case-specific text printed on the covers, with a cut-out showing any case-specific text on the title page underneath. This would allow the covers to potentially be re-used in many Hearings, saving paper and time. These changes would be made in consultation with the Contractor.

3.5 Type of Paper

    3.5.1   The printed transcript shall be produced on a high quality laser printer of sufficient clarity to permit reproduction of sharp, legible copy by methods such as microfilm, microfiche, photocopier machine, or offset printer.

    3.5.2   The required recycled paper content for transcript pages and covers shall be as per standards set from time to time by the Government of Ontario. Currently, they are as follows:

        3.5.2.1   Minimum Post-Commercial Waste Paper: 40%

        3.5.2.2   Minimum Post-Consumer Waste Paper: 10%

        3.5.2.3   Minimum Total Recycled Paper: 50%

3.6 Electronic Format

    3.6.1   The Official Electronic transcript must be an ASCII text file, guaranteed to be 100% equivalent to the Official Printed transcript on a page-by-page, line-by-line basis. The electronic copy must contain upper/lower case text that is 100% equivalent to the official transcript, with appropriate headers, flags, matching page and line numbers in the proper sequential order, etc.

3.6.2   If the electronic copy is provided by way of diskette, the data must be stored on a 3½ inch dual-sided, high or low density diskette in MS-DOS format. Each diskette shall be clearly labelled to identify the file name and the transcript contents by case name, docket number, date, volume and page numbers. Where a transcript spans more than one diskette, the diskettes shall be clearly labelled in a sequential manner.

3.6.3   If the electronic copy is transmitted by high-speed modem, the following modem file transmission protocols may be used: ZMODEM, KERMIT, CIS-B, etc. The minimum acceptable file transfer speed is 9600 baud, using a V.32 compatible modem.

3.6.4   Over time, other electronic formats or transmission protocols may be arranged by the Board with the Contractor. These could include different disk formats, Electronic Mail, direct access to sub-sections of the Boards LAN system, etc.

3.6.5   While the Board requires electronic transcript to be an ASCII file equivalent to the ''Standard'' print format described above, it is recognized that other parties may prefer other electronic formats (e.g., ''Condensed'' format, WordPerfect files, etc.) or transmission methods. The Contractor is free to satisfy these parties as long as:

    3.6.5.1   It is clear in the monthly reports to the Board exactly what is being sent to whom and by what method;

    3.6.5.2   There is no deviation from the Applicable Pricing/Limits Grid;

    3.6.5.3   There is no impact upon the production process for the standard materials.

3.7 Audio Cassettes

3.7.1   Audio tape shall be recorded on a standard dual-sided audio cassette tape at standard speed. Each tape shall be clearly labelled to identify the contents by case name, matter number, date and sequential order.

APPENDIX B

Attached to and forming part of Agreement between   and
Her Majesty the Queen dated April 1, 1994.

RELATED CHARGES AND DISBURSEMENTS

Related Charges

The Pricing/Limits Grids are attached.

APPENDIX C

Attached to and forming part of Agreement between   and
Her Majesty the Queen dated April 1, 1994.

ONTARIO GOVERNMENT PURCHASE ORDER #

APPENDIX D

Attached to and forming part of Agreement between
and Her Majesty the Queen dated April 1, 1994.

The Notices of Election of Applicable Pricing/Limits Grid for years one through three of
the Agreement follow.

NOTICE OF ELECTION
Year 1 of Contract

The Board hereby elects to use Pricing/Limits Grid Option _____for the period beginning on April 1/1994, and ending on March 31/1995. This will be referred to as the
Applicable Pricing/Limits Grid for the above term.

DATE _____ _____

Designated Board Representative
Ontario Energy Board

NOTICE OF ELECTION
Year 2 of Contract

The Board hereby elects to use Pricing/Limits Grid Option _____for the period beginning on April 1/1994, and ending on March 31/1995. This will be referred to as the
Applicable Pricing/Limits Grid for the above term.

DATE _____ _____

Designated Board Representative
Ontario Energy Board

NOTICE OF ELECTION
Year 3 of Contract

The Board hereby elects to use Pricing/Limits Grid Option _____for the period beginning on April 1/1994, and ending on March 31/1995. This will be referred to as the
Applicable Pricing/Limits Grid for the above term.

DATE _____ _____

Designated Board Representative
Ontario Energy Board

APPENDIX 12.10

Confidentiality Provisions of the

Canadian International Trade Tribunal Act, R.S.C. 1985, c. C-18.3

45.—(1) Where a person designates information as confidential pursuant to paragraph 46(1)(a) and that designation is not withdrawn by that person, no member and no person employed in the public service of Canada who comes into possession of that information while holding that office or being so employed shall, either before or after ceasing to hold that office or being so employed, knowingly disclose that information, or knowingly allow it to be disclosed, to any other person in any manner that is calculated or likely to make it available for the use of any business competitor or rival of any person to whose business or affairs the information relates.

(2) Subsection (1) does not apply in respect of any summary of information or statement referred to in paragraph 46(1)(b).

(3) Notwithstanding subsection (1), information to which that subsection applies that has been provided to the Tribunal in any proceedings before the Tribunal may be disclosed by the Tribunal to counsel for any party to those proceedings or to other proceedings arising out of those proceedings for use by that counsel only in those proceedings, subject to such conditions as the Tribunal considers are reasonably necessary or desirable to ensure that the information will not, without the written consent of the person who provided the information to the Tribunal, be disclosed by counsel to any person in any manner that is calculated or likely to make it available to

    (a) any party to the proceedings or other proceedings, including a party who is represented by that counsel; or

    (b) any business competitor or rival of any person to whose business or affairs the information relates.

(4) In subsection (3), "counsel", in relation to a party to proceedings, includes any person, other than a director, servant or employee of the party, who acts in the proceedings on behalf of the party.

46.—(1) Where a person who provides information to the Tribunal for the purposes of proceedings before the Tribunal wishes some or all of the information to be kept confidential, the person shall submit to the Tribunal, at the time the information is provided,

    (a) a statement designating as confidential the information that the person wishes to be kept confidential, together with an explanation as to why that information is designated as confidential; and

    (b) a summary of the information designated as confidential pursuant to paragraph (a) in sufficient detail to convey a reasonable understanding of the substance of the information or a statement

        (i) that such a summary cannot be made, or

        (ii) that such a summary would disclose facts that the person has a proper reason for wishing to keep confidential,

    together with an explanation that justifies the making of the statement.

(2) A person who designates information as confidential pursuant to paragraph (1)(a) fails to comply with paragraph (1)(b) where

  (a) the person provides neither the summary nor the statement referred to in paragraph (1)(b);

  (b) the person provides a summary of the information designated as confidential pursuant to paragraph (1)(a), but the Tribunal is satisfied that the summary does not comply with paragraph (1)(b);

  (c) the person provides a statement referred to in paragraph (1)(b), but does not provide an explanation that justifies the making of the statement; or

  (d) the person provides a statement referred to in paragraph (1)(b), but the Tribunal is satisfied that the explanation given as justification for the making of the statement does not justify the making thereof.

47.—(1) Where a person has designated information as confidential pursuant to paragraph 46(1)(a) and the Tribunal considers that such a designation is warranted, but the person has failed to comply with paragraph 46(1)(b), the Tribunal shall cause the person to be informed of the failure, of the ground on which the person has so failed and of the application of subsection 48(3) if the person fails to take, within the time limited therefor by or pursuant to that subsection, such action as is necessary for the person to take in order to comply with paragraph 46(1)(b).

(2) Where a person has designated information as confidential pursuant to paragraph 46(1)(a) and the Tribunal considers that, by reason of its nature, extent or availability from other sources or of the failure of the person to provide any explanation as to why it was designated as confidential, the designation of that information as confidential is unwarranted, the Tribunal shall cause the person

  (a) to be notified of the fact that the Tribunal considers the designation to be unwarranted and of its reasons for so considering; and

  (b) where the person has failed to comply with paragraph 46(1)(b), to be informed as provided in subsection (1).

48.—(1) Where a person is notified pursuant to paragraph 47(2)(a) with respect to any information that the person has designated as confidential pursuant to paragraph 46(1)(a), the person may, within fifteen days after being so notified,

  (a) withdraw the designation, or

  (b) submit to the Tribunal an explanation or further explanation as to why the information was designated as confidential

and, where the person does neither of those things within those fifteen days, that information shall not thereafter be taken into account by the Tribunal in the proceedings for the purposes for which it was provided, unless the Tribunal obtains that information from a source other than that person.

(2) Where, pursuant to subsection (1), a person submits to the Tribunal, within the fifteen days referred to in that subsection, an explanation or further explanation as to why the information was designated as confidential, the Tribunal shall again consider whether, taking into account that explanation or further explanation, the designation of the information as confidential is warranted and, if it decides that it is not warranted, shall cause the person to be notified that the information will not thereafter be taken into account by the Tribunal in the proceedings for the purposes for which it was provided, in which case

the information shall not thereafter be taken into account by the Tribunal in those proceedings, unless the Tribunal obtains the information from a source other than that person.

(3) Subject to subsection (4), where a person who has been informed pursuant to section 47 that the person has failed to comply with paragraph 46(1)(b) with respect to any information does not, within fifteen days after being so informed or within such longer time not exceeding thirty days after being so informed as the Tribunal, either before or after the expiration of the fifteen days, in its discretion allows, take such action as is necessary for the person to take in order to comply with paragraph 46(1)(b), the Tribunal shall cause the person to be notified that the information will not thereafter be taken into account by the Tribunal in the proceedings for the purposes for which it was provided, in which case the information shall not thereafter be taken into account by the Tribunal in those proceedings, unless the Tribunal obtains the information from a source other than that person.

(4) Subsection (3) does not apply in respect of any information that the Tribunal is prohibited by subsection (1) or (2) from taking into account in the proceedings for the purposes for which the information was provided.

49. Where
    (a) information given or elicited in the course of any proceedings before the Tribunal is, in the opinion of the Tribunal, in its nature confidential, or
    (b) the Deputy Minister of National Revenue indicates to the Tribunal in writing that subsection 84(1) of the Special Import Measures Act applies to information filed with the Secretary pursuant to paragraph 38(3)(b) of that Act,

the information shall not knowingly be disclosed by any member or person employed in the public service of Canada who comes into possession of the information in any manner that is calculated or likely to make it available for the use of any business competitor or rival of any person to whose business or affairs the information relates.

(Continued on page APP-114)

APPENDICE 17

APPENDIX 17.1

Typical Curriculum Vitae

EXPERIENCE

1981–   INCORPORATED
          Executive Vice President

1977–81   INC.
          Principal

1976–77   RESOURCES, INC.
          Consultant

EDUCATION

1976   UNIVERSITY
          M.S. In Industrial Administration

1974   UNIVERSITY OF
          B.S. in Mathematics (Statistics)

_____is a co-founder and Executive Vice-President of _____ , Incorporated _____ . Prior to founding _____ , _____ was a Principal at _____Inc. and conducted studies in the firm's Public Policy Studies area. _____areas of expertise include regulatory economics, financial and strategic analysis, and public policy analysis. _____has testified in utility rate proceedings and generic hearings before state utility boards and federal commissions. A sample of the projects _____has directed is provided below.

- For the _____Board, _____prepared a study on the design of rates for the contract carriage of natural gas and testified on this study before the Board.

- For the staff of the Land Use Regulation Commission in the State of _____ , _____evaluated the effect of a proposed hydroelectric project on an industrial company's competitive position and their decision to invest in plant modernization.

- For the staff of the _____Board, _____analyzed the cost allocation methods and rate structures proposed by _____and _____ Gas Corporation, Ltd. and presented testimony on alternative rate designs.

- For the _____Board, _____conducted a seminar on the principles and methods of cost allocation.

- for the _____Ministry of _____ , _____ participated in a conference on the use of flexible rate structures for the pricing of _ to large industrial customers.

• For a major industry association, _____ analyzed alternative cost allocations and postal rate structures for third-class bulk mail, and presented testimony in the 1984 rate proceeding before the Postal Rate Commission.

• On behalf of the _____ Municipal Electric Association, _____ testified before the _____ Board on time-of-use rate structures in a generic hearing on electricity rate design.

• For the _____ Board, _____ evaluated alternative natural gas structures for industrial users who use gas as a feedstock rather than as a fuel.

• For the _____ Board, _____ prepared testimony on the effect of different cost allocation methods on the rates charged large industrial customers by Ontario's gas utilities.

• For _____, _____ evaluated the proposed cost allocations and rate designs of _____ major natural gas distributors with whom _____ competes.

• For the _____ Power Research Institute, _____ was a principal architect in the development of a methodology to base time-of-use rates on time-differentiated accounting costs.

• For a major industrial client, _____ prepared econometric models and analyses measuring the impact of price increases on the demand for telecommunication services for public utility rate cases. _____ prepared analyses for presentation before public utilities commissions in Connecticut, Florida, Georgia, Massachusetts, North Carolina, Ohio, Pennsylvania and South Carolina.

• For a major U.S. utility, _____ assisted in the design of a comprehensive production and financial planning model to be used in the preparation of materials for rate proceedings.

FINANCIAL AND STRATEGIC ANALYSIS

• For a major U.S. utility, _____ developed a linear programming model to simulate the long-run interaction of supply, demand, and physical and regulatory constraints on the decision to bring on additional gas supplies.

• For the _____ Environmental _____, _____ analyzed the effect of the Economic Recovery Tax Act in 1981 on the ability of public utilities to finance new construction.

• For the _____, _____ analyzed the major obstacles which are preventing the utilities in the Northeast United States from replacing oil-fired generation capacity with coal-fired capacity.

• For the _____, _____ analyzed the impact of alternative accounting and tax policies on a public utility's shareholders and ratepayers.

• For the _____, _____ analyzed the effect of the Public Service Company of _____ cost-of-service index on the ratepayers and the shareholders of the utility.

• For a major industrial firm, _____ assessed the effect of a proposed acquisition on the industry's structure and assisted in the preparation of an affidavit to prevent the acquisition.

- For a major industrial client, _____ co-authored a study on the economic impact of different levels of research and development spending (published by _____, Inc. in 19__).

- For a major industrial client, _____ analyzed the impact of energy prices on employment growth in manufacturing industries.

- For a major industrial client, _____ analyzed the effectiveness of the current investment tax credit system and the effect of making this credit refundable.

PUBLIC POLICY ANALYSIS

- For the _____, _____ prepared a detailed economic analysis of the financial assurance and liability insurance regulations promulgated under the Resource Conservation and Recovery Act (RCRA).

- For the _____, _____ analyzed the use of financial responsibility regulations for hazardous substance releases under Section 108 of the Comprehensive Environmental Response, Compensation and Liability Act (the "Superfund" Act).

- For the _____, _____ evaluated the impact of the additional regulation of polychlorinated biphenyls (PCBs) in use in food, feed, and agricultural chemical establishment.

- For the _____, _____ developed a cost-effective strategy to control toxic and conventional pollutants in the copper smelting industry in a manner which minimizes health and environmental risks.

- For the _____, _____ analyzed the reliability of alternative measures of the health risks of toxic pollutants.

PUBLICATIONS

-
-
-
-

INDEX

All references are to sections of the text and appendices.

INDEX